INTRODUCTION TO THE NEW TESTAMENT

INTRODUCTION
TO THE NEW TESTAMENT

Revised Edition

by
WERNER GEORG KÜMMEL

Translated by

HOWARD CLARK KEE

NASHVILLE • ABINGDON

EINLEITUNG IN DAS NEUE TESTAMENT

17TH EDITION

Copyright © 1973 by Quelle & Meyer

INTRODUCTION TO THE NEW TESTAMENT

Translation copyright © 1975 by Abingdon Press

Fourth Printing 1981

Library of Congress Cataloging in Publication Data

Kümmel, Werner Georg, 1905-
   Introduction to the New Testament.

   Revised and updated translation of Einleitung in das Neue Testament by P.
Feine and J. Behm.
   Bibliography: p.
   Includes index.
   1. Bible. N.T.—Introductions. I. Feine, Paul, 1859-1933. Einleitung in das
Neue Testament. English. II. Title.
BS2330.F413 1975   225.6   74-26804

ISBN 0-687-19575-6

MANUFACTURED BY THE PARTHENON PRESS AT
NASHVILLE, TENNESSEE, UNITED STATES OF AMERICA

CONTENTS

Part One

The Formation of the New Testament Writings
A. THE NARRATIVE BOOKS
I. The Synoptic Gospels and the Acts

II.

B. THE LETTERS

I. The Letters of Paul

Part Two

The Formation of the Canon of the New Testament

Part Three

The History and Criticism of the Text of the New Testament

Appendix

PREFACE TO THE SEVENTEENTH EDITION

Inasmuch as the revised edition of Feine-Behm had already been reprinted four times in unaltered form since its appearance in 1963 (except for a bibliographical supplement to the fourteenth edition in 1965), it was evident that yet another unrevised edition was indefensible. Only a complete revision could be considered if the aim stated in the preface to the twelfth edition were to be served and if possible improved upon. Accordingly in this, the seventeenth edition, not only has the text as a whole been revised, more clearly structured, and freed from outdated formulations, but in addition the voluminous literature which has appeared since 1963 has been taken into account, with the result that some questions are answered differently or more nearly unequivocally. (Literature which has appeared since December 1, 1971, or which has come to my attention since then could not be taken into consideration.) But above all, certain wishes and proposals which I received through reviews and correspondence from individuals have been taken into consideration with the aim of making the book more readable and more useful: references to bibliography and to sources have been for the most part removed from the text and placed in footnotes; the enumeration of authors and bibliography on individual questions have been more clearly arranged (see on this the Key to the Bibliographical References); the abbreviations have been uniformly adapted to those of the third edition of RGG, to the extent that corresponding references are found therein already.

In view of the mounting flood of scholarly publications, I have in this revision kept strictly to the principle enunciated in the twelfth edition with regard to listing the literature. Omission of this or that title should not lead to the conclusion that I missed the work in question, since I have excluded not a few studies or publications because on closer examination they did not warrant being taken seriously as works of scholarship or because they proved to be simply repetitious.

The new identification of authorship on the title page, too, contributes to bibliographical simplification and, moreover, accords with an oft-expressed wish. But it further corresponds to the fact that, as a result of the most recent revision of this book, so little remains of the work of Paul Feine and Johannes Behm—apart from the overall arrangement, which has been altered in only a few

instances—that I can say with Jerome, in his letter to Pope
Damasus on the occasion of the completion of the Vulgate of the
Gospels: *Novum opus facere me cogis ex veteri.* All the more, therefore, I want to stress that my wish, as I complete this work, coin-
cides with that expressed by J. Behm in the preface to the first
edition of his revision (8th ed., 1936): "May this Introduction
also in its new form serve the study of the New Testament as *the*
source of Christian faith and Christian theology!"

Marburg, 1972   Werner Georg Kümmel

FROM THE PREFACE TO THE TWELFTH EDITION

In 1826 Martin Leberecht De Wette began the preface to his
*Compendium of Historical-Critical Introduction to the Canonical
Books of the New Testament* with the words: "When I turn over
to the reading public this long-announced introduction to the New
Testament with the feeling of joy that the completion of so long
delayed a work inspires, I cannot on the other hand conceal that
I fear it will not come up to the expectations that seem to have
been cherished for this work. The friends of critical research will
not be satisfied on account of my indeterminate results; on the other
hand those who regard our Holy Scriptures only with the eyes of
pious devotion will feel themselves offended by the freedom of our
investigation." I could not express my own thoughts better concerning the revision of Feine-Behm. Some time ago, when I—
not without some hesitation—undertook to bring J. Behm's widely
used textbook up to date in relation to the present state of research, I perceived what a difficult and all-encompassing task I had
taken on; but the deeper I went into the work, the clearer it became
to me that the book must be extensively rewritten, although the
structure and the basic methodological aim of the book must be
retained. My aim in revising the book was to include in a comprehensive way the present state of international scholarship, and
at the same time to make clear-cut decisions on disputed matters.
Yet I have not avoided leaving open those questions on which a
positive answer cannot be given to any appreciable extent.

Of the older literature mentioned in the earlier editions up until
about 1940, only a few titles have been retained, and only those

which are really indispensable. To survey completely the literature of the last twenty-five years would be impossible on the grounds of space alone, and all specifically theological studies had to be left out of account. Even so, I have striven to be so nearly complete as not to omit anything that is really essential for questions of introduction. Where possible, indications are given of where further bibliography can be found.

Marburg, April 1963   Werner Georg Kümmel

Key to the Bibliographical References

In the bibliographical references at the beginning of the individual parts and sections, titles are given in the order of their year of publication, although the works of a single author are always placed together. In the bibliographical references in the footnotes, wherever possible* the following sequence is observed: (1) commentaries (see §41); (2) introductions to the New Testament (see §3), respectively in Parts II and III the bibliography which is cited at the beginning of each part; (3) the literature mentioned at the beginning of the section in question; (4) other literature that is cited with full title. In connection with this sequence commentaries and introductions are incorporated alphabetically; the literature mentioned at the beginning of a section is incorporated in the sequence given at the beginning of that section. A semi-colon separates the four types of bibliography from each other.

In the case of monographs which appear in a series, as a rule the series is indicated only when the first reference is given. Reprints or unchanged editions are on principle not mentioned. The indication "Cath. (-olic)" is employed only in the enumeration of commentary series and introductions in §§1 and 3.

---

* Translator's note: Attention must be drawn to the qualification "wherever possible," since at some points in the notes strict adherence to the scheme of punctuation (e.g., where indications of pages, publication dates, etc., are given in addition to the names of authors) would have been confusing to the reader of the translation. Elsewhere Dr. Kümmel's distinctions have been indicated by the punctuation.

LIST OF ABBREVIATIONS

Abba .... J. Jeremias, *Abba. Studien zur nt. Theologie und Zeitgeschichte,* 1966
Abr. .... *Abraham unser Vater. Festschrift O. Michel,* AGSU 5, 1963
AGaJU .... Arbeiten zur Geschichte des antiken Judentums und des Urchristentums
AGG .... Abhandlungen der Gesellschaft der Wissenschaften zu Göttingen, philosophisch-historische Klasse
AGSU .... Arbeiten zur Geschichte des Spätjudentums und Urchristentums
AHG .... *Apostolic History and the Gospel: Festschrift for F. F. Bruce,* 1970
AKG .... Arbeiten zur Kirchengeschichte
AJA .... *American Journal of Archeology*
AnBibl .... Analecta Biblica
Anchor .... Anchor Bible
AnLov .... Analecta Lovanensia
ANTF .... Arbeiten zur nt. Textforschung
apost. .... apostolic
aram. .... Aramaic
armen. .... Armenian
art. .... article
ASNU .... Acta Seminarii Neotestamentici Upsaliensis (formerly: Arbeiten und Mitteilungen aus dem Nt. Seminar zu Uppsala)
ASTI .... *Annual of the Swedish Theological Institute*
AT .... Altes Testament (OT)
ATh .... Arbeiten zur Theologie
AThANT .... Abhandlungen zur Theologie des Alten und Neuen Testaments
ATR .... *Anglican Theological Review*

Barn. .... Barnabas, Letter of
Bauer .... W. Bauer, *Griech.-Deutsches Wörterbuch zu den Schriften des NT* . . . , ⁵1958. Eng. tr. by Arndt and Gingrich, 1957
Bb .... *Biblica*
BBB .... Bonner Biblische Beiträge
BeO .... *Biblica et Orientalia*
Beginnings .... Foakes-Jackson and Lake, *The Beginnings of Christianity* I, *The Acts of the Apostles,* Vols. I–V, 1920–33

Bh. .... *Beiheft* = supplementary volume
BevTh .... Beiträge zur evangelischen Theologie
BFChTh .... Beiträge zur Förderung christlicher Theologie
BhHw .... *Biblisch-historisches Handwörterbuch*
BHTh .... Beiträge zur historischen Theologie
bibl. .... bibliography
BJRL .... *Bulletin of the John Rylands Library*
Bl-Debr .... Blass-Debrunner, *Grammatik des nt. Griechisch,* [7]1943. Eng. tr. by R. W. Funk, 1961
BMS .... *The Bible in Modern Scholarship*, ed. by J. P. Hyatt, 1965
BR .... *Biblical Research*
BSt .... Biblische Studien
BThB .... *Biblical Theology Bulletin*
BU .... Biblische Untersuchungen
Buck-Taylor .... Ch. Buck and G. Taylor, *Saint Paul*, 1969
BWANT .... Beiträge zur Wissenschaft vom Alten und Neuen Testament
BZ .... *Biblische Zeitschrift*

ca. .... circa
cath. .... Catholic, including Catholic epistles
CB .... The Century Bible (New Edition)
CBL .... *Calwer Bibellexikon,* [5]1959
CBQ .... *Catholic Biblical Quarterly*
CGTC .... Cambridge Greek Testament Commentary
Ch. .... chapter
I and II Chron ..... I and II Chronicles
Clem. .... Clement of Alexandria
  Strom. .... *Stromata*
I and II Clem ...... I and II Clement
Col .... Colossians
Comm. .... Commentary
copt. .... Coptic
I, II Cor .... I and II Corinthians
cor. .... Corinthian
CN .... Conjectanea Neotestamentica
CNT .... *Commentaire du Nouveau Testament*
CSCO .... Corpus Scriptorum Christianorum Orientalium
CSEL .... Corpus Scriptorum Ecclesiasticorum Latinorum, pub. by the Vienna Academy of Sciences

d. .... died
Dan .... Daniel
DBS .... Dictionnaire de la Bible, Supplément
Did .... Didache
diss. .... dissertation

DLZ .... *Deutsche Literaturzeitung*
Dt .... Deuteronomy

ed. .... edited by, editor, or edition
e.g. .... for example
EHPR .... *Études d'histoire et de philosophie religieuses*
EKK .... Evangelisch-Katholischer Kommentar zum NT
EKL .... *Evangelisches Kirchenlexikon*
EnchB .... *Enchiridion Biblicum,* ⁴1961
Ep. .... epistle(s)
Eph .... Ephesians
ErgH .... *Ergänzungsheft* = supplementary volume
Esth .... Esther
Ét. bibl. .... *Études bibliques*
Eth. Enoch .... Ethiopic Book of Enoch
EThL .... Ephemerides Theologicae Lovanienses
Eus. (HE) .... Eusebius (*Church History*)
Ev, Evv .... *Evangelium, Evangelien* (Gospel[s])
EvK .... *Evangelische Kommentare*
EvTh .... *Evangelische Theologie*
Ex .... Exodus
ExpT .... *Expository Times*
Ezek .... Ezekiel

f, ff .... following page(s)
Festschr. .... *Festschrift* (for)
Festschr. Coppens ... *De Jésus aux Évangiles: Tradition et rédaction dans les Évangiles synoptiques,* Bibliotheca Ephemeridum Theologicarum Lovanensium 25: Donum natalicium Josepho Coppens, Vol. II, 1967
fr .... fragment
fr. .... French
FRLANT .... Forschungen zur Religion und Literatur des Alten und Neuen Testaments

Gal .... Galatians
GANT .... *Gestalt und Anspruch des NT,* ed. by J. Schreiner with the collaboration of G. Dautzenburg, 1969
GCS .... *Die griech. christlichen Schriftsteller der ersten drei Jahrhunderte,* ed. by the Berlin Academy of Sciences
Gen .... Genesis
GGA .... *Göttingische gelehrte Anzeigen*
Gn .... *Gnomon*

Hab .... Habakkuk
Heb .... Hebrews, Letter to

hebr. .... ⁚ hebrew
hellen. .... Hellenistic
Herm .... Shepherd of Hermas
   Mand. .... *Mandata*
   Sim. .... *Similitudines*
   Vis. .... *Visiones*
Jerome, *Vir. ill.* .... *De viris illustribus*
HNT .... Handbuch zum NT
HNTC .... Harper NT Commentary (in England, Black's NT
                Commentaries)
HThK   Herders Theologischer Kommentar zum NT
HTR .... *Harvard Theological Review*
HTS .... Harvard Theological Studies

ICC .... International Critical Commentary
idem .... by the same author
i.e. .... that is
Ign. .... Ignatius
   Phila .... To the Philadelphians
   Magn .... To the Magnesians
   Polyc .... To Polycarp
   Sm .... To the Smyrnaeans
in loc. .... see on the passage cited
Int .... *Interpretation*
IntB .... The Interpreter's Bible
Intr. .... Introduction
Iren. .... Irenaeus
   Haer. .... *Against Heresies*, cited according to Harvey's ed.
Isa .... Isaiah
II Isa .... Second, or Deutero-Isaiah

Jas .... James, Epistle of
JB .... Jerusalem Bible
Jb .... *Jahrbuch*
JbAC .... *Jahrbuch für Antike und Christentum*
JBL .... *Journal of Biblical Literature*
Jer .... Jeremiah
Jh. .... *Jahrhundert* (cent.)
JJSt .... *Journal of Jewish Studies*
Jn (or *joh.*) .... John (Johannine)
I, II, III Jn .... I, II, III Letters of John
Joh. .... Johannes (John)
Jos. .... Josephus, cited according to the ed. of Niese
   Ant. .... *Antiquities of the Jews*
   Ap. .... *Contra Apionem*
   Bell. .... *Jewish Wars*
   Vit. .... *Life*

JR	*Journal of Religion*
JTS	*Journal of Theological Studies*
Jub	Book of Jubilees
Just.	Justin
Apol.	*Apology*
Dial.	*Dialogue*
KBANT	Kommentare und Beiträge zum Alten und Neuen Testament
KuD	*Kerygma und Dogma*
lat.	Latin
lit.	literature; sometimes indicates bibliography
Lk	Luke, either as historical figure, as author, or the Gospel According to Lk
LThK	*Lexikon für Theologie und Kirche*, 2nd ed.
LXX	the Septuagint
Mal	Malachi
Manson, *St.*	T. W. Manson, *Studies in the Gospels and Epistles*, 1962
MBE	Monumenta biblica et ecclesiastica
MbThSt	Marburger Theologische Studien
Meyer	*Kritisch-exegetischer Kommentar über das NT*, founded by H. A. W. Meyer
Mk	Mark or the Gospel According to Mk
Moffatt	Moffatt NT Commentary
MPTh	*Monatsschrift für Pastoraltheologie*
MThS	Münchner Theologische Studien
MThZ	*Münchner Theologische Zeitschrift*
Mt	Matthew or the Gospel According to Matthew
n., nn.	note(s)
NAG	Nachrichten der Akademie der Wissenschaften in Göttingen, Philologisch-historische Klasse
NeP	*Neotestamentica et Patristica, Freundesgabe O. Cullmann*, Suppl. NovTest VI, 1962
NF	Neue Folge
NIC	New International Commentary on the NT=The New London Commentary on the NT
NovTest	*Novum Testamentum*
No.	number
NRTh	*Nouvelle Revue Théologique*
NS	New Series
NT	New Testament (in German, Latin, English, French, or Italian)
nt.	*neutestamentlich*
NTA	Neutestamentliche Abhandlungen

NTD .... Das Neue Testament Deutsch. Neues Göttinger Bibelwerk
NTF .... Neutestamentliche Forschungen
NTS .... *New Testament Studies*
NTTS .... New Testament Tools and Studies
NZSTh .... *Neue Zeitschrift für Systematische Theologie*

OrChr .... *Oriens Christianus*
OrChrA .... *Orientalia Christiana Analecta*
OLZ .... *Orientalistische Literaturzeitung*

Pap. .... Papyrus
par. .... parallel(s)
Past. .... Pastoral Epistles
Perspective .... *Jesus and Man's Hope*, Perspective Book I, 1970
I, II Pet .... I and II Peter
Phil .... Philippians
Phlm .... Philemon
Plsbr. .... Letters of Paul
pl. .... plural
Polyc. .... Polycarp
p., pp. .... page(s)
Preuschen, *Analecta* . E. Preuschen, *Analecta* II, ²1910 (=Sammlung ausgewählter kirchen- und dogmengeschichtlicher Quellenschriften, I, 8)
Pro .... Proverbs
Ps .... Psalms
PW .... Pauly-Wissowa, *Real-Encyklopädie der klassischen Altertumswissenschaft*

1QS .... Manual of Discipline from Qumran 1

RAC .... *Reallexikon für Antike und Christentum*
RB .... *Revue Biblique*
RBén .... *Revue Bénédictine*
RdQ .... *Revue de Qumran*
RE .... *Realenzyklopädie für protestantische Theologie und Kirche*, 3rd ed.
RechB .... Recherches Bibliques
RechSR .... Recherches de Science Religieuse
Rev .... Revelation
rev. .... revised
RGG .... *Die Religion in Geschichte und Gegenwart*
RHPhR .... *Revue d'Histoire et de Philosophie Religieuses*
RHR .... *Revue de l'Histoire des Religions*
RNT .... Regensburger NT = *Das NT übersetzt und kurz erklärt*, ed. by A. Wikenhauser and O. Kuss

Rom . . . . Romans
RQ . . . . *Römische Quartalschrift*
RThL . . . . *Revue Théologique de Louvain*
RThPh . . . . *Revue de théologie et de philosophie*
RVV . . . . Religionsgeschichtliche Versuche und Vorarbeiten

I, II Sam . . . . I and II Samuel
SAB . . . . Sitzungsberichte der Preussischen (or Berlin) Akademie der Wissenschaften, Philosophisch-historische Klasse
SAH . . . . Sitzungsberichte der Heidelberger Akademie der Wissenschaften, philosophische-historische Klasse
SBS . . . . Stuttgarter Bibelstudien
SBT . . . . Studies in Biblical Theology
Sch., Tr. U. . . . . H. Schürmann, *Traditionsgeschichtliche Untersuchungen zu den syn. Evangelien,* 1968
SGV . . . . Sammlung gemeinverständlicher Vorträge und Schriften aus dem Gebiet der Theologie und Religionsgeschichte
Sir . . . . Sirach, Ben Sira, Ecclesiasticus
SJT . . . . *Scottish Journal of Theology*
Slav Enoch . . . . Slavic Book of Enoch
SNTS . . . . Bulletin of Studiorum Novi Testamenti Societas
SNTSMS . . . . Monograph Series of Studiorum Novi Testamenti Societas
SPIB . . . . Scripta Pontificii Instituti Biblici
SStW . . . . *Synoptische Studien für A. Wikenhauser,* 1953
StANT . . . . Studien zum Alten und Neuen Testament
StBSt . . . . Stuttgarter Bibelstudien
StBM . . . . Stuttgarter Biblische Monographien
StD . . . . Studies and Documents
StEv . . . . *Studia Evangelica*
StG . . . . *Studies in the Gospels: Essays in Memory of R. H. Lightfoot,* 1955
StLA . . . . *Studies in Luke-Acts: Essays presented in Honor of P. Schubert,* 1966
StN . . . . Studia Neotestamentica
StNT . . . . Studien zum NT
StPB . . . . Studia Post-Biblica
StTh . . . . Studia Theologica
StUNT . . . . Studien zur Umwelt des NT
suppl. . . . . Supplement, supplemental, supplementary
SyBU . . . . Symbolae Biblicae Upsalienses
Synpt. . . . . synoptic
syr. . . . . Syriac

TDNT .... *Theological Dictionary of the New Testament,*
                  Eng. tr. of Kittel-Friedrich, *Theologisches Wörter-*
                  buch zum NT
Tert. .... Tertullian
  Adv. Marc. ......   *Adversus Marcionem*
  De pud. ....   *De pudicitia*
  Praescr. haer. .....   *De praescriptione haereticorum*
Test XII .... Testaments of the XII Patriarchs
ThB .... Theologische Bücherei
ThBl .... *Theologische Blätter*
ThE .... *Theologische Existenz heute*
I, II Thess .... I and II Thessalonians
ThF .... *Theologische Forschung*
ThHK .... *Theologischer Hand-Kommentar zum NT*
ThJ .... *Theologische Jahrbücher*
ThLZ .... *Theologische Literaturzeitung*
ThR .... *Theologische Rundschau*
ThRv .... *Theologische Revue*
ThSt .... Theologische Studien
ThStKr .... *Theologische Studien und Kritiken*
ThViat .... *Theologia Viatorum*
ThZ .... *Theologische Zeitschrift* (Basel)
I, II Tim .... I and II Timothy
Tit .... Titus
Torch .... Torch Bible Commentary
tr. .... translated, translator, translation
Trajectories .... H. Köster and J. M. Robinson, *Trajectories Through*
                  Early Christianity, 1971
TSt .... Texts and Studies
TU .... Texte und Untersuchungen zur Geschichte der
                  altkirchlichen Literatur
Ty .... Tyndale NT Commentaries
TZTh .... *Tübinger Zeitschrift für Theologie*

UB .... *Die Urchristliche Botschaft*
UNT .... Untersuchungen zum NT

v., vv. .... verse(s)
VE .... *Vox Evangelica: Biblical and Historical Essays by*
                  Members of the London Bible College
VF .... *Verkündigung und Forschung*
VigChr .... *Vigiliae Christianae*
v.l. .... variant readings

WA .... Weimar Edition of the Works of Martin Luther
Wisd .... Wisdom of Solomon

WGK, NT .... W. G. Kümmel, *The New Testament: The History of the Investigation of its Problems*, Eng. tr. 1973

WMANT .... Wissenschaftliche Monographien zum Alten and Neuen Testament

WuD .... *Wissenschaft und Dienst*

WUNT .... Wissenschaftliche Untersuchungen zum NT

Zahn .... *Komm. zum NT*, ed. Th. Zahn

ZAW .... *Zeitschrift für die at. Wissenschaft*

Zech .... Zechariah

ZKG .... *Zeitschrift für Kirchengeschichte*

ZKTh .... *Zeitschrift für katholische Theologie*

ZNW .... *Zeitschrift für die nt. Wissenschaft und die Kunde der älteren Kirche*

ZRGG .... *Zeitschrift für Religions- und Geistesgeschichte*

ZsTh .... *Zeitschrift für systematische Theologie*

ZThK .... *Zeitschrift für Theologie und Kirche*

ZüB .... *Zürcher Bibelkommentare* (earlier known as: *Prophezei*)

INTRODUCTION

§1. The Most Important Tools for the Study of the New Testament

Editions of the Greek New Testament

Most useful manual edition: Eberhard Nestle, *Novum Testamentum Graece*, 1898, rev. Erwin Nestle (^{13}1927), ^{25}1963 (with Kurt Aland). In addition, B. F. Westcott–F. J. A. Hort, *The New Testament in the Original Greek*, 1886; A. Souter, *Novum Testamentum Graece* (1910), ^{2}1947; H. J. Vogels, *Novum Testamentum Graece* (1920), ^{4}1955; A. Merk, *Novum Testamentum Graece* (1933), ^{9}1964 (SPIB); J. M. Bover, *Novi Testamenti Biblia Graeca et Latina* (1943), ^{3}1953 (on this see B. M. Metzger, JBL 66, 1947, 415 ff); Η ΚΑΙΝΗ ΔΙΑΘΗΚΗ, *2nd Ed. with Revised Critical Apparatus*, ed. D. Kilpatrick and E. Nestle, 1958; *The Greek New Testament*, ed. K. Aland, M. Black, B. M. Metzger, A. Wikgren, 1966.

Critical editions of the New Testament for special scholarly study: C. Von Tischendorf, *Novum Testamentum Graece, ad antiquissimos testes denuo recensuit* . . . Editio octava major I, 1869, II, 1872, III (*Prolegomena, scripsit* C. R. Gregory), 1894; B. F. Westcott–F. J. A. Hort, *The New Testament in the Original Greek* I (1881) ^{2}1898, II (1882) ^{2}1896; Herm. von Soden, *Die Schriften des NT in ihrer ältesten erreichbaren Textgestalt hergestellt auf Grund ihrer Textgeschichte* I, 1–3 (studies), 1902-10, II (text with apparatus), 1913; *Novum Testamentum Graece secundum textum Westcotto-Hortianum: Ev. Secundum Marcum (um apparatu critico novo plenissimo* . . . ed. S. C. E. Legg, 1935; *Ev. secundum Matthaeum* . . . ed. S. C. E. Legg, 1940 (the edition is inadequate; see on this H. J. Vogels, ThRv 34, 1935, 305 ff; T. W. Manson, JTS 43, 1942, 83 ff. As a result it has not been carried further).

Dictionaries, Concordances, Bible Lexicons

Dictionaries and concordances to the Greek New Testament: W. Bauer, *Griechisch-Deutches Wörterbuch zu den Schriften des NT und der übrigen urchristlichen Literatur* (^{2}1928), ^{5}1958 (=A *Greek-English Lexicon of the NT and other Early Christian Literature*, tr. Wm. F. Arndt and F. W. Gingrich from 4th ed., 1952, 1957); F. Zorrell, *Lexicon Graecum Novi Testamenti* (1911), ^{3}1961; H. Cremer, *Biblisch-theologisches Wörterbuch der Nt. Gräzität* (1867), 11th ed., completely revised and much altered by J. Kögel, 1923 (=*Biblical-Theological Lexicon of NT Greek*, tr. from 2nd ed. by Wm. Urwick, 1878); Supplement to the BThL, based on the 3rd and 4th eds., 1886; G. Kittel–G. Friedrich, *Theologisches Wörterbuch zum NT*, Vols. I-IX, 1933-73, X in preparation (=*Theological Dictionary of the New Testament*, tr. and ed. G. W. Bromiley, 1964-73, Vols. I-IX); *Theologisches Begriffslexikon zum NT*, ed. L. Coenen, E. Beyreuther, H. Bietenhard, I, 1967; II, 1, 1969, continuation in preparation; J. H. Moulton–G. Milligan, *The Vocabulary of the Greek Testament Illustrated from the Papyri and Other Nonliterary sources*, 1914-29; R. C. Trench, *Synonyms of the NT*, 1854, frequently reprinted.—C. H. Bruder, TAMEION . . . *sive Concordantiae omnium vocum Novi Testamenti Graeci* (1842), [7]1913; A. Schmoller, *Handkonkordanz zum griechischen NT* (1869), [13]1963; W. F. Moulton–A. S. Geden, *A Concordance of the Greek Testament According to the Texts of Westcott and Hort, Tischendorf and the English Revisers* (1897), [8]1953; R. Morgenthaler, *Statistik des Nt. Wortschatzes*, 1958.

On the Greek Old Testament: E. Hatch–H. A. Redpath, *A Concordance to the Septuagint and the other Greek Versions of the Old Testament*, 1892-97, suppl. 1906. On the earliest patristic literature: E. J. Goodspeed, *Index Patristicus sive Clavis Patrum Apostolicorum operum*, 1907; *idem, Index Apologeticus sive Clavis Justini Martyris operum aliorumque Apologetarum pristinorum*, 1912; H. Kraft, *Clavis Patrum Apostolicorum*, 1963.

Historical and theological dictionaries of the Bible: *Calwer Bibellexicon*, ed. Th. Schlatter (1893), [5] 1959; *Stuttgarter Biblisches Nachschlagewerk*, suppl. to the Stuttgart Jubilee Bible, 1932; T. K. Cheyne–J. S. Black, *Encyclopaedia Biblica*, 1899-1903; J. Hastings, *A Dictionary of the Bible*, 1898, rev. ed. by F. C. Grant and H. H. Rowley, 1963; J. Hastings, *A Dictionary of Christ and the Gospels*, 1906-8; *idem, Dictionary of the Apostolic Church*, 1915-18; F. Vigouroux *Dictionnaire de la Bible*, 5 vols., 1905-12, suppl. I-VII, 1928-66, to be continued; K. Galling, *Biblisches Reallexicon*, Handbuch zum AT, I, 1, 1937; E. Osterloh and H. Engelland, *Biblisch-theologisches Handwörterbuch zur Lutherbibel*, 1954; J. B. Bauer, *Bibeltheologisches Wörterbuch* (1958), [2]1962; *Deutsches Wörterbuch zum NT* (based on the original Greek text) by G. Richter, RNT 10, 1962; *Vocabulaire Biblique*, published under the direction of J.-J. von Allmen, 1954) tr. from 2nd ed. (1956) by P. J. Allcock as *Vocabulary of the Bible*, published in England, 1958, and in USA as *A Companion to the Bible*, 1958); *Wörterbuch zur bibl. Botschaft*, ed. P. Léon-Dufour, 1964; *Biblisch-historisches Handwörterbuch*, ed. B. Reicke and L. Rost, I-III, 1962-66; *The Interpreter's Dictionary of the Bible*, I-IV, 1962; *Bibel-Lexikon*, ed. H. Haag, [2]1968.

Grammars

G. B. Winer, *Grammatik des Nt. Sprachidioms* (1822), 8th ed. (since 1894) newly rev. by P. W. Schmiedel (incomplete); F. Blass, *Grammatik*

des Nt. Griechisch (1896), rev. since 4th ed. (1913) by A. Debrunner,
[12]1965 (with suppl. vol. by L. Tabachovitz); the Eng. tr. by R. W.
Funk, 1961, contains corrections prepared by Debrunner for a new edi-
tion; L. Radermacher, *Nt. Grammatik. Das Griechisch des NT im Zu-
sammenhang mit der Volkssprache dargestellt* (1911), [2]1925 (=HNT I);
A. T. Robertson, *A Grammar of the Greek NT in the Light of Historical
Research* (1914), [4]1923; *idem* and W. H. Davis, *A New Short Grammar
of the Greek NT*, 1931; J. H. Moulton, *A Grammar of NT Greek* I
(*Prolegomena*), (1906), [3]1908, II (*Accidence and Word-Formation*, ed.
W. F. Howard), 1929, III (*Syntax*, ed. N. Turner), 1963; J. H. Moulton,
An Introduction to the Study of the Greek NT (1941), [4]1952; F.-M.
Abel, *Grammaire du grec biblique, suivie d'un choix de Papyrus*, [2]1927
(=Ét. bibl.); M. Zerwick, *Graecitas Biblica*, [4]1960 (SPIB 92); C. F. D.
Moule, *An Idiom Book of NT Greek* (1953), [2]1959; K. Beyer, *Semitische
Syntax im NT* I, 1, StUNT I (1962), [2]1968.

Hermeneutics

F. Schleiermacher, *Hermeneutik und Kritik mit besonderer Beziehung
auf das NT*, ed. F. Lücke, 1838; F. D. E. Schleiermacher, *Hermeneutik*,
ed. H. Kimmerle, 1959; E. von Dobschütz, *Vom Auslegen des NT*, 1927;
J. Wach, *Das Verstehen* I, 1926, II, 1929, III, 1933; E. Fascher, *Vom
Verstehen des NT*, 1930; F. Torm, *Hermeneutik des NT*, 1930; R. Bult-
mann, "Das Problem der Hermeneutik," ZThK 47, 1950, 47 ff (=R. B.,
Glauben und Verstehen II, 1952, 211 ff); E. Lerle, *Voraussetzungen der
nt. Exegese*, 1951; E. Fuchs, *Hermeneutik* (1954), [2]1958; G. Ebeling,
art. "Hermeneutik," RGG[3] III, 1959, 242 ff (lit.); A. N. Wilder, "NT
Hermeneutics Today," in *Current Issues in NT Interpretation: Essays in
Honor of O. A. Piper*, 1962, 38 ff; J. D. Smart, *The Interpretation of
Scripture*, 1961; E. Fuchs, *Marburger Hermeneutik*, 1968; F. Mussner,
Geschichte der Hermeneutik von Schleiermacher bis zur Gegenwart, Hand-
buch der Dogmengeschichte I, 3c, 2, 1970. See also H. Zimmermann, *Nt.
Methodenlehre, Darstellung der historisch-kritischen Methode*, 1966; K.
Romaniuk, *Wegweiser in das NT. Einführung in die nt. Wissenschaft*
(1965), [2]1967.

Complete Commentaries on the NT

Still worthy of mention among the scholarly commentary series in
German Protestant theology are:
Kritisch exegetischer Kommentar über das NT, founded by H. A. W.
Meyer; begun in 1832, 16 divisions, whose up to nineteen editions possess
a strongly scholarly character and thus reflect the changing methods of
NT exegesis (cited as Meyer [10]I, etc.). Eng. tr. by various translators of
the 3rd–6th eds. have appeared as *Critical and Exegetical Handbook to*

the NT, 1884-89; most recently, *The Gospel of John*, by R. Bultmann, tr. G. R. Beasley-Murray *et al.* from the 14th ed., 1971.

Die heilige Schrift NTs zusammenhängend untersucht [The Holy Scripture of the NT comprehensively examined], by J. C. K. Hofmann, 1862 ff, 11 vols.; a masterpiece of penetrating exegetical skill ("salvation-history") with many arbitrary features.

Hand-Commentar zum NT, ed. by H. J. Holtzmann, 1889 ff; brief exposition from a sharply historical-critical viewpoint, now out of date.

Kommentar zum NT, ed. by Th. Zahn, 1903 ff, 17 vols. appeared; grandly conceived work of conservative exegesis with some outstanding essays, especially on textual criticism and the history of exegesis (cited as Zahn [4]I, etc.).

Handbuch zum NT, ed. by H. Lietzmann, 1906 ff; by G. Bornkamm, 1949 ff; exegetically concise, theologically inadequate in the older editions; noteworthy for the richness of comparative material in contemporary history and history of religions and of languages (cited as HNT).

Kommentar zum NT aus Talmud und Midrasch, by (H. L. Strack)— P. Billerbeck, 1922-61; comprehensive, superior collection of comparative rabbinic material, though not a detailed commentary.

Theologischer Handkommentar zum NT mit Text und Paraphrase, 7 vols., 1928-39, ed. by E. Fascher, 1957 ff; basically conservative standpoint, but open to all modern critical questions; seeks to expound the religious content of the NT (cited as ThHK).

Works for a general readership on a scholarly basis:

Erläuterungen zum NT [Explanations of the NT], by A. Schlatter (1887 ff), [4]1928; simple, biblicist interpretation of Scripture.

Die Schriften des NT übersetzt und für die Gegenwart erklärt (so-called "Göttinger Bibelwerk"), ed. by J. Weiss (later by W. Bousset and W. Heitmüller), (1906), [3]1917-18; the biblical study produced by the history-of-religions school.

Das NT Deutsch. Neues Göttinger Bibelwerk, ed. by P. Althaus and J. Behm, 1932 ff, ed. by P. Althaus and G. Friedrich, 1957 ff, now by G. Friedrich, with a supplemental series, 1969 ff; seeks to present the present state of NT research and at the same time to make the NT accessible as a living authority for Christians today (cited as NTD).

Die urchristliche Botschaft, an introduction to the writings of the NT, ed. by O. Schmitz (1929 ff), [2-7]1951 ff; seeks to express the primitive Christian message in its uniqueness (cited as UB).

Prophezei, Schweizerisches Bibelwerk für die Gemeinde, 1943 ff, since 1960 *Zürcher Bibelkommentare*; for a general readership; partly very scholarly and partly more devotional (cited as ZüB).

In preparation is *Evangelisch-katholischer Kommentar zum NT* (Preparatory Studies Vols. I-III have appeared, 1969-71; cited as EKK).

The most important English-language commentary is the equivalent and counterpart of the Meyer commentary, *The International Critical Commentary on the Holy Scriptures of the Old and New Testament*, 1895 ff (cited as ICC).

Conservative in slant is the very careful, more popularly aimed *New International Commentary* (in the British edition, *The New London Commentary*), 1951 ff (cited as NIC).

Brief but very careful exegesis of the Greek NT is offered by the *Cambridge Greek Testament Commentary*, 1957 ff (cited as CGTC).

Black's NT Commentaries, 1957 ff, contain detailed exegesis, which, though thoroughly scholarly, is intended for wider audiences. Published in U.S.A. as *Harper NT Commentary* (cited as HNTC).

Scholarly and homiletical exposition are offered side by side in *The Interpreter's Bible*, 1951 ff (cited as IntB).

Bible study for better-educated persons is offered by *The Moffatt NT Commentary*, 1928 ff (cited as Moffatt).

Tyndale NT Commentaries are conservative, strongly theological in aim, and have detailed historical introductions (cited as Ty).

Torch Bible Commentaries, 1949 ff, offer detailed introductions and a short commentary with the emphasis on religious significance (cited as Torch).

Peake's Commentary on the Bible, ed. by M. Black and H. H. Rowley, 1962, offers very short, popular expositions.

The Anchor Bible, 1964 ff, contains strictly scholarly commentaries by Protestant, Catholic, and Jewish scholars (cited as Anchor).

The Century Bible (also known as *The New Century Bible*), 1966 ff, offers independent scholarly commentaries which are also of use for a popular readership, based on the English text (cited as CB).

Very independent and worthwhile is the commentary series of French-speaking Protestantism, *Commentaire du NT*, 1949 ff (cited as CNT).

The most important Catholic commentary series on the NT are:

Cursus Scripturae Sacrae, Sectio Tertia, Commentarii in NT, 1890 ff.

The commentaries of the French *Études bibliques*, 1907 ff, are comprehensive, for the most part very basic exegesis with full citation of bibliography (cited as Ét. bibl.).

Herders Theologischer Kommentar zum NT, ed. by A. Wikenhauser, now by A. Vögtle, 1953 ff, offers strictly scholarly exegesis (cited as HThK).

Intended for a wider readership:

Die Heilige Schrift des NTs übersetzt und erklärt, ed. by F. Tillman (1913 ff), ²1931 ff, now replaced by:

Das NT übersetzt und kurz erklärt, ed. by A. Wikenhauser and O. Kuss (1938 ff), ³⁻⁵1959 ff, the so-called "Regensburger NT" (cited as RNT).

La Sainte Bible Traduite en francais sous la direction de l'École Biblique de Jérusalem, 1948 ff, contains in separate editions careful introductions and short explanations of the translated text (cited as JB). A shorter complete edition (*Le NT traduit . . .*), 1958, has appeared in a German translation (ed. by D. Arenhoevel, A. Deissler, A. Vögtle), 1968, and the English translation, *The Jerusalem Bible*, ed. by Alexander Jones.

Bibliographies

A systematic bibliography of all new publications, essays and reviews in the field of NT scholarship is offered regularly by the journal *Biblica* of the Pontifical Biblical Institute; since Vol. 49, the bibliography has appeared independently under the title *Elenchus Bibliographicus Biblicus*. Information about the contents of all journal articles in all languages is contained in the *Internationale Zeitschriftenschau für Bibelwissenschaft und Grenzgebiete*, 1951 ff, and in *NT Abstracts*. See also B. M. Metzger, *Index of Articles on the NT and the Early Church Published in Festschriften*, 1951; also, *Supplement to Index . . .* , 1955.

§2. Conception and Classification of the Introduction to the New Testament

F. C. Baur, "Die Einleitung ins NT als theologische Wissenschaft. Ihr Begriff und ihre Aufgabe, ihr Entwicklungsgang und ihr Organismus" [Introduction to the NT as a theological science: its conception and its task, the course of its development and its inner organic structure], ThJ 9, 1850, 462 ff; 10, 1851, 291 ff (excerpted in WGK, NT, 127 ff 139 f); Th. Zahn, art., "Einleitung in das NT," RE V, 1898, 261 ff; W. G. Kümmel, " 'Einleitung in das NT' als theologische Aufgabe," EvTh 19, 1959, 4 ff (=W. G. K., *Heilsgeschehen und Geschichte*, MbThSt 3, 1965, 340 ff); W. Marxsen, "Die Bedeutung der Einleitungswissenschaft für die Predigtarbeit," MPTh 49, 1960, 1 ff. Cf. also the introductory paragraphs of the various introductions to the NT.

The scholarly discipline of "introduction to the NT" is concerned with the historical questions of the origin and collecting of the NT writings, and of the textual tradition of both the writings and the collection. It presupposes the existence of the NT canon, in which the church of the second-fourth centuries brought together those writings which served the church as norm in its preaching and which were read in connection with worship. Accordingly the science of introduction is a strictly historical discipline which, by illuminating the historical circumstances of the origin of the individual writings, provides for exegesis the necessary presuppositions for understanding the writings in their historical uniqueness. Through the study of the development and preservation of the collection, it furnishes a sure historical foundation for the question of the doctrinal content of the NT. As a historical science the discipline of introduction has at its service the methods of historical research, and it is therefore a wholly justifiable goal for such research to treat the investigation of the circumstances of the origin of the individual writings and the literary connections between them as an older part of the history of early Christian literature and to regard the illumination of the rise of the canon as part of church history and the history of dogma.[1] G. Krüger (in *Das Dogma vom NT*, 1896) raised objections on historical grounds against the study in isolation of the twenty-seven writings collected in the NT canon under the designation "introduction to the NT." But in spite of this, the point of view is to be maintained, because through their belonging to the canon demarcated by the early church the NT writings possess a special character which has been recognized in faith by Christians, with the result that it is an especially important task for Christian theologians to lay the groundwork for exegesis of them on a sure historical basis. Also, theological reflection on the limits of the dogmatic validity of the canon as norm cannot be appropriately carried on without a clear insight into the antecedents and aims of the formation of the canon. "Introduction to the NT" is a theological discipline, not through its scholarly methods, but through the distinctive nature of its objectives. In keeping with its historical character, research moves appropriately from (1) the origins of the individual writings through (2) the rise of the collection to (3) the preservation of the text of the collection.

§3. HISTORY AND LITERATURE OF NEW TESTAMENT INTRODUCTION

W. G. Kümmel, *The New Testament: The History of the Investigation of its Problems*, tr. S. M. Gilmour and H. C. Kee, 1972 (cited as WGK, NT); *The Cambridge History of the Bible* III, ed. S. L. Greenslade, 238 ff, 294 ff; S. Neill, *The Interpretation of the NT 1861–1961*, 1964; W. G. Kümmel, *Die exegetische Erforschung des NT in diesem Jahrhundert*, in *Bilanz der Theologie im 20 Jh.* II, 1969 (=WGK, *Das NT im 20. Jh.*, SBS 50, 1970); see also the appropriate sections in the NT introductions of H. J. Holtzmann, A. Jülicher, M. Meinertz, and the survey of literature by Ph. Vielhauer, ThR, NF 31, 1965/66, 97 ff, 193 ff.

[1] Cf. H. Jordan, *Geschichte der altchristlichen Literatur*, 1911, 69 ff; P. Wendland, *Die urchristlichen Literaturformen*, HNT I, 3, [2,3]1912; O. Stählin, "Christliche Schriftsteller," in W. Christ, *Geschichte der griech. Literatur*, rev. by W. Schmid and O. Stählin II, 2, [6]1924, 1105 ff; M. Dibelius, *Geschichte der urchristlichen Literatur* I, II, Sammlung Göschen 934-935, 1926; D. W. Riddle–H. H. Hutson, *NT Life and Literature*, 1946; C. F. D. Moule, *The Birth of the NT*, HNTC, Companion Vol. I, 1962; A. N. Wilder, *The Language of the Gospel: Early Christian Rhetoric*, 1964; W. Beardslee, *Literary Criticism of the NT*, 1970, and studies of the history of dogma.

As a scholarly discipline, "introduction" has existed in the contemporary sense only since the Enlightenment. The main stages of its development are as follows:

1. The ancient church and that of the Middle Ages only rarely expressed interest in historical questions about the authorship of the NT books in connection with questions about the canon (prologues to the Pauline books and the Gospels, Muratorian Canon, Origen, Dionysius of Alexandria). The *Introductores scripturae divinae* collected by Cassiodorus (Tyconius, Augustine, Adrianos, who wrote an *Introduction to the Divine Scriptures ca.* 450, Eucherius, Junilius Africanus) are concerned with questions of exegesis rather than of introduction.

2. Since the Reformation period there have appeared studies of the origins of the canonical NT books written on the basis of dogmatic or polemical interests—especially in the Catholic church.

3. Starting with text-critical studies, the Oratorian Richard Simon opened the way for introduction to the NT as a scholarly discipline with his three books on the *Histoire critique* of the NT (1689-93). In striving to recover the original text of the NT, he posed questions about the manuscript tradition and the origin of the individual writings. The first great work of introduction in which the problems of the origin of the various writings and of the canon were handled in a consciously historical manner, although with the aim of defending the canon, was produced by rationalism: J. D. Michaelis, *Einleitung in die göttlichen Schriften des Neuen Bundes* (1750), [4]1788, stimulated by R. Simon. (An English translation of the 4th ed. by Herbert Marsh, *Introduction to the NT,* was published in 1793; [2]1802.) At the same time J. S. Semler traced the historical origin of the canon in his *Abhandlung von freier Untersuchung des Canon* (1771-75). The first really free investigation of the origin of the canonical Scriptures and of the NT text was provided by J. G. Eichorn's five-volume *Einleitung in das NT* (1804-27). With different handling of similar critical standards, there followed the works of De Wette, Schleiermacher, Credner, Reuss, Hug, and others.

4. The science of introduction received a new direction from F. C. Baur and his Tübingen School (A. Schwegler, E. Zeller, A. Hilgenfeld, A. Ritschl [in his beginning stages]). Baur defined "introduction" as criticism of the canon, or as scholarly research on the origin and the original character of the canonical Scriptures. The formation of the individual NT Scriptures is to be conceived in broad relation with the conceptual conflicts of the apostolic and postapostolic periods and their resolution in the unity of

early Catholicism. The foundation of Baur's view of history is the schema borrowed from Hegelian logic: thesis, antithesis, synthesis. Baur thought that the apostolic age was dominated by the opposition between the narrow-minded Jewish-Christianity of the original apostles and the law-free, universalistic gospel of Paul. In the post-apostolic period the opposition was eased: through concessions and compromises the two parties came closer together and united on a middle way over against the Gnosticism and Montanism of the second century. The ambiguous designation "tendency-criticism" [*Tendenzkritik*] meant to the Tübingen critical school that it considered each NT scripture to have been written on the basis of a specific tendency. Witnesses to a pure Pauline gospel are Gal, Cor, Rom; Rev is a monument to the rigid Ebionitism of the original apostles. Only these five writings are genuine. In the Synoptic Gospels and Acts the unifying tendency is making its appearance; they belong to the period of mediation and smoothing out of differences. The synthesis and the peaceful resolution is perfected in Jn. Baur's *Kirchengeschichte der 3 ersten Jahrhunderte* (1853), [3]1863 (tr. and ed. A. Menzies, *Church History of the First Three Centuries*, 1878-89) offers a comprehensive presentation of his theory. Baur's overall constructive point of view, already modified in many ways by his pupils, has not stood the test of time. The majority of his literary hypotheses fared no better; only the so-called "radical critics" who contested the Pauline authorship of even his major letters—at least in their traditional form—attempted to surpass them. (See on this A. Jülicher, *Einleitung in das NT*, [7]1931, 22 ff.) From Baur's work there has survived the basic recognition that the literature of primitive Christianity can be studied only in closest association with the external and internal history of early Christianity.

5. Since that time and down to the present, the scholarly discipline of introduction has developed among German-speaking Protestants partly along critical, partly along conservative lines: H. J. Holtzmann, *Lehrbuch der historisch-kritischen Einleitung in das NT* (1885), [3]1892 (comprehensive presentation of the entire work of the nineteenth century); A. Jülicher, *Einleitung in das NT* (1894), [7]1931 (rev. in collaboration with E. Fascher); R. Knopf, *Einführung in das NT* (1919), [5]1949, ed. H. Weinel and H. Lietzmann; O. Pfleiderer, *Das Urchristentum, seine Schriften und Lehren* (1886), [2]1902 (tr. as *Primitive Christianity* by W. Montgomery, rp. 1965); A. Harnack, *Geschichte der altchristlichen Literatur* I, 1893, II, 1897; B. Weiss, *Lehrbuch der Einleitung in das NT* (1886), [3]1897; Th. Zahn, *Einleitung in das NT* (1897-

99), [3]1906-7; *idem, Grundriss der Einleitung in das NT*, 1928;
C. R. Gregory, *Einleitung in das NT*, 1909; F. Barth, *Einleitung
in das NT* (1908), [4/5]1921; P. Feine, *Einleitung in das NT* (1913),
[7]1935, since [8]1936 rev. J. Behm, [9]1950; H. Appel, *Einleitung in
das NT*, 1922; W. Michaelis, *Einleitung in das NT* (1946), [3]1961
(with suppl. vol.); M. Albertz, *Die Botschaft des NT* I, 1, 1947;
I, 2, 1952; W. Marxsen, *Einleitung in das NT. Eine Einführung in
ihre Probleme*, 1963 (Eng. tr., *Introduction to the NT*, 1968).

For the general reader: A. Schlatter, *Einleitung in die Bibel*
(1889), [5]1933; Herm von Soden, *Urchristliche Literaturgeschichte*,
1905; M. Dibelius, *Geschichte der urchristlichen Literatur* I, II,
1926; K. Koch, *Das Buch der Bücher. Die Entstehungsgeschichte
der Bibel*, 1963; G. Haufe, *Vom Werden und Verstehen des NTs*,
1968; G. Bornkamm, *Bibel. Das NT*, Themen der Theologie 9, 1971.

Among English and American works, the following may be
mentioned: B. W. Bacon, *An Introduction to the NT*, 1900; J.
Moffatt, *An Introduction to the Literature of the NT* (1911),
[3]1918; A. H. McNeile, *An Introduction to the Study of the NT*
(1927), [2]1953, ed. C. S. C. Williams; E. F. Scott, *The Literature of
the NT*, 1932; E. J. Goodspeed, *An Introduction to the NT*, 1937;
idem, New Chapters in NT Study, 1937; K. and S. Lake, *An Introduction to the NT*, 1938; F. B. Clogg, *An Introduction to the
NT*, 1937; M. S. Enslin, *Christian Beginnings*, 1938; D. Guthrie,
NT Introduction I, *The Pauline Epistles*, 1961; II, *Hebrews to
Revelation*, 1962; III, *The Gospels and Acts*, 1965; C. F. D. Moule,
The Birth of the NT, HNTC, Companion Vol. I, 1962; R. M.
Grant, *A Historical Introduction to the NT*, 1964; E. F. Harrison,
Introduction to the NT, 1964; A. F. J. Klijn, *An Introduction to
the NT*, 1967; R. H. Fuller, *A Critical Introduction to the NT*,
1966.

For general readership: D. W. Riddle–H. H. Hutson, *NT Life
and Literature*, 1946; R. Heard, *An Introduction to the NT*, 1950;
T. Henshaw, *NT Literature in the Light of Modern Scholarship*
(1952), [2]1957; H. F. D. Sparks, *The Formation of the NT*, 1952.

Among works in French: F. Godet, *Introduction au NT*, 1893 ff
(German ed. by E. Reineck I, 1894, II, 1, 1905); M. Goguel,
Introduction au NT I-IV, 1/2, 1922-26 (incomplete).—Among
Dutch works: J. de Zwaan, *Inleiding tot het NT* I-III (1941/42),
[2]1948.—Among Italian works: F. Lo Bue, *Che cosa è il NT?* 1954.

Catholic literature: R. Cornely, *Introductionis in Sacram Script-
uram compendium . . . novis curis retractavit* A. Merk II: *Introductio specialis in singulos Novi Testamenti libros*, [12]1940; A. Schaefer,
Einleitung in das NT (1898), rev. M. Meinertz ([4]1933), [5]1950;

F. Gutjahr, *Einleitung zu den heiligen Schriften des NT*, [6/7]1923; J. Belser, *Einleitung in das NT*, [2]1905; E. Jacquier, *Histoire des livres du NT* I-IV, [6-11]1928-35; J. Sickenberger, *Kurzgefasste Einleitung in das NT* (1916), [5/6]1939; H. J. Vogels, *Grundriss der Einleitung in das NT*, 1925; H. Höpfl–B. Gut, *Introductionis in sacros utriusque Testamenti libros compendium*, Vol. III: *Introductio specialis in NT* ([4]1938), [6]1962, curavit A. Metzinger; P. Gaechter, *Summa Introductionis in NT*, 1938; K. Th. Schäfer, *Grundriss der Einleitung in das NT* (1938), [2]1952; A. Wikenhauser, *Einleitung in das NT* (1953), [4]1961, slightly rev. by A. Vögtle (tr. into English by J. Cunningham, 1958, from 2nd ed.); B. Mariani, *Introductio in Libros Sacros Novi Testamenti*, 1962; *Introduction à la Bible*, ed. A. Robert and A. Feuillet, 1959; K. H. Schelkle, *Das NT. Seine literarische und theologische Geschichte* 1963, [3]1966; A. Vögtle, *Das NT und die neuere kath. Exegese. I Grundlegende Fragen zur Entstehung und Eigenart des NT*, 1966; W. J. Harrington, *Record of the Fulfilment: The NT*, 1968; *Gestalt und Anspruch des NT*, ed. J. Schreiner in collaboration with G. Dautzenberg, 1969 (cited as GANT).

6. Research in the nineteenth century was largely dominated by the literary-critical approach, with its inquiries about the sources and literary links of the NT writings. But alongside this approach, building on the ideas of Herder and of Old Testament scholarship, there developed the literary-historical approach, which devoted its attention to the literary forms and stylistic patterns in the NT. In this investigation of the history of the literary forms and of the tradition, the objective concern was not with the literary achievement of the individual writers but with the prehistory of the form of the material as they received it, with the preliterary growth of the primitive Christian tradition on the analogy of the development of folk tradition in general, and with the precipitate of traditional forms in primitive Christian writings. Work on the literary history of the NT, which was influenced by the Old Testament scholar H. Gunkel (see RGG[3] II, 1958, 1908 f; WGK, NT, 330, n. 405), by such theologians as G. Heinrici (*Der literarische Charakter der Nt. Schriften*, 1908), A. Deissmann (*Light from the Ancient East*, tr. L. Strachan, 1910), and by ancient-history scholars such as U. von Wilamowitz ("Die griech. Literatur des Altertums," in *Die Kultur der Gegenwart* I, 8 [1905], [4]1924), E. Norden (*Die antike Kunstprosa* [1898], [2]1909-15; *idem, Agnostos Theos* [1913], [2]1926), is still at the beginning stages. The comprehensive studies (see bibl. in §2) are still inadequate. Consideration of the form- and tradition-history is essential for understanding early Christian litera-

ture as an expression of the life of primitive Christianity, and for an insight into its religious motivations. But form-history will never render superfluous critical, historical scholarship, the aim of which is a comprehensive history of the formation of a literature.

Corresponding to the historical-critical method, which is the only valid approach to the discipline of introduction, it would seem to be appropriate to reconstruct the historical development of the individual NT writings in chronological sequence, beginning with the Pauline letters (thus, e.g., Jülicher, Meinertz, Marxsen). But since a sure date can be given for almost none of the other NT writings, it seems wise on the ground of objectivity to stay with the order as given in the NT canon, except to take Lk and Acts, Jude and II Pet together, and to proceed chronologically with the genuine Pauline letters.

PART ONE

The Formation of the New Testament Writings

A. THE NARRATIVE BOOKS

I. The Synoptic Gospels and the Acts

§4. GOSPEL AND GOSPELS

On the concept "gospel," cf. J. Schniewind, *Euangelion. Ursprung und erste Gestalt des Begriffs Ev.*, BFChTh II, 13, 25, I, 1927, II, 1931; G. Friedrich, TDNT II, 1964, 721 ff; R. Asting, *Die Verkündigung des Wortes im Urchristentum*, 1939, 300 ff; J. Huby–X. Léon-Dufour, *L'Évangile et les Évangiles*, 1954; W. Marxsen, *Mark, the Evangelist*, 1969, 117 ff; H. Köster, *Synoptische Überlieferung bei den apostolischen Vätern*, TU 65, 1957, 6 ff; Bauer, 318; W. Schmauch, EKL II, 1956, 1213 ff; J. Schmid, LThK III, 1959, 1255 ff; P. Stuhlmacher, *Das paulinische Evangelium I. Vorgeschichte*, FRLANT 95, 1968 (bibl.).—On the literary form, cf. K. L. Schmidt, "Die Stellung der Evv. in der allgemeinen Literaturgeschichte," in *Eucharisterion*, Studies Presented to H. Gunkel, 1923, II, 50 ff; M. Albertz, *Die Botschaft des NT* I, 1947, 165 ff; G. Bornkamm, art. "Evangelien," in RGG[3] II, 1958, 749 ff (bibl.); R. V. G. Tasker, *The Nature and Purpose of the Gospels* (1944), [7]1962; G. Theissen, in R. Bultmann, *Geschichte der synoptischen Tradition*, suppl. vol., [4]1971, 124 f. (Eng. tr. by J. Marsh, *History of the Synoptic Tradition*, 1963).

Gospel (τὸ εὐαγγέλιον; also plural τὰ εὐαγγέλια) means in Greek, "reward for bringing [good] news," but also "the good news" itself. *Euangelion* achieved religious significance in the imperial cult above all; the appearance of the divine world-ruler, the inauguration of his reign, his decrees are tidings of joy (see TDNT II, 721 ff). Concerning the birthday of Augustus one reads in a calendar inscription of *ca.* 9 B.C. from Priene in Asia Minor (text from Stuhlmacher, p. 186): ἦρξεν δὲ τῷ κόσμῳ τῶν δι' αὐτὸν εὐαγγελί[ων ἡ γενέθλιος ἡμέρα] τοῦ θεοῦ="The birthday of the god was for the world the beginning of tidings of joy which have been proclaimed for his sake."

In the NT, gospel has the special meaning of "message of salvation." It is based on the verb εὐαγγελίζεσθαι, in Hebrew *bissar*, "to announce the news of salvation," Isa 40:9; 52:7; 61:1; Ps 96:2. For Second Isaiah there was a firm link with the messenger of God who proclaimed the joyous eschatological message of the inbreaking of God's royal rule. In Jesus' word (Mt 11:5) "gospel" —in direct dependence on Third Isaiah—is the message of the salvation which he himself brings. Elsewhere in the NT, and especially in Paul, "gospel" means the proclamation concerning Christ and the redemption which has come in him: Rom 1:1 ff; I Cor 15:1 ff, etc. Always in the NT, *euangelion* is the living word of preaching, corresponding to "evangelist" as the designation for the itinerant preachers: Acts 21:8; Eph 4:11; II Tim 4:5. Accordingly, *euangelion* always appears in the singular; at the beginning of the second century when εὐαγγέλιον came to be the designation for the written message of salvation, (Did 15:3; II Clem 8:5) the phrase is ἐν τῷ εὐαγγελίῳ. Justin (*Apol.* 66.3) for the first time used the plural for the writings which treat of the words and deeds, the passion and resurrection of Jesus (ἐν τοῖς . . . ἀπομνημονεύμασιν, ἃ καλεῖται εὐαγγέλια), but even then the conception still remains living that what is involved is a message of good news. So by the end of the second century an individual gospel book is designated as εὐαγγέλιον κατὰ Ἰωάννην ($\mathfrak{P}^{66}$; Iren., *Haer.* III. 11. 10), or one speaks of the *tertium evangelii librum* ("third book of the Gospels") (Muratorian Canon, 2). In the third century we find for the first time "evangelist" in the sense of "the author of a gospel" (Hippolytus, Tertullian; see TDNT II, 736 ff). In view of the presupposed unity of the gospel, Tatian —as late as 170—could be the first to write a harmony of the Gospels, the Diatessaron (see below §38.2a, and B. M. Metzger, RGG³ II, 769 f).

The order of the Gospels varies in the ancient church, in canon lists and in manuscripts. The customary order was probably conceived chronologically. It is found in the Muratorian Canon, in Origen, Irenaeus, etc., in most Greek and Syriac MSS. In D, W, and the Old Latin version of the NT (Vetus Latina), the Gospels connected with the name of an apostle stand first: Mt, Jn, Lk, Mk. For further variations in the order see E. Nestle–E. von Dobschütz, *Einführung in das Griech. NT*, ⁴1923, 9.

The first three Gospels are grouped under the name *Synoptics* (from σύνοψις, "to view at the same time"). The name was introduced in 1776 by J. J. Griesbach in his *Synopse*, where the parallel texts of the first three Gospels are printed beside one another for comparison (see WGK, NT, 75 f). In fact, this threefold tradition demanded such a comprehensive perspective in order for it to be recognized and evaluated in its unity and its diversities.

In the Synoptic Gospels we meet for the first time a new and distinctive literary genus. Viewed as a literary form, the Gospels are a new creation. They are in no way lives after the manner of Hellenistic biographies, since they lack the sense of internal and external history (as in lives of heroes), of character formation, of temporal sequence, and of the contemporary setting. Neither do the Gospels belong to the genre, memoirs, in which the collected stories and sayings from the lives of great men are simply strung together. Nor do they belong to the genus, miracle stories, in which the great deeds of ancient wonder-workers are glorified in a more or less stylized manner. The aim of the Gospels is not recollection about Jesus nor glorification of his miracles—these form only one aspect among others of the Gospels' content—but the main concern is rather to evoke faith and to strengthen it. Jesus' words and deeds are brought together from out of his life and reproduced in the form of a simple narrative in order to show to the early Christian church the ground of its faith and to provide firm support in its mission for preaching, instruction, and debate with its opponents. The Gospels are books for use in the community: for reading the Scriptures in worship. They are missionary writings in which the authors have wholly retreated behind the subject matter, even when they give expression to their theology in the form of a gospel. We are concerned with popular writings [*Kleinliteratur*] rather than with sophisticated literature [*Hochliteratur*], so that Justin's designation of the Gospels as "apostolic memoirs" (Just., *Apol.* 66. 3) is a misunderstanding by that onetime philosopher.

The Apocryphal Gospels stand more strongly under the influence of Hellenistic literary forms. This is less true of the older ones of which only fragments have survived than of the more recent Apocryphal Gospels such as the Protevangelium of James and the Infancy Gospel of Thomas, etc. The texts are accessible in the best form in C. von Tischendorf, *Evangelia Apocrypha*, [2]1876; E. Klostermann, *Apocrypha* I, [2]1908 and II, [3]1929 (=H. Lietzmann, *Kleine Texte* 3 and 8); H. B. Swete, *Zwei neue Evangelienfragmente*, 1908 (= *Kleine Texte* 31). English translation in E. Hennecke–W. Schneemelcher, ed. and tr. R. McL. Wilson, *NT Apocrypha*, I, 1963, II, 1965. See further J. Michl, art. "Apokryphe Evangelien," LThK III, 1959, 1217 ff (bibl.).

§5. The Synoptic Problem

Synopses: the most practical are: A. Huck, *Synopse der drei ersten Evv.*, [9]1936 (completely rev. by H. Lietzmann); K. Aland, *Synopsis quattuor evangeliorum* (1964), [5]1967; cf. further W. Rushbrooke, *Synopticon*, 1880 (very easy to survey, in multicolored print) and B. de Solages, *Greek Synopsis of the Gospels*, 1959 (contains in addition to the synopsis arranged according to the existing parallels, a complex analysis of the linguistic usage of each pericope. On this cf. J. Schmid, BZ, NF 5, 1961, 136 ff; P. Benoit, RB 67, 1960, 93 ff). Good schematic surveys in color are provided by J. Weiss, *Synpt. Tafeln zu den drei älteren Evv*, [3]1929, rev. R. Schütz; A. Barr, *A Diagram of Synoptic Relationships*, 1938; X. Léon-Dufour, *Concordance of the Synoptic Gospels*, 1957; W. R. Farmer, *Synopticon: The Verbal Agreement Between the Greek Texts of Matthew, Mark and Luke Contextually Exhibited*, 1969 (offers the texts of the three Synpt. successively with colored markings identifying agreement in wording). Good synoptic tables in Huck-Lietzmann, *Synopse*, XIII ff (based on this is *Gospel Parallels*, ed. B. Throckmorton, 1949); W. Michaelis, *Einl.*, 86 ff; Aland, *Synopsis*, 551 ff. Important linguistic-statistical aids in J. C. Hawkins, *Horae Synopticae*, [2]1909, above all in R. Morgenthaler, *Statistische Synopse*, 1971 (with synoptic statistics of wording of the three Synpt. and the sequence of sentences and pericopes).

Studies:
On the History of the Synoptic Problem: The works cited below by Holtzmann, Fascher, Grobel, Vaganay, Farmer, further J. Schniewind, ThR, NF 2, 1930, 134 ff; J. Schmid, ThRv 52, 1956, 49 ff; X. Léon-Dufour, RechSR 42, 1954, 549 ff; 46, 1958, 237 ff; J. Heuschen, RechB II, 1957, 11 ff; O. E. Evans, "Synoptic Criticism Since Streeter," ExpT 72, 1960/61, 295 ff.
On Source Analysis and Literary Criticism: H. J. Holtzmann, *Die synpt. Evv.*, 1863; P. Wernle, *Die synpt. Frage*, 1899; J. Wellhausen, *Einleitung in die drei ersten Evv.*, [2]1911; A. Harnack, *Sprüche und Reden Jesu; Beiträge zur Einleitung in das NT*, II 1907; B. H. Streeter, *The Four Gospels*, 1924; W. Bussmann, *Synopt. Studien* I 1925, II, 1929, III, 1931; V. Taylor, *Behind the Third Gospel*, 1926; *idem*, "The Order of Q," JTS, NS 4, 1953, 27 ff (=V. T., *NT Essays*, 1970, 90 ff); *idem*, "The Proto-Luke Hypothesis," ExpT 67, 1955/56, 12 ff; *idem*, "Methods of Gospel Criticism," ExpT 71, 1959/60, 68 ff; *idem*, "The Original Order of Q," *NT Essays in Memory of T. W. Manson*, 1959, 246 ff (=V. T., *NT Essays*, 1970, 95 ff); J. Schmid, "Mt und Lk. Eine Untersuchung des Verhältnisses ihrer Evv.," BSt 23, 2-4, 1930; *idem*, "Mk und der aram. Mt," SStW, 148 ff (=J. B. Bauer, *Evangelienforschung*, 1968, 75 ff); J. Schmid, art. "Synoptiker," LThK IX, 1964, 1240 ff; J. Jeremias, "Zur Hypothese einer schriftlichen Logienquelle," ZNW 29, 130, 147 ff (=Abba, 90 ff); C. C. Torrey, *The Four Gospels*, 1933; J. H. Ropes,

The Synoptic Gospels, 1934; K. Grobel, *Formgeschichte und synpt. Quellenanalyse*, FRLANT, NF 35, 1937; E. Hirsch, *Frühgeschichte des Ev.* I, *Das Werden des Mk* (1940), 1951; II, *Die Vorlagen des Lk und das Sondergut des Mt*, 1941 (on this see E. Haenchen, ThLZ 67, 1942, 129 ff); M. Lehmann, *Synoptische Quellenanalyse und die Frage nach dem historischen Jesus. Kriterien des Jesusforschung untersucht in Auseinandersetzung mit E. Hirschs Frühgeschichte des Evangeliums*, Bh. ZNW 38, 1970); B. H. Throckmorton, "Did Mark Know Q?" JBL 67, 1948, 319 ff; B. P. W. Stather Hunt, *Primitive Gospel Sources*, 1951; A. M. Perry, "The Growth of the Gospels," IntB VII, 1951, 60 ff; B. C. Butler, *The Originality of St. Matthew*, 1951; P. Parker, *The Gospel Before Mark*, 1953; H. Helmbold, *Vorsynpt. Evv.*, 1953 (on this see P. Winter, ZRGG 6, 1954, 355 ff and P. Vielhauer, Gn 26, 1954, 460 ff): H. G. Wood, "The Priority of Mark," ExpT 65, 1953/54, 17 ff; F. Bussby, "Is Q an Aramaic Document?" *ibid.*, 272 ff; J. Levie, "L'évangile araméen de S. Matthieu est-il la source de l'évangile de S. Marc?" NRTh 76, 1954, 689 ff, 812 ff; L. Vaganay, *Le problème synoptique*, 1954 (on this see J. Schmid, ThRv 52, 1956, 56 ff and P. Vielhauer, ThLZ 80, 1955, 647 ff); E. L. Bradby, "In Defence of Q," ExpT 68, 1956/57, 315 ff; A. M. Farrer, "On Dispensing with Q," StG, 1957, 55 ff; *La formation des évangiles*, RechB II, 1957 (contains essays by L. Cerfaux, J. Levie, J. W. Doeve, X. Léon-Dufour, N. van Bohemen); F. C. Grant, *The Gospels: Their Origin and Their Growth*, 1957; W. L. Knox, *The Sources of the Synoptic Gospels* I, *St. Mark*, 1953; II, *St. Luke and St. Matthew*, 1957 (on this see R. Bultmann, Gn 30, 1958, 274 ff); G. Bornkamm, art. "Evangelien, synpt.," RGG³ II, 1958, 753 ff (bibl.); Cassian, "The Interrelation of the Gospels: Matthew-Luke-John," StEv I, TU 73, 1958, 129 ff; N. Turner, "The Minor Verbal Agreements of Mt and Lk Against Mark," *ibid.*, 223 ff; *idem*, "Q in Recent Thought," ExpT 80, 1968/69, 324 ff; H. E. Tödt, *Der Menschensohn in der synpt. Überlieferung*, 1959, 215 ff (on Q); S. Petrie, " 'Q' Is Only What You Make It," NovTest 3, 1959, 28 ff; J. P. Brown, "An Early Revision of the Gospel of Mark," JBL 78, 1959, 215 ff; *idem*, "Mark as Witness to an Edited Form of Q," JBL 80, 1961, 29 ff; T. R. Rosché, "The Words of Jesus and the Future of the 'Q' Hypothesis," JBL 79, 1960, 210 ff; H. Schürmann, "Sprachliche Reminiszenzen an abgeänderte oder ausgelassene Bestandteile der Spruchsammlung im Lk und Mt," NTS 6, 1959/60, 193 ff (=Sch., Tr.U., 111 ff); W. R. Farmer, "A 'Skeleton in the Closet' of Gospel Research," BR 6, 1961, 18 ff; *idem*, "Notes on a Literary and Form-Critical Analysis of Some of the Synoptic Material Peculiar to Luke," NTS 8, 1961/62, 301 ff; *idem*, *The Synoptic Problem: A Critical Analysis*, 1964 (on this see F. W. Beare, JBL 84, 1965, 295 ff; M. Rese, VF 12, 1967, Part 2, 34 ff); W. R. Farmer, "The Two-Document Hypothesis as a Methodological Criterion in Synoptic Research," ATR 48, 1966, 380 ff; *idem*, " 'The Lachmann Fallacy,' " NTS 14, 1967/68, 441 ff; A. W. Argyle, "Agree-

ments Between Matthew and Luke," ExpT 73, 1961/62, 19 ff; *idem,*
"Evidence for the View That St. Luke Used St. Matthew's Gospel,"
JBL 83, 1964, 390 ff; R. North, "Chenoboskion and Q," CBQ 24,
1962, 154 ff; F. W. Beare, *The Earliest Records of Jesus,* 1962; M.
Styler, "The Priority of Mark," in C. F. D. Moule, *The Birth of the
NT,* 1962, 223 ff; N. B. Stonehouse, *Origins of the Synoptic Gospels:
Some Basic Questions,* 1963; R. L. Lindsey, "A Modified Two-Docu-
ment Theory of the Synoptic Dependence and Interdependence," Nov-
Test 6, 1963, 239 ff; J. M. Robinson, "ΛΟΓΟΙ ΣΟΦΩΝ, Zur Gattung
der Spruchquelle Q," *Zeit und Geschichte, Festschr. R. Bultmann,*
1964, 77 ff, expanded in *Trajectories Through Early Christianity,* 1972,
71 ff; E. M. Dalmau, *A Study on the Synoptic Gospels,* 1964; Št.
Porúbčan, "Form Criticism and the Synoptic Problem," NovTest 7,
1964/65, 81 ff; F. G. Downing, "Towards the Rehabilitation of
Q," NTS 11, 1964/65, 169 ff; R. T. Simpson, "The Major Agreements
of Matthew and Luke Against Mark," NTS 12, 1965/66, 273 ff; F.
Rehkopf, art. "Synpt.," BhHw III, 1966, 1910 ff; W. Wilkens, "Zur
Frage der literarischen Beziehung zwischen Matthäus und Lukas,"
NovTest 8, 1966, 48 ff; J. Lambrecht, "Die Logia-Quellen von Markus
13," Bb 47, 1966, 321 ff; M.-E. Boismard, "Évangile des Ébionites et
problème synoptique (Mc 1,2-6 et par.)," RB 73, 1966, 321 ff; N.
H. Palmer, "Lachmann's Argument," NTS 13, 1966/67, 368 ff; *idem,
The Logic of Gospel Criticism,* 1968, 112 ff; X. Léon-Dufour, "In-
terprétation des Évangiles et problème synoptique," *Festschr. Coppens,*
17 ff; S. McLoughlin, "Le problème synoptique. Vers la théorie des
deux sources. Les accords mineurs," *Festschr. Coppens,* 41 ff; H. Meynell,
"The Synoptic Problem: Some Unorthodox Solutions," *Theology* 70,
1967, 386 ff; H. Ph. West, "A Primitive Version of Luke in the
Composition of Matthew," NTS 14, 1967/68, 75 ff; A. M. Honoré,
"A Statistic Study of the Synoptic Problem," NovTest 10, 1968,
95 ff; E. P. Sanders, "The Argument from Order and the Relationship Between Matthew and Luke," NovTest 10, 1968, 95 ff; *idem,
The Tendencies of the Synoptic Tradition,* SNTSMS 9, 1969; D.
Lührmann, *Die Redaktion der Logienquelle,* WMANT 33, 1969; P.
Hoffmann, "Die Anfänge der Theologie in der Logienquelle," GANT,
134 ff; E. Bammel, "Das Ende von Q," *Verborum Veritas, Festschr.
G. Stählin,* 1970, 39 ff; A. Gaboury, *La structure des évangiles synop-
tiques. La structure-type à l'origine des Synoptiques,* Suppl. NovTest
22, 1970; H. C. Kee, *Jesus in History: An Approach to the Study of
the Gospels,* 1970; D. L. Dungan, "Mark—The Abridgement of
Matthew and Luke," *Perspective* I, 51 ff; J. A. Fitzmyer, "The
Priority of Mark and the 'Q' Source in Luke," *Perspective* I, 131 ff;
C. E. Carlston and D. Norlin, "Once More—Statistics and Q," HTR
64, 1971, 59 ff; A. Fuchs, "Sprachliche Untersuchungen zu Mt and
Lk. Ein Beitrag zur Quellenkritik," AnBibl 49, 1971.

On the Problems of Oral Tradition and Form Criticism: Bibliography:
E. Fascher, *Die formgeschichtliche Methode,* Bh. ZNW 2, 1924; P.

Benoit, "Réflexions sur la 'Formgeschichtliche Methode,'" RB 53, 1946, 481 ff; G. Bornkamm, see §4; G. Iber, "Zur Formgeschichte der Evv.," ThR, NF 24, 1956/57, 283 ff; J. Heuschen, see above; J. de la Potterie, Introduction to *Festschr. Coppens.*—Most important lit.: Th. Soiron, "Die Logia Jesu," NTA 6, 4, 1916; M. Dibelius, *From Tradition to Gospel,* 1935; idem, "Zur Formgeschichte der Evv.," ThR, NF I, 1929, 185 ff; K. L. Schmidt, *Der Rahmen der Geschichte Jesu,* 1919; R. Bultmann, *The History of the Synoptic Tradition,* 1963; idem, *Die Erforschung der synpt. Evv.* (1925), Aus der Welt der Religion, NF I, ³1960 (=R. B., *Glauben und Verstehen* IV, 1965, 1 ff); M. Albertz, *Die synpt. Streitgespräche,* 1921; G. Bertram, *Die Leidensgeschichte Jesu und der Christuskult,* FRLANT, NF 15, 1922; O. Perels, *Die Wunderüberlieferung der Synpt. in ihrem Verhältnis zur Wortüberlieferung,* 1934; V. Taylor, *The Formation of the Gospel Tradition,* 1933; R. H. Lightfoot, *History and Interpretation in the Gospels,* 1935; E. B. Redlich, *Form Criticism,* 1939; L. J. McGinley, *Form Criticism of the Synoptic Healing Narratives,* 1944; G. Schille, "Bemerkungen zur Formgeschichte des Ev.," NTS 4, 1957/58, 1 ff, 101 ff; 5, 1958/59, 1 ff; idem, "Der Mangel eines kritischen Geschichtsbildes in der nt. Formgeschichte," ThLZ 88, 1963, 491 ff; H. Riesenfeld, *The Gospel Tradition and Its Beginnings. A Study in the Limits of 'Formgeschichte,'* 1957 (=H. R., *The Gospel Tradition,* 1970, 1 ff); D. E. Nineham, "Eye-Witness Testimony and the Gospel Tradition," JTS, NS 9, 1958, 13 ff, 243 ff; NS 11, 1960, 253 ff; C. F. D. Moule, "The Intention of the Evangelists," *NT Essays in Memory of T. W. Manson,* 1959, 165 ff; R. Schnackenburg, art. "Formgeschichtliche Methode," LThK IV, 1960, 211 ff; idem, "Zur formgeschichtlichen Methode in der Evangelienforschung," ZKTh 85, 1963, 16 ff (= *Evangelienforschung,* ed. J. B. Bauer, 1968, 33 ff); B. Gerhardsson, *Memory and Manuscript,* ASNU 22, 1961, 253 ff (on this see M. Smith, JBL 82, 1963, 169 ff); B. Gerhardsson, *Tradition and Transmission in Early Christianity,* CN 20, 1964; A. Wilder, "Form-History and the Oldest Tradition," *Neotestamentica et Patristica, Freundesgabe O. Cullmann,* NovTest Suppl. 6, 1962, 3 ff; W. D. Davies, "Reflections on a Scandinavian Approach to 'The Gospel Tradition,'" *ibid.,* 14 ff (=W. D. D., *The Setting of the Sermon on the Mount,* 1964, 464 ff); E. Jüngel, "Paulus und Jesus," *Hermeneutische Untersuchungen zur Theologie* 2, 1962, 290 ff; J. Jeremias, *The Parables of Jesus,* 1963; G. Widengren, "Tradition and Literature in Early Judaism and in the Early Church," *Numen* 10, 1963, 42 ff; J. P. Brown, "Synoptic Parallels in the Epistles and Form-History," NTS 10, 1963/64, 27 ff; K. Koch, *Was ist Formgeschichte? Neue Wege der Bibelexegese,* 1964 (English translation, *The Growth of the Biblical Tradition,* 1969); V. Taylor, "Formgeschichte," ExpT 75, 1963/64, 356 ff; J. J. Vincent, "Did Jesus Teach His Disciples to Learn by Heart?" StEv III, TU 88, 1964, 105 ff; J. Rohde, *Rediscovering the Teaching of the Evangelists,* 1968; H. Zimmermann, *Nt. Methodenlehre. Darstellung der historisch-*

kritischen Methode, 1967, 128 ff, 214 ff; S. Schulz, *Die Stunde der Botschaft. Einführung in die Theologie der vier Evangelisten*, 1967; J. Blank, *Paulus und Jesus. Eine theologische Grundlegung*, StANT 18, 1968, 45 ff; N. Palmer, *The Logic* (see above), 163 ff; W. Wiefel, "Vätersprüche und Herrenworte," NovTest 11, 1969, 105 ff; E. V. McKnight, *What Is Form Criticism?* 1969; R. H. Stein, "What is Redaktionsgeschichte?" JBL 88, 1969, 45 ff; *idem*, "The 'Redaktions-geschichtlich' Investigation of a Markan Seam (Mk 1:21 f)," ZNW 61, 1970, 70 ff; J. Schreiber, *Die Markuspassion. Wege zur Erforschung der Leidensgeschichte Jesu*, 1969; W. G. Doty, "The Discipline and Literature of NT Form Criticism," ATR 51, 1969, 257 ff; N. Perrin, *What Is Redaction Criticism?* 1969; A. J. B. Higgins, "The Source of the Tradition about Jesus," in A. J. B. H., *The Tradition about Jesus*, SJT Occasional Papers 15, 1969, 1 ff; E. Güttgemanns, *Offene Fragen zur Formgeschichte des Ev. Eine methodische Skizze der Grund-lagenproblematik der Form- und Redaktionsgeschichte*, BevTh 54, 1970; J. Carmignac, "Studies in the Hebrew Background of the Synoptic Gospels," ASTI 7, 1970, 64 ff; G. Theissen in R. Bultmann, *Geschichte der Synoptischen Tradition*, suppl. vol., 1971, 9 ff (Eng. tr., *History of the Synoptic Tradition*, was published in 1963 and does not con-tain these supplemental remarks).

Comm. to Synpt. Gospels, see §41.

The synoptic problem is the question concerning the literary rela-tionship to one another of the three Synoptic Gospels: How can one explain the remarkable, complicated interrelationship of agreement and difference between Mk, Mt, and Lk? The situation is all the more striking in that Jn does not share in it.

1. The Problem

1. The content and the arrangement of the synoptic material are closely related. The course of the activity of Jesus is presented in a similar way. To the appearance of the Baptist are linked the baptism and temptation of Jesus as well as his appearance in public. Until the Passover at the time of his death, Jesus is active almost solely in Galilee, and his public activity is carried out in all the Gospels in the same sequence. Jesus' going to Jerusalem, his action there, and his trial are also described in quite similar fashion. All three accounts close with his crucifixion and resur-rection.

Mt and Lk have much more abundant material than Mk, but in their portrayal of the activity of Jesus all three of them con-verge again. In so doing they present no biography in the form of a continuous description, nor do they attempt to depict the personality of Jesus; rather, they give an account in colloquial language of the deeds and sayings of Jesus, together with the impact they made. The synoptic representation of Jesus consists of a mass of individual self-contained pieces of narrative and sayings material, which very frequently are placed beside each other with no chronological or spatial linking. At the same time, there are also sections which are in agreement, where items of similar content are placed together, e.g., the three controversy sayings (concerning forgiveness of sins, associating with sinners, and fasting): Mk 2:1-22 par.; the sabbath stories: Mk 2:23–3:6 par.; the parables: Mk 4 par. The sayings of Jesus in the Synoptics are very similar too, as distinct from Jn: there are no long discussions, but only short, sharply etched sayings, short speeches, and fragments of speeches, in addition to numerous parables.

2. The relationship extends even to details of style and language. In the pericope of the authority of Jesus (Mk 11:27 par.), in the narrative of the healing of the leper (Mk 1:40 par.), and in the eschatological discourse (Mk 13:5-8, 14-17, 28-32) large sections are word for word the same. Further examples are: Mk 8:34-36 par.; Mk 9:1 par.; Mk 10:13-15 par. The same holds true for texts for which there are parallels in only two of the Gospels (e.g., Mt 4:18-22a par. Mk 1:16-20a; Mk 1:21-25 par. Lk 4:31-35); above all is this true in the sayings sections which are found only in Mt and Lk (e.g., Mt 3:7b-10, 12 parallels Lk 3:7b-9, 17; Mt 23:37-39 par. Lk 13:34-35; Mt 11:4 ff par. Lk 7:22 ff). In many sections which are found in all three of the Gospels, two Gospels are in broad agreement while the third is divergent (e.g., Mt 20:24-28 par. Mk 10:41-45, against Lk 22:24-27; Mk 12:38-40 par. Lk 20:46 f, against Mt 23:6-13).[1]

3. On the basis of these agreements, the convincing conclusion seems to be that the Synoptics are in some way literarily dependent on one another. The situation is complicated, however, by the fact that the Gospels differ from one another sharply in both form and content. The infancy stories in Mt and Lk contradict each other in essential features: according to Mt, the birth story is told from the standpoint of Joseph; in Lk, from Mary's. In Mt, Jesus' family's residence is in Bethlehem; in Lk, it is in Nazareth. Neither the flight to Egypt (Mt 2:13 ff) nor the visit of the Magi (Mt 2:1 ff) is reported by Lk. The genealogy of Mt (1:1 ff) and that

---

[1] Further examples in W. R. Farmer, *Synoptic Problem*, 204 ff. Cf. also Farmer, *Synopticon*.

of Lk (3:23 ff) are wholly different, and the two are irreconcilable. Mk has none at all. Nor do the resurrection stories represent a unified tradition: Lk knows only the appearances of Jesus in Jerusalem; Mt reports them in Jerusalem and Galilee; Mk has no resurrection account at all. And of the material concerning the public activity of Jesus—of which Mt has twenty-five chapters, Lk has twenty-one, and Mk has only fifteen—there are differences at every step. Mk lacks almost completely the great sayings sections found in Mt (sermon on the mount, mission charge, woes on the Pharisees: Mt 5–7; 10; 23) as well as a portion of the parables. But in the parabolic material, even Mt and Lk diverge from each other. Mt presents the sayings material in his Gospel at various places in the form of addresses: sermon on the mount (5–7), mission address (10), first address to the Pharisees (12), the parables of the kingdom of heaven (13), the community address (18), the second address to the Pharisees (23), the eschatological discourse (24–25); by contrast, Lk lacks the greater part of the sayings material, but mingles it in with narrative, as in 6:20–8:3 and 9:51–18:14. Parts of the sermon on the mount are found in Lk in other settings and in other connections, but even so they are in wholly similar form. In comparison with Mt 5–7, Lk's sermon on the plain (6:20 ff) is strikingly short. Each of the three synoptists has material exclusively his own; this is especially true of Mt and Lk, while Mk has nothing of the infancy or resurrection stories. The special material of Mt and Lk is, however, closely tied in with material that they share in common, as in the sermon on the mount (Mt) and the sermon on the plain (Lk). In those pericopes which are found in all three Gospels, at times all three are in agreement, often Mt and Mk agree against Lk, and Mk and Lk against Mt, but sometimes also Mt and Lk agree against Mk.

How is this strange state of affairs to be explained?

2. The History of the Synoptic Problem

The real problem was first recognized in the second half of the eighteenth century. The ancient church and its opponents had already noticed the differences and contradictions among the Gospels,[1a] but the explanation was restricted to details. Augustine

---

[1a] See on this H. Merkel, *Die Widersprüche zwischen den Evv. Ihre polemische und apologetische Behandlung in der Alten Kirche bis zu Augustin*, WUNT 13, 1971, esp. 229 f.

was the first to develop ideas about the literary relationships between the various Gospels. In his *De consensu evangelistarum* I. 2 may be found historical observations about the Gospels: Augustine thought that the Gospels originated in the same order as they are found in the canon and that the later Gospels were not written without knowledge of the earlier ones, even though each one formulated the course of its narrative independently. His judgment that Mk was an abbreviation of Mt (*Marcus eum,* i.e., Mt, *subsecutus tamquam pedisequus et breviator eius videtur* ["Mark follows him (Mt) closely and seems to be his slave and epitomist"]) anticipated the synoptic criticism of the eighteenth century.

1. *The Primitive Gospel Hypothesis.* J. D. Michaelis thought he could explain the agreements between the Gospels by nothing else than their common use of "another apocryphal gospel" (*Einl.;* See above, §3.3; II, [3]1777, 793). Lessing was the first to advance the hypothesis [2] that our Gospels are different translations and excerpts of a very old, Aramaic apostolic writing, the Gospel of the Nazarenes, that Jerome found in the fourteenth century among a sect of the Nazarenes. This notion was given scholarly form by J. G. Eichhorn. In his book *Über die drei ersten Evangelien* [Concerning the first three Gospels] (1794), he first took the position that each evangelist had used the primitive gospel in a different form, but in his *Introduction* (*Einl. in das NT.* I, 1804), he reshaped his hypothesis independently (cf. WGK, *NT, 77* ff). He posited a primitive Aramaic gospel and derived from this writing nine different gospels, which together with other sources are supposed to underlie our present Gospels. Eichhorn's hypothesis was too artificial and worked with too many unknown factors to be able to find enduring acceptance in the form in which it was presented.[3] But its recognition that our canonical Gospels in specific instances represent the outcome of a prior literary process opened a new path, and the acknowledgement of a common source for Mt and Lk was the first insight into the necessity for a hypothesis about a sayings source.

2. *The Fragment or "Diēgēsis" Hypothesis.* H. E. G. Paulus had already assumed that Mt and Lk had grown out of depictions (memorabilia) of individual days in the career of Jesus. These ideas were taken up by Schleiermacher (*Über die Schriften des Lukas,*

---

[2] G. E. Lessing, *Theses aus der Kirchengeschichte,* 1776; *Neue Hypothesen über die Evangelisten als blos menschliche Geschichtsschreiber betrachtet,* 1778; both published posthumously; cf. WGK, NT, pp. 76 f.

[3] According to Št. Porúbčan all three Gospels are dependent on a Proto-Mk which originated *ca.* 36–40, rather than on each other.

ein kritischer Versuch, 1817). He conjectured that the original narrators—i.e., the apostles, as well as those who heard them—had sought to depict details of Jesus' words and acts. Outside of Palestine, a great yearning for such characterizations ("Diēgēses," as Schleiermacher called them) arose, as the first generation began to die off. These "depictors" soon became collectors. One collected miracle stories, another speeches, a third brought together accounts of the passion and resurrection. From these collections developed our Gospels. Here emerged the important insight that the Gospels contain worked-over material from a variety of sources, the origin of which is linked with the practical necessities of the primitive Christian community. But the agreements between the Gospels in structure and wording were not explained by this hypothesis, for which reason W. Knox's attempt to base the Synoptics on a large number of "tracts" arranged by content is not at all convincing (see the criticism of Bultmann). Still more important was the conjecture expressed by Schleiermacher in his research "Über die Zeugnisse des Papias von unsern beiden ersten Evv." (1832), in which he assumed that Mt included a collection of the sayings of Jesus that was to be traced back to the apostle Matthew; by this proposal the hypothesis of a sayings source reentered the picture.

3. *The Tradition Hypothesis.* While Eichhorn developed a literary hypothesis from Lessing's notion of a primitive gospel, Herder in connection with Lessing's proposal assumed that here was an oral primitive gospel which consisted of individual pieces (*Vom Erlöser der Menschen. Nach unsern drei ersten Evv. . . . Nebst einer Regel der Zusammenstimmung unserer Evv. aus ihrer Entstehung und Ordnung,* [Concerning the Reedeemer of Men. According to our first three Gospels . . . together with a rule for the agreement of our Gospels on the basis of their origin and order] 1796/97; see WGK, NT 79 ff). This hypothesis gained a stronger form in J. C. L. Gieseler's *Historisch-kritischer Versuch über die Entstehung und die frühesten Schicksale der schriftlichen Evv.* [Historical-critical essay concerning the origin and the earliest destinies of the written Gospels] (1818). According to this work, very quickly and quite spontaneously a uniform oral gospel was framed by the apostles in Jerusalem for the purpose of preaching. This primitive type of oral gospel was transmitted in an Aramaic tradition, but was preserved as well in two different Greek forms, on which the Synoptics are dependent. Indeed this hypothesis—to which J. W. Doeve in his theory still adheres—

that behind our Gospels lies the narrative detail [4] which is transmitted in conjunction with the exegesis of OT texts, represents a sound idea. Undoubtedly, the writing down of the Gospels was preceded by a period of oral traditions, within which the transition from Aramaic to Greek language took place. But that alone does not solve the complicated problem of parallels and disagreements between the Synoptics, especially since Luke expressly speaks of predecessors for his written report (Lk 1:1).

4. *The Utilization Hypothesis.* The three theories already described presuppose that the Synoptics originated without direct literary connections with each other. But the contacts between the three Gospels are so close that the acceptance of a literary dependence, which was propounded as early as Augustine, has at all times been championed. Although all theoretically possible combinations have found their supporters,[5] only three views can be seriously maintained.

a. The sequence adopted by Augustine, Mt-Mk-Lk, has its representatives today,[6] though mostly in an altered form, which considers Mk to be dependent on an earlier stage of Mt (see below, p. 48).

b. The assumption that the sequence was Mt–Lk–Mk, the so-called Griesbach hypothesis, was established by J. J. Griesbach (*Commentatio qua Marci evangelium totum e Matthaei et Lucae commentariis decerptum esse monstratur* [Treatise in which is demonstrated that the Gospel of Mark has been wholly derived from the commentaries of Matthew and Luke], 1789). Here it is maintained, as in Augustine, that Mk is the abbreviator of Mt, but Lk is also viewed as a predecessor for Mk. The outstanding proof for this is mentioned by F. Bleek in his *Einl. in das NT* [NT Introduction] (1862), 244 (with reference to his lectures of 1822): Mk 1:32 par., where Mk ὀψίας δὲ γενομένης, ὅτε ἔδυσεν ὁ

---

[4] J. W. Doeve in RechB II, 1957; Stather Hunt also places the linking of the Jesus narratives with the OT prophecies at the beginning of the process of gospel formation; P. Gaechter, *Das Mt*, 1962, 18, considers all three of the Gospels, independently of each other, to be dependent on the oral Greek tradition, while R. H. Gundry, *The Use of the Old Testament in St. Matthew's Gospel*, 182 ff, wants to make the Synoptics dependent on notes which the apostle Matthew wrote down during the lifetime of Jesus.

[5] See the enumeration in Höpfl-Gut, *Intr.*, 172. Unproved are the new theories of Lindsey (Lk is dependent on a primitive narrative and Q [see below §5.3.8]; Mk depends on Lk, the primitive narrative, and Q; Mt on the primitive narrative, Mk, and Q) and West (Mk and a primitive version of Lk are the sources of Mt; Lk is an expansion of the primitive version).

[6] Schlatter; Zahn; Butler; N. Walker, "The Alleged Matthean Errata," NTS 9, 1962/63, 394 (on the relationship of Mt to Mk).

ἥλιος is perhaps a conflation from Mt 8:16 ὀψίας δὲ γενομένης and Lk 4:40 δύνοντος δὲ τοῦ ἡλίου. D. F. Strauss and the Baur school adopted this thesis, and it has been revived by Farmer (with support from Dungan). De Wette and Bleek, however, consider Mk to be dependent on Mt and Lk, while denying any dependence of Lk on Mt. But the thesis must accept too many improbabilities and misjudges the literary independence of Mk.

c. The sequence Mk-Mt and Mk-Lk—i.e., the priority of Mk over Mt and Lk—was already occasionally represented in the eighteenth century (J. B. Koppe, 1782; G. C. Storr, 1786). The philologist C. Lachmann in the course of his work on the original text of the NT (see below, §39) observed that Mt and Lk agree in their sequence of material only when they are following the same sequence as Mk, and concluded from this that Mk presents the tradition in its most primitive form.[7] Mt must then have combined with the Markan material a sayings collection. Shortly after this C. G. Wilke and H. Weisse proved—at the same time (1838) but independently of each other (see WGK, NT, 148 ff)—that Mk represents the common source of narrative material for Mt and Lk, while Weisse expanded this position with the hypothesis that Mt and Lk joined with Mk a common collection of the sayings of Jesus. The two-source theory which was thereby established found its most active defender in H. J. Holtzmann (see WGK, NT, 151 ff), even though Holtzmann originally took the position adopted by many representatives of the two-source theory after him, that an *Urmarkus* [primitive Mk] distinct from our Mk was the source for Mt and Lk.

The two-source theory has gained wide acceptance in the last hundred years (even among Catholic scholars).[8] But again and again two factors have led many scholars to question the accuracy of this hypothesis.

a. Lk not only presents extensive special material, but in the material he has in common with Mk he shows striking departures, above all in the passion story. Accordingly it has been proposed that Lk, in addition to Mk and the sayings source drew on an

---

[7] C. Lachmann, *De ordine narrationum in evangeliis synopticis*, ThStKr 8, 1835, 570 ff; see WGK, NT, 146 f, and the English translation of the major part of this essay by N. H. Palmer, NTS 13.

[8] Cf. more recently, e.g., Albertz, Feine-Behm, Fuller, Heard, Henshaw, Jülicher, Klijn, McNeile-Williams, Marxsen, Michaelis, Vögtle; Filson, Geldenhuys, Grundmann, Haenchen, Johnson, Schniewind, Schweizer; de Solages, Schmid, Perry, Vielhauer, Bradby, Bornkamm, Beare, Dalmau, McLoughlin, Honoré, Fitzmyer, Carlston and Norlin, Morgenthaler.

additional narrative source[9] or at least on a special passion account,[10] or that Lk inserted Markan material into a "Proto-Lk" which he had already combined with the sayings source.[11]

b. Papias mentions in his reference to Mt[12] that Matthew collected the Logia in the Hebrew language and everyone translated them as he was able. On this basis it has been inferred that there must have been an Aramaic gospel of apostolic origin, and it has been affirmed that the agreements between Mt and Lk in the Markan material point to a common source for all three Synoptics. Benoit and Vaganay have accordingly offered the thesis that a version of Mt that had been translated into Greek in different forms was used by all three synoptic writers; Mt and Lk are supposed to have used in addition a special source written for expanding the Aramaic Mt, besides the Greek Mk. Mt is said to be the best witness for the Aramaic Mt, while Mk has abbreviated the Aramaic Mt even while expanding it with some details drawn from the preaching of Peter in Rome. Parker has proposed a similar hypothesis, according to which Mk is dependent on Mt, who best preserved the Aramaic primitive gospel, while Lk is dependent on Mk.[13] While Vaganay's form of the Aramaic primitive Mt hypothesis has been largely rejected,[14] other scholars have also postulated that behind the three Synoptics lies an oral or a written Aramaic gospel or several such written sources.[15]

In addition to these two forms of an altered two-source theory, various "multiple-source theories" (Grant) have been offered,[16] none of which has found broad support, least of all the especially arbitrary theories of Hirsch and Helmbold. §§6–8 offer discussion

[9] Grundmann, Rengstorf, Schlatter.

[10] Klijn (in a restricted form); Schürmann, Tyson, Rehkopf (see bibl. for §8); E. Trocmé, *La formation de L'Évangile de Marc*, 1963, 174 f.

[11] Fuller, Henshaw, de Zwaan; Streeter, Taylor, Perry, F. C. Grant; Evans, Jeremias.

[12] Eus., HE III. 39. 16; see below §7.4.

[13] Meynell goes on to propose that Mk has been brought into agreement with Mt and Lk, and G. Gander, *L'Évangile de l'Église*, 1970, wants to show that Mt is the best reproduction of the Aramaic primitive Mt, while Mk and Lk are secondary reworkings of the primitive Mt (cf., e.g., pp. 113, 123, 144).

[14] E.g., by Wikenhauser; Léon-Dufour, Schmid, Vielhauer, Levie, in RechB II, Bornkamm; E. Trocmé (see n. 10), 11 ff.

[15] Harrington; Léon-Dufour, Cerfaux, and Levie in RechB II.

[16] Cf Streeter, Bussmann, Hirsch, Helmbold, F. C. Grant, Boismard, among others. Also unconvincing is Gaboury, who developed by the method of *Strukturgeschichte* the hypothesis that all three Synoptics are dependent on, and have expanded in various ways, an essentially common source which is preserved only in Mk 1:1-13 and 6:14-16:8 (also X. Léon-Dufour in *Perspective*, 9 ff).

of the sources that have been proposed for the Synoptic Gospels individually.

5. *The Prehistory of the Gospel Material.* In addition to the literary-critical approach to the Synoptics, which was dominant in the nineteenth century especially, but which up to the present continues to propound new hypotheses, gospel research has since the end of the eighteenth century always given attention to the history of the oral transmission of the gospel material.[17] At the beginning of this century it was above all W. Wrede, *Das Messiasgeheimnis in den Evv.* [The Messianic Secret in the Gospels] (1901), and J. Wellhausen in his commentaries on the Synoptic Gospels (1903/4), who drew attention to the influence of the community's faith on the formation and transformation of the synoptic tradition and to the theology of the individual evangelists. But a methodical investigation of the gospel tradition was first undertaken following the First World War by the so-called form-critical approach (see WGK, NT, 282 ff). This approach transferred to the synoptic tradition observations which had been developed in literary-critical research in other fields, especially that of the Old Testament (H. Gunkel, H. Gressmann). Popular tradition follows set rules in the reproduction and reformulation of material. The rules vary in relation to the literary type: tale, saga, historical narrative, song, saying with this or that intention, etc. The same is true for small individual pieces of tradition out of which have grown the Gospels or their literary predecessors. To analyze these units form-critically and to arrange them properly is at the same time to discover their historical origin, since the individual form or type is not an accidental or arbitrary creation, but arises under certain historical presuppositions: the units have a *Sitz im Leben* [a "life situation" out of which they arose] (Gunkel). The way to form-critical research of the synoptic material was paved by K. L. Schmidt through his demonstration that in Mk the framework of the narrative was the creation of the author, so that behind it lay no original consecutive narrative, but only a loosely assembled collection of individual stories and sayings which had previously circulated independently. Dibelius, Bultmann, and their followers,[18] have carried out in detail the form-critical investigation of the gospel tradition. The essential results were the organization by Dibelius of the transmitted gospel material into parables and sayings of various types, paradigms,

[17] On the tradition hypothesis, see above, §5.2.3, and cf. the ideas of C. Weizsäcker and F. Overbeck in WGK, NT, 167 ff, 199 ff.
[18] F. C. Grant, Albertz, Bertram, Taylor, Lightfoot, Jeremias, Sanders, etc.

stories, cultic and personal legends; by Bultmann, into *apophtheg-mata* (i.e., a short unit whose point is contained in the saying of Jesus placed in a concise framework), unstructured sayings of the Lord, parables, miracle tales, historical narratives, and legends. According to this view, only the passion narrative was at an early stage structured as a consecutive narrative. The initial impetus for the formulation and transmission of the gospel tradition came from the early Christian preaching and not from interest in a biography of Jesus. The oldest tradition has been altered in many ways through dogmatic and apologetic concerns, and in the interest of ethical instruction and community discipline within the Palestinian or Hellenistic communities, as well as by the accretion of foreign material from the surrounding culture that originally had nothing to do with Jesus and by the introduction of place and time references. The gathering of this independent material in presumably preliterary groupings and their arrangement in the literary form of a "gospel"—created by Mark, but adapted by each of the evangelists to serve his own theological aims—represents the second stage of the history of the synoptic tradition.

The form-critical approach to the Gospels has prevailed broadly in its basic principles (see below, §5.2.9), but it has encountered fundamental opposition and, even more widely, rejection of the historical judgments bound up with the theory (see the account by Iber). Most recently Riesenfeld and Gerhardsson have sought to show the fallacy of form criticism's presupposition that the formulation of the tradition took place within the community. They maintain that the narrative and the sayings tradition go back to Jesus himself, who, on the analogy of the teacher-pupil relationship in the rabbinical schools, passed on to his disciples the tradition in fixed form.[19] Against this view it has rightly been objected [20] that the traditional technique of rabbinism hardly existed before the destruction of the temple (A.D. 70) and, further, Jesus was no pharisaic rabbi, nor was the oldest community the bearer of a "holy word." It is much more likely that before the formation of the Gospels there was a shaping and restructuring of the tradition through the community,[21] which in no way ex-

[19] Similarly Guthrie; G. Bouwman, *Das dritte Ev.*, 1968, 98; in a limited way, Vincent.

[20] See Nineham, Smith, Wilder, Davies, Widengren, Higgins. Further, in W. G. Kümmel, ThR, NF 31, 1965/66, 25 f.

[21] General considerations about suitable presuppositions for the tradition of original Jesus material (Wiefel) do not help any further here. Sanders, *Tendencies*, 294 ff, shows that we have no evidence for rabbinic traditional practices in Hellenistic Christianity.

cluded the possibility that the tradition or parts of it may go back
to the testimony of eyewitnesses for the beginning of its formation.
Therefore, the correctness of the point of departure of form-
critical research is in no way contradicted.

On the other hand, after the Second World War, research quite
rightly questioned one of the consequences of form-critical study
of the Gospels. In opposition to the form critics' position that the
evangelists were "collectors, bearers of tradition, redactors" (Dibelius), gospel criticism, taking up leads offered by earlier re-
searchers,[22] focused attention on the literary, sociological, and
theological presuppositions, methods, and tendencies of the individual evangelists, and in this way demonstrated a third *Sitz im
Leben* for the gospel tradition in addition to the history of Jesus
and the formation of the tradition in the community: redaction
criticism [*Redaktionsgeschichte*]. This mode of investigation,
which was first used by G. Bornkamm in 1948 on Mt and by H.
Conzelmann on Lk (1954), is as significant for the understanding
of the individual Gospels as it is for the history of the synoptic
tradition in detail, but it has not yet been able to develop a
dependable method,[22a] as will appear in our discussion of the individual Gospels.

The way to form-critical consideration of the Gospels can only
lead backward: first one must pose the literary-critical question
concerning the relationship of the Gospels to one another and concerning the supposed sources behind our Gospels. In this way the
redactional method of each of the evangelists can be examined.
Only then can the problem of the material that has been worked
over in the Gospels and in their sources be tackled.

3. Attempt at a Solution of the Synoptic Problem

The way to a solution of the synoptic problem will be found
most readily if one starts with what has been rendered more or less
certain through tradition and research, and then seeks to press on
to the limits of what can be known. But first three negative
determinations must be made:

1. We cannot be sure that the Synoptic Gospels have been pre-

---

[22] See Rohde, *Rediscovering the Teaching* . . ., 31 ff; Stein, *Redaktionsgeschichte*, 46 f; Perrin, *Redaction Criticism*, 7 ff, 21 ff (W. Wrede and R. H.
Lightfoot).
[22a] Cf., however, the discussion of criteria by R. H. Stein (ZNW 1970);
J. M. Robinson (in *Perspective,* 101) would prefer to speak of *Gattungs-
geschichte.*

served for us in their original wording. In the first two centuries the text of them was not yet incontestably established. In the process of their dissemination for the practical uses of worship, instruction, and evangelism, no importance was attached to exact, word-for-word copying. Furthermore, the Gospels underwent manifold changes quite spontaneously, as well as through intentional expansions, abbreviations, or accommodations of one Gospel to another. Thus the text of Lk used by Marcion seems to have already been conformed to the text of Mt and Mk. Dogmatic corrections too occurred down into the second century, e.g., in Mt 1:16; 11:27. Since, therefore, the text of the Synoptics cannot be reconstructed with certainty about every word, it is often not possible to determine where agreements or differences between two or three of the Synoptics are original or are the result of correction of the text.

2. The oldest tradition about the origin of Mt and Mk is in Eusebius' report (HE III. 39. 15 f) of the information from Papias. Admittedly the meaning of the words used by Papias to characterize Mt and Mk, and accordingly the translation of the passage as a whole, are highly disputed, so that it is methodologically inappropriate to try to clarify the literary relationships between the Synoptics, and the origin of Mt and Mk, by appeal to the information from Papias, as is widely done even today. It can readily be shown that Papias had no clear information that makes us more certain about the origin of Mt and Mk than does the scholarly examination of the Gospels themselves. Papias, of whom even the chronological setting is disputed,[23] declared in the preface to his work Λογίων κυριακῶν ἐξήγησις [Interpretation of the words of the Lord], thought to have been written in the first quarter of the second century, that he had given attention to the oral tradition of the Lord and had determined what was said by the specifically enumerated presbyters and disciples of the Lord, "and what Aristion and John the presbyter and the Lord's disciples say" (Eus., HE III. 39. 3 f). Later we shall discuss this proem in greater detail (see below, §10.6; 32.3); here it will suffice to establish that Papias refers to a certain John by the title of ὁ πρεσβύτερος (presbyter) and probably has this authority in mind (Eus., HE III. 39. 14) when introducing his statements about Mk and Mt with the phrase καὶ τοῦθ' ὁ πρεσβύτερος ἔλεγεν: "Mark was an interpreter [ἑρμηνευτής] of Peter and wrote down carefully what he remembered—though not in order [τάξει]—what was

[23] See bibl. in B. Altaner–A. Stuiber, *Patrologie*, [7]1966, 52 f; E. Bammel, RGG V, [3]1961, 47 f; J. Kürzinger, LThK VIII, 1963, 34 ff.

said or done by the Lord. He had, in fact, neither heard the Lord nor been a follower of him, but—later on—of Peter, as I said. The latter formulated his teachings as was needed [πρὸς τὰς χρείας], though not as though he wanted to create a compendium of accounts about the Lord, so that Mark made no mistake in writing down some as he remembered them. He took care, however, not to leave out or to falsify anything that he had heard. . . . Matthew collected the accounts in the Hebrew language ['Εβραΐδι διαλέκτῳ] and each one interpreted [ἡρμήνευσεν] it as he could."

It is clear that Papias draws his own interpretive conclusions about Mark from the statement that he has taken over from the presbyter. What the presbyter had said about Mk was twofold: (1) As ἑρμηνετής (interpreter) of Peter, Mark wrote down his statements from memory; (2) in spite of his carefulness, his account did not correspond to the order (τάξις) of the words and acts of Jesus. Thus the presbyter knows that it is as a pupil of Peter that Mark has written his Gospel, and this Gospel is reproached for its lack of order. Papias excuses Mark on the ground of the unsystematic mode of instruction of his authority, Peter, and certifies his care in the reporting of what he had heard. The interpretation of the statement about the presbyter raises two questions: (a) how is the relationship of Peter and Mark understood? (what does ἑρμηνευτής mean?) and (b) why is Mark charged with a lack of τάξις (order)? It is unlikely that Peter used an interpreter in his preaching, and so frequent attempts have been made to understand ἑρμηνευτής as "middleman," [24] though that is scarcely possible as a meaning for ἑρμηνεύειν in the statement about Mt. Whether, therefore, the presbyter was correctly informed about the relationship of Mk to Peter is an open question (see below, §6.2). The complaint against Mk about his lack of order (τάξις) in relation to the history of Jesus implies a comparison of Mk either with a sequence of the life of Jesus known to the presbyter from another source or with another Gospel.[25] Since the presbyter could scarcely have had independent knowledge of the

---

[24] Thus J. Behm, ThW II, 1935, 659 n. 3; J. Kürzinger, "Das Papiaszeugnis und die Erstgestalt des Mt," BZ, NF 4, 1960, 27; idem, "Irenaeus und sein Zeugnis zur Sprache des Mt," NTS 10, 1963/64, 109 n. 2. The interpretation of ἑρμηνευτής in the sense of interpreter of the didactic lectures in the synagogue (E. Stauffer, "Der Methurgeman des Petrus," NT Aufsätze, Festschr. J. Schmid, 1963, 283 ff) is contradicted by Papias' forms of expression, which are based on Greek conceptualizations (cf. W. C. van Unnik, "Zur Papias-Notiz über Markus," ZNW 54, 1963, 276 f).

[25] τάξις when used in connection with the words and deeds of Jesus can scarcely refer to the "literary art-form" (so Kürzinger, see n. 24).

sequence of events in the career of Jesus, Mk is being compared with another Gospel, and then rather with the most influential Gospel at the end of the first century: Mt.[26] That does not imply that the presbyter actually knew of a better chronological order for Mt, and the comment of the presbyter on this point is also hardly helpful. Moreover the defense of Mk added on by Papias does not display any better knowledge of the literary relationships, nor can this judgment be avoided by supposing that—contrary to the clear sense of the text of Papias—the reference is to the sayings source Q[27] or to additions by Mark to a written representation by Peter.[28]

The situation is no better with regard to the statement about Mt. Because our Mt is certainly not a translation from the Aramaic, it has often been supposed since Schleiermacher (see above, §5.2) that the statements of Papias refer to the hypothetical sayings source Q or to a primitive Aramaic gospel. But there can be no serious doubt that Papias (or the presbyter; it is not clear which) meant the canonical Mt (τὰ λόγια refers to records of Jesus)[29] and on grounds unknown to us assumes that behind that lies a primitive Aramaic text. If that understanding is correct,[30] then this statement does not in any way correspond to the actual literary situation. Rather, as "the first Christian man of letters," [30a] Papias applies to the Gospels a false standard, so that it is in order to leave the Papias references out of consideration—in spite of their great age—when studying the literary relationships between the Gospels.

3. *Aramaic Predecessors of the Greek Gospels.* It is incontrovertible that in the earliest period there was only an oral record

[26] J. Munck's theory that the comparison of Mt is with Lk is hardly justifiable ("Das Mt bei Papias," NeP, 250); even less so is that of a comparison of Mt with Jn (R. M. Grant, *Intr.*, 106, 119; H. Merkel, *Widersprüche zwischen den Evv.* [Contradictions between the Gospels], WUNT 13, 1971, 47 ff). E. Haenchen doubts completely that the presbyter compares Mk with another Gospel; *Der Weg Jesu*, 1966, 7.

[27] R. G. Heard on Q and Mark, NTS 2, 1955/56, 114 ff.

[28] T. Y. Mullins, "Papias on Mark's Gospel," VigChr 14, 1960, 216 ff.

[29] On this see recently Grundmann, *Comm. on Mt*, 41; Guthrie, *Intr.* I, 31 ff; J. Munck, "Presbyters and Disciples of the Lord in Papias," HTR 52, 1959, 228; J. Kürzinger (see n. 24), BZ 1960, 37 f.

[30] Kürzinger's position (see n. 24) that Papias is speaking, not of the Aramaic language, but of Mt's Jewish forms of expression is scarcely tenable • and cannot be defended on the evidence from Irenaeus; Klijn, *Intr.*, 200 f, maintains that suitable interpretation of the statements of Papias about Mt is simply impossible.

[30a] M. Dibelius, art. "Papias," RGG IV, [2]1930, 892 f.

of the narratives and sayings of Jesus. The original language of this tradition was Aramaic; our Greek Gospels still show the Aramaic tradition clearly in the background. In all probability the stream of oral tradition, first in Aramaic and then in Greek as well, continued for a long time, even when the literary fixing of the tradition had already taken place. It is extremely probable, therefore, that material from the oral tradition flowed even into the Synoptic Gospels, so that the influences of the Aramaic oral tradition or of translation variants that go back to this tradition are recognizable even in the later Gospels.

But everything refutes the hypothesis of Eichhorn, revived by Torrey, that the Synoptic Gospels as a whole are translations of primitive Aramaic documents, since the numerous alleged translation errors are only in a small degree convincing and can offer no evidence for the translation of the Gospels in their entirety from the Aramaic. Above all, the literary relationship of the Gospels to one another is comprehensible only as the relation between Greek texts, and in the case of Mk as the oldest Gospel nothing points to a translation from the Aramaic.[31] Papias' comment about Mt cannot serve as the basis for a hypothesis of an Aramaic gospel source (see above, §5.2). Earlier Aramaic stages of our Gospels are therefore to be posited with certainty only for the oral tradition.[32]

4. A comparison of all three Gospels with each other shows strikingly extensive agreement as regards extent of material between Mt and Mk and between Lk and Mk. Only three short accounts (Mk 4:26-29, the seed growing of itself; 7:31-37, the healing of the deaf-mute; 8:22-26, the blind man of Bethsaida) and three quite short texts from Mk (3:20, Jesus' relatives consider him to be mad; 9:49, salt with fire; 14:51, the fleeing young man) are found neither in Mt nor in Lk (i.e., about 30 verses out of 609). This attests that the Markan material is to be found

[31] Cf. the dependence of Mk 7:6 ff on the Greek OT, and E. J. Goodspeed, "Greek Idiom in the Gospels," JBL 63, 1944, 87 ff. Carmignac's alleged proof (mistranslations, play on words, misreadings) of an original Hebrew language for the document employed by Mk and of the eyewitness accounts used by Mt and Lk is untenable.

[32] Cf. the review of research by F. Rosenthal, Die aramaistische Forschung seit Th. Nöldekes Veröffentlichungen, 1939, 111 ff; S. Schulz, "Die Bedeutung der neuen Targumforschung für die synoptische Tradition," Abr., 425 ff (bibl.), and the comprehensive presentation by M. Black, An Aramaic Approach to the Gospels and Acts, ³1967, esp. 186 ff. N. Turner, ExpT 80, 1968/69, 325 ff, has shown that no proof can be adduced for a translation of the Q source from the Aramaic. Cf. also the list of translation variants in Sanders, Tendencies, 286 ff.

almost totally in both Mt and Lk, or indeed in either Mt or Lk. This set of facts based on the pericopes as a whole is also confirmed by word count. In sections common to Mt and/or Lk there are 10,650 words of Mark, 8,189 of which are in both other Gospels (7,040 in Lk and 7,678 in Mt).[32a] In the material that is common to all three, Mt and Lk have extensive congruence with Mk. On the basis of the resulting presupposition indicated by this evidence—that Mk could be the common source for Mt and Lk— the omission of small bits of Markan special material by Mt and Lk is thoroughly comprehensible: the two healings (by means of magical manipulations) and the position adopted by the relatives of Jesus are offensive; Mk 9:49 is incomprehensible; the note in 14:51 is no longer of any interest; only the omission of the seed parable is inexplicable, although Mt 13:24 ff does have at this place in the Markan structure the parable of the tares among the wheat. That Mt and Lk must have used a very similar source is implied in any case by a comparison of the extent of the material. For the dependence of Mk on Mt and/or Lk, or of Mt on Lk, or of Lk on Mt is inconceivable, since the omissions which would have to be assumed are incapable of explanation.[32b]

5. Decisive is the comparison of the sequence of the accounts in the Gospels: within the material that they have in common with Mk, Mt and Lk agree in sequence only insofar as they agree with Mk; where they diverge from Mk, each goes his own way.[33]

For example, in the section Mk 2–3 par. all three Gospels proceed together at first: Mk 2:1-22; Mt 9:1-17; Lk 5:17-39. In 9:18, however, Mt goes off on his own, and presents several healings, the mission discourse (9:35–10:42), and pericopes about Jesus and the Baptist, about woes, thanksgiving, and salvation (11:2-30), all of which are units that Lk has too, though in different places. Mk 2:23–3:6 once again agrees in essence with Mt 12:1-14 and Lk 6:1-11, but now Lk, with his sermon on the plain (6:20-49)

[32a] De Solages, 1049, 1052. By a somewhat different count, Morgenthaler asserts that Mt has 8,555 of Mk's 11,078 words, while Lk has 6,737.

[32b] Dungan's reference to Marcion's abbreviation of the gospel text also does not prove that Mark could have mishandled the tradition in the same way.

[33] Sanders (NTS 15, 1968/69, 255) names four exceptions to this rule, of which three concern only single verses, however, and one is an OT citation. That Mt and Lk unite together in divergence from Mk quite sporadically proves nothing (contrary to Sanders, 256). The statistical investigation of Honoré also comes to the same result: that no common divergences of Mt-Lk from Mk are present. However, on the expert information of Frau Prof. A. Hampe that the method employed in this work is unclear, I leave to one side the essay in the following discussion. On the other hand Morgenthaler, 283 f, is instructive.

and the material from 7:1–8:3, diverges from the sequence common
to Mk 3:7-35 and Mt 12:15-50 (except that Mk 3:13-19 = Mt
10:1-14, and Mt 12:33-45 is lacking in Mk). Only in 8:4 does
Lk return to the sequence of pericopes followed by Mt and Mk.

This fact—that Mk's sequence of material represents the common term between Mt and Lk—was first recognized by Lachmann
(see above, §5.2.4.c), who concluded from this that Mk had
best preserved the primitive gospel. Though later scholars have
drawn from this correct observation of Lachmann's the conclusion that the common term was Mk itself, that is by no means a
"Lachmann fallacy," [34] if indeed the divergence of Mt and Lk
from Mk can be rendered comprehensible, but not the divergence
of Mk from Mt and Lk.

And that is indeed the case. Since from Mk 6:7 on, Mt and Lk
practically never deviate from Mk's sequence, even though at
completely different points they offer substantial supplements to
Mk (an exception is Lk 22:21-23, 56-66), the only section of Mk
for which the sequence needs to be checked in relation to the
parallels in Mt and Lk is 1:1–6:6.[35]

It is readily apparent that Lk presents only four deviations from
the Markan order:

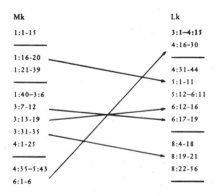

Mk	Lk
1:1-15	3:1–4:15
	4:16-30
1:16-20	
1:21-39	4:31-44
	5:1-11
1:40–3:6	5:12–6:11
3:7-12	6:12-16
3:13-19	6:17-19
3:31-35	
4:1-25	8:4-18
	8:19-21
4:35–5:43	8:22-56
6:1-6	

[34] By dispensing with the *Urmarkus* hypothesis, Butler, Farmer, Palmer,
Sanders, and Dungan have characterized the argument based on word order as
a "fallacy," since it proves only that—in this view—Mk is the middle point
between Mt and Lk. Even though Lachmann rejected the conclusion that Mt
and Lk were directly dependent on Mk, he at times comes close to implying it
(see WGK, NT, n. 212). And this conclusion obtrudes itself since it makes
readily comprehensible the deviations of Mt and Lk from Mk in some instances.
Farmer has not shown that Mk, when he agrees with one of the other two
Gospels in word order, also agrees in exact wording (*Synoptic Problem,* 218;
see also Morgenthaler, 292).

[35] In this the *Diagram* of Barr is very helpful, further Morgenthaler, 227 ff.

(*a*) The rejection of Jesus in Nazareth (Mk 6:1-6) is made into a programmatic scene for the inception of Jesus' activity; (*b*) the call of the disciples (Mk 6:16-20) is placed after the first of Jesus' works because in this way the response of those called is more plausible; (*c*) the call of the twelve (Mk 3:13-19) is placed before the crowding of the people around Jesus (Mk 3:7-12), because in this way Lk has hearers on hand for the sermon on the plain which he inserts at 6:20 ff; (*d*) the transposition of the rejection of Jesus' family (Mk 3:31-35) before the parable speech provides the crowds necessary for the scene. Thus in all four cases Lk's alteration of the Markan sequence is readily explicable, and furthermore detailed features show that Lk had the Markan sequence before him: Lk 4:23 speaks of miracles that took place in Capernaum which Lk does not report until 4:31 ff, even though he has placed Mk 6:1 ff before Mk 1:21 ff (par. Lk 4:31 ff) and in this connection has mentioned the miracles that took place in Capernaum. In Lk 4:38 Simon is mentioned, although his call is first narrated in 5:1 ff (transposed from Mk 1:16 ff).

Basically Mt diverges from the Markan order only in a twofold way:

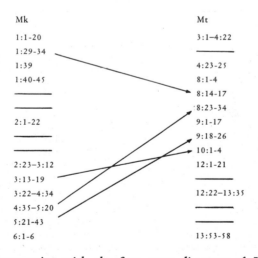

Mk	Mt
1:1-20	3:1–4:22
1:29-34	———
1:39	4:23-25
1:40-45	8:1-4
———	8:14-17
———	8:23-34
2:1-22	9:1-17
———	9:18-26
———	10:1-4
2:23-3:12	12:1-21
3:13-19	———
3:22–4:34	12:22–13:35
4:35–5:20	———
5:21-43	———
6:1-6	13:53-58

(*a*) In connection with the first great discourse of Jesus (Mt 5-7), there follows a string of ten miracle stories by way of illustrating 4:23; thus Mt brings together in Chs. 8 and 9 miracles that are scattered throughout the first half of Mk (1:29 ff; 4:35 ff; 5:21 ff). (*b*) Mt attaches to these miracle chapters a mission address (10:5 ff), as an introduction to which he has moved forward the call of the twelve (Mk 3:13 ff). Here also can be observed in detail Mt's alteration of Mk's sequence: the two controversy sayings in Mt 9:9-17 are out of place in a cycle of miracles and can be accounted for only on the ground that this is where they occur in Mk. Very significant likewise is the comparison of the parable chapter, Mk 4:1-34, with Mt 13:1-52: because Mt 13:36-52 has been added even though the Markan sequence has been maintained, the explanation of the parable of the weeds has been separated from the parable itself by the parables of Mt 13:31-33 and by a concluding statement in Mt 13:34 f; further, a second concluding statement follows in Mt 13:51.

The opposite position—that Mk has altered the sequence of Mt or Lk—offers no clarification in any of the cases mentioned (Wood offers other examples), so that the hypothesis of Griesbach, according to which Mk has excerpted the other two synoptists, is disproved, as well as the theory that Mk has used and abbreviated either Mt or Lk.[36]

6. Decisive, however, for the recognition of the priority of Mk over Mt and Lk is the comparison of language and content.[37] The strict agreement between the synoptists in the text that they share with Mk (see above, §5.1.2) proves in the first instance only that a literary relationship exists. But when the word usage of Mt and Lk is compared with Mk, it is apparent either that Mt and Lk have in large measure changed the colloquial or Semitic text of Mk into better Greek, and have done so in the same or similar ways, or that only Mt or Lk has effected any such alteration: cf. the replacement of κράβατος (Mk 2:4) by κλίνη (Mt) or κλινίδιον (Lk), or the change of the difficult construction τί οὗτος οὕτως λαλεῖ; βλαφημεῖ (Mk 2:7) in different ways by Mt and Lk.[38] That in every case Mk is primary cannot be doubted, so that the

---

[36] The attempt to show that Mt has improved on the logical sequence of Mk and therefore is dependent on Mk (Dalmau) is based on a false allegorical interpretation of the parable of the sower and is therefore not demonstrable. On the redactional reworking of Mk 1:29–6:11 by Mt, see F. Neirynck, "Rédaction et structure de Matthieu," *Festschr. Coppens*, 65 ff.

[37] See on this recently Styler and Guthrie, *Intr.* I, 126 ff.

[38] Lists of such changes in Wernle, *Synpt. Frage*, 11 ff, 18 ff, 131 ff, 146 ff; Hawkins *Horae*, 131 ff. The eight Aramaic words in Mk (Hawkins, 130) are entirely lacking in Lk, and Mt has only two (27:33, 40). Sanders, *Tendencies*, 10, 190 ff, contests that these linguistic differences could prove the priority of Mk, but he investigates only features which could be characterized as semitisms, and even then he can explain the dominance of parataxis and the historical present in Mk, which is supposedly secondary as contrasted with Lk and Mt, solely on the ground of Mk's personal preference!

thesis of Vaganay is untenable that on the basis of the oral tradition of Peter's preaching Mk has expanded the Aramaic Mt which lies behind Mk and Mt, but which is preserved in a better text by Mt.

More decisive than the purely linguistic alterations of the Markan text are the indications of substantive changes. In Mt 3:16, εὐθύς before ἀνέβη ἀπὸ τοῦ ὕδατος is incomprehensible, but is readily explained on the basis of Mk 1:10 εὐθὺς ἀναβαίνων . . . εἶδεν. In Mt 9:2, the reason for the remark "Jesus saw their faith" cannot be discerned; Mk 2:4, however, reports the most unusual undertaking of bringing the sick man to Jesus by digging a hole in the roof, a detail which Mt has obviously omitted. In Mt 14:1 the correct title for Antipas is used, τετράρχης, instead of the popular βασιλεύς in Mk 6:14, but in 14:9, Mt has βασιλεύς (=Mk 6:26), which can only be understood as a careless taking over of the Markan text. Still more striking is the replacement of Mk 10:18 τί με λέγεις ἀγαθόν by the inoffensive τί με ἐρωτᾷς περὶ τοῦ ἀγαθοῦ in Mt 19:17, and the strengthening of ἐθεράπευσεν πολλούς (Mk 1:34) to πάντας (Mt 8:16) and ἐνὶ ἐκάστῳ (Lk 4:40). Here, as in other places, Lk appears to be secondary: instead of the ambiguity of the subject in Mk 2:15, "As he sat at table in his house," Lk 5:29 has the clarification "Levi arranged a great feast in his house." In Lk 23:18 it is incomprehensible why the crowd suddenly asks for Barabbas to be freed, especially since he is not even identified until the following verse, but Lk has omitted the information given in Mk 15:6 about Pilate's custom of releasing a prisoner.[39]

On the basis of all these facts it may be inferred from a comparison of the material common to all three Synoptics that Mk has been used by Mt and Lk as a common source.

7. But is it really Mk and not a pre-Markan source that Mt and Lk—as well as Mk—have used? Earlier Lachmann and H. J. Holtzmann took the position that Mt and Mk were dependent on an earlier version of Mk, and the hypothesis of an *Urmarkus* which in different forms was used by Mt and Lk has often been defended,[40] especially the view that Mk as well as Mt and Lk is dependent on an Aramaic Mt (see above, §§5.2.4). In support of the theory, it is asserted that (*a*) the fact that Mk 6:45–8:26 is

[39] Further examples of this kind in Styler, 228 f.

[40] Older advocates in Taylor, *Comm.*, 67 ff. More recently, Hauck; Feine-Behm, Bornkamm; E. Barnikol, *Das Leben Jesu der Heilsgeschichte*, 1958, 264 ff; C. Masson, *L'Évangile de Marc et l'Église de Rome*, 1968, 525 f, 117 f. A. Fuchs tries to show that Mt and Lk have used an edited Deutero-Mk rather than our Mk.

lacking in Lk (the so-called "greater omission") can be explained only if Lk did not have this section in his copy of Mk; (*b*) the negative and positive agreements of Mt and Lk against Mk in texts otherwise common to them and Mk force the conclusion that they used a common version different from Mk; (*c*) cases in which Mt represents an older form of material shared in common with Mk lead to the same conclusion.

None of these arguments is persuasive, however.[41] (*a*) Numerous individual pericopes of Mk are missing in Lk, and in many cases the omission of a Markan text or the replacement of a Markan text by a parallel text can be explained objectively.[42] That Mk 6:45–8:26 is lacking is admittedly "enigmatic," but at the same time Lk gives evidence that he has read this section (Schürmann).[42a] The view that Lk had access to a truncated version of Mk is as unsatisfactory an explanation for the evidence as any hypothesis of an *Urmarkus*. (*b*) The agreements of Mt and Lk over against Mk in the Markan material are of very different sorts: (i) Some of these agreements are only the consequence of textual corruption and disappear when the text is corrected.[43] But as a consequence of the uncertainty of the wording in the Synoptics the explanation is also uncertain in many cases. (ii) By far the majority of the agreements concern grammatical or stylistic improvements over against Mk (see the list in de Solages, 1055 ff), by which a convergence is either unavoidable or easily explicable. Furthermore, at least as often variations such as these are found only in Mt or in Lk, or were carried out for different purposes.[44] These agreements cannot therefore be used as the basis for a *Vorlage* differing from Mk that was used by Mt and Lk. (iii) Finally there

---

[41] Opposed to the *Urmarkus* or primitive document hypothesis are Fuller, Klijn, Marxsen, Michaelis, Vögtle, Johnson, Taylor, Heuschen, Streeter, F. C. Grant, Schürmann, NTS 6, 1959/60, 196; Schnackenburg, SStW 205; T. Schramm, *Der Mk-Stoff bei Lk,* SNTSMS 14, 1971, 5 and n. 2; see esp. Schmid, *Mt und Lk,* 70 ff, 170 ff; SStW 159 ff; LThK IX, 1242.

[42] See H. Schürmann, "Die Dublettenvermeidungen im Lk" [The avoidance of doublets in Lk], ZKTh 76, 1954, 83 ff (= Sch., Tr.U., 279 ff).

[42a] According to Morgenthaler, 248 f, Lk recognized the close relationship of some texts with the texts taken over from Mk and wanted to leave room for his own special material.

[43] Thus κύριε is surely to be read in Mk 1:40 (=Mt-Lk; another view though not persuasive, in T. Schramm (see n. 41), 92 n. 3; and τοῦ κρασπέδου in Lk 8:44 (=Mk against Mt; cf. Streeter, 306 ff); and possibly in Mk 9:19 διεστραμμένη belongs in the Markan text (=Mt-Lk, cf. McLoughlin, 30).

[44] Lists are in Hawkins, 129 f, 135 f, 139 ff, and Schmid, *Mt und Lk,* 38 f, 41 f, 66 f. Cf. Morgenthaler, 301 ff, who erroneously traces the agreements to a subsequent dependence of Lk on Mt.

are a small number of agreements which can scarcely be depicted as accidental:[45] e.g., Mt 13:11 par. Lk 8:10 ὑμῖν δέδοται γνῶναι τὰ μυστήρια against ὑμῖν τὸ μυστήριον δέδοται in Mk 4:11; Mt 26:68 par. Lk 22:64 τίς ἐστιν ὁ παίσας σε which is lacking in Mk 14:65. These few instances may be explained through the influence of the oral tradition and are not extensive enough to justify the hypothesis of an *Urmarkus* or the theory that Mt and Lk have used a version of Mk that preserved the "Caesarean" text (so Brown).[45a] (c) There remain only those cases in which Mt is supposed to present an older form of the tradition than Mk. Especially pointed to in this connection are Mk 7:1 ff, 24 ff; 10:1 ff and par. because here Mt evidences a more Jewish version; but Schmid[46] has shown convincingly that in all these texts Mt has reworked—in the direction of judaizing—texts which in Mk are radically critical of the Law.

Since none of the arguments for an *Urmarkus* or for a document used also by Mk is convincing, by far the most probable conclusion is that in the form handed down to us Mk served as a source for Mt and Lk.

8. Eichhorn was the first to postulate a common source for Mt and Lk, while Schleiermacher inferred the existence of a sayings source from the Papias reference. Weisse linked these proposals with the thesis of the priority of Mk (see above, §5.2.1,2,4). The two-source hypothesis—that Mt and Lk used Mk as a source as well as a second common source, customarily called Q[47]—builds on the

[45] Lists are in Hawkins, 210 f. McLoughlin in his outstanding study tests forty-six instances of "remarkable agreements" and concludes that the only convergence which cannot be accounted for as an unambiguously text-critical or independent alteration is Mt 26:28 = Lk 22:64 (against Mk 14:65) τίς ἐστιν ὁ παίσας σε; even here McLoughlin, on the basis of a conjecture, wants to eliminate these words as secondary, but if that seems too problematical it is still the case that the number of agreements between Mt and Lk against Mk that lack explanations is very small.

[45a] T. F. Glasson, "An Early Revision of the Gospel of Mark," JBL 85, 1966, 231 ff, wants to consider that there was a version of Mk into which the "Western" readings intruded.

[46] Schmid, SStW, 171 ff; cf. also R. Hummel, *Die Auseinandersetzung zwischen Kirche und Judentum im Mt*, BevTh 33, 1966, 46 ff. When the texts which are supposed to be secondary in Mk are assembled, at the most one (Mk 1:29) can be shown to be secondary in Mk as compared with Mt and Lk.

[47] The usual view that the abbreviation "Q" is from the German word for source, *Quelle*, has been characterized by C. F. D. Moule as improbable (*The Birth of the NT*, 84 n. 1); but this meaning for the abbreviation is indeed rendered probable by the first attestation of its use (J. Weiss, *Die Predigt Jesu vom Reiche Gottes*, 1892, 8), where "Mk and Q" and "LQ" (=Lk's special material, *Lukasquelle*) are mentioned together. (Contrary to Lührmann, 1 n. 1, Wernle is not the first witness for this term.)

observation that Mt and Lk have extensive common material but that Lk could not have drawn directly from Mt nor Mt from Lk. The dependence of Mt on Lk is no longer defended today and can drop from consideration. On the other hand, that Lk took his common material over directly from Mt is championed again and again.[48] This position is completely inconceivable, however.[49] What could possibly have motivated Lk, for example, to shatter Mt's sermon on the mount, placing part of it in his sermon on the plain, dividing up other parts among various chapters of his Gospel, and letting the rest drop out of sight? How could anyone explain the fact that not once does Lk place material that he has in common with Mt at the same point in the Markan framework,[50] apart from the baptism texts and the temptation stories in Lk 3:7-9, 17, if he took that material from Mt and was therefore dependent on the Markan order that is likewise encountered in Mt?[51] Is it conceivable that Lk would have taken over none of Mt's additions to the text of Mk?[52] On this question Schmid and Vaganay[53] have shown that Mt and Lk alternate in offering the original form of the material they have in common, so that with respect to all these arguments the assumption of a direct dependence of Lk on Mt must be described as untenable.

Though it must therefore be accepted that there was a common source for the material common to Mt and Lk, the hypothesis of a written Q source is disputed from various points of view and it is accordingly assumed to be much more likely that a common oral tradition is involved.[54] This position is based on the claim that the supposed source has been imagined on the basis of personal

[48] Rengstorf, Schlatter, Ropes, Butler, Farrer, Cassian, Turner, Farmer, Argyle, Simpson, Wilkens, Sanders.

[49] The attempt by Argyle and Wilkens to make Lk's method of composition understandable by means of Lk's alleged use of Mt proves on the contrary that this assumption is untenable. See the arguments against Lk's use of Mt in J. Fitzmyer, 148 ff.

[50] Sanders, NTS 1968/69, 257 f, mentions several exceptions from this rule, but none of his examples is capable of proof.

[51] The state of affairs is clearly discernible in the colored tables of J. Weiss–R. Schütz and in de Solages, 1089 ff.

[52] Cf. Schmid, *Mt und Lk*, 25 ff; Bradby. Downing has shown convincingly that Lk knows the material he has in common with Mt only in a form that lacks the additions Mt has made to the material that he—in common with Lk —has taken over from Mk.

[53] Schmid, 183 ff; Vaganay, 293 ff.

[54] Ellis; R. M. Grant, Guthrie, Höpfl-Gut; Jeremias, Vaganay, W. L. Knox, Petrie, Rosché, Argyle, North, Rehkopf; O. Betz, *What Do We Know About Jesus?* 1968, 22; H.-Th. Wrege, *Die Überlieferungsgeschichte der Bergpredigt*, WUNT 9, 1968, 1 ff, 57, 108 f, 131, 172.

preference and cannot be reconstructed accurately, that the verbal agreements are fewer in the sayings of Jesus than in the text taken over from Mk, that a sayings source without a passion story would be inconceivable, and that the verbal associations point to an oral tradition. But the indications of the use of a common written source are so clear that the majority of scholars consider this position to be inescapable.[55] Decisive are the following facts:

a. The word-for-word agreements between Mt and Lk in their common text are in part so thoroughgoing (e.g., Mt 3:7-10; 7:7-11; 11:4-6; 12:43-45; 24:45-51 par.) as to force the assumption of a common text archetype, but in part also rather slight (e.g., Mt 10:26-33; 25:14-30 par.). Furthermore, the common vocabulary in all the sections which come under consideration is over 50 percent,[55a] which can hardly be accounted for by simple oral tradition.

b. Mt and Lk have inserted into the Markan framework the sayings material that goes beyond Mk, and have done so in quite different ways. Mt presents large sayings sections: 5–7; 10; 11; 18:10 ff; 23; 24:37 ff; 25; when this material is set aside, what remains is on the whole the Markan material. Lk presents the material that goes beyond Mk for the most part in 6:20–8:3 and 9:51–18:14, the so-called lesser and greater insertions. In view of the very different arrangement of this common material by Mt and Lk one would expect no community of sequence of these texts in Mt and Lk. The opposite is the case, however. If the sections in Lk for which Mt has a more or less equivalent parallel are numbered in their Lukan order and placed beside the Matthean parallels with the numbers of Mt's sequence (omitting individual sayings) the following picture results:[55b]

Lk			Mt	
1	3:7-9,16 f	Baptist's Preaching	3:7-12	1
2	4:2-13	Temptation of Jesus	4:2-11	2
3	6:20-23, 27-30, 32-36	Sermon on the Plain I	5:3-6, 11 f, 39-42, 45-48	3

[55] Recently, in addition to the supporters of the two-source hypothesis (see above, n. 8), Cole, Gilmour, Grundmann, Leaney; Riddle-Hutson, Sparks, Wikenhauser; Evans, Taylor, Hirsch, Throckmorton, Helmbold, Bussby, Tödt, Brown, Schürmann, Hoffmann, Lührmann; F. Neirynck (*Festschr. Coppens*), 65; E. Schweizer, *Jesus Christus im vielfältigen Zeugnis des NT* (Siebenstern-Taschenbuch 126), 1968, 124 f.

[55a] Thus de Solages, 1047; similarly Morgenthaler, 165. Carlston and Norlin, 71, 77, estimate a verbal agreement in the material common to Mt and Lk at 71 percent—27 percent higher than in the Markan material they have in common.

[55b] See the tables in Appel, 251 f; V. Taylor, JTS, NS 4, 1953, 29 f (=V.T., *NT Essays*, 1970, 92 f); Morgenthaler, 250 ff.

	Lk		Mt	
_4_	6:37 f, 41-49	Sermon on the Plain II	7:1-5, 16-21, 24-27	_7_
_5_	7:1-10	Centurion from Capernaum	8:5-13	_9_
_6_	7:18-35	John the Baptist's Sayings	11:2-19	_13_
7	9:57-60	Sayings on Discipleship	8:19-22	10
8	10:1-12	Mission Discourse	9:37—10:15	11
_9_	10:13-15, 21 f	Woes and Joys	11:21-23, 25 f	_14_
10	11:1-4	Lord's Prayer	6:9-13	5
11	11:9-13	On Prayer	7:7-11	8
_12_	11:14-23	Beelzebub Controversy	12:22-30	_15_
_13_	11:24-26	Saying on Backsliding	12:43-45	_17_
14	11:29-32	Against Request for Miracles	12:38-42	16
15	11:33-35	Sayings on Light	5:15; 6:22 f	4
_16_	11:39-52	Against the Pharisees	23:4, 23-25, 29-36	_19_
17	12:2-10	Summons to Confession	10:26-33	12
18	12:22-34	Cares and Treasures	6:25-33, 19-21	6
19	12:39-46	Watchfulness	24:43-51	22
20	13:18-21	Mustard Seed and Leaven	13:31-33	18
_21_	13:34 f	Predictions Concerning Jerusalem	23:37-39	_20_
_22_	17:22-37	Discourse on the Parousia	24:26-28, 37-41	_21_
_23_	19:11-28	Parable of the Talents	25:14-30	_23_

In spite of the different methods of composition, the texts under-
lined appear in the same order in Mt and Lk. Taylor has shown
that the same holds true for numerous details as well, if one compares the individual sayings of Mt with the Lukan order, rather
than working from the entire sequence of Mt.[56] Such agreement
can be no accident and proves a common, written source.

   c. The decisive evidence for a common, written source for Mt
and Lk is offered by the doublets, or double traditions (double
traditions are texts presented by both evangelists, but in different
forms; doublets are texts which one evangelist presents twice). It
is noteworthy that Lk reports the sending of disciples twice: Lk
9 and Lk 10, the first time in parallel with Mk 6:7-13 and the
second in parallel with Mt 10. Of course, in Lk 10:1 there are
seventy disciples, but as Lk 22:35 shows, the saying in Lk 10:4
was originally addressed to the twelve. Mt 10:1-16 makes contact
alternately with Mk 6:7-13 and Lk 10:1-12. Similarly there are
doublets in Mt, some of which parallel Mk while others parallel Lk's
sayings material, e.g., Mt 18:8 f and 5:29 f; 19:9 and 5:32.

[56] See also the *Diagram* of Barr.

Furthermore, there is a string of sayings of Jesus appearing twice in Mt and Lk, once in a setting which Mk also has, a second time in a sayings setting which is found only in Mt and Lk. The most important examples of this are:

a) "He who has, to him will be given" (Mt 13:12; Mk 4:25; Lk 8:18; cf. Mt 25:29; Lk 19:26).

b) "If any man will follow me, he must deny himself" (Mt 16:24 f; Mk 8:34 f; Lk 9:23 f; cf. Mt 10:38 f; Lk 14:27; 17:33).

c) The eschatological retribution for the rejection of Jesus (Mt 16:27; Mk 8:38; Lk 9:23 f; cf. Mt 10:32; Lk 12:8 f).

d) Persecution of the disciples on account of Jesus (Mt 24:9, 13; Mk 13:9, 13; Lk 21:12, 17; cf. Mt 10:19 f, 22; Lk 12:11 f).

e) Mk 3:23-30 is lacking in Lk; but Lk 11:17-23 offers a different version of the defense of Jesus against the charge of complicity with the demons. Mt 12:25-31, however, recalls alternately Mk 3 and Lk 11.[56a]

When this evidence of doublets and double traditions in Mt and Lk is placed beside the fact that Mk presents a single doublet (Mk 9:35; 10:43 f),[56b] it is incontrovertibly proved that Mt and Lk must have used a second source in addition to Mk. That this source was available to Mt and Lk in written form cannot be doubted in view of the extensive common sequence and the doublets, including Mt's mingling of sources. The linguistic agreements demonstrate that this source was in Greek. Though among the sayings of Jesus transmitted in Q there are indubitable Aramaisms or translation variants, it cannot be inferred from that that the Greek Q source as a whole was translated from Aramaic,[57] since the transition from Aramaic to Greek may very well have taken place at the oral stage of the tradition.

Attempts have often been made to reconstruct Q,[58] but without any certain, agreed-upon results. That merely goes with the fact that we have as little certain knowledge of the exact extent of Q as we have of the wording of Q in detail. For if we can infer the existence of Q from the points of contact between Mt and Lk in material lacking in Mk, what belongs to Q can be indicated only where there is extensive agreement in wording. But does that mean

[56a] See the complete list of doublets in Hawkins, 80 ff; de Solages 928 ff; and esp. Morgenthaler, 128 ff.

[56b] See de Solages, 1069; Morgenthaler, 140.

[57] Thus Bussby; in opposition, Turner, ExpT 1968/69; Lührmann, 85 ff; H.-W. Kuhn, "Der irdische Jesus bei Paulus als traditionsgeschichtliches und theologisches Problem," ZThK 67, 1970, 309 f.

[58] Cf., for example, Harnack, Streeter, Bussmann, Taylor, Hirsch. Lührmann seeks to reconstruct the wording of Q for many individual pericopes.

that texts such as the beatitudes (Mt 5:3 ff and Lk 6:20 ff), that
are transmitted in the same context, or the parable of the talents
(or pounds), which in both Mt and Lk comes at the end of the
Q material, cannot stem from Q, since here, in spite of similar
structure, the wording is only occasionally identical? And if we
know on the basis of Mt's and Lk's working over of the Markan
material that each of them has omitted a string of Markan texts,
could not Mk and Lk have preserved Q texts in their special sources,
especially in those sections (such as Mt 11:28-30 or Lk 9:61 f)
where on the whole the texts are reproduced in both Gospels?
Because no unambiguous answer can be given to these questions,
possible proof has been sought, and Schürmann, for example, thinks
he can show by means of words used rarely or not at all in Lk
or Mt, that Mt or Lk has read a certain text in Q but has omitted
it. But that is entirely too hypothetical to lead to a sure conclusion
about the extent of Q. Even if by stylistic, linguistic, or conceptual
arguments we can infer an original text lying behind Mt and Lk
corresponding to a saying of Jesus that we find in Mt or Lk,[59]
it remains uncertain whether that version of the text stood in Q
or is to be assumed as lying behind Q. Although the exact compass
and order of Q is beyond our reach, some conjectures about its
literary character may be advanced.

Examination of the material which must be seriously considered
as Q shows that mostly sayings material is involved, but that Q
must have included some narrative material (cf. Lk 4:2-13; 7:1-
10; 7:18-23; 11:14-23; 11:29-32). But the claim that Q was a
complete gospel (Hirsch, Helmbold) is an undemonstrable postulate.
It is probable that from the beginning the arrangement of the material in Q was based on content, since this "gospel" seems to have
been created for the practical needs of the church. We know from
the letters of Paul that the sayings of the Lord in the apostolic
age were assigned normative authority (cf. I Thess 4:15; I Cor
7:10, 12, 25; 9:14; 11:23 ff). But then one must reckon with the
fact that the need arose very early for a fixed form of the words
of Jesus. The beginnings of the process of fixation certainly reach
back into the primitive Palestinian community, probably into its
early period. As the arrangement of the sayings into sayings groups
in Q indicates, this arrangement was done on the basis of content,
probably because such an organization corresponded most closely to
the purpose which this "gospel document" was to serve. But, for

[59] Thus, e.g., Mt 13:16 f par. Lk 10:23 f. Cf. W. G. Kümmel, *Verheissung
und Erfüllung*, AThANT 6, ³1956, 105 n. 21 (=*Promise and Fulfillment*,
1957, 112 n. 21).

the arrangement of the writing as a whole, no conceptual principle may be inferred other than the fact that in Q as in Mk an account of the Baptist comes at the beginning and the parousia/judgment comes at the end.[59a] By observing the differing ways in which Mt and Lk have introduced the Q material into the Markan framework, we find that Mt has strung the Q material throughout the whole of his Gospel, while Lk has it largely in two great blocks (6:20–7:35; 9:57–13:34), so that Lk preserves the sequence of Q better than Mt. And Taylor's investigation of the sequence of Q material in the speeches in Mt confirms the conjecture that Lk has followed the Q order on the whole, while Mt has many times departed from the Q order, in keeping with the systematic recasting of his sources.

Even if this theory about the sequence of Q material as a whole is propounded, nothing generally valid can be said for the wording itself, because at times in Mt (e.g., 4:22 ff), at other times in Lk (6:20 ff), the more original tradition can be recognized. This circumstance, together with the presence of translation variants in Mt and Lk [59b] and the sharp difference between common texts (Mt 25:14 ff par. Lk 19:11 ff), often leads to the conjecture that Mt and Lk had Q before them in somewhat different forms. If this conjecture were made more precise, i.e., that Q consists only of a stratum of tradition in the process of growth,[60] that would clearly not be adequate to explain the state of affairs mentioned above in §5.3.8.a-c. But if it is supposed that the written source Q developed in different directions,[60a] so that perhaps on occasion the Greek form of one text or another was replaced by a divergent form from the oral tradition, this assumption best corresponds to the observations about a common text for Mt and Lk.

If the attempt is made to classify the Q source historically and form-critically, no stress need be placed on the fact that the author is completely unknown to us. The oft-repeated hypothesis that the author was the apostle Matthew[61] is based entirely on

[59a] Bammel would like to see in Lk 22:29, 30b (the transfer of power to the disciples before Jesus' death) the ending of Q and infers from this the influence of the "testament" literature on the formation of Q. But the evidence that Lk 22:29, 30b in its Lukan form stems from Q and stood at the end of it is hardly convincing.

[59b] Cf. Black (see n. 32), 186 ff.

[60] Fuller, Klijn, Meinertz, Bornkamm; Dibelius, *From Tradition*, 235; Léon-Dufour, (*Festschr. Coppens*) 16; E. Fascher, *Textgeschichte als hermeneutisches Problem*, 1953, 76.

[60a] Lührmann, 111 ff, where it is made clear that Mt used a form of Q expanded along Jewish-Christian lines.

[61] E.g., Cole, Lagrange; Albertz, Michaelis, McNeile-Williams.

Schleiermacher's problematical interpretation of the Papias witness about Mt (see above, §5.2.2). Q probably arose in Palestine, because it obviously consists of a collection influenced by the oral tradition of the sayings of Jesus even after the first written record was made.[61a] In attempting to fix a time when Q was written, the question has been asked whether Q is older or more recent than Mk and whether a literary link between the two gospel documents exists. Since a detailed comparison of those texts where Mk and Q converge[62] shows that often Mk offers older tradition (e.g., 3:28 f; 6:7 ff), but occasionally Q is older (e.g., Lk 3:16; Mt 7:2 par.), it cannot be proved in a general way whether Mk or Q is the older text. That there is some sort of traditional connection between Mk and Q cannot be denied, but that does not lead to the assumption that this connection—which concerns only an extremely small part of the material in Q and Mk—is to be explained on the basis of a literary link between the two.[63] The assumption of literary dependence, which in view of the strong linguistic differences between Mk and Q in the double tradition (cf. e.g., Mk 4:30-32 with Lk 13:18 f) is an extremely remote possibility, and is a consequence of the mistaken presupposition that the contacts among the traditional material can be explained solely on the basis of literary dependence. We have to perceive the relationship of the gospel writings to each other and to the oral tradition in an essentially looser way (see below, §5.3.9).

Since any literary link between Mk and Q is improbable, the time of writing of Q cannot be determined in this way. Especially since Wellhausen, the attempt has been made to fix a *terminus a quo* by means of Lk 11:50 f (par. Mt 23:35), where we read that "of this generation [will be required] the blood of all the prophets that has been poured out since the creation of the world, from the blood of Abel [Mt adds, the righteous] to the blood of Zachariah [Mt adds, the son of Berechaiah] who fell [Mt: was murdered] between the altar and the house [Mt: between the temple and the

[61a] Lührmann, 85 ff, suggests a Syrian provenance, because Mt 11:27 par. stems from a Greek-speaking Hellenistic church and Q presupposes the Gentile mission; but both presuppositions are appropriate in the same way for the Palestinian church "in the 50s and 60s" (Lührmann).

[62] See list of double traditions in F. C. Grant, *Gospels,* 108 f.

[63] According to Jülicher and Wellhausen, Q is dependent on Mk; similarly Schmithals, "Kein Streit um des Kaisers Bart," EvK 3, 1970, 80; according to Goguel, F. C. Grant, Brown (1961), Lambrecht, Schulz (*Stunde der Botschaft,* 363), Mk is dependent on Q; any literary relationship is rejected, e.g., by Albertz, Feine-Behm, Goodspeed, W. Michaelis; Strecker, Bussmann, Throckmorton, Güttgemanns, Stein.

altar]." In this threatening statement, which is essentially preserved in an older form in Lk,[64] Mt's version mentions "Zachariah, the son of Berechaiah," who has been identified with a certain Ζαχαρίας υἱὸς Βάρεις whose murder in the temple in A.D. 68 is reported by Josephus.[65] If it is considered probable that this man is intended,[66] it is hardly likely that mention of the father's name would have been omitted by Lk; rather, it must have been inserted by Mt. The Zechariah named in the Q version of the saying, without indication of the father, can then only be the prophet Zechariah, son of Jehoida, whose stoning in the forecourt of the temple under King Joaz is recounted in II Chron 24:20 f.[67] Even though questions still remain concerning this, it may be said with a high degree of probability that in the textual form in which it stood in Q this warning saying does not refer to the event of the year 68, so that from this passage no *terminus a quo* can be inferred for the editing of the sayings source.

Even though any possibility of a more exact dating of Q is impossible, it is unlikely that this document was completed later than *ca.* 50 to 70.

In what historical connection are we to understand the origin of this source? Since the material in Q is largely sayings material arranged topically, and since allusion to the passion story is completely lacking in what may be recognized as Q material, it has already been maintained in connection with a purely literary-critical consideration of the Gospels that the Q source displays a didactic or catechetical character, so that it was probably intended for the instruction of Christians on the religious, moral, and communal life and pursued no evangelistic aims.[68] The form-critical approach too has contented itself with establishing that this collection of the sayings of Jesus was arranged in the interests of paraenesis. But since

---

[64] Cf. the outstanding analysis by O. H. Steck, *Israel und das gewaltsame Geschick der Propheten* [Israel and the violent fate of the prophets], WMANT 23, 1967, 29 ff, 33 ff, where all the older lit. is given.

[65] Jos., *Bell.* IV, 335-43. The name of the father, Βάρεις, is not transmitted consistently in the tradition, so its Hebrew equivalent is uncertain; see *De bello judaico*, ed. O. Michel and O. Bauernfeind, II, 1, 1963, 54, n. 137, and 219, n. 86.

[66] So Steck (see n. 64), 37 ff.

[67] So once again Steck (see n. 64), 33 ff.

[68] Goguel, Jülicher; Wernle. While T. W. Manson, *The Sayings of Jesus*, 1949, 15 f, has noted the almost complete absence of polemic in Q, Lührmann would like to demonstrate that Q directs its polemic against all who close their minds to the preaching of the disciples. But the attempt at proof of a redaction of Q has hardly achieved its goal. On "more recent research on the sayings source," see Tödt, *Son of Man*, 235 ff.

the fundamental importance of the Easter faith has been recognized,
this collection of the sayings of Jesus could only be thought to have
arisen and to have been made to serve paraenetic aims as a consequence of a progressive development of the primitive Christian
community (Dibelius). With some justification the opponents of a
hypothesis of a Q source (see above, p. 64) have objected that a
source of this type is nowhere attested and one cannot conceive
that in early Christianity there would be a collection of words of
Jesus that left the passion story out of account. Accordingly Bornkamm and Tödt represent another historical understanding: a not
inconsiderable part of the Q material cannot be shown to be
paraenetic, but serves outspokenly christological aims (cf. only Lk
10:21 f), even though it does not presuppose a passion kerygma.[69]
The words of Jesus were collected rather with the aim of extending the proclamation of the message of Jesus about the coming of
God's kingdom and of the Son of man. Robinson[69a] went a step
farther and attempted to show by drawing together numerous
parallels that sayings collections of this type were designated by the
title of λόγοι, and that in Q Jesus was "considered as the Agent
of Wisdom," so that the taking over of Q into the frame of Mk
by Mt and Lk implied a criticism of this genre [Gattung]. And
according to Köster,[70] Q domesticated the logoi, in that the collector has carried out an equation of Jesus with the coming Son of
man, while in the original λόγοι collection used by the Gospel of
Thomas, sayings which speak of Jesus christologically and apocalyptic pronouncements are lacking. But it must be said first of all
against Robinson and Köster that neither through Jewish parallels
nor through linguistic usage in the Synoptic Gospels is it demonstrable that the sayings source was designated as λόγοι and Jesus was
represented as wisdom teacher, even though some of the Jesus words
in Q can be characterized as "wisdom words." Köster can support
his assumption of a more original λόγοι collection earlier than Q,
and not yet containing the apocalyptic expectation of the Son of
man, only by asserting that only the message of the coming kingdom of God corresponds to the preaching of Jesus and to the oldest

[69] Among those in agreement, Fuller, *Intr.*, 73 f. Cf. also Kee, 62 f., esp.
101 f, 105.

[69a] J. M. Robinson, *Trajectories*, 71 ff, esp. 86 f. Similarly H.-W. Kuhn
(see n. 57), 310 f; M. J. Suggs, *Wisdom, Christology and Law in Matthew's
Gospel*, 1970, 7 f.

[70] H. Köster, ΓΝΩΜΑΙ ΔΙΑΦΟΡΟΙ, in *Trajectories*, 114 ff; *idem*, "One
Jesus and Four Primitive Gospels," 158 ff.

gospel tradition.[71] But this thoroughly dubious reduction of the message of Jesus[72] can in no way prove the existence of this original collection, nor can it show that faith is here understood to be faith in the word of Jesus. Bornkamm, Tödt, and Hoffmann have far more justification for their thesis that the words of Jesus were collected with the aim of continuing proclamation and through faith in their enduring validity, so that Q's taking over of the self-utterances of Jesus (e.g., Mt 12:32; 13:16 f par.) serves the same kerygmatic goal as in Mk. It is questionable, however, whether the lack of any reference to the suffering of Jesus or to any passion story of whatever kind may be made to mean that Q presupposes no passion kerygma. Even if the *argumentum e silentio* is given weight—in reality, of course, we know nothing certain about the original extent of Q!—we must consider that in the Palestinian community in which Q must have originated (cf. Hoffmann) the passion kerygma repeated by Paul (I Cor 15:3 ff) was formulated at a very early date and that it attests the redemptive significance of the death of Jesus. In that case the collecting of the words of Jesus could not have taken place in conscious disregard of this basic confession (see also I Cor 11:25). It is much more likely that Käsemann[73] is right and that the *Sitz im Leben* of the sayings source is in the oldest Christian community, who believed in the resurrection of the One crucified, and who sought and found in the words of Jesus instructions for their missionary preaching and for their life as disciples. Others have rightly drawn attention[74] to the fact that the words of Jesus were collected under the presupposition that the risen Lord is giving his community instructions in full exercise of his authority, so that coping theologically with the death and resurrection of Jesus is the presupposition for the formation of the sayings source. The sayings source also presupposes the interpre-

---

[71] So Köster, *Trajectories*, 171 ff, where he invokes Ph. Vielhauer, *Aufsätze zum NT*, 1965, 55 ff, 92 ff, and N. Perrin, *Rediscovering the Teaching of Jesus* 1967, 164 ff.

[72] See my objections against Perrin in JR 49, 1969, 59 ff (esp. 64 f) and W. G. Kümmel, *The Theology of the NT According to Its Major Witnesses*, 1973, 76 ff.

[73] E. Käsemann, "On the Subject of Primitive Christian Apocalyptic," in *New Testament Questions for Today*, 1969, 108 ff.

[74] H. R. Balz, *Methodische Probleme der nt. Christologie*, WMANT 25, 1967, 167 ff; W. Thüsing, "Erhöhungsvorstellung und Parusieerwartung in der ältesten nachösterlichen Christologie," BZ, NF 12, 1968, 60 ff (=W. Thüsing, "Erhöhungsvorstellung . . ." SBS 42, 1969, 55 ff); Th. Boman, *Die Jesusüberlieferung im Lichte der neueren Volkskunde*, 1967, 103 ff; K. Lehmann, "Auferweckt am dritten Tag nach der Schrift," *Quaestiones disputatae* 38, 1968, 123 f.

tation of the death of Jesus as a victorious conflict (cf. Lk 12:20 par.; 13:34 f par.; 14:27 par.). The question why the community which stands behind the Q collection "did not make the passion and resurrection part of its proclamation" (Tödt) takes the absence of statements about the passion and resurrection from what can be surely identified as Q material as sure evidence of the original compass of Q, and is itself accordingly problematical. As a hypothesis one can still refer to the theory that apparently Q was organized for the need of the community itself, for whose existence the primitive Christian kerygma was a presupposition.[74a] Beyond this we have no knowledge as to whether or not the oldest literary form of "gospel" as it is accessible to us in Mk emerged in the same community and at the same time. In any case, the source Q owes its existence to the need of a Christian community that separated itself from Judaism, to strengthen its faith in the Advent and the awaited fulfillment of the kingdom of God by appeal to the traditional words of the risen Jesus and to provide guidelines for its preaching.

Even if the formation of a collection of sayings of Jesus and stories about him without a passion narrative is conceivable in this way, the attempt has been made to dismiss the further objection that a collection of this sort with no narrative framework has no parallel, by pointing to the Coptic Gospel of Thomas, which belongs to the Gnostic papyrus discovery from Nag Hammadi.[75] The text, which is designated at the conclusion as "The Gospel according to Thomas," consists of 114 sayings of Jesus, placed after each other disconnectedly; in a majority of cases they are introduced with the words "Jesus said," but occasionally a disciple's question is answered or even a completely detached saying is linked with an

---

[74a] In view of the already mentioned interpretation of the death of Jesus as a victorious conflict and the presence of such christological expressions as Mt 13:16 f par.; Lk 12:8 f par.; Mt 11:27 par., the assumption is false that for Q "the continuity between Jesus and the church is provided in eschatology, not in the kerygma," and that not Jesus but the coming judgment was the content of the preaching (Lührmann, 96 f). The assertion that "the passion kerygma . . . must lie behind Q" is by no means "an impermissible harmonization" (against H.-W. Kuhn (see n. 57), 309) and the absence of a passion narrative cannot be accounted for on the basis of a postulated genre, "words of a wise man" (against M. J. Suggs (see n. 69a), 9).

[75] English translations by A. Guillaumont et al., Gospel of Thomas (with Coptic text), 1959; by B. M. Metzger, in K. Aland, Synopsis, 517 ff; in Hennecke-Schneemelcher, N.T. Apocrypha I, (ed. R. McL. Wilson), 1963, 286 ff. Survey of bibl. by E. Haenchen, ThR, NF 27, 1961, 147 ff, 306 ff; by H. Quecke in La Venue du Messie, RechB 6, 1962, 217 ff; by K. Rudolph, "Gnosis und Gnostizismus, ein Forschungsbericht," ThR, NF 34, 1969, 181 ff.

indication of the circumstances. In addition to catchwords, the organizing principle of the sequence of sayings can be recognized almost solely at the beginning. A portion of the sayings are purely Gnostic, but a larger part more or less agree with the synoptic words of Jesus, or at least strongly resemble the type of sayings of Jesus in the Synoptics. It has often been asserted that the possibility of the existence of a sayings source has been demonstrated by this discovery.[76] And many scholars have sought to demonstrate that the Gospel of Thomas is dependent, not on the Synoptics, but on a tradition of the words of Jesus which is independent of the Synoptics, perhaps even of the transmission process which underlies them.[77] The case for basing the Gospel of Thomas on a tradition independent of the Synoptics is by no means convincing. It is much more likely that the Gospel of Thomas cites the canonical Gospels according to the oral tradition and freely alters them, and that in this way non-Gnostic sayings of Jesus have been taken up throughout from the free tradition.[78] But from this it follows that the Gospel of Thomas is undoubtedly not a later form of the same

[76] Thus, e.g., C.-H. Hunzinger, "Aussersynopt. Traditionsgut im Thomas-Evangelium," ThLZ 85, 1960, 843 f; O. Cullmann, "Das Thomas-Evangelium und die Frage nach dem Alter der in ihm enthaltenen Tradition" [The Gosp. of Thos. and the question of the age of the tradition it contains], ThLZ 85, 1960, 330 f; H. K. McArthur, "The Gospel according to Thomas," N.T. Sidelights: Essays in Honor of A. C. Purdy, 1960, 44; F. V. Filson, "N.T. Greek and Coptic Gospel Manuscripts," Biblical Archaeologist 24, 1961, 17; Downing, see lit. in §5, 181.

[77] Thus, e.g., Hunzinger, Cullmann (see n. 76); G. Quispel, "Some Remarks on the Gospel of Thomas," NTS 5, 1958/59, 277; R. McL. Wilson, " 'Thomas' and the Growth of the Gospels," HTR 53, 1960, 231 ff; R. Haardt, "Das kopt. Thomasev. und die ausserbiblischen Herrenworte," in Der historische Jesus und der Christus unseres Glaubens, ed. K. Schubert, 1962, 277; H. Montefiore in H. Montefiore and E. W. Turner, Thomas and the Evangelists, SBT 35, 1962, 78; H. Quecke (see n. 75), 237; J. B. Bauer, "The Synoptic Tradition in the Gospel of Thomas," StEv III, TU 88, 1964, 314; T. Schramm, Der Mk-Stoff bei Lk, SNTSMS 14, 1971, 9 ff; J. M. Robinson, Kerygma und historischer Jesus, [2]1967, 130 (with reservation); H. Köster, Trajectories, 1971, 129, 163 ff (according to Köster, no one has weakened Bultmann's contention that Saying 31 in the Gospel of Thomas is more original than Mk 6:1-6; but H. Schürmann, "Das Thomasev. und das luk. Sondergut," BZ, NF 7, 1963, 237 f, has shown that this saying is dependent on Lk 4:22 ff); A. J. B. Higgins, "The Gospel of Thomas," in A. J. B. H., The Tradition about Jesus, SJT Occasional Papers 15, 1969, 30 ff.

[78] Cf. H. K. McArthur (see n. 76), 61, 65; E. Haenchen, ThR, NF 27, 1961, 314; H. E. W. Turner (see n. 77), 39; H. Schürmann (see n. 77), 253; W. Schrage, Das Verhältnis des Thomas-Ev. zur synopt. Tradition und zu den kopt. Evangelienübersetzungen [The Relation of Thos. to the syn. Gospels and to the translations of the Gospels into Coptic] Bh. ZNW 29, 1964; K. Rudolph (see n. 75), 189 f; E. P. Sanders, Tendencies, 42.

literary genre as Q, but is a later, wholly different stage in the development of the tradition of the words of Jesus.[79] That conclusion results not only from the lack of any narrative or of any conceptual order, but above all from the lack of any Christology and so of any sort of relationship with the development of the gospel that is for the first time evident in Mk. The Gospel of Thomas presupposes the transformation of Jesus into the role of a Gnostic revealer, and shows in this way that it is a literary form of a later period.

Although the Gospel of Thomas can teach us nothing about the origin and the literary character of Q, by juxtaposition and blending of altered synoptic texts with texts taken from the tradition, it nevertheless shows us a phenomenon which is of great importance for the understanding of the Synoptic Gospels.

9. If it is considered certain that Mk and the hypothetical source Q served as the basic source for the two larger Gospels, Mt and Lk, the origin of something more than a fifth of Mt and more than a third of Lk still remains unexplained. Various sources have been postulated out of which this material may have been taken, but critical testing of these hypotheses (see §§7 and 8) shows that there is little probability that Mt and Lk used other written sources: "source-critical work on the Synoptics has reached an end in the two-source theory." [79a] The special material of Mt and Lk is much too dissimilar to make it seem probable that they used one or more written sources. Only thoroughgoing scrutiny of the oral tradition, together with the insights of the form-critical method, will enable us to understand entirely the formation of the Synoptics.

The form-critical method (see above §5.2.5) takes its departure from the fact demonstrated by K. L. Schmidt that the framework— i.e., the narrative material in the Synoptics which links together the individual accounts and sayings or groups of sayings—is secondary. The separating out of the framework from the tradition placed within that frame reveals that many times the narrative accounts represent self-contained individual narratives, but even when they have been expanded, as is often the case, this can easily be detected (cf. Mt 8:5-13 par.; Lk 7:1-10, from which Mt 8:11, 12 par. Lk 13:28, 29 can be shown to be an expansion). And the sayings tradi-

---

[79] Thus rightly R. McL. Wilson, *Studies in the Gospel of Thomas*, 1960, 143; J. B. Bauer in R. M. Grant and D. N. Freedman, *The Secret Sayings of Jesus*, 1960, 106 ff; E. Haenchen, ThR, NF 27, 1961, 316; B. Gärtner, *The Theology of the Gospel According to Thomas*, 1961, 30; K. Rudolph (see n. 75), 186; Lührmann, *Redaktion*, 91.

[79a] Ph. Vielhauer, ThLZ 80, 1955, 652.

tion likewise evidences correspondingly that the groups of sayings are secondary (see Mk 4:21-25 par.). If in these instances the original form of the individual tradition can be reconstructed through the tracing of the synoptic parallels, this insight also leads to the possibility of separating out texts into the units of tradition for which we have no such parallels (e. g., Mk 7:1-23; or Lk 16:1-12).[80] This analytical method, which already operates in part on the presupposition of literary criticism, offers the possibility of arranging the individual traditions according to literary form and thus to trace them back to their historical connection in which they received their form or modified form.

The insight that folk tradition shapes its material according to fixed rules, corresponding to the fixed aim in effect at that time, for the first time made it possible to arrange the units of gospel tradition—only the Gospels are here under consideration—according to their various "forms" and by this means to gain insight into their historical value. This is especially the case with the narrative material, which, apart from the passion narrative,[81] may be seen to fall into three different classes of narrative forms. First there are accounts like the healing of the blind man (Mk 8:22-26) in which the miracle and its accomplishment stand at the center of attention and which is interested in Jesus only as a wonder-worker (called by Dibelius, *Novellen*, "tales"). On the other hand there are narratives, such as the healing of the man with a lame hand on the sabbath (Mk 3:1-5) in which the person of Jesus, and his position in relation to God, to the Law, etc., play a decisive role (called by Dibelius "paradigms"—i.e., examples of preaching—but more appropriately by Taylor "pronouncement stories"). Closely

[80] Cf. on these texts W. G. Kümmel, "Jesus und der jüdische Traditionsgedanke," ZNW 33, 1934, 122 f (=W. G. K. *Heilsgeschehen und Geschichte*, 1965, 28 f) and Jeremias, *Parables*, 41 ff.

[81] It has been widely recognized since the beginning of form-critical investigation (see the history of research in Schreiber, *Markuspassion*, 13 ff) that the passion story was already a connected account in the old oral tradition. Schreiber's counterthesis that the passion story was first created by the evangelist Mark employing a redactional process through the use of sayings material, is based on a *petitio principii*: that the evangelist was in every line composing in a consciously literary and theologically reflective manner by which he presented his message "in coded form." On the basis of this same *petitio principii*, Schreiber infers that the gospel tradition could not be an account of what happened which then became a basis for preaching. The negative answer to the question whether Mk "already had before him a connected passion narrative or not" (E. Linneman, *Studien zur Passionsgeschichte*, FRLANT 102, 1970, 9 f, 54 ff, 132, 170 ff) also presupposes the unenlightening thesis that Mk combined individual traditions into independent, purely kerygmatic accounts, on the basis of which he subsequently formed a consecutive passion story.

related to paradigms are "controversy dialogues" in which the point is not an action but argument [*Auseinandersetzung*]; here too the important thing is the opinion expressed by Jesus (cf. the controversy about divorce, Mk 10:2-9). Finally there is a string of narratives which have been described as "myths" or "legends," such as the baptism and the transfiguration of Jesus (Mk 1:9-11; 9:2-9), but since these designations have nothing to do with form, Taylor's neutral description[82] is more appropriate. The classification of the sayings tradition has led to less unambiguous results, but with some certainty the following may be distinguished: parables (e.g., Mk 4:3-8), words of wisdom (e.g., the golden rule, Lk 6:31), prophetic words (Lk 12:32; Mk 9:1), legal opinions (cf. Mk 7:15), christological sayings (Mt 10:34).

By grouping the gospel tradition on the basis of its literary "forms" which have shaped it into a respective characteristic "style," [83] it is possible to draw conclusions about the interests which led to the development of the individual "forms" and "genres." From this one can move to the *Sitz im Leben*, i.e., to the historical situation and the aims of the community that the various "forms" serve. Combined with the analysis of the traditional material must be the reconstruction of the life of the community, which accounts for the development of the various forms. In this way it becomes clear that the interest of the oldest community was directed to the proclaimed account of the crucified and risen Jesus (cf. I Cor 15:3-5; Acts 10:38), and to this interest in preaching correspond the paradigms, the stories about Jesus, and the passion story. In addition, however, there is evident in the life of the community a twofold necessity: to give the community members direction for their life (cf. I Cor 7:10; I Thess 4:15), and to prepare the community for controversy with its opponents (I Thess 2:15 f; Acts 3:12 ff). Accordingly the sayings tradition, including the controversy dialogues, is strongly shaped by catechetical and polemical interests. Wholly lacking in the older community, however, is real biographical interest, apart from hints in other connections (e.g., Mk 6:3). On this evidence the *Novellen* can scarcely be included in the older gospel tradition, and where Jesus appears as purely a wonder-worker (Mt 17:24-27) or the ground of the Pales-

[82] Taylor, ExpT 75, 1963/64, 357 f ("stories about Jesus").
[83] "Under the word 'style' must be understood the whole way of speaking which . . . is determinative of its category. . . . Hence the style characterizes the category" (Dibelius, *Formgeschichte*, 7; Eng. tr. in *From Tradition to Gospel*, 7).

tinian legal presuppositions is abandoned (as in Mk 10:12), we are hardly dealing with old tradition.

Recently the viewpoints of the first representatives of form-critical research—"that the process of formation of the tradition was set in action primarily through the preaching needs" [84]—has been fundamentally questioned. Instead, the *Sitz im Leben* of the gospel tradition has been identified as a Christian school enterprise,[85] preaching and teaching (Schille), the mission (Moule), the rule of God which gains linguistic expression in the preaching of Jesus (Jüngel).[86] The thesis of Jüngel is in any case wanting, because it explains an item of faith as a historical step in the formation of the tradition; the other theses are correct to the extent that "preaching" is not adequate as a description of the virgin soil for the growth of the gospel tradition.[87] With greater justification it has been stressed that the units of tradition have several *Sitze im Leben*,[88] and that it is by scrutiny of these at the outset that the formation and modification of the individual traditions become comprehensible.

In the present context we can no more discuss the history of the synoptic tradition in detail than we can handle questions as to how from this history we can draw historical conclusions concerning the tradition of the eyewitnesses, of the life, and of the preaching of Jesus, or of the history of primitive Christianity. Nevertheless the findings of form criticism indicate on the synoptic question not only that the oral tradition was the decisive source for the fixing of the gospel material in written forms, but also that the oral tradition played a decisive role in the further reworking of the oldest gospel writing into the canonical Gospels. The use of

[84] Iber, ThR 24, 315, building on Dibelius.

[85] Stendahl, *The School of St. Matthew*, 1954.

[86] The perceptions of form-critical research up to that time were basically called into question by Schille (1963); Palmer, *Logic*, 175 ff; Sanders, *Tendencies*, 21 ff (esp. 26); R. H. Gundry (see n. 4), 189 ff; H. M. Teeple, "The Oral Tradition That Never Existed," JBL 89, 1970, 56 ff.

[87] For criticism of the concept "preaching," see Güttgemanns, 190 ff.

[88] Blank, *Paulus und Jesus*, 52, distinguishes for the sayings tradition: the situation in the life of Jesus, the situation of the disciples, the tradition of the post-Easter community, the gospel under consideration, and the situation of the community for which it is intended. The *Instruction Concerning the Truth of the Gospels* of the Pontifical Biblical Commission of April 21, 1964 (see J. A. Fitzmyer, "The Truth of the Gospels," ThSt 25, 1964, 386 ff), which recommends the form-critical method explicitly, although with some limitations (§5), also distinguishes three *tempora traditionis* (phases of the tradition): Christ and his disciples, the apostles, the biblical authors (§6:2-9). Completely arbitrary and undemonstrated is the thesis of H. M. Teeple (see n. 86) that there was no oral tradition at all going back to the life of Jesus.

the older sources by the later evangelists undoubtedly did not proceed in such a way that the written sources were simply written down or consciously altered. Freehand reproduction of sources was already taken for granted in Greek historical writing,[89] and in the Christian communities the written Gospels were known chiefly through being read in worship; the preservation or alteration of the written sources thus used no doubt took place for the most part on the basis of recall by memory, by means of which the influence of the still living oral tradition on the larger Gospels of Mt and Lk took place almost inevitably. This is true as much for the impact of detailed alterations of traditional units as for the taking over of comprehensive material, the so-called "special material" of Mt and Lk.[90] In connection with the discovery of the "Unknown Gospel" in Egerton Papyrus 2, Jeremias has shown that in view of the constant shifting of influences the four canonical Gospels are used by this gospel only on the basis of memory.[91] The Gospel of Thomas shows the same state of affairs, together with the continuing effect of the oral tradition.

If this assumption is also correct for the literary relationship between the three Synoptic Gospels, then these Gospels are the fixing of a specific stage of the oral tradition at a certain level; but beyond that, in their skill in taking over and modifying their written sources, they are the work of an author capable of design and theologically developed. The special nature of each of the Gospels can be understood only against the background of the synoptic question, but to that must be added the research into the redactional and theological history of each of the Gospels if we are to understand their particular characteristics.

§6. The Gospel of Mark

Commentaries: see §41. Studies: cf. in addition to lit. in §5, M. Werner, *Der Einfluss paulinischer Theologie im Mk*, Bh. ZNW 1, 1923; E. von Dobschütz, "Zur Erzählerkunst des Mk," ZNW 27, 1928, 193 ff; C. H. Dodd, "The Framework of the Gospel Narrative," ExpT 43, 1932, 396 ff (=C. H. D., *NT Studies*, 1953, 1 ff); R. Thiel, *Drei Markus-Evv.*, Arbeiten zur Kirchengeschichte 26, 1938 (on this see W. G. Kümmel, ThLZ 64, 1939, 118 ff); C. C. Torrey, "The Date

[89] See H. J. Cadbury, *The Making of Luke-Acts*, 1927, 155 ff.
[90] Cf. J. Schniewind, ThR, NF 2, 1930, 141 f; W. A. Beardslee, *Literary Criticism of the NT*, 1970, 73 f.
[91] J. Jeremias, ThBl 15, 1936, 43 f; also in Hennecke-Schneemelcher, *NT Apocrypha* I, 94 ff.

of Mark," in C. C. T., *Documents of the Primitive Church*, 1941, 1 ff;
F. C. Grant, *The Earliest Gospel*, 1943; T. W. Manson, "The Founda-
tion of the Synoptic Tradition: The Gospel of Mark," BJRL 28, 1944,
119 ff (=Manson, *St.*, 28 ff); D. F. Robinson, "The Sources of Mark,"
JBL 66, 1947, 153 ff; R. H. Lightfoot, *The Gospel Message of St. Mark*,
1950; A. Farrer, *A Study in St. Mark*, 1951; P. Carrington, *The
Primitive Christian Calendar*, 1952 (on this see W. D. Davies, "Reflections on Archbishop Carrington's *The Primitive Christian Calendar*,"
The Background of the NT and Its Eschatology, 1956, 124 ff = W. D. D,.
Christian Origins and Judaism, 1962, 67 ff); G. H. Boobyer, "Galilee
and Galileans in St. Mark's Gospel," BJRL 35, 1953, 334 ff; *idem*,
"The Secrecy Motif in St. Mark's Gospel," NTS 6, 1959/60, 225 ff;
H. A. Guy, *The Origin of the Gospel of Mark*, 1954; H. Riesen-
feld, "Tradition und Redaktion im Mk," *Nt. Studien für R. Bult-
mann*, Bh. ZNW 21, 1954, 157 ff; W. Marxsen, *Mark the Evangelist*, tr.
R. Harrisville, 1969 (on this see G. Strecker, ZKG 72, 1961, 141 ff);
D. E. Nineham, "The Order of Events in St. Mark's Gospel—An
Examination of Dr. Dodd's Hypothesis," StG, 1957, 223 ff; J.-B. Colon,
DBS V, 1957, 935 ff; A. Kuby, "Zur Konzeption des Mk," ZNW 49,
1958, 52 ff; O. Michel, CBL, 848 ff; T. A. Burkill, "Anti-Semitism
in St. Mark's Gospel," NovTest 3, 1959, 34 ff; *idem*, "The Hidden
Son of Man in Mark's Gospel," ZNW 52, 1961, 189 ff; *idem, Mysterious
Revelation: An Examination of the Philosophy of St. Mark's Gospel*,
1963; *idem*, "Mark 3:7-10 and the Alleged Dualism in the Evangelist's Miracle Material," JBL 87, 1968, 709 ff; C. Beach, *The Gospel of
Mark: Its Making and Meaning*, 1959; H. E. W. Turner, "The Tradition of Mark's Dependence upon Peter," ExpT 71, 1959/60, 260 ff;
S. F. G. Brandon, "The Date of the Markan Gospel," NTS 7, 1960/61,
126 ff; *idem*, "The Apologetic Factor in the Marcan Gospel," StEv
II, TU 87, 1964, 35 ff; J. B. Tyson, "The Blindness of the Disciples
in Mark," JBL 80, 1961, 261 ff; M. Karnetzki, "Die galiläische Redaktion im Mk," ZNW 52, 1961, 238 ff; *idem*, "Die letzte Redaktion
des Mk," in *Zwischenstation. Festschr. K. Kupisch*, 1963, 161 ff; J.
Schreiber, "Die Christologie des Mk," ZThK 58, 1961, 154 ff; *idem,
Theologie des Vertrauens. Eine redaktionsgeschichtliche Untersuchung
des Mk*, 1967; S. Schulz, "Mk und das AT," ZThK 58, 1961, 184 ff;
idem, "Die Bedeutung des Mk für die Theologiegeschichte des Urchristentums," StEv II, TU 87, 1964, 135 ff; E. Schweizer, "Anmerkungen
zur Theologie des Mk," NeP, 34 ff (=E. S., *Neotestamentica*, 1963,
93 ff); *idem*, "Zur Frage des Messiasgeheimnisses bei Mk," ZNW 56,
1965, 1 ff (=E. S., *Beiträge zur Theologie des NT,* 1970, 11 ff); J.
Blinzler, LThK VII, 1962, 95 ff (bibl.); E. Trocmé, *La formation de
l'Évangile selon Marc*, EHPR 57, 1963; Ph. Vielhauer, "Erwägungen
zur Christologie des Mk," *Zeit und Geschichte. Dankesgabe an Rudolf
Bultmann*, 1964, 155 ff (=Ph. V., *Aufsätze zum NT*, ThB 31, 1965,
199 ff); G. Strecker, "Zur Geheimnistheorie im Mk," StEv III, TU 88,
1964, 87 ff; U. Luz, "Das Geheimnismotiv und die markinische Chris-

tologie," ZNW 56, 1965, 9 ff; J. Bowman, *The Gospel of Mark: The New Christian Passover Haggada*, StPB 8, 1965 (on this see E. Haenchen, ThLZ 92, 1967, 275 f); N. Q. Hamilton, "Resurrection Tradition and the Composition of Mark," JBL 84, 1965, 415 ff; L. E. Keck, "Mark 3:7-12 and Mark's Christology," JBL 84, 1965, 341 ff; *idem*, "The Introduction to Mark's Gospel," NTS 12, 1965/66, 352 ff; J. L. Moreau, "Rome and the NT—Another Look," BR 10, 1965, 38 ff; E. Best, *The Temptation and Passion: The Markan Soteriology*, SNTSMS 2, 1965; K. Tagawa, *Miracle et l'Évangile*, EHPR 62, 1966 (on this see G. Strecker, ThLZ 94, 1969, 33 ff); K. Niederwimmer, "Johannes Markus und die Frage nach dem Verfasser des 2. Ev.," ZNW 58, 1967, 172 ff; L. S. Hay, "Mark's Use of the Messianic Secret," *Journal of the American Academy of Religion* 35, 1967, 16 ff; C. Maurer, "Das Messiasgeheimnis des Mk," NTS 14, 1967/68, 515 ff; R. S. Barbour, "Recent Study of the Gospel According to St. Mark," ExpT 79, 1967/68, 324 ff; G. Minette de Tillesse, *Le secret messianique dans l'Évangile de Marc*, Lectio Divina 47, 1968 (bibl. 527 ff); Ch. Masson, *L'Évangile de Marc et l'Église de Rome*, Bibliothèque Théologique, 1968; H.-D. Knigge, "The Meaning of Mark," Int 22, 1968, 53 ff; Th. K. Weeden, "The Heresy That Necessitated Mark's Gospel," ZNW 59, 1968, 145 ff; R. P. Martin, "A Gospel in Search of a Life-Setting," ExpT 80, 1968/69, 361 ff; J. Roloff, "Das Mk als Geschichtsdarstellung," EvTh 27, 1969, 73 ff; R. Pesch, *Naherwartungen. Tradition und Redaktion in Mk 13*, KBANT 7, 1969; *idem*, "Anfang des Evangeliums Jesu Christi. Eine Studie zum Prolog des Mk (Mk 1, 1-15)," *Die Zeit Jesu*, Festschr. H. Schlier, 1970, 108 ff; K.-G. Reploh, *Markus—Lehrer der Gemeinde. Eine redaktionsgeschichtliche Studie zu den Jüngerperikopen des Mk*, StBM 9, 1969; K. Kertelge, "Die Epiphanie Jesu im Ev. (Mk)," GANT, 153 ff; E. Grässer, "Jesus in Nazareth, (Mark VI:1-6a). Notes on the Redaction and Theology of St. Mark," NTS 16, 1969/70, 1 ff; K. Kertelge, *Die Wunder Jesu im Mk. Eine redaktionsgeschichtliche Untersuchung*, StANT 23, 1970; J. M. Robinson, "On the Gattung of Mark (and John)," *Perspective* XII (1971), 99 ff; N. Perrin, "The Literary Gattung 'Gospel'—Some Observations," ExpT 82, 1970/71, 4 ff; D. Blatherwick, "The Markan Silhouette?" NTS 17, 1970/71, 184 ff; H.-W. Kuhn, *Ältere Sammlungen im Mk*, StUNT 8, 1971; N. Perrin, "The Christology of Mark: A Study in Methodology," JR 51, 1971, 173 ff; R. H. Stein, "The Proper Methodology for Ascertaining a Markan Redaction History," NovTest 13, 1971, 181 ff.

1. Contents

Introduction 1:1-13: The message of the Baptist, baptism and temptation of Jesus.[1] *Part One: Jesus in Galilee* 1:14–5:53: Jesus

---

[1] Keck, NTS 12, 1965/66, and R. Pesch want to end the introduction to Mk with 1:15: in 1:16-20 the Gospel would then begin with the preaching of Jesus. Although the intention of the evangelist cannot be discerned with cer-

in and around Capernaum (the message of Jesus, the first disciples, preaching and exorcism in the synagogue, healings, start of the itinerant preaching in Galilee, healing of a leper) 1:14-45; controversy conversations, conflict scenes (the lame man and the forgiveness of sins, Jesus and the tax collector, question of fasting, two sabbath conflicts, Jesus and his relatives, defense against the reproach of the scribes, the charge of Jesus' league with Beelzebub) 2:1–3:35 (in between is inserted, following a portrayal of the pressure of the crowds 3:7-12, the choice of the twelve 3:13-19); preaching in parables (four kinds of seed with interpretation, aim of veiled communication, seed growing of itself, mustard seed) 4:1-34; Miracle at the Lake of Gennesaret (calming of the storm on the Lake, the Gerasene, Jairus' daughter and the hemorrhaging woman) 4:35–5:43. *Part Two: Jesus as Itinerant Within and Outside Galilee* 6:1–9:50: rejection in Nazareth (6:1-6a); sending out of the disciples (6:6b-13); Herod and Jesus (6:14-16) (attached is the execution of the Baptist by Herod, 6:17-29); feeding of the five thousand (6:30-44); Jesus' walking on the lake (6:45-52); brief stay in Gennesaret (6:53-56); discussion of clean and unclean (7:1-23); the Syrophoenician woman (7:24-30); the healing of a deaf-mute (7:31-37); feeding of the four thousand (8:1-10); demand for a sign (8:11 f); discussion of the need for bread and the feedings (8:13-21); healing of the blind man of Bethsaida (8:22-26); confession of Peter at Caesarea Philippi and first prediction of the passion (8:27-33); the way of suffering of the disciples and the coming of the rule of God (8:34–9:1); transfiguration and discussion during the descent (9:2-13); healing of the epileptic boy (9:14-29); second prediction of the passion (9:30-32); discussion of discipleship (9:33-50). *Part Three: Jesus on the Way to Jerusalem* 10:1-52: Jesus' position on marriage (10:1-12); on children (10:13-16); on wealth (10:17-31); third prediction of the passion (10:32-34); Jesus and the sons of Zebedee (10:35-45); healing of a blind man at Jericho (10:46-52). *Part Four: Jesus in Jerusalem* 11:1–13:37: messianic procession (11:1-10); withdrawal to Bethany (11:11); cursing of the fig tree and explanation (11:12-14, 20-25); in between, the cleansing of the temple (11:15-19); controversy and instructional conversations (question of authority, parable of the evil vineyard-workers, tribute money, resurrection, the greatest commandment, David's son

tainty, 1:14 as exposition (contrary to R. Pesch) makes a more convincing impression of a new motif than does 1:16 (so also Reploh, 13). 6:1-6a could also be attached to the first part—the rejection would then close Part One, as Schweizer and Grässer hold—but for this also there is no unambiguous criterion.

and Messiah, warning concerning the scribes) 11:27–12:40; the widow's mite (12:41-44); eschatological discourse (13:1-37). *Part Five: Passion and Resurrection Narrative* 14:1–16:8: the death plot 14:1 f; anointing in Bethany 14:3-9; betrayal by Judas 14: 10 f; the last meal (preparation, announcement of the betrayal, institution of the Supper) 14:12-25; walk to the Mount of Olives, announcement of Peter's denial (14:26-31); Gethsemane (14:32-42); the capture of Jesus (14:43-52); Jesus before the high council (14:53-65); denial by Peter (14:66-72); Jesus before Pilate (15:1-5); condemnation (15:6-15); mocking (15:16-20); going to Golgotha and the crucifixion (15:21-32); the death of Jesus (15:33-41); burial (15:42-47); the empty tomb and the message of the resurrection (16:1-8).

2. Literary Character and Theological Aim of the Gospel of Mark

Since literary comparison of the Synoptics leads to the conclusion that Mk is the basic source for the two other Gospels, Mk is accordingly the oldest form directly attainable by us of the literary genre "gospel." The confidence with which "liberal" theology deduced from this fact that what we encounter in Mk must be the most original form of the Jesus tradition (see WGK, NT 151 ff, 174, 176 ff) was severely shaken when W. Wrede (1901) showed that Mk was constructed on the basis of the dogmatic theory of a messiahship that was to be kept secret; the confidence became wholly untenable when K. L. Schmidt (1919) showed that "the framework of the history of Jesus" in Mk stemmed from the arbitrarily shaped linking together of the material handed on as single units in the tradition. The view developed further by form-critical research, that behind Mk only singly transmitted tradition units may be discerned—such as the controversy conversations 2:1–3:35; the parables 4:1-32; the miracle on the lake 4:35–5:43; the passion story—is by no means accepted on all sides. Attempts have been made in various ways to determine the sources of Mk: Thiel finds three complete gospels that have been absorbed, one of which goes back to Peter; Hirsch supposes that a Gospel of Peter has been joined with a version of this Gospel revised through the use of a twelve source; W. Knox assumes at least nine "tracts" to have been sources; D. F. Robinson postulates a shorter Mk, combined from two sources, to which were added two other sources and the additions of a redactor; Parker thinks that an Aramaic Jewish-Christian gospel was worked over by a Gentile Christian; according to Karnetzki a Galilean redactor expanded a historical source used by Mt and Lk, and a second redactor produced the final version of Mk by the use of the oral tradition; Guy sees in Mk the assembling of individual papyrus sheets out of which a redactor has made a coherent book; and H. Köster considers the use of a "miracle source" by Mk to be indubitable.[2] But none of these hypotheses is convincing, since there is neither an objective criterion present for arranging the various bits of Mk into one or more prior written sources, nor can difficulties in the text serve adequately as a basis for the assumption that there has been a secondary redaction of utilized sources. We cannot go beyond declaring that Mk is probably based on no extensive written sources, but that more likely the evangelist has woven together small collections of individual traditions and detailed bits of tradition into a more or less coherent presentation.[3]

On the basis of which leading ideas has the evangelist conceived this blending of his material? The question is extremely difficult to answer, since it must be answered exclusively on the ground of an analysis of Mk itself, and as a result the answers range far and wide. That Mk has no biographical-chronological interest is shown by the widespread use of wholly flaccid links between individual texts, καί, πάλιν, ἐκεῖθεν, ἐν ἐκείναις ταῖς ἡμέραις, ἐξελθών, etc.,[4] and the lack of any direct geographical or pragmatic connections (on this see Guy). Dodd, to be sure, wants to show that the order of the narratives in Mk is basically and essentially the traditional sequence of events of the history of Jesus, which is discernible in Acts 10:37-41; in this Dodd has found some support.[5] But Nineham has shown that neither the existence of such a chronological framework nor the insertion of individual traditions into such a framework can be convincingly demonstrated.[6]

Others have sought to demonstrate schemata based on content as the organizing principle of Mk. According to Farrer the narratives in Mk are arranged according to a theological scheme, which

[2] H. Köster, "One Jesus and Four Gospels," in *Trajectories*, 164 f.

[3] More recently Cole, Cranfield, Johnson, Taylor, Michaelis; F. C. Grant, Trocmé, H. W. Kuhn; J. Jeremias, *Eucharistic Words of Jesus*, [3]1966, 90 f; cf. also E. Güttgemanns, *Offene Fragen zur Formgeschichte des Evangeliums*, 1970, 226 ff; P. J. Achtemeier, "Toward the Isolation of Pre-Markan Miracle Catenae," JBL 89, 1970, 265 ff.

[4] Cf. R. Bultmann, *History of the Synoptic Tradition*, 1963, 322 ff.

[5] E.g., Taylor; T. W. Manson, Riesenfeld.

[6] Similarly also Trocmé, 23 ff; Best, 112; J. M. Robinson, *Kerygma und historischer Jesus*, [2]1967, 123 f; E. Güttgemanns (see n. 3), 201 ff.

often repeats itself in the sense of a typological fulfillment of OT texts.[7] Carrington sees the sequence in Mk as determined by the liturgical calendar, according to which the individual pericopes were read in worship on set Sundays, and thinks he can find traces of such liturgical sectioning in the oldest manuscripts.[8] Beach thinks he can discern six stages of revelation of the messiahship of Jesus which build on one another as in a Greek drama, and Mk is thought to be the originator of this dramatic scheme.[8a] Bowman claims to have discovered in Mk parallels to the Jewish Passover Haggada in the form of the proclamation of the new history of deliverance.[9] Close examination of all these schemes leads to no proof based on the text itself.

Research in redactional history has recognized that the author of Mk was not indeed simply a "composer, collector, editor," [10] but a writer who consciously shaped the tradition. The unique literary features of his composition are apparent as well. Although Mk writes in a simple, popular style and takes over incidental features of the tradition (4:38; 6:39 f; 8:22 ff; 10:21; 14:51 f), he does not simply place the individual traditions next to each other. Rather, he employs literary artifice in many ways, telescoping pericopes in order to fill out certain time intervals: 3:22-30 into 3:21, 31-35; 5:25-34 into 5:21-24, 35-43; 6:14-29 into 6:6-13, 30 f; 11:15-19 into 11:12-24, 20-25; 14:3-9 into 14:1 f, 10 f; 14:55-64 into 14:53 f, 66-72;[11] he makes preparations in advance for later events: 3:9 before 4:1 ff; 11:11 before 11:15 ff; 14:54 before 14:66 ff; 15:27 before 15:32b;[12] above all, he evokes an impression of a more comprehensive event by frequently inserting summary accounts between individual narratives (1:32-34; 3:7-12; 6:53-56), and the few indications he gives of the teachings of Jesus he depicts as illustrations: 1:14 f, 22, 35; 2:2, 13; 10:1; 12:38a.

Beyond that, on the basis of a superficial survey it will already be evident that Mk indicates in broad strokes a geographical arrangement (Galilee—Galilee and surrounding regions—journey to Jerusalem—Jerusalem; see above, pp. 82 ff). Nevertheless, during

---

[7] Opposed by H. E. W. Turner, *Historicity and the Gospels*, 1963, 45 ff.

[8] See the objections of W. D. Davies.

[8a] Blatherwick constructs five sections which build on one another theologically; the result is not convincing.

[9] See the criticism by Haenchen.

[10] M. Dibelius, *From Tradition to Gospel*, n.d., 219 f; similar statements by Güttgemanns (see n. 3), 74 f.

[11] On this hybridization of the pericopes, see Roloff, 79 f; Stein, 193 f.

[12] See von Dobschütz, 196 ff.

the period of time depicted in 6:1–9:50 Jesus is mostly in Galilee (including places on the east shore of the Lake of Gennesaret), and only in 7:24 (Tyre), 7:31 (Tyre, Sidon), 8:27 (Caesarea Philippi) are brief sojourns outside Galilee mentioned.[13] Against this, from 10:1 on, Mk describes in clear-cut manner Jesus' way to Jerusalem and his final stay there. It surely corresponds with the actual situation as well as with the tradition that Jesus, who came from Galilee, carried on most of his activity there, and his journey to Jerusalem shortly before his death in Jerusalem was undoubtedly also preserved in the tradition.[14] It is highly probable that the geographical hints concerning places outside Galilee (7:24, 31; 8:27) stem from the tradition (Marxen). On the other hand, it is questionable whether Jesus, as Mk supposes (adopted by Mt and Lk; otherwise in Jn), had never been in Jerusalem before the journey there described in Mk 10:1 ff, since, in addition to the saying in Mt 23:37 par. Lk 13:34, a string of indications in Mk presuppose that Jesus had been active earlier on in Jerusalem.[15] From this it is evident that Mk himself has essentially created the itinerary of Jesus, so it may also be inferred that the pervasive concentration in Galilee of the activity of Jesus arises from a theological motive. The idea that Mk could not have Jesus journey to Jerusalem more than once because the way to Jerusalem is for Jesus the anabasis into the heavenly sanctuary, or that "Galilee of the Gentiles" for Mk includes the pagan places such as Tyre, Sidon, and Caesarea Philippi, is completely contrived.[16] Nothing in

[13] Contrary to the division proposed on pp. 82 ff (which Guthrie also follows), 1:14–9:50 can therefore be lumped together as "Galilean Activity" (so, e.g., Harrison), while others propose other divisions (e.g., Harrington: 1:1–8:26; 8:27–16:8). But it can scarcely be contested that Mk uses a geographical set of divisions as his means of structuring (contrary to Roloff, 80 f). The proposal to divide Mk into six sections—carried out in various ways, recently by Trocmé, 63 ff (bibl.), and Pesch, 48 ff—with the supposedly confirming evidence of symmetrical subdivisions is not convincing.

[14] The thesis of Schreiber (*Theologie des Vertrauens*, 190) that "the journey signalized by means of the ὁδός-motif begins already in 8:27 and . . . has no support in the tradition" does not fit the facts: the first linking of the motif of the way with the goal of Jerusalem is in 10:32 f; and the position that the journey to Jerusalem shortly before his death was already contained in the oldest Jesus tradition is no "modernistic interpretation of reality," but corresponds to the tradition which is also contained in Lk 13:33 (cf. W. G. Kümmel, *Promise and Fulfillment*, 1957, 72, and K. Lehmann, "Auferweckt am dritten Tag nach der Schrift," *Quaestiones Disputatae* 38, 1968, 231 ff).

[15] See K. L. Schmidt, *Der Rahmen der Geschichte Jesu*, 1919, 271 ff, 301 ff; Marxsen, *Mark*, 63 ff.

[16] Against Schreiber, ZThK 1961, 160 f; *idem, Theologie des Vertrauens*, 170 ff, 190 ff. Mk has nothing to say about an anabasis of the Redeemer into

the text suggests either that for Mk Galilee is the land of Jesus because Jesus is active there in the presence of the evangelist through the preaching of the Christian community, or that according to 14:28 and 16:7 his parousia has been promised in Galilee.[17] Yet the promise "After my resurrection I will go before you into Galilee" (14:28; cf. 16:7) is far more likely to be linked with the appearances of the risen Lord.[18] On the other hand, it is surely true that apart from the two instances mentioned and the quite different reference to Galilee in 6:21, Galilee is always inserted by the evangelist (Lohmeyer), and that all the decisive declarations about the activity of Jesus are linked with Galilee:[19] Jesus comes from Galilee (1:9) and begins his preaching there (1:14, 39). There he gains his first disciples (1:16) and followers (1:28; 3:7), announces his passion (9:30), and promises his return as the Risen One to Galilee (14:28). Just as Galilee is for Mk the place of Jesus' eschatological revelation, so it is also the point of departure for the Gentile mission: 7:24, 28, 37; 14:28 (cf. 4:32; 13:10; 14:9).[20] Basically therefore it was the tradition that shaped the structure of Mk according to geographical locales, but the Gospel receives its characteristic stamp through the theological idea of the significance of Galilee as the place of Jesus' eschatological activity and the point of departure of the Gentile mission which is guided into its ways by the risen Lord.[21] In precisely the same way, Jerusalem appears, not only as the place of Jesus' death, as

---

the heavenly sanctuary: ἀναβαίνειν is used in the everyday sense. Only an arbitrary combining of texts can sustain the assertion that Mk counts Tyre, Sidon, and Decapolis as part of Galilee, and in this way "intentionally juxtaposes historically incompatible elements in order to point the reader to his theology" (p. 177).

[17] Marxsen, 92 ff; Lohmeyer, *Galiläa und Jerusalem*, FRLANT 52, 1936, 26 ff. Trocmé, 186 n. 44, also understands 14:28; 16:7 to refer to the parousia; thus also H. W. Bartsch, *Entmythologisierende Auslegung* [Demythologizing Exegesis], ThF 26, 1962, 79; L. Gaston, *No Stone on Another*, 1970, 482.

[18] Cf. Schweizer; Knigge; W. G. Kümmel (see n. 14), 77 ff; H. Grass, *Ostergeschehen und Osterberichte*, 2 1962, 117, 300 f; U. Wilckens, "Der Ursprung der Überlieferung der Erscheinungen des Auferstandenen," in *Dogma und Denkstrukturen*, Festschr. E. Schlink, 1963, 78 f; J. Rohde, *Rediscovering the Teaching of the Evangelists*, 1968, 117. An improbable literary construct is the position that Mk in 16:7 "is demanding a rereading of the Gospel so that the risen Lord may be encountered" (thus M. Horstmann, *Studien zur markinischen Christologie*, NTA, NF 6, 1969, 131 f).

[19] Marxsen, Masson 37 ff; Schulz, *Die Stunde der Botschaft*, 1967, 28.

[20] Lightfoot, Boobyer, Karnetzki.

[21] Cf. Niederwimmer, 182 f; Pesch, 233 f. Stress on the central place of Galilee by Mark scarcely serves the aim of dissociating Jesus for the reader from politically involved Jerusalem (against Masson, 40 f).

the historical tradition undoubtedly affirmed, but also as the place of origin of the Jewish obduracy toward Jesus (3:22; 7:1; 10:33; 11:18). The reverse side of Mk's stress on the Gentile mission is the repeated indication of the unbelief of the Jews, especially of the Jewish rulers who delivered him up, and of God's judgment on such unbelief (cf. 3:6; 7:6, 8; 9:31; 10:33; 12:12; 13:2; 14:41; 15:38).[22] Thus by the way he divides the story of Jesus between Galilee and Jerusalem, Mk demonstrates the theological idea of the transfer of salvation from the unbelieving Jews to the believing Gentiles, and thereby discloses that he is addressing himself to Gentile Christianity, which no longer has any relationship with Jerusalem and the Jews there. However, any sort of polemic "against Jewish theology of the primitive community and specifically against Peter," simply cannot be demonstrated in Mk.[23]

But there overlaps with this "geographical-theological" structuring of Mk another kind of structure which is "of a systematic or christological type and which exhibits a clear break between 8:26 and 8:27."[24] Although there are occasional indications of the significance of Jesus in 1:1–8:26 (1:34; 2:10, 17b, 19, 28; 3:11; 4:41; 6:2, 14-16), it is in 8:27 that for the first time the question about the nature of Jesus is directly posed and answered, and at the same time the salvific necessity of his death and resurrection is referred to (8:27-31, 38; 9:2 ff, 12, 31, 41; 10:33 f, 45; 11:1 ff, 27 ff; 12:6 ff, 35 ff; 13:26 f, 32; and the passion narrative). This concentration of the christological and soteriological material in the second half of the Gospel is without doubt the conscious construction of the evangelist: "Now the gospel really begins for the first time as the apostles preached it; prior to this, little of it can be discerned."[25] It is manifest already in this compositional concentration on the christological material that "Mk is conceived completely from the perspective of the post-Easter kerygma."[26] This fact can be even more clearly perceived through the motif of the messianic secret employed in this literary construction. Wrede was the first to prove that this concept was

[22] See on this Boobyer, "Galilee," 340 ff; Burkill, NovTest 1959, and *Revelation*, 119 ff, 224 f, 323; Schweizer, ZNW 1965, 3 n. 17.

[23] Against Tyson, 267; Schreiber, ZThK 1961, 177; Schulz, ZThK 1961, 190; similarly Trocmé, 86 ff, 101; Tagawa, 179 ff.

[24] Riesenfeld, 160; Schulz (see n. 19), 61 (the caesura does not occur before 8:21, as Kuby proposes). This suggestion is rejected by Roloff, 83.

[25] J. Wellhausen, *Das Ev. Marci*, [2]1909, 62.

[26] Thus with methodologically persuasive support E. Schweizer, *Anmerkungen*, 46 (=*Neotestamentica*, 104). Cf. also Burkill, ZNW 1961, 197 f, and Marxsen, *Intr.*, 140.

characteristic of Mk by pointing to the commands to silence (1:34, 44; 3:12; 5:43; 7:36; 8:26, 30; 9:9), to the private instruction of the disciples (7:17 f; 9:30 f, 33; 10:10), and to the hidden meaning of the parables (4:10 ff, 34b). He saw in this a dogmatic equating, taken over by Mk, of the unmessianic reality of the historical Jesus and the messianic faith of the primitive community since the resurrection (see WGK, NT 284 ff). This explanation of the situation (adopted by Bultmann) does not work for Mk and has no validity for the tradition taken over by Mk either, if it is the case that an element in the preaching of the historical Jesus was the claim that he was designated by God as the "bearer of salvation" for the End-time.[27] In any case Mk knows nothing of an unmessianic Jesus tradition; rather, the demand for keeping the secret about the dignity of Jesus stands in constant tension with the breaking of the secret through the demons (1:24; 3:11), through the sick (10:27), and even through Jesus himself (2:19; 9:2 ff; 11:1 ff, 27 f; 14:62),[28] because "for Mk it is actually the messianic material that gives him more trouble than the unmessianic." [29] Above all, the comprehensive discussion of the problem of the messianic secret, which has gone on since Wrede's[30] time and is by no means over yet, has shown that the viewpoint represented by Mk is essentially more complicated than Wrede supposed. Even if we assume that it can be proved for certain that the secrecy motif belongs to the evangelist's redaction and not to the material he has taken over,[31] still the statements which belong to this complex of ideas are contradictory. On the one hand the disciples appear as a chosen group who have been informed of the secret in 4:11 f, 34, so that one cannot speak of a complete holding back of the secret.[32] On the other

---

[27] See W. G. Kümmel, *Theology* (see §5 n. 72), 1973, 58 ff.

[28] Burkill, *Revelation,* 123, 164, 180, 188 ff, 322; Minette de Tillesse, 83, 104.

[29] Schweizer, ZNW 56, 1965, 8 (=*Beiträge zur Theologie,* 19); cf. Strecker, 93, and Grässer, 18 (with bibl., n. 2).

[30] On the history of research cf. H. J. Ebeling, *Das Messiasgeheimnis und die Botschaft des Marcus-Evangelisten,* Bh. ZNW 19, 1939; E. Percy, *Die Botschaft Jesu,* Lunds Universitets Årsskrift, N.F.I, Vol. 49, No. 5, 1953, 271 ff; E. Sjöberg, *Der verborgene Menschensohn in den Evv.,* Skrifter utgivna av Kungl. Humanistiska Vetenskapssamfundet i Lund 53, 1955, 100 ff; Minette de Tillesse, 14 ff; cf. also D. E. Aune, "The Problem of the Messianic Secret," NovTest 11, 1969, 1 ff.

[31] Cf., e.g., Minette de Tillesse, 41, 72, 81, 92, 108, 187, 251, 292 f, 506. The denial by Trocmé (99 n. 97, 123 n. 63) that the "messianic secret" is a characteristic concept for Mk is contradicted by these clear-cut observations.

[32] Schweizer, *Anmerkungen,* 41, 99; Percy (see n. 30), 293 f.

hand Jesus and his disciples act differently with regard to the secret before 8:26 than they do from 8:27 on: up to 8:26 Jesus says nothing of the necessity of his suffering or of his resurrection, and the disciples do not comprehend at all who Jesus is; from 8:27 on, Jesus speaks of both and airs the secret. The disciples, however, misunderstand the secret disclosed to them of the suffering Messiah.[33] And finally the demand for secrecy does not always have the same meaning: the command to silence in the miracle stories is meant to show that the miracle and therefore the miracle-worker cannot be kept hidden; in this case, it is not a matter of a messianic secret at all (1:44 f; 5:43; 7:36 f). The command to silence addressed to the demons (1:34; 3:12) and that to the disciples (8:30; 9:9), however, forbid making known the dignity of Jesus without making clear why making it known should be forbidden.[34]

As a consequence of these contradictions and of the lack of any proof, the aim of the evangelist in introducing this dogmatic theory is in no way clearly perceptible. The attempt has been made to show that the secret can be explained through "the union of the Hellenistic kerygma about Christ, whose essential content consists of the Christ myth . . . with the tradition of the story of Jesus," [35] which combination would carry with it the necessary hiddenness of the Redeemer.[36] But the joining of the Hellenistic Christ myth with the Palestinian Jesus tradition is in no way represented in Mk, any more than is the portrayal of the history of Jesus as an enthronement process, since Mk knows of neither the preexistence of Jesus, nor of the ascent of the Redeemer from the cross, nor of

[33] Sjöberg, 102 ff; Kuby, 54; Burkill, ZNW 52, 1961, 190 ff; idem, Revelation, 145 ff, 168 ff; Schweizer, ZNW 56, 1965, 7 (=Beiträge zur Theologie, 17); Luz, 23 f; Weeden, 145 ff; Minette de Tillesse, 218 ff, 291, 303 ff. The contesting of this situation by Schreiber, Theologie, 197; Tagawa, 52, 156 f; G. Strecker, "Die Leidens-und Auferstehungsvoraussagen im Mk," ZThK 64, 1967, 35 f n. 50, denies the clear facts.

[34] Luz, 11 ff, 28; Roloff, 84 ff.

[35] R. Bultmann, History of the Synoptic Tradition, 347.

[36] Marxsen, Mark, 130 f; Schreiber, ZThK 58, 1961, 155 f; idem, Theologie, 218 ff; Schulz, StEv II, 144. Akin to this is the position that Mk portrays the history of Jesus as a necessarily hidden enthronement process (Vielhauer, 167 f, 212 f; Strecker, 103; Güttgemanns (see n. 3), 259; C. Burger, Jesus als Davidssohn, FRLANT 98, 1970, 67. Wholly untenable is the fantastic hypothesis that Mk represents a missionary attempt to win over to the church's kerygma the Jesus communities of Galilee which had taken no notice of the Easter event (W. Schmithals, "Kein Streit um des Kaisers Bart," EvK 3, 1970, 80).

the crucifixion as enthronement.[37] It has been proposed that the intentional hiddenness of the Messiah is to be understood as the mode of expressing the divine rejection of the unbelieving Jews,[38] but then there is no explanation as to why the hidden messianic dignity breaks through here and there and why the elect disciples do not comprehend the secret that has been disclosed to them. According to Sjöberg, the hiddenness of the Messiah corresponds to the apocalyptic conception of the Son of man who is first revealed in the parousia; but after his appearance the apocalyptic Son of man is no longer concealed, and the hiddenness in Mk is only very limited. Neither is the thesis illuminating that the messianic secret seeks to keep the reader from assuming that the individual pericopes are full revelations of Jesus' messianic dignity.[39] Further, if the messianic secret is taken as an expression of the conviction that faith in Jesus as Son of God is possible initially on the basis of faith in the act of God in the crucifixion and resurrection of Jesus,[40] that offers only a partial explanation of the change in behavior of Jesus toward his disciples after 8:27. Finally, the claim that the messianic secret is a literary means used by the evangelist to emphasize for the reader the significance of the person of Jesus[41] leaves unexplained why Mk allows the prohibition against making Jesus known to be repeatedly violated.

A clear explanation that takes into account all the facts concerning the christological aim of the evangelist has not yet been elicited from the text. Nevertheless the objective of the evangelist will best be determined correctly if his portrayal of the Son of man who wants to be hidden and yet cannot remain so, is understood as an expression of faith which perceives—already in the earthly life of Jesus—the hidden dignity of the Son of God who goes through death to resurrection, and which can account for the unbelief of the Jews, and the misunderstanding of the disciples, only as resulting from intentional concealment.

Although ultimately a cloud remains over the question of Mk's

[37] Cf. Schweizer, *Anmerkungen* 44 n. 1, cf. also 102 n. 35; Strecker, 95; Best, 125 ff; Keck, JBL 84, 1965, 356 f; Knigge, 61 f; Grässer, 14 n. 4.

[38] Dibelius, F. C. Grant, Lightfoot, Boobyer, Burkill, *Revelation,* 186 f.

[39] Thus Fuller, *Intr.,* 110. Similarly Marxsen, *Intr.,* 137 (the impression is to be avoided that what is involved is an account of a revelation which is fully open to view) and M. Horstmann (see n. 18), 134 (the message of the risen Lord is to appear even after Easter as being open to misunderstanding).

[40] Percy (see n. 30); Boobyer, Schweizer, ZNW 56, 1965, 8 (=*Beiträge zur Theologie,* 18 f); Strecker, 104; Luz, 26, 30; Hay; Maurer, 524 f; Barbour, 327; Minette de Tillesse, 319 f, 506; Reploh, 97 f; Kertelge, 156, 197; W. Egger, "Die Verborgenheit Jesu in Mk 3:7-12," Bb 50, 1969, 484 ff.

[41] Ebeling, Minette de Tillesse, 187, 251, 506.

aim in taking up the dogmatic motif of concealment of the true essence of Jesus, it may be asked further whether Mk has not pursued further objectives in writing his "Book of Secret Epiphanies." [42] (a) Mk defends Jesus against the charge that he has abandoned the Jewish Law and against the suspicion of Jewish nationalism; he ascribes all human guilt in the crucifixion of Jesus to the Jewish leaders (2:6-8; 3:6; 7:7 f, 13; 12:13 ff, 28 ff; 14:1 f, 55).[43] By these apologetic arguments Mk seeks to make his Gentile readers understand the riddle of the Jewish unbelief, and to make them aware of the grace given to them in their calling. (b) Although Mk without doubt writes with the object of proclaiming "the Good News of Jesus Christ, God's Son," and so pursues no biographical-chronological goal, the oft-repeated view does not hold up that Mk has no interest in the history of Jesus as an event of the past.[44] Rather Mk represents the history of Jesus as a chronological sequence between the coming of the Baptist and the crucifixion under Pilate (1:9; 15:1 ff). He rebukes the disciples for their lack of understanding in the pre-Easter situation, and in 9:9 stresses this chronological difference. The temporal references backward in 6:17 ff; 11:30 (cf. 1:14) show the consciousness of the chronological sequence of the activity of Jesus and that of the Baptist. That is, "in his Gospel Mk proves the relevance of the earthly Jesus for the kerygma to be history," [45] and thus he is the creator of the literary genre, gospel. (c) But the attempt has been made to point out still more concrete aims in the writing of Mk. According to Weeden (similarly Martin), Mk is fighting Christians in the Christian communities who puff themselves up with spiritual claims on the basis of their understanding of Jesus as wonder-worker and θεῖος ἀνήρ (13:6, 22; 3:10 f, 14 f; 6:7). But it is in no way shown as probable that the understanding of Jesus as wonder-worker is presented as a view to be abandoned or that there is any connection between this picture of Jesus and

[42] M. Dibelius, *From Tradition to Gospel,* n.d., 230. The story of the transfiguration (9:2 ff) shows this with special clarity. Cf. Burkill, *Revelation,* 164, 180.

[43] See Burkill, *Revelation,* 38 f, 119 ff, 224 f, 323; Brandon, StEv II, 42; Schweizer, ZNW 56, 1965, 3 n. 17 (=*Beitr. zur Theologie,* 13 f n. 17); Minette de Tillesse, 323 f; Masson, 22, 77, 90; Pesch, 231 ff.

[44] E.g., Schreiber, *Theologie,* 89; Tagawa, 122; Minette de Tillesse, 502.

[45] Schulz (see n. 19), 42, cf. 36 ff; further Marxsen, *Intr.,* 130 ff; Strecker, 103; Roloff, 78 ff, 89 ff; Kertelge, 137, 187 ff, 193, 202; also E. Käsemann, "The Beginnings of Christian Theology," NT Questions, 1969, 82 ff; and R. H. Stein, "The 'Redaktionsgeschichtlich' Investigation of a Markan Seam (Mc 1:21 f)," ZNW 61, 1970, 93. According to Perrin, 7, in Mk past, present, and future flow together into a single account of the past.

the prophesied False Messiahs.[45a] Mk does clearly warn of an error which proclaims that the End has already begun (13:6 f, 21-23) and puts in the place of this "near expectation" the claim of an incalculable proximity of the End (13:28 f, 30, 32-37).[46] On this point we probably do have an actual objective of the evangelist in writing his Gospel. It is probable that, by means of his method of arranging and reworking the Jesus tradition that he has adopted, Mk pursues the further objective of providing "for the community the standard and orientation for present decisions." [46a] But that objective can be perceived in detail only in highly conjectural fashion.

On the basis of these observations two frequently represented theses show themselves to be false. (*a*) Since Papias asserted that Mk was based on the preaching of Peter (see above, §5.3.2), attempts have often been made to show that Mk presents Peter in some special way, or at least to trace some of the material adopted by Mk back to Peter.[47] But neither the mention of culpable features in the picture of Peter (8:33; 9:5; 14:30 f, 66 ff) nor the evidence concerning Peter's role as spokesman for the disciples (1:36; 5:37; 8:29; 9:2; 11:21; 13:3; 14:33; 16:7) can support the assertion that this information could go back only to Peter's reporting. Since nothing suggests the contrary, all of it simply comes out of the tradition which has been taken over. What we can learn from the material that lies behind Mk and from his composing of it in no way leads us back to eyewitnesses as the chief bearers of the tradition. "Without the stimulus from Papias, we should scarcely have advertised Peter as the guarantor for the material in the Markan narrative" (Jülicher-Fascher). There was thus not likely to be any special connection of Mk with Peter.[48]

(*b*) Since Volkmar (1857) the thesis has been defended—at first in opposition to the Tübingen school—that Mk stands under

---

[45a] According to J. M. Robinson (*Perspective*, 102 f; also in *Trajectories*, 189), Mk has combined an aretalogy cycle with a passion narrative.

[46] Marxsen, *Intr.*, 142; Masson, 105 f; Pesch, 181 ff, 218 ff, 235 ff; *idem*, GANT, 320 ff. Without justification Schulz rejects any near expectation in Mk (see n. 19), 98; so also M. Horstmann (see n. 18), 97 f.

[46a] Reploh, 185.

[47] Thus recently Cole, Cranfield, Grundmann, Johnson, Schniewind, Taylor; Albertz, Feine-Behm, Guthrie, Harrington, Harrison, Heard, Höpfl-Gut, Klijn, Mariani, Meinertz, Michaelis, Schäfer, Schelkle, Sparks, Wikenhauser; F. C. Grant, T. W. Manson, Guy, Colon, Michel, Turner, Bowman, among others.

[48] Cf. Fuller, Riddle-Hutson; Trocmé, 100 ff, 116; Niederwimmer, 175 ff; G. Bornkamm, RGG II, 761; D. E. Nineham, JTS 9, 1958, 20 f; F. W. Beare, *The Earliest Records of Jesus*, 1962, 13.

the influence of Pauline theology.[49] After Werner showed that Mk is much more dependent on Gentile Christianity, however, the thesis was reworked to claim that Mk combined "the Pauline kerygma and the (so-called) synoptic tradition."[50] But it is no more demonstrable that Mk was influenced by the Christ myth (see above, pp. 91 f) than there is ground for the supposition that Mk viewed the death of Jesus as redemptive under the influence of Paul. This evaluation of the death of Jesus was already the view of the primitive community according to I Cor 15:3, and both the characteristically Pauline term κύριος and the Pauline concept of the humiliation of the Son of God are missing in Mk. It is clear that Mk shaped the Palestinian Jesus tradition on the basis of Gentile-Christian presuppositions; it is scarcely demonstrable that he had any connection with Paul or with Pauline-influenced Gentile Christianity.[51]

3. Author

The identity of the writer of Mk is not disclosed anywhere in his Gospel. That he is recounting a "personal experience"[52] in mentioning the young man who fled naked when Jesus was taken prisoner (14:51 f) is a strange and wholly improbable conjecture. Even if it were accurate, no name could be deduced from it. But the oldest tradition, attested by Papias, offers as writer of this Gospel Μᾶρκος, who wrote down the account of Peter from memory (see above, §5.3.2). We have already seen that no special connection with Peter can be inferred from Mk, and that Papias, or the elder cited by him, had no reliable knowledge of the connection of Mk with Peter.[53] Furthermore Papias' representation of the reproduction of the preaching of Peter by Mk is false, because the material in Mk "is the product of a complicated, in part con-

---

[49] On the history of this thesis see Werner, 1 ff.

[50] Marxsen, 147; similarly Tyson, Schreiber; Bultmann (see n. 4), 372; Percy (see n. 30), 295 f.

[51] Thus, e.g., Feine-Behm; F. C. Grant; Guy.

[52] Thus Grundmann, Schniewind, Wohlenberg; Albertz, Feine-Behm, Harrison, Henshaw, Höpfl-Gut, Meinertz, Michaelis, Zahn; W. Neil, *The Life and Teaching of Jesus*, 1965, 41.

[53] No help is offered by the conjecture of τάχει instead of τάξει, or the resulting translation, "Mk wrote down what [Peter] had kept in his memory, not hastily, however" (H. A. Rigg, "Papias on Mk," NovTest 1, 1956, 161 ff); for the supposition of a change of subject from ἐμνημόνευσεν to ἔγραψεν is as arbitrary as the assumption that the τάξει of Papias was wrongly heard as τάχει.

tradictory tradition history." [54] Although Papias' account about the relation of the author to Peter is on these grounds useless, his information that the author of Mk was named Mark could still be correct. Of course, Papias is the only independent witness for this information, since the other reports about Mk as "the recollections of Peter" (Just., *Dial.* 106. 3) and about the circumstances that occasioned Mark's writing down the preaching of Peter[55] are all dependent on Papias and have no independent value as testimony. The Latin prologue to Mk, in the past often dated in the second century, according to which Mk, Peter's interpreter, wrote his Gospel in Italy after the death of Peter, is now shown by more recent research to be in no case earlier than the Vulgate; i.e., not before the fourth century (see below, §35).

The Mark who is named by Papias as the author of Mk is surely identical with the John Mark frequently mentioned in Acts.[56] He was the son of a certain Mary, in whose house in Jerusalem a part of the primitive community came together (Acts 12:12). His cousin Barnabas (Col 4:10) and Paul took him to Antioch after the collection journey (Acts 12:25) and had him with them on the so-called first missionary journey (Acts 13:5). Because of him Barnabas later separated from Paul and went with Mark to Cyprus (Acts 15:37 ff). Later Mark again belonged to the Pauline circle: in Phlm 24 Paul names Mark among his co-workers; in Col 4:10 he recommends him to the community at Colossae to be received as a guest; and according to II Tim 4:11, Timothy is to bring Mark with him to Rome. In view of the pseudonymity of I Pet, it is impossible to say how the mention in I Pet 5:13, Μᾶρκος ὁ υἱός μου, is related to these reports of occasional collaboration of Mark with Paul. On the other hand the conclusion of the sentence about Mk contained in the Muratorian Canon (*quibus tamen interfuit et ita posuit*: "on some [occasions] he was nevertheless present and thus set down [a record]") can be readily understood as saying that Mark was present at some of the events which he narrates. Mark presumably grew up in Jerusalem and lived there during the time of Jesus' activity and death there, even though he was not a follower of Jesus.

---

[54] Niederwimmer, 185.

[55] Irenaeus, Clement of Alexandria, Origen, Jerome (texts in Huck-Lietzmann, *Synopsis*,[9] VIII ff, and Aland, *Synopsis*, 533-39 f, 546.

[56] It is scarcely possible that *Marcus* is the name of an otherwise unknown Roman Christian (F. C. Grant), or that the author is indeed named Mark, although he is not identical with John Mark (Schweizer).

As justification for the tradition attested by Papias that John Mark is the author of Mk, one can adduce the fact that obviously the tendency to attribute the Gospels to personal followers of Jesus arose quite early, even though in Papias' time we can prove this for Mt alone (see below, §7.4). Consequently the secondary attribution of Mk to a non-apostle and non-disciple would simply not suggest itself, and for this reason the great majority of scholars consider it certain that John Mark was the author of Mk.

Yet the considerations against this assumption carry weight.[57] The author obviously has no personal knowledge of Palestinian geography, as the numerous geographical errors show.[58] He writes for Gentile Christians, with sharp polemic against the unbelieving Jews. He does not know that the account of the death of the Baptist (6:17 ff) contradicts Palestinian customs. Could a Jewish Christian from Jerusalem miss the fact that 6:35 ff and 8:1 ff are two variants of the same feeding story? The tradition that Mk was written by John Mark is therefore scarcely reliable. The reference to I Pet 5:13 ("The elect in Babylon and my son Mark also greet you") [59] does not account for the tradition, but only the subsequent linking up of the author of Mk with the preaching of Peter. Accordingly, the author of Mk is unknown to us.[60]

4. Place and Time of Writing

That Papias asserts that Mk was written in Rome can be deduced from Eusebius only with great uncertainty (HE II. 15. 2), but Clement of Alexandria (Eus., HE VI. 14. 6) unambiguously attests this traditon, which is followed today by the majority of scholars. In support of this tradition the use of many Latin words is pointed to: e.g., μόδιος 4:21; λεγιών 5:9, 15; σπεκουλάτωρ 6:27; δηνάριον 6:37; ξέστης = sextarius (jug) 7:4; κῆνος = census 12:14; φραγελλοῦν = flagellare 15:15; κεντυρίων 15:39, 44 ff; the explanations λεπτὰ δύο, ὅ ἐστιν κοδράντης (quadrans) 12:42; αὐλῆς, ὅ

[57] Thus Johnson; Heard, Marxsen; F. C. Grant, Beach, Niederwimmer; G. Bornkamm, RGG II, 761; E. Haenchen, Der Weg Jesu, 1966, 8; Schulz (see n. 19), 9.

[58] Cf. 5:1; 7:31; 10:1; on this see Niederwimmer, 178 ff.

[59] Thus Marxsen, Intr., 143; Moreau; Haenchen (see n. 57); J. Regul, Die antimarcionitischen Evangelienprologe, 1969, 96.

[60] The wholly groundless conjecture of Trocmé (202 f) that Philip is the author of Mk 1–13, collapses with the undemonstrable assumption that Mk 14–16 is a secondary supplement, attributed to Mark, added to the original Mk, which lacked a passion narrative (ibid., 193 f). Masson (115) has rightly stressed that the passion story belongs of necessity to Mk 13.

ἐστιν πραιτώριον 15:16; expressions such as τὸ ἱκανὸν ποιῆσαι = satisfacere 15:15 or ῥαπίσμασιν αὐτὸν ἔλαβον = verberibus eum acceperunt 14:65. But here we are dealing largely with technical military terminology, just as in Ign., Polyc. 6:2.[61] Lk-Acts has just as many Latinisms.[62] If the reference in 10:12 to the right of a woman to dissolve the marriage—which, in conformity with the Jewish regulations, is missing in Mt 5:32 and 19:9—is an expansion by Mk in consideration of his Gentile readers, he could as well have in mind Hellenistic as Roman legal rights. The argument that Mk could have found general churchly acceptance alongside Mt and Lk only if an important Christian community stood behind it can be adduced in relation to any larger Christian community—if it has any weight at all. Otherwise nothing points to Rome, and a Gentile Christian community in the East is much more likely.[63]

The time of writing is difficult to determine. An early origin is improbable,[64] because the development of the gospel tradition has already progressed far, and Mk 13 shows traces of the threatening nearness of the Jewish war. Most scholars assign a date in the years 64–70, since the destruction of Jerusalem in the year 70 is mentioned not unambiguously, but some scholars consider a date after 70 more likely for the composition.[65] Brandon would like to see reflected in Mk 13 the situation of the Roman Christians in the year 71,[66] but his evidence is scarcely convincing. Since no overwhelming argument for the years before or after 70 can be adduced, we must content ourselves with saying that Mk was written ca. 70.

5. The Ending of Mark

Today it is generally accepted that the account of the resurrection and the ascension which is found in most manuscripts and

[61] See on this Blass-Debrunner, suppl. to 12th ed., 7, p. 6 n. 1.

[62] See C. F. D. Moule, Idiom Book of NT Greek, [2]1959, 192. M. Hengel, "Mk 7:3 πυγμῇ," ZNW 60, 1969, 197 f, wants to regard πυγμῇ = pugno = "with a handful" also as a Latinism.

[63] Thus, e.g., Schweizer; Klijn. Syria is suggested by Fuller; Karnetzki, Schreiber, Kertelge. Less likely are Galilee (Marxsen) or Transjordan, (Schulz [see n. 19], 9).

[64] Ca. 40: Torrey; ca. 50–60: Albertz, Höpfl-Gut, Mariani, Meinertz; Trocmé.

[65] Johnson; Beach, Brandon, Hamilton, Minette de Tillesse, Masson, Pesch; N. Walter, "Tempelzerstörung und synopt. Apokalypse," ZNW 57, 1966, 41 ff.

[66] S. G. F. Brandon, Jesus and the Zealots, 1967, 222 ff, and Masson, 103, 110.

versions (16:9-20) was not part of the original Mk.[67] This is confirmed not only by the absence of this account from an essential part of the oldest tradition (ℵ B 304 k sy[sin], MSS of other Eastern versions, Clement of Alexandria, Origen, and the testimony of Eusebius and Jerome), but also by the divergent character of the text of the other Gospels.[68] Mk 16:9-20 is obviously not a self-contained composition (so Helzle), but combines (according to Linnemann) allusions to Lk and Jn (vv. 9-14), sayings of Jesus in direct address (vv. 15-18), and an announcement of the ascension and the mission of the disciples (vv. 19-20). But Linnemann's hypothesis that Mt 28:16 f + Mk 16:15-20 was the original ending of Mk requires too many arbitrary assumptions, and would even so be no more than a probability (Mt 28:16 f goes back to a Markan *Vorlage* which has not been preserved; Mt 28:18-20 is dependent on Mk 16:15-20; the linguistic usage in Mk 16:15-20 conforms to that of Mk. But on the contrary: ὁ κόσμος ἅπας 16:15 against ὁ κόσμος ὅλος in 8:36 and 14:9; παρακολουθέω 16:17 and ἐπακολουθέω 16:20 against the frequent ἀκολουθέω; ὁ κύριος 16:19 in the narrative; why 16:9-14 is brought in instead of the introduction allegedly used in Mt 28:16 f remains wholly unexplained). Furthermore on the basis of Linnemann's hypothesis it remains incomprehensible why in the textual tradition, in addition to the ending at 16:8 which is attested in many groups of texts, there are found only witnesses for the

D. L. Dungan, *Perspective* I, 97, considers any date from 70 to Tatian to be possible!

[67] Otherwise still Mariani, *Intr.*, 73. Curiously, K. W. Clark, "The Theological Relevance of Textual Variation in Current Criticism of the Greek NT," JBL 85, 1966, 9 f, considers the question to be presently insoluble because 16:9 ff is already found in Justin and in Old Latin, Old Syriac, and Coptic manuscripts.

[68] Bibl. on the question of the ending of Mk in W. G. Kümmel, ThR 17, 1948/49, 9 n. 2; 18, 1950, 23 n. 1; J. Duplacy, *Où en est la critique textuelle du NT?*, 1959, 44; R. Bultmann, *History of Synoptic Trad.*, 1963, 284 ff. See further E. Helzle, "Der Schluss des Mk und das Freer-Logion," TLZ 85, 1960, 470 ff (Tübingen diss.); F. Gils, "Pierre et la foi au Christ ressuscité," EThL 38, 1962, 18 ff; H.-W. Bartsch, *Das Auferstehungszeugnis*, ThF 41, 1965, 9 ff; H. Waetjen, "The Ending of Mk and the Gospel's Shift in Eschatology," ASTI 4, 1965, 114 ff; B. Thiering, "Opening and Closing Narratives in the Gospels and Acts," *Abr-Nahrain* 4, 1963/64, 1965, 50 ff; K. Aland, "Bemerkungen zum Schluss des Mk," *Neotestamentica et Semitica: Festschr. M. Black*, 1969, 255 ff; idem, "Der wiedergefundene Markusschluss? Eine methodologische Bemerkung zur textkritischen Arbeit," ZThK 67, 1970, 3 ff; E. Linnemann, "Der (wiedergefundene) Markusschluss," ZThK 66, 1969, 255 ff; R. P. Meye, "Mk 16:8— The Ending of Mk's Gospel," BR 14, 1969, 33 ff; H. R. Balz, art. Φοβέω κτλ, TDNT IX, 1970, 206 f.

appended 16:9-20 or the "shorter Markan ending" (see below) or for the combination of the two, but nowhere is there to be found evidence of the allegedly original ending of Mk. On the other hand the section 16:9-20 must have originated as early as the second century since it is known to Tatian and Irenaeus (who knows it as the end of Mk). It is not attested in the Greek manuscripts of the NT, however, before the fifth century (Codex W). Equally old is the so-called "shorter Markan ending," which is attested in a few Greek manuscripts and versions (L Ψ 099 *et al.*, syr., and Coptic MSS) between 16:8 and 9, and in the Vetus Latina MS k instead of 16:9 ff. And it could have originated only so long as 16:9 ff was not yet known (Aland).[69] The so-called Freer Logion,[70] which in W is inserted between 16:14 and 16:15 and consists of a defense of the eleven with reference to the power of Satan and the answer of Christ, arose in the second or third century as an expansion of 16:9 ff. It is clearly evident from these various attempts to discover an ending of Mk beyond 16:8 that early on there was an uneasy feeling that Mk could not end at 16:8. Mt and Lk must have had the same uneasiness as well, since their divergence beyond Mk 16:8 shows that, though they expanded Mk, it already ended at 16:8. Was that in fact the original ending of Mk? That is debated by many to the present day, especially since it seems that the appearance of the risen Lord in Galilee predicted in 14:28 and 16:7 ought to be reported. Frankly, no one has yet been able to explain how the original ending was lost. A loss resulting from a leaf breaking off would hardly have gone unremedied. And no one can say why anyone would intentionally discard the ending—which would have had to take place before Mt and Lk! "The manuscript evidence leads to no other supposition than that Mk circulated from the beginning with the short ending, i.e., ending at 16:8, as it began its literary existence through being copied from the original exemplar." [71] As a result there is an increasingly strong inclination to the view that 16:8 is the intended ending of Mk.[72] In this con-

[69] See the convincing evidence in Aland (see n. 68), ZThK 1970, 10 ff.

[70] Translation in Hennecke-Schneemelcher, *NT Apocrypha* I, 188.

[71] Aland (see n. 68) *Festschr. Black,* 160.

[72] Among others, Grundmann, Lohmeyer; Heard, Klijn, Marxsen, Michaelis; F. C. Grant, R. H. Lightfoot, Farrer, Carrington, Guy, Burkill, Tyson, Schreiber, Trocmé, Tagawa, Kertelge, Blatherwick, Bartsch, Waetjen, Thiering, Meye (see n. 68); W. C. Allen, "St. Mark 16:8. They Were Afraid. Why?" JTS 47, 1946, 46 ff; 48, 1947, 201 ff; L. J. D. Richardson, "St. Mark 16:8," JTS 49, 1948, 144 f; U. Wilckens, *Auferstehung,* 1970, 50; P. Stuhlmacher, "Kritische Marginalien zum gegenwärtigen Stand der Frage nach Jesus," *Fides et communicatio, Festschr. M. Doerne,* 1970, 346 f.

nection the two following questions must be answered: Can a book have ended with γάρ? What is the meaning of the abrupt ending ἐφοβοῦντο γάρ? The stylistic possibility of a book ending with γάρ has been demonstrated,[73] and the reference to the fear of the women means their timidity in view of the message of the resurrection.[74] As a means of stressing the message of the angels, which is for Mk decisive, the reference to fear is a wholly appropriate conclusion. Furthermore, the tension in the composition of 16:6-8 which Mk has created between the message of the angels (16:7) and the silence of the women (16:8)[75] permits no carrying the story further. There exists then some probability that the εὐαγγέλιον, which according to 1:1 Mk seeks to proclaim, has reached its goal in 16:7 f, so that we therefore have Mk preserved complete.

§7. THE GOSPEL OF MATTHEW

Commentaries: see §41. Studies: cf., in addition to lit. in §5, E. von Dobschütz, "Mt als Rabbi und Katechet," ZNW 27, 1928, 338 ff; B. W. Bacon, *Studies in Matthew*, 1930 (on this see W. G. Kümmel, ThLZ 57, 1932, 29 ff); C. C. Torrey, "The Biblical Quotations in Matthew," in C. C. T., *Documents of the Primitive Church*, 1941, 41 ff; S. E. Johnson, "The Biblical Quotations in Matthew," HTR 36, 1943, 135 ff; T. W. Manson, "The Gospel According to St. Matthew," BJRL 29, 1945/46, 392 ff (=Manson, *St.*, 68 ff); K. W. Clark, "The Gentile Bias in Matthew," JBL 66, 1947, 165 ff; C. H. Dodd, "Matthew and Paul," ExpT 58, 1946/47, 293 ff (=C. H. D., *NT Studies*, 1953, 53 ff); G. D. Kilpatrick, *The Origins of the Gospel According to St. Matthew*, [2]1950; S. G. F. Brandon, *The Fall of Jerusalem and the Christian Church*, 1951, 217 ff; K. Stendahl, *The School of St. Matthew*, ASNU 20, 1954 (=[2]1968 with expanded preface); *idem*, "Quis et unde? An Analysis of Mt 1-2," *Judentum, Urchristentum, Kirche, Festschr. J. Jeremias*, Bh. ZNW 26, 1960, 94 ff; B. Gärtner, "The Habakkuk Commentary (DSH) and the Gospel of Matthew," StTh 8, 1954, 1 ff; N. A. Dahl, "Die Passionsgeschichte bei Matthäus," NTS 2, 1955/56, 17 ff; F. V. Filson, "Broken Patterns in the Gospel of Matthew," JBL 75, 1956, 227 ff; L. Vaganay, DBS V, 1957, 940 ff;

---

[73] Cf. Richardson (see n. 72); Gils, (see n. 68), 18 n. 39. Meye (see n. 68), 37 ff, draws attention to the fact that the style of Mk is generally abrupt and that 16:1-8 announces the resurrection as the fulfillment of the word of Jesus himself.

[74] H. R. Balz (see n. 68), speaks without justification of "terror before God in view of the crucifixion"; according to 10:32, "fear" indicates fright in view of the miraculous event which in 16:7 has been announced to the reader as certain.

[75] See on this H. Grass, *Ostergeschehen und Osterberichte*, [2]1962, 16 ff, 289.

C. U. Wolf, "The Gospel of the Essenes," BR 3, 1958, 28 ff; P. Nepper-Christensen, *Das Mt, ein judenchristliches Ev?* Acta Theologica Danica I, 1958 (bibl.); O. Michel, CBL, 857 ff; J. Jeremias, "Die Muttersprache des Evangelisten Matthäus," ZNW 50, 1959, 270 ff (=Abba, 255 ff); H. W. Bartsch, "Die Passions- und Ostergeschichten bei Matthäus," *Basileia, W. Freitag zum 60. Geburtstag*, 1959, 28 ff (=H. W. B., "Entmythologisierende Auslegung," ThF 26, 1962, 80 ff); J. C. Fenton, "Inclusio and Chiasmus in Matthew," StEv, TU 73, 1959, 174 ff; E. P. Blair, *Jesus in the Gospel of Matthew*, 1960; G. Bornkamm, G. Barth, H. J. Held, *Tradition and Interpretation in Mt's Gospel*, 1963; J. M. Grintz, "Hebrew as the Spoken and Written Language in the Last Days of the Second Temple," JBL 79, 1960, 32 ff; G. Hebert, "The Problem of the Gospel According to Matthew," SJT 14, 1961, 403 ff; C. H. Lohr, "Oral Techniques in the Gospel of Matthew," CBQ 23, 1961, 403 ff; J. P. Brown, "The Form of 'Q' Known to Matthew," NTS 8, 1961/62, 27 ff; G. Strecker, *Der Weg der Gerechtigkeit. Untersuchung zur Theologie des Mt*, FRLANT 82, 1962 (=²1966, with suppl.); *idem*, "Das Geschichtsverständnis des Mt," EvTh 26, 1966, 57 ff; J. Schmid, LThK VII, 1962, 176 ff; X. Léon-Dufour, *Théologie de Matthieu* (survey of lit.), RechSR 50, 1962, 90 ff; C. F. D. Moule, "Translation Greek and Original Greek in Mt," in C. F. D. M., *The Birth of the NT*, 1962, 215 ff; *idem*, "St. Matthew's Gospel: Some Neglected Features," StEv II, TU 87, 1964, 91 ff; C. W. F. Smith, "The Mixed State of the Church in Matthew's Gospel," JBL 82, 1963, 149 ff; J. Kürzinger, "Irenäus und sein Zeugnis zur Sprache des Mt," NTS 10, 1963/64, 108 ff; W. Trilling, *Das wahre Israel. Studien zur Theologie des Mt*, StANT 10, ³1964; *idem*, "Mt, das kirchliche Ev. Überlieferungsgeschichte und Theologie," GANT, 186 ff; E. Krentz, "The Extent of Matthew's Prologue," JBL 83, 1964, 409 ff; J. Smit Sibinga, "Ignatius and Matthew," NovTest 8, 1966 (=*Placita Pleiadia, Festschr. G. Sevenster*), 263 ff; R. Hummel, *Die Auseinandersetzung zwischen Kirche und Judentum im Mt*, BevTh 33, ²1966; R. Pesch, "Der Gottessohn im matthäischen Evangelienprolog. Beobachtungen zu den Zitationsformeln der Reflexionszitate," Bb 48, 1967, 395 ff; R. Walker, *Die Heilsgeschichte im ersten Ev*, FRLANT 91, 1967; R. H. Gundry, *The Use of the Old Testament in St. Matthew's Gospel*, Suppl. NovTest 18, 1967; W. Schmauch, "Die Komposition des Mt in ihrer Bedeutung für seine Interpretation," in W. S., *Zu achten aufs Wort. Ausgewählte Arbeiten*, 1967, 64 ff; D. R. A. Hare, *The Theme of Jewish Persecution of Christians in the Gospel According to St. Matthew*, SNTSMS 6, 1967; O. H. Steck, *Israel und das gewaltsame Geschick der Propheten*, WMANT 23, 1967, 289 ff; F. Neirynck, "La rédaction Matthéenne et la structure du premier Évangile," *Festschr. Coppens*, 41 ff; M. P. Brown, "Mt as ΕΙΡΗΝΟΠΟΙΟΣ," in *Studies in the History and Text of the NT in Honor of K. W. Clark*, StD 29, 1967, 39 ff; C. S. Petrie, "The Authorship of the Gospel According to Mt: A Reconsideration of the External Evidence," NTS 14, 1967/68, 15 ff; H.

P. West, "A Primitive Version of Luke in the Composition of Mt,"
NTS 14, 1967/68, 75 ff; H. Merkel, "Jesus und die Pharisäer," NTS
14, 1967/68, 197 ff; H. B. Green, "The Structure of St. Matthew's
Gospel," StEv IV, TU 102, 1968, 47 ff; R. P. Martin, "St. Matthew's
Gospel in Recent Study," ExpT 80, 1968/69, 132 ff; W. Rothfuchs,
Die Erfüllungszitate des Mt, BWANT V, 8, 1969; J. D. Kingsbury,
The Parables in Mt 13: A Study in Redaction Criticism, 1969; K.
Tagawa, "People and Community in the Gospel of Mt," NTS 16,
1969/70, 149 ff; E. Schweizer, "Gesetz und Enthusiasmus bei Mt," in
E. S., *Beiträge zur Theologie des NT*, 1970, 49 ff; A. Sand, "Die Polemik
gegen 'Gesetzlosigkeit' im Ev nach Mt und bei Paulus. Ein Beitrag
zur nt. Überlieferungsgeschichte," BZ, NF 14, 1970, 112 ff; P. Bonnard,
"Matthieu, éducateur du peuple chrétien," *Mélanges Bibliques en hommage au R. P. B. Rigaux*, 1970, 1 ff; X. Léon-Dufour, "Redaktionsgeschichte of Matthew and Literary Criticism," *Perspective*, 9 ff; K. M.
Fischer, "Redaktionsgeschichtliche Bemerkungen zur Passionsgeschichte
des Mt," *Theologische Versuche* II, ed. J. Rogge and G. Schille, 1970,
190 ff; E. L. Abel, "Who Wrote Matthew?" NTS 17, 1970/71, 138 ff.

1. Contents

Prologue 1:1–4:16. Chs. 1–2: names and places of origin of
Jesus (see Stendahl, *Jeremias Festschr.*); genealogy of Jesus (1:1-
17); birth and naming of Jesus (1:18-25); homage of the Magi
in Bethlehem (2:1-12); flight to Egypt (2:13-15); slaughter of
the children in Bethlehem (2:16-18); return from Egypt and
residence in Nazareth (2:19-23). 3:1–4:16: preparation for the
activity of Jesus: John the Baptist (3:1-12); baptism of Jesus
(3:13-17); temptation of Jesus and residence in Capernaum (4:1-
11).

Part One: The Proclamation of the Kingdom of God in Galilee
4:17–16:20. After the account of the call of Jesus' first disciples
(4:18-22) and his first teaching and healing activity (4:23-25),
portrayal of his action through word (5–7: sermon on the mount)
and act (8–9): ten miracles, interrupted by conversations (8:18-
22; 9:9-17): healing of the leper (8:1-4); healing of the servant
of the official from Capernaum (8:5-13), of Peter's mother-in-law
and of many sick (8:14-17); dismissal of unsuitable followers;
stilling the storm (8:23-27); healing the Gadarene demoniac
(8:28-34), of a lame man (9:9-13); question of fasting (9:14-17);
healing of Jairus' daughter and of the hemorrhaging woman
(9:18-26), of two blind men (9:27-31), and of a mute demoniac
(9:32-34). Conversations follow in Chs. 11 and 12, framed by
the discourses of Chs. 10 and 13 and introduced by a new descrip-

tion of the teaching and healing work of Jesus (9:35-38). Sending
out of the twelve and address to the disciples: instructions for the
mission; words concerning the fate of the disciples; warning about
fearless confession and suffering (10:1–11:1); Jesus and the
Baptist (11:2-19); pronouncement of woe on the cities of Galilee
(11:20-24); shout of joy and summons of the Savior (11:25-30);
conflict conversations with the Pharisees (sabbath conflict; defama-
tion of Jesus as being in league with Beelzebub, demand for signs)
12:1-45; the true relatives of Jesus 12:46-50; seven parables of
the kingdom of God (sower, with explanation; mustard seed,
leaven; treasure; pearl; fishnet) 13:1-52; rejection in Nazareth
(13:53-58). Then follows a series of reports which show Jesus as
itinerant, beginning and ending with the question who Jesus is
(14:1–16:20): Herod's opinion about Jesus (14:1-2); arrest of the
Baptist (14:3-12); feeding of the five thousand (14:13-21);
Jesus' walking on the lake and Peter's sinking (14:22-23); healings
in Gennesaret (14:34-36); discourse on clean and unclean (15:1-
20); Jesus and the Canaanite woman (15:21-28); healings of the
sick (15:29-31); feeding of the four thousand (15:32-39); demand for signs (16:1-4); warning about the leaven of the Pharisees (16:5-12); Peter's confession at Caesarea Philippi (16:13-20).

*Part Two: Jesus on the Way to Jerusalem and the Predictions of
the Passion* 16:21–25:46. First prediction of the passion (16:21-23);
sayings about the sufferings of the disciples and the coming of the
Son of man (16:24-28); transfiguration and conversation about
the return of Elijah (17:1-13); healing of the epileptic boy
(17:14-21); second passion prediction (17:22-23); question about
the temple tax (17:24-27); discourse on discipleship (sayings about
behavior toward the "little ones," about offenses, about behavior
within the community, parable of the roguish servant, 18:1-35);
conversations about marriage and divorce (19:1-12); blessing of
children (19:13-15); the rich young man (19:16-26); reward
for following Jesus (19:27-30); parable of the workers in the
vineyard (20:1-16); third passion prediction (20:17-19); Jesus
and the sons of Zebedee (20:20-28); healing of the two blind
men near Jericho (20:29-34); procession toward Jerusalem (21:1-
11); cleansing the temple (21:12 f); homage of the children in
the temple (21:14-17); cursing of the fig tree (21:18-22); question of authority (21:23-27); parable of the dissimilar sons (21:28-
32), of the evil vineyard-workers (21:33-46), and of the royal
marriage (22:1-14); question of the Pharisees about the tribute
money (22:15-22); question of the Sadducees concerning the
resurrection (22:23-33); question of the Pharisees about David's

son as Messiah (22:41-46); discourse against the Pharisees and scribes, including seven woes (23:1-36); lament over Jerusalem (23:37-39). Eschatological chapters: 24–25; destruction of the temple (24:1 f); warning signs of the End (24:3-14); the great tribulation (24:15-28); the parousia of the Son of man (24:29-31); determining the End (24:32-36); parables of the flood, of the watchful master of the household, of the faithful and slothful servants, of the ten maidens, of the entrusted talents (24:37–25:30); prediction of the judgment of the world by the Son of man (25:31-46).

Conclusion: Passion Narrative and Resurrection Report 26:1–28:20. Passion narrative (26:1–27:56): decree of death (26:1-5); anointing in Bethany (26:6-13); Judas' betrayal (26:14-16); preparation of the Passover (26:17-19); identification of the betrayer and institution of the Lord's Supper (26:20-30); prediction of the denial, Gethsemane, capture of Jesus, hearing before the high council, denial of Peter (26:31-75); handing over Jesus to Pilate, death of Judas, proceedings before Pilate, condemnation, mocking, way to Golgotha, crucifixion and death of Jesus (27:1-56); burial (27:57-61); guard at the tomb (27:62-66). Resurrection report (28:1-20): message of the resurrection at the empty tomb (28:1-8); appearance of the risen Lord to the women (28:9 f); the Jewish lie about the theft of the body of Jesus (28:11-15); final word of the risen Lord to his disciples on a mountain in Galilee: command to evangelize and to baptize (28:16-20).

2. Literary Character and Theological Aim of the Gospel of Matthew

The question how the divisions of Mt were intended to be by the evangelist cannot be answered with certainty. The structure offered in section 1 above builds on the observation that the formula ἀπὸ τότε ἤρξατο ὁ Ἰησοῦς or Ἰησοῦς Χριστός is found only in 4:17 and 16:21 and in each case clearly indicates the beginning of a new phase of the activity of Jesus,[1] though in divergence from that structuring 26:1–28:20 is to be considered an independent concluding section. Nevertheless this structure cannot be proved

---

[1] Lohmeyer; Schmauch; especially Krentz (in agreement, Strecker, *Geschichtsverständnis*, 62 f; in disagreement, Walker, 115 n. 2). Krentz has shown that 3:1–4:16 clearly belongs to 1–2 and that in 1:1–4:16 there are seven "fulfillment citations," of which 3:3 and 4:15 f carry forward the geographical interests of Mt 2.

unambiguously any more than can the division based on Mk's
structure (prehistory and preparation for the activity of Jesus:
1:1–4:11; Jesus in Galilee: 4:12–13:58; Jesus on the way to Jerusalem: 14:1–20:34; Jesus in Jerusalem: 21:1–28:20).[2] In view of
this uncertainty numerous other outlines have been proposed (based
on the number seven,[3] or on thematic points of view[4]). But most
common is the attempt to show—following Bacon's proposal—
that the similar conclusions to discourses in 7:28; 11:1; 13:53;
19:1; 26:1 (καὶ ἐγένετο ὅτε ἐτέλεσεν ὁ Ἰησοῦς τοὺς λόγους τούτους
or the like) are meant to form five books, which combine the discourses in 5–7; 10; 13; 18; 24–25 with the narrative material that
precedes each discourse. The pattern corresponds to the Five Books
of Moses.[5] But it is rightly maintained to the contrary that this
assumption of a fivefold structure leaves out of account Ch. 23
with its discourse,[6] and wrongly designates Chs. 1–2 and 26–28
as prologue and epilogue. There is really no foundation for the
notion that Mt tries to portray Jesus as the "New Moses," quite
apart from the fact that the reader is never notified that Mt is
using five similar endings for the discourses, or that the narratives
that precede the discourses in each case belong with them.[7] It must
suffice us to state that Mt has essentially taken over the Markan
framework and has employed it as the base for his own expanded
presentation,[8] since it obviously seemed to him best suited for
achieving his goal.

Mt has basically reworked the Markan account by means of detailed modifications, by major abbreviations and new formulations,
but especially by inserting extensive material. It has already been
shown that the rearranging of the material that Mt took over
from Mk 1–5 contributes to the systematic bringing together of
similar material (see above, §5.3.5). The systematization is further
evident in the fact that in the discourses composed and inserted

[2] Also in the twelfth-sixteenth editions of this *Intr.*; further, Michaelis,
Wikenhauser; similarly, Harrison, Mariani; Neirynck.

[3] E.g., Gaechter, Lohmeyer; Albertz; Schmauch. Green proposes a chiastic
division into eleven sections.

[4] In various ways, e.g., Grundmann; Harrington, Léon-Dufour in Robert-
Feuillet.

[5] Johnson; Fuller, Harrington, Höpfl-Gut; Kilpatrick, Stendahl, Dahl; J. P.
Brown, M. P. Brown; H. Kee, *Jesus in History*, 1970, 151 f; hesitantly W. D.
Davies, *The Setting of the Sermon on the Mount*, 1964, 14 ff, 92 f.

[6] Harrington, 144, therefore considers Ch. 23 a subsequent insertion by the
evangelist.

[7] Cf. Guthrie, Klijn; Blair, Bornkamm, Barth, Lohr, Strecker, Moule, Trilling,
Walker, Rothfuchs.

[8] See Nierynck, esp. 66 f.

by Mt, the material has been arranged from the standpoint of subject matter and catechetical aims:[9] the six antitheses (5:21-48); the three texts about proper cultic performance (6:1-18); the eschatological parables (24:37–25:46, etc.), especially when it can be shown from the Lukan parallels that the material did not have such an order in the tradition. To this systematization, which is evident from a comparison with Mk and Q, corresponds Mt's fondness for the repetition of formulas 4:23; 9:35; 10:1/9:13; 12:7/8: 12; 13:42, 50; 22:13; 24:51; 25:30/3:7; 12:34; 23:33; for the introductory formulas of the fulfillment citations (see below, pp. 110 ff, etc.); for the use of schematic numbers: seven parables (Ch. 13); ten miracle stories (Chs. 8–9); seven woes against the Pharisees (Ch. 23), etc.; for the stereotyped formulas at the beginning and end of the miracle stories, and thus for the overall impressive presentation.[10] Furthermore Mt has significantly improved Mk's Greek[11] and shortened his narrative; above all, the healing miracles are accommodated to the controversy- and scribal conversations (Held). In addition, Mt has increased the number of links between individual traditions—mostly missing in Mk—and has in this way strongly increased the impression of a chronological or spatial connection in the narrative (cf., e.g., 12:46; 13:1; 14:1) without actually changing anything in the juxtaposition of the narratives. The secondary character of these links in comparison with Mk is evident in 14:12, where Mt has overlooked the fact that the account of the death of the Baptist (Mk 6:17-29) is a chronological retrospective supplement, and so he erroneously links the end of this account to the following story of the feeding of the five thousand (Mk 6:30 ff par.; Mt 14:13 ff).[12]

Mt has also undertaken substantive alterations of his Markan prototype—but almost nothing in the sayings of Jesus that he has taken over from Mk![13] We have already noted that he assimilated the healing stories with the controversy- and scribal conversations by means of abbreviation; by setting aside concrete individual

[9] Bonnard, *Festschr. Rigaux*, 5 f.

[10] See the collected evidence in von Dobschütz, in Held, 241 ff, and the lists in Lohr, which are to be sifted critically.

[11] Cf. P. Wernle, *Die synopt. Frage*, 1899, 146 ff. In addition, scattered Semitisms are to be found in the language of Mt (Moule, "Translation Greek," 217 f) at the same time that Semitisms have been eliminated (Strecker, *Weg der Gerechtigkeit*, 19 ff).

[12] On these alterations, see R. Bultmann, *History of Synopt. Tradition*, 351 f.

[13] See T. R. Rosché, "The Words of Jesus and the Future of the 'Q' Hypothesis," JBL 75, 1960, 214; confirmed by C. E. Carlston and D. Norlin, "Once More—Statistics and Q," HTR 64, 1971, 64, 68 ff, and R. Morgenthaler, *Statistische Synopse*, 1971, 163.

features he conveys an even greater emphasis on the figure of Jesus, who "heals all sickness and all infirmities among the people" (4:23; 9:35), and on faith as the prerequisite for receiving help from Jesus ("Woman, your faith is great; may it happen to you as you will," 15:28, against Mk 7:29). Held [13a] conjectures quite rightly that Mt has omitted the two healings (Mk 7:31 ff; 8:22 ff) because he found no point of connection in them for his theological interpretation. Furthermore, Mt has strongly assimilated the figure of Jesus the Son of God to faith in the exalted Lord, in that he strikes out or alters the emotional reactions of Jesus (ὀργισθείς Mk 1:41 par. Mt 8:3; ἠγανάκτησεν Mk 10:14 par. Mt 19:14) and offensive features in the narrative about Jesus (ἐξέστη Mk 3:21; οὐκ ἐδύνατο ἐκεῖ ποιῆσαι οὐδεμίαν δύναμιν Mk 6:5 par. Mt 13:58 οὐκ ἐποίησεν ἐκεῖ δυνάμεις πολλάς). And he has Jesus addressed as Kurios.[14] Similarly, the disciples are strongly idealized, so that blame or evidence of failure is eliminated (the blame of Mk 4:13 is replaced by blessedness in Mt 13:16 f; Mk's "they did not understand, because their hearts were hardened" [6:52] becomes in Mt 14:33 "they worshiped him and said, 'Truly you are the Son of God' ").[15] To contest this state of affairs by appeal to the quite valid evidence that Mt has several times introduced against the disciples a charge of deficient faith or obedience[16] (cf. ὀλιγόπιστοι 16:8 against Mk 8:17; or σκάνδαλον εἶ ἐμοῦ [Peter] 16:23 against Mk 8:33) is to ignore that Mt has not proceeded in consistent fashion, but has occasionally taken over elements of the tradition that are prejudicial to the disciples and then has made them stronger in order to stress the saving power of Jesus (cf. 14:30-33).

The distinctive theological aim of Mt in his reworking of the Markan material is discernible if we focus attention on the extensive expansion of Mk by Mt. About half of Mt has no parallel in Mk; from this half, about five-ninths is found also in Lk, and the remaining four-ninths is Mt's special material.[17] If, as established in §5, the material he has in common with Lk is assumed to have been taken over from Q, where did he get his special material? Even if we give up the notion that Mt and Mk are dependent on a common Urmatthäus [primitive Mt] and that the special material is

[13a] Held, 199 ff.

[14] Cf. also the examples mentioned above, pp. 60 f, and in Strecker, Der Weg der Gerechtigkeit, 120 ff; Fischer, 109 f, 113 f.

[15] Cf. Strecker, Weg der Gerechtigkeit, 193 f; Trilling, Das Wahre Israel, 91 f; Fischer, 122.

[16] Barth, 114 ff.

[17] According to the word count in de Solages, Synopse Grecque des Évangiles, 1959, 1049.

from that source (see against this §5.3.6), the origin of the special material has to be explained in one of two ways from the use of one or more written sources. According to the one assumption, Mt would have had to use the Q source in a form that was expanded in comparison with that used by Lk, so that the non-Markan material, or at least a great part of it, would have come from Q^{Mt}.[18] Obviously the possibility exists that this or that text which is found only in Mt came from Q; but this assumption cannot be based on evidence to the effect that the Gentile Christian author of Mt could not have inserted into his Gospel explicitly Jewish Christian texts such as 5:20; 10:23 without their having been in his *Vorlage* (J. P. Brown), or that the expansion of Lk 17:3 f (par. Mt 18:15, 21) by means of the community regulations (Mt 18:16-20) must have taken place already in Q (Strecker). If Mt's use of Mk and Q is to be conceived as a dependence based on more or less oral transmission rather than a purely literary reworking (see above, §5.3.9.b), then the strong possibility exists that the evangelist has taken over details of various origin and has placed them wherever it seemed suitable, even in a Q context. Filson[19] has shown convincingly that Mt has no reluctance in destroying the form of literary series by insertions (see the insertion of 6:7-15 in the midst of 6:1-18, or the scattering of Mk 4 in Mt 13).[20] The theory of the origin of Mt's special material from Q becomes still more dubious when its advocates find themselves compelled to attribute a part of the special material to still other sources (J. P. Brown, the parables; Strecker, the fulfillment quotations), because there is no place for them in Q. Accordingly, it is most unlikely that the Matthean special material was taken over as a whole, or even largely, from Q.

More common is the assumption that Mt has used a third source (M) in addition to Mk and Q.[21] But this supposition could be supported only if it could be presupposed as self-evident that extensive material must come from a written source; actually, the form-critical and theological disparities of the special material can by no means be accounted for if we suppose them to have stemmed

---

[18] Bacon, J. P. Brown, Strecker.

[19] F. V. Filson, "Broken Patterns."

[20] On the relation of Mt 13 to Mk 4 see Kingsbury, 12 f.

[21] Above all, B. H. Streeter, *The Four Gospels,* 1924; further, Johnson; Henshaw; Kilpatrick, Smit Sibinga; E. Hirsch, *Frühgeschichte des Ev.* II, 1941; T. W. Manson, *The Sayings of Jesus,* 1949, 21 ff; V. Taylor, "The Original Order of Q," *NT Essays in Memory of T. W. Manson,* 1959, 246 ff; F. G. Downing, "Towards the Rehabilitation of Q," NTS 11, 1964/65, 169 ff, and others.

from a common written source. If Mt 1 and 2 turn out to be the
evangelist's own composition with aim of showing the names and
places of origin of Jesus (Stendahl), and if in the passion narrative no scriptural source in addition to Mk is evident (Dahl), then
it is only the special material in Chs. 3–25 which could have come
from the postulated source M, and it would be impossible to declare
what literary character this source must have had.

The most probable supposition, therefore, is that Mt has used only
oral tradition in addition to Mk and Q.[22] It is quite likely that a
part of this tradition had been arranged into groups according to
form or subject matter before Mt, but that cannot be
demonstrated in detail. It has certainly been conjectured that an
oral or written source must have been used for one complex: namely
for the so-called "formula quotations" or, better, "fulfillment
quotations."[23] This is the customary designation for the quotations
found only in Mt (1:23; 2: [6], 15, 18, 23; 4:15 f; 8:17; 12:18-
21; 13:35; 21:5; 27:9 f) which are introduced by the formula
ἵνα πληρωθῇ τὸ ῥηθὲν ὑπὸ κυρίου διὰ τοῦ προφήτου λέγοντος (2:15)
or similarly, and are thus differentiated from all other quotations.
These quotations are said to be distinguished from all the other quotations in Mt not only by the introductory formula, but also by
their text. Yet the situation as a whole and the explanation for it are
extraordinarily under dispute. Surely Torrey's thesis is misguided
(cf. Johnson) that Mt has inserted OT quotations from the Hebrew into his Aramaic text; from this our Greek text would then
be a translation, which accidentally or under the influence of Mk
occasionally makes contact with LXX. Recent research is much
more united in its conclusion that Mt has taken over from his
sources in Greek the quotations which he shares with Mk or Lk,
and that occasionally he assimilates them to LXX in details (cf.
Mt 3:3 par. Mk 1:3 = LXX word for word; Mt 4:6 f par. Lk 4:
10 f = LXX word for word). Also in those quotations which are
found in Mt alone, but where the introductory formula of the

---

[22] Thus, e.g., Albertz, Guthrie, Heard, Michaelis; Dahl; F. W. Beare,
The Earliest Records of Jesus, 1962. The supposition is unnecessary that Mt
has used a second tradition, also known to Lk, as source for some of his Markan
material (Grundmann, 18).

[23] Though it has been used customarily since at least the beginning of this
century (see W. Soltau, ZNW 1, 1900, 221), the designation *Reflexionszitate*
to characterize Mt's formula for introducing scriptural quotations is a poor one.
"Formula quotations," the designation proposed by S. Johnson (in "Biblical
Quotations," 135) is also still too general, whereas the term of Rothfuchs
(20 f), *Erfüllungszitate* (="fulfillment quotations"), indicates well the pecu-
liarity of the introductory formulas.

"fulfillment citations" is not used, Mt as a rule follows LXX (Mt 21:16 = LXX, which is exclusively the text that could be used in this connection). There are exceptions, however: Mt 11:29 εὑρήσετε ἀνάπαυσιν ταῖς ψυχαῖς ὑμῶν follows in part the Hebrew text of Jer 6:16 against LXX, but this may have been taken over with the logion 11:28-30; in 16:27, however, Mk 8:38 has been expanded through use of Prov 24:18 according to the Hebrew text and against LXX; and in 11:29 the quotation from Jer 6:13 is partly based on LXX but in the word ἀνάπαυσιν corresponds to the Hebrew text (though once more it is uncertain whether the quotation came with the logion 11:28-30). Even though it cannot be deduced from these isolated examples that the evangelist Matthew himself knew the Hebrew text, it is evident in any case that in the tradition available to him there were OT quotations which came, not from LXX, but from other translations of the Hebrew text.

As for the fulfillment citations already mentioned that are found in Mt, investigation of the form of their text shows that their Greek text stands much closer to the Hebrew text than is the case with the other quotations, but that an influence of LXX cannot be denied. For example, in Mt 8:17, Isa 53:4 is quoted exactly according to the Hebrew text and in total divergence from LXX and every other Greek version; on the other hand, the reference to Isa 7:14 in Mt 1:23 follows LXX, especially in the translation of hā'almāh by ἡ παρθένος, while the choice of καλέσουσιν as against qārā't of the Hebrew text or καλέσεις of LXX better suits the context of the quotation: the parents do not give to the child the name Immanuel. The divergent character of the text and the special introductory formulas has been accounted for on the assumption that Mt took over these scriptural quotations from an oral[24] or a written source.[25] Stendahl argues against the notion that these quotations come from a source, and proposes as much more likely that they are to be traced to the exegetical activity of a Christian "school," which performed exegesis in a manner similar to that of the Habakkuk commentary found at Qumran. The similarity in exegetical method is denied by Gärtner, however, who assumes that the fulfillment citations grew out of the endeavor to have on hand suitable scriptural references for use in preaching to the Jews and that Mt took over his citations from this tradition. Now it has been proved convincingly[26] that the introductory formulas come from the

[24] Grundmann, Lohmeyer; Bacon, Strecker, Rothfuchs.
[25] Kilpatrick; with caution, Nepper-Christensen.
[26] Strecker, 50; Pesch, 398 f; Rothfuchs, 44, 55; S. Schulz, *Die Stunde der Botschaft*, 1967, 165.

evangelist, but then the question arises whether the quotations thus introduced were taken from a source.[27] Without doubt the quotation in Mt 21:5 has caused the peculiar misunderstanding that Jesus sat on an ass *and* her foal (21:7), but just as clearly the context in 1:23 has caused the alteration of the quotation (see above; similarly in 2:6). On the other hand it is improbable that Mt created the fulfillment quotations himself, as the scanty Matthean linguistic material in them evidences,[28] and nothing can be found in them to indicate the activity of an exegetical school. Gärtner's position[29] probably comes closest to the truth: these quotations owe their origin to the missionary preaching tradition, and in no case do the quotations point to a written or fixed oral source which Mt used in addition to Mk and Q. If Mt on this assumption is not dependent on a source of any particular sort, then the strength is gone from the argument that the quotation in 13:14 f is to be eliminated as a later interpolation because its introductory formula is different from that of the fulfillment citations and its text is pure LXX.[30]

But then if Mt follows no source even for the quotations cited in his Gospel, but takes them out of the tradition as he does his other special material and inserts it all, together with the Q material, into his reworked Mk, the question arises as to his aim in expanding and thus transforming Mk. Since the fulfillment citations have as their goal to stress the "fulfillment" of the word of Scripture in the person of Jesus and thus to show Jesus as the obvious goal of the revelation of God in the OT, they have often been viewed in connection with related phenomena in Mt: (*a*) Mt does not explain Jewish customs, regulations, or modes of expression (hand-washing, 15:2 par. Mk 7:2 f; φυλακτήρια [see below, p. 115], and fringed clothing, 23:5; straining out gnats, 23:24; whitewashed graves, 23:27); Hebrew expressions are untranslated, 5:22; 27:6. (*b*) He reworks narratives in the form of a specifically rabbinic formulation of the issue: instead of the general question "Can a man divorce his wife (Mk 10:2), he writes (Mt 19:3), "Can a man divorce

---

[27] See on this Guthrie, 154 ff; Stendahl, [2]viii; Pesch, 403; Schweizer, 59 n. 37.

[28] Otherwise, Pesch, 399 n. 4, 403; Gundry, 172; Rothfuchs, 92 f, according to whom Mt formulated the fulfillment citations himself, though no adequate evidence for this is offered.

[29] So Schulz (see n. 26), 165.

[30] Against Torrey, 66 f; Johnson, 137 f; Stendahl, 129 ff; Strecker, 70 n. 3, 248; Kingsbury, 38 f; J. Gnilka, "Das Verstockungsproblem nach Mt 13:13-15," in *Antijudaismus im NT?* Abhandlungen zum christlich-jüdischen Dialog 2 1967, 127. Counterargument in Gundry, 116 ff.

his wife κατὰ πᾶσαν αἰτίαν?" and accommodates it to the basic casuistic discussion about the permitted grounds for divorce. Correspondingly, he introduces into the unconditional saying of Jesus "Whoever divorces his wife and marries another, commits adultery against her" (Mk 10:11) the unchastity proviso μὴ ἐπὶ πορνείᾳ (19:9, also in 5:32), and so has Jesus represent the strict though conditional view of the Shammaites.[31] (c) He presents sayings which represent the unconditional validity of the Law: "Whoever relaxes one of the least of these commandments . . . will be called least in the kingdom of God" (5:19);[32] "everything that the scribes and Pharisees say to you do and maintain" (23:3). (d) Mt presents sayings of Jesus which explicitly limit the activity of Jesus to Israel: "Do not go into the way of the Gentiles and enter no city of the Samaritans" (10:5); "I am sent only to the lost sheep of the house of Israel" (15:24; cf. 10:6); addition to Mk 7:24 ff, "you will not have gone through all the cities of Israel before the Son of man comes" (10:23). (e) Mt accommodates the language of Jesus to Jewish linguistic formulas: with the exception of 12:28; 19:24; 21:31, 43, Mt has regularly ἡ βασιλέια τῶν οὐρανῶν instead of ἡ βασιλεία τοῦ θεοῦ that is used exclusively in Mk and Lk; ὁ πατὴρ ὑμῶν ὁ ἐν τοῖς οὐρανοῖς, which is found only once in Mk (11: 25) and not at all in Lk, occurs fifteen times in Mt, of which 6:9; 7:11; 10:32 f; 12:50 are at variance with the synoptic parallels; the behavior demanded of the disciples is only in Mt designated as δικαιοσύνη (5:6, 10, 20; 6:1, 33; 21:32); Mt presents the Lord's Prayer in a form much closer to Jewish liturgical usage by means of the address, the sevenfold petitions, and the formulation of the prayer for forgiveness (6:12, ὀφειλήματα instead of ἁμαρτίας Lk 11:4).[33] From this it has been concluded that Mt has reworked Mk

[31] See on this Hummel, 49 ff, Neirynck, 59 f; J. Dupont, *Mariage et divorce dans l'évangile*, 1959, 27 ff, 85 ff. Further examples of casuistic reworking by Mt in C. E. Carlston, "The Things That Defile (Mk 7:15) and the Law in Mt and Mk," NTS 15, 1968/69, 86 ff.

[32] Also Mt 5:18, "Until heaven and earth pass away, not an iota or a stroke will pass away from the law," is reformulated by Mt, at variance with the certainly original parallel (Lk 16:17), so that still more clearly stressed is the binding validity of the Law in every detail until the end of the age, the more so since the ambiguous phrase "until all takes place" may signify "until the law is done in each and every way," as suggested, e.g., by Strecker, *Weg der Gerechtigkeit*, 143 ff, and Trilling, *Das wahre Israel*, 167 ff.

[33] Walker, 134 ff, argues that these features of Mt were formed in the strongly Jewish-oriented tradition that he drew upon, but that they are anachronisms which have been "eliminated by Mt effectively and frequently in other places"; but most of these features are recognizable as Mt's own redactional alterations!

with the help of Jewish-Christian tradition that he has adapted in order to defend Christianity in the eyes of Jewish-Christian readers, to make it acceptable to them, and to prove to them that Jesus was the Jewish Messiah. The author would have been a Jewish Christian who had at his disposal rabbinic knowledge.[34] Even beyond this is the supposition that the community whose outlook Mt represents is in association with Judaism and interprets the Law in Jewish fashion: 12:1 shows by the addition to the pericope of plucking grain on the sabbath—the disciples "were hungry" (in contrast to Mk 2: 23)—that the sabbath was still observed. The recasting of Lk 16:16a ("The law and the prophets [are in effect] until John") into Mt 11:13 ("All the prophets and the law prophesy until John") shows that the Law is still regarded as valid. Since Mt 24:9 runs, "You will be hated by all people" (against Mk 13:13), it is evident that, according to Mt, the disciples must suffer the fate of "the Jews" among the Gentiles.[35] Support for the second of these suppositions, to be sure, rests on a forced and scarcely convincing exegesis. That the church of Mt sees itself as over against Judaism and not linked with the synagogue is shown by these facts: Mt again and again speaks of "your synagogues, their synagogues, their scribes," etc. (7:29; 9:35; 23:34),[36] and above all there is the saying inserted by Mt, "The kingdom of God will be taken from you and given to a people who produce its fruits" (21:43).[37]

Recently the view that Mt displays a Jewish-Christian character and is intended for Jewish Christians has been generally disputed, and scholars have sought to prove that the author of Mt was not a birthright Jew and did not write for Jewish Christians; rather, it is said, he was a Gentile Christian and devoted his efforts to the Gentile-Christian church, which was in the majority.[38] The arguments which are advanced for this view are obviously of very different weight. That Mt did not reproduce a few Semitic words from Mk (Mk 3:17; 5:41; 7:11, 34; 10:46, 51; 14:36) does not

---

[34] So in various ways Bonnard, Gaechter, Grundmann, Schlatter, Schmid; Feine-Behm, Heard, McNeile-Williams, Meinertz, Michaelis, Wikenhauser; von Dobschütz, Kilpatrick, Stendahl, Gärtner, Blair, Wolf, Hummel, Merkel, Kingsbury.

[35] Thus, e.g., Bornkamm, Barth, Hummel.

[36] Cf. Kilpatrick, 110 f; Hare, 104 f, 113, 125, 127; W. Schrage, TDNT VII, 830 ff.

[37] See further 28:15, "This word is spread abroad among the Jews to this day," and cf. Grundmann, 33, 112; Klijn, 32 f; Schelkle, 58; Steck, 314; Martin, 136; Tagawa, 160; J. Rohde, *Rediscovering* . . . , 96 f; S. Schulz (see n. 26), 162, 211.

[38] Thus in various ways Clark, Nepper-Christensen, Hebert, Strecker, Trilling, Walker; S. Schulz (see n. 26), 161 f.

prove that he did not understand them, since he generally abbreviates the texts but does take over other Semitic words (Mt 6:24; 10:4, 25; 27:33) or introduce them ('Εμμανουήλ 1:23; ῥακά 5:22; κορβανᾶν 27:6). That he uses the grecized form Ἰσκαριώτης (10:4; 26:14) instead of the correct Semitic form Ἰσκαριώθ (Mk 3:19; 14:10) proves only that he is writing in a region where Greek is spoken. If it cannot in this way be shown that the author knew no Semitic languages, neither can the opposite be proved.[39] Even if Mt wrote for former Jews (Nepper-Christensen), it is not conclusive that he had to write in the language of the Jews, either Hebrew or Aramaic, if in fact his readers spoke Greek. The argument that πλατύνουσι τὰ φυλακτήρια αὐτῶν could have been written only by a Gentile Christian who confused tefillin (Jewish prayer bands) with amulets (Clark) is fallacious, since it is probable that in this text Jesus is polemicizing against the ostentation of wearing amulets.[40]

All these arguments for (or against) a Gentile-Christian origin for Mt are not convincing, but the assertion is true that Mt's position is in no way particularistic; rather, the message of Jesus is valid for all people. That is implied not only by the command of the risen Lord "to make disciples of all people" (28:19), but also from the explanatory phrase ὁ ἀγρός ἐστιν ὁ κόσμος (13:38); the prediction "This gospel of the kingdom will be preached ἐν ὅλῃ τῇ οἰκουμένῃ εἰς μαρτύριον πᾶσιν τοῖς ἔθνεσιν" (24:14); the expansion of the parable of the wedding feast, πορεύεσθε οὖν ἐπὶ τὰς διεξόδους τῶν ὁδῶν (22:9).[41] In no way does Mt represent the point of view that the gospel is chiefly or exclusively for the Jews, as might be inferred from the sayings of Jesus mentioned above on p. 113: 10:5 f, 23; 15:24. More frequently a few texts are pointed to which are said to indicate that for Mt Christianity has superseded Judaism, and that according to Mt the Jews will ultimately be cast out: "The sons of the kingdom will be cast into outer darkness" (8:12); "The kingdom of God will be taken from you" (21:43); the Jews pronounce upon themselves their final condemnation: "His blood be on us and on our children"; "the Jews" stand over against the church (28:15). The features in Mt which contradict the seemingly crude anti-Jewish viewpoint of Mt—speaking

---

[39] Thus Jeremias, who according to Abba, 260, no longer advances the linking of ὡσαννά 21:9, 15 with the dative as evidence that the native language of the evangelist was Aramaic.

[40] So J. Bowman, "Phylacteries," StEv I, TU 73, 1957, 523 ff.

[41] Further in Trilling, Das wahre Israel, 124 ff. On the universalism of Mt see R. M. Grant, 132; Guthrie, 23 f; J. Rohde, Rediscovering . . . , 52 f, 58 f, 80 ff, 93 ff.

of preference for the Jews and seeking to prove that Jesus is the Messiah of the Jews—are interpreted by supporters of this view as tradition that has been taken over by Mt but not assimilated to his own point of view.[42] But that is a completely untenable position. It is in the first place not the case that according to Mt all the Jews are finally rejected: πάντα τὰ ἔθνη in the mission instruction includes the Jews as does πάντα τὰ ἔθνη in the judgment of the world (25:32). In the parable (21:33 ff) when the vineyard is taken away from the workers because of the murder of the son, that means (21:43) that the kingdom of God will be given, not to the unbelieving Jews who lay in wait for Jesus and before that John the Baptist (21:23, 31 f 45 f), but to ἔθνει ποιοῦντι τοὺς καρποὺς αὐτῆς. That is, the unbelieving Jews are replaced by the eschatological people of God, who are identified by bringing forth fruits, so that the distinction between Jew and Gentile is no longer significant. Mt 23:39, "You will not see me again until you say, 'Blessed is he who comes in the name of the Lord,' " does not presuppose the conversion of Israel in the End-time, but implies that there are Jews who will greet with praise the risen Lord when he appears at the parousia.[43] The church is not the "new" but the "true" Israel.[44]

If in Mt's view the Jews are not already finally condemned, only by forced argument can one attribute to tradition which the evangelist has not assimilated to his own view all those texts which display an outspoken Jewish-Christian tendency. The strongly Jewish formulation of the material he has taken over, the emphatic reporting of the fulfillment citations, and the insertion of texts which represent the enduring validity of the Law and the special role of Israel—all these factors belong together and show that the author not only lived in a Jewish-Christian tradition, but also wanted to present to his readers the message of the authority of the risen Lord and of salvation through baptism, as well as the keeping of his commandments, and to do so in a manner that would lead them as Jewish Christians to recognize Jesus Christ as son of David and son of Abraham (1:1), whose gospel of the kingdom was to be proclaimed before the End "in all the inhabited world as a witness to all people" (24:14).

The evangelist could not carry out this objective free from

---

[42] Cf. esp. Strecker, *Weg der Gerechtigkeit*, 16 ff; Walker, 82, 108; Hare, 148; Fischer, 118 ff; S. Schulz (see n. 26), 214.

[43] On Mt's interest in the conversion of the Jews, see Steck, 313; Kingsbury, 26 f; Tagawa, 160.

[44] Trilling, *Das wahre Israel*, 96, 213; Kingsbury, 72, 154; Tagawa, 159, 162; wrongly contested by Hare, 157.

contradictions,[44a] and these contradictions are the source of the
contradictory interpretations of which we have been speaking.
But if the aim of the evangelist is clearly discerned and the probability is taken seriously that the sayings of Jesus in 10:5, 23;
15:24 (see above, p. 113) go back to Jesus himself [45] and so belong
to the oldest Palestinian tradition, then it follows that Mt does
not belong to a Jewish Christianity that calls into question the
Gentile church, but to a Jewish Christianity that—in spite of its
general recognition of the universal validity of Jesus' mission—
weakened his radical criticism of the Law, as it was expressed in
the antitheses partly taken over by Mt and partly formulated
by him (5:21-48),[46] and that did so by stressing the enduring
validity of the Law (cf. 5:18 f; 23:3, 23b). Yet Mt presents this
interpretation of Jesus' stance toward the Law as being nearer the
traditional Jewish understanding of the Law, not because he is
battling Palestinian-Christian enthusiasm or Gentile-Christian antinomianism[47]—for this there is not adequate evidence; rather his
opposition is to unbelieving Judaism, viewed as a unity and with
its pharisaic interpretation of the Law (15:3 ff, 13 f; 23:3 f, 13,
23 f). "Mt feels that the Pharisees have altogether missed the true
meaning of the Scriptures." [48] Obviously the real interest of Mt
lies not in his relationship to Judaism or to Jewish Christianity
or to Gentile Christianity, but on the one hand in the proof that
Jesus is the "Messiah" long promised by God, "the Son of the
living God" (16:16), who "will save his people from their sins"

[44a] Abel offers the untenable view that a Jewish-Christian-oriented Mt was
subsequently expanded along Gentile-Christian lines.

[45] See on this J. Jeremias, *Jesus' Promise to the Nations*, 26 ff; W. G.
Kümmel, "Eschatological Expectation in the Proclamation of Jesus," *The
Future of Our Religious Past, Essays in Honour of R. Bultmann*, 1971, 41 ff;
M. Künzi, *Das Naherwartungslogion, Mt. 10:23. Geschichte seiner Auslegung*,
Beiträge zur Geschichte der biblischen Exegese 9, 1970, 177.

[46] Cf. G. Barth, 93; W. G. Kümmel, "Jesus und der jüdische Traditionsgedanke," ZNW 33, 1934, 125 (=W. G. K., *Heilsgeschehen und Geschichte*,
MbThSt 3, 1965, 31).

[47] In various ways and with reference to 5:17 ff; 7:15 ff; 13:41; 23:8 ff;
24:11 ff; Grundmann, 33 ff; Barth 64 ff; 159 ff; Hebert, Hummel 64 f, 169;
Steck, 312; E. Käsemann, "The Beginnings of Christian Theology," *New Testament Questions of Today*, 82 ff. Rightly opposing these theses are Stendahl,
²xii; Moule, StEv II, 93; Trilling, *Das wahre Israel*, 211; Walker, 134 f;
Schweizer, 53 n. 13; Sand, 124; Rohde, *Rediscovering . . .* , 58, 100 ff.

[48] Blair, 141. Similarly Hummel, 12 ff; Hare, 96; Tagawa, 161; Sand, 124.
Hummel shows that Mt makes no clear distinction between different groups
within pharisaic Judaism; but it cannot be concluded from this that for Mt
the Pharisees are only a literary "topos" (so Strecker, EvTh 1966, 68; Walker,
16, 20).

(1:21), and on the other hand in his ever-repeated stress on the fact that such salvation is to be gained only in the ἐκκλησία of Christ (16:18 f; 18:17 f) and as a member of the people that bring forth the fruits of the kingdom of God (21:43). It was a mistake to dispute about the *Sitz im Leben* of Mt and to try to comprehend its origin in relation to liturgical reading,[49] or catechetical instruction,[50] or scribal exegesis of Scripture.[51] None of these theses can adduce more than a part of the material in their own support. Trilling was quite right when he declared "that a totally satisfactory answer to the question of the 'Sitz im Leben' has not been found to this day." [52] Mt writes an expanded form of Mk as a "community book" [53] which is to provide for the needs of a particular Christian community as follows: for its debate with contemporary Judaism, strength in its knowledge of Jesus as the Christ (10:17); for the realities of community life and ethical decisions (18:15 ff; 19:1 ff), advice conveyed through the sayings of Jesus. The assumption is not true that Mt has abandoned the near expectation of the parousia,[54] as the uncorrected use of such texts as 4:17; 10:23; 16:28; 24:33 f shows.[55] But unremitting expectancy (24:42 ff) demands, in view of the uncertainty of the time, advice for the church and for the individual Christians in the interim ἕως τῆς συντελείας τοῦ αἰῶνος (28:20).[56] Mt offers to the church these counsels by pointing back to the OT predictions, which for the church of the present find their complete fulfillment in the authoritative history and teaching of Jesus.[57] But the history and teaching of Jesus are authoritative not because Jesus as a "New Moses" has proclaimed a "New Law," [58] but because the risen Lord has commanded that

---

[49] Kilpatrick; cf. against this Guthrie, 24 f.

[50] Von Dobschütz, Schille; to a limited degree Guthrie, 25 f.

[51] Stendahl.

[52] Trilling, *Das wahre Israel*, 220.

[53] A. Harnack, *The Acts of the Apostles*, tr. J. R. Wilkinson, 1909, xv n. 1.

[54] Thus Strecker, *Weg der Gerechtigkeit*, 41 ff; Trilling, *Das wahre Israel*, 44 f; Schulz (see n. 26), 229.

[55] Cf. Blair, 141; Hummel, 159 f; M. P. Brown, 47.

[56] See E. Grässer, *Das Problem der Parusieverzögerung in den synopt. Evv. und in der Apg*, Bh. ZNW 22, 1957, 200 ff.

[57] On the historicizing character of the portrayal of the story of Jesus in Mt, see Marxsen, *Intr.*, 132, 135; Strecker, *Weg der Gerechtigkeit*, 185, 192 ff; *idem*, EvTh 1966, 63 ff; Trilling, *Das wahre Israel*, 218; Hummel, 169; Pesch, 411; Schulz (see n. 26), 167 ff. Against this, but without any proof, H. Thyen, *Studien zur Sündenvergebung*, FRLANT 96, 1970, 235 n. 4.

[58] See those named in n. 5; further, Fuller, *Intr.*, 117 f; Blair, 131 ff; H. Anderson, *Jesus and Christian Origins*, 1964, 341. Rightly critical are G.

"all that I have commanded you" is to be taught to all people, and this teaching has promised his help until the end of the age (28:20). This is the teaching that Mt presents in his community book; it remains to ask what community Mt has written it for.

3. Place and Time of Writing

On the basis of the evidence presented thus far, it is certain that the author of Mt lived in a Greek-speaking area and wrote for Greek-speaking Christians most of whom were of Jewish origin. (Nothing indicates that the readers came out of the Qumran sect.) [59] It is scarcely to be assumed that Mt was written in Palestine.[60] On the basis of the report of the flight of Jesus' parents to Egypt (2:13 ff) it cannot be inferred that Mt wrote in Alexandria (Brandon to the contrary). Most scholars assume, relying on Streeter, that Mt was written in Antioch or, more generally, in Syria. They can adduce for this theory the fact that the oldest witness for knowledge of Mt is Ignatius.[61] Occasionally Phoenicia is proposed, [62] and there is no evidence against that conjecture. On the matter of the time of writing, the point of departure is Mt's dependence on Mk; on that basis, a date before 70 is excluded.[63] A time of origin after 70 is surely to be inferred from the supplement to the parable of the wedding feast (22:7): "Then the king became angry and sent his officer and condemned those murderers and burned their city." Here obviously the destruction of Jerusalem is alluded to; even if this is a stylized reference to the ancient practice of sending punitive expeditions, the author of Mt can hardly have introduced it here as an expansion of the parable (it is missing in Lk 14:16 ff) unless he meant the destruction of Jerusalem to be conceived as a punishment by God for the unbelief of the Jews.[64] Even if, indeed, Mk and Mt

---

Barth, 153 ff; Trilling, *Das wahre Israel*, 186; Walker, 146; Carlston (see n. 31), 83; Schulz (see n. 26), 184 f, 189.

[59] Against Wolf. There is also no trace (Strecker, *Weg der Gerechtigkeit*, 250 f) of a polemic against the influence of former adherents of the Qumran sect in the Christian community (thus C. W. F. Smith, 168).

[60] Gander, Schlatter; Albertz, Guthrie, Michaelis.

[61] Cf. Ign., Eph 17:1; Sm. 1:1; 6:1; Polyc. 1:3; 2:2. Smit Sibinga is unable to show that Ign. is dependent rather on a source of Mt.

[62] Kilpatrick; Blair.

[63] Mariani: 48–50; Höpfl-Gut, Meinertz: 50–60; Gander: not later than 62; Michaelis, Cassian, StEv I, TU 73, 129 ff: 60–70.

[64] K. H. Rengstorf, "Die Stadt der Mörder," *Judentum, Urchristentum, Kirche*, Festschr. J. Jeremias, Bh. ZNW 26, 1960, 160 ff, esp. 125 f, has been

originated in different regions, precisely in his reworking of Mk Mt shows so clear a development of community relationships and theological reflection (see, e.g., 18:15 ff and 28:19) that a date of writing shortly after Mk[65] seems less likely than a time between 80 and 100.[66] A date of origin after 100 is excluded by Mt's having been used by Ignatius.

4. Author

Since Mt contains no direct evidence about its author, we must consider the external tradition in determining the author. The oldest evidence is the account of Papias: Ματθαῖος . . . Ἑβραΐδι διαλέκτῳ τὰ λόγια συνετάξατο ἡρμήνευσεν δ'αὐτὰ ὡς ἦν δυνατὸς ἕκαστος (Eus., HE III. 39. 16; on this see above, §5.3.2). Only since Schleiermacher has the question been raised whether Papias' account refers to the canonical Mt,[67] because our Mt is not a translation from a Semitic language, but was written in Greek in dependence on a Greek Mk. No doubt Papias meant our Mt, but he had no more seen a Mt in a Semitic language than had those later witnesses who depended on Papias.[68] The oft-repeated thesis that Matthew was the author of a main source of Mt (the "Logion source" or an Aramaic Mt) and that accordingly the whole was named for the part Κατὰ Ματθαῖον[69] is a completely groundless assumption. We must concede that the report that Mt was written by Matthew

---

rightly refuted by Grundmann, in loc.; Strecker, Weg der Gerechtigkeit, 35; Trilling, Das wahre Israel, 85; Walker, 56 f; E. Linnemann, Gleichnisse Jesu, [5]1969, 167.

[65] Ca. 75 is assumed, e.g., by Schmid, Tasker; Harrison, Klijn, Schelkle, Wikenhauser; Michel, Hare; J. H. Ropes, The Synoptic Gospels, 1934.

[66] Thus Bonnard, Grundmann, Johnson; Feine-Behm, Fuller, Heard, Henshaw, Marxsen, McNeile-Williams, Riddle-Hutson; Kilpatrick, Bornkamm, Blair, Strecker, C. W. F. Smith, Walker; Schulz (see n. 26), 163.

[67] On this see most recently Guthrie, Intr., I, 31 ff. R. Gryson, "À propos du témoinage de Papias sur Matthieu. Le sens du mot ΛΟΓΙΟΝ chez les Pères du deuxième siècle," EThL 41, 1965, 530 ff, shows that Christian usage in the second century supports the theory that by τὰ λόγια Papias means the whole of Mt.

[68] See the evidence in Nepper-Christensen, 37 ff; also, 210 f, the witnesses from the early church.

[69] Thus recently in various forms Feine-Behm, Harrington, Meinertz, Schelkle, Sparks, Wikenhauser; Gundry, Abel; Vaganay, Le problème synoptique, 1954. Aramaic as the original language of Mt is defended by Mariani; Hebrew by Gaechter; Grintz; J. Carmignac, Recherches sur le "Notre Père," 1969, 33 ff.

"in the Hebrew language" is utterly false, however it may have arisen.[70]

All that remains of the tradition passed on by Papias is the name, Matthew. This must refer to the Μαθθαῖος who is included in the list of "the twelve" (Mt 10:3; Mk 3:18; Lk 6:15; Acts 1:13). In Mt 10:3 he is designated as a "tax collector," but this must be considered alongside the fact that in Mk 2:14 par. Lk 5:24 the tax collector is named Levi (Mk adds, "son of Alphaeus"), while in the parallel, Mt 9:9, his name is Matthew. We have no way of accounting for these differences in name,[71] and we know nothing beyond this of the Matthew who is in the circle of the twelve. Is it possible that Mt indeed originated with Matthew, one of the twelve, and thus from an eyewitness and member of the most intimate circle of Jesus' disciples? The dependence of Mt on the Greek Gospel of a non-disciple, the systematic and therefore nonbiographical form of the structure of Mt, the late-apostolic theological position and the Greek language of Mt make this proposal completely impossible. Today it is represented by only a scattering of scholars,[72] and most reject it.[73] But if the author of Mt cannot be a member of the twelve, he is completely unknown to us and we do not know how the tradition of Matthew as author of Mt originated. The author of Mt—whose name is unknown to us—was a Greek-speaking Jewish Christian who possibly had some rabbinic knowledge but who in any case felt obligated to a form of the Jesus tradition which potently accommodated the sayings of Jesus to Jewish viewpoints. He was himself concerned to proclaim for the church gathered from all peoples the importance of Jesus as Messiah. Accordingly Mt has become in a real sense the Gospel of the *church*.

[70] J. Munck, "Die Tradition über das Mt bei Papias," NeP, 249 ff, considers it probable that the assumption concerning a "Hebrew" Mt developed in connection with the early formation of the canon as a way to explain the differences between the Synoptics.

[71] R. Pesch, "Levi-Matthäus (Mc 2:14/Mt 9:9; 10:3). Ein Beitrag zur Lösung eines alten Problems," ZNW 59, 1968, 40 ff, shows that the author of Mt has replaced the name Levi with Matthew, and proposes that Mt thought a μαθητής must be one of the twelve, but he cannot explain why Mt chose the name Matthew.

[72] Gaechter; Mariani; Gundry; in a more limited way, Guthrie, Harrison.

[73] E.g., Filson, Grundmann, Johnson, Rigaux, Schmid, Tasker; Fuller, Harrington, Heard, Henshaw, Michaelis, Vögtle, etc., as well as those mentioned on p. 49 who claim the name for one of Mt's sources.

§8. THE GOSPEL OF LUKE

Commentaries: see §41. Studies: in addition to the lit. in §5, W. K. Hobart, *The Medical Language of St. Luke*, 1892; A. Harnack, *Luke the Physician*, 1907; H. J. Cadbury, *The Style and Literary Method of Luke*, HTS 6, 1920; *idem, The Making of Luke-Acts*, 1927; V. Taylor, *Behind the Third Gospel*, 1926; *idem*, "The Proto-Luke Hypothesis," ExpT 67, 1955/56, 12 ff; *idem*, "Methods of Gospel Criticism," ExpT 71, 1959/60, 68 ff; *idem*, "The Narrative of the Crucifixion," NTS 1962/63, 77 ff; *idem*, "Theologians of Our Time: F. Rehkopf," ExpT 74, 1962/63, 262 ff; *idem*, "Rehkopf's List of Words and Phrases Illustrative of Pre-Lukan Speech Usage," JTS, NS 15, 1964, 59 ff; M. Dibelius, "Jungfrauensohn und Krippenkind. Untersuchungen zur Geburtsgeschichte Jesu im Lk," SAH 1932, 4 (=M. D., *Botschaft und Geschichte* I, 1953, 1 ff); M. Goguel, "Luke and Mark," HTR 26, 1933, 1 ff; G. D. Kilpatrick, "A Theme of the Lucan Passion Story and Luke 23:47," JTS 43, 1942, 34 ff; *idem*, "The Gentiles and the Strata of Luke," *Verborum Veritas, Festschr. G. Stählin*, 1970, 83 ff; H. Sparks, "The Semitisms of St. Luke's Gospel," JTS 44, 1943, 129 ff; T. E. Bleiben, "The Gospel of Luke and the Gospel of Paul," JTS 45, 1944, 134 ff; T. W. Manson, "The Work of St. Luke," BJRL 28, 1944, 382 ff (= Manson, *St.*, 60 ff); H. Sahlin, *Der Messias und das Gottesvolk*, ASNU 12, 1945; *idem, Studien zum 3. Kap. des Lk*, Uppsala Universitets Årsskrift, 1949, 2; S. M. Gilmour, "A Critical Re-examination of Proto-Luke," JBL 67, 1948, 143 ff; R. Morgenthaler, *Die lukanische Geschichtsschreibung als Zeugnis* I.II, AThANT 14, 15, 1948 (on this see W. G. Kümmel, ThR, NF 22, 1954, 197 ff); E. Schweizer, "Eine hebraisierende Sonderquelle des Lukas?" ThZ 6, 1950, 161 ff; L. Girard, *L'évangile des voyages de Jésus*, 1951; P. Vielhauer, "Das Benedictus des Zacharias (Lk 1,69-79)," ZThK 49, 1952, 255 ff (= P. V., *Aufsätze zum NT*, ThB 31, 1965, 28 ff); R. Koh, *The Writings of St. Luke*, 1953; J. Blinzler, "Die literarische Eigenart des sog. Reiseberichts im Lk," SStW 1953, 20 ff (lit.) (=J. B., *Aus der Welt und Umwelt, Gesammelte Aufsätze* I, 1969, 62 ff); J. Schneider, "Zur Analyse des lukanischen Reiseberichts," SStW, 207 ff; H. Schürmann, "Die Dubletten im Lk," ZKTh 75, 1953, 338 ff (=Sch., Tr.U., 272 ff); *idem*, "Die Dublettenvermeidungen im Lk," ZKTh 76, 1954, 83 ff (= Sch., Tr.U. 279 ff); *idem, Der Paschamahlbericht Lk 22, (7-14) 15-18*, NTA, 19, 5, 1953; *idem, Der Einsetzungsbericht Lk 22, 19-20*, NTA 20, 4, 1955; *idem, "Jesu Abschiedsrede, Lk 22, 21-38,"* NTA 20, 5, 1957; *idem*, "Protolukanische Spracheigentümlichkeiten?" BZ, NF 5, 1961, 266 ff (=Sch., Tr.U., 209 ff); E. Lohse, "Lukas als Theologe der Heilsgeschichte," EvTh 14, 1954, 256 ff; P. Schubert, "The Structure and Significance of Luke 24," *Nt. Studien für R. Bultmann*, Bh. ZNW 21, 1954, 165 ff; P. Winter, "Some Observations on the Language in the Birth and Infancy Stories of the Third Gospel," NTS 1, 1954/55, 111 ff; *idem*, "Magnificat and Benedictus—Maccabaean

Psalms?" BJRL 37, 1954, 328 ff; *idem*, "The Treatment of His Sources by the Third Evangelist in Luke XXI–XXIV," StTh 8, 1955, 138 ff; *idem*, "The Proto-Source of Luke 1," NovTest 1, 1956, 184 ff; *idem*, "On Luke and Lucan Sources," ZNW 47, 1956, 217 ff; *idem*, "The Main Literary Problem of the Lucan Infancy Story," ATR 40, 1958, 257 ff; H. Russell, "Which Was Written First, Luke or Acts?" HTR 48, 1955, 167 ff; C. F. Evans, "The Central Section of St. Luke's Gospel," StG 1955, 37 ff; N. Turner, "The Relation of Lk. I and II to Hebraic Sources and to the Rest of Luke-Acts," NTS 2, 1955/56, 100 ff; P. Benoit, "L'enfance de Jean-Baptiste selon Luc I," NTS 3, 1956/57, 169 ff; (=P. B. *Exégèse et théologie* III, 1968, 165 ff); H. F. D. Sparks, "St. Luke's Transpositions," NTS 3, 1956/57, 219 ff; E. Grässer, *Das Problem der Parusieverzögerung in den synpt. Evv. und in der Apg*, Bh. ZNW 22, 1957 (=²1960 with supplement), 178 ff, 204 ff; L. Cerfaux et J. Cambier, DBS 5, 1957, 545 ff (bibl.); R. Laurentin, "Structure et théologie de Luc I–II," Ét. Bibl. 1957 (bibl.); J. Jeremias, "Perikopen-Umstellungen bei Lukas?" NTS 4, 1957/58, 115 ff (=J. J., Abba, 1966, 93 ff); *idem*, *The Eucharistic Words of Jesus*, 1966, 96 ff, 139 ff; A. Strobel, "Lukas der Antiochener," ZNW 49, 1958, 131 ff; A. Hastings, *Prophet and Witness in Jerusalem: A Study of the Teaching of Saint Luke*, 1958; O Michel, CBL, 819 ff; J. C. O'Neill, "The Six Amen Sayings in Luke," JTS, NS 10, 1959, 1 ff; *idem*, *The Theology of Acts in Its Historical Settings* (1961), ²1970 (on this see H. Conzelmann, ThLZ 87, 1962, 753 ff; H. F. D. Sparks, JTS, NS 14, 1963, 457 ff); B. Reicke, "Instruction and Discussion in the Travel Narrative," StEv I, TU 73, 1959, 206 ff; R. M. Wilson, "Some Recent Studies in the Lucan Infancy Narratives," StEv I, TU 73, 1959, 235 ff; J. Tyson, "The Lucan Version of the Trial of Jesus," NovTest 3, 1959, 249 ff; W. Grundmann, "Fragen der Komposition des lukanischen 'Reiseberichts,'" ZNW 50, 1959, 252 ff; F. Rehkopf, *Die lukanische Sonderquelle*, WUNT 5, 1959 (on this see H. Conzelmann, Gn 32, 1960, 470 f); H. Conzelmann, *The Theology of St. Luke*, 1960 (on this see P. Winter, ThLZ 81, 1956, 36 ff; 85, 1960, 929 ff); H. Conzelmann, "Luke's Place in the Development of Early Christianity," StLA 298 ff; L. Gaston, "Sondergut und Markusstoff in Lk 21," ThZ 16, 1960, 161 ff; *idem*, *No Stone on Another: Studies in the Significance of the Fall of Jerusalem in the Synoptic Gospels*, Suppl. NovTest 23, 1970, 244 ff; U. Luck, "Kerygma, Tradition und Geschichte Jesu bei Lukas," ZThK 57, 1960, 51 ff; H. C. Snape, "The Composition of the Lucan Writings: A Re-Assessment," HTR 53, 1960, 27 ff; W. C. Robinson, "The Theological Context for Interpreting Luke's Travel Narrative (9, 51 ff)," JBL 79, 1960, 20 ff; *idem*, *Der Weg des Herrn. Studien zur Geschichte und Eschatologie im Lk*, ThF 36, 1964; J. Schmid, LThK VI, 1961, 1207 ff (lit.); H. W. Montefiore, "Does 'L' Hold Water?" JTS, NS 12, 1961, 59 f; C. K. Barrett, *Luke the Historian in Recent Study*, 1961; C. S. C. Williams, "Luke-Acts in Recent Study," ExpT 73, 1961/62, 133 ff; R. Leaney,

"The Birth Narratives in St. Luke and St. Matthew," NTS 8, 1961/62, 158 ff; J. Gnilka, "Der Hymnus des Zacharias," BZ, NF 6, 1962, 215 ff; G. Braumann, "Das Mittel der Zeit. Erwägungen zur Theologie des Lk," ZNW 54, 1963, 117 ff; S. Schulz, "Gottes Vorsehung bei Lk," ZNW 54, 1963, 104 ff; H. H. Oliver, "The Lucan Birth Stories and the Purpose of Luke-Acts," NTS 10, 1963/64, 202 ff; J. H. Davies, "The Purpose of the Central Section of St. Luke's Gospel," StEv II, TU 87, 1964, 164 ff; A. Q. Morton and G. H. C. Macgregor, *The Structure of Luke and Acts*, 1964; H. Flender, *St. Luke: Theologian of Redemptive History*, 1967; W. C. van Unnik, "Luke-Acts, a Storm Center in Contemporary Scholarship," StLA, 15 ff; U. Wilckens, "Interpreting Luke-Acts in a Period of Existentialist Theology," StLA, 60 ff; P. Minear, "Luke's Use of the Birth-Stories," StLA, 111 ff; P. Borgen "Von Paulus zu Lk," StTh 20, 1966, 140 ff; A. George, "Tradition et rédaction chez Luc. La construction du troisième évangile," *Festschr. Coppens*, 100 ff; S. Aalen, "St. Luke's Gospel and the Last Chapters of I Enoch," NTS 13, 1966/67, 1 ff; W. B. Tatum, "The Epoch of Israel: Luke I, II and the Theological Plan of Luke-Acts," NTS 13, 1966/67, 184 ff; C. H. Talbert, *Luke and the Gnostics: An Examination of the Lucan Purpose*, 1966; *idem*, "An Anti-Gnostic Tendency in Lucan Christology," NTS 14, 1967/68, 259 ff; *idem*, "The Redaction Critical Quest for Luke the Theologian," *Perspective*, 171 ff; A. Vögtle, "Hochverehrter Theophilos," *Tätigkeit im rechten Sinne, Festschr. H. Rombach*, 1967, 29 ff; T. Holtz, *Untersuchungen über die at. Zitate bei Lk*, TU 104, 1968; D. R. Jones, "The Background and Character of the Lukan Psalms," JTS, NF 19, 1968, 19 ff; G. Bouwman, *Das dritte Ev.*, 1968; I. H. Marshall, "Recent Study of the Gospel According to St. Luke," ExpT 80, 1968/69, 94 ff; *idem*, *Luke: Historian and Theologian*, 1970; F. Schütz, *Der leidende Christus*, BWANT, 5th series 9, 1969; G. Schneider, *Verleugnung, Verspottung und Verhör Jesu nach Lk 22,54-71. Studien zur lukanischen Darstellung der Passion*, StANT 22, 1969; J. D. Kaestli, *L'eschatologie dans l'oeuvre de Luc. Ses caractéristiques et sa place dans le développement du Christianisme primitif*, Nouvelle série théologique 22, 1969; F. O. Francis, "Eschatology and History in Luke-Acts," *Journal of the American Academy of Religion* 37, 1969, 49 ff; M. Rese, "At. Motive in der Christologie des Lk," StNT 1, 1969; S. G. Wilson, "Lukan Eschatology," NTS 15, 1969/70, 330 ff; K. Löning, "Lk—Theologe der von Gott geführten Heilsgeschichte (Lk, Apg)," GANT, 200 ff; D. Gill, *Observations on the Lukan Travel Narrative and Some Related Passages*, HTR 63, 1970, 199 ff; W. G. Kümmel, "Luc en accusation dans la théologie contemporaine," EThL 46, 1970, 205 ff; T. Schramm, *Der Markusstoff bei Lukas. Eine literarkritische und redaktionsgeschichtliche Untersuchung*, SNTSMS 14, 1971; G. Ogg, "The Central Section of the Gospel According to St. Luke," NTS 18, 1971/72, 39 ff.

1. Contents

The structure of Lk differs from that of Mk and Mt in that, in place of the section "Jesus' journeying within and outside Galilee" (Mk 6:1–9:50 and par. Mt 14:1–20:34), which continues the account of Jesus' activity in Galilee in a slightly deviating geographical form, Lk has an extensive section (9:51–19:27) which shows Jesus on the way to Jerusalem and which incorporates only shortly before its end (18:15-43) the Markan (10:13-52) "journey of Jesus toward Jerusalem." It is debated whether Lk offers any sort of evidence of subsections of this extensive so-called "travel narrative" (on this see below, §8.3.6), but with good reason reference has been made to the fact that the aim of Jesus to go to Jerusalem (9:51) is stressed anew in 13:31-35, so that a new section begins at 14:1, or better yet at 13:31.[1] If that is the case, then with all due caution Lk may be divided into five main parts: prehistory and preparation for the activity of Jesus (1:5–4:13); Jesus' activity in Galilee (4:14–9:50); Jesus on the way to Jerusalem (9:51–13:30 and 13:31–19:27); Jesus in Jerusalem (19:28–24:53). Placed prior to this is a prologue (1:1-4).[2] This gives us in detail the following sequence for Lk's account:

Following the prologue (1:1-4), the first main part (1:5–4:13) begins with the historical antecedents: announcement of the birth of John (1:5-25); announcement of the birth of Jesus (1:26-38); Elizabeth's visit to Mary (1:39-56, which includes Mary's song of praise, the Magnificat, 1:46-55); birth of John (1:57-80, including Zachariah's song of praise, the Benedictus, 1:68-79); the birth of Jesus (2:1-20); circumcision and presentation in the temple (2:21-40, including Simeon's hymn, the Nunc Dimittis, 2:29-32); the twelve-year-old Jesus in the temple (2:41-52). The preparation for the public appearance of Jesus includes the appearance of the Baptist and his preaching (3:1-18), his imprisonment by Herod (3:19 f), the baptism of Jesus (3:21 f), Jesus' ancestry back from Joseph to Adam and God (3:23-38); Jesus' temptation (4:1-13).

The second main part (4:14–9:50), Jesus' activity in Galilee, begins after a short description of Jesus' appearance in Galilee (4:14 f) with his inaugural sermon in Nazareth (4:16-30; 4:31–6:19). Lk follows Mk: healings in Capernaum, preaching in

[1] O'Neill, Reicke.
[2] Schürmann, *Comm.* I, 146, would like to find a threefold structure in Lk: (3:1–4:44, the beginning in Galilee; 5:1–19:27, Jesus' public activity and teaching in the land of the Jews; 19:28–24:53, the consummation in Jerusalem). But in fact 5:1 does not mark a new beginning, whereas 9:51 does.

Galilee (4:31-44); the first disciples (5:1-11); the healing of
the leper, the lame man and the forgiveness of sins, Jesus and the
tax collectors, the question of fasting (5:12-39); plucking grain
and healing on the sabbath (6:1-11); choice of the apostles and
pressure of the crowds (6:12-19). The sermon on the plain (6:12-
19) corresponds to Mt's sermon on the mount; to it are attached
other bits from other traditions: the official of Capernaum (7:1-
10); the young man of Nain (7:11-17); the Baptist and Jesus
(7:18-35); the anointing of Jesus by a sinful woman (7:36-50);
the women in attendance on Jesus (8:1-3). The next two units—
the parable of the four kinds of soil with explanation and attached
sayings (8:4-18), and the true relatives of Jesus (8:19-21)—
stand in Lk in reverse order from Mk, but 8:22—9:50 resumes the
Markan order. Missing from Lk, however, are Mk 6:1-6, 17-29;
9:9-13 and the whole section Mk 6:45—8:26. Storm on the lake,
demoniac at Gerasa, Jairus' daughter, and the hemorrhaging woman
(8:22-56); sending of the twelve, decision of Herod, feeding of
the five thousand (9:1-17); confession of Peter with passion prediction and sayings about discipleship (9:18-27); transfiguration
and healing of the epileptic boy (9:28-43a); second passion prediction, quarrel over rank, and rejection of the strange exorcist
(9:43b-50).

The third main part (9:51—13:30): beginning of the journey
to Jerusalem. This offers chiefly material common to Mk, but some
special tradition as well: at the outset is the narrative of the village
in Samaria which refuses to receive Jesus because of his goal of
Jerusalem (9:51-56). There follow conversations about discipleship (9:57-62), the sending of the seventy (10:1-20), the shout of
joy and the pronouncement of the blessedness of the eyewitnesses
(10:21-24), the question about attaining eternal life and the
parable of the merciful Samaritan (10:25-37); Mary and Martha
(10:38-42); the Lord's Prayer (11:1-4); sayings about prayer,
including the parable of the importunate friend (11:5-13). Controversy speeches: reproach of Jesus' league with Beelzebub, the
blessedness of Jesus' mother, the demand for signs, sayings about
light, speech against the Pharisees (11:14-54). Warnings to the
disciples: fearless confession, freedom from anxiety, the heavenly
treasure, watchfulness, fidelity, the time of division, with the
addition of the conversation about conflict over an inheritance and
the parable of the rich grain-grower (12:1-53). Warnings to the
people about repentance: the signs of the time, the necessity of
repentance, the parable of the unfruitful fig tree, Jewish resentment
at the healing of the woman on the sabbath, parables of the mustard

seed and the leaven, the impending judgment on the Jews (12:54–13:30).

The fourth main part (13:31–19:27):[3] resumption of the journey to Jerusalem. Until 18:14 this offers mostly special material, but also some Markan material. In 18:15-43 it again follows Mk 10:13-52, closing with special material and with material shared with Mk. First stressed is the necessity of Jesus to go to Jerusalem (13:31-35). There follow discourses by Jesus as guest at meals: healing of a man with dropsy on the sabbath, warning about modesty and selflessness, parable of the great feast (14:1-24). To this are added the sayings about discipleship, the parables of the tower-builder and the warrior (14:25-35), the parables of the lost sheep, the lost coin, and the two sons (15); instructions concerning attitude toward earthly goods: the parable of the unjust householder and related sayings about the pride of the Pharisees, the Law, and the kingdom of God, parable of the rich man and poor Lazarus (16); instructions to the disciples: offense, reconciliation, faith, obligation of servants, the grateful Samaritan among the ten lepers (17:1-19); the little eschatological address (the coming of the kingdom of God, the advent of the Son of man) 17:20-37; parables of the rich man and of the widow (18:1-8), of the Pharisee and the tax collector (18:9-14). 18:15-43 builds on Mk 10:13-52 (blessing of the children, question about eternal life, third prediction of the passion, healing of the blind man). From other tradition come the story of Zacchaeus (19:1-10) and the parable of the pounds (19:11-27).

The fifth main part (19:28–24:53): Jesus in Jerusalem. Until 22:53, the Markan sequence is essentially followed; Lk then diverges several times as he proceeds with the passion story, and from 24:13 on he offers special material: entry into the temple and temple cleansing (19:28-48), with which is linked the question of authority, the parable of the vine-dressers, the questions of the tribute money, the Sadducees, of David's son, the warning about the scribes, the widow's mite (20:1–21:4), the eschatological discourse (21:3-36), the conclusion of the activity in Jerusalem (21:37, 38). In the passion narrative (22:1–23:56) the betrayal by Judas is followed by the Last Supper and the farewell discourse (22:7-38), Jesus on the Mount of Olives and his arrest (22:39-53); the denial of Peter, the mocking of Jesus, the hearing before the Sanhedrin (22:54-71) the hearing before Pilate (23:1-25; and in between, the sending of Jesus to Herod Antipas, 23:6-16); the

---

[3] The proposal to end this section at 19:46 (J. H. Davies, 168; Talbert, NTS 14, 1967/68, 264) is not at all helpful, since 19:47 is not a new beginning.

way to Golgotha and the words of Jesus to the women of Jerusalem (23:26-32), the crucifixion and death of Jesus (23:33-49),
the burial (23:50-56). To the account of the Easter message at
the empty tomb (24:1-11 [?]) Lk adds: the disciples at Emmaus
(24:13-35), the appearance of the risen Lord to the eleven in
Jerusalem (24:36-49), farewell to the disciples and the ascension
(24:50-53).

2. The Literary Aim of the Gospel of Luke According to Luke's Own Statement

Luke is the only one of the evangelists who has prefaced his
Gospel with a prologue (1:1-4) according to the literary custom of
the time, in which he mentions his sources and predecessors and
the basic reasons for his writing.[4] The prologue, which is written
in good Greek and according to contemporary literary conventions,
may be recognized in the first instance as a foreword to Lk. But
not only the probability that from the outset the author had in
view the carrying forward of the narrative beyond the death of
Jesus into the history of the church, but also the statement that
"among us these events have come to fulfillment" (1:1), attests
that Luke intended his prologue (1:1-4) to serve for both books.[5]
If Lk 1:1-4 is read from this perspective and with a consideration
for literary usage, the author tells us the following concerning
his sources and aims:

1. Lk is relying on the tradition of those "who from the beginning
were eyewitnesses and servants of the word," as did the other
evangelists.

"From the beginning" with reference to the eyewitnesses cannot
include the infancy stories, but must begin with the public activity
of Jesus, and to introduce the preparation for this, namely, the
appearance of the Baptist, Lk sets forth his first great synchronism

---

[4] In addition to the commentaries and Lohse: H. J. Cadbury, "Commentary
on the Preface of Lk," *Beginnings* I, 2, 1922, 489 ff; E. Haenchen, "Das 'wir'
in der Apg und das Itinerar," ZThK 58, 1961, 362 ff (=E. H., *Gott und
Mensch*, 1965, 260 ff); G. Klein, "Lk 1, 1-4 als theologisches Programm,"
Zeit und Geschichte, Festschr. R. Bultmann, 1964, 193 ff; S. Schulz, *Die Stunde
der Botschaft,* 1967, 242 ff; H. von Campenhausen, *The Formation of the Christian Bible,* tr. J. A. Baker, 1972; 124-28; A. J. B. Higgins, "The Preface to Lk
and the Kerygma in Acts," AHG, 78 ff.

[5] E.g., Ellis, Grundmann, Feine-Behm; Lohse, Russell, Luck, Marshall,
Luke, 40; Cadbury, Klein, Schulz (see n. 4); A. J. B. Higgins (see n. 4), 49.
Other viewpoints in Rigaux, Schürmann; Michaelis; Conzelmann, Flender;
Haenchen (see n. 4).

(3:1). What Lk and his predecessors report comes from men who to some extent participated in these things from the beginning and who were the first proclaimers of the gospel. Whether this tradition was handed on orally or in writing Lk does not say, but he does not presuppose the existence of a complete gospel from the hand of an apostle, judging by his distinction between the tradition of the original witnesses (1:2) and the gospel writings which he knows (1:1).

2. Based on the tradition of the eyewitnesses, "many" before Lk have undertaken to give a presentation of the "events" which "have been fulfilled among us" (ἐν ἡμῖν).[6] By this expression, which conceals more than it reveals, Lk means the connected facts of the life, death, and resurrection of Jesus, as preserved in the gospel writings known to Lk, facts that were concluded with the resurrection and which continue to be efficacious in the "preaching of the kingdom of God" and in the "teaching concerning our Lord Jesus Christ" (Acts 28:31). With his historical work Lk joins their ranks, though he was not himself a witness from the beginning, because he feels the works of his predecessors to be in some way inadequate.[7] The stylized πολλοί tells nothing about the number of predecessors known to Lk.

3. The goal of Lk's work was to arouse full confidence in the content of the Christian teaching in the mind of Theophilus—and his readers as a whole—through the reliable passing on of the narratives. To this end he had researched [8] the history wrought by God "from the beginning" (ἄνωθεν) and took pains to give full (πᾶσιν) and accurate (ἀκριβῶς) information (see below, pp. 146 f) so that he could present the things "in good order" (καθεξῆς).

4. The book receives a still stronger literary character through the dedication to κράτιστος Θεόφιλος, since the person addressed is to be regarded "as representative of a wide circle of readers—i.e., if possible of all Christians." [8a] Κράτιστος could be the title of a

---

[6] ἐν ἡμῖν in v. 1 indicates the generation of the End-time; ἡμῖν in v. 2 indicates the generation of the writer; cf. Schürmann, Comm I, 5, 8; Flender, St. Luke, 64 ff n. 138; von Campenhausen (see n. 4), 125 n. 84.

[7] Thus Klein (see n. 4), 195.

[8] Perhaps ἄνωθεν is intended to include the infancy stories explicitly, as claimed by Klein (see n. 4), 209, and Schürmann, Comm. I, 11. That with ἄνωθεν Lk is trying to score a point against Jn, which he has used, and which has no infancy stories and no genealogy, is a fantastic proposal (against W. Gericke, "Zur Entstehung des Joh," ThLZ 90, 1965, 816).

[8a] Vögtle, Festschr. Rombach, 39, who has shown that the recipient of the dedication was in no way obligated "to distribute the writing in question, and surely not in any public way" (38).

high official, but it was also used as a polite form of address.[9] This form of address offers nothing concerning the position of the completely unknown Theophilus; even κατηχήθης is ambiguous, so that it cannot be decided whether Theophilus was a Christian or had merely heard about Jesus and the Christians.

From all this it may be inferred that Luke knew himself to be a man of the third stage of the Christian tradition and pursued the objective of giving a reliable presentation of the events of the tradition he had tested from the first generation. In his view, more certain knowledge of "the events which have been fulfilled among us [by God] was essential for the critical examination of the Christian λόγοι. And Luke claimed to be creating through his presentation of the narrative a work that would lay claim to literary quality,[10] and he expresses this claim by means of the prologue with its dedication. It must be asked in what manner Luke has carried out his objective.

3. Literary Character and Theological Aim of the Gospel of Luke

So far as we can determine, when Lk wants to give his account καθεξῆς = "in good order, according to the sequence" 1:3 (on καθεξῆς cf. 8:1; Acts 3:24; 11:4; 18:23), this does not mean that he presents the traditional material in an essentially different order than he found in his sources. Obviously the situation can be clearly determined only for the relationship to Mk, and Lk 1:1–22:53 matches Mk, with the already mentioned exceptions (§5.3.5): Mk 6:1-6 is moved forward (Lk 4:16-30); Mk 1:16-20 is moved back (Lk 5:1-11); Mk 3:7-12 changes places with 3:13-19; Mk 3:31-35 is moved back (Lk 8:19-21); while Lk 22:54–23:49 follows an essentially different sequence from Mk 14:53–15:41. For the relationship to Q only the well-founded conjecture can be offered that Lk has on the whole preserved the sequence of this source as well (see above, p. 69). Yet the justification of this position depends on how Lk's use of his sources is evaluated as a whole, and on this the views diverge widely.

The situation is as follows. Lk follows the Markan sequence extensively, except in the passion narrative, but uses only seven-tenths of the material from Mk in three large blocks (3:1–6:19; 8:4–9:50; 18:15–24:11). In between is the non-Markan tradition:

[9] Bauer, *Lexicon*, 424 f, and Cadbury (see n. 4), 505 ff.
[10] One can scarcely think of a "free book-market" (against von Campenhausen [see n. 4], 124); see Vögtle, *Festschr. Rombach*, 40 ff.

6:20–8:3 (the so-called "small insertion") and 9:51–18:14 (the so-called "large insertion"). Non-Markan material is also found within the Markan blocks: larger pieces are Lk 3:23–4:13; 4:16-30; 5:1-11; 19:1-27; 22:14-18, 24-38; 23:6-16, 27-31, 39-43; and the pre- and posthistories, Lk 1–2 and 24:12-53, contain exclusively special material.[11] The non-Markan material includes approximately three-fifths of the entire Gospel and more than one-third of Lk has no parallels in Mk, and thus is special material. The large extent of the special material, the fact that about three-tenths of Mk is missing from Lk, the sharp differences in the passion story between Lk and Mk, and the considerable linguistic deviations of Lk from Mk when they are parallel (cf. Lk 21:12-26 with Mk 13:9-25), led Streeter in more recent times[12] to the newly substantiated theory that Mk was not a basic source for Lk that he expanded by use of Q and his special material, but that the author first fashioned a gospel from Q and L (=special material) which began at 3:1 ("Proto-Luke"), and then subsequently inserted portions of Mk and added Chs. 1 and 2. This thesis was made still more precise by some scholars, in the main by Streeter himself: "Proto-Luke" was written by Luke, a pupil of Paul, on the basis of inquiry among the eyewitnesses during Paul's imprisonment in Caesarea (Acts 23:35–27:1), and later, when Luke went with Paul to Rome, the work was expanded on the basis of the Roman Mk.[13] Other scholars maintain that it is only for the passion narrative that a special source behind the account is demonstrable,[14] or they represent the related position that the whole of Lk's special material comes from one apostolic narrative source, but they do not consider this special source to be the foundation of Lk.[15] Many scholars, however, have rejected the assumption of a

[11] According to the word count of de Solages, *Synopse Grecque des Évangiles*, 1049; similar relative numbers on the basis of counting entire pericopes in Goguel, *Intr.* I, 494.

[12] On the prehistory of the Proto-Luke hypothesis see K. Grobel, *Formgeschichte und synoptische Quellenanalyse*, 1937, 67 ff, and Gaston, *No Stone* . . . , 244 f.

[13] Cf. in addition to those mentioned in §5 n. 11: T. W. Manson, Koh, Lohse, Rehkopf, Gaston, Williams, Morton, Marshall, Kilpatrick (1970, for Chs. 3–20); Jeremias and Winter would like to distinguish between the author of Lk and of Proto-Luke.

[14] Thus those mentioned in §5 n. 10; further George, Schütz, G. Schneider, Schramm; E. Bammel, "Das Ende von Q," *Festschr. G. Stählin*, 1970, 45.

[15] Thus in various ways those mentioned in §5 n. 9; further Schramm; earlier representatives of views like that in Schürmann, ZKTh 1954, 90 n. 64 (= Sch., Tr. U., 286 n. 64); a Hebrew special source is proposed by Schweizer; Sahlin, with the support of Gaston, *No Stone* . . . , 254, proposes a Hebrew-Aramaic "Proto-Luke" extending from Lk 1:5 to Acts 15.

Proto-Luke[16] or have described as inadequate the claim for a special source for Lk's passion narrative.[17]

In fact, the assumption of a Lukan special source or a Proto-Luke is as questionable as is a special source for the passion narrative in Lk.

a. Leaving aside the proto-history in Lk 1–2, the comparison of Lk with Mk shows that on the whole Lk follows the Markan sequence, but occasionally does not shrink from alterations in the sequence (see above, §5.3.5). The claim that as compared with Mk Lk has no rearrangement of the pericopes outside the passion narrative,[18] can be maintained only (1) if it is disputed—without adequate reason—that the events narrated in Lk 4:16-30 and 5:1-11 (rejection in Nazareth; call of the first disciples) have received from Lk a different position in the sequence of narratives. (It is all the same whether these pericopes were taken over by Lk already formulated, or whether, as is more likely, they were formed by Lk in reliance on Mk but with the help of other traditions.) Or (2) if—in similarly unsupported manner—the transposition of Mk 3:7 ff and 3:31 ff by Lk is called a "supplement" (the advancing of the story of John's imprisonment to Lk 3:19 f instead of its position in Mk 6:17 f par. can scarcely be called an addendum!). There is therefore no adequate ground for disputing the possibility that Lk has rearranged material in the passion narrative (Sparks).

b. The supposition that Lk has inserted four blocks of Markan material (Mk 1:21–3:6; 4:1–9:40; 10:13-52; 11:1–14:16) secondarily into his special source (see the tables in Jeremias, *Eucharistic Words*, 97 f) collides with two facts: (1) In the places where the small (Lk 6:17–8:3) and large (9:51–18:14) interpola-

---

[16] E.g., Ellis, Rigaux; Goguel, Klijn, Michaelis; Kilpatrick (1942), Gilmour, Schürmann, Hastings, O'Neill, Conzelmann, Montefiore, Leaney, Talbert, Schramm; K. Grobel (see n. 12), 118 f; E. Trocmé, *La formation de l'évangile selon Marc*, 1963, 173 f; J. A. Bailey, *The Traditions Common to the Gospels of Luke and John*, Suppl NovTest 7, 1963, 18 ff.

[17] Among others, J. Finegan, *Die Überlieferung der Leidens- und Auferstehungsgeschichte Jesu*, Bh. ZNW 15, 1934, 35 ff; R. H. Lightfoot, *History and Interpretation in the Gospels*, 1935, 164 ff; G. Iber, "Zur Formgeschichte der Evangelien," ThR, NF 24, 1957/58, 301 f; R. Bultmann, *History of the Synoptic Tradition*, 435 (cf. 282); A. Vööbus, *The Prelude to the Lukan Passion Narrative. Tradition-, Redaction-, Cult-, Motif-Historical and Source-Critical Studies*, Papers of the Estonian Theological Society in Exile 17, 1968, *passim*; J. Schreiber, *Die Markuspassion*, 1969, 49 f; J. Blinzler, *Der Prozess Jesu*, ⁴1969, 170 ff (bibl.); H. C. Kee, *Jesus in History*, 1970, 183 f.

[18] Schürmann, Jeremias, Rehkopf; C. Burchard, "Das doppelte Liebesgebot in der frühen christlichen Überlieferung," *Der Ruf Jesu und die Antwort der Gemeinde, Festschr. J. Jeremias*, 1970, 42.

tions interrupt the sequence that Lk has taken over from Mk, there is in each case a section from Mk (3:20-30; 9:42–10:12) omitted by Lk. Similarly, where Lk inserts the material in 19:39-44, the Markan section (Mk 11:11-14) is lacking. This can hardly be accounted for if Markan blocks were inserted in a Lukan special source.[19] (2) When Lk presents doublets (of non-Markan origin but with content similar to Mk) or another version of a text he has omitted from Mk, the Markan text always precedes the doublet, and in the majority of cases the position of the omitted Markan text is prior to that of the Lukan version.[20] This also can be explained only if Mk was used as a basic source for the composition of Lk.

c. The so-called "travel narrative" (9:51–19:27) is a creation of Luke, as recent work on the subject has shown (see below, §8.3.6). Luke has introduced material of various origins into a not fully developed framework of a journey to Jerusalem. In this "central section" we have, not an original tradition taken over directly by Luke, but a composition of the evangelist, who has expanded on the situation presented in Mk 10:1, 11:1 by arranging disparate material.

d. Rehkopf's effort at isolating non-Lukan vocabulary in Lk has not succeeded (in spite of support from Taylor) in proving the existence of a coherent special tradition in Lk or the blending of this special tradition with Q prior to the insertion of the Markan material.[21] No more successfully have others been able to show[22] that the various bits and pieces of special tradition in the Lukan passion narrative represent an originally coherent source into which Luke has inserted individual verses from Mk. On the one hand, the grounds adduced for an originally connected narrative consisting of the individual elements of the Lukan special material (e.g., from 22:15-20 and 22:24-32) are something less than obvious; and on the other hand, the alternatives are not limited to a "connected written source" or a "free invention" of Luke.[23] That Luke has enriched the Markan passion narrative by orally transmitted fea-

[19] So Schürmann, ZKTh 1954, 83 f. The objection that Lk could have omitted such Markan pericopes "for the reason . . . that they were already in his first sketch" (J. Schmid, ThRev 62, 1966, 304) would be worth considering at most for Mk 3:22-27.

[20] See Schürmann, ZKTh 1953, 341 f. The few exceptions are Lk 4:16-20 instead of Mk 6:1-6; Lk 7:36 instead of Mk 14:3-9; Lk 10:25-28 instead of Mk 12:28-31; Lk 16:18 instead of Mk 10:11. (I here respond to objections raised in a letter from J. Jeremias.)

[21] Cf. Conzelmann, Gn, 1960, and Schürmann, BZ 1961.

[22] E.g., Schürmann, Tyson, Rehkopf.

[23] Thus Schürmann, *Jesu Abschiedsrede*, 140 n. 476.

tures or that he has reworked Mk on the basis of such tradition, is much more seriously to be considered—certainly until more really persuasive evidence is provided for the dependence of Luke on a connected special source for his passion narrative.[24] It is significant that V. Taylor latterly shifted to conceding that Mk furnished the framework for the Lukan passion narrative.

e. Winter and Gaston try to show that Mk is not the basic source for the apocalyptic discourse of Lk 21 or for the passion narrative, but that, as in the passion narrative, individual verses from Mk 13 have been inserted into an already existing connected source. The basis for this assumption is, on the one hand, that when the passages in agreement with Mk are removed, the result is said to be a clearer continuity of meaning, which would then be original; on the other hand, the claim is that the contradictions in the Lukan text (e.g., 21:20 against 21:21, and 21:27 against 21:28) can only be explained as meaningfully coherent by removal of the verses in agreement with Mk which Lk has allegedly inserted. But against this it should be said that the exclusion of the Markan verses does not make the original continuity more comprehensible (e.g., 21:20, 21b, 22), while the contradictions between the apocalyptic traditions that have been combined can be explained as well on the basis of Mk's having been expanded by other traditions as through the interpolation of Markan verses in a postulated sequence from a special source. When one considers how thoroughly Lk has reworked the Markan wording in the sense of a greater stress on the timeline until the parousia—where Lk's dependence on Mk cannot be contested (cf. Lk 21:8 with Mk 13:5 f)—it is more reasonable to assume that in Lk 21 the text of Mk 13 has been used as the basic source together with further units of tradition.[25]

f. That Lk has used Mk as a basic source is shown conclusively in the breaking up of the Markan structure in the process of Lk's expansion. Especially striking is Lk's separation of the passion predictions, which Mk inserted at equal intervals (Mk 8:31 f; 9:30 ff par. Lk 9:22, 43 ff; but Mk 10:32 ff par. Lk 18:31 ff, because the "great interpolation" [Lk 9:51–8:14] has been placed in between). Also the insertion of the genealogy (Lk 3:23 ff) between the baptism and the temptation of Jesus (Mk 1:9-11, 12 f) separates in a secondary way items that belong together. And Lk's bracketing of the public ministry of Jesus by the temporary distancing of the Devil from the temptation of Jesus to the beginning

[24] ExpT 1959/60, 69.
[25] Cf. Grässer, 152 ff, Schmid, LThK VI, 1209, Barrett, 65.

of the passion narrative—which is inserted in Q material at 4:13 and in Markan material at 22:3—shows that the evangelist has created out of Mk and Q a deliberate conjoining.[26]

All this implies that the theories of a Lukan special source and a "Proto-Luke" comprising Q + special material are untenable, and that Lk can scarcely have had a consecutive special tradition for the passion narrative. The great age and the Palestinian origin of the Lukan special tradition cannot be ascertained on the basis of undemonstrable assumptions about a Lukan source or a Proto-Luke.[27] (Indeed Montefiore wants to confirm this conclusion by referring to the fact that the alleged Proto-Luke could not have been brought to Rome by Luke, since the papyrus manuscript would have been lost in the shipwreck off Malta [Acts 27:41 ff]!) If, then, Luke did not derive from a consecutive special source the extensive material that goes beyond Mk and Q, the possibility cannot be excluded that he—as has already been conjectured for Mk—found assembled in oral or even written form some of the special traditions that he employed. But that can hardly be demonstrated with certainty. (Farmer would like to derive, e.g., 13:1-9 and 15:1-32 from the same source, but he is unable to make a convincing case.) In no instance is it illuminating to attempt to account for the undoubtedly conscious LXX style of Luke (Sparks) by assuming there were Hebrew or hebraizing sources.[28] And the search for various traditional sources[29] and bearers of tradition[30] is a worthless enterprise. We can seek to determine only the historical origin of individual units of tradition and the mode of their modification and arrangement by Luke.

In connection with the question about the sources of Lk, a problem is still presented by the prehistories in Lk 1 and 2.[31] The problem arises not only from the chronological synchronism (3:1 f), which shows that the actual reporting begins only at that point, but also from the unmistakable fact that, following the literarily stylized prologue (1:1-4), the narratives and the songs

[26] Thus Conzelmann, 16,22,53.

[27] Thus also Rigaux, *Comm.*, 79 f.

[28] Sahlin, Schweizer; *contra*, Michaelis, *Einl.*, 71 ff; Aalen points to the linguistic and conceptual contacts of Lk with the Greek text of Ethiopic Enoch (97 ff), without being able to offer a clear explanation for this connection.

[29] Albertz: women tradition; relatives tradition; Hellenistic tradition.

[30] Hastings: the evangelist Philip, Simon of Cyrene; Joanna, the wife of Chuza (8:3; 24:10) transmitted accounts about Herod!

[31] On the history of research, see R. M. Wilson, Oliver, 205 ff; St. Benko, "The Magnificat: A History of the Controversy," JBL 86, 1967, 263 ff; W. Wink, *John the Baptist in the Gospel Tradition*, SNTSMS 7, 1968, 60 ff, and the bibl. in Schürmann, *Comm.* I, 18 ff, 70, 84, 140 ff.

1:5–2:52) pass over immediately into a kind of Greek that is strongly reminiscent of the semiticizing LXX language. Many adherents of the Proto-Luke hypothesis have drawn from these observations the conclusion that it was only at the final composition of Lk that the prehistories—based on written sources—were prefixed to Proto-Luke, which originally began with 3:1. Related to this is the position that the strongly Semitic language of these chapters is conceivable only by supposing that Hebrew sources were translated and expanded by the author of Lk, or at least he employed Greek sources that had been translated out of Hebrew. In this connection different views have arisen as to whether the hymns (1:46 ff; 68 ff; 2:29) were taken up along with these sources or whether they were introduced from other traditions.[32] Others are of the opinion that Lk himself composed this narrative on the basis of older oral or written traditions in conscious accommodation to the language of LXX.[33] On this Winter has sought to show in many works[34] that a great part of Lk arose in Baptist circles and was only secondarily applied to Jesus.[35] He wants to see in the hymns (1:46 ff, 68 ff) Maccabean battle songs, sung before and after battle. By the addition of 1:76-79 they were then linked with the Baptist. Opinions vary especially widely about the original character of the Benedictus (1:68 ff): some see in the hymn as a whole a song about the Baptist,[36] while others regard it as a Christian poem with reference to the Baptist (Benoit) or to Jesus,[37] as a Jewish messianic psalm (Gaston), or as a combination of a messianic psalm and a nativity song about John from Jewish-Christian circles (Gnilka). Linguistic observations[38] show that the postulation of a translation of both chapters from Hebrew is not compelling. Even though many features in the story of John's birth and the Benedictus (cf. 1:16 f, 76) seem to indicate

[32] Thus in various ways, e.g., Schürmann; Schelkle; Sahlin, Winter, Laurentin, Hastings, Wilson, Gaston; Wink (see n. 31), 61 f.

[33] R. M. Grant; Dibelius, Turner, Benoit, Sparks, Minear; C. Burger, *Jesus als Davidssohn*, FRLANT 98, 1970, 137.

[34] Complete enumeration in NTS 10, 1963/64, 209 n. 4.

[35] The position that the nativity story of the Baptist originated in the Baptist's circles has long had its representatives; cf. Wink (see n. 31), 60; in addition, Benko (see n. 31), 274.

[36] Vielhauer; Benko (see n. 31), 274; Burger (see n. 33), 131; H. Thyen, Βάπτισμα μετανοίας εἰς ἄφεσιν ἁμαρτιῶν, Zeit und Geschichte, Festschr. R. Bultmann, 1964, 115 f.

[37] Sahlin, Leaney, Jones; Wink (see n. 31), 67 f.

[38] See Schürmann, *Comm.* I, 141, 144; Turner, Benoit, Sparks.

the origin of these texts in Baptist circles, recent research[39] has made it seem probable that as a whole the material which underlies Chs. 1 and 2 arose in Jewish-Christian circles under strong influence of OT language and concepts. Above all, the observation is important that in 1:26-37 and 2:1-10 we encounter two completely different representations of the birth of Jesus (Dibelius; Leaney) which have been placed secondarily into a combination that is not free from contradictions. Although at present a final decision cannot be reached about the origin and the homogeneity of the individual elements of tradition in Lk 1 and 2, nevertheless the observations just mentioned speak against the assumption that in Lk 1 and 2 larger source units were drawn upon. The probability points rather to Lk's having worked over various traditions which had in part already received a linguistically fixed form. These he prefixed to his presentation of the public activity of Jesus, which assumption also explains the theological agreements between Lk 1-2 and Lk 3-24.[40] The few linguistic deviations between Lk 1-2 and Lk 3-24 can perhaps be traced back —if an explanation is required at all—to the fact that the prehistory was written later than the rest of the Gospel.[41]

If on this basis it must be considered probable that Lk originated from the insertion of material from Q and from a special tradition into the Markan sequence, which has been essentially maintained, then the claim is confirmed (see above, p. 130) that "Lk does not offer a more exact historical sequence of events than Mk, so that his intention to write everything 'in the right order' (καθέξης) cannot indicate a strict chronological order, which his sources would not have permitted him to do."[41a] The goal to which Luke aspired of καθεξῆς γράψαι he attains, not by a chronologically more reliable sequence, but through other kinds of editing of Mk and by the interpolation of other abundant tradition. (1) the revision of Mk (and, as may be inferred, of Q and the special tradition as well) was accomplished as in the case of Mt by closer coupling of individual accounts with each other and by occasional creation of larger connections in the course of the narrative: links by means of expressions such as μετὰ ταῦτα, καὶ ἐγένετο ἐν μία τῶν ἡμερῶν, ἀναστὰς δέ (5:27, 17; 4:38); in contrast to Mk 2:13 ff, 18 ff, Lk 5:27-39 becomes a single narrative by means of pre-

---

[39] Cf. above all, Wink (see n. 31), 60 ff (esp. 71 f, 81 f) and Schürmann, Comm. I, 143 ff.

[40] Cf. Oliver; Wink (see n. 31), 79 f.

[41] Thus Schürmann, Comm. I, 141; Benoit, NTS 1956/57, 175 f; Benko (see n. 31), 275.

[41a] J. Schmid, LThK VI, 1208.

senting Jesus' interrogators as identical (5:30, 33 as against Mk 2:16, 18); in 19:11, in contrast to Mt 25:14, the parable of the pounds is placed in the context of the biography of Jesus by referring to his proximity to Jerusalem and the expectations of the crowds; in 4:13 the remark about the temporary restraint of the Devil anticipates 22:3; 8:2 f names in a preparatory way the women who are to be present at the crucifixion and the discovery of the empty tomb (23:49, 55; 24:10).[42] In addition to other grounds these numerous combinations of two reports refute the assumption of Morgenthaler that Luke arranges his material consistently on a principle of duality. (2) Luke has significantly altered the wording of Mk and that of his other tradition as well, by replacing colloquial words and expressions and forming better Greek sentences.[43] Especially noteworthy is Luke's elimination of all foreign-language words, except for ἀμήν; even this word has several times been omitted by Luke or replaced by a Greek word, though he does use it six times in speeches which involve direct instruction for the life of Christians (4:24; 12:37; 18:17, 29; 21:32; 23:43).[44] Luke undoubtedly writes in more elevated language than do his sources, but then this tendency is combated by his inclination to closely match the biblical Greek of LXX (see Sparks). And Luke has not exercised this linguistic renovation of the tradition in a comparable way throughout the whole of his material: in the narrative material, especially in the introduction .to the pericopes, the Lukan linguistic peculiarities are four times as frequent as in the sayings of Jesus, and correspondingly the number of words agreeing with Mark in the Jesus sayings exceeds that in the narrative sections.[45] And in the prehistory Luke more closely approximates the LXX style than in the rest of the Gospel. From this it may be inferred that Luke has shaped the tradition quite consciously for the Greek-speaking reader, but has imposed on himself narrower limits for the passing on of the sayings of the Lord.

(3) Like Mt, Lk has also set aside offensive features that were

---

[42] On these features, cf. R. Bultmann, History, 334 ff, 358 ff; Dibelius Tradition, 199 ff.

[43] Cf. Klostermann, HNT, 243 ff; P. Wernle, Die synpt. Frage, 10 ff.

[44] O'Neill, JTS 1959. The claim that Lk has not eliminated any "Amen" sayings can be supported only by the arbitrary assumption that Amen appeared nowhere in Lk's source, Mk (against K. Berger, Die Amen Worte Jesu, Bh. ZNW 39, 1970, 35.

[45] Schürmann, Paschamahlbericht, 2; Rosché, "The Words of Jesus . . . ," JBL 79, 1960, 212 (confirmed by C. E. Carlston and D. Norlin, "Once More— Statistics and Q," HTR 64, 1971, 64, 68 ff).

in the Markan text: instead of the healing of "many" (Mk 1:34; 3:10) there is the healing of "all" (Lk 4:40; 6:19); Jesus' emotions disappear (Lk 6:10; 18:22, in contrast to Mk 3:5; 10:21); also lacking are the explanation by Jesus' relatives that he is out of his mind (Mk 3:20) and his healing by touch (Lk 4:39; 9:42 against Mk 1:31; 9:27); Jesus' cry of "My God, My God! Why hast thou forsaken me?" (Mk 15:34) is replaced by "Father, into thy hands I commit my spirit" (Lk 23:46). In keeping with this, Jesus in Lk knows himself to be the Messiah from the outset (4:21), and so is greeted by Peter as κύριε (5:8) and often in the narrative called ὁ κύριος by the evangelist (7:13; 10:1, 41; 22:61; among others), because in the activity of Jesus the time of salvation has already broken in σήμερον σωτηρία τῷ οἴκῳ τούτῳ ἐγένετο (19:9, spoken to Zacchaeus). That does not exclude Luke's especial delight in bringing to the fore Jesus' moving human traits: Jesus talks with the women on the way to the cross (23:27 ff) and with a fellow victim of crucifixion (23:40 ff); he heals the ear of the high priest's slave who was wounded by one of his disciples (22:51); and from the house of the high priest looks at Peter in the act of denial (22:61).

(4) With this stress on the human, moving features of Jesus is to be associated the fact that according to Lk Jesus expresses more emphatically than in Mk or Mt God's love for the despised, both by his behavior and by his message: to sinners (5:1 f; 5:8 [ἀνὴρ ἁμαρτωλός εἰμι says Peter]; 7:36 ff; 15:1 ff; 18:9 ff; 19:1 ff ["the Son of man came to seek and to save the lost"]; 22:31); to the Samaritans (10:30 ff; 17:11 ff); to women (7:12, 15; 8:2 f; 10:38 ff; 23:27 ff). With this belongs also the stronger rejection of wealth (12:15 ff; 16:19 ff), with the warning about the μαμωνᾶς τῆς ἀδικίας (16:9, 11) and the woes over "the rich and those now satiated" (6:25 f), as well as with the blessing of the "poor" and those "now hungering" (6:20 f). It has been proposed that, by his emphasis on the poor, Lk "has given to the preaching of Jesus a slight Ebionite coloration" (Feine-Behm), but in view of the totality of the features mentioned above, that is false: Lk has so strongly emphasized the influence on Jesus of late Jewish "piety of the poor," as well as his repudiation of the religious scorn toward certain groups of persons, solely on the presupposition that in Jesus the divine love had really become present redemption for those who in the eyes of men were lost.[46]

[46] On Lk's valuing of the poor, see Schürmann, *Comm.* I, 327; L. E. Keck, "The Poor Among the Saints in the NT," ZNW 56, 1965, 108 ff; H.-J. Degenhardt, *Lukas Evangelist der Armen,* 1965.

(5.) Still more important is the fact that Luke has placed the history of Jesus in a clearly recognizable link with the history of his own time. That has occurred in three ways: (a) By the reference to the connection between the birth of Jesus in Bethlehem and the census decree of Caesar Augustus under Quirinius (2:1 f), and by the chronological grounding of the appearance of the Baptist, based on dates from Roman and Jewish history (3:1 f), the history of Jesus is made known as a part of the general course of history. In keeping with this, in the NT as a whole it is only in Lk that names of Roman caesars are mentioned (cf. in addition Acts 11:28; 18:2). And Luke explicitly emphasizes that "this" (i.e., the history of Christ as the fulfillment of the prophetic promises) "did not happen in a corner" (Acts 26:26). According to Luke, the history of Jesus Christ belongs to world history. (b) Obviously Luke is the first to place the history of Jesus as the beginning of the ongoing history of the church (Lk 19:11; 21:8), in that he has Acts, his second book, serve as a historical sequel to Lk. Yet by this tactic Luke is not the first to make the history of Jesus into past history, nor is his account of the history of Jesus the first "Life of Jesus." [47] For Mk and Mt also look back on the history of Jesus as past (see above, §6.2, with n. 45; §7.2, with n. 57). The history of Jesus is for Lk only the beginning of the eschatological redemptive history, in which the Jesus event is carried forward through preaching.[48] The history of Jesus therefore has finally reached its real goal when Paul in Rome preaches τὰ περὶ τοῦ κυρίου Ἰησοῦ (Acts 28:31). (c) Luke is eager to prove the political innocence of Jesus in the eyes of the Romans, especially of Pilate (Lk 23:4, 14, 20, 22; 23:47, "This man was innocent"), while the Jews appear as those who sanction the disturbance and seek unjustly to condemn Jesus as a political insurrectionist (20:20, 26; 23:2, 5, 18 f, 23, 25). There can be no doubt [49] that here we face a political apologetic, which exonerates the Romans from guilt for the crucifixion of Jesus (Pilate does not condemn Jesus: Lk 23:25 against Mk 15:15 par. Mt 27:26), and thus is prepared the defense of the Christians against political suspicion in Acts (e.g., Acts 17:7; see

---

[47] Thus Käsemann, "The Problem of the Historical Jesus," in *Essays on NT Themes*, 1964, 15 ff; similarly, Marxsen, *Intr.*, 156 f; Conzelmann, 16 f; Robinson, 28, Barrett, 64; Löning, 203; U. Wilckens, *Die Missionsreden der Apg*, 1961, 202; E. Haenchen, *Acts*, 90 ff; R. Bultmann, *Theology of the NT* II, 117, 126; Schulz (see n. 4), 238, 284.

[48] Cf. Flender, *St. Luke*, 73, 146; O. Betz "The Kerygma of Luke," Int 22, 1968, 138.

[49] See Kilpatrick (1942); Conzelmann, 138 ff; Schütz, 126 ff; Manson, *St.*, 60 f.

below, p. 163). In this political defense too the connection between
the history of Jesus and world history appears.

(6) The decisive motive in Luke's reworking of Mk, however,
is theological. That is evident in the alteration of the geographical
framework of Mk. The author of Lk obviously has no accurate
conception of Palestinian geography,[50] and knows nothing of other
journeys of Jesus to Jerusalem (Girard). Rather, he has expanded
the Markan account of Jesus' journey to Jerusalem after concluding his activity in Galilee and vicinity by representing Jesus
in 9:51–19:27 as always being on the way to Jerusalem (9:51;
13:22, 33; 17:11; 18:31; more general are the allusions to Jesus'
journey in 9:57; 10:1, 38; 14:25). The reference in 17:11, διήρχετο
διὰ μέσον Σαμαρείας καὶ Γαλιλαίας, is incomprehensible, but demands
no conjecture.[51] In putting together the journey to Jerusalem,
Luke has introduced material from Q, from his special tradition,
and from the Markan Jerusalem journey (Mk 10), which for the
most part has no recognizable connection with the biographical
situation (Blinzler, Reicke).[51a] This emphatic alteration of the
Markan source allows the conjecture that in his account of the
journey to Jerusalem Luke has created more than merely the framework for bringing together further material from his tradition.

Recent work on the "travel narrative" has attempted to discover the leading objective behind this composition: teaching for
disciples with instructions for the life and work of disciples and
the future missionary work of the community of disciples;[52]
material arranged by analogy with Dt;[53] instruction of the apostles
and discussion with their opponents;[54] Jesus' awareness of the
passion is expressed as a journey;[55] the way to the passion is united
with Jesus' activity as the prophetic teacher ordained to be Messiah;[56] the progress of redemptive history portrayed as "Way";
preparation for the apostolic witness;[57] journey as the first stage

[50] See Conzelmann, 19 ff., who with too much assurance describes the concepts of Lk.

[51] Against Blinzler.

[51a] Ogg tries to explain on literary-critical and historicizing—but wholly
arbitrary—grounds the travel narrative as resulting from the juxtaposition of
two parallel accounts of the journey to Jerusalem (9:51–10:42 and 17:11–19:28)
together with an expansion in 11:1–17:10 and recurrent interpolation between
9:50 and 19:29.

[52] J. Schneider, Gill.

[53] Evans.

[54] Reicke, Marshall.

[55] O'Neill, Conzelmann; Schulz (see n. 4), 240.

[56] Grundmann; similarly George, 110 f.

[57] Robinson.

in the ascension of Jesus;[58] the journey portrays Jesus' claim to authority and his rejection;[59] the representation of Jesus' journey to Jerusalem is influenced by the tragic course of Paul to Jerusalem.[60] But the multiplicity of these attempts shows that the main perspectives of this composition are not clearly presented, so that the insight must suffice that in 9:51–19:27 the Lord who is on his way to suffer according to the will of God is equipping his disciples for carrying on his preaching after his death (9:60; 10:3, 16; 17:22-25).[61] The scope of this composition and its position prior to the actual passion narrative lend to this section on the activity of Jesus a special weight; thus it becomes clear that through this alteration to the form of Mk, Luke wants to report the history of Jesus as preparation for the work of the disciples after Easter.

In this way the dominant theological objective of the structuring of the history of Jesus in Luke's work is touched upon; the integration of the history of Jesus into God's redemptive history. It has long been observed that "for Luke, eschatology is not represented in the preaching of Jesus with the acuteness that it is in Mk and Mt," and that "the expectation of the nearness of the End seems dampened in comparison with Mk and Mt (19:11; 9:27; 22:69)" (Feine-Behm). More recent research on the theology of Luke[62] has shown, however, that this receding of the expectation of the near End is only an especially striking indication of the fact that Luke "propounds a Christian view of history, which comprehends as the fulfillment of the divine promises the activity of Jesus, his death and resurrection, but then extends the line beyond this event so that redemptive history continues on in the course of the history of the church until the end of time." [63] Above all, there are three ideas by which Luke's basic theological view gives a new direction to the history of Jesus:

a. The expectation of the nearness of the End was shunted from its dominant position: the summary of the message of Jesus "Soon to come is the kingdom of God" (Mk 1:15) was replaced by the initial preaching of Jesus in Nazareth (Lk 4:21): "Today is this scripture [concerning the eschatological sending of the Spirit upon

---

[58] Davies, similarly Flender.

[59] Schütz, 70 ff.

[60] Bouwman, 74.

[61] Rigaux, 201, would like to understand the travel narrative simply as a "collection of the deeds and words of Jesus."

[62] Cf. esp. Lohse, Grässer, O'Neill, Conzelmann, Luck, Kaestli, Francis, Wilson, Löning; Haenchen, Acts.

[63] Lohse, 265.

Jesus] fulfilled in your hearing." In place of the promise "Some of you who are standing here will not taste death until they see the kingdom of God having come in power" (Mk 9:1), we find (Lk 9:27) "Some who stand here will not taste death until they have seen the kingdom of God." The parable of the entrusted pounds is spoken, according to the Lukan introduction (Lk 19:11) "because they thought that the kingdom of God was coming immediately." The warning in Mk 13:6, "Many will come in my name and say 'I am he' and lead many astray," is expanded in Lk 21:8: "Many will come in my name and say 'I am he' and 'The time is at hand'; do not follow after them." Indeed, the question "When is the kingdom of God coming?" is rejected, because there are no signs given on the basis of which it can be answered and because "the kingdom of God is among you" (Lk 17:20).[64] But does Luke reject the question about setting a time for the End because "the time lies in the distant future," because "Luke has decisively repudiated the adherence to the expectation of a near End"? [65] This approach is contradicted by some texts in which are proclaimed the nearness of judgment (3:9, 17, spoken by the Baptist), the nearness of the kingdom of God (10:9, 11 as Jesus' commission to the seventy), the speedy judgment of God (18:7 f), and the danger of counting on the delay (12:45 f). Lk 21:32 echoes the saying in Mk 13:30, "All this will happen before this generation has passed." These texts cannot be explained away only by the claim that Luke has "simply taken over" these sayings but that the overall sense rather than the individual saying is decisive,[66] since in Lk 10:11 ἤγγικεν ἡ βασιλεία τοῦ θεοῦ has obviously been added (cf. Mt 10:14) and the reference to the fate of Sodom "on that day" (i.e., on the Day of Judgment) in the next verse (10:12) shows that Luke must have understood the kingdom of God, not as present, but as threateningly future. In Lk 18:7 f, the reference to the speedy setting things right by God comes probably from Luke himself. It is hardly justifiable, therefore, to say that Luke has abandoned completely the expectation of the End as near,[67] but for him it has lost its pressing character and

---

[64] On the translation of this enigmatic word, cf. W. G. Kümmel, *Promise and Fulfillment*, 1957, 32 ff, and F. Mussner, "Wann kommt das Reich Gottes?" BZ, NF 6, 1962, 107 ff.

[65] Grässer, 194; Conzelmann, 132; similarly Marxsen, *Intr.*, 158; Haenchen, *Acts*, 95 f; Schulz (see n. 4), 237, 292 f.

[66] Grässer, 190; similarly Conzelmann, 104 f.

[67] Wilson proves that in Lk the delay of the parousia and references to the near End conflict with one another, which Wilson accounts for on the basis of the pastoral situation; according to Francis (59), Lk stresses the threatening

the present is stressed more heavily as the time of salvation.

  b. If it is not the case that Luke replaced the near expectation of the End by the concept of redemptive history,[68] there can be no doubt that he pictures the history of Jesus as the beginning of redemptive history and not as *the* eschatological event. Lk 16: 16 is particularly characteristic of this view: the saying of Jesus as found in its original form (Mt 11:12) "From the days of John the Baptist until now the kingdom of God has suffered violence," becomes in Lk 16:16 "The law and the prophets [are in effect] until John. From this time on the good news of the kingdom of God is preached, and everyone is earnestly urged to enter it." [69] On the basis of this saying, Conzelmann has been the chief representative of the view that Luke is picturing the history of Jesus as "the midpoint of time," which presupposes the time of the Law and the prophets, and which is followed by the time of the church. He alleges that growing consciousness of the failure of the parousia to occur led to the replacement of eschatology by redemptive history.[70] There can indeed be no doubt that the delay of the parousia affected Luke's reproduction of the message of Jesus. That is apparent not only in the suppression of the near expectation, as already mentioned (cf. also 21:9 οὐκ εὐθέως τὸ τέλος), but also strikingly in the separation of still affirmed temporal expectation of the End from the events within history: the persecution of the disciples and the destruction of Jerusalem (21:12 ff, 20 ff) are—in contrast to Mk 13:9 ff, 14 ff—events in history which are differentiated from and have no chronological relationship with the signs of the parousia and the parousia itself (Lk 21:25 ff par. Mk 13: 24 ff; cf. πρὸ δὲ τούτων πάντων Lk 21:12 [71]). Even if the growing

---

approach of the End, but denies its immediate coming. That Lk is unaware of the problem of the delay of the parousia but is only warning against equating the ascension of Jesus with the coming of the kingdom of God (Talbert, *Perspective,* 173 ff, 184 ff) is no more accurate than the claim that Lk has replaced the chronological nearness of the End with "a spatial nearness of the Kingdom" (Robinson, *Weg des Herrn,* 66; similarly Francis, 63).

  [68] See n. 65; further Barrett, 64; U. Wilckens, *Die Missionsreden der Apg.,* 1961, 93.

  [69] See on this W. G. Kümmel, " 'Das Gesetz und die Propheten gehen bis Johannes'—Lk 16:16 im Zusammenhang der heilsgeschichtlichen Theologie der Lukasschriften," *Verborum Veritas, Festschr. G. Stählin,* 1970, 89 ff (bibl.), and Ph.-H. Menoud, "Le sens du verbe BIAZETAI dans Lc 16:16," *Mélanges Bibliques en hommage au R. P. B. Rigaux,* 1969, 207 ff.

  [70] Cf. Conzelmann, 17, 149 ff, 185 ff, 208 f; similarly those mentioned by W. G. Kümmel, EThL 1970, nn. 14-16; further Tatum, 186; Bouwman 52, Schneider 209.

  [71] On the editing of Mk in Lk 21:12 ff see Grässer, 158 ff; Kaestli, 41 ff.

consciousness of the delay of the parousia did have the result that "in place of a short, limited time there appeared the extended time of the church," [72] it does not follow that Luke has introduced the concept of redemptive history as a substitute for actual eschatology. It is to be noted that "Lk's sketch of redemptive history is not yet developed nor is it treated expressly as a theme," [73] and that Lk stresses only the difference between the period of the Law and the prophets and the period from John the Baptist until the parousia (Lk 16:16; 21:27 f).[74] At the same time it must be said that Luke is by no means the first to introduce the concept of redemptive history into the reproduction of the gospel tradition, since the proclamation of the presence of redemption that endures into the future, until the End, has formed the fundamental viewpoint of the gospel proclamation since the preaching of Jesus.[75] What led Luke to his inclusion of the history of Jesus within redemptive history was not the distressing problem of the delay of the parousia,[76] but the fact that the experience of the protracted yet ever threateningly short time brought to the center of attention the presence of the still expected consummation, so that the history of Jesus became the ἀρχή of the events which have been fulfilled "among us" (Lk 1:1 f).

c. For Luke it is a theological necessity that he report the "life of Jesus" as the beginning of his more extensive history of the church (see above, §8.3.5). For the experience of the Spirit as the power of the End-time in the church of the present (Acts 1:8; 2:1 ff; 5:32; 10:44 ff) makes it possible to see the history of Jesus as being dominated by the same Spirit of God which came upon Jesus σωματικῷ εἴδει (Lk 3:22) and dominated him until the final prayer (Lk 23:46; cf. 4:1, 18 and δύναμις 4:14, 36; 5:17). The history of Jesus is therefore consciously recounted by Luke looking backward from the church of the present (Acts 10:36), but his account "does not intend to historicize, but is proclamation as address in the present." [77] Lk cannot be represented as "the first

---

[72] Grässer, 197.

[73] Luck, 53.

[74] See W. G. Kümmel (see n. 69), 97 ff and EThL 1970, 274 f; further Marshall, Luke, 146, 221; Wilson, 333 ff; W. Wilkens, "Wassertaufe und Geistempfang bei Lk," ThZ 23, 1967, 31.

[75] Cf. W. G. Kümmel (see n. 64), passim; also in "Futuristic and Realized Eschatology in the Earliest Stages of Christianity," JR 43, 1963, 303 ff; O. Cullmann, Christ and Time, 1964, 1 ff; Kaestli, 79 ff.

[76] Thus correctly Wilckens, StLA, 66 f; Borgen, 147, 155 f; George, 122; Talbert, Perspective, 196.

[77] Schulz (see n. 4), 251; cf. Talbert, Perspective, 211 f.

representative of nascent early Catholicism" because "he attempt[s]
to present the history of Christianity including that of Jesus as secu-
lar history."[78] Indeed it is extremely questionable whether the oft-
represented thesis that early Catholicism is characteristic of Luke[79]
is in fact true. Even though the concept of "early Catholicism"
itself cannot be clearly defined,[80] it may still be said unambiguously that the views which may with certainty be indicated as
"early Catholic—the church as institution of salvation, ordained
church officers, apostolic succession, sacramental priesthood, authoritative interpretation of Scripture, linking of the Spirit to the
institution—are not encountered in the Lukan writings.[81]

Thus it should have become clear that Luke seeks to reach his
goal—καθεξῆς γράψαι, the traditions of the eyewitnesses—in such
a way that he depicts the history of Jesus, dominated by the Spirit
of God, as the basis for the apostles' witness "in Jerusalem and all
Judea and Samaria, and to the end of the earth" (Acts 1:8) in order
to offer to the believer ἀσφάλεια, which is for him indispensable
(Lk 1:4).

In this connection it is probable that Luke wants to make this
ἀσφάλεια perceptible to Theophilus because he sees the church of
his time as threatened by "wild wolves" from without and by "men
who speak distortions" from within (Acts 20:29 f). The striking
stress on the reality of the death and resurrection of Jesus (Lk 23:
55; 24:3, 39), the connection of the journeys of the earthly Jesus
with his ascension (9:51), and the integration of the history of
Jesus into world history (1:5; 2:1 f; 3:1 f) obviously serve to ward
off Gnostic and especially Docetic false teaching which endangers
the ἀσφάλεια of the Word concerning which Theophilus is in-

[78] E. Käsemann, *Questions*, 21.

[79] Thus first in 1949 E. Käsemann, *Exegetische Versuche und Besinnungen* I,
1962, 132 f; see further, those mentioned by W. G. Kümmel, EThL 1970, 270
nn. 21-25; O'Neill, *Theology*, 174.

[80] Cf. F. Mussner, art. "Frühkatholizismus," LThK VI, 1961, 89 f (bibl.);
Conzelmann, StLA, 304; Kaestli, 94. On the basic problem of "early Catholi-
cism" in the NT: H. Schürmann, "Das Testament des Paulus für die Kirche
Apg 20:18-35," *Theologisches Jahrbuch* 1964, 58 ff; St. Neill, *The Interpreta-
tion of the NT 1861–1961*, 1964, 186 ff; J. H. Elliott, "A Catholic Gospel:
Reflections on 'Early Catholicism' in the NT," CBQ, 1969, 213 ff; W. G.
Kümmel, *Das NT im 20. Jahrhundert*, StBSt 50, 1970, 82 f.

[81] Cf. those named by W. G. Kümmel, EThL 1970, 277 nn. 60, 61; also
Marxsen, Michaelis, *Einl.*, 141, ErgH, 21 f; Kaestli, 93 ff; Löning, 223; Talbert,
Perspective, 220 n. 146; Marshall, *Luke*, 20, 219 f; W. Eltester, "Lukas und
Paulus," *Eranion, Festschr. H. Hommel*, 1961, 7 f; W. Schneemelcher, "Die
Apg des Lukas und die Acta Pauli," *Apophoreta, Festschr. E. Haenchen*, Bh.
ZNW 30, 1964, 236.

structed.[82] The theological revision of the Jesus tradition thus apparently has a current objective as well.

4. Author

Through the dedication to the same Theophilus and the reference backward in Acts 1:1, Lk and Acts present themselves as the works of one author. They undoubtedly belong together in language, style, and theological position. But neither Lk nor Acts allows us to determine directly or indirectly who the author was. The tradition of the ancient church is first encountered in the Muratorian Canon, since a testimony in Papias is lacking, and since it is very questionable whether the erroneously designated "anti-Marcionite prologue to Lk" is of great age (see below, §35.3). The Muratorian Canon runs: "The third gospel according to Luke. After the ascension of Christ, Luke, whom Paul had taken with him as an expert in the way [= teaching; read *itineris* instead of *juris*], wrote under his own name and according to his own understanding. He had not, of course, seen the Lord in the flesh, and therefore he begins to tell the story from the birth of John on, insofar as it was accessible to him" (lines 3-8).[83] Later tradition[84] has not been able to add any further early information: the claim that Luke was from Antioch,[85] is first met for certain in Eusebius, HE II 4. 6; the so-called "anti-Marcionite prologue" is not a usable source (see above), and the "we" in a part of the "Western" text tradition of Acts 11:28, which presupposes the Antiochian tradition, does not occur once in a Western text that is demonstrably old (see below, p. 176). Thus there remains as the single account going back to the second century that Luke the physician is the author of Lk-Acts. This can only mean "Luke, the beloved physician" (Col 4. 14; Phlm 24; II Tim 4:11), who was born a Gentile, since Paul in Col 4:14 explicitly excludes Luke from his "fellow-workers of the circumcision." An identification with Lucius (Rom 16:21; Michaelis) is extremely unlikely, since probably by συγγενής μου Paul would designate a member of his own people, and therefore a

---

[82] More precise evidence in Schürmann (see n. 80), 26 ff, and Talbert, who, however, without justification would like to see Docetism being combated, in particular of a kind attested at Corinth (NTS 14, 1967/68, 270 f).

[83] Translation based on E. Hennecke-Schneemelcher, *NT Apocrypha* I, ³1963, 42 f.

[84] Reproduced in *Beginnings* II, 210 ff.

[85] Thus still Rigaux; Schelkle; Strobel; G. Stählin, Apg., NTD 5, 1962, 2; R. Glover, " 'Luke the Antiochene' and Acts," NTS 11, 1964/65, 97 ff.

Jew. According to the mention made in Col and Phlm, Luke must have been at the place of Paul's imprisonment, from which these letters came, but since the location cannot be determined with certainty (see §21.5), no clear biographical information can be deduced from it. Whether the "we-narrative" of Acts provides information of a kind about Luke's participation in the missionary journeys will be discussed in §9.

With regard to the second-century tradition about Luke the physician as the author of Lk-Acts, we must first ask whether we are really dealing here with an old tradition. H. J. Cadbury has noted[85a] that, as early as the end of the second-century, the presupposition that a canonical Gospel must have an apostolic author (see Tert., *Adv. Marc.* IV. 2) could have led to the inference that Luke was the author on the basis of comparing the "we" in Acts with the allusions by Paul to his companions during his imprisonment (Col 4:10-12; Phlm 23 f; II Tim 4:9-12). Though this cannot be proved, it is not certain either that the tradition from the end of the second century is based on ancient information. It is the more questionable, therefore, whether the inferred or traditional assumption that Luke the physician is the author of Lk-Acts can be brought into harmony with the information from Lk and Acts.

The question has often been discussed whether the books of Luke in their language and outlook allow us to perceive that the author was a physician. Hobart especially came to the conclusion on the basis of a comprehensive comparison of Lukan vocabulary with the language and characteristic expressions of Greek physicians that both Lukan writings clearly manifest a familiarity with medical technical language and leave no doubt about the vocation of the author.[86] The methodological untenability of this thesis has been revealed by Cadbury, who showed that almost all the allegedly purely medical expressions in Lk are to be found, e.g., in LXX, Josephus, Plutarch, Lucian, and that the style of Lk evidences no more medical language or medical interests than the style of contemporary writers who were not physicians. The use of individual words and expressions which have parallels predominantly in the medical literature of the Greeks—e.g., συνεχομένη πυρετῷ μεγάλῳ Lk 4:38 (cf. Mk 1:30 πυρέσσουσα); ἀνὴρ πλήρης λέπρας Lk 5:12 (cf. Mk 1:40 λεπρός); ἔστη ἡ ῥύσις τοῦ αἵματος αὐτῆς Lk 8:44 (cf. Mk 5:29 ἐξηράνθη ἡ πηγὴ τοῦ αἵματος αὐτῆς); ἐκψύχω Acts 5:5, 10;

[85a] Cadbury, *Beginnings* II, 250 ff.

[86] Thus also, with greater or lesser certainty, Ellis, Geldenhuys, Rigaux; Albertz, Feine-Behm, Harrison, Höpfl-Gut, Mariani, Meinertz, Michaelis, Moffatt, Wikenhauser, Zahn; Harnack.

12:23; ἀνακαθίζω Lk 7:15; Acts 9:40—shows only that Luke writes
a more literate Greek than Mk, the more so since all these expressions are found elsewhere (cf. W. Bauer, *Lexicon*, on the individual
words). Even less is proved by the diagnoses of illnesses, such as
Lk 4:35 (different from Mk), the depiction of the care of the
injured man (Lk 10:34), or the expunging of the harsh condemnation of medical art (Mk 5:26, against Lk 8:43) or the addition
of δεξιός in Lk 6:6; 22:50.

It has been asserted that Lk shows a striking affinity with the
theology of Paul and so must have originated with a pupil of Paul.[87]
Indicative of this are said to be the universalism (4:27; 24:47),
the stress on faith (8:12; 18:8), God's love for sinners (15:1 ff),
the gospel of joy (2:10; 10:20), and such common concepts as
σωτηρία (19:9), κύριος for the earthly Jesus (see above, p. 139),
δικαιόω (18:14). But all these instances involve general Gentile-
Christian concepts and words, and the specifically Pauline *theo-
logumena* are lacking. Even if we leave out of consideration for the
moment the portrayal of Paul in Acts, in Lk the author is obviously
a total stranger to the theology of Paul (cf. Bleiben). This can be
perceived most clearly in that the death of Jesus is understood as a
transition to heavenly glory in accordance with divine necessity
(9:22; 17:25; 24:26) but only a single time is there mention of an
expiatory death (Mk 10:45 is omitted; the cry of being abandoned
by God on the cross in Mk 15:34 is lacking; the death of Jesus is
seen as a martyr's death, 23:47). Only in the eucharistic word
(22:19 f) is the death of Jesus said to be "for you" [88] (similarly
Acts 20:28). In view of this different interpretation of the death
of Jesus by Luke[89] nothing can be said about the proximity of Lk
to the theology of Paul; indeed it only raises the question about
the tradition that Luke is the author of Lk.

The only thing that can be said with certainty about the author,
on the basis of Lk, is that he was a Gentile Christian. This is confirmed by the facts mentioned above, that he has no knowledge of
the geography of Palestine and, with the exception of ἀμήν, avoids

[87] Thus, e.g., Feine-Behm, Höpfl-Gut, Léon-Dufour in Robert-Feuillet; cf.
also Bouwman, 98 ff; Marshall, *Luke, passim*.
[88] The so-called "shorter" text of Lk 22:19 f is repeatedly defended as
original, but unjustifiably; see most recently Talbert, *Luke and the Gnostics*, 73;
A. Vööbus (see n. 17), 77 ff; also "A New Approach to the Problem of the
Shorter and Longer Text in Luke," NTS 15, 1968/69, 457 ff.
[89] Cf. on this Conzelmann, *Theology*, 199 f; Barrett, 59; Talbert (see n.
89), 73, 75; Schütz, 80 ff; E. Lohse, *Märtyrer und Gottesknecht*, FRLANT 64,
1955, 187 ff; Schulz (see n. 4), 289; G. Voss, "Die Christologie der luk.
Schriften in Grundzügen," StN, Studia 2, 1965, 99 ff, esp. 130.

Semitic expressions. That he is writing for Gentile Christians may be inferred on the ground of his omission of the characteristic traditions about the struggle of Jesus against the pharisaic understanding of the Law, and his modification of Palestinian into Hellenistic features. Lacking are Mt 5:17, 20, the antitheses (Mt 5:21-48), the sayings against false ritual piety (Mt 6:1-8, 16-18), the controversy about clean and unclean (Mk 7:1-23), the narrative of the Canaanite woman (Mk 7:24 ff), etc. Lk 5:19 par. Mk 2:4 and Lk 7:36 ff presuppose Hellenistic circumstances. But this insight into the Gentile origin of the author of Lk does not decide the question whether the author really was Luke the physician, and speaks decisively against his being a pupil of Paul, though it is only on the basis of Acts that this possibility can be denied with certainty (see §9.4).

5. Time and Place of Writing

It has been repeatedly asserted that Lk and Acts were written at the end of the decade of the sixties, before the end of the trial of Paul.[90] This date is scarcely compatible with Lk 1:1 ff, however, since by the year 60 "many" gospel writings could not have been in existence, including Mk. Decisive against the early date is the fact that Lk looks back on the fall of Jerusalem—in 70. A prediction by Jesus of judgment on Jerusalem according to Mk 13:2 par. Lk 13:34 f must be regarded as historical, but in Lk 21:20, 24 there appears an apocalyptic prediction which has been reworked from the "abomination of desolation" (Mk 13:14 ff) into a prediction of doom on Jerusalem that has been formulated *ex eventu:* presupposed are the events of the year 70, including the siege and destruction of the city by the Romans, the slaughter of innumerable Jews, and the carrying off of the survivors into Gentile prisons. The same is true of the portrayal in 19:43 f: the wall which the enemies throw up around the city, the siege and blockade, the delivery of the conquered city and its inhabitants to the victors, the complete destruction of the city—all these correspond exactly to the descriptions which contemporary accounts offer of the action of Titus against Jerusalem. Accordingly, Lk was in any case written after 70. From Lk itself it cannot be decided how late the date must be brought down. On the other hand, the writing of Acts is without doubt a *terminus ad quem,* since Acts 1:1 looks back to

[90] So, e.g., Ellis, Geldenhuys; Albertz, Guthrie, Harrison, Höpfl-Gut, Mariani, Meinertz, Schäfer; Sahlin, Koh, Cerfaux-Cambier, Hastings.

Lk as the πρῶτος λόγος.[91] O'Neill's attempt to date Lk in the period 115–135 comes to grief on the date of Acts (see below, p. 186).[92] Probably the date of Lk's writing is between 70 and 90.

No ancient tradition is available for the place of writing: suggestions have been Caesarea,[93] Achaia,[94] the Decapolis,[95] Asia Minor,[96] and, above all, Rome.[97] But there is no convincing argument for any of these conjectures, and we can say for certain only that Lk was written outside Palestine.

§9. ACTS

Commentaries: see §41. Bibliography: W. G. Kümmel, ThR, NF 14, 1942, 162 ff; 18, 1950, 16 ff; 22, 1954, 194 ff; J. Dupont, "Les problèmes du Livre des Actes entre 1940 et 1950," in J. D., *Études sur les Actes des Apôtres*, Lectio Divina 45, 1967, 11 ff; *idem*, *Les sources du Livre des Actes*. État de la question, 1960; W. Bieder, *Die Apg in der Historie. Ein Beitrag zur Auslegungsgeschichte des Missionsbuches der Kirche*, ThSt 61, 1960; E. Grässer, ThR, NF 26, 1960, 93 ff; D. Guthrie, "Recent Literature on the Acts of the Apostles," VE 2, 1963, 33 ff; E. Haenchen, *Apg*, Meyer III,[14] 1965, 13 ff, 670 ff; Eng. tr. by R. McL. Wilson, *Acts*, 1971, 14–50; A. J. and M. B. Mattill, *A Classified Bibliography of Literature on the Acts of the Apostles*, NTTS 7, 1966; I. H. Marshall, "Recent Study of the Acts of the Apostles," ExpT 80, 1968/69, 292 ff.—Studies: J. Weiss, *Über die Absicht und den literarischen Charakter der Apg*, 1897; A. Harnack, *The Acts of the Apostles* III, 1907; C. C. Torrey, *The Composition and Date of Acts*, HTS 1, 1916; F. J. Foakes-Jackson, K. Lake *et al.*, "Prolegomena and Criticism," in *Beginnings* I, 1, 1920; I, 2, 1922; A. Wikenhauser, *Die Apg und ihr Geschichtswert*, NTA 8, 3-5, 1921; *idem*, LThK I, 1957, 743 ff; M. Dibelius, "Zur Formgeschichte der Apg," ThR, NF 3, 1931, 233 ff; *idem*, *Aufsätze zur Apg*, FRLANT 60, 1951; Eng. tr. *Studies in the Acts*, 1956 (cf. on this A. D. Nock, Gn 25, 1953,

---

[91] The assumption that Acts was written after Proto-Luke and that Lk was written after Acts (Koh; C. S. C. Williams, HNTC on Acts, 12 f; P. Parker, "The 'Former Treatise' and the Date of Acts," JBL 84, 1965, 52 ff) collapses with the hypothesis of Proto-Luke; Russell has shown that there is no unambiguous witness for Acts' having been written after 70, but can adduce no grounds for the writing of Acts *before* Lk; and Bouwman's assertion that Acts was in various ways the *Vorlage* for Lk is unconvincing. (See criticism in Marshall, *Luke*, 157 n. 1.)

[92] Decisive grounds against the late date in Sparks, JTS 1962, 457 ff.

[93] Klijn; Michel.

[94] T. W. Manson; Conzelmann, StLA, 302; Bouwman.

[95] Koh.

[96] Löhning.

[97] E.g., Geldenhuys; Michaelis; Hastings.

497 ff); B. S. Easton, *The Purpose of Acts*, 1936 (=B. S. E., *Early Christianity* 1955, 33 ff); J. Jeremias, "Untersuchungen zum Quellenproblem der Apg," ZNW 36, 1937, 205 ff (=J. J., Abba, 1966, 238 ff); M. H. Shepherd, "A Venture in the Source Analysis of Acts," *Munera Studiosa, Festschr. W. H. P. Hatch*, 1946, 91 ff; W. L. Knox, *The Acts of the Apostles*, 1948; P. Benoit, "Remarques sur les 'sommaires' des Actes, II, IV et V," *Aux sources de la tradition chrétienne, Festschr. M. Goguel*, 1950, 1 ff (=P. B., *Exégèse et théologie* II, 1961, 181 ff); *idem*, "La deuxième visite de Saint Paul à Jérusalem," Bb 40, 1959, 778 ff (=P. B., *Exégèse et théologie* III, 1968, 285 ff); H. F. D. Sparks, "The Semitisms of Acts," JTS, NS I, 1950, 16 ff; Ph. Vielhauer, "Zum 'Paulinismus' der Apg," EvTh 10, 1950/51, 1 ff (=Ph. V., *Aufsätze zum NT*, ThB 31, 1965, 9 ff); E. Hirsch, *Frühgeschichte des Ev.* I, [2]1951, XXX ff; A. W. Argyle, "The Theory of an Aramaic Source in Acts 2,14-40," JTS, NS 3, 1952, 213 f; Ph.-H. Menoud, "Remarques sur les textes de l'ascension dans Luc-Acts," *NT Studien für R. Bultmann*, Bh. ZNW 21, 1954, 148 ff; *idem*, "Le Plan des Actes des apôtres," NTS 1, 1954/55, 44 ff; *idem*, "Pendant quarante jours (Actes 1,3)," *Neotestamentica et Patristica, Freundesgabe O. Cullmann*, NovTest Suppl. 6, 1962, 148 ff; O. Bauernfeind, "Zur Frage nach der Entscheidung zwischen Paulus und Lukas," ZsTh 23, 1954, 59 ff; E. Haenchen, "Tradition und Komposition in der Apg," ZThK 52, 1955, 205 ff (=E. H., *Gott und Mensch*, 1965, 206 ff); *idem*, RGG[3] I, 1957, 501 ff; *idem*, "Quellenanalyse und Kompositionsanalyse in Act 15," *Judentum, Urchristentum, Kirche, Festschr. J. Jeremias*, Bh. ZNW 26, 1960, 153 ff; *idem*, "Das 'Wir' in der Apg und das Itinerar," ZThK 58, 1961, 329 ff (=E. H., *Gott und Mensch*, 1965, 227 ff); *idem*, "Judentum und Christentum in der Apg," ZNW 54, 1963, 155 ff (=E. H., *Die Bibel und wir*, 1963, 338 ff); *idem*, "Die Apg als Quelle für die christliche Frühgeschichte," in E. H., *Die Bibel und wir*, 312 ff; H. J. Cadbury, *The Book of Acts in History*, 1955; *idem*, "Acts and Eschatology," *The Background of the NT and Its Eschatology, Festschr. C. H. Dodd*, 1956, 300 ff; *idem*, "'We' and 'I' Passages in Luke-Acts," NTS 3, 1956/57, 128 ff; C. F. Evans, "The Kerygma," JTS, NS 7, 1956, 25 ff; *idem*, "'Speeches' in Acts," *Mélanges Bibliques, Festschr. B. Rigaux*, 1970, 287 ff; B. Reicke, *Glauben und Leben der Urgemeinde. Bemerkungen zu Apg 1-7*, AThANT 32, 1957; E. Käsemann, *NT Questions of Today*, 1969, 1 ff; E. Schweizer, "Zu den Reden der Apg," ThZ 13, 1957, 1 ff (=E. Sch., *Neotestamentica*, 1963, 418 ff); E. Trocmé, *Le "Livre des Actes" et l'histoire*, EHPR 45, 1957; G. Klein, review of E. Haenchen, *Apg.*, Meyer III,[10] 1956 and Meyer III,[13] 1961, ZKG 68, 1957, 362 ff; 73, 1962, 358 ff; G. Klein, *Die Zwölf Apostel*, FRLANT 77, 1961, 115 ff; A. Ehrhardt, "The Construction and Purpose of the Acts of Apostles," StTh 12, 1958, 45 ff (=A. E., *The Framework of the NT Stories*, 1964, 64 ff); *idem*, *The Acts of the Apostles*, 1969; A. E. Haefner, "The Bridge Between Mark and Acts," JBL 77, 1958, 69 ff; U. Wilckens, "Kerygma und

Ev. bei Lukas (Beobachtungen zu Acta 10,34-43)," ZNW 49, 1958, 223 ff; *idem, Die Missionsreden der Apg. Form- und traditionsgeschichtliche Untersuchungen,* WMANT 5, 1961 (lit.; cf. on this J. Dupont, RB 69, 1962, 37 ff = J. D. *Études sur les Actes des Apôtres,* Lectio Divina 45, 1967, 133 ff); G. Schille, "Die Fragwürdigkeit eines Itinerars der Paulusreisen," ThLZ 84, 1959, 165 ff; O. Michel, CBL, 1959, 71 ff; R. Bultmann, "Zur Frage nach den Quellen der Apg," *NT Essays in Memory of T. W. Manson,* 1959, 68 ff (=R. B., *Exegetica,* 1967, 412 ff); J. Dupont, "Le salut des gentils et la signification théologique du livre des Actes," NTS 6, 1959/60, 132 ff (=J. D., *Études sur les Actes . . . ,* 393 ff); W. C. van Unnik, *The "Book of Acts" the Confirmation of the Gospel,* NovTest 4, 1960, 26 ff; *idem,* "Die Apg und die Häresien," ZNW 58, 1967, 240 ff; J. T. Townsend, "The Speeches in Acts," ATR 42, 1960, 150 ff; H. Conzelmann, review of E. Haenchen, *Apg,* Meyer III,[12] 1959, ThLZ 85, 1960, 241 ff; H. Zimmermann, "Die Sammelberichte der Apg," BZ, NF 5, 1961, 71 ff; *idem, Nt. Methodenlehre,* 1967, 243 ff; J. C. O'Neill, *The Theology of Acts in Its Historical Settings* (1961), 1970 (on this see H. F. D. Sparks, JTS, NS 14, 1963, 457 ff); W. Eltester, "Lukas und Paulus," *Eranion, Festschr. H. Hommel,* 1961, 1 ff; J. Cambier, "Le voyage de S. Paul à Jérusalem en Act 9,22 ff et le schéma missionaire théologique de S. Luc," NTS 8, 1961/62, 249 ff; S. S. Smalley, "The Christology of Acts," ExpT 73, 1961/62, 358 ff; G. Strecker, "Die sogenannte zweite Jerusalemreise des Paulus," ZNW 53, 1962, 67 ff; J. Jervell, "Zur Frage der Traditionsgrundlage der Apg," StTh 16, 1962, 25 ff; *idem,* "Paulus—der Lehrer Israels. Zu den apologetischen Reden in der Apg," NovTest 10, 1968, 164 ff; F. V. Filson, "Live Issues in Acts," BR 9, 1964, 26 ff; J. H. Crehan, "The Purpose of Luke in Acts," StEv II, TU 87, 1964, 354 ff; M. D. Goulder, *Type and History in Acts,* 1964; R. A. Martin, "Syntactical Evidence of Aramaic Sources in Acts I-XV," NTS 11, 1964/65, 38 ff; M. Wilcox, *The Semitisms of Acts,* 1965 (on this see J. A. Emerton, *Journal of Semitic Studies* 13, 1968, 282 ff); P. Parker, "The 'Former Treatise' and the Date of Acts," JBL 84, 1965, 52 ff; G. Lohfink, "Paulus vor Damaskus," SBS 4, 1965; R. R. Williams, "Church History in Acts. Is It Reliable?" in *Historicity and Chronology in the NT,* Theological Collections 6, 1965, 145 ff; D. P. Fuller, *Easter Faith and History,* 1965, 192 ff; E. R. Goodenough, "The Perspective of Acts," StLA, 51 ff; J. Knox, "Acts and the Pauline Letter Corpus," StLA, 279 ff; P. Schubert, "The Final Cycle of Speeches in the Book of Acts," JBL 87, 1968, 1 ff; *idem,* "The Place of the Areopagus Speech in the Composition of Acts," *Transitions in Biblical Scholarship,* ed. J. C. Rylaarsdam, 1968, 235 ff; Ch. Burchard, *Der dreizehnte Zeuge. Traditions- und kompositionsgeschichtliche Untersuchungen zu Lukas'. Darstellung der Frühzeit des Paulus,* FRLANT 103, 1970; A. J. B. Higgins, "The Preface to Luke and the Kerygma in Acts," AHG, 78 ff; A. J. Mattill, "The Purpose of Acts: Schneckenburger Reconsidered," AHG, 108 ff; D. F. Payne, "Semitisms in the Book of Acts," AHG, 134 ff; I. H. Marshall, *Luke: Historian and Theologian*, 1970.

On the text of Acts: Th. Zahn, *Die Urausgabe der Apg des Lukas*, Forschungen zur Geschichte des nt. Kanons IX, 1916. J. H. Ropes, *The Text of Acts, Beginnings* I, 3, 1926; A. C. Clark, *The Acts of Apostles*, 1933; W. G. Kümmel, ThR, NF 11, 1939, 96 ff; *idem*, "Die älteste Form des Aposteldekrets," *Spiritus et veritas, Festschr. K. Kundsin*, 1953, 83 ff (=W. G. K., *Heilsgeschehen und Geschichte*, MbThSt 3, 1965, 278 ff); M. Dibelius, "The Text of Acts: An Urgent Critical Task," JR 21, 1941, 421 ff (in German in *Aufsätze*, 76 ff); L. Cerfaux, "Citations scripturaires et tradition textuelle dans le Livre des Actes," *Aux sources de la tradition Chrétienne, Festschr. M. Goguel*, 1950, 43 ff (=*Recueil Lucien Cerfaux* II, 1954, 93 ff); Ph.-H. Menoud, "The Western Text and the Theology of Acts," SNTS II, 1951, 19 ff; C. C. Williams, *Alterations to the Text of the Synoptic Gospels and Acts*, 1951, 54 ff; E. Haenchen, "Schriftzitate und Textüberlieferung in der Apg," ZThK 51, 1954, 153 ff (=E. H., *Gott und Mensch*, 1965, 157 ff); *idem*, "Zum Text der Apg," ZThK 54, 1957, 22 ff (=E. H., *Gott und Mensch*, 172 ff); *idem, Apg*, Meyer III, [14]1965, 47 ff, 50 ff, 656 f (lit.), 666 ff; Eng. tr. 1971, 50 ff, 60 (bibl.), references to textual issues in index, 737. A. F. J. Klijn, *A Survey of Researches into the Western Text of the Gospels and Acts (1949–1959)*, NovTest 3, 1959, 169 ff; *idem*, "In Search of the Original Text of Acts," StLA, 103 ff; *idem, A Survey of the Researches into the Western Text of the Gospels and Acts II, 1949–1969*, Suppl. NovTest 21, 1969, 56 ff; H. C. Snape, "The Composition of the Lucan Writings," HTR 53, 1960, 34 ff; E. J. Epp, *The Theological Tendency of Codex Bezae Cantabrigiensis in Acts*, SNTSMS 3, 1966 (on this see R. P. C. Hanson, NTS 14, 1967/68, 282 ff); G. D. Kilpatrick, "An Eclectic Study of the Text of Acts," *Biblical and Patristic Studies in Memory of R. P. Casey*, 1963, 64 ff; W. Thiele, "Ausgewählte Beispiele zur Charakterisierung des 'westlichen' Textes der Apg," ZNW 56, 1965, 51 ff; R. P. C. Hanson, "The Provenance of the Interpolator in the 'Western' Text of Acts Itself," NTS 12, 1965/66, 211 ff; E. Haenchen and P. Weigandt, "The Original Text of Acts?" NTS 14, 1967/68, 469 ff.

1. Contents

The widely practiced division of Acts into two main parts of unequal length (1–12, from Jerusalem to Antioch=Peter's section; 13–28, from Antioch to Rome=Paul's section) is scarcely the intention of the author, who pursues no biographical aims. Rather the book can be divided at 15:35/36: expansion from Jerusalem up to the assurance of the Gentile mission (1:15–15:35); the expansion to Rome (15:36–28:31).[1] Or the attempt has been made to

---

[1] Thus, e.g., Harrington, Vögtle; Menoud; similarly, but with a division at 8:4, 21:7, Haenchen, *Die Bibel und wir*, 313 f.

divide the book into five sections, geographically determined in connection with the missionary command (1:8): 1:15–8:3, Jerusalem; 8:4–11:18, Samaria and the coastal region; 11:19–15:35, Antioch and the Antiochene mission; 15:36–19:20, lands of the Aegean Sea; 19:21–28:31, from Jerusalem to Rome.[2] The following overview, along the lines of the third proposal, should naturally also be considered a hypothetical structuring.

After the prologue, with the account of the ascension (1:1-14), comes the first main section (1:15–8:3) concerning the spread of the gospel in Jerusalem: 1:15-26, completion of the circle of the twelve by the choice of Matthias; 2:1-41, Pentecost (1-13, the outpouring of the Spirit; 14-36, the preaching of Peter and, 37-41, the results); 2:42-47, first summary; 3:1–4:22, healing of a lame man by Peter, Peter's preaching in the temple, Peter and John before the council; 4:23-31, prayer of the community after the apostles' release; 4:32-35, second summary, followed by the example of Barnabas (4:36, 37) and the counterexample of Ananias and Sapphira (5:1-11); 5:12-16, the third summary; 5:17-42, the apostles before the council; 6:1–8:3, Stephen and the first persecution (6:1-7, the choice of the seven; 6:8-15, charge against Stephen; 7:1-53, address of Stephen; 7:54–8:3, death of Stephen as martyr and the persecution of the Gentile Christians in Jerusalem).

The second main section (8:4–11:8) describes the spread of the gospel in Samaria and the coastal regions: 8:4-25, preaching in Samaria; 8:26-40, Philip and the Ethiopian official; 9:1-9, conversion of Paul; 9:10-30, Paul in Damascus and Jerusalem; 9:31-43, Peter in Lydda and Joppa; 10:1–11:18, Peter in Caesarea and the conversion of Cornelius.

The third main section (11:19–15:35) narrates the spread of the gospel to Antioch and from Antioch outward: 11:19-26, the first Christians in Antioch (the name Χριστιανοί); 11:27-30, 12:25, the collection journey of Paul and Barnabas from Antioch to Jerusalem—in between, 12:1-19, the persecution of the primitive church by Herod Agrippa I (martyrdom of James, son of Zebedee; rescue of Peter), 12:20-24, death of Herod—13:1–14:28, mission centering in Antioch (13:1-3, sending of Paul and Barnabas; 13:4-12, preaching in Cyprus; 13:13-52, journey to Antioch in Pisidia, address of Paul, expulsion of the missionaries; 14:1-6a, preaching in Iconium and flight; 14:6b-20a, preaching and miracle of healing in Lystra, persecution; 14:20b-28, return from Derbe to Antioch);

---

[2] Thus O'Neill, 66 f; similarly Dupont, NTS 6, 1959/60, 135 (= *Études*, 397); Filson wants to make six divisions, each of which closes with a summary: 6:7; 9:31; 12:24; 16:5; 19:20; 28:30 f.

15:1-35, Apostolic Council (conflict in Antioch (1 f), negotiations in Jerusalem (3-21), apostolic decree (22-29), return to Antioch of those commissioned (30-35).

The fourth main section (15:36–19:20) describes the spread of the gospel in the Aegean lands: 15:36-40, the separation of Paul and Barnabas; 15:41–16:10, journey of Paul through Asia Minor to Troas; 16:11–17:14, Paul in Macedonia (Philippi, 16:11-40; Thessalonica, 17:1-9; Berea, 17:10-14); Paul in Greece (Athens, 17:15-34; Corinth, 18:1-17); 18:18-22, return to Antioch by way of Ephesus; 18:23–19:20, resumed journey through Asia Minor (18:23, Galatia and Phrygia; 18:24-28, Apollos in Ephesus; 19:1-20, Paul in Ephesus [disciples of John, 1-7; preaching and miracle of Paul, 8-20]).

The fifth main section (19:21–28:31) presents the spread of the gospel from Jerusalem to Rome: 19:21 f, resolution to travel to Rome by way of Jerusalem; 19:23-40, Demetrius' disturbance in Ephesus; 20:1-6, journey to Macedonia, Greece, and back to Troas; 20:7-12, Troas; 20:13-16, journey from Troas to Miletus; 21:1-14, journey from Miletus to Caesarea; 21:15-26, arrival in Jerusalem; 21:27-39, arrest and imprisonment of Paul; 21:40–22:21, address of Paul on the steps of the temple court; 22:22-29, hearing before the Roman officer; 22:30–23:11, Paul before the council; 23:12-22, Jewish plot against Paul; 23:23-35, transfer of Paul to Caesarea; 24:1–26:32, Paul's imprisonment in Caesarea (24:1-26, plot and Paul's defense before the procurator Felix; 24:27, Festus, the successor of Felix; 25:1-12, appeal of Paul to Caesar; 25:13-27, visit of Herod Agrippa II to Festus in Caesarea; 26:1-32, Paul before Agrippa); 27:1–28:16, transporting Paul to Rome (27:1-12, voyage to Crete; 27:13-26, voyage in the storm; 27:27-44, the ship breaks up; 28:1-10, the stay on Malta; 28:11-16, journey to Rome); 28:17-31, Paul under custody in Rome.

2. Acts as the Second Part of Luke's Historical Work

Acts is not a literary work that can stand on its own: as the dedication to Theophilus shows, it constitutes the carrying forward of Lk and belongs with it as the second part of a complete historical work. The prologue to Acts (1:1) makes reference to Lk as the "first book," and ties in at the end of Lk with the appearances of the risen Lord to the apostles and his farewell (1:2 ff). In a fuller statement, it tells once again of his last meeting with the disciples and the ascension (1:6 ff).

The reference back and the repetition are not without their own difficulties, it must be acknowledged: there is no ὁ δὲ δεύτερος λόγος to correspond to τὸν μὲν πρῶτον λόγον (1:1), and so we lack the expected indication of the contents of the second volume that is introduced with these words; the sentence in 1:2 is scarcely translatable; the account of the ascension in 1:9 ff reaches back to the time period which according to 1:2 was already concluded in volume 1; according to Lk 24:50 f, the ascension took place on the day of resurrection near Bethany,[3] but according to Acts 1:3, 12, it took place on the Mount of Olives forty days later. Accordingly various explanations for the secondary alteration of the beginning of Acts have been proposed. According to one assumption, the lack of an indication of contents and the repetition of the ascension narrative may be accounted for if the information about the forty-day period before the ascension and the new ascension account— i.e., Acts 1:3-14—have been interpolated.[4] Related with this is the somewhat less broad proposal that at least the first verses of Acts have been destroyed by interpolation without the ascension narrative (1:6 ff) having been included in the interpolation.[5] According to the other position, Lk 24:50-53 proves to be linguistically and substantively as much in contradiction with Lk as Acts 1:1-5 is with the rest of Acts. By contrast, Lk 24:49 and Acts 1:6 link together well, so it must be supposed that Lk and Acts originally constituted a continuous work which first became separated in the process of canonization, at which point Lk 24:50-53 and Acts 1:1-5 were added on.[6] This second hypothesis of an original unity of Lk-Acts is in any event untenable. On the one hand, there is by no means sufficient ground for the assertion that Lk 24:50-53 is a secondary addition, and, on the other hand, we know nothing of Lk and Acts having come together into the canon, where the two books are never together, while everything indicates that Lk came to be regarded as canonical essentially earlier than Acts. Three facts, however, speak decisively against this hypothesis: (a) If Lk 24:50-

[3] καὶ ἀνεφέρετο εἰς τὸν οὐρανόν (Lk 24:51) is to be left in the text with 𝔓75 and the majority of the "Egyptian" witnesses (against ℵ*, and the majority of "Western" witnesses); cf. J. Jeremias, Eucharistic Words, 1955, 99; K. Aland, "Die Bedeutung des 𝔓75 für den Text des NT," in Studien zur Überlieferung des NT und seines Textes, ANTF 2, 1967, 158, 170 f.

[4] Thus W. G. Kümmel, ThR, NF 17, 1948, 9 n. 1 and the scholars cited there; Clark, 407 f; Ph. Vielhauer, ThR 31, 1965/66, 125.

[5] Bauernfeind; Albertz, Feine-Behm; E. Norden, Agnostos Theos, 1913, 310 ff.

[6] Menoud, Bultmann Festschr., Trocmé, 31 ff; Lake, Beginnings V, 1 ff; A. N. Wilder, "Variant Traditions of the Resurrection in Acts," JBL 62, 1943, 311; H. Sahlin, Der Messias und das Gottesvolk, 1945, 11 ff; H. Conzelmann, Theology, 203 n. 4, considers only Lk 24:50-53 to be an addition.

53 and Acts 1:1-5 were first added as a conclusion for the separated half of the total work and as the beginning of the second half, it would be inconceivable that the originator of these two additions would have brought about these contradictions, the existence of which this hypothesis is supposed to explain. (*b*) At the time of the writing of Lk, the literary form "gospel" was so firmly set that the author of Lk could scarcely have included in his Gospel the spread of the Christian message to Rome. Furthermore, from the standpoint of bookmaking technique, the combined work Lk-Acts was too long, while Lk and Acts are of nearly the same length and of normal compass.[7] (*c*) Acts 1:6 ff in fact does not tie in smoothly with Lk 24:49, since the disciples, according to Lk 24:33, are in a house in Jerusalem, into which Jesus enters (24:36), while according to Acts 1:12 the ascension, without change of locale, takes place in the open air on the Mount of Olives. Further, οἱ μὲν οὖν συνελθόντες in Acts 1:6 conflicts with εὗρον ἠθροισμένους τοὺς ἕνδεκα in Lk 24:33. The view that Acts 1:1-5 must be an addition because Lk 24:50 originally linked up with Acts 1:6 must accordingly be rejected as impossible.[8]

But the hypothesis that Acts 1:3-14, or a part of it, has been interpolated is similarly quite unlikely. Acts 1:8 is so apt a statement of the theme of Acts that it can hardly be from another hand; and an interpolator who wanted to pass on a tradition divergent from Lk 24—a period of forty days between the resurrection and the ascension—would scarcely have mentioned it in so unemphatic a manner as in Acts 1:3. Above all, one would have expected an interpolator to have added in a stylistically correct manner a summary of contents of volume 2 to correspond to the recapitulation in 1:1-2. Besides, in 1:1-5 a few inconspicuous stylistic peculiarities of Luke are encountered which an interpolator could scarcely have noted and copied.[9] The fewest difficulties are offered, then, by the assumption that the beginning of Acts, in spite of its stylistic offenses, comes from the author of Acts. That the time given for the ascension in Lk is different from that in Acts is a fact that cannot be done away with, certainly not by the totally unconvincing claim that the round number forty has nothing to do with the date of the ascension but is intended merely to characterize the unique authority of the resurrection witnesses.[10] But these divergences be-

[7] Cadbury, *Book of Acts*, 138 f.

[8] Cf. Haenchen; Dupont, *Les sources* . . . , 24 n. 2; van Unnik, NovTest 1960; Wilckens, *Missionsreden*, 57 n. 1; Menoud, *Cullmann Festschr.*; Conzelmann (see n. 6); H. Anderson, *Jesus and Christian Origins*, 1964, 343 f.

[9] See the evidence in Haenchen *in loc.*

[10] Thus Menoud, *Cullmann Festschr.*

come comprehensible if it is clearly seen that Lk obviously portrays the ascension in Lk 24 as the terminus of the life of Jesus, and in Acts the ascension, together with the forty days of instruction and the message of the angel (1:11), is the beginning of the time of the church.[11]

If the author of Acts gave a title or superscription to it, it is not preserved and we know nothing of it. The name πράξεις [τῶν] ἀποστόλων or, briefly, πράξεις, acta or actus apostolorum, is attested since the time of Clement of Alexandria and Irenaeus (Muratorian Canon: acta omnium apostolorum, "acts of all the apostles"),[12] but it is scarcely original and does not fit the contents of the book.[13] For Luke, apostles are consistently the twelve (except for 14:4, 14), but in Acts only Peter appears prominently, and from 13:4 on Paul plays the major role—though he is not called an apostle, except in 14:4. Otherwise the author has no biographical interests. The name Acts of the Apostles, which must have emerged in the second century in connection with the formation of the NT canon, corresponds to the ancient church's interest in Peter and Paul as the two chief apostles and to a misunderstanding of Acts as a work of literature in the period of the apologists. The changing designations of the book in Irenaeus (Haer. III. 31. 3: Lucae de apostolis testificatio, "Luke's witness to the apostles") and Tertullian (De jejunio 10: commentarius Lucae, "Luke's commentary") also show that an authentic title was lacking.

Because Acts breaks off abruptly with a mention of the two-year-long preaching activity of Paul while imprisoned in Rome (28: 30 f), it has been conjectured that the end is accidental, or that it has been intentionally broken off, or that Lk wanted to write a third book.[14] But since there is no evidence anywhere that a third book was planned or ever existed (τὸν πρῶτον λόγον in 1:1 indicates nothing more than two volumes),[15] and since 28:30 can be understood as a purposeful ending to the book, these conjectures are worthless.[16]

---

[11] Haenchen; Vögtle, Das NT . . . , 107; D. P. Fuller, 197 f; C. K. Barrett, Luke the Historian in Recent Study, 1960, 56 f; A. George, "Tradition et rédaction chez Luc," EThL 43, 1967, 119. Another view in H. Flender, St. Luke, 33 f.

[12] Bauernfeind, Comm., 16.

[13] Otherwise in Höpfl-Gut, Meinertz, Schäfer; Wikenhauser is uncertain.

[14] Thus Zahn; Goguel, de Zwaan; W. L. Knox; J. Jeremias, NTD IX, [8]1963, 2.

[15] See Bauer, Lex., 733.

[16] Cf. Trocmé, 34 ff.

3. Literary Distinctiveness and Theological Character of Acts

Research into the literary character of Acts and its aims[17] received its decisive impulse from F. C. Baur, who for the first time (in 1838) propounded the thesis that Acts originated in the late period of primitive Christianity and sprang from the intention to weaken the conflict between Jewish Christianity and Gentile Christianity that is perceptible in the genuine Pauline letters and to do so by accommodating both parties to each other (see WGK, NT, 132 f). In conjunction with these ideas, M. Schneckenburger, in *Über den Zweck der Apg* (1841), saw Acts as an apology for Paul against the Judaists: Luke consciously passes over everything that recalls the real opposition of Jewish Christianity to Paul and deliberately highlights whatever places Paul and Peter on the same line. In a book which was fundamental for his comprehensive historical outlook, *Paulus, der Apostel Jesu Christi* (1845), Baur himself took a decisive further step: while Schneckenburger found no objectively incorrect features in the portrait of Paul in Acts and held Lk to be the author, Baur explained that Acts was a product of the second century which had falsified history in the interests of setting aside the opposition between Peter and Paul and thus, as opposed to the genuine Pauline letters, represented no reliable historical source (see WGK, NT, 133 ff). This view of a "tendency" of the author of Acts to conciliate by falsifying the facts was sharpened still more by Baur's pupils, E. Zeller and A. Schwegler (see WGK, NT, 144 ff). The result not only provoked opposition from conservative theologians, but also led scholars employing a fundamentally critical approach (esp. E. Reuss and A. Ritschl) to question it by showing that the early period of Christianity by no means evidences only the antitheses Jewish Christianity and Gentile Christianity, as claimed by Baur (see WGK, NT, 155 ff, 160 ff). Even though it then appeared that the assumption of a conciliating "tendency" and a conscious falsification of history on the part of Acts was unfounded, the perception could not be dismissed that numerous contradictions—of a kind not easily resolved—exist between Paul and Acts. These contradictions were explained on the ground that Acts manifests a unified picture of early Christian history as it took possession of the Gentile world in the postapostolic period: "Paul is not judaized nor Peter paulinized, but Peter and Paul are lucanized,

---

[17] On the history of research, see Goguel, *Intr.* III, 37 ff; Trocmé, 1 ff; A. C. McGiffert and J. W. Hunkin, *Beginnings* I, 2, 363 ff; and see bibl. mentioned below, pp. 163 f.

i.e., catholicized." [18] In 1870 F. Overbeck had characterized the position of Acts in a similar way and in addition had attributed to Acts the aim of defending Christianity against political suspicions.[19] J. Weiss found no intra-Christian "tendencies" in Acts, and interpreted it as an apology for Christianity against Jewish accusations, addressed to Gentile society with the aim of showing that the world mission of the church had superseded Judaism.

Although the "tendency criticism" of the "Tübingen school" was shown to be a wrong approach, the task still remained of perceiving the aim that the author had pursued in writing Acts, and at the same time to determine the theological standpoint of the book. Only in this way could the historical value and the message of the book be grasped reliably. Although research at the beginning of the twentieth century devoted itself primarily to the question of the sources of Acts (see below, §9.4), as early as 1912 P. Wendland [20] sought to prove that Acts was to be understood as a "natural expression of developing church relationships and of the change of historical outlook associated with them" and to assign it literarily a "middle position between a history and a book of heroes." The question of the literary character and the interests of its author in writing Acts was first tackled methodologically by M. Dibelius (1923).[21] The result of this and subsquent research by Dibelius was not only the extracting of small units and a travel diary from the continuous narrative of Acts but, above all, the demonstration of the methods used by the author for editing the tradition and his aim "to make clear the meaning which these events contain" (*Studies*, 125). This line of investigation has been taken up pre-eminently by E. Haenchen. In association with work on Lukan theology (see above, §8.3), above all, the problems of the factual relationship of the Lukan portrait of Paul to Paul and of Lk's view of redemptive history have been dealt with frequently.

Three views of the literary aim of Acts must at the outset be dismissed as false: (*a*) Although the author shows himself to be familiar with the literary usages of his time and in inserting speeches employs a literary method of ancient historians, Acts is not "a real historical work" [22] nor is its author "the first Christian historian." [23] The fact that Luke as volume 1 of a double work goes before Acts

[18] A. Jülicher, *Einl.*, 1894, 263; see WGK, NT, 174 ff.
[19] See Haenchen, *Acts*, 23.
[20] P. Wendland, *Die urchristlichen Literaturformen*, HNT I, 3, [2,3]1912, 321, 325.
[21] M. Dibelius, *Studies*, 1 ff.
[22] E. Meyer, *Ursprung und Anfänge des Christentums* III, 1923, 7.
[23] Dibelius, *Studies*, 123 ff; Vielhauer, 14 = 25; Wilckens, *Missionsreden*, 92.

speaks against such an assumption. Furthermore, so many of the marks of real historical writing are missing—completeness of material, exactitude of historical detail, consistent chronology, biographical interest—that a reportorial account, or even reporting with a set "tendency," cannot be the aim of Acts.[24] (b) The conjecture that Acts was written to serve as a defense of Paul at his trial in Rome,[25] is untenable. Not only does it presuppose an impossibly early date for the origin of the book (ca. 62; see below, §9.5), but it cannot account for the greater part of the material in Acts nor of its presentation there (Chs. 1–12; thrice-repeated account of the conversion of Paul: 9; 22; 26), and it overlooks the fact that Acts is book 2 of Lk. (c) In a twofold way the attempt has recently been made to picture Acts as a document of a controversy within the church. (i) According to Trocmé, in the years after 52, Acts seeks to defend Pauline Christianity against the Jewish claims that Pauline Christianity is a peril to the state and signifies an apostasy from original Christianity. But we do not know that at the end of the first century such an anti-Pauline Judaistic polemic existed, nor is there evident in Acts more than an isolated echo (21:20 ff) of Judaistic accusations against Paul, so that a defense of this kind is out of the question. (ii) According to others,[26] Acts seeks to snatch Paul from the clutches of the Gnostics by showing that he is orthodox (Barrett) or that he is dependent on the original apostles (Klein). In the first place it must be said that only in Acts 20:29 f is there polemic against the Gnostics, and there Paul is by no means in need of differentiation from the Gnostics. Above all, it is not true that the importance of Paul in Acts is diminished in favor of the twelve (Klein; see below, p. 170). And even if it is the case that "Luke carefully avoids Gnostic ideas and language" (Barrett), the repudiation of Gnostic ideas is only indirect and does not lead to any polemic.[27] An anti-Gnostic defense of Paul is certainly not the aim of the author of Acts.[28]

Even though in Acts no apologetic within the Christian community is evident, the aim of defending the Christians against the

[24] Van Unnik, NovTest 1960, 44; Haenchen, *Die Apg als Quelle* . . . , 314.

[25] Thus most recently Munck; Sahlin, Koh; earlier representatives in Sahlin, 35 f; according to Mattill, Acts was written during Paul's two-year imprisonment in Rome as a defense against the Jewish-Christian attacks against Paul; numerous alleged parallels between Jesus (or Peter) and Paul are said to prove this.

[26] Klein; Barrett (see n. 11), 62 f.

[27] See van Unnik, ZNW 1967, 240 ff.

[28] Thus Trocmé, 56 f; Haenchen, *Acts*, 596 f.

charge of enmity toward the state is unmistakable. Against the charge of the Jews, "All of them are acting contrary to the decrees of Caesar by saying that there is another king, Jesus" (17:7; cf. 17:6; 24:5), the defense of Paul is juxtaposed: "Neither against the law of the Jews, nor against the sanctuary nor against Caesar am I guilty of any sort of violation" (25:8). Thus Luke shows again and again that the Roman officials must attest to the complete lack of guilt of the Christians and, above all, of Paul (16:39; 18:15 f; 19:37; 23:29; 25:25; 26:32), and that they do not hinder Paul from preaching the gospel while he is being detained for questioning in Rome (28:30 f). The apologetic aim of this and related texts is as unmistakable here as the same feature is in Lk (see above, §8.3). Such apologetic would have been pointless for Christians and must have had pagan readers in view.[29] We have already seen that Paul's judges in Rome were surely not to be reached by this means. ("No Roman official would ever have sifted through so much that in his view was theological and ecclesiastical rubbish in order to gain so small a grain of relevant apology.") [30] It is hardly likely that the general public would have been addressed.[31] It is much more likely that the author is hoping to reach individual Gentile readers and to win them over to Christianity.[32] His effort is not to demonstrate the unity of Christianity and Judaism in order to allow Christianity to enjoy the same recognition that the state granted to the Jewish religion.[33] Rather the Christians are set in opposition to the Jews, and in light of the Jewish slander are portrayed as politically harmless (25:7 f) and as the true heirs of the OT revelation of God (26:6 f, 22 f; 28:28).[34]

This apologetic aim is only one goal in Lk-Acts, secondary, but not unimportant; the greatest amount of the material, especially in the speeches, is proclamation and has Christian readers in view. Acts, then, undoubtedly, has a twofold aim: it "tells of the apostolic time in order to edify the Christians and to convert the pagans." [35] What the actual theme of this edifying narrative of apostolic

[29] In addition to those mentioned by Dupont, NTS 1959/60, 133, see van Unnik, NovTest 1960, 40 f; O'Neill, 171 f; Haenchen, *Acts*, 403 f, 624 ff, 657 f.

[30] Barrett (see n. 11), 63.

[31] Against J. Weiss; Evans, "Speeches," 302; O'Neill, 176 f, 181.

[32] See Burchard, 184; Marshall, *Luke*, 38, 219.

[33] Thus Haenchen; Easton. Just as unsuitable is the idea that Acts seeks to defend the right of Christians to live in Israel (so Jervell, NovTest, 1968).

[34] Cf. O'Neill, 179 f; Conzelmann, ThLZ 1960, 244 f.

[35] Haenchen, RGG; similarly O'Neill.

times is[36] has been much contested, but the multiplicity of goals for the book that have been proposed on good grounds[37] is such as to raise the question whether a clear answer is possible. On the basis of most of these proposals, it may be inferred that the geographical structuring of the account in Acts in the sense of an expansion of missionary territory (see above, §9.1) includes the actual, step-by-step expansion: from the preaching to the Jews in Jerusalem to the final self-exclusion of the Jews from God's redemption and the unhindered proclamation to the pagans in Rome: "They will listen" (28:28-31). And Dupont [38] has correctly shown that in Lk 24:46 f already the risen Lord proclaims as the meaning of both writings, not only the suffering and resurrection of Christ, but also the preaching "to all the people, beginning from Jerusalem." And the same risen Lord (Acts 1:8) conveys to the disciples more precisely the charge "You will be my witnesses in Jerusalem and in all Judea and in Samaria and to the ends of the earth." [39] The theme of 1:8 is carried through in Acts, and the declaration in 28:31 that Paul in Rome "preaches the kingdom of God and teaches about the Lord Jesus" to all who come to him μετὰ πάσης παρρησίας ἀκωλύτως strikes a "triumphal note" (Nock), which corresponds precisely to the author's aim in Acts and proves to be the intended end of the book: "in fact the two-volume work, Lk-Acts, is brought to a dramatic close and epitomized in an adverb." [40]

By carrying out his objective of portraying God's worldwide redemptive work in Christ as coming to its goal in the preaching to the pagans in Rome,[41] the author of Acts created a literary form

[36] See survey in van Unnik, NovTest 1960, 39 ff; D. P. Fuller, 202 ff.

[37] Recent proposals include the victorious course of the gospel to the capital of the empire (Feine-Behm, Wikenhauser; Filson); the breaking down of religious, racial, and national barriers to unhindered preaching of the gospel (Stagg); the entire work, Lk-Acts is a Gospel (Trocmé, Eltester); the gospel of the Holy Spirit (Ehrhardt); chief aim is the preaching of the gospel for unbelievers (O'Neill); God's witness of his own work of salvation for the world (van Unnik); Acts is to confirm the faith of the recently converted Theophilus (Crehan); Acts seeks to show that the Gentile mission was the fulfillment of the Christ event that had its high point in the resurrection and ascension (D. P. Fuller).

[38] Dupont, NTS 1959/60, 139 ff (=Études, 401 ff).

[39] Cf. Cambier, NTS 1961/62.

[40] I.e., ἀκωλύτως (Stagg, Comm., 1).

[41] W. C. van Unnik, "Der Ausdruck ῾ΕΩΣ ᾿ΕΣΧΑΤΟΥ ΤΗΣ ΓΗΣ (Apg 1:8) und sein at. Hintergrund," Studia Biblica et Semitica, Festschr. T. C. Vriezen, 1966, 355 ff, shows that Lk may have understood "to the ends of the earth" according to the OT linguistic usage only in the sense of the witness "to the entire world." But that does not exclude the idea that Lk has obviously

which had no real prototype either in Christianity or in the surrounding world, and also no successor. (The Apocryphal Acts of
the second century are from the literary standpoint completely
different.) [42] Attention has been drawn to the fact that in form
Acts has contacts with the Hellenistic portraits of divine men
(Barrett), but this contact is evident only in individual narratives
and features, since Acts does not present any sort of religious
biography. With greater justice, reference has been made to the
kinship which Acts displays, in the manner of its missionary
narrative, to the mission literature of Hellenistic Judaism, but it
was scarcely familiarity with that literature that led the author
to choose the form of a historical narrative for his work (O'Neill).
This form is rather the outcome of the author's basic theological
view, according to which the history of Jesus is the beginning of
the still expanding history of the church (see above, §8.3). The
decisive question, however, is by what literary method the author
represents this history and with what theological intention he has
shaped it.

First it must be affirmed that the author is in a different position
as the writer of Lk than he is as the writer of Acts. In writing Lk,
according to his own indication (Lk 1:1-4) and as may be confirmed by literary criticism, he had predecessors whose works he
could supplement in the greater compass of his own presentation.
But in Acts he was faced with a completely new task. Even if the
author used sources of wider compass—and we shall see that it is
quite unlikely that he did—it is generally acknowledged that none
of these sources encompassed the whole of the time period presented
by the author, and the linking up of the history of the primitive
community with the Pauline Gentile mission as far as Rome was
in any event first carried out by the author of Acts. By no means
did he strive for anything like completeness. He prefers giving
pictures of details to a continuous narrative with greater comprehensiveness, and weaves acts and speeches of the chief characters
into his representation. He does not enter into the struggles between
Paul and his opponents that are known to us from the Pauline
letters. In his portrayal of the activity of Peter and the development of the primitive community, as well as in the history of the
Pauline mission, huge gaps yawn between significant, instructive
narrative details. What we learn about the community in Jeru-

---

seen the promise of Jesus fulfilled with the unhindered preaching in Rome.
"Salvation is then finally—and for Lk exclusively as well—sent to the Gentiles"
(R. Pesch, *Der Anfang der Apg: Apg 1:1-11*, EKK, Vorarbeiten 3, 1951, 32).
    [42] Cf. the survey by J. Michl, LThK I, 1957, 747 ff.

salem, its common life, its worship, its relationship to Judaism, its groups (Hebrews and Hellenists), its mission, about the actions and the fate of the circle of the twelve, etc., is very meager. Important events such as the attack of Herod Agrippa I on the Christians (12:1 ff) or the beginning of Christianity in Antioch (11:19 ff) are only touched upon. Yet there is plenty of space to repeat other material, such as the two identical scenes before the council (4:1 ff; 5:17 ff) and the Cornelius story (10:1–11:18). Concerning Paul we do not learn the things that are most important historically; of the chief centers of his activity, Corinth and Ephesus, where he spent years, only a few detailed features are conveyed. By contrast, the experiences of the imprisoned Paul, from his arrest in Jerusalem through the hearings before Felix, Festus, and Agrippa and the voyage up to his arrival in Rome and his dealings with the leaders of the Jews in Rome, are narrated in great and minute detail. The author leaves aside what seems unsuited to the achieving of his literary and missionary goals, and he repeats with characteristic variation what he wants to make especially impressive: the twice-told tale of the vision of Peter (10:9 ff; 11:5 ff); the three accounts of Paul's conversion (9:3 ff; 22:5 ff; 26:12 ff). His account, therefore, is dependent in its choice of what to tell, and whether in brief or extended narrative, not only on the tradition that is available, but at least as much on his own aims.

The aims come into focus above all in those sections which have most surely been shaped by the author: the summary narratives and the speeches.

The summary narratives as a literary means were already taken over from Mk in Lk (Lk 4:40 f; 6:17 ff). But in Acts they are employed only in the portrayal of the primitive community (2:42 ff; 4:32 ff; 5:12 ff), if one leaves out of consideration the generalized sentences such as 9:31; 16:5. These three comprehensive depictions of worship life, of the prohibition against private property, and of the miracles of the apostles, are congruent and repeat themselves in a remarkable way, but how they were built up is not clear. Various assumptions have been made as to how they were developed secondarily: a shorter summary narrative was expanded in its final redaction by the use of another summary narrative;[43] all three narratives were expanded in their central parts by an unknown editor on the basis of another summary narrative;[44] the author of Acts developed and idealized detailed narratives that were

---

[43] Jeremias, ZNW 1937, 206 f (=Abba, 240 f).
[44] Benoit, Festschr. Goguel.

handed on to him.[45] But none of these theories is persuasive, since nothing implies the taking over and reworking of detailed accounts, and certainly not by any unknown editor. Rather the summary narratives as a whole come from the author of Acts, which explains the linguistic kinship of these texts. The goal they pursue is to generalize on the basis of the traditional detailed narratives, which explains why there is so little logical structure in these texts.[46] If that is the case, then these summary accounts may indeed utilize traditional narrative detail, but primarily they attest the author's representation of the primitive church as the ideal community which in complete harmony and with common possessions leads its life of prayer- and table-fellowship, respected by everyone and guarded by its miraculous deeds. That is the picture of the original Christian period as it was seen in the time of the author, not the result of a conscious idealization.

Essentially more difficult is the answer to the question about the origin of the speeches in Acts.[47] By Haenchen's reckoning, the speeches comprise "about 300 of the roughly 1,000 verses of the book."[48] Their significance in the mind of the author is evident in that they appear at every decisive turning point in the narrative, and the facts which in the author's opinion are important are reported more than once in the speeches. This interest of the author in the speeches does not go so far as to prove that he had no sources or reliable accounts of any kind available in formulating the speeches. Since the Stephen speech (Acts 7), the mission speeches of Peter (2:14 ff; 3:12 ff; 4:9 ff; 5:30 ff; 10:34 ff) and of Paul, addressing the Jews (13:16 ff), the addresses of Paul to the Gentiles (14:15 ff; 17:22 ff) and to Christians (20:18 ff), his defense speeches (22:1 ff; 26:2 ff), and his speech attacking his opponents (28:25 ff) represent completely different types of speeches, it has been concluded that the speeches in Acts transmit to us essentially accurate information about what was said in the particular situations.[49] Those who have not been willing to go that far have at least elicited [50] from the missionary speeches in Acts 2–13 kerygmatic formulas of the primitive church,[51] and have deduced from

[45] Zimmermann, BZ 1961; also in Nt Methodenlehre, 1967, 243 ff.

[46] Thus Conzelmann, Apg, HNT, 7 f; Haenchen, Acts, 193 ff.

[47] On the history of research, see Grässer, ThR 1960, 133 ff; Wilckens, Missionsreden, 7 ff.

[48] Haenchen, Acts, 104 n. 1.

[49] E.g., Bruce, Williams; Feine-Behm.

[50] In connection with M. Dibelius, Tradition, 21, and C. H. Dodd, The Apostolic Preaching and Its Developments, 1936, 29 ff.

[51] See most recently Smalley.

Stephen's speech (esp. 7:44 ff) the views of Stephen and the Hellenists,[52] and from the Areopagus speech (17:22 ff) the missionary theology of Paul (see below, p. 182).

A few general observations raise questions about this view, however. In the first place, Schweizer and Wilckens have proved that the missionary speeches of both Peter and Paul in Acts have the same basic scheme, in spite of the different circumstances. This points to the shaping hand of the same writer. Furthermore, Townsend has shown that the speeches in Acts were created by the author and that they are dependent on one another: the reader does not notice gaps in the argument of the speeches because he unconsciously fills them in from other speeches in the same book. Thus the connection of David with the quotation from the psalm in Acts 13:35, though it is presupposed in 13:36, makes no sense in its setting, but is easily comprehensible if the line of thought in 2:15 ff is already known. Finally, Evans has drawn attention to the fact that no *Sitz im Leben* can be posited for the repetition and preservation of the apostolic speeches into the late apostolic times—in contrast to the Jesus tradition—in terms of which this speech tradition could be accounted for: "One does not remember the argument of a speech twenty, thirty or forty years afterwards unless it has been constantly repeated in the meanwhile. But why would it be repeated?" [53] At the time that these speeches were given no one was taking stenographic notes (Bruce notwithstanding); and that Paul had his speeches in manuscript (Blaiklock) is an irresponsible assertion.

In this connection two basic ascertainments are more essential: (*a*) Dibelius[54] has shown that the author built on the literary usage of ancient historical writing by placing speeches in the mouths of certain participants at crucial points in the narrative in order to explain for the reader the significance of the events.[55] A close analysis of all the larger speeches shows that they are aimed primarily at the reader and thus take into account to only a limited degree the special situation of the hearer in the scene in question (cf., e.g., calling the Christians "saints," 26:10; the mention of the collection, 24:17; the enumeration of the nations, 2:9 ff; the historical midrash, 7:2 ff). The repetition of certain facts and

[52] E.g., M. Simon, *St. Stephen and the Hellenists in the Primitive Church,* 1958; M. H. Scharlemann, "Stephen: a Singular Saint," AnBibl 34, 1968.

[53] Evans, JTS 1956, 25 ff; Lohfink, 46 f.

[54] M. Dibelius, "The Speeches in Acts and Ancient Historiography," *Studies in Acts,* 1965, 138 ff.

[55] Cf. also earlier H. J. Cadbury, "The Speeches in Acts," in *Beginnings* I, Vol. 5, 402 ff, and recently Evans, *Festschr. Rigaux.*

ideas in several speeches, the literary device of interrupting a speech at an effective point in the sequence of thought (7:53 f; 17:31 f; 19:27 f; 23:6 f; 26:23 f), the Hellenistic coloration of the Areopagus speech and the speech before Agrippa II (optative in 17:27; 26:29; citation of profane authors in 17:28; 26:14) show the shaping activity of the writer in his formulation of the speeches. The speeches in Acts originate, therefore, with the author, even when in some case or another he may have reworked records or traditional items. Dibelius has correctly stressed that in these speeches the author of Acts is not expressing his personal opinion, but wants to preach: "He found a new way to present material which up until then had not been literarily handled; by the art of composing speeches he seeks to illuminate not merely the situation but the way of God; he does not want to attest the capabilities of the author, but the gospel." [56]

(b) Through his research on the missionary speeches in Acts, Wilckens has confirmed and extended the results of Dibelius' work. Wilckens has proved that the missionary speeches in Acts 2–13 exhibit a common schema (cf. also Schweizer). But he has also shown that the traditional character and the antiquity of this schema cannot be proved. Further he has shown that these speeches have not been inserted as already existing wholes into a connected narrative, but that all has been formulated by the author, including the connected narrative. From this it can be inferred that "the apostolic speeches in Acts . . . [are] to be valued as proofs, not for early, or the earliest, primitive Christian theology, but for Lukan theology from the end of the first century." [57] But when Wilckens tries to show that the detailed material too does not stem from old tradition but from the theology of the time of the author, some objection may be raised, especially if the remaining speeches in Acts are kept in view. For example, Stephen's speech (7:1 ff) is inexplicable without assuming a tradition, even though it is also uncertain whether this tradition goes back to the primitive church. Similarly, the παῖς title for Jesus is not created for the first time by Luke's exegesis of Scripture. But it is incontestable that the speeches of Acts are the decisive literary means by which the author of Acts stamps his own theological meaning on the narrative tradition that he has employed.

It may now be asked further whether the author of Acts did not

[56] Dibelius, *Studies*, 183; cf. Schubert, JBL 1968, 16: "Lk makes the speeches into an essential part of the narrative itself: the narrative of the proclamation of the Word of God."
[57] Wilckens, *Missionsreden*, 186.

express his own theological ideas by means of his shaping of the narrative and by his choice of the material he recounted. The answer to this question is extraordinarily difficult, since, unlike Lk, no source or traditions have been preserved that he might have used. The comparison with Paul's letters alone allows an occasional comparison. Since the author did not know the letters of Paul (see below, p. 186), we do not know in any case whether the author knew a fact that came to us from Paul at all if he did not report it, and conclusions from the lack of certain facts in the Acts account are highly problematical. For example, it is highly questionable[58] whether the author consciously concealed the hostility (that may be inferred from Paul) of the primitive church against the Gentile mission because that was the only way he could clearly associate the Gentile mission with Jesus. And necessary as it is to attempt to discover the motives which dominate the composition of individual narratives if we are to understand the theological intention of the narrative, it is also dangerous to try to identify these motives too exactly. Thus Haenchen has scarcely interpreted correctly the origin of, and Luke's intention for, the account of the attempt in Lystra to worship Paul and Barnabas (14:11 ff) in assuming that the author tried to create in this narrative "a high point in the development of apostolic power," which was then to outshine the passion of Paul that follows (14:19 f). And the assertion that the author of Acts in 14:4, 14 calls Paul and Barnabas "apostles," contrary to his terminology used elsewhere, in order to conceal from his readers the fact that elsewhere he denies to Paul the apostolic title,[59] without any basis attributes to the author of Acts a cunning deception of his readers. It is only the summary narratives and the speeches that can be used with methodological certainty in determining the theological ideas of the author of Acts that dominate his account.

In our investigation of the theological aims that dominate the Gospel of Lk we have already seen that it interprets the history of Jesus as the beginning of the redemptive history that moves continuously through the present to the end of time (see above, p. 145). This conception naturally dominates Acts as well, and it has been assumed correspondingly that its redemptive-historical conception is the logical outcome of the delay of the parousia: "The expectation of an imminent End has vanished, and the problem of the delay of the parousia is no longer a problem. . . . The time between Pentecost and the parousia is the period of the Holy

---

[58] Against Barrett (see n. 11), 60 f.
[59] Klein, *Die zwölf Apostel*, 212.

Spirit and the progressive evangelism of the world, and thus the
enhancement of the redemptive history." [60] As proof of the correctness of this position is adduced the existence of Acts itself, and in
addition the principal rejection of the question about setting a
time for the parousia (1:7), the replacement of the imminent
return by the commissioning for world mission (1:8), the idea of
long periods of time (26:29), the presentation of the Spirit as
substitute for the coming of the kingdom of God (1:8).[61] Now
it is surely true for Acts that the expectation of the End does not
stand in the central position, but it cannot be denied that for the
author of Acts eschatology has not become merely a *locus de
novissimis* [a formal doctrine of the last things].[62] This is shown
by the quotation from Joel 3:1 in Acts 2:17 where, instead of
καὶ ἔσται μετὰ ταῦτα, (LXX in conformity with the Hebrew text)
appears the version καὶ ἔσται ἐν ταῖς ἐσχάταις ἡμέραις.[63] This alteration of the OT text makes it clear that for the author the coming
of the Spirit signifies the inbreaking of the eschatological time of
redemption. This eschatological importance of the present is indicated in the first speech in Acts, but in the second speech (3:20 ff)
there is an even clearer reference to the parousia: "Repent . . . ,
so the times of renewal will come from the Lord and he will send
his Anointed who has been previously appointed for you, Jesus,
whom heaven must receive until the times of the restoration of all
things, which God has declared through the mouth of the prophets
from the beginning onward." To interpret the speech about Jesus'
reception in heaven as an expression of the delay of the parousia is
completely groundless.[64] Neither is it true that the eschatological
idea in 3:20 f interrupts what would otherwise be a good line of
thought, so it is unlikely that eschatological speculation about
Elijah has been taken over from Baptist circles, transferred

---

[60] Vielhauer, EvTh 1950/51, 13 = *Aufsätze*, 24. Similarly those mentioned
in §8 nn. 65 and 68, and R. Bultmann, *Theology* II, 116 f.

[61] See the assembling of the evidence in E. Grässer, *Das Problem der Parusieverzögerung in den synopt. Evv. und in der Apg*, Bh. ZNW 22, 1957, 204 ff.

[62] Thus Vielhauer, EvTh 1950/51, 12 (=*Aufsätze*, 23).

[63] This reading, attested by ℵ, A, 096, 81; D, Lat., Iren., Tert., by "Egyptian" as well as "Western" witnesses, is undoubtedly correct as against the
reading accommodated to LXX in B 076 (thus, e.g., Conzelmann, *in loc.*; Wilcox, 47 f; Burchard, 182 n. 27; Marshall, *Luke*, 161; Kilpatrick, 65; F.
Mussner, " 'In den letzten Tagen' (Apg 2:17a)," BZ, NF 5, 1961, 263 ff;
Talbert, *Perspective*, 176, against Ropes, *in loc.*; Haenchen, ZThK 1954, 162
(=*Gott und Mensch*, 166); T. Holtz, *Untersuchungen über die at. Zitate
bei Lk*, TU 104, 1968, 7 f; M. Rese, "At. Motive in der Christologie bei Lk,"
StNT 1, 1969, 51 f.

[64] Haenchen, *in loc.*, Grässer (see n. 61), 213 f.

to Jesus, and, by tying in a scriptural proof for the past appearance of Jesus, (3:22 ff) in fact extenuated.[65] For the Jewish expectation in Mal 3 that is connected with Elijah—that all things will be restored at the end of days—is modified and used in Acts 1:6 ff; 15:16 f also,[66] which shows that the author saw eschatological fulfillment begun in the present, inaugurated by the sending and exaltation of Jesus, just as he awaited its ultimate completion in the parousia. This is confirmed by the link that is established in 1:11 between the ascension and the parousia by reference to the commanding appearance of the risen Lord as judge of the world in central texts (10:42; 17:31) and by the declaration that "we must enter the kingdom of God through many tribulations" (14:22).[67] Although it is correct that the concept of the βασιλεία is "no longer a vehicle of preaching" [68] and that the expectation of an imminent End is no longer encountered in explicit terms, Acts reports clearly and regularly the preaching of Jesus Christ that is being spread as far as Rome and does so in the consciousness that the End is approaching. The expectation of the parousia and of the inbreaking of the kingdom of God lives out of the conviction that the risen Lord has been exalted with this purpose by God.[69] The existence of Acts itself does not argue against this position, because this account does not aim to be a historical document for later generations, but proclamation and edification for the present, together with and in confirmation of Lk.

Therefore it is not true either with regard to Acts that Lk is "the first representative of nascent early Catholicism" because he describes "the hour of the church as the midpoint of time." [70] Of course, there are to be found in Acts, as in Lk, concepts typical of the late period of early Christianity: ascension in addition to the resurrection of Jesus, the risen Lord's eating food, punitive miracles, magical healings, communication of the Spirit by the laying on of

[65] Bauernfeind; Schweizer, Wilckens.

[66] Cf. F. Mussner, "Die Idee der Apokatastasis in der Apg," *Lex tua veritas, Festschr. H. Junker,* 1961, 293 ff (=*Praesentia Salutis,* 1967, 223 ff).

[67] The contesting of an eschatological connection between θλῖψις and βασιλεία τοῦ θεοῦ (Conzelmann, Haenchen) is based on a circular argument; cf. Cadbury, Dodd Festschr., 311, and R. Schnackenburg, *Gottes Herrschaft und Reich,* 1959, 183 f.

[68] Schnackenburg (see n. 67); Acts 1:3; 8:12; 19:8; 20:25; 28:23, 31 (cf. also 24:25) show that an exact meaning for "the rule of God" or for "the coming judgment" cannot be perceived.

[69] Cf. Cadbury, *Dodd Festschr.;* van Unnik, NovTest 1960, 45 f; Marshall, *Luke,* 175 ff.

[70] Thus Käsemann, *New Testament Questions of Today,* 1969, 21. On the question of the "early Catholic" character of Lukan theology, see above, pp. 145 f.

the apostles' hands (1:9 ff; 1:4; 10:41; 5:1 ff; 13:9 ff; 5:15; 19:11 f; 8:7; 19:6, among others), but, for the author of Acts, the epoch of the church is not the midpoint of time; rather, the present of the church is the End-time, which has been announced since the setting in action of the kingdom of God in Jesus, and which has begun since Pentecost in the Spirit. The completion of the End-time is expected—no longer feverishly but with certainty—in the appearance of the Christ who is now waiting in heaven. It may be said that for the author the theological task was to resolve "the problem of historical time in Christianity, which had been everywhere operative from the beginning and which thus became obtrusively evident." [71] But it is by no means true that for the author of Acts redemption was present in the past history of Jesus, while faith is directed backward to the past life of Jesus and "participation in redemption" is understood "consistently as historically transmitted sharing in a specific past." [72] This completely ignores the fact that the author not only involves the risen Lord again and again in the spread of the gospel (9:4 ff; 18:9 f; 22:18 ff; 23:11), but also knows the experience that the Spirit, which, as the power of the End-time, is granted by Christ to Christians at Pentecost (1:8; 2:3 f, 33), is again and again being granted to believers (2:38; 5:32; 10:44 ff; 15:8 f), and makes itself discernible in the life of the Christian community (4:8, 31; 6:3; 7:55; 9:31; 11:24, 28; 13:4, 9; 15:28; 20:28).[73] From the standpoint of faith in the presence of the Spirit granted by the exalted Lord, the author of Acts shapes the history of the eschatological redemption which is being extended through preaching, and seeks by this means to prepare for the awaited coming of the promised Christ. Though the author is the theologian of the redemptive history that began with Christ, in his hope of the fulfillment already begun in Christ he takes his stand within the framework of a primitive Christian view of history, even if by including the Christ who is continually at work in the spread of the gospel in his narrative "of the things which have been fulfilled among us" (Lk 1:1), he takes seriously, from a theological viewpoint, the historical reality of the Christianity of his time.

But where did he get the information for his account, and when was he writing?

[71] Wilckens, *Missionsreden*, 200.
[72] Wilckens, *Missionsreden*, 202, 205 ff.
[73] Cf. Schweizer, TDNT VI, 404 ff.

4. The Sources and the Author of Acts

On the basis of the occasional occurrence of a "we" in the narrative, it has been conjectured that the author of Acts used written sources in the composition of his work, though that can also be inferred from the prologue, according to which the author was not "an eyewitness from the beginning." [73a] At the outset, however, three hypotheses can be rejected. (*a*) At the end of the nineteenth and the beginning of the twentieth century either a thorough reworking of a primitive document by a redactor was assumed (most recently by Loisy), or the compilation of Acts out of several sources,[74] but neither of these theories can be sustained. (*b*) Nor are the assumptions more persuasive that a source used in Lk 24 is continued in Acts 1:15 ff (Hirsch), or that a source that begins at Acts 3 originally linked up with Mk 16:8 though Acts 1:13 f (Haefner). (*c*) The hypothesis presented by Torrey, that the author of Acts 15:36 ff has prefaced his account with the translation of an Aramaic document that he has taken over (1:1b–15:35), and the similar assumption of Sahlin that Acts 1:6–15:35 is the conclusion of an Aramaic Proto-Luke that the author has translated and expanded,[75] are both exploded by the composite character of Acts 1–15, and especially by the fact that several of the OT quotations were usable for the context only in the LXX wording (e.g., 2:17 ff; 15:17), and in this section we find LXX language consistently.[76]

By contrast, three theories have found numerous supporters down to the present. (*a*) Harnack found in Acts 2–5 two parallel sources, one of which (3:1–5:16) is the beginning of the Jerusalem-Caesarean narrative (8:5-40; 9:32–11:18; 12:1-23) and is historically valuable, while the other (2:1-47 + 5:17-42) is a

---

[73a] On the history of research, see esp. Dupont, *Sources.*

[74] Most recently Shepherd: a Petrine source, an Antiochene source, Acts of Paul; Macgregor: three sources for Chs. 1–15; Buck-Taylor: Hellenistic source, travel source, ship's log.

[75] In agreement is L. Gaston, *No Stone on Another,* Suppl. NovTest 23, 1970, 254. Also Ehrhardt, *Acts,* 1, assumes Aramaic sources for 1–15.

[76] Cf. W. G. Kümmel, ThR 1942, 168 n. 1; 1950, 17 f; Dupont, *Sources,* 25 ff; Sparks, Argyle, Townsend. Lohfink, 53 ff, has shown that the "appearance conversations" (9:4 ff; also 22:7; 26:14 ff) are patterned after an LXX form of presentation. The research of Martin and Wilcox has shown at most the possibility that individual sections within 1–15 were originally composed in a Semitic language, but according to Emerton that could be accounted for on the assumption of LXX influence. Payne warns against overevaluation of the LXX influence.

worthless doublet. The rest of the narrative up to 15:35 (i.e., 6:1–8:4; 11:19-30; 12:25–15:35) Harnack attributed to an Antiochene source (see below, under b). This division of Acts 2–5 into two sources has been modified in various ways.[77] According to Reicke, 2:42–4:31 and 4:32–5:42 are two primitive church traditions that parallel each other down to details and have been juxtaposed, while Trocmé sees a written account used in 3:1–5:42, which the author has expanded by means of speeches, summary narratives, and the single account in 5:1-11. Not only its artificiality speaks against Reicke's construction, however, but also the proof by Jeremias that the two reports of hearings (4:1 ff; 5:17 ff) are by no means parallel, but describe substantively different proceedings. Furthermore, the summary narratives in 2:42 ff and 4:32 ff come from the author himself. Trocmé's view is countered by the fact that the account which he assumes to be basic cannot be differentiated linguistically from the alleged supplements by the author, and that an account of a trial, stripped of any kerygmatic elements, has no conceivable *Sitz im Leben* within the primitive community.

(*b*) Essentially better grounded is the proposal of an Antiochene source in Acts 6–15. Harnack based his thesis about the Antiochene source (see above) on an argument for the homogeneity of the contents. Jeremias has provided a new base with his assertion that sections 8:5-40; 9:31–11:18; 21:1-24; 15:1-33 were interpolated into the otherwise cohesive account from Acts 6:1–15:35; in addition, this underlying missionary account may be seen from 15:35 to the end of Acts as well.[78] Independently, these hypotheses were taken up by Benoit and Bultmann in 1958. According to Bultmann there is an Antiochene source—written originally in the "we" style—which may be discerned in 6:1-12a; 7:54–8:4; 11:19-26; 12:25, and a travel narrative beginning at 11:28 (where the "we" is original) and at 13:2 (where the "we" has been replaced by the author with the third person); the interpolations by the editor (Paul and Barnabas are inserted in 15:1-35; and 2:14-21, 24-31, 33-35 are examples of other interpolations) show that he employed written sources. Benoit postulates that the original source continuity between the Antiochene account in 11:27-30 and 15:3 ff was interrupted by a Palestinian and a Pauline tradition (12:1-23; 13; 14) —12:25 and 15:1, 2 are then redactional!—from which it is inferred that Paul's journey to Jerusalem in 11:27 ff is identical with the visit in 15:3 ff, and that in the source thus identified

---

[77] Cf. Kümmel, ThR 1942, 168 f; Dupont, *Sources,* 37 ff; recently Reicke; Trocmé; Ehrhardt, 24 f (according to whom 3:12–5:11 is interpolated).

[78] For criticism see Kümmel, ThR 1942, 170.

there is agreement with the narrative of the journey in Gal.[79] But Bultmann's proposal of an original "we" in 11:28; 13:2 is untenable.[80] And as little support can be adduced for an original literary link between 6:12a and 7:54 or between 11:26 and 12:25 having been destroyed as for the shifting from first to third person plural in an alleged Antiochene source in Chs. 6–12. The case for insertions in the speech of Peter (2:14 ff) and the narrative in 15:1 ff has not been successful either.[81] Benoit's reconstruction of the sources is weak, in that 11:27-30 cannot come from a single source, but represents a combining by the author of Acts;[82] nor can his theory explain why the editor would have created, by means of redactional links (12:25; 15:1, 2) together with the interjecting of Chs. 12 and 13, a further Pauline journey in conflict with one of his basic sources. Hence also the assumption of an Antiochene source is rendered improbable.

(*c*) The hypothesis that has gained the most supporters is that the author used a written source in the second half of his book. Belonging to this source would have been in any event the texts narrated in the first person plural (the so-called "we" texts): 16: 10-17 (the journey from Troy to Philippi); 20:5-15 (the journey from Philippi to Miletus); 21:1-18 (the journey from Miletus to Jerusalem); 27:1–28:16 (the journey from Caesarea to Rome). The we-sections begin in each case without warning in the middle of the narrative, and just as unexpectedly cease. They narrate exclusively journeys by sea with their beginning and ending on land. The "we" usually indicates "Paul and his companions" including the narrator, but in 16:17; 21:18 at the point of transition to the third person, Paul is placed side by side with the ἡμεῖς.[83] The assumption is ready to hand and has been adopted repeatedly since antiquity that by the "we," the author signifies that he was a personal participant in the indicated section. The "we" is therefore simply a redactional stylistic usage of the author. Yet the author nowhere indicates that directly, and this assumption became in-

---

[79] Thus also Harrington, *Intr.* 205 f.

[80] As early as 1899 Harnack indicated the secondary character of the "we" in 11:18; see A. von Harnack, "Über den ursprünglichen Text Act. Apost. 11, 27,28," *Studien zur Geschichte des NT und der Alten Kirche* I, AKG 19, 1931, 33 ff; Dupont, *Sources,* 66 n. 1, shows that in 13:2 λειτουργούντων cannot have the community as its subject.

[81] On Ch. 15 cf. Haenchen, *Jeremias Festschr.*

[82] See M. Dibelius, *Wochenschrift für klassische Philologie* 36, 1919, 5 ff, and the convincing evidence of Strecker.

[83] 28:16 can be understood in the same way. See Cadbury, NTS 1956/57, 129.

stantly problematical as people began to doubt the possibility that
Acts originated with a traveling companion of Paul. Thus since
the beginning of the nineteenth century in various forms the
hypothesis has been championed of a we-source employed by the
author of Acts, who is then assumed to be Luke, in keeping with
the tradition of the ancient church, though other traveling companions of Paul have been proposed as well.[84] On the other hand,
where the intention is to hold on to the traditional position that
Luke the physician was the author of Acts as well as Lk (see
above §8.4), frequently the hypothesis of a we-source is given the
twist that in these sections Luke used his own notes.[85] Most of these
scholars refer to the fact that the reports in the first person plural
cannot be distinguished stylistically from the other accounts in
the third person plural, and moreover are quite fragmented. This
then raises the question whether in the other reports that are not
in the we-form there may not be notes which originate with the
author of Acts as well.

Consonant with this consideration is the hypothesis of Dibelius,
built on the work of Norden, that in Chs. 13–21 the author of
Acts had as the basic source for his account an itinerary, to which
the we-sections belonged. As evidence for this, Dibelius adduces
that several stops are mentioned of which we are told nothing
(e.g., 14:24-26; 17:1; 20:13-15) and that frequently the insertions of speeches and detailed accounts into a travel narrative could
explain the unevenness of the narrative (cf. the double mention of
Derbe in 14:6, 20). Dibelius assumed that the "we" was not taken
from a travel diary of one of Paul's companions, but that Luke the
physician as the author of Acts had utilized this diary and indicated
by the "we" where he had personally participated. Scarcely anyone
has adopted this thesis of Dibelius.[86] On the other hand, a string
of scholars have accepted Dibelius' supposition of an itinerary, but
have not identified the author (Luke?) of the itinerary with the
author of Acts.[87] More recently the assumption of an itinerary

[84] See the summary by Dupont, *Sources,* 77 n. 2; further Stählin, Comm., 215.

[85] Thus recently, e.g., Blaiklock, Macgregor; Cerfaux, in Robert-Feuillet,
Feine-Behm, R. M. Grant, Harrington, Henshaw, Klijn, McNeile-Williams,
Meinertz, Michaelis, Wikenhauser; Dupont, W. L. Knox, D. P. Fuller, Ehrhardt,
Mattill, Marshall.

[86] See, however, Vögtle; S. Schulz, *Die Stunde der Botschaft,* 1967, 241.
Trocmé has altered the thesis: a diary of several of Paul's companions was employed, but that of Luke, the author of Acts, is used only where the "we"
occurs; Nock suggests several diaries.

[87] Grässer, ThR 1960, 126 f; Haenchen, ZThK 1955, 220 ff (=*Gott und
Mensch,* 221 ff); Klein, ZKG 1957, 365; 1962, 359 f.

has been vigorously contested. Ehrhardt[88] considers the existence of such a document impossible, because papyrus was too expensive, because Paul could not have carried such a burden with him, and because no parallels for it exist. Schille regards the evidence for the use of an itinerary by the author of Acts as completely unconvincing, just as he considers it impossible that the author of Acts obtained his knowledge through an eyewitness account, since the author has an entirely false picture of Paul's missionary activity. And in view of Paul's expectation of an imminent End, the keeping of a diary is unthinkable. Now Haenchen[89] has abandoned the assumption of an itinerary and discusses in a quite fanciful way the possibilities by which the author of Acts could have gathered his information: visits to churches, inquiries, the diary of one of the men who accompanied Paul from Philippi to Jerusalem on his last journey.

The problem of the sources underlying Acts 13–28 is therefore completely open, though it cannot be separated from the question of the author.[90] Investigation of the we-sections has shown that they cannot be separated stylistically from their present context and, further, that they are fragmentary. It could be demonstrated by literary means whether the author is speaking in the we-sections only if it could be shown that the reader can assign this meaning to the "we," even though it is not referred to in the context, because he was prepared to do so by the prologue. Otherwise there remains only the possibility of finding out, by discussion of the authorship question, whether the assumption is correct that by the "we" the author wants to reveal his participation in the events.

Cadbury and Dupont,[91] it is true, have sought to show that the prologue (Lk 1:1-4) prepares for the "we" in Acts 16 ff. While the author in 1:2 (οἱ ἀπ' ἀρχῆς αὐτόπται) mentions the men who can attest Jesus' activity from the beginning—which is not applicable to him—he says of himself in 1:3, "From my standpoint, I, who have for a long while carefully participated in all the events, determined to write it out for you in sequential order, most worthy Theophilus." This translation (Dupont) is based on the claim that

---

[88] Ehrhardt, "The Construction . . . ," 78 n. 3 (=Framework, 101 n. 2).

[89] ZThK 1961, 329 ff (=Gott und Mensch, 227 ff). Also critical of the assumption of an itinerary, Conzelmann, Comm., 5; Marxsen; W. Schmithals, Paul and James, SBT 46, 1965, 85.

[90] In spite of the protest of Dupont, Sources, 161.

[91] Cadbury, NTS 1956/57; Dupont, Sources, 99 ff; Cf. also Nock, 502 f; Trocmé, 126 f; Buck-Taylor, 208 ff. Higgins, AHG, 82, wants to interpret παρακολουθηκότι for Lk as "search out," but for a part of Acts also as "participate."

παρακολουθέω never means "to pursue a matter" but "to participate in something," and that ἄνωθεν (1:3) means "for a long time" in contrast to ἀπ᾽ ἀρχῆς (1:2) = "from the beginning on." The author of the double work Lk-Acts would then be explaining here that he took part personally in the matters reported and is pointing ahead to the "we" in Acts 16 ff. This translation of Lk 1:3 is undoubtedly wrong.[92] In the first place, πᾶσιν ἀκριβῶς as a qualification of παρηκολουθηκότι speaks against it: one cannot take part "carefully" in events, and if the "we" were to refer back to παρηκολουθη-κότι in the sense of "participate," the author of Acts would by no means have taken part in "all things." Furthermore the author of Acts juxtaposes ἀπ᾽ ἀρχῆς and ἄνωθεν in Acts 26:4 f without making any substantive distinction,[93] and the reader could not perceive a change of meaning from 1:2 to 1:3, since the meaning "from the beginning on" was without doubt current for ἄνωθεν.[94] Most importantly, παρακολουθέω certainly can mean "to pursue a thing"[95] and in association with ἄνωθεν πᾶσιν ἀκριβῶς no reader could give the word another meaning. Accordingly, Lk 1:3 is to be translated, "I, who from the beginning had followed everything carefully, resolved." Thus there is lacking any hint of participation by the author of Lk-Acts in any of the events, and any preparation for the "we" in Acts 16 ff.

This "we" therefore remains unexplained for the reader, and whether the author of Acts wanted to indicate his participation in a part of the Pauline journeys or not can only be clarified by an answer to the question whether Acts can actually have been written by a companion of Paul. Since Vielhauer has tried to show that "in his Christology the author of Acts is pre-Pauline; in his natural theology, his conception of the Law and his eschatology, he is post-Pauline" and that he stands at an "obvious conceptual distance from Paul,"[96] the question of the relation of the theology of Acts to that of Paul has been much discussed. But important as

[92] Cf. Haenchen, ZThK 1961, 362 ff (=Gott und Mensch, 260 ff); also in ThLZ 87, 1962, 43.

[93] See Haenchen, ZThK, 1961, 364 (=Gott und Mensch, 262) and Conzelmann, Comm., in loc. The distinction between the two concepts in 26:4 f by G. Klein, "Lk 1:1-4 als theologisches Programm," Zeit und Geschichte, Festschr. R. Bultmann, 1964, 207 f, is arbitrary.

[94] Philo, Vita Mosis II, 48: the author of the Book of Moses ἠρχαιολόγησεν ἄνωθεν ἀρξάμενος ἀπὸ τῆς τοῦ παντὸς γενέσεως; i.e., "he told ancient things from the beginning on, starting with the creation."

[95] See Bauer, Lexicon, 624, and the reference there to Demosthenes. The Vetus Latina understands this in the same way: adsecuto a principio omnibus diligenter.

[96] Vielhauer, EvTh 1950/51, 15 (=Aufsätze, 26).

this question is in this connection, it must be broadened by another question: How does the information reported in Acts relate to what we can extract about Paul's activity from his letters? Neither question can here be discussed comprehensively, but for the decision about the authorship of Acts a few essential facts will suffice.

a. If we start with the matter of information about Paul's activity, we have already noted (p. 175) that the report of his second visit to Jerusalem (Acts 11:27 ff) originated as a combination by the author of Acts, that in any case Acts is wrong in saying that Paul had been in Jerusalem twice before the Apostolic Council (Acts 15 = Gal 2). Yet Paul attaches great importance in Gal 2:1 to the fact that the visit to the Apostolic Council was the second he had made to Jerusalem.

b. According to Acts 10:1–11:18, Peter had accomplished the first conversion of a pagan through his preaching, and by his report in Jerusalem he had achieved the sanction of the "apostles and brothers" there for engaging in table fellowship with the Gentiles. And when Paul was under attack in Jerusalem owing to his law-free Gentile mission he obtained (15:7 ff) from Peter and James a defense of the Gentile mission. But Paul reports in Gal 2:1 ff that he had to defend the Gentile mission before the δοκοῦντες, and finally succeeded in having the "pillars," James, Peter, and John, unite with him in dividing up the missionary objectives.

c. This settlement concerning the missionary objectives is missing in the report of the Apostolic Council in Acts 15; instead we are told (15:22 ff) that the gathering in Jerusalem had decided with the participation of Paul and Barnabas to issue the injunction to the Gentile Christians of Antioch, Syria, and Cilicia "to abstain from meat offered to idols, from blood, from things strangled, and from unchastity." Paul says nothing of this so-called "Apostolic Decree" in Gal 2, and his οὐδὲν προσανέθεντο in 2:6 excludes the possibility; in discussing the question about the right of Christians to eat meat sacrificed to idols in I Cor 8–10 he gives no indication of such an agreement. Attempts have been made to evade the facts here, either by stressing that the agreement was effective only for a special problem in Antioch, Syria, and Cilicia, so that Paul had no need to mention it to the Corinthians,[97] or it is asserted that the noncultic version of the Apostolic Decree attested in witnesses for the "Western" text (without καὶ πνικτῶν) is the original

[97] E.g., Höpfl-Gut; Filson, 35; Y. Tissot, "Les prescriptions des presbytres (Actes 15:41 D)," RB 76, 1970, 321 n. 3.

text of Acts (15:20, 29; 21:25) and that this moral requirement
for abstinence from worship of idols, murder, and unchastity was
not an "injunction" that Paul would have been obligated to mention.[98] But even if it could be established that the formulation of
the letter (15:22 ff) and thus the address of the author has been
taken over word for word—which is thoroughly questionable—
there can be no doubt that the requirement proposed in 15:19-21
and passed on in 15:28 f has in view Gentile Christians in general.
And only the four-member cultic form of the Apostolic Decree
can be shown to be the starting point for the complicated textual
development of this passage.[99] The Apostolic Decree in the form
reported in Acts cannot have been decided upon with Paul as
participant, quite apart from the question how its origin is to be
accounted for historically.[100]

There can be no doubt that, on the three essential points that
have been mentioned concerning the information about Paul's activity, the author of Acts is so misinformed that he can scarcely
have been a companion of Paul on his missionary journeys. This
is confirmed when one considers the representation of Paul's theology in Acts. It is not completely astounding that "not a single
specifically Pauline idea" [101] is to be found in Acts, since we cannot
tell how much of Paul's theology would have been understood by
one of his companions. Nor can we take it as merely self-evident
that the thinking of the author of Acts followed the lines of
Pauline theology. One may ask, however, whether he presents
Paul and his message in such a way that we can perceive from this
representation that he was acquainted with the most pregnant
features of the historical Paul. That cannot be answered affirma-
tively if the following three points are taken into consideration:

a. In the prescript to most of his letters Paul calls himself
ἀπόστολος Χριστοῦ Ἰησοῦ or the like, and stresses that he can claim

[98] Thus, e.g., Feine-Behm.

[99] See Kümmel, Festschr. Kundsin=Heilsgeschehen, 278 ff; Williams, Alterations, 72 ff; Epp, 107 ff. Y. Tissot (see n. 97), 321 ff, considers the four-member
cultic form in 15:29 to be Lukan, while καὶ πνικτοῦ in 15:20 is a gloss; the
"Western" text of 15:29 and 21:25 is therefore a secondary accommodation to
the original text of 15:20 and is also to be interpreted cultically. That is as
untenable as the renewed defense of the ethically understood "Western" text of
the Apostolic Decree by Th. Boman, "Das text-kritische Problem des sog. Aposteldekrets," NovTest 7, 1964/65, 26 ff.

[100] Cf. the survey in Conzelmann, Comm., 84 f; Haenchen, Acts, 468 ff;
Kümmel, ThR, NF 17, 1948, 32 ff; 18, 1950, 28, and response in Y. Tissot
(see n. 97) 321 n. 3, 341 n. 61a.

[101] Vielhauer, EvTh 1950/51, 15, (=Aufsätze, 26), in agreement with
Bauernfeind, ZsTh 1954, 74.

this title because he has seen the Lord and that the Corinthians must recognize his dignity even when it is contested by his opponents (I Cor 9:1 f; 15:9 f; II Cor 12:11 f; Rom 11:13). In Acts, however, Paul has the title of apostle only in 14:4, 14, together with Barnabas, and in a completely unemphatic way. Elsewhere the twelve are designated as apostles and contrasted with Paul (1:26; 15:2, 6, 22 f; 16:4). It is difficult to say why as a rule the author does not count Paul among the apostles and why that view breaks down in 14:4, 14. (Possibly this exception could be traced back to a record that was incorporated, but it was certainly not intentional; see above, p. 170.) Elsewhere in Acts the avoidance of the apostolic title for Paul is surely not intended to make Paul appear subordinate to the twelve: the whole structure of Acts speaks against that.[102] However this situation is to be explained, it shows in any event that the author of Acts does not know of Paul's emphatic claim to the title of apostle.

b. Paul's preaching of God's saving act in Christ which forgives sins and grants life has as its presupposition the conviction that "all men sinned," that they have rejected the knowledge of God and of works of Law that they might have attained and have thereby lost their share in the divine glory (Rom 3:23; 1:19-21; 2:14 f). Neither Jew nor Gentile can of himself attain salvation (Rom 1:22 ff; 2:17 ff; 9:31 f); the mission of Christ first makes salvation possible for the believers (Rom 3:21 f, 25; II Cor 5:18 ff; Gal 4:4 f; I Thess 1:9 f). But in the Areopagus address (Acts 17:22 ff) there is a reference to a pagan poet which declares that human beings are of the divine race, nor are they far from God, whom they are to seek; on the other hand, the role of Christ in relation to them is that of judge of the world, the significance of which fact has become evident through God's raising Jesus from the dead. There can be no doubt that the author has placed this in the mouth of Paul as a characteristic example of a missionary address to the heathen—"a hellenistic speech about the true knowledge of God"[103]—although this has been often contested.[104] Even if we

---

[102] Against the thesis of Klein that Acts wants to depreciate Paul, Burchard has shown (*passim*, esp. 135 f, 173 ff) that "Luke insists on placing Paul's witness, though nonapostolic, on the same level as that of the twelve apostles" (174).

[103] Dibelius, *Studies,* 138 ff.

[104] See bibl. on the Areopagus speech in B. Gärtner, *The Areopagus Speech and Natural Revelation,* ASNU 21, 1955; Dupont, NTS 1959/60, 152 n. 4 (= *Études,* 416 n. 76); W. G. Kümmel, *Man in the NT,* 1963, 87 ff; further O'Neill, 160 ff; J.-Ch. Lebram, "Der Aufbau der Areopagrede," ZNW 55, 1964, 221; H. Flender, *St. Luke,* 69 ff; Schubert, "The Place of the Areopagus Speech . . ."; T. D. Barnes, "An Apostle on Trial," JTS, NS 1969, 407 ff.

were to concede that Paul, in missionary preaching to the pagans, linked up with their conceptual world, it would still be unthinkable that in place of the eschatological message of redemption that was fundamental for him he would have placed a Stoic doctrine of the kinship of men to the divine. And it is equally unthinkable that a missionary companion of Paul could have attributed to him these radically different views of salvation and of God.

c. At the center of Paul's theology stands the message that through Christ's death for us God has wrought salvation (Rom 3:24 ff; 5:6 ff; I Cor 1:18 ff; 15:3; II Cor 5:18 ff; Gal 3:13). In the Pauline speeches of Acts, however, there is only one mention of the death of Jesus according to Scripture (13:27-29) and one of "the church of God which he bought by his blood" (20:28). And even in the last-named instance there is no reference to the redemptive significance of the death of Jesus for believers. This situation, which corresponds to what we found in Lk (see above, §8.4), shows that at most the author knows by hearsay something of the central features of Paul's doctrine of redemption, but he cannot have learned about it through any personal contact.

From the facts adduced there is a sufficient base for inferring that the author of Acts was not a missionary companion of Paul, so that the "we" in Acts 16 ff cannot be expressing his participation in the missionary journeys of Paul. This conclusion cannot be evaded by claiming that in the we-passages Luke has been with Paul only briefly and therefore has insufficient knowledge:[105] the deviation from the historical situations and from the central features of Paul's theology makes it impossible to trace Acts back to Paul himself, not because the connection is inadequate but because it is completely lacking. Furthermore, the author would have had to be with Paul for a long period during the journey from Jerusalem to Rome and in Rome. The misconception of Paul's theology cannot, as Eltester would like, be explained on the basis that Luke was Paul's companion by assuming that Luke, as a Greek, could not understand the Jewish-based theology of Paul, or that Acts' concept of apostleship arises from Luke's having written the Gospel of Lk, in which the guarantees of the gospel tradition are seen in the disciples of Jesus alone. Even a Greek, if he were at the same time a personal pupil of Paul, would know that in the Apostolic Council Paul took on no obligations. Even the third evangelist as pupil of Paul would have known Paul's

---

[105] Nock, Trocmé, 143 ff. R. H. Fuller, *Intr.*, 130, thinks that Luke may be writing at a temporal remove from the events and that in the interim his theology has developed.

claim to be an apostle and his understanding of the death of Jesus. And the third argument as well, that Acts must have originated with Luke the physician, proves nothing. Against the assertion[106] that Acts must have carried the name of its author because its dedication (1:1) shows that it was intended for the book trade, it may be said that a dedication in no way has this significance (see §8 n. 8a) and Acts was scarcely intended for a broad public and thus for the book trade.[107] It is therefore firmly established that, in spite of the opposing view of many scholars, Acts cannot have been written by a companion of Paul, and thus not by Luke the physician, to whom the tradition refers it (see above, §8.4).[108]

As explanation of the we-sections there remain only two possibilities: either an editor unknown to us took the "we" over from a source, or he interpolated it into his account on his own. The second supposition[109] is most unlikely, since the author would scarcely have inserted the "we" in such sporadic fashion if he wanted to give his report the appearance of an eyewitness record. It is far more likely that he already found the "we" in a source that he employed. That is especially probable if[110] there is reasonable ground for the assumption that in Acts 13–28 there was a travel narrative as a basic source. And that is the case. The general reasons against this assumption signify little, since we have no facts on the necessity or possibility of making notes on the stages of journeys. And naturally we cannot say anything as to whether the basic narrative thread is composed of one or several sources. The observations remain that there are numerous place references concerning which nothing of consequence is recounted, and that the progress of the narrative is often interrupted by unmistakably inserted narrative units. The probability is very great, therefore, that in Acts 13–28 or at any rate a large part of this section of Acts, something like a travel narrative, a diary, a list of places visited, or such, has been used, although this basic narrative thread cannot be separated out in detail and with exactitude. The we-sections in all probability belonged to this narrative thread, and the conjecture that Luke the physician is the spokesman there

---

[106] Thus Goodspeed; Dibelius, Dupont.

[107] See nn. 30-32. Even H. von Campenhausen, *The Formation of the Christian Bible*, 1972, 126 f n. 92, cannot demonstrate that a work with a dedication must have named its author.

[108] Thus Conzelmann, Haenchen; Marxsen; Vielhauer, Klein, Evans, O'Neill.

[109] Thus, e.g., Conzelmann, *Comm.*, 6; Marxsen, *Intr.*, 168.

[110] In spite of frequent disputing; see above, p. 178.

might adduce in its support the fact that apart from such a situation the non-apostle Luke would not have been hit upon as the author of Lk-Acts. Yet this argument is not persuasive, since this name could have been arrived at by deduction (see above, §8.4). That such travel descriptions and narratives existed—narrated partly in the first, partly in the third person—has been demonstrated.[111] It is often assumed that the account of the voyage in 27:1–28:14 could not have belonged to this narrative thread, since the references to Paul can easily be separated out from a profane account of a shipwreck.[112] But it has been correctly asserted to the contrary[113] that the source underlying the narrative and clearly expanded by the author speaks of a transport of prisoners so that it is even more probable that also in 27:1–28:16 a travel account from the context of Paul has been used. Therefore even here, at least in places, the "we" belongs to the underlying source.

Other sources than the travel narrative(s) in 13–28 cannot be ascertained in Acts, which calls attention to the significant fact noted since Harnack that Acts represents a linguistic unity.[114] That is not to say that here and there individual texts have not been taken over verbatim (e.g., the speech of Stephen, 7:1 ff, or that of Tertullus, 24:2 ff, or parts of the Areopagus speech or the letter from the Apostolic Council),[115] but nothing more than conjectures can be advanced. The much-favored guessing game as to which persons could have provided the author with his information[116] is a pointless enterprise.

5. Time and Place of Writing

Since Acts, as the second part of the Lukan double work, must have been written later than Lk, which was written after 70 (see above, §8.4), it could not have been produced before 80; the

---

[111] Norden, 316 ff; Nock, 500 ff; Schmithals (see n. 89), 71, would rather think of a missionary narrative that included the "we."

[112] Thus Grässer, Dibelius, Klein, ZKG 1956, 366; 1962, 360; Bultmann; Conzelmann, ThLZ 1960, 248 f.

[113] Nock; Haenchen, ZThK, 1961, 358 ff (=Gott und Mensch, 356 ff); also "Acta 27," Zeit und Geschichte, Festschr. Bultmann, 1964, 235 ff.

[114] Thus, most recently, Dupont, Sources, 85.

[115] On the speeches of Peter see E. Schweizer, Lordship and Discipleship, 58, 95 f.

[116] Cf. Stagg; Albertz, Feine-Behm, Höpfl-Gut, Michaelis, Schäfer, Wikenhauser; Reicke, Ehrhardt, The Acts; even Haenchen, Acts, 86.

linguistic differences between Lk and Acts[117] require a certain time lapse between the two writings by the same author. The attempts to assign the production of Acts to before the death of Paul at the beginning of the sixties[118] or *ca.* 70[119] are accordingly untenable. On the other hand the earlier frequent assumption of Acts' dependence on Josephus has rightly been given up,[120] so that a date *ca.* 95 cannot be based on this theory. Klein[121] would like to locate Acts in the second century, based on the early Catholicism of the book. But that is not at all convincing (see above, p. 172) because this designation for the theology of Acts is problematical and in any case provides no more exact dating possibility. O'Neill wants to prove the period between 115 and 130 as the time of writing, by pointing to Justin as the theologian with whom Acts has the closest relationship. But his contention that Justin knew Acts is forced,[122] and his early dating of Justin is arbitrary. Besides, the alleged parallels between the theology of Acts and Justin are by no means convincing. Against Klein's and O'Neill's second-century dating is the decisive evidence that by nearly universal judgment the author of Acts does not know the letters of Paul,[123] which by all appearances were collected toward the end of the first century (see below, §35). The theory, which has been offered in various forms, that the author of Acts knew the letters of Paul, but chose not to use them[124] is utterly improbable. The most likely assumption, therefore, is a date for Acts between 80 and 90, but a date between 90 and 100 is not excluded.[125]

Where the author wrote cannot be ascertained. On the basis of the traditional interpretation of "we," some have guessed Rome,[126]

[117] Cf. Clark, 396 ff; J. C. Hawkins, *Horae Synopticae*, ²1909, 177 ff; cf. also Stählin, 4; S. G. Wilson, "Lukan Eschatology," NTS 16, 1969/70, 347.

[118] See n. 25; further Blaiklock, Bruce; Harrison; Parker, Goodenough, Marshall; G. Bouwman, *Das dritte Ev.*, 1968, 65.

[119] E.g., Williams, Stagg; Michaelis, Wikenhauser; Michel.

[120] Most recently, Ehrhardt, StTh 1958, 64 f (=*Framework*, 85 f).

[121] Klein, ZKG 157, 371. Thus also M. S. Enslin, "Once Again, Luke and Paul," ZNW 61, 1970, 253, 271.

[122] The texts adduced by O'Neill, 31 f, are not taken seriously. Cf. Sparks, JTS 1963, 464.

[123] M. S. Enslin (see n. 121), 253 ff, seeks to show—against all probability—that the author of Acts knows and uses the letters of Paul, but does not mention them because of their misuse by false teachers.

[124] Knox; Klein, *Zwölf Apostel*, 189 ff; Burchard, 155 ff; C. H. Talbert, *Luke and the Gnostics*, 1968, 88.

[125] Thus, e.g., Fuller, Goodspeed, Marxsen, Schelkle, Vögtle.

[126] Hanson, NTS 1965/66, 224 ff, thinks he can prove that Acts was written in Rome, and that it ends before the end of the first (!) Roman imprisonment of Paul because the Roman readers already knew everything further about Paul.

but Antioch, Ephesus, a Pauline community in Macedonia, Achaia, or Asia Minor have all been proposed.[127]

6. The Text of Acts

In all critical editions of the NT, the text of Acts is that of the oldest majuscules ($\mathfrak{P}$ [45,47], B, ℵ, A, C) and the Alexandrian church fathers, which is attested as early as the first part of the third century in $\mathfrak{P}$[45]. In addition, there exists a significantly different, longer[128] form of the text in the "Western" witnesses, such as D[e,a], the Old Latin versions, the Vetus Syra (insofar as it can be inferred from Ephraem's commentary on Acts, which survives only in Armenian), the marginal notes of the Harklean Syriac version, Latin church fathers such as Irenaeus (when preserved in Latin), Tertullian, Cyprian, Augustine, but also in textual witnesses from Egypt, such as $\mathfrak{P}$[38,41,48] and a Coptic manuscript.[129] The great majority of the Greek MSS represent the Koine text of Acts.[130] Since the large number of variants in the "Western" text cannot simply be traced back to the corruption of an original text, the question is raised whether the "Western" text is a modification of the "Egyptian" text (or its presupposition) or whether both text forms developed from a supposedly primitive text that lies behind them. Zahn's thesis that the "Western" text was the original edition of Luke, of which the "Egyptian" text was a second edition by the same author, has not been sustained, since the differences between the two textual forms involve in part contradictory evidence (cf. the stipulations in the Apostolic Decree; see above, p. 180). But again and again it has been assumed that the "Western" text of Acts is closest to the original text.[131] But today, in the light of $\mathfrak{P}$[48], there can no longer be any doubt that the "Western" text is as old as the "Egyptian" text, and it may be ascertained

---

[127] Goodspeed: Ephesus; Trocmé: Macedonia, Achaia, or Asia Minor; Conzelmann, StLA, 30,1, points to the Aegean as the center of his presentation; Glover notes the information about Antioch.

[128] According to F. Kenyon, *The Western Text in the Gospels and Acts*, 1938, 26, the text of the "Western" witnesses is about 8½ percent longer.

[129] Cf. the list of "Western" witnesses in Epp, 28 ff. The Coptic MS mentioned is a mixed text; see Haenchen and Weigandt, NTS 1967/68.

[130] Cf. the text-critical information in §38. In his text edition, Ropes presents on facing pages the text of B and D with associated witnesses, so far as they were known in 1925.

[131] E.g., by A. C. Clark, Snape; P. Glaue, "Der älteste Text der geschichtlichen Bücher des NT," ZNW 45, 1954, 90 ff; for the LXX quotations, Cerfaux.

that the "Western" text is not simply a text run wild. It may be demonstrated that a large number of the additions and variants of the "Western" text, relative to the "Egyptian" text, can be accounted for as smoothing out difficulties or substantive alterations (cf. the "we" in 11:28, the cultic form of the Apostolic Decree, and the related insertion of the golden rule in 15:29; the motivation for the officials' change of mind in 16:35, the journey of Apollos to Corinth in 18:27). Other variants serve to strengthen the divine leading (19:1), the activity of the missionaries (14:25), the theological predicate (28:31), but also the intensification of the guilt of the Jews.[132] There can be no doubt, therefore, that a greater part of the variants of the "Western" text in Acts arose as a conscious editing of the text attested in B, ℵ, and the related MSS.[133] This process was undoubtedly aided by Acts' receiving its canonical status later than the Gospels, so that its text was guarded less (Dibelius). This does not preclude the fact that the "Western" text of Acts has preserved certain readings which can scarcely be understood as secondary alterations and may well represent the original text (cf. the geographical information in 12:10; 20:15; the indications of time in 19:9; 27:5; $\Delta o \nu \beta[\epsilon] \rho \iota o s$ in 20:4 as the place of origin of the Macedonian Gaius). But as a whole the "Egyptian" text form is the more original, so that an eclectic method is the only means of determining the individual original readings in the "Western" text,[134] which occasionally rests on a single attestation ($\tau o \hat{\iota} s \psi \alpha \lambda \mu o \hat{\iota} s$ 𝔓[45] in 13:33) or a conjecture.[135]

§10. The Gospel of John

Commentaries: see §41. Bibliography: L. Schmid, "Joh. und Religionsgeschichte," diss. Tübingen, 1933; Ph.-H. Menoud, *L'évangile de Jean d'après les recherches récentes*, Cahiers théologiques de l'actualité protestante 3, [2]1947; *idem*, "Les études johanniques de Bultmann à Barrett," RechB III, 1958 (see below) 11 ff; E. Haenchen, ThR, NF 23, 1955, 295 ff; W. F. Howard, *The Fourth Gospel in Recent Criticism and Interpretation*, rev. C. K. Barrett, 1955; J. A. T. Robinson, "The New Look on the Fourth Gospel," StEv, TU 73, 1959, 338 ff (=J. A. T. R., *Twelve NT Studies*, SBT 34, 1962, 94 ff); A. M. Hunter, "Recent Trends in NT Studies," ExpT 71, 1959/60, 164 ff, 219 ff; R. Schnackenburg, *Nt. Theologie. Der Stand der Forschung*, Biblische Handbibliothek I,

---

[132] Cf. 13:27 (D) with 17:30 and the works of Menoud and Epp.

[133] See the evidence in Thiele.

[134] Thus Wilcox, 185, Williams, Klijn; exaggerated by Kilpatrick.

[135] On 4:25 cf. Haenchen, ZThK 51, 1954, 156 f (=*Gott und Mensch*, 160 f); and Conzelmann *in loc*.

1963, 107 ff; English translation, *New Testament Theology Today*, London, 1963; E. Malatesta, *St. John's Gospel 1920–1965*, AnBibl 32, 1965 (bibl.); H.-O. Metzger, "Neuere Johannes-Forschung," VF 12, 1967, 2,12 ff; B. Vawter, "Some Recent Developments in Johannine Theology," BThB 1, 1971, 30 ff. Studies: W. Baldensperger, *Der Prolog des 4. Ev.*, 1898; A. Schlatter, *Die Sprache und Heimat des 4. Evangelisten*, BFChTh VI, 4, 1902; W. Wrede, *Charakter und Tendenz des Joh*, SGV 37, 1903; E. Schwartz, *Über den Tod der Söhne Zebedäi*, AGG, NF 7, 5, 1904; *idem*, "Aporien im 4. Ev.," NAG 1907, 341 ff; 1908, 115 ff, 149 ff, 497 ff; J. Wellhausen, *Erweiterungen und Änderungen im 4. Ev.*, 1907; W. Heitmüller, "Zur Johannes-Tradition," ZNW 13, 1914, 189 ff; C. F. Burney, *The Aramaic Origin of the Fourth Gospel*, 1922; C. C. Torrey, "The Aramaic Origin of the Gospel of John," HTR 16, 1923, 305 ff; H. Windisch, "Der joh. Erzählungsstil," ΕΥΧΑΡΙΣΤΗΡΙΟΝ, Festschr. *H. Gunkel* II, FRLANT, NF 19, 1923, 174 ff; *idem, Johannes und die Synpt.*, UNT 12, 1926; *idem*, "Die Absolutheit des Joh," ZsTh 5, 1928, 3 ff; K. Kundsin, *Topologische Überlieferungsstücke im Joh*, 1925; *idem, Charakter und Ursprung der joh. Reden*, Acta Universitatis Latviensis, Theological Series I, 4, 1939; R. Bultmann, "Die Bedeutung der neuererschlossenen mandäischen und manichäischen Quellen für das Verständnis des Joh," ZNW 24, 1925, 100 ff (=R. B., *Exegetica*, 1967, 55 ff); *idem*, RGG³ III, 1959, 840 ff; B. W. Bacon, "The Elder John in Jerusalem," ZNW 26, 1927, 187 ff; *idem*, "John and the Pseudo-Johns," ZNW 31, 1932, 132 ff; *idem, The Gospel of the Hellenists*, 1933; M. Dibelius, "Joh 15, 13. Eine Studie zum Traditionsproblem des Joh," *Festgabe A. Deissmann*, 1927, 168 ff (=M. D., *Botschaft und Geschichte* I, 1953, 204 ff); *idem*, RGG² III, 1929, 349 ff; E. Lohmeyer, "Aufbau und Gliederung des vierten Ev.," ZNW 27, 1928, 11 ff; F. Büchsel, *Johannes und der hellen. Synkretismus*, BFChTh 2, Reihe 16, 1928; E. C. Colwell, *The Greek of the Fourth Gospel*, 1931; W. von Loewenich, *Das Johannesverständnis im zweiten Jh.*, Bh. ZNW 13, 1932; G. Hoffmann, *Das Joh als Alterswerk*, NTF IV, 1, 1933; T. Sigge, *Das Joh und die Synpt.*, NTA 16, 2/3, 1935; E. Hirsch, *Studien zum vierten Ev.*, BHTh 11, 1936; *idem, Das vierte Ev. in seiner ursprünglichen Gestalt verdeutscht und erklärt*, 1936; *idem*, "Stilkritik und Literaranalyse im vierten Ev.," ZNW 43, 1950/51, 129 ff; L. Vaganay, "La finale du quatrième évangile," RB 45, 1936, 512 ff; H. Preisker, "Das Ev. des Johannes als erster Teil eines apokalyptischen Doppelwerkes," ThBl 15, 1936, 185 ff; P. Gardner-Smith, *Saint John and the Synoptic Gospels*, 1938; *idem*, "St. John's Knowledge of Matthew," JTS, NS 4, 1953, 31 ff; E. Schweizer, *Ego eimi . . .*, FRLANT, NF 38, 1939; E. Percy, *Untersuchungen über den Ursprung der joh. Theologie*, 1939 (on this see R. Bultmann, OLZ 43, 1940, 150 ff; M. Dibelius, DLZ 61, 1940, 1 ff); J. Schniewind, "Über das Joh" (1939), in H. J. Kraus, *Julius Schniewind. Charisma der Theologie*, 1965, 187 ff; J. Jeremias, "Joh. Literar-Kritik," ThBl 20, 1941, 33 ff; R. M. Grant, "The Fourth Gospel and the Church," HTR 35, 1942, 95 ff; *idem*, "The Odes of Solomon and the Church of

Antioch," JBL 63, 1944, 363 ff; *idem,* "The Origin of the Fourth Gospel," JBL 69, 1950, 305 ff; E. C. Broome, "The Sources of the Fourth Gospel," JBL 63, 1944, 107 ff; H. A. Fischel, "Jewish Gnosticism in the Fourth Gospel," JBL 65, 1946, 157 ff; T. W. Manson, "The Fourth Gospel," BJRL 30, 1946/47, 312 ff (=Manson, *St.,* 105 ff); E. Käsemann, review of Bultmann, *Comm.,* VuF 1942/46, 1946/47, 182 ff; *idem,* review of Howard, *Fourth Gospel,* and Barrett, *Comm.,* GGA 211, 1957, 145 ff (=E. K., *Exegetische Versuche und Besinnungen* II, 1964, 131 ff); *idem, The Testament of Jesus: A Study of the Gospel of Jn in the Light of Jn 17,* 1968 (on this see G. Bornkamm, EvTh 28, 1968, 8 ff=G. B., *Gesammelte Aufsätze* III, 1968, 104 ff); M.-E. Boismard, "Le chapitre XXI de saint Jean," RB 54, 1947, 473 ff; *idem,* "Clément de Rome et l'Évangile de Jean," RB 55, 1948, 376 ff; *idem,* "L'évolution du thème eschatologique dans les traditions johanniques," RB 68, 1961, 507 ff; *idem,* "Saint Luc et la rédaction du quatrième évangile," RB 69, 1962, 185 ff; *idem,* "Les traditions johanniques concernant le Baptiste," RB 70, 1963, 5 ff; C. M. Connick, "The Dramatic Character of the Fourth Gospel," JBL 67, 1948, 159 ff; W. G. Wilson, "The Original Text of the Fourth Gospel," JTS 50, 1949, 59 ff; J. Bonsirven, "Les aramaïsmes de saint Jean l'évangéliste," Bb 30, 1949, 405 ff; C. Maurer, *Ignatius von Antiochien und das Joh,* AThANT 18, 1949; N. Uricchio, "La teoria delle trasposizioni nel vangelo di S. Giovanni," Bb 31, 1950, 129 ff; E. Ruckstuhl, *Die literarische Einheit des Joh,* Studia Friburgensia, NF 1, 1951; S. Mendner, "Joh. Literarkritik," ThZ 8, 1952, 418 ff; *idem,* "Die Tempelreinigung," ZNW 47, 1956, 93 ff; *idem,* "Zum Problem 'Joh und die Synpt,'" NTS 4, 1957/58, 282 ff; *idem,* "Nikodemus," JBL 77, 1958, 293 ff; H. P. V. Nunn, *The Authorship of the Fourth Gospel,* 1952; H. F. D. Sparks, "St. John's Knowledge of Matthew; The Evidence of John 13:16 and 15:20," JTS, NS 3, 1952, 58 ff; C. H. Dodd, *The Interpretation of the Fourth Gospel,* 1953 (on this see R. Bultmann, NTS 1, 1954/55, 77 ff; P. Winter, ThLZ 80, 1955, 141 ff); C. H. Dodd, "Some Johannine 'Herrnworte' with Parallels in the Synoptic Gospels," NTS 2, 1955/56, 75 ff; *idem, Historical Tradition in the Fourth Gospel,* 1963 (on this see G. Strecker, Gn 36, 1964, 773 ff); C. K. Barrett, "Zweck des 4. Ev.," ZsTh 22, 1953, 257 ff; *idem,* "The Theological Vocabulary of the Fourth Gospel and the Gospel of Truth," *Current Issues in NT Interpretation,* Festschr. O. Piper, 1962, 210 ff; *idem,* "Das Joh und das Judentum," *Franz Delitzsch-Vorlesungen 1967,* 1970; B. Noack, *Zur joh. Tradition,* Publications de la Société des Sciences et des Lettres d'Aarhus, Série de Théologie 3, 1954 (on this see R. Bultmann, ThLZ 80, 1955, 521 ff); R. A. Edwards, *The Gospel According to St. John: Its Criticism and Interpretation,* 1954; R. Gyllenberg, "Die Anfänge der joh. Tradition," *Nt. Studien für R. Bultmann,* Bh. ZNW 21, 1954, 144 ff; L. Mowry, "The Dead Sea Scrolls and the Background for the Gospel of John," *The Biblical Archaeologist* 17, 1954, 78 ff; C. Goodwin, "How Did John Treat His Sources?" JBL 73, 1954, 61 ff; H. C. Snape, "The Fourth Gospel, Ephesus and Alexandria," HTR 47,

1954, 1 ff; J. N. Sanders, " 'Those whom Jesus loved': St. John XI:5," NTS 1, 1954/55, 29 ff; I. Buse, "John V:8 and Johannine-Marcan Relationship," NTS 1, 1954/55, 134 ff; idem, "St. John and the Marcan Passion Narrative," NTS 4, 1957/58, 215 ff; idem, "St. John and the Passion Narratives of St. Matthew and St. Luke," NTS 7, 1960/61, 65 ff; K. Aland, "Der Montanismus und die kleinasiatische Theologie," ZNW 46, 1955, 114 ff; K. Weiss, "Der westliche Text von Lc. 7,46 und sein Wert," ZNW 46, 1955, 241 ff; F.-M. Braun, "L'arrière-fond judaïque du Quatrième Évangile et la Communauté de l'Alliance," RB 62, 1955, 1 ff; idem, "Hermétisme et Johannisme," Revue Thomiste 55, 1955, 22 ff, 259 ff; idem, "La 'Lettre de Barnabé' et l'Évangile de saint Jean," NTS 4, 1957/58, 119 ff; idem, Jean, le théologien, et son évangile dans l'église ancienne, Ét. Bibl., 1959 (on this cf. M.-E. Boismard, RB 67, 1960, 592 ff); F.-M. Braun, "Saint Jean, la sagesse et l'histoire," Neotestamentica et Patristica, Freundesgabe O. Cullman, suppl. NovTest 6, 1962, 123 ff; R. M. Wilson, "The Fourth Gospel and Hellenistic Thought," NovTest 1, 1956, 225 ff; E. Stauffer, "Probleme der Priestertradition," ThLZ 81, 1956, 135 ff; idem, "Historische Elemente im vierten Ev.," in Bekenntnis zur Kirche, Festschr. E. Sommerlath, 1960, 33 ff; H. Becker, Die Reden des Joh und der Stil der gnostischen Offenbarungsrede, ed. R. Bultmann, FRLANT 68, 1956 (on this see C. K. Barrett, ThLZ 82, 1957, 911 f); P. Parker, "Two Editions of John," JBL 75, 1956, 303 ff; idem, "John and John Mark," JBL 79, 1960, 97 ff; idem, "John the Son of Zebedee and the Fourth Gospel," JBL 81, 1962, 35 ff; idem, "Luke and the Fourth Evangelist," NTS 9, 1962/63, 317 ff; W. F. Albright, "Recent Discoveries in Palestine and the Gospel of St. John," The Background of the NT and Its Eschatology: Festschr. C. H. Dodd, 1956, 153 ff; E. K. Lee, "St. Mark and the Fourth Gospel," NTS 3, 1956/57, 50 ff; Cassian, "John XXI," NTS 3, 1956/57, 132 ff; R. E. Brown, "The Qumran Scrolls and the Johannine Gospels and Epistles," in The Scrolls and the NT, ed. K. Stendahl, 1957, 183 ff (=R. E. B., NT Essays, 1965, 102 ff); R. E. Brown, "The Problem of Historicity in John," CBQ 24, 1962, 1 ff (=R. E. B., Essays, 143 ff); G. D. Kilpatrick, "The Religious Background of the Fourth Gospel," in Studies in the Fourth Gospel, ed. F. L. Cross, 1957, 36 ff; G. D. Kilpatrick, "What John Tells Us About John," Studies in John, Festschr. J. N. Sevenster, suppl. NovTest 24, 1970, 75 ff; S. Schulz, Untersuchungen zur Menschensohn-Christologie im Joh, 1957 (bibl.); idem, Komposition und Herkunft der joh. Reden, BWANT, 5, Series 1, 1960 (bibl.); H. Strathmann, EKL II, 1958, 357 ff; R. Schnackenburg, "Das vierte Ev. und die Johannesjünger," Historisches Jahrbuch 77, 1958, 21 ff; idem, LThK V, 1960, 1101 ff; idem, "Zur Herkunft des Joh," BZ, NF 14, 1970, 1 ff; idem, "Der Jünger, den Jesus liebte," EKK Vorarbeiten [preparatory vols.] 2, 1970, 97 ff; G. Baumbach, Qumran und das Joh, Aufsätze und Vorträge zur Theologie und Religionswissenschaft 6, 1958; L'Évangile de Jean. Études et Problèmes, RechB 3, 1958 (contains essays by M.-E. Boismard, H. van den Bussche, F.-M. Braun, G. Quispel); W. Wilkens,

Die Entstehungsgeschichte des vierten Ev., 1958 (on this see J. M. Robinson, JBL 78, 1959, 242 ff; C. K. Barrett, ThLZ 84, 1959, 828 ff); W. Wilkens, "Evangelist und Tradition im Joh," ThZ 16, 1960, 81 ff; P. Borgen, "John and the Synoptics in the Passion Narrative," NTS 5, 1958/59, 246 ff; O. Michel, CBL, 658 ff; E. Haenchen, "Joh. Probleme," ZThK 56, 1959, 19 ff (=E. H., *Gott und Mensch* 1965, 78 ff); *idem, Das Joh und sein Kommentar*, ThLZ 89, 1964, 881 ff (=E. H., *Die Bibel und wir*, 1968, 208 ff); A. Kragerud, *Der Lieblingsjünger im Joh*, 1959 (on this see W. Michaelis, ThLZ 85, 1960, 667 ff; M.-E. Boismard, RB 67, 1960, 405 ff); R. D. Potter, "Topography and Archeology in the Fourth Gospel," StEv, TU 73, 1959, 328 ff; W. C. van Unnik, "The Purpose of St. John's Gospel," StEv, TU 73, 1959, 382 ff; T. C. Smith, *Jesus in the Gospel of John*, 1959; J. A. T. Robinson, "The Destination and Purpose of St. John's Gospel," NTS 6, 1959/60 (= J. A. T. R., *Twelve NT Studies*, 1962, 107 ff); *idem*, "The Relation of the Prologue to the Gospel of John," NTS 6, 1962/63, 120 ff; A. Guilding, *The Fourth Gospel and Jewish Worship*, 1960 (on this see E. Haenchen, ThLZ 86, 1961, 670 ff); A. J. B. Higgins, *The Historicity of the Fourth Gospel*, 1960; *idem*, "The Words of Jesus According to St. John," BJRL 49, 1967, 363 ff; W. Grundmann, *Zeugnis und Gestalt des Joh*, ATh 7, 1960; H. M. Teeple, "Qumran and the Origin of the Fourth Gospel," NovTest 4, 1960, 6 ff; *idem*, "Methodology in Source Analysis of the Fourth Gospel," JBL 81, 1962, 279 ff; S. Temple, "The Two Traditions of the Last Supper, Betrayal, and Arrest," NTS 7, 1960/61, 77 ff; *idem*, "A Key to the Composition of the Fourth Gospel," JBL 80, 1961, 220 ff; *idem*, "The Two Signs in the Fourth Gospel," JBL 81, 1962, 175 ff; K. A. Eckhardt, *Der Tod des Johannes als Schlüssel zum Verständnis der joh. Schriften*, 1961; G. H. C. Macgregor and A. Q. Morton, *The Structure of the Fourth Gospel*, 1961 (on this see E. Haenchen, ThLZ 87, 1962, 487 ff); O. Merlier, *Le Quatrième Evangile. La Question johannique*, 1961; E. D. Johnston, "The Johannine Version of the Feeding of the Five Thousand—an Independent Tradition," NTS 8, 1961/62, 151 ff; H. Braun, "Qumran und das NT," ThR, NF 28, 1962, 192 ff (=H. B., *Qumran und das NT* 1, 1966, 96 ff; II, 1966, 118 ff); K. G. Kuhn, "Joh und Qumrantexte," *Neotestamentica et Patristica*, Festschr. O. Cullmann, suppl. NovTest 6, 1962, 111 ff; A. Bailey, *The Tradition Common to the Gospels of Luke and John*, suppl. NovTest 7, 1963; D. M. Smith, "John 12:12 ff and the Question of John's Use of the Synoptics," JBL 82, 1963, 58 ff; *idem, The Composition and Order of the Fourth Gospel: Bultmann's Literary Theory*, 1965; H. Balmforth, "The Structure of the Fourth Gospel," StEv II, TU 87, 1964, 25 ff; E. D. Freed, "Variations in the Language and Thought of John," ZNW 55, 1964, 167 ff; *idem, Old Testament Quotations in the Gospel of John*, suppl. NovTest 11, 1965; *idem*, "Samaritan Influence in the Gospel of John," CBQ 30, 1968, 580 ff; *idem*, "Did John Write His Gospel Partly to Win Samaritan Converts?" NovTest 12, 1970, 241 ff; S. Brown, "From Burney to Black: The

Fourth Gospel and the Aramaic Question," CBQ 26, 1964, 323 ff;
E. Grässer, "Die antijüdische Polemik im Joh," NTS 11, 1964/65, 74 ff;
J. W. Bowker, "The Origin and Purpose of St. John's Gospel," NTS
11, 1964/65, 398 ff; O. Böcher, *Der joh. Dualismus im Zusammenhang
des nachbiblischen Judentums,* 1965; J. Blinzler, *Joh. und die Synpt.,*
SBS 5, 1965; W. Gericke, "Zur Entstehung des Joh," ThLZ 90, 1965,
807 ff; C. Dekker, "Grundschrift und Redaktion im Joh," NTS 13,
1966/67, 66 ff; W. A. Meeks, *The Prophet-King: Moses Traditions and
the Johannine Christology,* suppl. NovTest 14, 1967 (on this see R.
Schnackenburg, BZ, NF 13, 1969, 136 ff); F. M. Cross, *The Ancient
Library of Qumran,* 1961, 195 ff; F. Neugebauer, *Die Entstehung des
Joh. Altes und Neues zur Frage seines historischen Ursprungs,* ATh I,
36, 1968; H. Leroy, *Rätsel und Missverständnis, Ein Beitrag zur Formgeschichte des Joh,* BBB 30, 1968; J. L. Martyn, *History and Theology
in the Fourth Gospel,* 1968 (on this see T. A. Burkill, JBL 87, 1968,
439 ff); J. L. Martyn, "Source Criticism and Religionsgeschichte in the
Fourth Gospel," *Perspective,* 427 ff; A. M. Hunter, *According to John,*
1968; G. W. Buchanan, "The Samaritan Origin of the Gospel of John,"
Religions in Antiquity: Festschr. E. R. Goodenough, suppl. Numen 14,
1968, 149 ff; D. Deeks, "The Structure of the Fourth Gospel," NTS
15, 1968/69, 107 ff; J. Roloff, "Der joh. 'Lieblingsjünger' und der
Lehrer der Gerechtigkeit," NTS 15, 1968/69, 129 ff; J. H. Charlesworth,
"A Critical Comparison of the Dualism in 1 Q S III, 13-IV, 26 and
the 'Dualism' Contained in the Fourth Gospel," NTS 15, 1968/69, 389 ff;
G. Dautzenberg, "Die Geschichte Jesu im Joh," GANT, 229 ff; J. Colson,
L'énigme du disciple que Jésus aimait, Théologie historique 10, 1969;
J. Becker, "Aufbau, Schichtung und theologiegeschichtliche Stellung
des Gebetes in Joh 17," ZNW 60, 1969, 56 ff; *idem,* "Wunder und
Christologie. Zum literarkritischen und christologischen Problem der
Wunder im Joh," NTS 16, 1969/70, 130 ff; *idem,* "Die Abschiedsreden
Jesu im Joh," ZNW 61, 1970, 215 ff; R. Fortna, *The Gospel of Signs:
A Reconstruction of the Narrative Source Underlying the Fourth Gospel,*
SNTSMS 11, 1970; *idem,* "Source and Redaction in the Fourth Gospel's
Portrayal of Jesus' Signs," JBL 89, 1970, 151 ff; L. Morris, *Studies in
the Fourth Gospel,* 1970; F. L. Cribbs, "A Reassessment of the Date of
Origin and the Destination of the Gospel of John," JBL 89, 1970, 38 ff;
G. W. McRae, "The Fourth Gospel and Religionsgeschichte," CBQ 32,
1970, 13 ff; F. Hahn, "Der Prozess Jesu nach dem Joh," EKK Vorar-
beiten 2, 1970, 97 ff; L. Schottroff, *Der Glaubende und die feindliche
Welt. Beobachtungen zum gnostischen Dualismus und seiner Bedeutung
für Paulus und das Joh,* WMANT 37, 1970; B. Rigaux, "Les déstinataires
du quatrième évangile à la lumière de Jean 17," Revue théologique de
Louvain 1, 1970, 289 ff; J. M. Robinson, "The Johannine Trajectory,"
in *Trajectories,* 232 ff; S. S. Smalley, "Diversity and Development in
John," NTS 17, 1970/71, 276 ff; G. Richter, "Die Fleischwerdung des
Logos im Joh," NovTest 13, 1971, 81 ff.

1. Contents

The Gospel of John is divided into two main sections: (1) Jesus' work in the world: 1:19–12:50. (2) His return to the Father: 13:1–20:29. Preceding is a prologue (1:1-18), and at the end is a supplement (Ch. 21). If this division once strikes the eye, any further dividing up of Jn becomes uncertain. While many scholars think that Jn has not been handed down in its original form, others have sought to show in the text as transmitted an ingenious arrangement according to the numbers 7, 3, and 5.[1] But none of this ingenious structuring can be demonstrated from the text,[2] and it may be appropriate to reject such a process.

The prologue announces the incarnation in Jesus Christ of the Logos that was with God "in the beginning," who brought grace and truth and who as "the only God of the kind" has made God known. In 1:6-8, 15 we hear of John the Baptist.

The first main section is introduced by the Baptist's testimonies to Jesus (1:19-34), and by accounts of the gathering of the first disciples around Jesus (1:35-51). At the wedding in Cana, Jesus discloses his majesty by means of his first sign, the changing of water into wine (2:1-11). He passes through Capernaum on the way to Jerusalem for the Passover, demonstrates his authority in cleansing the temple (2:12-22), and through his signs finds faith among many of the people (2:23-25). At night he instructs a Pharisee, Nicodemus, about entering the kingdom of God (3:1-21), Nicodemus dropping out of sight in 3:11. Jesus baptizes in the Jordan, receives testimony once more from John the Baptist (3:22-30), which in 3:31-36 is no longer clearly indicated as the words of the Baptist. On the way to Galilee he reveals himself at the well to a Samaritan woman as the dispenser of "living water" and the Messiah, but he finds faith among her fellow countrymen simply at his word (4:1-42). In the healing of the son of the royal official, Jesus performs his second sign in Galilee (4:43-54). At a feast in Jerusalem Jesus' first great controversy with the Jews over his authority as the Son arose as a result of his healing at the pool of Bethesda a man who had been lame for thirty-eight years (5:1-18, 19-47). Prior to the Passover (6:4) he is back in Galilee, where he feeds the five thousand on the eastern shore of the lake

---

[1] Thus in various ways Albertz; Lohmeyer; Hirsch (for the reconstructed basic document); Dodd (for Chs. 2–12); van den Bussche in RechB III, 108 f; Grundmann. Cf. also F.-M. Braun, *Jean*, 13 ff, and Deeks, who seeks to demonstrate four parts with 3x7 subdivisions, in the second half in reverse order.

[2] Cf. also Haenchen, ThR 1955, 311 ff.

(6:1-13). He withdraws as a result of the enthusiasm of those who had been fed, is overtaken by the crowd, and disputes with the Jews in the synagogue at Capernaum about the "bread of life" —that is, the eating of the flesh and drinking of the blood of Jesus (6:25-59). At that point the mass of disciples leave him (6:60-66), but through the mouth of Peter the twelve confess him to be the "Holy One of God," while Jesus predicts Judas' betrayal (6:67-71). At the Feast of Tabernacles, Jesus again goes to Jerusalem (7:1-13) and discusses his mission with the Jews (7:14-30). The council wants to arrest him (7:31-36); on the last day of the feast Jesus calls for faith in himself (7:37-44); the arrest miscarries, but the Jewish leaders reject him as a Galilean (7:45-52; 7:53–8:11, concerning the woman taken in adultery, is an interpolation). In further controversies (light and darkness; being from above and being from below; freedom and slavery; children of God and children of the Devil; Abraham and Jesus) the antipathy between him and the Jews comes to its sharpest point (8:12-59). The healing on the sabbath of the man born blind brings to light the blindness of the Pharisees (9:1-41). In the parable of the shepherd and the flock Jesus indicates himself as the true shepherd, and is thereupon declared to be obsessed (10: 1-21). When at the Feast of Dedication of the Temple he openly declares himself to be the Messiah, who is one with the Father, he is threatened with stoning and withdraws to Peraea (10:22-42). After the raising of Lazarus from the dead, in which Jesus reveals himself as "the resurrection and the life" (11:1-44), there follows the council's sentence of death against him (11:45-53; prior to the Passover, Jesus once more withdraws into isolation with his disciples (11:54-57), is anointed in Bethany by Mary (12:1-11), and greeted in Jerusalem by the people as King of Israel (12:12-19). When the Greeks want to see him, however, he speaks of the glorification through death which he is confronting (12:20-36a). After the report that Jesus has hidden himself again comes the accounting for the unbelief of the majority by reference to the fulfillment of prediction and a summary of the preaching of Jesus (12:36b-50) for which no situation is indicated.

The second main section[3] portrays (Chs. 13–17) Jesus' farewell to his disciples: the foot-washing at the meal as a symbol of puri-

---

[3] Hahn, 27 f, adduces noteworthy arguments for the assumption that the author intends Chs. 11–12 to serve as a bracket linking the earthly activity of Jesus with his suffering and death; G. Johnston, *The Spirit-Paraclete in the Gospel of John*, SNTSMS 12, 1970, 156 f, would also like to see 11:55–12:50 as a "bridge" between the public and the private activity of Jesus.

fication and serving love (13:1-20); designation of the betrayer (13:21-30); farewell address (13:31–16:33: departure from the disciples, commandment to love; allusion to Peter's denial, 13:31-38; consolation for his own: he is going to the Father but will return to them anew through the Spirit, Ch. 14; Jesus as the vine, 15:1-17; the hatred of the world, 15:18–16:4a; the coming of the Spirit, 16:4b-15; Jesus comes to his own in the perfected fellowship, 16:16-33); farewell or high-priestly prayer (Ch. 17:[4] petition for glorification, 17:1-8; prayer for the disciples, 17:9-19; prayer for those who come to faith through the disciples' word, 17:20-23; prayer for union with him, the glorified One, 17:24-26). Chs. 18–20 show the perfecting of Jesus: the passion narrative (Chs. 18–19: Jesus taken to prison, 18:1-11; Jesus in the house of Annas and the denial of Peter, 18:12-27; hearing before Pilate, 18:28-40; scourging, crowning with thorns, Pilate's delivering Jesus over to be crucified, 19:1-16a; crucifixion and death, 19:16b-30; piercing the side, with reference to the witnesses, 19:31-37; removal from the cross and burial, 19:38-42. Revelations of the risen Lord (20:1-29); discovery of the empty tomb (20:1-11); Jesus encounters Mary Magdalene (20:11-18); the risen Lord among his disciples, without Thomas (20:19-23) and with Thomas (20:24-29).

Conclusion: the aim of the book (20:30 f).

Postscript: Ch. 21: the revelation of the risen Lord by the Lake of Tiberias (21:1-14); the risen Lord with Peter and the beloved disciple (21:15-23); equating of the author with the beloved disciples, and the new conclusion (21:24, 25).

2. The History of the Johannine Question

Since the beginning of the third century it has been widely accepted that Jn originated with John the son of Zebedee, a member of the twelve, and that like Mt, it had as its author an eyewitness of the life of Jesus. But this view, which is attested as early as the end of the second century (see below, §10.6), has from the outset not been free from dispute. Irenaeus (*Haer.* III. 11. 12) knows of people who reject the Johannine promise of the Spirit-Paraclete (Jn 14:16 f; 15:26; 16:7) and thus "reject the Gospel [of Jn] as well as the prophetic Spirit." Caius, the Roman presbyter who wrote at the beginning of the third century, obviously

[4] On the structure cf. Rigaux, 293 f.

sharing the same aim of depriving the Montanists of the scriptural support for their doctrine of the present Paraclete, designated both Jn and Rev as works of the Gnostic Cerinthus, and in so doing exploited as an argument the deviation of Jn from the Synoptics.[5] The same origin of Jn is represented by a group of anti-Montanists within the church, to whom Epiphanius (*Panarion* 51) assigned the epithet "Alogoi." [6] This criticism of the apostolic authorship of Jn, which arose from polemic against heretics, had little enduring effect, but shows that the wording of Jn permitted such a criticism and that the comparison of Jn with the Synoptics had in this connection a decisive importance. It was in the eighteenth century that once again individual voices began to be raised against Jn's having originated with an apostle; by the beginning of the nineteenth century several theologians had adopted this view and, in addition to the differences between Jn and the Synoptics, showed the contradictions within the text of Jn, which led to the theory of the use of sources or of secondary editing (see WGK, NT, 85 f). K. G. Bretschneider, a general superintendent in Gotha, in a writing which appeared in 1820, *Probabilia de evangelii et epistularum Joannis, apostoli, indole et origine* [Probabilities concerning the nature and origin of the Gospel and Epistles of John], adduced—in addition to the difference between the teaching of Jesus in the Synoptics and that in Jn—the non-Jewish character and the late attestation of Jn as arguments against the apostolic origin of Jn. The strong opposition that arose led Bretschneider four years later to withdraw his critical view (see WGK, NT, 86). But in spite of the great influence of Schleiermacher, who on the basis of its spiritual content attributed Jn to an eyewitness, the critical objections could no longer be silenced. D. F. Strauss in his *Life of Jesus* (1835/36) sought to show that in Jn was presented a more developed form of "myth" compared to the Synoptics, so that the question of Jn as a historical source was not to be considered (cf. WGK, NT, 124 ff). Though it was widely perceived as negative, Strauss's criticism was made methodologically certain by F. C. Baur's *Kritische Untersuchungen über die kanonischen Evv.* (1847), in which he maintained that Jn, written in the later second century, contained no historically valuable tradition; but at the same time he stressed that Jn did not aim to be a historical account but sought to present an idea (see WGK, NT, 128 f). If in this way the distinctive historical ques-

[5] Cf. F.-M. Braun, *Jean*, 147 f.
[6] See Goguel, *Intr.* II, 158 ff; Schnackenburg, Comm. I, 180 f; H. Merkel, *Widersprüche zwischen den Evv.*, WUNT 13, 1971, 34 ff.

tion about the aim of Jn and its relations to its origins displaced the ordinary criticism of the tradition, the discussion concentrated first of all on the question of the authenticity and historical value of Jn. Baur's late dating of Jn in the second century evoked little reaction, while his contesting of the apostolic origin and his assertion that the sources of Jn were of lesser value than those of the Synoptics persuaded many,[7] though conservative scholarship defended the eyewitness testimony and the apostolic origin of Jn.[8]

This discussion, which has continued to the present, has since the middle of the nineteenth century moved concurrently with other questions which to some extent aroused interest among the critics at the beginning of the nineteenth century.[9] In order to explain or to dismiss the numerous difficulties which the course of the narrative as well as the sequence of ideas in Jn offers, four basic theses have been proposed or interlinked: (a) Since 1871 many adherents have been gained by the view, occasionally represented in the Middle Ages, that the text of Jn as we have received it is out of order because of shuffling of the sheets, or that it was left unfinished by its author and incorrectly organized by his pupils. The task of the present-day scholar, therefore, and the indispensable prerequisite for suitable exegesis, is to restore the sequence intended by the original author.[10] (b) Since the beginning of the nineteenth century the view has often been proposed that the traditional text of Jn achieved its present form through the merging of several sources or through the extensive expansion of a basic apostolic document.[11] Since these partition theories have proved to be methodologically inadequate and accordingly have long been abandoned, we need go into them no further here. (c) Methodologically related to the partition theories is the proposal, which since the time of Schwartz and Wellhausen (1907) has been presented in the most varied forms, that a redactor, or redactors, have expanded the original Gospel, rearranged it, adapted it to the church situation. The points of departure for such theories are items which are literarily and doctrinally offensive.[12] (d) The juxtaposition of narratives

---

[7] Cf., e.g., Weizsäcker, Jülicher; see WGK, NT, 172, 177.

[8] E.g., Schlatter, B. Weiss, Zahn.

[9] Cf. the rather overdrawn distinctions in the methodological history by Schulz, *Untersuchungen,* 39 ff.

[10] See the history of these theories in Howard, 111 ff, 303; Uricchio; F.-M. Braun, *Jean,* 23; Schnackenburg, *Comm.* I, 41 ff.

[11] See Schulz, *Untersuchungen,* 48 ff.

[12] See the surveys by Howard, 95 ff, 297 ff, Schweizer, 84 ff, Schulz, *Untersuchungen,* 62 ff. In addition, most recently Dekker, according to whom a basic

and extensive speeches, and the occasional, though infrequent, contacts of Jn with the Synoptics, have since the beginning of the nineteenth century led to the question whether Jn is dependent on the Synoptics, but at the same time they have led to the conjecture that the author of Jn has used not only individual traditions but large, comprehensive sources.[13] Recently the tenability of such source theories has been fundamentally challenged by means of word statistics.[14]

Since the beginning of the present century the history-of-religions approach to Jn has been added to those of historical and literary criticism. Besides the usually posed alternatives, "Jewish or Greek background" for the conceptual world of Jn, in the twentieth century the supposition has been advanced that Near Eastern Gnosticism is the intellectual context in which Jn belongs, and since the discovery of the writings of the Qumran community the influence on Jn of the thought world of Qumran has been asserted with more or less certainty.[15]

On the answer to the history-of-religions questions hangs in large measure the decision concerning a problem with which research on Jn has been keenly occupied and which points up the theological issue in the narrower sense: the question of the aim of Jn and the readers for whom it was written. This question was often posed as an alternative: Jewish or Hellenistic readers? Beyond that, since Baldensperger first proved that there was in Jn a recognizable polemic against the disciples of John the Baptist, a polemical goal for Jn has been sought on various fronts. Recently the long-abandoned assumption of a missionary aim for Jn has been presented several times.[16] Here there can only be summary reference to the intensive research into Johannine theology over recent decades.[17]

---

document with Palestinian-Jewish linguistic characteristics has been expanded by a redactor, who exhibits non-Palestinian-Jewish linguistic characteristics (e.g., Ch. 6 is a non-Jewish addition).

[13] Cf. Menoud, *L'Évangile*, 16 ff; Ruckstuhl, 10 ff; Haenchen, ThR 1955, 302 ff.

[14] Esp. Menoud, Schweizer, Ruckstuhl.

[15] See the accounts in L. Schmid; Menoud, *L'Évangile*, 30 ff, and RechB III, 20 ff; Haenchen, ThR 1955, 313 ff; Schulz, *Untersuchungen*, 43 ff, and recently Schnackenburg, *Comm.* I, 101 ff; McRae.

[16] See below, p. 229.

[17] Cf. the reports in Menoud, *L'Évangile*, 51 ff; Haenchen, ThR 1955, 326 ff; Schnackenburg, *NT Theology*; Vawter; W. G. Kümmel, *Das Nt im 20. Jh.*, SBS 50, 1970, 105 ff.

3. The Literary Character and the Sources
of the Gospel of John

Jn belongs to the same literary genre, "gospel," as the Synoptics, just as in this writing too the activity of Jesus is narrated from the time of his association with John the Baptist until his death, and the account of the resurrection of Jesus is attached as a conclusion. In Jn as in the Synoptics there are stories of Jesus' miracles side by side with those about his instructional activity. In spite of this, on purely external grounds Jn is to be distinguished from the Synoptics in three ways: (*a*) While in the Synoptics Jesus' ministry is confined to Galilee and vicinity with the one final journey to Jerusalem that ends in the crucifixion, in Jn's account Jesus goes three times from Galilee to Jerusalem (2:13; 5:1; 7:10). And while Jesus' stay in Jerusalem is about a week long according to Mk 11–15, according to Jn he remains in Jerusalem and Judea from 7:10 on. (*b*) This stay in Jerusalem continues from a Feast of Tabernacles (7:2) through a Feast of Dedication (10:22) to the Passover (11:55; 12:1; 18:28), or about half a year. Furthermore, Jn 2:13 mentions a Passover and 6:4 speaks of the nearness of the Passover; 5:1 (according to the best-attested text) mentions only "a feast," and whether a Passover is meant or not cannot be determined. But even if 5:1 is left out of consideration, the ministry of Jesus according to Jn 2–19 encompasses more than two years, of which the last half-year is in Judea and Jerusalem. The chronological inferences from Mk 2:23—ripening of the grain between Passover and the Feast of Weeks—and Mk 14:1 suggest a ministry of Jesus lasting not more than a year. The chronological and topographical framework of Jn is quite different from that of the Synoptics, therefore. (*c*) The report of the acts and teachings of Jesus in the Synoptics is composed from individual accounts and individual sayings or groups of sayings, which are linked together in a sequence of actions and sayings. Only the passion story forms a larger connected account (see above, §5.2.5). Sporadically Jn also includes individual narratives (2:1-10, 13-21; 4:46-53; 12:1-9, 12-15; 13:36-38), and the passion story forms a large connected narrative. But in the main Jn consists of large sayings complexes which often take off from a preceding narrative (Chs. 4, 5, 6, 9, 11). And these sayings complexes are not formed by juxtaposing individual sayings, but revolve around a theme or several themes, partly in dialogue

form, so that with some justification one may speak of the
"dramatic" character of the Johannine accounts.[18]

Just as Jn differs sharply from the Synoptics in the framework
of his account and in the manner of his presentation, so also
he differs in material. Jn has only a few narratives in common
with the Synoptics: call of the disciples (1:35 ff); the healing of
the official's son (4:46 ff); the feeding of the five thousand and
the walking on the lake (6:1 ff, 16 ff); the confession of Peter
(6:66 ff); the entrance into Jerusalem (12:12 ff); the Last Supper
with the prediction of the betrayal (13:1 ff), and a few sections
of the passion story. The cleansing of the temple (2:13 ff) and the
anointing in Bethany (12:1 ff) correspond to pericopes in the
Synoptics, but they stand in other contexts. On the other hand,
Jn offers a few miracle stories not transmitted in the Synoptics:
the marriage at Cana (2:1 ff); the healing of the lame man at the
pool of Bethesda (5:1 ff); the healing of the man born blind (9:
1 ff), and the resurrection of Lazarus (11:1 ff); the stories of
Nicodemus (3:1 ff) and the Samaritan woman (4:5 ff) are also
found only in Jn. Frequently Jn presupposes a situation narrated
in the Synoptics without telling it himself: the baptizing activity
of the Baptist (1:25); the sayings of the Baptist (1:26 f); the
baptism of Jesus (1:32); the imprisonment of John the Baptist
(3:24); the circle of the twelve (6:67 ff); 20:24; the Gethsemane
scene (12:27). Sayings of Jesus are occasionally reminiscent of
synoptic sayings: cf. Jn 2:19 = Mk 14:58 par.; 3:3 = Mt 18:3;
3:35 = Mt 11:27 par.; 4:44 = Mk 6:4 par.; 5:23b, 13:20 = Lk 10:
16 par. Mt 10:40 and 12:5 = Mk 8:35 par.; 13:16, 15:20 = Mt 10:24;
15:7b = Mk 11:24 par.; 16:23 = Mt 7:7 par.; 16:32 = Mk 14:27
par.; 18:11 = Mk 14:36 par.; 20:23 = Mt 18:18. Yet these sayings
are scarcely ever in the same setting as in the Synoptics. The great
majority of the Johannine sayings have no parallel in the Synoptics,
and the language of the Johannine speeches is completely different
from that of the Synoptic Jesus.

In view of the occasional contacts of Jn with the Synoptics,
leaving aside the fact that the Johannine narratives are vastly
different, the question arises whether there is any literary link
between Jn and the Synoptics.[19] The opinion was long dominant
that Jn knew and presupposed the Synoptics, or at least Mk, but
since Gardner-Smith's research (1938) the view that Jn knew
none of the Synoptics and that he created his Gospel from a com-

---

[18] Windisch, *Erzählungsstil*; Connick, Noack, 116 f; Martyn, *History and
Theology*, xxi, 5 ff.
[19] On the history of the problem, see Blinzler, 16 ff.

pletely independent tradition has gained many adherents.[20] Still more common is the assumption that Jn knew none of our Gospels but did know the tradition that these Gospels preserve.[21] The arguments that have been adduced against the connection between Jn and the Synoptics are in the main two: (a) The number of texts in which Jn's dependence on the Synoptics can with some justification be defended is astonishingly small, and closer examination shows that even in these texts the differences are far greater than the agreements. (b) The overall framework of Jn differs from that of the Synoptics and shows that Jn's acquaintance with the tradition that shows affinities with the Synoptics could not have been through the medium of the Synoptics, and that perhaps Jn did not know the same tradition in a single instance. We cannot consider the additional arguments that are advanced—that a Gospel which is by an eyewitness cannot be dependent on a source which is not from an eyewitness, and that the superiority of Jn's account in historical detail can only be explained if Jn preserves a tradition independent of and partly superior to the Synoptics (thus, e.g., Michaelis)—because the premises of this line of argument must themselves be ascertained if the conclusions are to be allowed.

But even the two arguments mentioned above are scarcely sufficient to exclude the possibility that Jn knew or used the Synoptics, and so many scholars summarily assert that Jn knew the Synoptics,[22] while others accept Jn's dependence on Mk and Lk[23] or on Mk alone.[24] Supporting Jn's knowledge of Mk is the fact that several scenes and brief historical notes appear in Jn in the same sequence as in Mk, and that in many of these places there are clear verbal echoes.[25] Especially striking is the agreement of Jn 6:7 with Mk 6:37 διακοσίων δηναρίων ἄρτοι; of Jn 5:8 with Mk 2:11 ἆρον τὸν κράβατόν σου; of Jn 12:3 with Mk 14:3 (λίτραν)

[20] Sanders; Michaelis; Menoud; J. A. T. Robinson, Manson, Wilkens, Higgins.
[21] Among others, Bultmann, R. E. Brown, Schnackenburg; Feine-Behm, Feuillet in Robert-Feuillet, Fuller, Harrington, Heard, Klijn; Hunter, Schniewind, Käsemann, Connick, Mendner, Dodd, Noack, Parker, Borgen, Haenchen, Grundmann, Johnston, D. M. Smith, Böcher, Martyn, Fortna, Morris, Hahn, Rigaux, Robinson. Buse and Temple assume Jn's knowledge of one of the sources of Mk.
[22] Lightfoot, Strathmann; Höpfl-Gut, McNeile-Williams; Hirsch, Maurer, Goodwin, Freed. The "proof" of a relationship between Jn and all three Synoptics offered by K. Hanhart, "The Structure of Jn 1:35–4:54," *Studies in John: Festschr. J. N. Sevenster,* Suppl. NovTest 24, 1972, 22 ff, is sheer fantasy.
[23] Barrett; Sparks; Howard, Teeple, Bailey; B. H. Streeter, *The Four Gospels,* 1924.
[24] Meinertz; R. M. Grant, HTR, 1942; Lee, Balmforth, Blinzler, Gericke. Only Sparks, JTS 1952, has explicitly defended Jn's knowledge of Mt.
[25] Cf. the lists in Barrett, *Comm.,* 34 ff; Blinzler, 52 ff.

μύρου νάρδου πιστικῆς πολυτελοῦς (or πολυτίμου; in all three cases only Jn and Mk have this wording). In a series of other instances the contact of Jn with Mk is just as unmistakable (Jn 4:44 par. Mk 6:4; Jn 6:20 par. Mk 6:50; Jn 12:7 f par. Mk 14:7 f; Jn 19:17 par. Mk 15:22; Jn 19:29 par. Mk 15:36), but in these cases Mt is paralleling Mk, so that only a contact with Mt or Mk can be asserted.[26]

The literary connection of Jn with Lk is also very probable. Indicative of this is the prominence of the same names (Mary and Martha, Lazarus, Annas) and detailed features (Jn 13:2, 27 par. Lk 22:3; Jn 13:38 par. Lk 22:34; Jn 18:10 par. Lk 22:50), but above all the story of the anointing (Jn 12:3 ff par. Lk 7:36 ff). For the Johannine account of the senseless act of the anointing by Mary (she anoints the feet of Jesus and dries them with her hair) can be explained in one of two ways: (1) Either Jn has combined the story (Mk 14:3 ff par. Mt 26:6 ff) of the anointing of Jesus' head by a woman with the story (Lk 7:36 ff) in which (according to the majority of MSS) a sinful woman wets Jesus' feet with her tears and dries them with her hair;[27] or (2) in line with the illuminating argument of K. Weiss, Jn in the copy available to him did not read τοὺς πόδας μου in Lk 7:46,[28] so that Lk originally described only the wetting, drying, and kissing of Jesus' feet and the anointing of Jesus—that is, his head (cf. also Jn 11: 2!). Jn misunderstood this account, and said that the woman had anointed Jesus' feet and dried them (Jn 12:3). In either case, however, Jn's knowledge of Lk must be assumed.[29]

Less clear is the decision whether Jn also knew Mt. Those features where there is similarity in content (Jn 18:11 par. Mt 26:52; Jn 20:23 par. Mt 18:18) differ greatly linguistically. The saying about the slave and the master (Jn 15:20, cf. 13:16) has a clear link not only with Mt 10:24 f but also with its wider context (see Sparks), but this link is not close enough to be considered evidence for literary dependence.[30] Only on the basis of the texts

[26] Further examples in Lee.

[27] Thus Bailey, 1 ff.

[28] These words are missing in the "Western" textual witnesses D, W, 079, b, q.

[29] Parker wants to recognize a tradition common to Jn and Lk only ("the fourth evangelist must somewhere, some time have been associated with Lk in the Christian missionary enterprise," 336), while Bailey points out the kinship in the passion section between Jn and the Lukan alterations of Mk, but in addition he postulates the common use by Lk and Jn of written individual narratives. Blinzler, 57 f, considers it likely that Jn knew Lk only.

[30] Cf. Gardner-Smith, JTS 1953; C. H. Dodd, NTS 1955/56, 76 f; Blinzler, 58 f.

cited above for the dependence of Jn on Mk as well as Mt can the assumption be made of a literary link between Jn and Mt.

Though the question whether Jn knew Mt must remain undecided, Jn's knowledge of Mk and Lk can be asserted with greater probability, and knowledge of the Synoptics as a genre can be presupposed for Jn in any case.[31] As is true of the question of the literary relationship between the Synoptics (see above, §5.3.8b), this dependence is not to be represented as direct reworking of a written copy. Obviously the author knew the Gospels of Mk and Lk from memory and utilized them as seemed to him useful, according to his recollection (cf. Lee). But he used them in a very different way from the Synoptics' use of their sources. On the one hand, he took only a small part of the material known to him from the Synoptic Gospels, did not use these earlier Gospels as an exemplar, but occasionally inserted material known to him from these Gospels into his own presentation. On the other hand, Jn treated the materials he took over with complete freedom, as is shown by the manner in which he employs OT quotations from memory, shapes them anew, and combines them.[32] Thus the texts taken over from the Synoptics are extensively incorporated in language and form into the Johannine account and comprise only one woof in the fabric of the entire Gospel. Establishing the literary relationship of Jn to Mk and Lk therefore accounts for the echoes of the Synoptics in Jn, but does not enable us to understand the literary character of Jn.

The comparison of Jn with the synoptic material has shown a difference, not only of material, but in the chronological structure as well. If this framework is examined more closely a series of contradictions is immediately apparent.[33] Jn 6:1 presupposes that Jesus is in Galilee, although in 5:1 he is in Jerusalem. 7:3 f seems to presuppose that Jesus has not yet been in Jerusalem, in spite of 2:23 and 5:1. 7:19-23 refers back to the death plot of the Jews reported in 5:18 at least a half-year earlier. In 10:19-29a controversy arises on account of an event (9:1 ff) that took place three months before, and 10:33 ties in to a statement made by Jesus a half-year earlier (5:18). At the end of the farewell discourse (14:31) is the concluding sentence "Arise; let us go on our way," although the discourse proceeds for two more chapters (15–16) on the same themes. In addition to these contradictions

[31] Thus Dautzenberg, 232.
[32] See the evidence in Noack, 84, and Goodwin.
[33] Cf. Schnackenburg, *Comm.* I, 34 ff; Wellhausen, *Comm.,* 5 f; Schweizer, 84 ff.

in the narrative sequence, there are breaks in the line of thought: 3:31 ff fits poorly on the lips of the Baptist, but well on the lips of Jesus in connection with 3:21; 12:44 ff, following after the conclusion, 12:36b-43, leads into a speech without a situation. Jesus' self-designation as "the door" (10:7, 9) fits poorly the shepherd discourse (10:1-6, 11 ff). Since the time of Tatian, who reversed the order of Chs. 5 and 6, and the Sinaitic Syriac, which interchanges the Annas and Caiaphas scenes (18:13-24),[34] these and similar difficulties have led to the assumption that the text of Jn has not reached us in the sequence intended by the author, either because the author died before the work was completed, or because subsequent to completion pages were switched round or a similar disorganization occurred. By rearranging Ch. 5 after 6, or 10:19-29 before 10:1, etc., the attempt has been made to restore the original, sensible sequence.[35] But there are weighty considerations against this assumption.[36] Above all, it is paleographically most unlikely.[37] If it were a matter of switching round entire leaves, the contents of the interchanged leaves would have to be of about the same length. But attempts to prove this[38] fail, since in no case is the space occupied by these allegedly interchanged sheets of the same extent or a multiple of it.[39] There are some isolated examples from antiquity of the interchange of sheets,[40] but it never occurs in a series of sections from the same work. And if one feels compelled to assume the displacement of sections of varying lengths, there is no evidence that it was at all customary to write out drafts on single sheets. If one assumes that the

---

[34] See the apparatus in the Nestle-Aland edition of the NT or in Aland's *Synopsis* (on 18:13).

[35] Recently rearrangements of greater or lesser extent have been proposed by, e.g., Bernard, Bultmann, Schnackenburg; Dautzenberg, R. M. Grant, Wikenhauser; Menoud, Howard, Hirsch, Schweizer, Jeremias in ThBl 1941, Käsemann, Mendner, Wilkens, Guilding, Grundmann, Eckhardt, Macgregor, Merlier, Becker, Hahn. D. M. Smith has reconstructed what Bultmann proposed as the original order of the text, *Composition*, 179 ff.

[36] Cf. Barrett, R. E. Brown, Lightfoot, Sanders; Goodspeed, Guthrie, Harrington, Klijn, Michaelis, W. G. Wilson, Dodd; Parker in JBL 1956; Teeple in JBL 1962; Deeks.

[37] See on this Haenchen, ThLZ 1964, 805 f (=*Die Bibel und wir*, 214 f); D. M. Smith, *Composition*, 176 f; J. Jeremias, TDNT VI, 494 f; K. Aland, "Glosse, Interpretation, Redaktion und Komposition in der Sicht der nt. Textkritik," *Apophoreta*, Festschr. E. Haenchen, Bh ZNW 30, 1964, 22 f (=K. Aland, *Studien zur Überlieferung des NT und seines Textes*, ANTF 2, 1967, 49 ff).

[38] See Schweizer, 110 f.

[39] Cf. W. G. Wilson; Parker, JBL 1956.

[40] Schweizer, 109 n. 161; Jeremias, TDNT VI, 495.

sheets of the original MS were assembled in random sequence, it is strange not only that the sections allegedly out of sequence always begin and end with complete sentences, but also that the redactor with the sheets in his hand could not arrange them in proper order while we who lack the sheets are supposedly able to do so.

If it is assumed there was interchange, not only of the larger sections but also of smaller units as well (Bultmann, for example, thinks the original sequence in 6:27-59 was: 27, 34 f, 30-33, 47-51a, 41-46), it is completely impossible to determine the form in which the redactor must have found these small bits of text. The assumption of a secondary transposition in very many cases presupposes what must first be proved a justifiable presupposition: that the author intended to present a structure free of topographical and chronological contradictions and a logical setting forth of the discourses of Christ. But in fact a meaningful arrangement of the material by the evangelist is not always discernible, and in these cases the exegete who rejects the theory of secondary transpositions should "settle for establishing the difficulties [aporiai]." [41] But on the whole "no one has shown convincingly that the Gospel has been disarranged," [42] so that hypotheses of secondary transposition cannot solve the literary problem of Jn.

Occasionally the secondary transposition of Jn has been assigned to the evangelist himself, and in this case the paleographical difficulty would not obtain. According to Wilkens, the basic Gospel of the author was a "Gospel of signs" which contained only the narratives and, like the Synoptics, traced the path of Jesus from Galilee to Jerusalem. The evangelist expanded this basic Gospel with discourses which he shaped first and then inserted in the Gospel without altering its basic outline. Finally, by rearranging the combined Gospel and adding further material, he reworked the whole into a passion Gospel, without being able to bring the project to completion. But this history of the origin of Jn is neither demonstrable nor probable,[43] since why would the author have subsequently and systematically wrecked his beautifully constructed Gospel and thus have created the difficulties whose origin this theory is intended to explain? The same objection is valid for Parker's theory (JBL 1956); he rejects transpositions, but assumes that the author has added not only Ch. 21 but also 2:1-12 and Chs. 4 and 6 subsequent to completion of the Gospel, and that he

[41] Bultmann, NTS 1954/55, 86.
[42] Teeple, JBL 1962, 286.
[43] Cf. the criticism in Barrett, ThLZ 1959.

has not checked whether the additions fit their contexts. Other scholars have attempted to solve the literary problem of Jn by assuming a later redaction of the Gospel, in part with the conjecture of systematic transpositions. As a rule the starting point for these hypotheses is the observation that there are additions in Ch. 21 and 7:53–8:11. The pericope of the woman taken in adultery (7:53–8:11) does not belong in the original tradition of Jn, as shown by the manuscript evidence,[44] the linguistic form, and the uncertain position (disruptive in some MSS and variable in others). Perhaps it was introduced as an illustration of 8:15.[45]

That Ch. 21 represents a supplement is incontestable, because 20:30 is unmistakably the end of the book. The question is only whether this supplement originates with the evangelist or with someone else. On the basis of the MS tradition available to us, Jn never circulated without Ch. 21. Yet Jn 21 offers some striking differences from Jn 1–20: in 21:2 the sons of Zebedee, elsewhere missing, suddenly appear; the Christophany in 21:3 takes place in Galilee, while Ch. 20 is set in Jerusalem; in 21:23 the death of the beloved disciple is presupposed, but in 21:24 he is attested as author of Jn. While the author could say of himself in 21:24a, "This is the disciple who bears witness of this and has written it," 21:24b, "And we know that his witness is true," could not come from him and does not fit with the indication of his death in 21:23. 21:25 also, with its exaggerated, aretalogical style, is a complete departure from the style of Jn. The attempt has been made to link the assumption that the evangelist wrote 21:1-23 with the assumption that 21:24, 25 (or at least 21:25) is not authentic in such a way that 20:30 is said to be the original ending of Jn which stood first after 21:23; from there it was displaced to its present position by a pupil of the evangelist who wanted to insert a witness to him (21:24-25).[46] But this resolution of the difficulty is impossible: it does not explain why anyone would have inserted 20:30 f before 21:1, nor could 21:23 or 21:24a be a tolerable ending to the book. 21:24b is in no way possible on the lips of the author. Most authors who want to consider Jn 21 a supplement by the author of Jn 1–20 explain 21:24 f

[44] It is lacking in the oldest Greek MSS, from $\mathcal{P}^{66,75}$ on and from the oldest witnesses for the Latin, Syriac and Coptic versions, but even in more recent Greek MSS it is not always present.

[45] Cf. the excurses by Barrett, Bauer, R. E. Brown (bibl.), Zahn (*in loc.*); Aland (see n. 37), 11 ff, cf. also 39 ff; U. Becker, *Jesus und die Ehebrecherin. Untersuchungen zur Text- und Überlieferungsgeschichte von Joh 7,53-8:11*, Bh. ZNW 28, 1963 (bibl.).

[46] Lagrange; Menoud, Vaganay (who considers 21:24 genuine).

as an addition by a pupil of the author.[47] But the assumption that Jn 21 is by the author encounters considerable difficulties. The fact that v. 24 must be separated out in order to assert the same authorship for 1–20 and 21:1-23 is precarious, since on other grounds there is no occasion for the insertion. But then arise the already mentioned substantive difficulties and the improbability that the same author would have added a supplement of this kind without relocating or removing the concluding words in 20:30 f. But above all there are linguistic difficulties. Scholars[48] have referred to linguistic agreements between Ch. 21 and the rest of Jn (e.g., ἀνθρακιά, ὀψάριον, μέντοι, 21:24, cf. with 5:32), but these contacts can be understood as conscious or unconscious literary adaptation. In fact, the linguistic differences are more numerous:[49] there are not only words which are never used in Jn (e.g., ἰσχύειν), but also divergent linguistic habits (e.g., ἀπό in the partitive sense, ἐπιστραφείς instead of στραφείς) which are scarcely conceivable in the same author.[50] All these observations show that with a high degree of probability, Jn 21 must be regarded as an addition by a later hand.[51] A conjecture about the purpose of this supplement can be offered only when we have considered the question of authorship.

If Jn 21 was added by a later hand, the question arises whether the hand of this redactor is to be traced elsewhere. Since in 19:35 the trustworthiness of the witness for the death of Jesus is spoken of in a manner similar to mention of the writer in 21:24 and interrupts the logical connection, 19:35 has often been regarded as an insertion by the author of the supplement.[52] If a redactor has been at work on the Gospel at all, then one may ask why other

---

[47] Tenney; Grant, Höpfl-Gut, Meinertz, Schäfer; Howard, Jeremias, Ruckstuhl, Wilkens, Grundmann; C. F. D. Moule, "The Individualism of the Fourth Gospel," NovTest 5, 1962, 177. According to Tasker only v. 25 is an addition by a pupil of the author; according to Sanders, *Comm.*, 48, only καὶ ὁ γράψας ταῦτα is added. According to Bauer, Schlatter; Mariani; Cassian, Kragerud, the whole of Ch. 21 comes from the author of 1–20.

[48] Schweizer, 108 n. 158; Boismard, RB 1947, 474 ff.

[49] Cf. Boismard, RB 1947, 484 ff; Merlier, 151 ff.

[50] Ruckstuhl's objections (143 ff) against these conclusions are evasions; yet Freed, ZNW 1964, 192 ff, has noted that the linguistic variations between Jn 1–20 and 21 must be placed in comparison with similar variations within 1–20.

[51] Thus, e.g., Barrett, R. E. Brown, Bultmann, Lightfoot, Mastin, Schnackenburg, Strathmann; Albertz, Dautzenberg, Feine-Behm, Fuller, Goguel, Goodspeed, Harrington, Klijn, McNeile-Williams, Marxsen, Michaelis, Schelkle, Wikenhauser; Dibelius, Hirsch, Käsemann, Dodd, Teeple, Eckhardt, H. Braun, D. M. Smith; R. Pesch, *Der reiche Fischfang*, 1969, 39, 102. Feuillet in Robert-Feuillet; Jülicher and Schweizer consider a decision impossible.

[52] Bultmann; Goguel, Marxsen, Wikenhauser; Bacon, Hirsch. Jeremias considers only 19:35 and 21:24 to be redactional.

passages which disturb the flow of thought or which resemble
the Synoptics (e.g., 1:22-24, 27, 32; 3:24; 4:2; 11:2; 16:5b; 18:9,
13b, 14, 24, 32) or texts which in terms of content stand in tension with Johannine teachings (the future eschatological sayings
in 5:28 f; 6:39 f, 44b, 54; 12:48, and the references to baptism
and the Lord's Supper in 3:5 [ὕδατος καί]; 6:51b-58; 19:34b)
could not also be additions by a redactor. Indeed linguistic arguments in support of some of these can be advanced.[53] Others go
farther and try to reconstruct a basic document which a redactor
has expanded by using synoptic and other material.[54] Preisker
reconstructs a primitive eschatological Gospel; according to Eckhardt, Ignatius worked over a Johannine sketch, and this writing
was then expanded a second time. Boismard (RB, 1962) deduces
from the contradictions in Jn and the echoes of Lk that Luke
has joined the Johannine material to an account, expanded individual scenes, and reintroduced material that he had earlier excluded.[55] J. Becker assumes there were expansions by various hands
—"anonymous growth"[56]—in Chs. 14–17, while Brown[57] wants
to discern five steps in the development of Jn, of which the
fourth and fifth represent the insertion of material originally
excluded by the evangelist and further introduction by a redactor
of this and alien material. Richter wants to exclude all texts which
presuppose the incarnation as being anti-Docetic corrections supplied by a redactor (1:14-18; 5:28 f; 6:51b-58, etc.) on the basis
of the intention expressed in 20:31. Naturally it is quite possible
that interpolations were made in the text before the MSS were
written on which our entire MS tradition is based. Understandably
the text reads more smoothly when the disruptive textual passages
are removed. Though there are no fundamental considerations
against assuming that there were individual redactional additions,
it is highly questionable whether ineptitude in presentation could
be assigned as well to the evangelist as to a redactor. On substantive grounds it is highly improbable that the futuristic eschatological passages are interpolated, because futuristic eschatology is found
also in uncontested places (3:5; 10:9; 12:32; 14:3; 17:24) and

[53] Bultmann, Schnackenburg; Marxsen; Bacon, Jeremias, Käsemann, Temple,
JBL, 1961; Teeple, JBL, 1962; G. Klein, "Das wahre Licht scheint schon,"
ZThK 68, 1971, 296 n. 144.

[54] Cf. n. 12; further Schwartz, Wellhausen, Hirsch, Mendner, Temple in
JBL 1961, Merlier.

[55] Boismard, RB 1962 and 1963.

[56] J. Becker, ZNW 1969, 76.

[57] R. E. Brown, *Comm.* I, xxiv ff.

is theologically indispensable.[58] The passage relating to the Lord's Supper (6:51b-58), which has repeatedly been designated as a sacramental insertion,[59] is linguistically thoroughly Johannine.[60] The passage is suspect on the basis of its content only if, on what are surely inadequate grounds, one is already convinced that Jn is to be interpreted along spiritualizing or existentialist lines and that he has no interest in the sacraments. There is good reason, therefore, to regard 6:51b-58 as an original part of Jn,[61] so that the words ὕδατος καί in 3:5 and the reference to the baptism and the Lord's Supper in 19:34b are in no way to be regarded as interpolations. The assumption that a redactor is responsible for the present order of material in Jn cannot be demonstrated as probable on the basis of redactional inserts, but neither is the reverse true.

The still more far-ranging hypotheses according to which Jn developed through the extensive expansion of a basic document[62] can only be characterized as arbitrary and undemonstrable. The insoluble difficulties [aporiai], as recently Mendner and Merlier would like to describe them, are difficulties only if one applies to the text a completely inappropriate standard of logic and narrative sequence. If the conversation with Nicodemus recounted in Jn 3 originally stood between 7:45-52a and 8:13 f, and included only 3:13a, 7b, 9 f, 12b, 13a, 31a, 32a, 33, 34a, 35 (so Mendner, JBL 1958), then Streeter's warning[63] concerning the older source

[58] Cf. Ruckstuhl, 159 ff; Barrett, *Joh und Judentum*, 73; Charlesworth, 406 f; McRae, 18 f; Hahn, 91; W. G. Kümmel, "Die Eschatologie der Evv.," (1936), 21 ff (=*Heilsgeschehen und Geschichte*, 1964, 60 ff); *idem*, *Theology of NT*, 1973, 293 f; L. van Hartingsveld, *Die Eschatologie des Joh*, 1962, 194, 200 ff; G. Klein (see n. 53), 309 n. 215, declares that such views are simply "methodologically inadequate." And Boismard's assumption (RB 1961) that the redactor has joined together different drafts by the same author, which differ among themselves as a consequence of a development from a traditional futuristic eschatology to a present eschatology, does not explain why the redactor should simply have placed side by side texts that differ.

[59] See those mentioned by Schulz, *Untersuchungen*, 115 f; further, Richter, 108 f; G. Bornkamm, "Die eucharistische Rede im Joh," ZNW 47, 1956, 161 ff (=*Geschichte und Glaube* I, *Gesammelte Aufsätze* III, 1968, 60 ff); also "Vorjohanneische Tradition oder nachjohanneische Bearbeitung in der eucharistischen Rede Joh 6?" *Geschichte und Glaube* II, *Gesammelte Aufsätze* IV, 1971, 51 ff; E. Lohse, "Wort und Sakrament im Joh," NTS 7, 1960/61, 117 ff.

[60] Cf. Ruckstuhl, 169 ff; 220 ff.

[61] See recently H. Schürmann, "Joh 6:51c—ein Schlüssel zur grossen joh. Brotrede," BZ, NF 2, 1958, 245 ff (=*Ursprung und Gestalt*, 1970, 151 ff); P. Borgen, "The Unity of the Discourse in John 6," ZNW 50, 1959, 277 f; H. Klos, "Die Sakramente im Joh," SBS 46, 1970 (bibl.), esp. 11 ff, 59 ff.

[62] See n. 12.

[63] B. H. Streeter, *The Four Gospels*, 1924, 377.

theories must be raised for the literary critics who propound such theories: "If the sources have undergone anything like the amount of amplification, excision, rearrangement and adaptation which the theory postulates, then the critic's pretence that he can unravel the process is grotesque. As well hope to start with a string of sausages and reconstruct the pig." Eckhardt's multi-stage hypothesis, which claims to know that Ignatius saved the unfinished copy of the Gospel before the destruction of Jerusalem and reworked it in Antioch, etc., requires so many undemonstrable concatenations that it cannot be presented in connection with serious historical research. Boismard's conjecture that Luke edited Jn rests on observations to be taken seriously, but in the first place he lays too much stress on the standard of logical sequence in the Johannine account, and in the second place he leaves out of consideration the fact that the author very probably knew Lk, so that linguistic and substantive echoes of Lk are more readily understandable on that basis. Finally, J. Becker cannot account for the many who have manipulated the text of the Gospel, nor can Brown adduce compelling arguments for his complicated expansion hypothesis.

It may be said that "neither displacement theories nor redaction theories are necessary to explain the present state of the gospel," [63a] without any need to speak of the "unity" of Jn. If the difficulties are not to be explained on the basis of a later alteration of Jn 1–20, then the question of the sources and aim of the gospel forces itself on us more urgently. For that the author created it out of his own recollection as an eyewitness and therefore needed no sources[64] is scarcely convincing in view of the contradictions in his account, and is therefore to be rejected. As we saw, Jn knew Mk and Lk at least, and occasionally used them. Knowledge of the collection of Pauline letters[65] cannot be demonstrated, and the OT is cited relatively seldom in a direct way, and then in a very free manner from memory.[66] The greatest part of the material in Jn is taken over from neither the OT nor the synoptic tradition, and the question arises whether Jn has used sources for this material. The attempt of Macgregor and Morton to establish (by means of statistical computation based on the concept of standard line and page sizes) a second source which the author has joined with his Gospel in alternating blocks founders on the

---

[63a] Barrett, *Comm.*, 20.

[64] Guthrie, Michaelis; Edwards proposes some notes of the author.

[65] Goodspeed; Hirsch; R. M. Grant, JBL 1950; by contrast, Feine-Behm.

[66] See Goodwin; Freed, *Old Testament Quotations.*

fact that neither the character of the second source nor the intention in putting the two sources together can be explained.[67] In another direction, the source theory of Bultmann is much debated.[68] It arose from the observation that the numeration of the σημεῖα in 2:11 and 4:54 could not originate with the evangelist, since a larger number of signs were attributed to Jesus in 2:23 and 4:45, and since 20:30, "Jesus did many other signs in the presence of his disciples," does not suit as an ending to Jn, but would serve well as the conclusion to a signs source (cf. also 12:37). On the basis of stylistic observations, which he first made in I John (see below, p. 438), Bultmann concluded, therefore, that the evangelist used as his basic source for Jesus' speeches a revelatory-speech source (originally Gnostic), which he had then modified and expanded with glosses. As a third source Bultmann hypothesized a collection of passion and resurrection stories, the existence of which can be discerned in the redactional additions of the evangelist (e.g., 18:13b, 14, 24).[69] The supposition of a "sign source" has found many adherents.[70] In connection with that J. Becker postulated a two-part source with seven miracles,[71] and Fortna expanded this hypothesis into positing a "Sign Gospel," which begins with the Baptist and ends with the resurrection of Jesus. On the basis of these source hypotheses an attempt has been made to differentiate theologically between the θεῖος ἀνήρ Christology of the Sign Gospel and the interpretation of miracles as "signs" by the evangelist.[72] Following Bultmann, though critically, H. Becker has attempted to reconstruct the source of the "revelatory speeches" against the background of Gnostic parallels, but the assumption of such a speech source has on the whole been rejected.[73] On the other hand, a special written source for the Johannine pas-

[67] Against this see Haenchen, ThLZ 1962. The alleged discovery of seven sources by Broome is even less convincingly based (cf. Ruckstuhl, 17 ff).

[68] See the summary in RGG[3] III, 842 f.

[69] See the reconstruction of Bultmann's sources in D. M. Smith, Composition, 23 ff, 38 ff, 48 f.

[70] See the lists in J. Becker, NTS 1969/70, 132 n. 1; Fortna, Gospel of Signs, 24 n. 2; J. M. Robinson, Trajectories, 51 ff; further in Schottroff, 246 ff, and Robinson, Trajectories, 235 ff.

[71] J. Becker, NTS 1969/70, 135.

[72] Martyn, Perspective, 248, 250 ff; J. Becker, NTS 1969/70; Fortna, Gospel of Signs, 228 ff, and JBL 1970; J. M. Robinson.

[73] See Schnackenburg, Comm. I, 54 f; Dautzenberg, 234; Haenchen, ThR 1955, 306 f; Käsemann, VuF 1946/47, 187 f; D. M. Smith, Composition, 110 ff. K. Rudolph supports such a source in "Problems of a History of the Development of the Mandaean Religion," History of Religion 8, 1969, 224.

sion story has been often proposed, both before and since Bult-mann.[74]

In order to test and refute the possibility of and justification for this and earlier source theories, scholars have sought to establish the linguistic and stylistic peculiarities of Jn and then to show that these can be observed straight through all the supposed sources. The conclusion has been drawn with more or less certainty that the positing of written sources for Jn is contradicted by the lin-guistic and stylistic evidence.[75] In opposition to these methods it has been objected that the detailed linguistic indicators are of very different weight, and could well have been introduced by the evangelist in the process of adapting portions of his sources, so that on the basis of these observations nothing decisive can be said about source hypotheses.[76] This research undoubtedly proved that the linguistic characteristics are distributed over the entire Gospel, so that separating out connected sources solely on the basis of linguistic and stylistic arguments is hardly possible. On the other hand, in individual pericopes it is so evident that what may be designated as characteristic features of Jn are missing, that one must accordingly assume that at those points other traditions have been taken over.[77] But even with this assumption, the ques-tion is by no means decided whether the evangelist has used a connected written "signs source" or a complete "Sign Gospel," as Fortna would like to show by tracing the "aporiai" and by means of linguistic and stylistic evidence. (Fortna actually recon-structs the Greek of the "Sign Gospel" word for word.) The separating out of this source edited, according to this hypothesis, by the evangelist takes place mostly on the basis of overrefined logical and conceptual claims about the continuity of the text: Fortna's arguments for the sequence of seven miracles in the source can only be characterized as purely subjective, and the stylistic observations proposed as a base for the original combining of the

[74] Goguel, *Intr.* II, 436 ff; M. Dibelius, "Die at. Motive in der Leidensge-schichte des Petrus- und Johannes-Ev.," Bh. ZAW 33, *Festschr. W. Baudissin* (=M. D. *Botschaft und Geschichte* I, 1953, 221 ff); V. Taylor, *The Formation of the Gospel Tradition,* 1933, 53 f; more recently, Sanders-Mastin; D. M. Smith, *Composition,* 114; Fortna, *Gospel of Signs,* 113 ff; Hahn, 25 f.

[75] Menoud, *L'Évangile,* 15 f; Schweizer, 87 ff; Jeremias, 35 ff; Ruckstuhl, 190 ff; a summary of these Johannine "characteristica" in F.-M. Braun, *Jean le théologien,* 401 ff.

[76] Hirsch, ZNW 1950/51, 134 ff; Haenchen, ThR 1955, 307 ff. Cf. the basic discussion by Schulz, *Untersuchungen,* 51 ff; Teeple, JBL, 1962; D. M. Smith, 107.

[77] Schweizer, 100; Schulz, *Untersuchungen,* 56 f. This is especially true for 2:1-10, 13-19; 4:46-53; 12:1-8, 12-15.

account of the Baptist and the passion narrative with the miracles
in a single narrative complex are incapable of demonstration.[78]
The recasting of a sign source or a Sign Gospel by the evangelist
is by no means likely, but the evidence for a special tradition for
the passion narrative is also insufficient to demonstrate a connected
written source in addition to Jn's knowledge of Mk and Lk.[79]

Most difficult is the question of the origin of the Johannine
speeches. Three decisive objections tell against the hypothesis of a
"revelatory-speech" source: (*a*) Käsemann[80] has drawn attention
to a strictly constructed hymn that can be perceived behind the
prologue of Jn and that has nothing corresponding to it in the
rest of Jn, so that stylistic analysis has no sure evidential base
in the rest of Jn. (*b*) The features of style adduced by Bultmann
are not sufficiently clear to distinguish source from adaptation,[81]
especially as Bultmann repeatedly deems it necessary to see an influence on the evangelist from his source. And against H. Becker's
reconstruction of the source it is to be objected that the arguments proffered for any such construct often can lead to precisely
the opposite conclusion: "If Jn used a source, and if he reshaped
it as radically as Becker thinks he did, that source can no longer
be recovered." [82] (*c*) If the evangelist adapted a revelatory-speech
source consisting of couplets, in his own new complex he must
have broken it up into tiny pieces and interspersed it with his
own perceptions, which is wholly unlikely.[83] That the speeches
of Jn are taken from a written source is thus unproved; rather,
all the evidence points to the fact that the author himself is speaking in the greater part of the Gospel, utilizing his own speech in
the dialogic structuring and in the explanation of the narratives.
So if to all appearances neither the narrative nor the sayings material comes from written sources, then the oft-represented assertion

---

[78] The greater part of the *characteristica* of Jn mentioned by Fortna, 105 ff,
are missing in the reconstructed text of the source, because the source should
not have contained any of Jesus' addresses, and the list of the notable stylistic
features encountered only in the source (214 ff) proves nothing, either because
the purely occasional occurrence of a word is not a noteworthy feature, or
because most of the words adduced are qualified by the particular context or are
not characteristic at all. Objections against Bultmann's "sign source" in D. M.
Smith, *Composition*, 111 n. 183.

[79] Cf. Barrett, *Comm.*, 118; Bailey, 21.

[80] VuF, 1946/47, 187.

[81] See Noack, 18 ff.

[82] Barrett, ThLZ 1957, 912.

[83] D. M. Smith, *Composition*, 111, 113.

that Jn is based on two different layers of tradition[84] is extremely doubtful, since frequently in Jn the narratives form the point of departure for the speech complexes.

If no connected written sources for Jn—apart from the Synoptics —can be demonstrated with any probability, that does not mean that the author is dependent on no tradition at all. If the awkward turns in the course of the narratives and discourses are not the result of later insertions in the original Gospel, then they force one to the assumption that the author has utilized alien or unique traditions. We have already seen how on the basis of linguistic evidence certain narrative details show that they have been adopted. This is indubitably true for the prologue of the Gospel as well. The recent comprehensive discussion of the origin and original form of Jn 1:1-18[85] supports the view that a Logos hymn constructed in strophes has been expanded by the evangelist and reworked as the prologue to the Gospel.[86] In behalf of this theory is adduced the fact that within some of the relatively few verses of the prologue there are numerous religious words that are not used elsewhere in Jn (λόγος, σκηνοῦν, χάρις, πλήρωμα, ἐξηγεῖσθαι), while other verses evidence Johannine stylistic peculiarities and thus may be inferred to come from the evangelist.[87] There are differences of opinion as to which verses are to be regarded as added by the evangelist (most often mentioned are vv. 6-8, 12 f, 15), just as there are different judgments about the origin of the hymn expanded by the author.[88] Many scholars maintain that the

---

[84] Käsemann, VuF 1946/47, 185; Wilkens, Grundmann, 14 f; older representatives of this view in Schweizer, 85 n. 22; *contra*, Barrett, *Comm.*, 17; Teeple, JBL 1962, 280 f.

[85] See the bibl. up to 1966 in A. Feuillet, art. "Prologue du Quatrième Évangile," DBS VIII (Fascicle 44, 1969), 685 ff. Since then, C. Demke, "Der sog. Logos-Hymnus im joh. Prolog," ZNW 58, 1967, 45 ff; A. Feuillet, *Le prologue du Quatrième Évangile*, 1968; J. C. O'Neill, "The Prologue to St. John's Gospel," JTS, NS 20, 1969, 41 ff; P. Borgen, "Observations on the Targumic Character of the Gospel of John," NTS 16, 1969/70, 288 ff; M. D. Hooker, "John the Baptist and the Johannine Prologue," NTS 16, 1969/70, 354 ff; G. Richter, "Ist ἐν ein strukturbildendes Element im Logoshymnus Joh 1:1?" *Biblica* 51, 1970, 539 ff; C. K. Barrett, *Joh und Judentum*, 1970, 28 ff; also *The Prologue of St. John's Gospel*, The E. M. Wood Lecture 1970, 1971.

[86] Surveys of the various hypotheses in R. E. Brown, *Comm.* I, 21 ff; Schulz, *Komposition*, 12 ff; Feuillet, DBS VIII, 656 ff; also *Prologue* (see n. 85), 179 ff.

[87] See Schulz, *Komposition*, 11 f; Teeple, JBL 1962, 284; R. Schnackenburg, "Logoshymnus und joh. Prolog," BZ, NF, 1957, 77 ff.

[88] According to most scholars, the author has utilized a Christian hymn that was written in Greek; according to a few, the author subsequently added and expanded a hymn of his own (R. E. Brown; J. A. T. Robinson, NTS 1962/63, 125; Smalley, 287; Feuillet, DBS VIII, 662; Hooker, 358 (see n. 85). E.

prologue is a unity and was composed by the evangelist.[89] Although the supposition that there is a hymnic base for the prologue seems quite probable, the exact form of this source remains uncertain, which exemplifies the fact that, although large sections of the narrative and discourse material of Jn can with great probability be perceived to have come from tradition that has been taken over, it is scarcely possible to determine the exact compass and form of the tradition that has been utilized. When we inquire about the history-of-religions background of this tradition, it becomes evident that the insight concerning Jn's dependence on tradition does not signify that "the beginnings of the Johannine tradition are as old as those of the Synoptics."[90]

But first we must consider once more how the presence in Jn of numerous contradictions and gaps in the logic is to be explained. Two theses may be mentioned here which attempt to solve this problem without positing later insertions into the Gospel. According to the one view, these difficulties can be explained by the fact that we are dealing with the work of an old man.[91] It is questionable whether this view would ever have been hit upon on the basis of the Gospel itself if there were not an early church tradition that the apostle John wrote the Gospel at a great age. But this tradition is relatively recent (see below, §10.6), and the psychology of age can scarcely account for the topographical and chronological non sequiturs. To be taken more seriously is the assumption that at his death the author left behind an incomplete work.[92] Methodologically there is nothing to be said against this conjecture, though it is difficult to understand why the editor

---

Haenchen, "Probleme des joh. Prologs," ZThK 60, 1963, 325 ff, conjectures that the prologue was expanded by the man who wrote Ch. 21; O'Neill (see n. 85) also assumes secondary interpolations by another hand. A Hellenistic-Jewish (O'Neill), Baptist, or Gnostic origin of the supposed hymn (Bultmann, Comm.; Schulz, Komposition, 66 ff; H. Thyen, ΒΑΠΤΙΣΜΑ ΜΕΤΑΝΟΙΑΣ. ΕΙΣ ΑΦΕΣΙΝ ΑΜΑΡΤΙΩΝ, Zeit und Geschichte, Festschr. R. Bultmann, 1964, 117 ff; R. Macuch, "Anfänge der Mandäer" [see n. 120 below], 108 f) is in any case highly unlikely.

[89] Barrett, Comm., 126; Joh und Judentum, 33; Prologue (see n. 85), 27; Ruckstuhl, 63 ff; Dodd, Interpretation, 292 ff; Borgen (see n. 85); W. Eltester, "Der Logos und sein Prophet," Apophoreta, Festschr. E. Haenchen, 1964, 116 ff; H. N. Ridderbos, "The Structure and Scope of the Prologue to the Gospel of John," NovTest 9, 1966 (=Festschr. G. Sevenster), 180 ff.

[90] Gyllenberg, 146.

[91] Grundmann, Strathmann; Albertz, Michaelis; Hoffmann.

[92] Strathmann; Feine-Behm; F.-M. Braun, Jean, 24 f; Schnackenburg, LThK V, 1101; Wilkens, D. M. Smith, Composition, 239 with n. 79, questioning Käsemann, GGA 1957, 147 (=Exegetische Versuche und Besinnungen II, 1964, 134).

did not remove the all too clear difficulties (6:1!). If this conjecture remains as a possibility, the question must still be asked whether the intention of the author may not offer another possible clarification.

4. The History-of-Religions Setting of the Gospel of John

The most striking distinction between the speeches of the Johannine Jesus and those of Jesus in the Synoptics is the completely different language which Jesus speaks in Jn. It is not so much a matter of language in the grammatical-stylistic sense as of its conceptual world. Of course, the language of Jn in the narrower sense raises problems too: indeed, on the basis of the strongly Semitic character of the language of Jn, it has often been conjectured that Jn as a whole is a translation from Aramaic.[93] Occasionally it has been proposed that only one of the sources drawn upon by the author was written in the Aramaic language.[94] Bonsirven, however, has drawn attention to the many features in the Greek of Jn which cannot be accounted for on the basis of translation from Aramaic, while Colwell has shown kinship of the language of Jn to Epictetus, and Kilpatrick has pointed out the similarity to the language of the LXX. Barrett has shown that it is not necessary to adduce mistranslations; but even in rejecting the idea of a translation of Jn from the Aramaic, it must be acknowledged either that the author thought in Aramaic while writing in Greek,[95] or at least that he came from a bilingual area.

The real historical problem, however, is the origin of the conceptual world in which, in Jn, the evangelist himself is speaking, as well as Jesus, the Baptist, and the Jews. This language is characterized by the opposition of light and darkness, lie and truth, above and below; the contrast of ὁ πατήρ and ὁ υἱός; the numerous ἐγώ εἰμι-sayings of Jesus; redemptive concepts, such as water of life, bread of life, light of the world; and the description of Jesus as "the one whom the Father has sent," who has gone up to heaven, etc. In all these there is a difference from the Palestinian-Jewish conceptual world of the synoptic Jesus. In spite of this evidence, the

[93] De Zwaan; Burney, Torrey, Eckhardt; Boismard, RechB III, 41 ff, offers wildly speculative examples of "Aramaisms" in the MS tradition variants.
[94] Hunter, ExpT 1959/60; Bultmann, RGG III, 844; T. W. Manson; cf. also Feuillet in Robert-Feuillet, 659.
[95] Thus Barrett, Bultmann, Schnackenburg, *Comm.* I, 89 ff; Dodd; Hunter, *According to John,* 22. Cf. R. E. Brown, *Comm.* I, cxxx.

attempt has been made to explain Jn exclusively on the basis of
the OT and rabbinic Judaism,[96] but to do so is to overlook the
fact that the Johannine Christology, with its myth of the Son
who returns to the Father, has no more root in pharisaic Judaism
than does the dualistic language. And nowhere in Jn is there any
sort of familiarity with the views of the rabbis.[97] The language
of Jn is no more readily to be accounted for against the background of the Greek world or of Hellenistic philosophy. The older,
much-esteemed view that the λόγος concept of the prologue of Jn
and the God-mysticism have their closest parallel in Philo[98] is today
represented chiefly by C. H. Dodd: Jn "certainly presupposes a
range of ideas having a remarkable resemblance to those of Hellenistic Judaism, as represented by Philo." [99] But it is significant
that Dodd also assumes a decisive kinship of Jn with the Hermetic
literature,[100] since Jn's indubitable similarity to some of the ideas
of this late Hellenistic philosophical-mystical religiosity[101] does
not rest, any more than do his contacts with Philo, on the fact
that Jn is related to the Hellenistic understanding of the world
and to ecstatic religiosity, to which he strives to accommodate the
Christian message in order to make it appealing to educated
Greeks.[102] Contradicting this notion are the absence of the basic
Hermetic concepts from Jn[103] and the impersonality of the changing λόγος concept in Philo, which thus cannot account for the
personal λόγος in Jn. The striking kinship of Jn with Philo and
the Hermetica shows rather that the Hellenistic Jew, like pagan
mystics, had taken over that form of religion of late antiquity
which had also influenced Jn: namely, Gnosticism.[104]

[96] Büchsel (see WGK, NT 389 ff); Hoskyns; Schlatter; F.-M. Braun, RB
1955; also *Jean le Théologien II. Les grands traditions d'Israël et l'accord des
Écritures selon le Quatrième Évangile*, 1964.

[97] Against Dodd, *Interpretation*, 75 ff; P. Borgen, "God's Agent in the Fourth
Gospel," *Religions in Antiquity, Festschr. E. R. Goodenough*, Suppl. *Numen*
14, 1968, 137 ff. Rightly, Haenchen, ThR 1955, 322 f; Schulz, *Komposition*,
151 f.

[98] Older views in L. Schmid, 14 ff.

[99] Dodd, *Interpretation*, 73. Cf. also Goodspeed, *Intr.*, 308 ("In fact, the
Gospel [of John] may be said to be intensely Greek from Prologue to Epilogue
in every fiber of both thought and language"), Heard, Klijn.

[100] Cf. on this Schnackenburg, *Comm.* I, 118 ff.

[101] See the parallels in Dodd, *Interpretation*, 34 f, 50 f, and F.-M. Braun,
Revue Thomiste 1955, 259 ff, 275 ff.

[102] "Jn sets forth a synthesis of Jewish and Greek thought," Barrett, *Comm.*,
32.

[103] See Kilpatrick, "Religious Background," 40.

[104] Thus Bultmann, NTS 1954/55, 78 f.

Since the conceptual world of Jn can be accounted for neither in terms of orthodox Palestinian Judaism nor in terms of Hellenistic philosophy and mysticism, in recent decades research has more and more brought up two other phenomena in order to make conceivable the emergence of the Johannine thought world: pagan gnosis, especially that of the Mandaeans, and heterodox Judaism, specifically as attested in the Qumran documents. As early as 1788, J. D. Michaelis[105] observed in Jn a polemic "against the disciples of John, Mandaeans"; i.e., he noted a polemical relationship with non-Christian Gnosticism. In 1903 W. Wrede advanced the conjecture "that the Gospel of Jn is based on gnostically influenced views." [106] But a Gnostic background for Jn first became a lively possibility when R. Bultmann in 1925 drew upon the newly accessible Mandaean writings translated by M. Lidzbarski, in addition to the half-Jewish, half-Christian-Gnostic Odes of Solomon and Manichaean texts, in order to reconstruct the Gnostic myth utilized by Jn. At the same time, in his commentary on Jn[107] W. Bauer used the Mandaean texts abundantly for the interpretation of Jn. A heated controversy arose in opposition to the adducing of the Mandaean texts, in which H. Lietzmann in particular made an impression in his "Beitrag zur Mandäerfrage" (1930) in which he asserted that the Mandaeans were a religious community that first arose in the Byzantine-Arab period in the vicinity of the Euphrates, so that primitive Christianity could have had no connection with them.[108] While most scholars have maintained a negative stance toward the assumption of a link between Jn and Oriental Gnosticism, especially of the kind documented among the Mandaeans, Odeberg (1929), Bauer (1933), and Bultmann (1941) have used the Gnostic background as the basis for their commentaries on Jn. Schweizer and H. Becker have shown in detail the closeness of the Johannine conceptual world to Oriental Gnosticism. The question has been raised, on the basis of later Jewish mystical texts, whether there was not at the time of primitive Christianity a Jewish gnosis closely related to the Mandaean conceptual forms, which could then have served as the intellectual basis for the Johannine conceptual world.[109]

A new situation was created when the scriptures of the Qumran

---

[105] J. D. Michaelis, *Einl. in das NT* II, ⁴1788, 1140.

[106] Wrede, *Charakter*, 29 f (see WGK, NT, 301 f).

[107] HNT, ²1925.

[108] On this discussion see WGK, NT, 350 ff.

[109] Odeberg, *Comm.*, 215 f; Fischel; H. Schlier, "Zur Mandäerfrage," ThR, NF 5, 1933, 32.

community became known (since 1948). On the basis of the first fragmentary publications K. G. Kuhn asserted, "In these new texts we are enabled to grasp the native setting of Jn, and that native setting is . . . a Palestinian-Jewish sectarian piety with a Gnostic structure." [110] The comparison of Jn with these texts, comprehensively published since 1948, has convinced many scholars that the author of Jn was in some way or other influenced by the Qumran community.[111] Some have thought that this connection could be clarified more precisely: the evangelist was a pupil of John the Baptist, who grew up in the Qumran community and was for a long time a member of it.[112] As an alternative it has been said that the evangelist, who wrote in Ephesus, came into contact with the thought world of Qumran through the disciples of John in Ephesus (Acts 19:1 ff), or through members of the Qumran community who came to Ephesus after 70 bringing with them their scriptures.[113] Cullmann tries to show that the "Hellenists" in Acts 6:1; 9:29 are identical with the ἄλλοι who according to Jn 4:38 launched the Samaritan mission, and that Jn also manifests the same hostility as these two groups toward the temple in Jerusalem. He would like to conclude from this that the author of Jn, like the "Hellenists," came from a syncretistic kind of Judaism closely akin to Qumran.

These efforts to render comprehensible a supposed influence on Jn from the thought world of the Qumran community are scarcely tenable. For the evangelist to have been a pupil of John the Baptist, it must be assumed that the evangelist is identical with the "beloved disciple" and that he in turn is identical with one of the two brothers presupposed in Jn 1:40—all of which is extremely doubtful (see below, §10.6). Moreover it is by no means likely that the Baptist was ever a pupil or a member of the Qumran community.[114] The Qumran influence on the evangelist in Ephesus is pulled out of thin air. And it is an undemonstrable conjecture

[110] K. G. Kuhn, "Die in Palästina gefundenen hebr. Texte und das NT," ZThK 47, 1950, 210.

[111] Cf. Boismard, JB; J. A. T. Robinson, StEv I; Hunter, ExpT 1959/60; Mowry; F.-M. Braun, RB 1955; Stauffer, ThLZ 1956; Albright; Schulz, Komposition, 161; Schnackenburg, LThK V; T. C. Smith, Grundmann, K. G. Kuhn, Böcher, Roloff, Charlesworth; O. Cullmann, "The Significance of the Qumran Texts for Research into the Beginnings of Christianity," in The Scrolls and the NT, ed. K. Stendahl, 1957, 25 ff. R. E. Brown (183 ff) sees indirect connections, as does Higgins.

[112] F.-M. Braun, Stauffer, R. E. Brown, J. A. T. Robinson.

[113] F.-M. Braun, R. E. Brown.

[114] H. Braun, Qumran und das NT I, 1966, 106 f; 113 f; II, 1966, 20 ff.

that the ἄλλοι are Samaritan missionaries and that they are identical with the "Hellenists," while the opposition to the temple in Jn 4 and that at Qumran are of wholly different character.[115] But even if the attempts to trace historical connections between Jn and the thought world of Qumran are not tenable, the question remains whether some connection is not actually forced upon us. Reference may be made to the ethical dualism, bound up with the idea of creation, to the predestinarian distinction between the "sons of light" and "those who remain in the darkness," between men "who are of the truth" and those who "are from their father, the devil," to concepts such as "bear witness to the truth," "light of life," etc.

It is not to be denied that striking parallels are present and that here and there an expression in Jn is found elsewhere only at Qumran (μαρτυρεῖν τῇ ἀληθείᾳ Jn 5:33; cf. "Witnesses to the truth," 1QS 8:6).[116] But beside that must be placed the fact that the parallels between the Qumran scriptures and Jn are in most cases found in other early Jewish writings as well,[117] especially in apocalyptic, and that the conceptual complex of dualism is completely different in the two settings: in Qumran it is a matter of a radical interpretation of the Law and the organized group, "community" (yaḥad); in Jn the issue is the decision to have faith in "the One sent," and the "being one" as "Christ and the Father are one" (17:22). The idea of the New Covenant, which is characteristic of Qumran, is lacking in Jn; conversely the figure of a divine redeemer plays no role in Qumran (the messianic expectation is wholly future), and the opposition of death and life is lacking there as well. Most importantly, the mythological Christology of Jn and the associated gnosticizing discourses in Jn, which speak of "coming from above" and "being born from above," as well as the ἐγώ εἰμι predications, have no point of connection in Qumran. It must be adjudged that both Jn and the Qumran community have a common background, but that the thought world of Qumran cannot be the native setting of Johannine thought forms.[118]

Since in the writings of the Mandaeans there are to be found not only numerous parallels for the dualistic language of Jn but

---

[115] H. Braun (see n. 114), I, 116, 118.

[116] H. Braun (see n. 114), I, 118 f.

[117] See the references in Teeple, NovTest 1960, 18 ff; and in H. Braun (see n. 114), I, 96 ff; II, 118 ff.

[118] Thus R. E. Brown, Bultmann, Schnackenburg; Harrington, Baumbach, Teeple, NovTest 1960, Morris; H. Braun (see n. 117).

also clear parallels with the Johannine conception of the One sent from heaven in the Mandaean myth of the heavenly redeemer, Bultmann, Bauer, and others have drawn extensively on the Mandaean mythological gnosis as an aid in reconstructing the conceptual background of Jn. They presuppose that the Mandaean religion—our earliest knowledge of which derives from seventh/ eighth century writings from the Euphrates region—goes back in its earlier stages to the time of late Hellenism and to western Syria. In addition to linguistic and historical evidence, these scholars adduce the relationship of the Odes of Solomon, which are preserved in Syriac, with Jn and the conceptual world of the Mandaeans. Lietzmann and many others have disputed the correctness of this line of argument.[119] But research since about 1940 has had a new and broader base through the texts published by Lady Drower, and as a result of the beginning of differentiation of strata within the Mandaean texts scholarship has reached the common opinion that the Mandaean religion, or at least its roots, belongs in spatial and temporal proximity to primitive Christianity and either developed out of gnosticizing Judaism or at any rate engaged in polemical exchange with a syncretistic Judaism: "The Mandaean religion in its fundamental state stands within the sphere of judaizing (Western) gnosis, which presents itself on the eastern borders of the Syro-Palestinian cultural territory in the form of a baptizing sect."[120] Through this insight it is confirmed that Jn could not have been influenced by the preserved Mandaean writings, so that there is no question of Jn's ties with Mandaean or even proto-Mandaean circles. But the oft-observed similarity of

[119] On the state of the discussion at that time cf. H. Schlier, "Zur Mandäerfrage," ThR, NF 5, 1933, 1 ff, 69 ff; and Schweizer, 46 ff; for another view, F. Rosenthal, *Die aramaistische Forschung seit Th. Nöldekes Veröffentlichungen,* 1939, 224 ff.

[120] K. Rudolph, *Die Mandäer. I. Prolegomena: Das Mandäerproblem,* FRLANT 74, 1960, 175. In addition to this fundamental work (bibl.!), surveys in W. Baumgartner, "Der heutige Stand der Mandäerfrage," ThZ 6, 1950, 401 ff; *idem,* "Zur Mandäerfrage," *Hebrew Union College Annual* 23, 1950/51, 41 ff; R. Macuch, "Alter und Heimat des Mandäismus nach neuerschlossenen Quellen," ThLZ 82, 1957, 401 ff; Schulz, *Komposition,* 170 ff; *idem,* "Die Bedeutung neuer Gnosisfunde für die nt. Wissenschaft," ThR, NF 26, 1960, 301 ff; C. Colpe, art. "Mandäer," RGG IV, [3] 1960, 709 ff; J. Schmid, art. "Mandäismus," LThK VI, 1961, 1343 ff; G. Widengren, "Die Mandäer," *Handbuch der Orientalistik* I, 8, 1961, 83 ff; R. Macuch, "Anfänge der Mandäer," in F. Altheim and R. Stiehl, *Die Araber in der Alten Welt* II, 1965, 76 ff; H.-M. Schenke, "Die Gnosis," in *Umwelt des Urchristentums,* ed. J. Leipoldt and W. Grundmann, I, 1965, 396 ff; K. Rudolph, "Problems of a History of the Development of the Mandaean Religion," *History of Religion* 8, 1969, 210 ff; *idem,* in Foerster, *Gnosis* II (see below, n. 129), 173 ff.

Jn to the Mandaean concepts[121] points to the conclusion that the Mandaean writings are late, deformed witnesses for a Jewish Gnosticism which was formed on the edge of Judaism and which is to be assumed as the intellectual background of Jn.

This problem of a pre-Christian Gnosticism and of a gnosticizing Judaism is still completely in a state of flux. Two facts may be established, however. (a) The Odes of Solomon,[122] which come from the first half of the second century, are without doubt documents of a Christian Gnosticism, but a Gnosticism whose dualism is weakened through Jewish influence (concept of creation; eschatology). The original language of these poems cannot be determined—they are preserved complete in Syriac, in part in Coptic, and one ode in Greek—but there is some evidence for Syriac as the original. It is incontrovertible that there are strong similarities between the conceptuality of the Qumran hymns and the Odes, on the one hand, and the Mandaean texts, Jn, and Ignatius, on the other. The assumption that the author of the Odes was a member of the Qumran community who was converted to Christianity[123] is very unlikely in view of the clearly Gnostic understanding of existence in the Odes and the strong contacts with Mandaean conceptuality.[124] And that the Odes of Solomon are dependent on Jn[125] is at the very least not clearly demonstrable. Rather, the Odes of Solomon, whose Gnostic Christianity undoubtedly represents an overlay, presuppose a gnosis influenced by Judaism which is as closely related to Jn and Ignatius as to the Mandaean writings.[126] (b) Without doubt there was a Jewish Gnosticism already in the first century A.D.; i.e., a strongly dualistic specula-

---

[121] Cf. Schnackenburg, Comm. I, 120. Also the works of Rudolph, Widengren, Macuch (see n. 120).

[122] Translation by W. Bauer in Hennecke-Schneemelcher (R. McL. Wilson, ed.) NT Apocrypha II, 1964, 808 ff (bibl.). In addition, Schulz, art. "Salomo-Oden," RGG V, ³1961, 1339 ff; J. Carmignac, "Un Qumrânien converti au Christianisme: l'auteur des Odes de Salomon," in Qumran Probleme, ed. H. Bardtke, Deutsche Akademie der Wissenschaften zu Berlin, Schriften der Sektion für Altertumswissenschaft 42, 1963, 75 ff; K. Rudolph, "War der Verf. der Oden Salomos ein 'Qumran-Christ'? Ein Beitrag zur Diskussion um die Anfänge der Gnosis," RdQ 4, 1963/64, 523 ff; also "Gnosis und Gnostizismus, ein Forschungsbericht," ThR, NF 34, 1969, 221 ff; J. H. Charlesworth, "Les Odes de Salomon et les manuscrits de la Mer Morte," RB 77, 1970, 522 ff.

[123] Thus Carmignac and Charlesworth (see n. 122).

[124] See the evidence in Rudolph, RdQ 1963/64 (see n. 122), esp. 553 ff.

[125] Thus J. Schmid, art. "Oden Salomos," LThK VII, 1962, 1094 f, and Schnackenburg, Comm. I, 126 f.

[126] Cf. also R. M. Grant, JBL 1944.

tion—even while maintaining the Jewish doctrine of creation—concerning the modes of divine revelation, the throne of Yahweh, journeys to heaven. Evidence for this is offered by various constitutive elements of older apocalyptic (e.g., Ethiopic Enoch 14; Slavic Enoch 30:8 ff), wisdom speculation, the Apocalypse of Abraham, as well as details from the talmudic traditions, without our being able to perceive in detail the rise or the history of this Jewish gnosis.[127]

On the basis of these considerations, which point to the existence of a Jewish Gnosticism as a peripheral phenomenon of Judaism in the first century and to the emergence of a prior stage of the Mandaean religion in the same time period as primitive Christianity and in spatial proximity to it, the denial of a "pre-Christian Gnosticism"[128] must be regarded as untenable. Admittedly, the question what should be understood by "Gnosticism" is as debatable as the question of the historical origins of this religious movement. But the recent comprehensive discussion of these questions, which has taken on a new lease of life especially through the discovery of a greater number of Gnostic documents in the

---

[127] On Jewish Gnosticism cf. Fischel; G. Scholem, *Major Trends in Jewish Mysticism*, 1941, 73 ff; R. Marcus, "The Qumran Scrolls and Early Judaism," BR I, 1956, 31 ff; O. Cullmann, "Das Rätsel des Joh im Lichte der neuen Handschriftenfunde," (1958) in O. C., *Vorträge und Aufsätze 1925–1962*, 1966, 262 f; M. Simon, *Die jüdischen Sekten zur Zeit Christi*, 1964, 94 f; H. M. Schenke, "Das Problem der Beziehung zwischen Judentum und Gnosis," *Kairos* 7, 1965, 133; G. Quispel, "Gnosticism and the NT," in *The Bible and Modern Scholarship*, ed. J. P. Hyatt, 1965, 268 f; H. Jonas, "Response," *ibid*, 292 ff; W. Schmithals, *Die Gnosis in Korinth*, FRLANT 66, [3]1969, 44, 279 f; English translation, *Gnosticism in Corinth*, 1971, 36-86, 293 ff; *idem*, "Das Verhältnis von Gnosis und NT als methodisches Problem," NTS 16, 1969/70, 379; K. Rudolph, "Randerscheinungen des Judentums und das Problem der Entstehung des Gnostizismus," *Kairos* 9, 1967, 112 ff; *idem*, "Gnosis und Gnostizismus," ThR, NF 36, 1971, 108 ff; M. Hengel, *Judentum und Hellenismus*, WUNT 10, 1969, 562; R. McL. Wilson, *The Gnostic Problem*, 1958, 172-255; O. Hofius, *Katapausis. Die Vorstellung vom endzeitlichen Ruheort im Hb*, WUNT 11, 1970, 20 f (radically critical); B. Vawter, BThB 1, 1971, 42. It is inappropriate to speak of "pre-Gnosticism" or "esotericism" (e.g., Quispel, Wilson, also Higgins); and Judaism and gnosis cannot be "treated as alternatives" in terms of history of religion (*against* Schottroff, 176).

[128] Thus, e.g., recently Brown, *Comm.* I, lv; K. G. Kuhn, 121 f; R. P. Casey, "Gnosis, Gnosticism and the NT," *The Background of the NT and its Eschatology: Festschr. C. H. Dodd*, 1956, 52 ff; A. Richardson, *An Introduction to the Theology of the NT*, 1958, 41 ff; C. Colpe, art. "Gnosis, Religionsgeschichtlich," RGG II, [3]1958, 1648 ff; J. Munck, "The NT and Gnosticism," *Current Issues in NT Interpretation: Festschr. O. Piper*, 1962, 224 ff; A. D. Nock, "Gnosticism," HTR 57, 1964, 276 ff.

Coptic language at Nag Hammadi,[129] permits the following two
assertions to be offered with some certainty:

1. The Gnostic concept of existence has at its root an anti-cosmic
dualism according to which evil is this world in which man finds
himself imprisoned, though in his essential being he is of divine
nature. The "I" that has forgotten its divine nature cannot free
itself from imprisonment in the world; rather a revelation from
the realm of divine light—as a rule, through a redeemer—opens
to him the knowledge (γνῶσις) of his true nature and thus makes
possible the return of the divine spark of light—proleptically in
the present and ultimately at the End—to the heavenly home.[130]
Texts and concepts which presuppose this view of reality and this
"knowledge" as the way to salvation can be described as being
under Gnostic influence, even though not all the concepts mentioned are attested in any particular context.[131]

2. For the rise of Gnostic religiosity, which is not derivable
from any other religion, we have no direct sources. But the observations already mentioned concerning the existence of Gnostic religiosity in the first century are, besides, supported by establishing
Gnostic features for the opponents of Paul in Corinth and Colossae
and for the false teachers in Jude and I Jn (see below, §§16.3;
21.3, 4; 29.2; 31.3), and by the not unchallenged probability that

[129] On more recent research on Gnosticism, see W. Foerster, "Das Wesen der
Gnosis," *Die Welt als Geschichte* 14, 1954, 100 ff; E. Haenchen, art. "Gnosis
und NT," RGG II, ³1958, 1652 ff; S. Schulz, "Die Bedeutung neuer Gnosisfunde für die nt. Wissenschaft," ThR, NF 26, 1960, 209 ff, 301 ff, esp. 329 ff;
Barrett, *Piper Festschr.*; H.-M. Schenke, "Die Gnosis," in *Umwelt des Christentums I, Darstellung des nt. Zeitalters*, ed. J. Leipoldt and W. Grundmann, 1965,
371 ff, esp. 395 ff; H.-M. Schenke, "Hauptprobleme der Gnosis," *Kairos* 7,
1965, 114 ff; W. Schmithals, *Gnosticism in Corinth*, 1971, 25 ff, 326 ff;
idem, NTS 1969/70 (see n. 127), 378 ff; J. M. Robinson, "The Coptic Gnostic
Library Today," NTS 12, 1967/68, 356 ff, esp. 372 ff; K. Rudolph, "Gnosis
und Gnostizismus, ein Forschungsbericht," ThR 34, 1969, 121 ff, 181 ff, 358 ff;
ThR 36, 1971, 1 ff, 89 ff (bibl.); R. McL. Wilson, *The Gnostic Problem*, 64 ff;
E. Lohse, *Umwelt des NT*, NTD Suppl. Series 1, 1971, 187 ff, 213. The most
important Gnostic texts in translation are presented with introduction and
bibl. by W. Foerster, *Die Gnosis* I. *Zeugnisse der Kirchenväter*; II. *Koptische u.
Mandäische Quellen*, with general index (Die Bibliotek der Alten Welt), 1969
1971.

[130] For a definition of Gnosticism, cf., from the lit. mentioned in n. 129:
Schenke, *Gnosis*, 374 ff; Schmithals, *Gnosis*, 23, 26 f; Rudolph, *Kairos* 1967,
109; Wilson, 11; Foerster, *Gnosis* I, 17; further, the proposals of the Messina
Congress on the Origins of Gnosticism: *Christentum und Gnosis*, ed. W. Eltester,
Bh. ZNW 37, 1969, 129 ff.

[131] The concept of the "redeemed redeemer" does not belong to Gnosticism,
from the beginning or of necessity, see (cf. n. 129) Schenke, *Gnosis*, 382;
Schmithals, *Gnosis*, 26; Rudolph, ThR 1971, 11 f.

some of the Gnostic texts found at Nag Hammadi show no or
hardly any Christian influence.[132] On the basis of these observations
the conjecture that the Gnostic religion arose in Syrian territory in
the first century in connection with some fringe developments in
Judaism is well founded,[133] especially since the earliest representative of Gnostic religion known to us by name seems to be the
Samaritan Simon Magus[134] (Acts 8:9 ff).

Since, as we have seen, the thought world of Jn cannot be
understood on the basis of pharisaic or Qumranian Judaism, or
Hellenistic mysticism or pagan Gnosticism or early Mandaeanism,
the most probable way to account for the history-of-religions setting of the Johannine conceptual world is a Jewish form of gnosis,
based in the region of Syria-Palestine, manifesting a stronger mythological character than the texts of Jewish Gnosticism known to
us or those from the Qumran community, and utilizing the myth
essential to Jn concerning the descending and ascending One
Sent.[135] That is to say, the Johannine thought world cannot be
explained by reference to a heterodox Judaism,[136] to apocalyptic
Judaism,[137] to a special mingling of modes of thought in Palestine

---

[132] Above all, the Adam Apocalypse is regarded as a non-Christian product
(A. Böhlig in *Koptisch-gnostische Apokalypsen aus Codex V von Nag Hamadi im
Kopt. Museum zu Alt-Cairo,* ed., tr., and arranged by A. Böhlig and P. Labib,
Wissenschaftliche Zeitschrift der Martin-Luther-Universität Halle—Wittenberg,
1963, Special Volume, 90, 95; K. Rudolph, ThLZ 90, 1965, 361 f; *idem,* ThR
1969, 160 ff; G. W. McRae, "Anti-dualistic Polemic in 2 Cor 4:6?" StEv IV,
TU 102, 1968, 428 f; M. Krause, in Foerster, *Gnosis* II (see n. 129), 20 (21 ff
for the text). Objections to this interpretation are listed by J. M. Robinson,
NTS 1967/68, 377 f, and K. Rudolph, ThR 1969, 162 ff; on this see R. McL.
Wilson (see n. 129), 67, 129 f. Possibly the "Letter of Eugnostos" is not in-
fluenced by Christianity either: thus M. Krause, "Das literarische Verhältnis des
Eugnostos-Briefes zur Sophia Jesu Christi," in *Mullus, Festschr. Th. Klauser*
(Jb. für Antike und Christentum, Ergänzungsband 1), 1964, 214 ff; *idem,* in
Foerster, *Gnosis* II (see n. 129), 35; J. M. Robinson, NTS 1967/68, 374 ff;
skeptical against this is R. McL. Wilson (see n. 129), 106 ff.
[133] Thus Schenke, *Umwelt* I, 395, 401; *idem, Kairos* 1965, 132 f; Rudolph,
Kairos 1967, 109; *idem,* ThR 36, 1971, 115 f; Wilson (see n. 129), 134.
[134] Cf. Foerster, *Gnosis* I (see n. 129), 38 ff.
[135] Thus, e.g., Bultmann; Haenchen, ThR 1955, 324 ff; Käsemann, VF
1946/47; R. M. Grant, JBL 1950, 321 f; Schulz, *Komposition,* 123, 186;
J. A. T. Robinson, NTS 1959/60, 130 (=J. A. T. R., *Twelve NT Studies,*
124); Schottroff, 242; Barrett, *Joh und Judentum,* 73; Robinson, 242 ff; F. C.
Grant, *The Gospels: Their Origin and Growth,* 1957, 58 f, 159; H. Braun,
Qumran und das NT I, 1966, 123; II, 1966, 119 ff, esp. 138, 140; C. H. Talbert,
Luke and the Gnostics, 1966, 57 f.
[136] Fuller, *Intr.,* 174; Cross, 195 (Jn is "the most Jewish among the gospels").
[137] Böcher, 164.

at that time,[138] and certainly not by the wholly unproved assertion that Jn was influenced by Samaritanism.[139] The decisive factor in this is that the concept of the descent and ascent of the redeemer, which is of fundamental importance for Jn, cannot be demonstrated in Judaism but is characteristic of Gnosticism.[140] The assertion that Jn relies on a form of Jewish Gnosticism for his linguistic and conceptual form can be supported by two further observations: (a) It has often been pointed out that the prologue of Jn and the Johannine presentation of Jesus' revelation of the divine secrets to his own recall the concepts and formulations of the Jewish wisdom literature.[141] As Bultmann has rightly shown, that holds true only because the statements concerning the descent of wisdom belong together with the conceptual complex of the descent of the revealer that is characteristic of Gnosticism. Jn could have found a part of the conceptions presupposed by Jewish Gnosticism even in the wisdom literature that had been influenced by Hellenism. But the weakened anti-cosmic dualism and the linking of a Christology of preexistence with the myth of a redeemer who descends and then ascends again cannot be accounted for in this way. (b) E. Schweizer earlier presented the thesis[142] that the christological self-predications using ἐγώ εἰμι have nowhere such close parallels as in the Mandaean texts, yet since then this thesis has been limited to the OT prototypes or called into question.[143] But the polemical character of the self-predications (Jn 10:11; 15:1) points rather to opposition to Gnostic redeemer figures,[144] and a considerable number of the ἐγώ εἰμι-predicates can now be shown in the Gnostic texts from Nag Hammadi.[145] So the fact remains that in this perspective also Jn appears to have been influenced by Gnostic language.

[138]   R. E. Brown, Comm. I, lxiv.
[139] Freed, CBQ 1968; idem, NovTest 1970; Meeks, 317 f; Buchanan.
[140] Schnackenburg, Comm. I, 443; Meeks, 297; Martyn, Perspective, 267; cf. Schottroff, 292 n. 3.
[141] R. Bultmann, "Der religionsgeschichtliche Hintergrund des Prologs zum Joh," Eucharisterion II, Festschr. H. Gunkel, FRLANT, NF 1923, 3 ff (= R. B., Exegetica, 1967, 10 ff); F.-M. Braun, Festschr. Cullmann; cf. also Sanders, Comm., 19; McRae, 22. Haenchen, ThLZ 1964, 684 (= Die Bibel und wir, 211 f) wants to derive even the style of the Johannine revelatory discourses from the Jewish wisdom literature.
[142] Schweizer, Ego eimi, esp. 36 ff; further, Schulz, Komposition, 119 f.
[143] E. Schweizer, Church Order in the NT, SBT 1961, 118 n. 447; Schnackenburg, Comm. I, 123; R. Borig, Der wahre Weinstock, StANT 16, 1967, 178 ff.
[144] G. Braumann, Theologisches Begriffslexikon zum NT II, 1, 1969, 740.
[145] G. W. McRae, "The Ego-Proclamation in Gnostic Sources," in The Trial of Jesus, Festschr. C. F. D. Moule, SBT II, 13, 1970, 122 ff, esp. 129 ff.

Although it has thus been shown to be overwhelmingly probable that Jn relies extensively for his thought world—especially in the discourses of Christ—on a Jewish-Gnostic milieu which we must suppose to have existed on the fringe of Palestinian Judaism and which had absorbed strong influences from a mythological Gnosticism, that does not by any means imply that "Jn offers Christian gnosis . . . in the sense that Christianity has been conformed to gnosis." [146] C. K. Barrett, in a comparison of Jn with the Gnostic Gospel of Truth,[147] has shown rather that Jn consciously employed pre-Christian Gnostic language in an anti-Gnostic sense, because "Gnosis raised questions that the theologian could not ignore." [148] A careful interpretation of Jn shows that Jn utilized in an emphatically anti-Gnostic way the Gnostic language taken over by him (cf. 1:14; 3:16; 17:15; 20:20).[149] Even if the history-of-religions setting of Jn can be determined in only a conjectural fashion, the insight is decisively helpful in ascertaining the theological aim and the circumstances of the origin of Jn.

5. The Aim and the Theological Character of the Gospel of John

The aim pursued by the author of Jn is expressed by him in the conclusion (20:30 f): "Many other signs Jesus did in the presence of his disciples which are not written in this book. These [signs], however, are written that you might believe that Jesus is the Christ, the Son of God, and that in believing, you might have life in his name." It cannot be decided with certainty whether in 20:31 πιστεύητε ($\mathfrak{P}$ [66 vid.], $\aleph^*$, Θ, 0250) or πιστεύσητε (the majority of MSS) is to be read (presumably the present tense). But even if πιστεύητε is original, the irregular use of tenses in Jn precludes certainty as to whether Christian readers are presupposed who are to be strengthened in the faith, or men who are to be won

---

[146] Schottroff, 277; cf. also *idem*, "Heil als innerweltliche Entweltlichung: Der gnostische Hintergrund der joh. Vorstellung vom Zeitpunkt der Erlösung," NovTest 11, 1969, 294 ff, esp. 317; and Käsemann, *The Testament of Jesus*, 1968, 63 ff.

[147] English translation of this document from the Nag Hammadi discoveries by K. Grobel, *The Gospel of Truth*, 1960.

[148] Barrett, *Festschr. Piper*, esp. 223.

[149] See Hahn, 94 ff; Smalley, 281, 291; W. G. Kümmel, *Theology of NT* (see n. 58), 263 ff, esp. 321; E. Schweizer, "Jesus der Zeuge Gottes. Zum Problem des Doketismus im Joh," *Studies in John: Festschr. J. N. Sevenster*, Suppl. NovTest 24, 1970, 161 ff. See also below, pp. 229 f, with n. 160.

for the faith.[150] Nevertheless it can be shown that in Jn and I Jn such ἵνα-clauses, independent of the tense, have as their aim instruction of members of the community.[151] On this basis it is extremely unlikely that the author of Jn is thinking primarily of non-Christians for whom he will illumine faith in Christ.[152] Just as it is the case that Jn is concerned to show that Jesus of Nazareth is "the one of whom Moses has written in the law and the prophets" (1:45), so is it the case that Jesus designates himself as the "true shepherd" and "vine" (10:11, 14; 15:1) and thereby distinguishes himself polemically from the thieves and mercenaries (10:8, 10, 12)—i.e., from the savior figures who unjustly claim these titles.[153] Though Jn seeks in this way to show Jesus as the fulfillment of Judaism as well as the true pagan religion, the missionary quality is wholly lacking in Jn.[154] That is evident not only in the way that the evangelist repeatedly alludes to events which are reported in the Synoptics (see below, p. 232), but even more in the way he demands in the gospel statements that the readers "remain in his word" (8:31; cf. 6:67 f; 15: 4 ff).[155] Thus Jn was written, at least primarily, to confirm and secure Christians in the faith.[156]

From this perspective the polemical touches evident in Jn are comprehensible. (1) Already in the time of Irenaeus (*Haer.* III. 11. 7) it was assumed that Jn is polemicizing against the Gnostic Cerinthus, and this view finds supporters today.[157] But what we know about Cerinthus—the separation of a God above from a

[150] See Barrett, ZsTh 1953, 258; Neugebauer, 11 f; esp. H. Riesenfeld, "Zu den joh. ἵνα-Sätzen," StTh 18, 1964, 216 f.

[151] Cf. Jn 5:34; 13:19; I Jn 1:4; 5:13, and Riesenfeld (see n. 150), 213 ff, esp. 220.

[152] Thus, e.g., Dodd; Smalley, 290; C. F. D. Moule, "The Intention of the Evangelists," NT *Essays in Memory of T. W. Manson,* 1959, 168. The Baptist communities are named as the recipients by Stauffer, ThLZ 1956, 146; Jewish sects by R. M. Grant, *Intr.,* 160; Jews and Gentiles under the influence of Hermetic religiosity by F.-M. Braun, *Revue Thomiste* 1955, 294; Klijn tries to show that Jn was a missionary tract for Jews, likewise van Unnik; T. C. Smith; J. A. T. Robinson, NTS 1959/60; Cribbs, 49, 55; H. van den Bussche, "Die Kirche im vierten Ev.," in *Von Christus zur Kirche,* ed. J. Giblet, 1966, 105 f.

[153] See Schulz, *Komposition,* 122 f.

[154] Cf. Schnackenburg, *Comm.* I, 148; Grässer, 87; Neugebauer, 12 ff; Riesenfeld, (see n. 150), 220.

[155] See J. Heise, *Bleiben. Menein in den Joh. Schriften,* Hermeneutische Untersuchungen zur Theologie 8, 1967, 173.

[156] Thus, e.g., R. E. Brown, *Comm.* I, lxxviii; Feine-Behm; Barrett, ZsTh 1953, 272; *idem, Joh. und Judentum,* 23, and those named in n. 154.

[157] Höpfl-Gut, Meinertz, Wikenhauser; Grundmann; Neugebauer, 34 ff.

God below; separation of the Spirit from Jesus before his passion[158] —is not the target of Jn's polemic (as is also the case in I Jn; see below, §31.3), so that the statement by Irenaeus is scarcely true.[159] It cannot be denied, however, that Jn contains polemic against Gnostic ideas, which is implied not only by the formulations which exclude Docetism (such as 1:14; 6:53 f; 19:34)[159a] but also by the exclusive claims of the redeemer-predicates in behalf of Jesus which were assigned to Gnostic revealer figures: shepherd, vine, the Sent One, etc.; Jn 10:11; 15:1; 5:36, etc.).[160] Jn lays claim to the language of gnosis in order to show Christians that Jesus is the true revealer.

(2) Some texts of Jn (1:7 f, 15, 20-27; 3:26-30; 5:33-36; 10:41) manifest a stance against John the Baptist and his followers, as Bretschneider noted and as has been widely accepted since Baldensperger.[161] The Baptist himself in Jn stresses repeatedly that he is not the Prophet, nor the Messiah, and points to Jesus, who alone must increase. That is clearly aimed at an overevaluation of the Baptist, as seems to have prevailed in the circles of the followers of the Baptist.[162] Since Jn polemicizes against such an honoring of the Baptist, that must have been a real danger for the reader; yet it is a subsidiary motif that receives relatively little emphasis.

(3) Since Weizsäcker first drew attention to the polemical opposition to Judaism in Jn, some have seen as the goal of Jn the warding off of Jewish attacks on Christianity,[163] though many see

[158] See R. M. Grant, JBL 1950; H. Rahner, LThK VI, 1961, 120.
[159] Thus R. E. Brown, Comm. I, lxxv; Schnackenburg, Comm. I, 151; Michaelis; R. M. Grant, JBL 1950; Michel.
[159a] Richter wants to eliminate as redactional all texts which rule out Docetism.
[160] Cf., e.g., Schnackenburg, Comm. I, 151 f; Schelkle, 95; Schniewind, 203; Bornkamm, EvTh 1968, 22 (=Aufsätze III, 118); Barrett, Joh und Judentum, 62, 72; C. H. Talbert (see n. 135), 58 ff; cf. also n. 149.
[161] E.g., Schnackenburg, Comm. I, 148 f; idem, Historisches Jahrbuch 1958; Feine-Behm, Henshaw, Michaelis, Wikenhauser; Howard, Michel; J. A. Sint, "Die Eschatologie des Täufers, der Täufergruppen und die Polemik der Evv.," in Vom Messias zum Christus, ed. K. Schubert, 1964, 126 ff; contra, T. C. Smith, 50 f; J. A. T. Robinson, NTS 1959/60, 130 (=Twelve NT Studies, 124).
[162] On the disciples of John, cf. Acts 19:1 ff, and Schnackenburg, Historisches Jahrbuch 1958; Sint (see n.161), 96 f, 148 f (bibl.).
[163] Jülicher-Fascher; Wrede; R. M. Grant, JBL 1950. According to Guilding, for the sake of Jewish Christians who were excluded from the synagogue, Jn reproduces the sermons of Jesus which were originally given in connection with the Jewish liturgical year and does so in their original liturgical pattern as proof that the Jewish system of worship has its fulfillment in Jesus (pp. 54, 213). But the lectionary cycle presupposed by Guilding was almost certainly not in existence at this time (see L. Morris, The NT and the Lectionaries, 1964;

this as only a secondary aim.[164] Supposing that Jn is a drama being
played out on two different levels,[165] Martyn tries to prove that
the controversy between Jesus and the Jews reflects in actuality
the situation of the Christian community in the evangelist's own
territory: the Christians who originally belonged to a synagogue
community have recently been officially excluded, and some have
been sentenced to death. On the basis of this debate with the
Jews of his own city, Jn wants to show that Jesus is the Messiah.
Now there can be no doubt that Jn polemicizes against "the Jews"
in the sharpest way and that from the beginning they want to
destroy Jesus (cf. 5:16, 18, 37 f, 45; 7:1, 19; 8:22-24, 37-59;
10:31-39; 19:7). This hostility is so keen that Jesus speaks to the
Jews about "your law" (8:17; 10:34; see also 7:19 and "the word
in their law" [15:25] in the words of Jesus!).[166] Jn 16:2, "They
will exclude you from their synagogues," shows that it was through
the actual animosity between Jews and Christians at the time of
the writing of Jn that this picture of opposition between Jesus
and the Jews who rejected him got its acuteness (though there
are in addition Jews who believe in him: 8:31; 11:45; 12:11). For
without doubt this exclusion is associated with the introduction
into the eighteen synagogal prayers of the curse on the Jewish
Christians at the end of the first century. If this polemic had
its origin, as is undoubtedly the case, in the historical circumstances
of the period, Martyn has hardly shown that the events in the
city of residence of the author of Jn are reflected in this polemic,
since his thesis about a two-level drama remains wholly unproved.[167]
At the same time by their enmity toward Christians Jews who hold
onto their religion give concrete expression to the enmity of the
κόσμος against Jesus and his own (note the connection of 15:18 f
with 16:1 f). Thus the polemic against the Jews is a real motif in
Jn, but this polemic passes over into the basic dualistic representation of the opposition between the ἄρχων τοῦ κόσμου τούτου and

---

L. Crockett, "Lk 4:16-30 and the Jewish Lectionary Cycle: A Word of Caution,"
JJSt 17, 1966, 13 ff), and the claim that the sermons of Jesus were presented
in connection with the OT readings for the synagogue year is sheer fantasy
(see Haenchen, ThLZ, 1961).
[164] Schnackenburg, *Comm.* I, 146 ff; Feine-Behm, Henshaw, Meinertz, Riddle-
Hutson, Wikenhauser; Grässer, esp. 86 ff; Meeks, 295, 300 f, 318; Neugebauer,
14 f; Leroy, 172; Hahn, 86 ff.
[165] Martyn, *History and Theology*, 17, 55, 127 ff; *idem, Perspective*, 258.
[166] On the ambiguous meaning of the designation "the Jews" in Jn cf. Grässer,
76 f; Hahn, 86 ff.
[167] See the justifiable objections of Schnackenburg, BZ 1970, 7 ff.

Christ, who has triumphed over the κόσμος (12:31; 16:33). At the same time, the polemic against the unbelief of the Jews is "also a warning to unbelievers within Christianity itself." [168]

If, then, Jn wrote to foster the faith of Christians and to protect it by polemical defense,[168a] the further question presents itself: How does the author of Jn want his so different representation of Jesus to be understood vis-à-vis the Synoptics? On the supposition that the author of Jn knew the Synoptics, Clement of Alexandria[168b] offered the thesis that Jn wanted to go beyond the Synoptics by supplementation: "Last of all, Jn, because he perceived that the bodily things [τὰ σωματικά] were presented in the other Gospels, in consultation with his friends and motivated by the divine Spirit, created a spiritual Gospel [πνευματικὸν ποίησαι εὐαγγέλιον]." This "supplemental hypothesis" has its representatives down to the present day;[169] a related view is that, on the basis of superior knowledge, Jn wanted to correct the Synoptics.[170] But against these proposals is the fact that Jn nowhere says he has anything new to add, much less anything to correct in the Synoptics. Windisch therefore tried to establish the thesis that Jn wanted to set the absolute Gospel in place of the others.[171] But, on the contrary, Jn often clearly relies on the synoptic accounts and thus unmistakably presupposes that his readers can enhance their understanding by their knowledge of the Synoptics, or at least the synoptic tradition, (cf. 1:25, the baptizing activity of John; 1: 32 f, the baptism of Jesus; 3:24, the imprisonment of John the Baptist; 6:67, 70; 20:24, existence of the circle of the twelve; 12:16, participation of the twelve in the entry of Jesus into Jerusalem; 18:40, alternatives—to release Jesus or Barrabas). If Jn is not an expansion of, nor an improvement of, nor a substitute for the Synoptics, which it knows and can presuppose that its readers know, the only remaining possibility is that it presupposes (without directly saying so) knowledge of the existing Gospels and on that basis gives its own representation of Jesus, which seeks to reveal in a complete way that Jesus is the Anointed One, the

---

[168] Hahn, 89; cf. Grässer, 90.

[168a] It cannot be demonstrated that Jn is aimed especially at initiated (Rigaux, 318 f) or gnosticizing Christians (Käsemann, *Testament*, 73).

[168b] According to Eusebius, HE VI. 14.7.

[169] Thus Boismard, JB; Goguel, Höpfl-Gut, Schäfer; Sigge; in a limited way, Meinertz. On the history of the problem, see Windisch, *Johannes*, 1 ff.

[170] Stauffer, "Historische Elemente," 33; Gericke, 812.

[171] In addition Riddle-Hutson; Bauer, ThR 1929, 139; R. M. Grant, HTR 1942, 95. Cf. *contra*, Blinzler, 65 ff.

Son of God (20:31). In this way it seeks "to express adequately
what was already contained in the earlier tradition." [172]

This independent representation of Jesus seeks to provide full
expression for Christian faith in Jesus, the Messiah and Son of
God, and so builds in a thoroughgoing way on faith's picture of
Jesus within the Christian community: Jn "offers in a systematic,
more independent and large-scaled way a representation, not of
what Jesus was, but of what the Christians have in Jesus." [173] That
is not to say that Jn does not intend to report historical occurrences
and that he includes no historical traditions. The opposite is undoubtedly the case, as the repeated topographical and chronological
information in Jn shows. But the oft-repeated assertion that the
author of Jn claims to write as an eyewitness[174] is simply not true
for Chs. 1–20: the first person plural in 1:14 ἐσκήνωσεν ἐν ἡμῖν,
ἐθεασάμεθα τὴν δόξαν αὐτοῦ is without doubt as in 1:16 ἐκ τοῦ πλη-
ρώματος αὐτοῦ ἡμεῖς πάντες ἐλάβομεν indicative of participation in
Christian faith;[175] and 19:35 recalls the witness of one ἑωρακώς,
but that does not indicate in any way that the witness is identical
with the writer. The thesis which is constantly being defended in
new forms, that the author proves himself to be a resident of Jerusalem and an eyewitness by his exact knowledge of geography and
chronology and of details of the story of Jesus,[176] rests on a faulty
inference and is at the same time objectively false. Although it
cannot be contested that Jn contains historically reliable information—that is possibly the case for the date of Jesus' death or for the
shift of the Baptist's disciples to Jesus—it can only be proved
from instance to instance and does not allow any inference about

[172] Barrett, ZsTh 1953, 269; similarly Bultmann, Lightfoot; Blinzler, 70 f.

[173] M. Dibelius, RGG⁹ III, 350; similarly Schnackenburg, Comm. I, 14;
Strathmann, Comm., 22 f; E. Gaugler, "Das Christuszeugnis des Joh," in Jesus
Christus im Zeugnis der Heiligen Schrift und der Kirche, Bh. EvTh 2, 1936,
41 f; F. Mussner, "Die joh. Sehweise und die Frage nach dem historischen Jesus,"
Quaestiones disputatae 28, 1965, 43, etc.

[174] E. g., Boismard, JB; Schnackenburg; Feine-Behm; Feuillet in Robert-
Feuillet, Meinertz, Michaelis; Nunn, Stauffer, Eckhardt, Morris; Mussner (see
n. 173), 19, 67.

[175] See Barrett and Bultmann on 1:14; E. Fascher, "Christologie und Gnosis
im vierten Ev.," ThLZ 93, 1968, 727.

[176] Thus in various forms R. E. Brown, Sanders; Schnackenburg, Comm.
I, 6, 78 f (see, however, n. 191); Feine-Behm, Guthrie, Mariani, Michaelis,
Schelkle; T. W. Manson, Gyllenberg, Stauffer, Albright, Potter, T. C. Smith,
Higgins; R. E. Brown, Essays, 145 ff; Blinzler, 72 ff; Cross, 195; Hunter, Ac-
cording to John, 49 ff, 56 ff; Morris, 108 ff. The authenticity of the speeches of
Jesus is stressed especially by Albright, Guilding, Higgins, BJRL 1967; Eckhardt.
See on the other hand Dautzenberg, 247; Barrett, Joh und Judentum, 39 ff.

the author's having been an eyewitness. It is false to say that the Johannine discourses of Jesus are "in truth Jesus' mode of speech" [177] because the gnosticizing language of the Johannine Jesus is obviously that of the evangelist and in any event could not be that of the Jesus of Nazareth whom we come to know in the traditions of the Synoptics. If it is history that Jn wants to communicate,[178] it is history that has been thoroughly reshaped from the standpoint of faith in the risen Lord. Accordingly the corresponding theological question concerning Jn is not the question— in itself justifiable—as to his contribution to the history of Jesus, but the question whether or not his portrayal from the standpoint of faith in Jesus as the Son of God who has come from heaven is an essentially suitable interpretation of God's historical work of redemption in Jesus. In answering this question it is immaterial that the author could not have been an eyewitness, as in any event his report of Jesus' discourses shows.

6. The Author

Since the days of the Alogoi, but especially since the beginning of the nineteenth century, the question about the authorship of Jn has been loaded. On the one hand, the theory that it was written by John the son of Zebedee as named in the tradition has been passionately defended, because it has been thought that on this tradition hangs the apostolic authority and the historical reliability of Jn. On the other hand, this tradition has been just as passionately contested, because the historical or theological doubtfulness of this Gospel is seen as based on the untruth of this tradition. Since both lines of argument are false, the discussion of the question of authorship should seek dispassionately to determine what we can know and what we cannot.

In Chs. 1–20 Jn does not name the author, and where the author includes himself with others in a "we" he does not indicate that he is an eyewitness, as we have already seen. In the second half of the Gospel we do meet the disciple ὃν ἠγάπα or ἐφίλει ὁ Ἰησοῦς (13:23-25; 19:26 f; 20:2-8), but the Gospel itself offers no help in identifying this person. All that is clear is that this "beloved disciple" stands in some sort of relationship with Peter. Beyond that one may ask whether the ἄλλος μαθητής (18:15 f) who, as

---

[177] Eckhardt, 52.
[178] Thus rightly, e.g., Schnackenburg, *Comm.* I, 8; J. Becker, NTS 1969/70, 70, 143.

an acquaintance of the high priest, leads Peter into the high priest's palace, is identical with the "beloved disciple," because in 20:3, 8 the latter is indicated as ὁ ἄλλος μαθητής. But since this designation in 20:3 refers back to τὸν ἄλλον μαθητὴν ὃν ἐφίλει ὁ Ἰησοῦς in 20:2, the question as to the identity of ἄλλος μαθητής in 18:15 f cannot be answered unambiguously. If the beloved disciple is meant here, then what is implied is the superiority of the beloved disciple to Peter. It does not help us further to learn that he is an acquaintance of the high priest. Potentially of greater significance would be another passage if its logical connection were more certain. In 19:26 the beloved disciple is mentioned as standing at the cross, together with the women; to him, Jesus entrusts his mother. Then are reported the death of Jesus and the determination of his death by the soldiers, at which time water and blood flow from Jesus' side opened by the lance thrust (19: 28-34). Then follows in 19:35 the statement "And he has seen it, has testified to it, and his witness is reliable, and he knows that he tells the truth, by which also you believe." Since the only one present at the cross in addition to the women is the beloved disciple, it is plausible to see him as the one mentioned in ἑωρακώς and the witness in 19:35, even though that is not directly stated. But it still remains unclear whether ἐκεῖνος in v. 35b and ἑωρακώς mean another person,[179] although the equating of ἐκεῖνος and ἑωρακώς is by far the most natural assumption.[180] If these two assumptions are correct—that in 19:35 the beloved disciple is meant, and that knowledge concerning the truth of what he attests is attributed to him—then it may be inferred that the evangelist can name an eyewitness (at least of the event of Jesus' death) as a guarantor. But even if all this is correct, to what extent we can presuppose that this beloved disciple was a witness of the scenes in which he is mentioned still remains completely open, and who he is remains unknown. According to 19:35, he can scarcely be identical with the author. In the perspective of Jn 1–20 we can go no farther, so that Jn is anonymous.

Of course, Jn has been handed down only in association with the supplement in Jn 21. We have seen that substantively and linguistically it is very likely that this supplement was written by another hand and that it was added to the Gospel (see above, pp. 207 ff). Yet the linguistic kinship shows that the person(s) who supplemented the Gospel was/were heavily dependent on the author of the Gospel. Here we must once more deal with the rela-

[179] Bultmann, Hoskyns, Strathmann suggest Jesus.
[180] Thus, e.g., Barrett on this verse.

tionship between Peter and the beloved disciple (21:7). Peter, to whom Jesus gave responsibility for leadership of the disciples, though he also predicted his martyrdom (21:15-19), now sees the beloved disciple, asks Jesus about him, and receives the enigmatic word "If I wish that he remains until I come, what is that to you?" (21:22). Since 21:23 stresses that Jesus did not intend to say that the beloved disciple would not die until the parousia had occurred, such a correction makes sense only if the beloved disciple had died in the interim. 21:24a builds on the statement that the beloved disciple "has attested this and written it"; in all probability περὶ τούτων as well as ταῦτα refers back to the whole of the Gospel. It is accordingly asserted that the beloved disciple, who has meanwhile died, is an eyewitness (so at least 19:35) as well as the author of the Gospel. 21:24b adds to that, "And we know that his witness is true," which can only mean that the Christians speaking there or the Christian community as a whole (3:11) can attest the veracity of the author of the Gospel. Since, then, the author himself cannot in any case be speaking after 21:23, and since there is no sufficient ground for separating this verse from the rest of Ch. 21, it is confirmed that the whole of Ch. 21 cannot have been written by the author of Jn 1–20. The author of Ch. 21 pursues the objective of designating the beloved disciple as the author of the Gospel by adding his supplement. But the author of Jn 1–20 did not do this, nor does it fit with the way in which the beloved disciple is mentioned in Chs. 13–20.

Ch. 21 is thus of no further help in identifying the beloved disciple. Indeed it may be concluded from 21:7 that the beloved disciple must belong to those named in 21:2 and to those disciples who went fishing together (21:3). In addition to the three disciples mentioned with names, there are enumerated "the [sons] of Zebedee and two other disciples." In view of this text, the claim—oft-repeated and based on the Synoptics—that the beloved disciple must be one of the sons of Zebedee[181] is completely without foundation. With equal justification the beloved disciple can be sought in one of the two disciples mentioned without names. The secret of the figure of the beloved disciple will therefore not be disclosed by Ch. 21. On the basis of information provided in Jn, the author of Jn remains unknown to us, even if, in spite of the tension with 1–20, it should be true that the author is the beloved disciple.

Of course, scholars have not been happy with the determination

---

[181] E.g., Feine-Behm, Guthrie, Mariani, Michaelis, Wikenhausr.

that the identity of the beloved disciple is unknown. The traditional argument tries to clarify his identity through comparison with the Synoptics. It is then pointed out that "the disciple whom Jesus loved" must be one of the disciples who according to Mk 5:37 par.; 9:2 par.; 14:33 were with Jesus when he took only the most trusted with him: Peter and the sons of Zebedee, James and John. Since Peter is mentioned in addition to the beloved disciple, and since James died in 44, only John the son of Zebedee can be considered as the beloved disciple and the author of Jn. Confirmation for this conclusion is found in 1:40 f, where πρῶτον is stressed, and then it is noted that first Andrew brought his brother Simon (Peter) to Jesus, from which it is inferred that the second of the disciples who shifted to Jesus from John the Baptist, and remains unnamed in 1:40, also brought his brother to Jesus. As in the Synoptics (Mk 1:16 ff), Jn would therefore presuppose the call of the sons of Zebedee at the outset of Jesus' activity.[182] But this circle of logic is extremely fragile. First it is highly doubtful whether Jn should be supplemented in any way from the Synoptics, and therefore whether we can presuppose (1) that the author of Jn could only have meant by "the disciple whom Jesus loved" one of the three disciples who according to the synoptic account were his most trusted followers; (2) that in referring to the second pair of brothers in 1:40 f he could only have had the sons of Zebedee in mind, even though he does not name them. On other grounds, it is scarcely comprehensible why the beloved disciple would begin to play a role only in Ch. 13, if he belonged to the circle of Jesus' followers from the beginning. And finally this logical circle does not explain why John the son of Zebedee is indicated by a pseudonym, nor does it make conceivable why the conversion of the second pair of brothers in 1:40 f would be referred to only in the πρῶτον of 1:41, which for all its heavy stress remains unclear. Approached in this way, the equating of the beloved disciple with John the son of Zebedee will not work.

Other identifications have been attempted. According to several scholars[183] the beloved disciple is Lazarus, whom Jesus raised from the dead, based on 11:3, where it is said, "Lord, see, he whom

[182] Thus, among others, Feine-Behm, Michaelis, Wikenhauser on the presupposition that the beloved disciple is the author of Jn; Tasker, McNeile-Williams, Hunter in rejection of this assumption.

[183] F. V. Filson, "Who was the Beloved Disciple?" JBL 68, 1949, 83 ff; Eckhardt (identifies Lazarus with John the son of Zebedee, which he accounts for by considering the name Lazarus in Jn 11 and 12 as an interpolation). According to Sanders, *Comm.*, 50 f, the author, John Mark, has taken up reminiscences of the beloved disciple *Lazarus*.

you love is ill." E. L. Titus proposes[184] Matthias (Acts 1:15 ff). More commonly the beloved disciple has been equated with the man who was host at the Last Supper,[185] although other names have also been supported.[186] Because all these attempts are unverifiable fancies and Jn seems strongly to protect the anonymity of the beloved disciple, some scholars would like to see in the beloved disciple an ideal figure,[187] which is extremely improbable.[188] His rivalry with Peter would then lead to the conclusion that Peter is also an ideal figure, and it is inconceivable that the author would have attributed to an ideal figure so small a role. If 18:15 f does in fact refer to the beloved disciple, that note, with reference to an ideal figure, would be utter nonsense. The author of the supplement (21:23) knew of the death of the beloved disciple and the considerations connected with it.

The fact remains that we have no possibility of breaking through the anonymity of this "disciple"; since, however, the texts in which he is called "the beloved disciple" are inserted by the author himself into the tradition that he has taken over,[189] he must have attached great value to being able to adduce as guarantor of his account of the passion of Jesus someone who was adjudged worthy of the title "the disciple whom Jesus loved." The often uttered conjecture that this man must have been a resident of Jerusalem[190] is not convincing, but he certainly did not belong to the twelve,[191] and the basis for his anonymity remains unknown

[184] E. L. Titus, "The Identity of the Beloved Disciple," JBL 69, 1950, 323 ff.

[185] Parker, JBL 1960; L. Johnson, "Who was the Beloved Disciple?" ExpT 77 1965/66, 157 f, suggests John Mark; Colon proposes a priest from Jerusalem, whom he identifies with the presbyter John.

[186] See the enumeration in Kragerud, 42 ff.

[187] The type of ideal discipleship, according to Jülicher-Fascher, Marxsen; Bacon, Dibelius, Festschr. Jülicher, 180 (=Botschaft I, 214); E. Kraft, "Die Personen des Joh," ExTh 16, 1956 18 ff; the ideal bearer of the apostolic witness, according to R. M. Grant, HTR 1942, 116; H. Lietzmann, Beginnings of the Christian Church, 1937, 311 f; E. Käsemann, "Ketzer und Zeuge," ZThK 48, 1951, 304 (=Exegetische Versuche und Besinnungen I, 1960, 180); Gentile Christianity as the real Christianity, according to Bultmann; Johannine prophetism in opposition to office in the community, according to Kragerud. Every mention of the beloved disciple is interpolated according to those mentioned by Kragerud, 11 f; further, Goguel, Intr. II, 362 ff; A. Harnack, Studien zur Geschichte des NT und der alten Kirche I, AKG 19, 1931, 126 n. 2; this assumption is wholly arbitrary.

[188] Cf. Schnackenburg, EKK 2, 108 f; Roloff, 139 ff.

[189] See the evidence in Schnackenburg, EKK 2, 99 ff; Roloff, 131 ff.

[190] Recently Colon and Schnackenburg, EKK 2.

[191] Schnackenburg, EKK 2, 122, now correctly stresses that "the anonymity speaks against authorship by the apostle John."

to us.[192] The question of the author cannot be clarified even with the help of the beloved disciple.

It remains to be asked whether the church tradition about the identity of the author of Jn is of any help. The tradition that John the son of Zebedee wrote Jn in Ephesus at an advanced age is first found definitely in Irenaeus, *Haer.* III. 1. 2. (=Eus., HE V. 8. 4): "Thereafter [after the first three Gospels] John, the Lord's disciple, who had leaned on his breast, published the gospel himself, as he was staying in Ephesus." In this information from his chief work, *Against Heresies*, written *ca.* 180, Irenaeus reproduced the tradition of his native territory, Asia Minor, and of Rome as well. Polycrates, Bishop of Ephesus, in a letter written *ca.* 190 to Victor, Bishop of Rome (preserved in Eus., HE V. 24. 2 ff), invokes the witness of the Asia Minor tradition and in the process mentions, "Furthermore, John also, who leaned on the Lord's breast . . . this one is buried in Ephesus." Melito, Bishop of Sardis (*ca.* 170) makes allusions to Jn in the same way as to the Synoptics,[193] and in the *Epistula apostolorum*, which is thought to have originated about the same time in Asia Minor, not only is Jn often used and cited, but John is also at the head of the list of apostles.[194]

Thus Irenaeus' information proves to be the tradition of Asia Minor from the last quarter of the second century, but the Muratorian Canon (lines 9 ff) shows the same to be true for Rome: "The fourth of the Gospels is by John, from among the disciples. When he was summoned by his fellow disciples and bishops he said: 'Fast with me for three days from today, and whatever is revealed to anyone, that we shall share with one another.' In the same night it was revealed to Andrew, one of the apostles, that John should write out in his name, to be checked by all [the other apostles], everything. . . . [In Jn 1:1] he declares himself not only to be an eye- and ear-witness, but also as recorder in sequential order of all the miracles of the Lord." [195] It was thus the tradition in both Asia Minor and Rome in the last quarter of the second century that the Fourth Gospel was written by John the beloved

---

[192] Roloff mentions as a parallel the "Teacher of Righteousness" of the Qumran community. But that fits only in a very limited sense, since the designation "the one whom Jesus loved" could scarcely be at the same time a designation of his function.

[193] Cf. Barrett, *Comm.*, 94.

[194] R. M. Grant, HTR 1942, 104, would like to deduce from this that the gospel alluded to in this document—Jn—is considered to be by the apostle John, which is by no means certain.

[195] Translation in Hennecke-Schneemelcher, *NT Apocrypha* I, 42 ff.

disciple, who is identical with John the disciple in Ephesus. There can be no doubt that Irenaeus means by "the disciple of the Lord" the son of Zebedee, since he quotes Jn 1:14 with the formula ὁ ἀπόστολος εἴρηκεν (*Haer*. I. 1. 19) and says concerning the church at Ephesus, "The church in Ephesus, which was founded by Paul, where John remained until the time of Trajan, is a true witness of the tradition of the apostles" (*Haer*. III. 3. 4 = Eus., HE III. 23. 4). Still more striking is the fact that Irenaeus almost always names this John "*the* disciple of the Lord," and this singular is not used for any other person.[196] And in the Muratorian Canon, the author of John is called *Johannes ex discipulis*.[197] This designation, "the disciple of the Lord," in the tradition that we meet at the end of the second century is thus clearly attached to the John who is regarded as the author of Jn. From the end of the second century on, the writing of Jn by John the son of Zebedee is undisputed.

This viewpoint, to be sure, was not universally recognized in the second half of the second century, as the attribution of Jn to the Gnostic Cerinthus by various anti-Montanists in this period shows (see above, §10.2). We must inquire as to the source of Irenaeus' knowledge about John the apostle and disciple of the Lord as the author of the Fourth Gospel. Irenaeus appeals to two traditional sources: (*a*) In a letter to the Gnostic Florinus (in Eus., HE V. 20. 4) he says: "These teachings were not transmitted to you by the elders before us, who associated with the apostles. I saw you when I was a child, with Polycarp in lower Asia Minor. . . . [I can remember precisely] how [the blessed Polycarp] told of his association with John and with the others who had seen the Lord, and how he remembered their words and what it was that he had heard from the Lord concerning his miracles and his teachings." From this information one can conclude no more than that Polycarp had known a John who had seen the Lord; that he was an apostle is not said, nor is it said that Polycarp had met this John in Asia Minor. According to his own information, Irenaeus was a παῖς when he met Polycarp;[198] and Polycarp himself in his letter to the Philippians does not appeal to his relationship with an apostle. In view of this, it is very much open to

---

[196] See Bernard, *Comm.* I, xlvii; Burney, 138 f.

[197] Line 9 (read *discipulis* instead of *decipolis*).

[198] A. Harnack calculated that at the death of Polycarp, Irenaeus could not have been more than fifteen (*Geschichte der altchristlichen Literatur bis Eusebius* II, 1, 1897, 342 ff). But this argument is weak if the death year of Polycarp was 161 (or later) rather than 155 (thus H. von Campenhausen, *Aus der Frühzeit des Christentums*, 1963, 253 f).

question whether Irenaeus may not be mistaken when he claims that the John whom he heard of from Polycarp as a child was an apostle and had moved to Asia Minor. (*b*) Irenaeus further appeals for his knowledge of the apostle John to "all the presbyters who met together in Asia with John, the disciple of the Lord. . . . Some have seen not only John but others of the apostles" (*Haer*. II. 33. 3; in part also in Eus., HE III. 23. 3). Who these presbyters were cannot be determined with certainty,[199] but whoever they may have been, it is not said of them that they knew John the disciple of the Lord. And it remains unclear whether the information that this meeting took place in Asia Minor is a tradition of the presbyters or whether it was added by Irenaeus, so that nothing more can be inferred than that Irenaeus knew of a disciple of the Lord, John, whom the presbyters of Asia Minor had heard of. Nothing is said in the presbyters' tradition about the apostle John, and neither by Polycarp nor by the tradition of the presbyters is this John, the Lord's disciple, designated—as Irenaeus reports—as the author of a Gospel. This means that the tradition acknowledged by Irenaeus as his source knows only of a disciple of the Lord, John; whether this John was in Asia Minor and was known as the author of a Gospel is uncertain.

What do we know about the view of Papias, a contemporary of Irenaeus' "presbyters"? Eusebius says nothing of a statement by Papias concerning Jn, and the so-called anti-Marcionite prologue to Jn, which claims to reproduce Papias' statement about Jn, is late and worthless.[200] We do not have a sure testimony that Papias knew Jn, and what has been adduced as evidence for Papias' acquaintance with Jn is unconvincing.[201]

Irenaeus clearly asserts that Papias was a hearer of John (Ἰωάννου ἀκουστής; Iren., *Haer*. V. 33. 4 = Eus., HE III. 39. 1), but this information does not tally with Papias' own words in the proem to his "Exposition of the Sayings of the Lord." This much-disputed

---

[199] Harnack's assumption (see n. 198), 133 ff, that the source of the testimony of the presbyters as alleged by Irenaeus is actually Papias' written testimony is untenable, since Irenaeus (*Haer*. V. 33. 3, 4; partially in Eus. HE III. 39. 1) mentions the presbyters in addition to Papias. See J. Regul, *Die antimarkionitischen Evangelienprologe*, Vetus Latina, Aus der Geschichte der Lateinischen Bibel 6, 1969, 134 ff.

[200] Thus Regul (see n. 199), 99 ff. esp. 195 ff. The text is in Regul, 34.

[201] See the careful presentation of evidence in Regul (see n. 199), 143 ff. Even if Papias knew I John (thus Eus., HE III. 39. 17), it cannot be inferred from this that he also knew Jn (against W. Bauer, *Orthodoxy and Heresy in Earliest Christianity*, tr. R. Kraft *et al.*, 1971, 204 f; Ph. Vielhauer, ThR, NF 31, 1965/66, 126 f).

text (in Eus., HE III. 39. 3 f) runs: "I shall shrink from no effort to present everything that I once learned well from the elders [παρὰ τῶν πρεσβυτέρων] and have well retained, together with the exposition [of the words of the Lord], the truth of which [αυτῶν ἀλήθειαν] I myself vouch for. For I found my joy, unlike the masses, not in those who make many words but in those who teach the truth; not in those who commit to memory strange commandments, but in those who have preserved in the mind the commands which were given by the Lord for the faith and which derive from the truth itself. But if someone else came who was a successor of the elders, I took care to search out according to the words of the elders what Andrew or Peter had said [εἶπεν], or what Philip or what Thomas or James or what John or Matthew or any other of the disciples of the Lord and what Aristion and the elder John, the disciple of the Lord, say [ἅτε Ἀριστίων καὶ ὁ πρεσβύτερος Ἰωάννης οἱ τοῦ κυρίου μαθηταὶ λέγουσιν]. For I did not consider what came out of books so valuable for me as what originated from the living and enduring voice."

In view of this text the discussion shifts chiefly to the appearance twice of the name of John and to the meaning of οἱ πρεσβύτεροι and τοῦ κυρίου μαθηταί. It is hard to conceive that the first question is disputed at all and that the assertion is repeatedly made that Papias mentioned only one John.[202] An unprejudiced exegesis of the text leaves no doubt that Papias says that as he had opportunity he inquired from the pupils of the πρεσβύτεροι about the sayings of the πρεσβύτεροι and that in this way he learned (1) what the seven mentioned by name and other disciples of the Lord said, and (2) what the Lord's disciples, Aristion and the πρεσβύτερος (elder) John are saying.[203] Papias therefore mentions two persons with the name of John into whose teaching he had inquired. The one is named together with the circle of the twelve and is obviously, like the others of this group, no longer living; accordingly, only the son of Zebedee can be meant. The other is obviously known by the designation "John the elder" and like Aristion is still living. Papias has heard of the two groups only through their pupils (παρακολουθηκώς τις τοῖς πρεσβυτέροις). From

[202] Thus, e.g., Feine-Behm, Meinertz, Michaelis; Nunn, Edwards; C. S. Petrie, "The Authorship of 'The Gospel according to Matthew' . . . ," NTS 14, 1967/68, 21 f; see further those mentioned in Regul (see n. 199), 147 n. 4.

[203] Thus already in Eus., HE III. 39. 5; recently, e.g., Barrett, R. E. Brown, Sanders, Schnackenburg; Klijn, Mariani; F.-M. Braun, *Jean*, 357 ff; Merlier, 224 ff; Colson, 47; Regul (see n. 199), 117 f; J. Munck, "Presbyters and Disciples of the Lord in Papias," HTR 52, 1959, 223 ff.

this it may be inferred that Irenaeus' information that Papias was "a hearer of John" is not correct.[204]

Although thus far the text from Papias is to be interpreted with some assurance, the second question cannot be answered with full certainty. The concept πρεσβύτεροι which we encounter as Papias' comprehensive designation for men whom he regards as bearers of the tradition and, in addition, as a distinguishing designation for the second John in our section, can in both cases indicate in Papias' sense only the generation of the bearers of the tradition. The "elder John" is thus the man who did not belong to the circle of the twelve, but who, like Aristion, could communicate "the commands given by the Lord for faith." Why he is called especially "*the* elder" we cannot know. It is also unclear what is meant by τοῦ κυρίου μαθηταί which is mentioned beside it, although that it is synonymous with οἱ πρεσβύτεροι is unlikely, judging by the context.[205] Probably the elder John was not a member of the inner circle of disciples of Jesus, but was some sort of personal disciple. Papias, however, has heard from the apostle John as well as from the elder John only through their pupils; we cannot infer by this means that Papias knew Jn.

The tradition which we can first lay hold of toward the end of the second century that Jn was written in Ephesus by the son of Zebedee can therefore hardly be traced farther back. Concerning the bearers of the tradition mentioned by Irenaeus—Polycarp and the elders—we have only the information that they enjoyed some relationship with a disciple of the Lord, John; and Irenaeus nearly always names as author of Jn "the disciple of the Lord," even though he considers him to be an apostle. From the tradition transmitted through Irenaeus, only the following information can be inferred: that John, a disciple of the Lord, was the author of Jn, though this conclusion is weakened by the ascertainment that in his letter, Polycarp betrays no knowledge of Jn.[206] It can no longer be determined whether this John, the disciple of the Lord, is identical with the disciple of the Lord, John the elder, mentioned by Papias.

Thus it is very questionable whether we can continue to reason

[204] Thus also Regul (see n. 199), 131 f; Munck (see n. 203), 229 proposes that Papias first heard the presbyters directly on his journey, and their pupils later in Hierapolis but that is read into the text.
[205] See Regul (see n. 199), 125. Possibly in this context "the disciples of the Lord" should be interpreted as "the personal disciples of Jesus." Thus Munck (see n. 203), 232.
[206] He does indeed know I John; see R. M. Grant, HTR 1942, 100.

in the following way: the only tradition that can be taken seriously concerning the author of Jn in the ancient church leads back to John, the Lord's disciple. Since the equating of this John with the son of Zebedee is not attested before Irenaeus and is impossible on other grounds (see below), then in all probability the author of Jn is to be sought in "the elder John," with whom Papias had some connection. This probability becomes a certainty if the Letters of Jn come from the same author, since the author of II John and III John calls himself ὁ πρεσβύτερος (see also § 32.3). Against the assumption and others like it that Jn comes from the elder John mentioned by Papias[207] is the fact that we can only *infer* that the tradition on which Irenaeus relies traces Jn back to John, the Lord's disciple, so that Papias' equating him with the elder John must remain uncertain. At most the elder John's authorship of Jn and the Johannine letters can be described as a possibility (Barrett).

Even though a great age cannot be proved for the tradition that John the son of Zebedee was the author of Jn, it yet remains to be asked whether this tradition may not in fact be correct, as a large number of scholars assert.[208] The question could of course be answered negatively if it could be proved that John the son of Zebedee died early as a martyr. As evidence for this, in addition to Jesus' prediction of the martyrdom of the sons of Zebedee (Mk 10:39 par.), it is adduced (1) that according to late accounts, Papias has passed on the tradition that "John the theologian and his brother James were put to death by the Jews," and (2) that some ancient martyrologies also mention the martyrdom of John.[209] The evidence for this thesis is of very uneven value. While it can hardly be explained why the prediction of Mk 10:39 would have been preserved if the facts contradicted it,[210] the Papias account is totally unreliable and the historical value of the lists of

[207] Bauer, Bernard, Henshaw, McNeile-Williams, Sparks; Dibelius, Grundmann, Merlier, Colon.

[208] Thus recently Lightfoot, Strathmann, Tenney; Feine-Behm, Guthrie, Harrington, Klijn, Mariani, Michaelis, Wikenhauser; Menoud, Edwards, Stauffer, Albright, Böcher, Gericke, Hunter, Morris.

[209] Since E. Schwartz, many take this view: recently, e.g., Bauer; Jülicher-Fascher; Bultmann, Dibelius, R. M. Grant, HTR 1942.

[210] The claim that Mk 10:39 does not predict martyrdom for the sons of Zebedee (thus Schnackenburg, *Comm.* I, 71 f; A. Feuillet, "La Coupe et le baptême de la passion," RB 74, 1967, 360 ff) is extremely improbable, at least for the text which Mk has taken over (Mk 10:35-40). Cf. E. Haenchen, *Der Weg Jesu*, 1966, 363 f; E. Schweizer, NTD 1, [11]1967, on Mk 10:35-45.

martyrs is contested.[211] Even if there is some probability that John
did die as a martyr, it still remains completely uncertain when and
where this occurred, so that this argument cannot speak decisively
against John the son of Zebedee having written Jn.

A few other facts, however, speak decisively against the correctness of this tradition. We have already seen that the Gnostic language of the Johannine discourses of Jesus makes Jn's having been
written by an eyewitness impossible. In addition it would be completely impossible to understand why Jn could have prevailed only
so slowly and against such great opposition, if it had been known
from the outset that it was written by an apostle.[212] Furthermore,
dependence on Mk by a member of the twelve is scarcely imagin-
able, and the schematic treatment of Jesus' conflict with "the
Jews" betrays no knowledge of the actual conflict of Jesus with
the Pharisees, Sadducees, and scribes. To all these arguments which
show it to be impossible that Jn was written by a member of
the twelve may be added the evidence which particularly excludes
John the son of Zebedee.[213] All the events in which John son of
Zebedee had a decisive role are omitted in Jn (call of the sons of
Zebedee, Mk 1:19 f; healing of Peter's mother-in-law, Mk 1:29;
choice of the twelve, Mk 3:13 ff; raising the daughter of Jairus,
Mk 5:37 par.; transfiguration, Mk 9:2 ff par.; request of the sons
of Zebedee with prediction of their martyrdom, Mk 10:35 ff par.;
Gethsemane, Mk 14:22 ff par.). John's brother, James, is never
mentioned. Although the sons of Zebedee were Galileans, in Jn all
interest in Galilee is lacking. Acts 4:13 reports that Peter and
John were ἄνθρωποι ἀγράμματοι ("illiterate men"); yet Jn is written
in Greek that is good, though semitizing. The authorship of Jn
by John the son of Zebedee is thus out of the question.

This tells us that we do not know who the author was. It is
often asserted that he must have been a Jew,[214] but that is by no
means a persuasive supposition, since the presentation in Jn of a
string of geographical references which are lacking in the Synoptics
can readily be explained by acknowledging that there were topographical traditions in the Christian community. If he was a
former Jew, one may conjecture that he had belonged to a gnosticizing group before he became a Christian, though that is pure
speculation. The only certain thing is that he had come into con-

---

[211] Cf. on this esp. Barrett, *Comm.*, 86 f; Schnackenburg, *Comm.* I, 71 ff;
F.-M. Braun, *Jean*, 375 ff; Morris, 280 ff.

[212] Thus Barrett; Käsemann.

[213] See the evidence in Parker, JBL 1962; Merlier, 200 ff.

[214] Most recently T. C. Smith, Grundmann.

tact with a Palestinian Christian who in some way or other communicated to him the passion story of Jesus and that he named his informant "the disciple whom Jesus loved," though we do not know whether this designation was part of the tradition as well. Nothing further is known about the author of Jn, and all further conjectures about the rise of the late tradition of John the son of Zebedee as author contribute nothing to our understanding.

7. Time and Place of Writing

Today it is possible to date Jn with some certainty within relatively narrow limits. The question which writers of the early second century knew Jn is now debated as before: I Clem scarcely knows Jn,[215] nor is knowledge by Barn. and Herm. any more certain.[216] On the other hand there is some evidence that Ignatius knew Jn.[217] But a decision on this basis is no longer essential for establishing a fixed *terminus ad quem* for the writing of Jn: Papyrus 52 from the early second century is a fragment of a MS of Jn (see below, §38.1.b), and a fragment of an "Unknown Gospel" [218] from about the same time knows Jn as well. Thus if Jn was known in Egypt in the first quarter of the second century, the beginning of the second century is a *terminus ad quem*. On the other hand, Jn's knowledge of Lk is extremely probable, so it could not have been written before *ca.* 80–90.[219] The assumption that Jn was written probably in the last decade of the first century is today almost universally accepted.

It is more difficult to determine the place of writing. Ephesus or Asia Minor as the place of writing is defended by those who depend on the church tradition, but also by others on different grounds.[220] Apart from the fact that the tradition is quite late, nothing in the Gospel itself points to an origin in Asia Minor, so scholars have sought to link the tradition with other hints about the origin of Jn: the tradition that John came from Alexandria

[215] In spite of Boismard, F.-M. Braun.
[216] Rightly Boismard, RB 1960, 593 ff, in opposition to F.-M. Braun.
[217] Thus Maurer, Nunn; F.-M. Braun; opposed by Barrett.
[218] See §5 n. 91; text in G. Mayeda, *Das Leben-Jesu-Fragment Papyrus Egerton 2 und seine Stellung in der urchristlichen Literaturgeschichte,* 1946.
[219] Earlier dates suggested by R. M. Grant; Gardner-Smith, Mendner, Gericke (before the death of Nero!), Cribbs, Hunter, Morris.
[220] Cf. recently, on one side R. E. Brown; R. M. Grant; Hunter; on the other side, Barrett; Aland, Neugebauer.

to Ephesus,[221] or that he was from Jerusalem, but went to Ephesus by way of Antioch.[222] These reconstructions cannot be proved, and the home of the Johannine thought world is clearly not Alexandria.[223] There are, however, substantive contacts with the Odes of Solomon, which presumably came from Syria, and with Ignatius of Antioch, who was probably the first to have used Jn. The linguistic form of Jn also leads us to think of a Greek-speaking author in a Semitic environment, just as the conceptual world manifests a kinship with gnosticizing circles on the fringes of Judaism. So the assumption that Jn arose somewhere in Syria is the best hypothesis.[224]

B. THE LETTERS

§11. THE LETTER AS A LITERARY FORM IN THE NEW TESTAMENT

A. Deissmann, *Bibelstudien*, 1895, 187 ff; *idem*, *Licht vom Osten*, 1923, 116 ff, Eng. tr. *Light from the Ancient East*, n.d., 146 ff; P. Wendland, *Die urchristlichen Literaturformen*, HNT I, 3, [2,3]1912, 342 ff; M. Dibelius, *Geschichte der urchristlichen Literatur* II, 1926, 5 ff; Eng tr., *A Fresh Approach to the New Testament and Early Christian Literature*, 1936, 137 ff; E. Lohmeyer, "Probleme paulinischer Theologie I: Die brieflichen Grussüberschriften," ZNW 26, 1927, 158 ff; O. Roller, *Das Formular der paulinischen Briefe*, BWANT, IV, 6, 1933; L. G. Champion, *Benedictions and Doxologies in the Epistles of Paul*, diss. Heidelberg, 1934; P. Schubert, *Form and Function of the Pauline Thanksgivings*, Bh. ZNW 20, 1939; J. T. Sanders, "The Transition from Opening Epistolary Thanksgiving to Body in the Letters of the Pauline Corpus," JBL 81, 1962, 348 ff; J. Schneider, RAC II, 564 ff; E. Fascher, RGG³ I, 1412 ff; B. Rigaux, "Paulus und seine Briefe," *Biblische Handbibliothek* 2, 1964, 164 ff; T. Y. Mullins, "Disclosure: A Literary Form in the NT," NovTest 7, 1964, 44 ff;

[221] Snape, Stauffer.

[222] Lightfoot; Schnackenburg, *Comm.* I, 134; Feuillet in Robert-Feuillet; R. M. Grant, JBL 1944; Manson, Eckhardt. Somewhat differently and hesitantly, Schnackenburg, EKK, 116.

[223] Alexandria as the place of writing is the conjecture of Martyn, *History and Theology*, 58.

[224] Thus Bauer; Jülicher-Fascher, Klijn; Burney, Schweizer, Haenchen, ZThK 1959; Regul (see n. 199), 104. It is not true that Ephraem's Commentary on the Diatessaron already offers this information (in spite of Bauer's appeal to an older Latin translation of the Armenian text). See L. Leloir, "L'original syriaque du commentaire de S. Éphrem sur le Diatessaron," *Biblica* 40, 1959, 165 f.

R. W. Funk, *Language, Hermeneutic and the Word of God*, 1966, 251 ff; *idem*, "The Apostolic Parusia: Form and Significance," *Christian History and Interpretation: Festschr. J. Knox*, 1967, 249 ff; G. J. Bahr, "Paul and Letter Writing in the 1st Century," CBQ 28, 1966, 465 ff; *idem*, "The Subscriptions in the Pauline Letters," JBL 87, 1968, 27 ff; C. J. Bjerkelund, *Parakalô: Form, Funktion und Sinn der parakalô-Sätze in den paulinischen Briefen*, Bibliotheca Theologica Norvegica 1, 1967; W. G. Doty, "The Classification of Epistolary Literature," CBQ 31, 1969, 183 ff; O. Güttgemanns, *Offene Fragen zur Formgeschichte des Ev.*, BevTh 54, 1970, 111 ff; J. L. White, "Introductory Formulae in the Body of the Pauline Letter," JBL 90, 1971, 91 ff.—Good comparative material from letters among the papyri is offered by S. Witkowski, *Epistolae privatae Graecae*, 1906; A. Deissmann, in loc.; B. Olsson, *Papyrusbriefe aus der frühesten Römerzeit*, 1925.

Twenty-one writings of the NT have the form of a letter. But not all are really letters, that is, a writing on a particular occasion directed to a specific person or circle of persons, written with the aim of a direct communication with no thought of any wider distribution. In James, for example, all the features appropriate to a letter are missing. Rev is set in an epistolary framework, but literarily it belongs to the genre, apocalypse. Opinions vary on whether Heb is to be regarded as a real letter or as an artificially constructed essay which is aimed at a wider public and which uses the form of a letter only as an external appearance. Of the Catholic epistles, only II and III John are specifically addressed.

The schema is on the whole the customary one for Hellenistic letters of the time: at the beginning, the name of the sender and recipient with a greeting formula (prescript), then thanks and petition to God (proem), followed by an introductory formula; at the end greetings are extended and benedictory wishes in the sender's own hand, which take the place of the signature that is customary for us (*eschatokoll*). The papyrus finds of recent decades have provided abundant illustrative material for this form. Paul, however, in his prescript formula has linked up more closely with the Oriental-Jewish usage, while James (and the letters in Acts 15:23; 23:26) follow Hellenistic usage. But the letters of Paul rise above the general run of letters as a result of the free, well-thought-out reshaping of these sections—especially the prescript and proem—which according to the situation presupposed by the letter varies the set formulas at the beginning and the end,[1] though the reshaping is also affected by the paraenesis and the

[1] Cf. Schubert, Sanders, Mullins.

communications concerning the journeys of Paul and his traveling companions.[2] Closest to the ancient private letters stand Phlm and II and III John. Surely such short, personal lines from Paul or from the presbyter would be fully comprehensible in their implications and allusions only to those immediately addressed. But like the longer letters of Paul, they are not private correspondence, but the instrument of early Christian missionary work. The letters of Paul which have survived are letters of the apostle in his official capacity; they serve the furthering of his missionary ministry at a distance. The form of the letter in the hands of the apostle exploits all the stylistic forms of the oral missionary address, especially the proclamation of the Word in worship, preaching, paraenesis, instructive exposition, prophetic witness, hymns; it became the form of recording for posterity edificatory or theological thought in the earliest church. Occasionally Paul has incorporated already shaped bits from the primitive tradition or from his own formulations (e.g., I Cor 15:3-5; Rom 1:3, 4; Phil 2:6-11; Col 1:15-20). But the exact wording and the origin of such fragments can be established only conjecturally.

As a result of the special manner of use of the letter form in the early Christian mission, the boundary between actual and artificial letters[3] in the NT cannot always be sharply drawn. An occasional letter, which was expressly to be read to all Christians in a certain place (I Thess 5:27), a letter to an individual community which was to be kept and exchanged with that sent to the neighboring community (Col 4:16), or letters to several communities (Gal 1:2; cf. II Cor 1:1) are on the way to becoming texts with an official character. On the other hand, in letters of such a general nature as I Pet and Heb a glimpse of special community and temporal situations is not wholly lacking. The actual requirement of the mission, edification and instruction, warning and care of souls, warning against heresy, and guarantee of ecclesiastical order, comprise the potent force for the independent transformation of the letter form into a means of internal communication for Christianity. Not even the form of the less private letters in the NT can be bracketed immediately with the Hellenistic epistle (cf. Epicurus, Seneca) or with the Jewish-Hellenistic letters (e.g., Letter of Aristeas).

---

[2] See Funk.

[3] Deissmann's distinction between "letter" and "epistle" does not match the special quality of the early Christian letter. Doty suggests that more or less private letters be distinguished.

I. The Letters of Paul

§12. General Background

W. G. Kümmel, "Paulusbriefe," RGG³ V, 1961, 195 ff (lit.); J. Cambier, art. "Paul," DBS VII, 1962, 329 ff; B. Rigaux, "Paulus und seine Briefe," *Bibl. Handbibliothek* 2, 1964, 164 ff; A. Q. Morton and J. McLeman, *Christianity in the Computer Age*, 1964, 24 ff, 92 ff; *idem, Paul, the Man and the Myth*, 1966 (on this see J. J. O'Rourke, JBL 86, 1967, 110 ff; C. Dinwoodie, SJT 20, 1967, 116 ff); H. K. McArthur, "Computer Criticism," ExpT 76, 1964/65, 367 ff; *idem,* "KAI Frequency in Greek Letters," NTS 15, 1968/69, 339 ff; A. Q. Morton, "The Authorship of the Pauline Corpus," *The NT in Historical and Contemporary Perspective: Festschr. G. H. C. Macgregor*, 1965, 209 ff; *idem,* "Computer Criticism: A Reply," ExpT 77, 1965/66, 116 ff; M. L. Stirewalt, "Paul's Evaluation of Letter-Writing," *Search the Scriptures: Festschr. R. T. Stamm,* Gettysburg Theological Studies 3, 1969, 179 ff. See further Bibl. in §11.

The NT canon contains thirteen letters which name Paul as author in the prescript. Heb, which was first considered Pauline in Alexandria, then generally in the East, and since the fourth century in the West, surely does not come from Paul. Among the Pauline letters the so-called Pastoral epistles (I Tim, II Tim, Tit) form a special group. Those letters which, according to their own statement, were written by Paul during an imprisonment (Phil, Col, Phlm, Eph) can also be grouped together as the "Imprisonment letters." Except for Phlm and the Pastorals, all Paul's letters are addressed to communities.

After the beginning of the nineteenth century, questions were raised about the Pauline origin first of the Pastorals, then of those to the Thessalonians, Eph, Phil, and Col. F. C. Baur and the Tübingen school considered only the four so-called chief letters— Gal, I and II Cor, Rom—to be authentic documents of the apostle, because only these letters could be understood as witnesses for the struggle of Paul against "judaizing." But it soon became evident that by this approach the historical picture of early Christianity was placed in too narrow a frame. The representatives of the "radical criticism" [1] denied the apostle even these four main letters, and explained them as being the precipitate of antinomian currents from the period *ca.* 140 A.D. But this view faded out, as did later

---

[1] Bruno Bauer, A. Pierson, S. A. Naber, A. D. Loman, W. C. van Manen, G. A. van den Bergh van Eysinga, R. Steck.

reconstructions,[2] as a result of untenable literary presuppositions and forced historical constructs. In addition to the four main letters, I Thess, Phil, and Phlm are to be regarded as genuine, while the Pauline authorship of the Pastorals is surely to be contested and that of the other three letters (II Thess, Col, and Eph) is debatable. The recently undertaken attempt to show with the aid of computers that only the four main letters and Phlm can come from Paul cannot be characterized as successful, because the probative force of these word counts is thoroughly uncertain.[3] On the other hand it remains in dispute whether the genuine letters may contain inauthentic sections and may in part be explained as combinations of several letters or parts of letters.

Without doubt Paul dictated his letters (Rom. 16:22), but, according to the custom of the time, indicated their authenticity by a concluding greeting in his own handwriting. That is surely the case for all the Pauline letters, but it is expressly noted in several, because when the letter was read aloud this was the only way the community could be aware that he had written the concluding greeting with his own hand (I Cor 16:21; Gal 6:11; Col 4:18; II Thess 3:17; Phlm 19).[4] The assumption that Paul assigned to secretaries the formulation of his letters[5] is impossible, in view of the frequent indications of breaks in the spoken word and the uniformity of the specifically Pauline language.[6]

All the preserved letters of Paul come from the period of the height of Paul's missionary activity and its end. From the first decade and a half of his work there is no testimony from his own hand. But in the second oldest of the preserved letters Paul speaks of his letter-writing custom (II Thess 3:17). Thus all the earlier letters have been lost.

Two letters to the Corinthians that have not been preserved

[2] J. G. Rylands, A. Loisy, H. Delafosse, among others.

[3] Against the evidence of Morton that the frequency of the theoretically unconscious use of καί is markedly less in the main letters than it is in the other Pauline letters, these objections may be raised: "Before the tests themselves are tested the judgment must be rendered: unproved" (Dinwoodie); on the basis of Morton's criterion, Rom 7 could not be by Paul (O'Rourke); on the other hand, McArthur has shown that similar differences in the frequency of καί could be shown, as in Paul, in the letters of Ignatius, Basil of Caesarea, and Synesius of Cyrene as well.

[4] There is no proof that the extent of letter conclusions written by Paul's own hand was larger than this.

[5] Thus chiefly O. Roller, *Das Formular der paulinischen Briefe*, 1933; but see also Bahr, CBQ 1966, 465 ff.

[6] See recently J. N. Sevenster, *Do You Know Greek?* Suppl. NovTest 19, 1968, 11 f.

are mentioned by the apostle himself (I Cor 5:9; II Cor 2:4), as well as a letter to Laodicea (Col 4:16). This reference has given occasion for the invention of a letter of Paul to the Laodiceans.[7] The editor of the apocryphal Acts of Paul (ca. A.D. 180) has contrived or taken over a letter from the Corinthians to Paul and his answer to it (III Cor), by linking up with I Cor 7:1; 5:9.[8] The exchange of letters—in Latin—between Paul (eight letters) and Seneca (eight letters) is a spurious product of the fourth century.[9]

§13. The Chronology of the Life of Paul

D. W. Riddle, *Paul, Man of Conflict*, 1940, 201 ff; J. Knox, *Chapters in a Life of Paul*, 1950, 47 ff; J. Dupont, "Chronologie Paulinienne," RB 62, 1955, 55 ff; Th. H. Campbell, "Paul's Missionary Journeys as Reflected in His Letters," JBL 74, 1955, 80 ff; M. J. Suggs, "Concerning the Date of Paul's Macedonian Ministry," NovTest 4, 1960/61, 60 ff; F. Hahn, *Das Verständnis der Mission im NT*, WMANT 13, 1963, 77 ff; J. Finegan, *Handbook of Biblical Chronology: Principles of Time Reckoning in the Ancient World and Problems of Chronology in the Bible*, 1964, 495 ff; B. Rigaux, "Paulus und seine Briefe," *Bibl. Handbibliothek* 2, 1964, 99 ff; E. Haenchen, *Acts*, 1971, 60 ff; D. Georgi, "Die Geschichte der Kollekte des Paulus für Jerusalem," ThF 38, 1965, 91 ff; A. Strobel, art. "Zeitrechnung," BhHw 3, 1966, 2224 ff; J. C. Hurd, "Pauline Chronology and Pauline Theology," *Christian History and Interpretation: Festschr. J. Knox*, 1967, 225 ff; *idem*, "The Sequence of Paul's Letters," *Canadian Journal of Theology* 14, 1968, 189 ff; G. Ogg, *The Chronology of the Life of Paul*, 1968; C. Buck and G. Taylor, *Saint Paul: A Study of the Development of His Thought*, 1969; R. Jewett, *Paul's Anthropological Terms*, AGaJU 10, 1971, 11 ff.—On the Gallio Inscription: A. Deissmann, *Paul*, 1957, 261 ff; DBS II, 1934, 355 ff (bibl.); B. Schwank, "Der sog. Brief an Gallio und die Datierung des I Thess," BZ, NF 15, 1971, 265 f.

Up to the present we have no certain fixed point for an absolute chronology of Paul: i.e., the arrangement of the events of his life within contemporary chronology. Even if the dates of Sergius Paulus as proconsul in Cyprus (Acts 13:7 ff) and of the transfer of the procuratorship of Judea from Felix to Festus (Acts 24:27)

---

[7] See this thoughtless juxtaposition of Pauline expressions, esp. from Phil, tr. in Hennecke-Schneemelcher, *NT Apocrypha* II (ed. R. Mcl. Wilson), 1965, 128 ff.

[8] In *NT Apocrypha* (see n. 7), 322 ff.

[9] In *NT Apocrypha* (see n. 7), 133 ff. On the whole issue, cf. K. Pink, "Die pseudo-Paulinischen Briefe," Bb 6, 1925, 68 ff, 179 ff; and D. Guthrie, "Acts and Epistles in Apocryphal Writings," AHG 338 ff.

could be clearly fixed—which is not the case[1]—we should not be greatly helped, because the order of the missionary journeys (Acts 13:14) is rendered uncertain as a result of the sketch of Paul's activity offered in Gal 1:16 ff, and because it cannot be decided whether the διετία mentioned in Acts 24:27 refers to the year of office of Felix or (as is more probable) to the imprisonment of Paul in Caesarea. On the other hand, help toward establishing an absolute chronology may be provided by the mention of Gallio, the governor before whom Paul was arraigned near the end of his ministry in Corinth, according to Acts 18:12-18. An inscription first published in 1905 reproduces a letter of the Emperor Claudius to the city of Delphi which was written when, following a military success, Claudius was for the twenty-sixth time acclaimed as emperor; in it he mentions Lucius Junius Gallio as predecessor of the proconsul of the province of Achaia at this time. The proconsuls had to remain in Rome until the middle of April in order to assume their office, and in the senatorial provinces, to which Achaia belonged, they were normally in office for a year. Since the twenty-sixth acclamation of Claudius must have occurred between January 1, 52, and August 1, 52, the period of office for Gallio must have been from the spring of 51 to 52.[2] The meeting between Paul and Gallio would then have taken place about May or June of 51. According to Acts 18:11, Paul had at this time already been in Corinth for about a year and a half, that is, since the end of 49. In Acts 18:2 it is reported that Paul resided with a married couple, Priscilla and Aquila, who had come to Corinth from Rome recently (προσφάτως) as a result of Claudius' edict against the Jews. The expulsion of the Jews from Rome, is reported by Suetonius without time indication in *Claudius* 25: "He [Claudius] expelled the Jews from Rome, since under the impetus of Chrestus they were persistently making disturbances." This would also have taken place in 49. With some probability, the chronology of Paul can therefore be worked out, backward and forward from this fixed point.

Of course, this procedure is legitimate only if it is presupposed that the chronological information that may be inferred from the letters of Paul is essentially compatible with the course of Paul's ministry as recounted in Acts. This presupposition has been questioned recently by the methodological claim that the sequence of the Pauline letters can be established only by first ignoring Acts,

---

[1] See Ogg, 60 ff, 146 ff.
[2] More recent discoveries make this determination still more certain. Cf. Schwank (bibl.).

then treating the letters of Paul as the primary sources, and that only in a secondary way may it be asked whether the sequence thus established can be associated with the information in Acts (Riddle; Knox; Suggs; Hurd; Buck and Taylor; Jewett). This methodological demand is basically correct, and various attempts to follow it through concretely[3] show that on the basis of Paul's statements about the collection for Jerusalem, the following sequence may be established with assurance: I Cor; II Cor 1–9; Rom. But the chronological arrangement of the other letters must then be based on problematical conjectures about the development of Paul's thought,[4] so by this method no sure result at all is offered for a comprehensive outline of Paul's mission. Yet Campbell has proved convincingly that the sequence of Paul's missionary activities that can be inferred from his letters is so remarkably compatible with the information from Acts that we have good grounds for deriving the relative chronology of Paul's activity from a critical combination of the information from Paul's letters with the account in Acts.

This approach produces the following chronology, though it is not exact down to the year: From the call of Paul to the Apostolic Council was sixteen years, according to Gal 1:18; 2:1, on the most probable chronological interpretation. Three years are scarcely too much for the period from the end of the Apostolic Council to the end of the eighteen months' activity in Corinth (Gal 2:1, 11; I Thess 2:2; Phil 4:15 f; I Thess 3:1; II Cor 11:7–9; Acts 15:30–18:18a). The time for the return from Corinth to Asia Minor by way of Palestine, for the more than two-year stay in Ephesus, the journey to Corinth through Macedonia with the three-month stay in Achaia and then the delivery of the collection to Jerusalem (I Cor 16:8; II Cor 2:12 f; 9:4; Rom 15:25–27; Acts 18:18b–21:15) must have encompassed more than three years. Calculated on the basis of the stay in Corinth from 49 to 51, the results are as follows:

[3] Hurd (1968) in a survey up to 1962 mentions as the majority view the sequence Thess; the so-called "earlier letter" (I Cor 5:9); I Cor; Phil; II Cor 1–9; Gal; Rom; Col; Eph, with the placement of II Cor 10–13 disputed. Buck and Taylor claim to have proved the sequence II Thess; I Thess; I Cor; II Cor 10–13; Phil; II Cor 1–9; Gal; Rom; Col; Phlm; Eph. Jewett tries to establish the sequence I and II Thess; Gal; Phil; six Corinthian letters; Phlm (between the fifth and sixth Cor letters).

[4] Thus esp. Hurd and Buck-Taylor, who, by means of a purely arbitrary source theory for Acts, assign to the journeys of Paul in Acts a completely mistaken order and assume that all the letters of Paul were written between 44 and 49–52.

From this point on, chronologically definite statements cannot be made, since we do not know how long Paul's trial in Caesarea lasted. It is only a likely assumption that Paul was freed after two years in a Roman prison (Acts 28:30) and that he then went to Spain (cf. Rom 15:24; I Clem 5:7); similarly inferential is his martyrdom (under Nero?; cf. I Clem 5:7; 6:1).

§14. THE FIRST LETTER TO THE THESSALONIANS

Commentaries: see §41. Research: W. Lütgert, *Die Vollkommenen in Philippi und die Enthusiasten in Thessalonich*, BFChTh 13, 6, 1909, 55 ff; W. Hadorn, *Die Abfassung der Thessalonicherbriefe in der Zeit der dritten Missionsreise des Paulus*, BFChTh 24, 3/4, 1919–20, 67 ff; W. Michaelis, *Die Gefangenschaft des Paulus in Ephesus und das Itinerar des Timotheus*, NTF I, 3, 1925, 65 ff; T. W. Manson, "St. Paul in Greece: The Letters to the Thessalonians," BJRL 35, 1952/53, 428 ff (=Manson, *St.*, 259 ff); C. E. Faw, "On the Writing of First Thessalonians," JBL 71, 1952, 217 ff; K.-G. Eckart, "Der zweite echte Brief des Apostels Paulus an die Thessalonicher," ZThK 58, 1961, 30 ff; W. G. Kümmel, "Das literarische und geschichtliche Problem des ersten Thessalonicherbriefes," *Neotestamentica et Patristica, Freundesgabe O. Cullman*, NovTest Suppl. 6, 1962, 213 ff (=W. G. K., *Heilsgeschehen und Geschichte*, MbThSt 3, 1965, 406 ff); K. Thieme, "Die Struktur des I Thess," Abr., 450 ff; W. Schmithals, "Die Thess als Briefkompositionen," *Zeit und Geschichte, Festschr. R. Bultmann*, 1964, 295 ff; *idem*, "Die historische Situation der Thess," *Paulus und die Gnostiker. Untersuchungen zu den kleinen Plsbr.*, ThF 35, 1965, 89 ff; B. Rigaux, art. "Thess," LThK 10, 1965, 105 ff.

1. Contents

Following the opening greeting (1:1) is an expression of thanks for the exemplary way in which the community has accepted the Christian faith (1:2-10). Then Paul in retrospect defends his missionary work in Thessalonica (2:1-12) and returns once more to the conduct of the reader (2:13-16). He concludes this opening part of the letter with a gratitude-filled expression concerning his relation with the community (2:17–3:10) and an intercession which is in the same framework as the opening of the letter. In Chs. 4–5 there follow warnings and instructions: a reminder of the ethical obligations of the Thessalonian Christians with a pagan past (4:1-12), an eschatological instruction concerning the fate of members of the community who have "fallen asleep" before the parousia, accompanied by a call for watchfulness on the part of the living (4:13–5:11), and a string of detailed advice for the community life (5:12-22). Concluding prayers and benediction (5:23-28).

2. The Founding of the Community

Thessalonica—until 1937, Saloniki—the capital of the Roman province of Macedonia, lay on the great military highway, the Via Egnatia, which led from Dyrrhachium to Byzantium and by which Rome was linked with the East. It was at that time a populous city which had a synagogue (Acts 17:1) with many non-Jewish "God-fearers" (Acts 17:4).

On the so-called second missionary journey, about the year 49, Paul came from Philippi to Thessalonica and founded there the Christian community, aided by Silvanus (or, as he is called in Acts, Silas) and Timothy (cf. I Thess 1:1, 5-8; 2:1-14; 3:1-6; Phil 4:16; and see Acts 17:1-10; 18:5). The community was almost entirely pagan (1:9; 2:14; Acts 17:4); Aristarchus (Acts 20:4) was a Jewish Christian from Thessalonica according to Col 4:10 f.

Acts 17:2 does not prove that Paul was active there for only three to four weeks. A relationship of trust, as is evident in 2:9-12, 17, 19 f; 3:6, could not have developed in so short a time, any more than the exemplary faith of the Thessalonians could have done (1:8 ff). According to Phil 4:16, the Christians of Philippi sent support more than once to the apostle at Thessalonica, so that his stay there must have been of longer duration. Paul did not create a strict community organization in Thessalonica: 5:12 is not speaking of officers in the formal sense (cf. I Tim 5:17), but of members of the community who voluntarily care for the brethren, and the imperatives (5:14) are not aimed at office-holders, but summon the community itself to responsibility for the spiritual welfare of its members.

The community must have developed quickly and in a gratifying way (1:3 f; 2:13); Paul characterizes them as examples (1:7 f) for the believers of Macedonia and Achaia. But the Jews incited the mob of the city against Paul and Silas, so that they had to flee by night to Berea (Acts 17:5 ff). Paul left there as well when effective preaching was forcibly hindered by the Jews from Thessalonica, journeying first to Athens and from there on to Corinth (Acts 17:13 f). According to Acts 17:14 f, Silas and Timothy remained in Berea but received orders from Paul in Athens to come to him as quickly as possible; coming from Macedonia, they met Paul in Corinth (Acts 18:5). These statements do not agree exactly with I Thess 3:1-6. There Paul says that in his desire for news of the young community, which he had had to leave so hastily, "we decided to stay on alone in Athens, and we have sent Timothy" (1 f) i.e., to Thessalonica. He says the same thing in v. 5: "I have sent," at which point v. 5 takes up again from v. 2 (editorial "we" = I, in 3:6 ff and elsewhere, referring to Paul). The expression "we decided to stay on alone in Athens" presupposes the presence there of Timothy. The various attempts to remove this contradiction are not capable of proof and are probably useless, since Acts is not informed precisely about the journeys of Paul's companions.[1]

3. Time of and Occasion for the Letter

I Thess offers statements which presuppose a situation whereby Paul has sent Timothy from Athens to Thessalonica (3:1 f) in order to learn something about the state of the community. Since, according to 1:1 and 3:6, Timothy and Silas are with Paul, and Timothy has brought news from Thessalonica, and since in addition Athens is mentioned in 3:1 as though Paul were no longer there, the predominant view is that I Thess was written in Corinth, where Paul had gone from Athens, and where, according to Acts 18:5, Timothy and Silas once more met Paul. Since time must be allowed for Timothy's journey from Athens to Thessalonica and back to Corinth, and for spreading the news about the state of the faith of the Thessalonians in Macedonia and Achaia (I Thess 1:8 f), I Thess must have been written about the year 50. I Thess is therefore the oldest surviving letter of Paul. Several objections have been offered against this proposal:[2] (a) The opponents whom Paul is fighting in I Thess represent the same views (according to Schmithals they are Jewish-Christian Gnostics) as do those attacked in Gal and II Cor, and Paul has to defend himself against the same reproaches. That leads to the assumption that I Thess must

[1] Cf. von Dobschütz, *Comm.*, 13 ff.
[2] See Lütgert, Hadorn, Michaelis, Schmithals; Buck-Taylor, 46 ff.

have been written during the same period of activity of Paul as Gal and II Cor.[3] (b) The reports concerning the spread of the news about the faith of the Thessalonians in Macedonia and Achaia, indeed in every place (1:8 f), concerning the persecution of the community (2:14) and the organization that already existed in it (5:12) imply a distance in time from the founding of the community which must have been longer than a few months. (c) The occurrence of several deaths within the community is inconceivable within so short a time. (d) Since according to Acts 17:14; 18:5, Timothy was not with Paul in Athens, although I Thess 3:1 presupposes that he was, the stay in Athens mentioned in I Thess cannot be identical with the one named in Acts. Consequently, I Thess must have been written during the third missionary journey, as Paul journeyed on his "interim visit" to Corinth (II Cor 2:1). We would then have to suppose a stay in Athens on this journey, at which time Paul was accompanied by Timothy. (e) At the beginning of his short stay in Athens (Acts 17:15 ff) Paul cannot have planned several times to travel to Thessalonica without then being able to carry out his plans (I Thess 2:17 f). (f) I Thess must have been written in Athens after Paul's departure from Corinth, because at the time of his stay in Corinth Paul still shared the expectation that all Christians would live until the parousia, while according to I Thess 4:15 ff, this no longer corresponds to his view at this time.

But these arguments are not convincing. (a) It is true that in I Thess 2:1 ff Paul defends himself against reproaches similar to those in Gal and I Cor: leading others astray (2:3 = II Cor 6:8); deceit (2:3 = II Cor 4:2); greed (2:5 = II Cor 12:16-18); seeking personal glory (2:6 = II Cor 10:17 f; 3:1; 4:5); not allowing the community to support him (2:7 = II Cor 11:9); flattery and ingratiating himself with people (2:4 f = Gal 1:10).[4] But this evidence does not demand that I Thess be dated in the period of the apostle's struggle against Judaizers and Gnostics. Jews, Judaizers, and Gnostics undoubtedly used the same weapons many times against Paul. In Thessalonica it was obviously the local Jews who persuaded the young Christian community that Paul was a magician of corrupt mind who by means of all sorts of tricks promoted his self-seeking, ambitious propaganda. In 2:1 ff, 18 f, and 3:9 f, Paul is guarding himself against such attacks and not against false doctrine that

---

[3] According to Schmithals I Cor, Phil, Rom 16 also.

[4] Cf. Schmithals, "Historische Situation," 100 ff. Schmithals cannot prove that the reproaches against Paul stem from Gnostic opponents who since Paul's departure have been represented in the church at Thessalonica.

has penetrated the community. If this is the historical background, then the sudden lunge against Judaism's hostility to Christians is readily explained (2:14-16). (*b*) The references to the widening fame of the Thessalonians' faith and the persecution they experienced do not require a long period of time, and there is no mention of an established organization (see above, p. 256). (*c*) A few deaths could have occurred even in a short time. (*d*) Acts could scarcely have been so precisely informed about the journeys of Paul's companions. (*e*) We do not know how long Paul's stay in Athens recounted in Acts 17 lasted, and we cannot determine what obstacles Paul meant when he said, "We wanted to come to you —I, Paul—once or twice, but Satan hindered us from doing so" (2:18). Consequently, the claim cannot be substantiated that in the situation in Athens described in Acts 17 Paul "could have traveled to the north instead of to Corinth," [5] so I Thess could not have been written at this time. (*f*) It is unproved that Paul at the time of his first visit to Corinth expected that all Christians would live until the parousia,[6] so this argument is simply useless.

But more important than these negative statements, what the letter tells us about Paul's relations with the community up to that time argues against I Thess's having been written several years after Paul's departure from Thessalonica. In 1:5–2:12 allusions to the time of Paul's first missionary activity in Thessalonica (1:5, 9; 2:2, 8 f, 12) and to his "arrival" among them (1:9; 2:1) point out how unobjectionable was his coming to Thessalonica, how the Thessalonians by their conversion became imitators of Paul and of Christ (1:6) and thus examples for others (1:7). With ever-changing turns of expression, the apostle reminds them of these facts: "You know" (1:5; 2:1 ff); "You yourselves recall" (2:9); "You are witnesses" (2:10). All these are fresh recollections. Furthermore (2:17 f), following his departure, Paul felt "πρὸς καιρὸν ὥρας deserted by reason of his separation" from his readers; therefore he must have been away from Thessalonica for only a short time. His longing for his community so overmastered him that he decided, not once but twice, to travel to Thessalonica in order to see whether the community was standing fast in the period of tribulation and persecution in which it found itself (3: 2 f), but "Satan hindered" him from doing so. Since he could not hold out any longer without news from Thessalonica, he sent Timothy there from Athens (3:1 f, 5), received with great gratitude and joy the good news that Timothy brought back to him,

---

[5] Schmithals, "Historische Situation," 133.

[6] Thus Buck-Taylor, 47.

and immediately wrote this letter (3:6 ff). Thus the letter can have been written only a few months after the founding of the community, the apostle's first letter to them after the separation.

According to 3:6, I Thess was written immediately after Timothy's return to Paul. Paul had journeyed on from Athens to Corinth and had begun to preach in the synagogue there, until Silas and Timothy met him once more (Acts 18:1-5). Accordingly, several months, but not more, elapsed between Paul's separation from the Thessalonians and the writing of this letter to them. Paul received the impetus to write the letter through his receipt of the fresh news which Timothy had brought from Thessalonica, which raises the possibility that Paul in Chs. 4 and 5 is answering a letter from the community (Faw, on the basis of περὶ in 4:9, 13; 5:1, 12). The news frees Paul from a heavy concern: the community stands firm in faith and love (3:6); his deep joy at this is expressed in terms which serve to strengthen the faith of the community and to ward off the suspicions brought against Paul. Evident here is the difficulty into which former pagans had fallen through the preaching of the imminent eschatological glory (cf. 4:11 f, 13 ff; 5:1 ff, 14), but also the necessity of bringing into vital harmony the still future responsibility before God and sober moral obligation in the present (5:6 ff; 4:3 ff; 5:12 f, 19 f). Although I Thess lacks any systematic instruction, it is all the more a real letter, which originated in a specific, unique situation, a personal testimony of Pauline missionary work.

4. Authenticity and Unity

This argument can only be validated, however, if one presupposes that I Thess originated with Paul in the form in which it has been handed down. The challenge to the genuineness of the letter offered by K. Schrader (1836) and then by F. C. Baur and a part of his school (Volkmar and Holsten) has no supporters today, nor does the inadequately grounded assumption that sections 2:13-16; 4:1-8, 10b-12, 18; 5:12-22, 27[7] are not of Pauline origin.[8]

---

[7] Eckart. Schmithals, "Historische Situation," 131, considers it difficult for 2:15 f to be genuine; according to B. A. Pearson, "I Thess 2:13-16: A Deutero-Pauline Interpolation," HTR 64, 1971, 79 ff, 2:13-16 is an interpolation from the time after 70, because the idea is un-Pauline and the section interrupts the connection between 2:12 and 2:17.

[8] Against Eckart, see Kümmel, Festschr. Cullmann, 215 ff (=Heilsgeschehen, 408 ff); cf. also Schmithals, "Historische Situation," 91 f; Pearson, "Interpolation" (see n. 7), can point to some difficulties in 2:13-16, but can explain neither the origin of the text nor why it was interpolated at precisely this point.

On the other hand, E. Fuchs,[9] Eckart, and Schmithals[10] would like to prove in various ways that I Thess was composed from two genuine letters to the Thessalonians.[11] Out of the two Thessalonian letters Schmithals reconstructs four "original" letters, of which the second includes I Thess 1:1–2:12 = 4:2–5:28, and the fourth includes I Thess 2:13–4:1. According to Schmithals there are two decisive grounds for this proposal: I Thess 2:13 begins with a second proem (the first is in 1:2), and 3:11 is a conclusion of a letter (with a second at 5:23). "A letter with two proems and two concluding formulae is not a letter, but a compounding of two letters." [12] But since Paul made a transition directly from proem to correspondence (2:2 ff), why should he not resume the proem at 2:13 ff? And before he shifts to paraenetic material (4: 1 ff), why should he not conclude the correspondence proper with a festive wish (3:11 ff; cf. also Rom 11:33 ff)? [13] We scarcely have the right to postulate that Paul must always have used the schema of a letter in the same way. But above all, there are two arguments against the hypothesis that I Thess was combined from two letters: (1) The letter I Thess 1:1–2:12 = 4:2–5:28 can be understood as a complete letter; but the redactor must have omitted the introductory section of the second letter (2:13–4:1) as well as the concluding remarks and the benediction. Then καὶ διὰ τοῦτο καὶ ἡμεῖς in 2:13a, which does not fit as an introductory remark, has to be explained away as a "redactional flourish." [13a] But this act of the redactor is incomprehensible. (2) Still more important is the objection that no illuminating explanation at all can be found for having combined the two reconstructed letters into the secondary composition of I Thess (and the same holds true for the hypotheses about secondary compositions of I and II Cor, Gal, Phil; see §§16–18, 20). The proposal is unconvincing that the splicing together into a single letter of two or more letters of Paul to the same community is to be explained on the ground of the intention

---

[9] E. Fuchs, "Hermeneutik?" ThViat 7, 1960, 46 ff (=E. F., *Glaube und Erfahrung*, 1965, 118 ff).

[10] In agreement with W. Schenk, "Der I Kor als Briefsammlung," ZNW 60, 1969, 243.

[11] Against Eckart's partition, see Kümmel (see n. 8), 220 ff (=412 ff).

[12] Schmithals, "Briefkompositionen," 302.

[13] C. J. Berkelund, *Parakalô*, 1967, 129, 133, stresses correctly that 3:11-13 concludes the proem, not a letter, and that 4:1 f cannot be interpreted as a conclusion to a letter.

[13a] Thus Schmithals, "Briefkompositionen," 305.

of the editor of the earliest collection of the letters of Paul to publish seven Pauline letters and to show by this number "the catholicity of the collection."[14] The fact is that the hypothesis of an original collection of seven Pauline letters is itself not proved (see §35.2). Above all, however, no one has adduced really convincing motives for someone other than the original author piecing together several of his letters, leaving out some parts and reworking other parts.[15] The parallel adduced by G. Bornkamm[16]—the probable combination in Polycarp's Letter to the Philippians of two letters: 1–12 and 13–14[17]—proves nothing in this connection, because in that case two letters are set side by side, while in the Thessalonians hypothesis the letters are interwoven. If it is a fact that "in antiquity there are no parallels" for such combining of letters,[18] on that basis the hypothesis that two letters to the Thessalonians were combined to form our I Thess must be considered unlikely.

§15. THE SECOND LETTER TO THE THESSALONIANS

In addition to bibl. in §14: W. Wrede, *Die Echtheit des 2 Thess*, TU, NF 9, 2, 1903; A. Harnack, "Das Problem des 2 Thess," SAB 1910, 560 ff; J. Wrzol, *Die Echtheit des 2 Thess untersucht*, BSt 19, 4, 1916; J. Graafen, *Die Echtheit des 2. Briefes an die Thessalonicher*, NTA 14, 5, 1930; E. Schweizer, "Der Thess ein Phil?" ThZ 1, 1945, 90 ff, 286 ff; 2, 1946, 74 f; see, on the other hand, W. Michaelis, ThZ 1, 282 ff; H. Braun, "Zur nichtpaulinischen Herkunft des zweiten Thessalonicherbriefes," ZNW 44, 1952/53, 152 ff (=*Gesammelte Studien zum NT und seiner Umwelt*, 1962, 205 ff); P. Day, "The Practical Purpose of Second Thessalonians," ATR 45, 1963, 203 ff; D. Lührmann, *Das Offenbarungsverständnis bei Paulus und in den paulinischen Gemeinden*, WMANT 16, 1965, 109 ff.

[14] W. Schmithals, "Zur Abfassung und ältesten Sammlung der paulinischen Hauptbriefe," *Paulus und die Gnostiker*, 1965, 191 ff.

[15] Cf. W. Michaelis, "Teilungshypothesen bei Paulusbriefen," ThZ 14, 1958, 321 ff.

[16] G. Bornkamm, *Die Vorgeschichte des sog. Zweiten Korintherbriefes*, SAH 1961, 2, 3, 34 n. 131.

[17] See B. Altaner, *Patrology*, tr. from the 5th German ed. by H. C. Graef, 1960, 111.

[18] Schmithals, "Briefkompositionen," 314. The reference of J. Schmid (ThRv 62, 1966, 305) to the writings of Simeon of Mesopotamia as an example leads nowhere, since what is involved here is not letters but probably conscious deception (see J. Quasten, *Patrology* III, 1960, 164 ff).

1. Contents

After the introductory greeting formula (1:1-2) Paul offers thanks for the preservation of the community in faith and love, especially for their patience in suffering. He warns them of the parousia and the last judgment, and closes the introduction to the letter with a petition for the community (1:3-12). The letter proper begins with an appeal for restraint in view of the report of an exaggerated expectation of the parousia in the Thessalonian community: the day of the Lord has not yet come; first "the Adversary" must come. He is already at work in secret, but will be restrained by a power known to the community. Following his disclosure he will be destroyed at the parousia (2:1-12).

This is followed by thanks for the Christians' election, warning about being steadfast, repeated intercession with reference to the trustworthiness of Christ and God (2:13–3:5). Then come special instructions relative to the disorderly, who are leading lazy lives in view of the nearness of the parousia (3:6-16). Closing greeting in Paul's own handwriting (3:17-18).

2. Chronological Sequence of I and II Thessalonians

Since Hugo Grotius (1641) it has been repeatedly proposed that II Thess was written before I Thess.[1] The grounds for this earlier dating of II Thess are: (1) I Thess was placed before II Thess in the canon because it was longer. (2) Timothy, on being sent to Thessalonica, would have taken a letter with him. (3) The distress in II Thess is in the present; in I Thess it is in the past. (4) The disorders in II Thess 3:11 are something new, but in I Thess 5:4 the disorderly are dealt with as already mentioned; I Thess 4:10, 12 is so brief that the warning can be understood only on the basis of II Thess 3:6 ff. (5) The reference to the personal signature in II Thess 3:17 makes sense only if this is the first letter. (6) The remark that the community has no need to be instructed about times and periods (I Thess 5:1) fits better if its members have already read II Thess 2:3 ff. (7) The references in I Thess 4:9, 13; 5:1, using περί, to questions which are problems in the community can best be explained if these questions were raised for

---

[1] Recently Albertz, Appel (II Thess was merely *sent* before I Thess); de Zwaan; Hadorn, 116 ff; T. W. Manson; J. Weiss, *The History of Primitive Christianity*, 1937, 151 ff; Buck-Taylor, 140 ff; Schmithals considers 2:1-12; 3:6-16 to be Paul's first letter to Thessalonica.

the community by statements in II Thess. (8) The eschatology
and the Christology in II Thess are more primitive than those in
I Thess.

These arguments are in no way convincing, however. (1) There
is no basis for conjecturing a transposition within the collection
of Pauline letters. (2) Timothy is a fellow sender, so he could not
have taken the letter with him. (3) The difficulties are still continuing, according to I Thess 3:3 f, and, given the conditions in
Thessalonica, could break out anew any day. As II Thess 1:4 ff
shows, that actually did occur. (4) Paul had already at the founding of the community warned against a propensity for idleness
arising from eschatological enthusiasm (I Thess 4:11); he deals
with it in I Thess 4:10 f and 5:14. Meanwhile in II Thess vigorous
measures had to be taken, for which Paul naturally appeals to
oral instruction given when the community was founded rather
than referring to I Thess 4:10 f; 5:14. (5) Paul recalls earlier
written communications not only in I Cor 5:9; II Cor 2:3 ff; 7:8,
12, but also in II Thess 2:15. And II Thess 2:2 perhaps presupposes
that a spurious letter from him is circulating in Thessalonica. This
conjecture, however, abundantly justifies the remark in II Thess
3:17 about his custom in letter-writing. (6) I Thess 5:1 f alludes
to oral instruction, as does I Thess 4:9. (7) Nothing indicates that
the questions current in the community were occasioned by a letter
from Paul. (8) II Thess does not mention those who die before
the parousia, but that implies nothing about an earlier eschatological
view than I Thess. And if the death and resurrection of Jesus are
lacking in II Thess, a purely futuristic eschatology cannot be inferred from that, especially since II Thess 3:18 presupposes an
already exalted Lord Jesus Christ. But the fact that I Thess 2:17–
3:10 could stand only in a first letter to a community speaks decisively against the supposition that I Thess is the second letter to
the community. The canonical sequence must therefore be the
original.

3. Authenticity and Unity

The first to contest the genuineness of II Thess[2] was J. E. Christian Schmidt in *Vermutungen über die beiden Briefe an die Thessalonicher* (1798): two admonitions in 2:1-12 to rely on a letter
written in his name in which he asserts the nearness of the parousia
are as un-Pauline as are the related fantasies about the Antichrist.

---

[2] On the history of criticism, cf. Rigaux, *Comm.*, 124 ff.

F. H. Kern[3] added to that theory the proposal that II Thess was literarily dependent on I Thess and pointed to the un-Pauline expressions and to II Thess 3:17. This reference betrays the attempt to gain for the inauthentic letter acceptance as a Pauline letter. Kern's research was for decades regarded as normative. W. Wrede in establishing the inauthenticity of the letter laid stress on the literary dependence of II Thess on I Thess: II Thess is almost completely dependent on I Thess; besides, if Paul had believed that his name had been misused in a forgery (II Thess 2:2; 3:17), he would have followed up on the matter. This criticism of Wrede's by and large lies at the basis of the denial today of the authenticity of II Thess, but in addition there are pointed out (a) the incompatibility of II Thess 2:1-12 with the eschatological passages I Thess 4:13 ff and I Cor 15:20 ff;[4] (b) the moralizing in II Thess 1:5 ff and 2:12 in comparison with Paul;[5] (c) the consistent focus of the argument in II Thess on the authority of the apostle.[6] The assumption of a post-Pauline origin for II Thess is widely regarded today as unavoidable.[7] In opposition to this W. Schmithals tries to show that "the single effective argument" against the Pauline origin of II Thess—the assumption of literary dependence by II Thess on I Thess—is weakened if it is recognized that II Thess also is composed of two letters and that the literary similarity between I and II Thess can be explained by the similar manner of combining two letters in both the canonical letters.

The assumption of non-Pauline origin for II Thess is challenged by important considerations, however. Arguments against the authenticity based on the difference of the expectation of the End in I and II Thess cannot be regarded as valid. The concepts employed in II Thess are traditional apocalyptic material: the Man of Lawlessness (II Thess 2:3) and the Restrainer ($\kappa\alpha\tau\acute{\epsilon}\chi\omega\nu$) in 2:7 are apocalyptic figures;[8] the events which 2:3 ff presupposes are as compatible and as incompatible with I Cor 15:23 ff in an es-

---

[3] "Über 2 Thess 2,1-12," TZTh 1839, 145 ff.

[4] Masson; Fuller, Marxsen; G. Ziener, GANT, 305; Lührmann.

[5] H. Braun.

[6] G. Dautzenberg, GANT, 97 ff.

[7] Cf., in addition to those mentioned in nn. 4-6, Jülicher; R. Bultmann, Theology, 1951, 190; H. J. Schoeps, Paul, 1961, 51; E. Fuchs, "Hermeneutik?" ThViat 7, 1960, 346 (=E. F., Glaube und Erfahrung, 1965, 119); K.-G. Eckart, "Der zweite echte Brief des Apostels Paulus an die Thessalonicher," ZThK 58, 1961, 30 f; P. Day, "The Practical Purpose of Second Thessalonians," ATR 45, 1963, 203 ff; G. Bornkamm, Paul, 1970, 243; B. A. Pearson, "I Thess 2:13-16: A Deutero-Pauline Interpolation," HTR 64, 1971, 88 f.

[8] See Dibelius, in loc.

chatological portrayal as I Thess 4:13 ff is with I Cor 15:51 ff. There is nothing surprising about the alleged tension between I Thess 5:2, where the parousia is expected to come like a thief in the night, and II Thess 2:3 ff, where anticipatory signs must first occur (apostasy, disclosure of the great transgressor, who sets up in the temple a blasphemous arrogance and presents himself as God, the shunting aside of the restraining power); it must be recalled that both conceptions—the End is coming suddenly, and it has historical antecedents—occur together in the apocalyptic of Judaism and early Christianity, and lie within the same perspective. Nor is it true that Paul nowhere else offers such apocalyptic detail (cf. I Thess 4:15-17; I Cor 15:23-28, 51 f). The "over-realized eschatology"[9] of the false teachers who proclaim, "The day of the Lord has already come" (II Thess 2:2)[10] must by no means be viewed as related to Gnosticism. Moreover Paul, in spite of references to events still delaying the End, presupposes, in II Thess 2:7 that "the mystery of lawlessness is already at work," and thus calculates that the eschatological events are beginning. Yet the reports that have reached him about the super-enthusiastic eschatological expectation of some Christians in Thessalonica understandably leads him to emphasize the factors in the delay even while he maintains the expectation of an imminent parousia.

The remaining objections to Paul's having written II Thess are not convincing either, and, indeed, some factors support his having written it. Clearly, on the basis of reports, Paul had reason to suppose that a spurious letter in his name was being circulated (2:2), and accordingly he refers in 3:17 to the characteristic feature of all his letters. But nothing justifies the postulate that he should have gone further in clearing up this matter, especially since in Gal 6:11 on other grounds he also pointed to the authenticity of Gal by reference to the signature in his own handwriting. Although Braun would like to see in II Thess a moralizing extension of the theology in I Thess because of the prediction of divine judgment on the oppressors of the community (1:5 ff), there is an analogous judgment on the Jews who oppose the mission in I Thess 2:16. And II Thess 1:11 shows that in II Thess there is by no means an expectation that there will be a general acceptance of Christians in the judgment merely because they are Christians.[11] To point to

---

[9] Thus R. H. Fuller, *Intr.*, 59.

[10] See Schmithals, "Historische Situation," 146 ff, on this translation of ἐνέστηκεν, which is the only one possible.

[11] Further arguments against Braun in Schmithals, "Briefkompositionen," 310 n. 35.

a more consistent kind of stress on the authority of the apostle
and of the tradition handed on by him (2:2, 15; 3:4, 6, 10, 12,
14) than in Paul's other letters is to overlook the fact that Paul
in I Thess 4:1 f; I Cor 7:25, 40; 14:37; Gal 5:2; Phil 2:12 places
no less explicit emphasis on his apostolic authority.

While the objections against Pauline authorship for II Thess
are by no means persuasive, there are several things that speak for
its authenticity. The language and style of II Thess are, apart from
a few words, thoroughly Pauline: ἐπιφάνεια for the parousia occurs
only in II Thess 2:8 and in the Pastorals, but it is not the sole
terminus technicus in II Thess. While occasionally in II Thess
(2:13; 3:16) κύριος is used instead of θεός (I Thess 1:4; 5:23),
a similar exchange is found elsewhere (I Thess 2:12; cf. Col 1:10).
The literary relationship of II Thess to I Thess is without doubt
very close,[12] but, contrary to the claim of Wrede, the points of
contact do not occur in the same sequence, throughout, and they
are spread over only about a third of the letter, so that nothing
compels the assumption of literary dependence. The change of tone
—compare II Thess 1:3; 2:13 εὐχαριστεῖν ὀφείλομεν with I Thess
1:2; 2:13 εὐχαριστοῦμεν—is understandable in view of the reproof
that Paul has to express in II Thess, and furthermore corresponds
to liturgical style (I Clem 38:4; Barn 5:3).

The hypothesis of inauthenticity creates its own difficulties, however. Since from the early second century on (Polyc., Phil 11:4;
Marcion) II Thess has belonged uncontestedly to the Pauline writings, it must have been written at the very latest in the opening
years of the second century. But the controversy over the "over-
realized eschatology" which forms the central point of the letter
cannot be accounted for on the basis of post-Pauline tendencies
in the first century. Indeed, II Thess 2:4 was obviously written
while the temple was still standing. The addition of μεθ' ἡμῶν in
1:7 is thoroughly Pauline[13] and speaks in favor of Pauline authorship, but it would be quite improbable in an imitator. Similarly,
the premature conclusion in 3:1-5 fits a living, dictating Paul
better than a consciously imitative author.

Of course, this argument is valid only if it is presupposed that
II Thess represents a literary unity in the form handed down.
Against that supposition Schmithals has objected that in II Thess
the proem (2:13 f) and the concluding formula (2:16–3:5) of a
second letter are also present, so that II Thess is a combination
of two letters: 1:1-12; 3:6-16; and 2:13 f, 1-12, 15-17; 3:1-3

[12] Cf. the table in Rigaux, *Comm.*, 133 f.
[13] Cf. I Thess 3:12; also von Dobschütz on this passage.

(5), 17 f. This theory assumes that the introductory formula was omitted from the second letter, that the concluding formula was omitted from the first letter, that the redactor transposed 2:1-12 after 2:13 f, since otherwise "the two proems would succeed one another directly," and finally that the undeniably difficult ἡμεῖς δέ (2:13) is a "redactional bracket." All these are arbitrary assumptions. The repetition of the proem formula in 2:13 is just as possible as the beginning of a concluding formula in 2:16 f in the original context of a Pauline letter, so long as the undemonstrable and unjustifiable demand is not advanced that Paul must always have kept to the same literary schema in all his letters. The whole of the evidence points rather to II Thess as a second letter of Paul to the community in Thessalonica.

Still to be explained is the striking circumstance that Paul should have had to write to the same community a letter that is similar in so many ways. Attempts have been made to avoid the force of this by assuming that it was addressed originally to a Jewish-Christian minority in Thessalonica,[14] or to a special group within the church,[15] or to the community in Berea[16] or Philippi.[17] But all these hypotheses are controverted by the fact that the original address must then have been altered (why?), and that according to II Thess 2:15 Paul had already written a letter to the same community.

II Thess is most comprehensible, therefore, if Paul himself wrote II Thess a few weeks after he had written I Thess, when the first letter was still fresh in his mind. The proem of II Thess also mentions, in addition to Paul, Silvanus and Timothy, although according to Acts Silvanus accompanied Paul only during the second missionary journey. Paul has received new information from Thessalonica ("we hear" 3:11; cf. 2:2). In spite of persecution and troubles, the community had not wavered (1:4), though alleged revelations (διὰ πνεύματος 2:2) had been presented there by a false teacher who appealed to oral or written statements of Paul for support of his view that the Day of the Lord had already arrived (2:2). This apocalyptic fanaticism led to the shunning of work in favor of "being busy" (3:11 f), so that Paul recommends measures for church discipline against such fanaticism (3:6 ff, 11 ff).

In this setting one can understand both the apocalyptic teaching, which builds on the oral missionary preaching and which stresses the reverse side of the eschatological preaching, and at the same

[14] Albertz; Harnack.
[15] Dibelius.
[16] Goguel.
[17] Schweizer.

time how it is that with the curious mixing of new material and borrowings from I Thess, I Thess 2:1–3:10 still remains essentially unused. Also comprehensible in this somewhat altered state of affairs is the strengthening of certain points of view which were treated in I Thess, such as the obligation to suffer, the threat of judgment against the persecutors of the community, the setting straight of the idlers and the fanatics. Even though details in II Thess as well as in I Thess are not completely transparent for us, that very fact is based on the nature of a real letter and gives no occasion for doubt about its authenticity.

If II Thess was written not long after I Thess, then it may be inferred that the probable place of writing was Corinth and the probable time was 50/51.

§16. THE FIRST LETTER TO THE CORINTHIANS

Commentaries: see §41. Research: W. Lütgert, *Freiheitspredigt und Schwarmgeister in Korinth*, BFChTh 12, 3, 1908; A. Schlatter, *Die kor. Theologie*, BFChTh 18, 2, 1914; H. von Soden, *Sakrament und Ethik bei Paulus*, MbThSt I, 1931, 1 ff (=H. v. S., *Urchristentum und Geschichte* I, 1951, 239 ff); T. W. Manson, "St. Paul in Ephesus: (3) The Corinthian Correspondence," BJRL 26, 1941/42, 101 ff (=Manson, *St.*, 190 ff, 210 ff); J. T. Dean, *Saint Paul and Corinth*, 1947; P. Cleary, "The Epistles to the Corinthians," CBQ 12, 1950, 10 ff; J. Munck, *Paul and the Salvation of Mankind*, 1959, 135 ff; W. Schmithals, *Die Gnosis in Korinth. Eine Untersuchung zu den Korintherbriefen*, FRLANT, NF 48 (1956), ³1969; U. Wilckens, *Weisheit und Torheit. Eine exegetisch-religionsgeschichtliche Untersuchung zu 1. Kor. 1 und 2*, BHTh 26, 1959; E. Dinkler, RGG³ IV, 1960, 17 ff; D. Georgi, review of Schmithals, *Gnosis*, VF 1958/59, 1960, 90 ff; C. K. Barrett, "Cephas and Corinth," Abr., 1 ff; *idem*, "Christianity at Corinth," BJRL 46, 1964, 269 ff; J. C. Hurd, *The Origin of I Corinthians*, 1965 (on this see W. G. Kümmel, ThLZ 91, 1966, 505 ff); R. Batey, "Paul's Interactions with the Corinthians," JBL 84, 1965, 139 ff; J. Harrison, "St. Paul's Letters to the Corinthians," ExpT 77, 1966, 285 ff; A. Feuillet, DBS VII, 1966, 171 ff; J. R. Richards, "Romans and 1 Corinthians: Their Chronological Relationship and Comparative Dates," NTS 13, 1966/67, 14 ff; N. A. Dahl, "Paul and the Church at Corinth According to 1 Corinthians 1:10–4:21," *Christian History and Interpretation: Festschr. J. Knox*, 1967, 313 ff; J. C. K. Freeborn, "The Development of Doctrine at Corinth," StEv IV, TU 102, 1968, 404 ff; R. Baumann, *Mitte und Norm des Christlichen. Eine Auslegung von 1 Kor 1,1–3,4*, NTA, NF 5, 1968; W. Schenk, "Der 1 Kor als Briefsammlung," ZNW 60, 1969, 219 ff; R. Jewett, *Paul's Anthropological Terms*, AGaJU 10, 1971, 23 ff.

1. Contents

After the proem and the expression of thanks for God's action among the community, Paul on the basis of reports (1:11) discusses conflicts within the community (1:10–4:21): in reaction to the mistakenly high estimate of individual primitive Christian leaders Paul makes reference to the nonessentiality of the individual preacher of the gospel, since the gospel is not human wisdom (1:13–3:17). [As a kind of excursus in 2:6-16 he notes that there is indeed a wisdom for the mature.] He combats human boasting by referring to the insignificance of the apostles (3:18–4:13) and draws attention to his own plans concerning the community (the sending of Timothy that has happened and his own plan for coming). On the basis of a further communication (5:1) comes a discussion of sexual questions: 5:1-13, the case of incest; 6:12-20, relations with prostitutes; in between is handled by means of catchwords the problem of legal disputes between Christians (6:1-11). On the basis of a written inquiry from the Corinthians (7:1), Paul discusses: marital problems (7:1-40); eating food offered to idols (8:1–11:1). (Excursus in 9:1-27 on the right of the apostle to receive support, his waiving support, and his adaptability for the sake of the mission; in 10:1-13 is treated the Fathers' peril in the desert and the analogous peril of Christians.) Transition to problems related to worship (11:2–14:40): in sequence are treated the problems of head-covering for women at worship (11:3-16), correct celebration of the Lord's Supper (11:17-34), and the place of the Spirit's gifts in the community meetings (12:1–14:40). (Another excursus in 13:1-13: a hymn describing ἀγάπη.) In 15:1-58 there follows a discussion of the resurrection of Christians; in 16:1-18 is a series of brief communications: the collection (16:1-4); travel plans (16:5-12); concluding warnings (16:13 f); communications (16:15:18). Greetings and benediction (16:19-24).

Clearly the letter has no consecutive development of ideas, but takes up different questions about the life and faith of the Christian community on the basis of reports from the community and in response to a letter from the community, and in so doing there is no connection between the individual sections. It may be conjectured that not only 7:1 ff, but also the sections introduced by the phrase περὶ δέ (8:1 ff; 12:1 ff; 16:1 ff), are responding to questions raised in the letter from the Corinthians mentioned in 7:1 ff. In 11:18 ff; 15:12 ff it is evident that Paul has taken reports from the community as his starting point. Strikingly and often, a connected theme is interrupted by an excursus (2:6-16; 6:1-11; 9:1-27; 10:1-13; 13:1-13).

2. Founding of the Community

In 146 B.C., the rich old city of Corinth[1] was destroyed. Caesar rebuilt the city as a Roman colony, and from 29 B.C. onward Corinth was the seat of a proconsul, and the capital of the senatorial province of Achaia. Located on two seas and with harbors on the east (Cenchreae) and west (Lechaeum), it was a natural trading center between East and West. In the colorfully mixed population, religious syncretism flourished. The city's addiction to vice was proverbial.[2] About the year 49, in the course of his so-called second missionary journey which had taken him through Macedonia and Athens, Paul reached Corinth with his preaching of the gospel. His helpers were Silvanus and Timothy (II Cor 1:19; Acts 18:5). Acts 18:1-17 offers a very fragmentary account of his activity there, but it can be supplemented extensively from I and II Cor. Paul taught first in a synagogue and then, following a conflict with the Jews, in the house of the proselyte Titius Justus (Acts 18:4 ff). Whereas he allowed the Philippians to support him in part during his stay in Thessaly, he undertook his own support by the labor of his hands in Corinth (Acts 18:2 f; I Cor 4:12; 9:1 ff; II Cor 11:7 ff). After a year and a half of Paul's ministry (Acts 18:11) there was a flourishing community, which consisted of Gentile Christians (I Cor 12:2), mostly from the lower classes (I Cor 1:26 ff), but the Jewish-Christian element was also represented (Acts 18:4; I Cor 7:18), as were the upper social and economic levels (11:21 ff; Acts 18:8; Rom 16:23). After Paul, Apollos—a rhetorically gifted Jew from Alexandria, won over to Christianity by Aquila and Priscilla (Acts 18:24 ff; I Cor 3:5 ff) —was active in Corinth for a long time and in a manner similar to Paul.

Prior to I Cor Paul had already written a letter to the Corinthians (I Cor 5:9 ff), in which he had forbidden the community to have any dealings with lascivious persons. In Corinth this had been in-

---

[1] Concerning Corinth, see T. Lenschau, PW Suppl. 4, 1924, 991 ff; 6, 1935, 182 ff; *Ancient Corinth: A Guide to the Excavations*, ⁶1960; R. M. Grant, BhHw II, 1964, 988 ff.

[2] The widespread assumption that in the Temple of Aphrodite on the Acrocorinth prostitution was extensively practiced does not correspond to the facts; see H. Conzelmann, *Korinth und die Mädchen der Aphrodite. Zur Religionsgeschichte der Stadt Korinth*, NAG 1967, 8.

terpreted as though the apostle meant immoral persons outside the
community. The question whether this "prior letter" is lost or
whether it may in part or as a whole be reconstructed out of
the preserved Corinthian letters can only be answered in connection
with the question about the unity of the two letters.

3. Occasion for the Letter

The most important occasion was a written inquiry from the
Corinthian community (7:1: "About which you have written")
to the apostle, presenting a series of questions. Perhaps the Corinthians Stephanus, Fortunatus, and Achaicus had brought this
letter to Paul (16:17 f). He had received information about the
community through Chloe's people (1:11), but we know nothing
further about that. The picture of the community that all this
information conveyed was not a happy one. In matters of sex,
on the one hand the community tolerated the fact that a Christian
was living with his own stepmother without interference from the
community (5:1 ff). And Paul had to underscore that for Christians to have relations with prostitutes was impossible (6:12 ff).
But, on the other hand, there was among the Christians of Corinth
an ascetic view which saw all sexual relationships as something
sinful (7:1, 28). In their day-to-day disputes the Christians turned
to pagan courts for justice (6:1 ff), accepted invitations to meals
at which meat which had been sacrificed to idols was served (10:
27 f), and took part in meals in pagan temples (8:10). At the
Lord's Supper the rich stuffed themselves with food and drink
that they had brought along, while the poor remained hungry (11:
17 ff). Worship degenerated into disorder, since glossolalia, which
practice was exalted as *the* Christian charisma, threatened to suppress all other workings of the Spirit (14). The whole idea of the
Christian belief in the resurrection of the dead was denied by a part
of the community (15:12).

But most of all Paul was troubled by the report of strife and
splits within the community. Because at the beginning of his comments on this situation in the community (1-4) Paul says that
there are those persons in the community who describe themselves
as "belonging to Paul, Apollos, Cephas, or Christ" (1:12), there
has been, ever since F. C. Baur,[3] discussion of "parties" in Cor-

[3] F. C. Baur, "Die Christuspartei in der korinthischen Gemeinde," etc., TZTh
4, 1831, 61 ff (=F. C. B., *Ausgewählte Werke in Einzelausgaben,* ed. K.
Scholder, I, 1963, 1 ff); excerpts in WGK, NT, 129 ff.

inth.[4] The attempt has been made to specify the individual "parties" and to apportion the polemic of this letter so as to correlate with the parties.[5] On the basis of the account in Gal (2:11 ff), it is easy to form the view that the supporters of Peter were the representatives of a Jewish Christianity that appealed to the original apostles from Jerusalem, although in I Cor we hear nothing of a demand to fulfill the Law and know nothing of Peter staying in Corinth.[6] On the basis of Acts 18:24 and I Cor 1:18 ff one could also maintain that Apollos was the representative of a kind of Christianity that developed rhetoric and demanded wisdom, and then see in the followers of Paul those Christians who identified with him and defended his version of Christianity. But it cannot be proved that Paul turns his attention in certain parts of I Cor to one or other of these "parties," and at the same time the listing of the names— Paul, Apollos, Cephas—in 3:4 f; 3:22; 4:6 varies for no perceptible reason and from Ch. 5 on there is no mention of groups forming.[7] Above all, it cannot be determined what view the group represented which said, ἐγὼ χριστοῦ. Guesses have included radical Jewish Christianity,[8] identification with James the Lord's brother,[9] pneumatics,[10] libertine Gnosticism,[11] the preaching of God, freedom, and immortality.[12] Others would like to see in this group a reaction against the Petrine group.[13] Still others, aware that all these are unprovable, conclude from the omission of the name of Christ in the related enumeration at 3:22 (cf. 1:12) and in I Clem 47:3 that the phrase ἐγὼ δὲ χριστοῦ is to be explained as a gloss.[14] But quite apart from the unanswerable question why this phrase

---

[4] W. Schmithals, The Office of Apostle, 1969, 204 n. 471, speaks of a "Petrine community.

[5] See the survey in Hurd, 96 ff.

[6] In addition to those named by Hurd (100 n. 5), a ministry of Peter or at least a stay in Corinth is represented by Barrett, "Cephas," 5 f, and Schmithals, Gnosis,³ 354 f.

[7] The proposal can only be described as fantastic that in I Cor Paul is polemicizing against an undermining of his authority by the adherents of Apollos, who employ to this end the Letter to the Hebrews which Apollos wrote to Corinth (against H. Montefiore, Comm. on Heb, HNTC 1964, 22 ff).

[8] F. C. Baur; Feine-Behm.

[9] C. Weizsäcker, Das Apostolische Zeitalter der christlichen Kirche, ²1892, 277 f; E. Bammel, ThZ 11, 1955, 412.

[10] Lietzmann; Jülicher-Fascher.

[11] Lütgert, Schmithals, Jewett.

[12] Manson, St., 207.

[13] Barrett, Christianity, 284.

[14] Heinrici, Héring, J. Weiss; Goguel, Michaelis; Wilckens; H. Mosbech, "Apostolos in the NT," StTh 2, 1949/50, 196.

should have been inserted, it must be objected against this hypothesis that in 1:13 μεμέρισται ὁ χριστός is best understood if it is preceded by the phrase objected to, ἐγὼ δὲ χριστοῦ. Others have disputed the fact that there was any factionalism in Corinth at all, and have presented the view that only opposition against Paul is at issue in Corinth, so that in the slogan ἐγὼ δὲ χριστοῦ he sets the only correct position against the "group" slogans he has himself formulated.[15] Yet nothing suggests that Paul has himself formulated the slogans in 1:12—and certainly not the last of them as his own viewpoint!

On the other hand it is thoroughly erroneous to assume that Paul is dealing with closed groups in the church. In 1–4 he is always polemicizing against the whole community, and in the rest of the letter he is speaking to the entire community. The split did not originate as a result of the mere presence of different teachers or tendencies in the community, but through undue esteem of human teachers, especially of those who performed baptisms among the Corinthians as a result of a mystery-like understanding of baptism (1:12 ff; 4:15; cf. 4:6: "In order that you might not be inflated one before the other, in opposition to the other"). We have no means of determining how the particularistic claim "to belong to Christ" relates to this joining together of certain circles in the Corinthian community around the person who baptized them (Paul, Apollos, Cephas). But neither do we know whether Paul evaluated such a claim differently from the slogans mentioned later. On the basis of the controversy in I Cor 1–4 it cannot be assumed, therefore, that in this letter Paul is polemicizing on two fronts (or more). On other grounds that is improbable. There is nothing in I Cor by way of a polemic against "Judaistic," that is, radically Jewish-Christian views.[16] Rather, the whole letter manifests a front against a Gnostic perversion of the Christian message which attributes to the pneumatics, as those liberated from the σάρξ, a perfect redemptive state and an unconditional moral freedom.[17] But it is very questionable whether, from the presupposition that Paul was inadequately informed about the views of the Gnostics, a genuine Gnostic Christology as held by

---

[15] Thus in various ways Munck; Dahl, 329; Baumann, 50, 54 f; R. Reitzenstein, *Die hellenistischen Mysterienreligionen,* [3]1927, 334; E. Käsemann, "Einführung zu F. C. Baur," *Ausgewählte Werke* I, 1963, x.

[16] Against Manson; H. J. Schoeps, *Paul,* 1961, 76 f.

[17] Thus among others Fuller, R. M. Grant, Marxsen; Schmithals, Dinkler, Freeborn, Jewett.

his opponents in Corinth can be reconstructed.[18] It is clear that Paul also engages in controversy over questions and views held within the community that can only in a forced way be attributed to Gnostic presuppositions: trials before a pagan court (6:1-11); abstinence from marriage (Ch. 7), women's aversion to covering their heads (11:3 ff). But this evidence does not alter the fact that in I Cor Paul sees himself as fighting on only one front: the enthusiastic-Gnostic front. But he regards the abandonment of Gnostic views as the prerequisite for standing true to the preaching of Jesus Christ, who was crucified and raised again.

4. Authenticity and Integrity

The genuineness of I Cor is not disputed: the letter is already clearly known in I Clem 37:5; 47:1-3; 49:5; Ign., Eph 16:1; 18:1; Rom 5:1; Phila 3:3. Repeatedly 1:2b[19] and 14:33b-35 (or 36)[20] have been pointed out as non-Pauline interpolations. Because this letter which is concretely aimed at the Corinthians could not have been intended for Christianity as a whole, the additional comment "with all who call upon the name of the Lord Jesus in every place, theirs and ours" is regarded as impossible. This "ecumenical" supplement is explained on the basis of the position of I Cor in the oldest collection of the Pauline letters. But since we know nothing for sure about the earliest collection of the letters of Paul (see below, §35.2), this explanation of the addition is not demonstrable. On the other hand, the difficulty cannot be avoided by limiting those ἐπικαλούμενοι to official liturgists[21] or by regarding sender and recipient as bracketed together in the addition "with all who call . . ." [22] Rather one must conclude that in 1:26 Paul has expanded the address by a liturgically

---

[18] Against Schmithals' reconstruction of the Christology of the Corinthian Gnostics, see recently Conzelmann, *Comm.*, 29; Baumann, 204 f, 280; H. R. Balz, *Methodische Probleme der nt. Christologie*, WMANT 25, 1967, 157 f.

[19] J. Weiss; Dinkler; Schmithals, *Paulus und die Gnostiker*, 1965, 188 f (bibl.) Eng. tr., *Paul and the Gnostics*, 1972, 258, bibl. in n. 46.

[20] Barrett (hesitantly); Conzelmann, J. Weiss, Dinkler; J. Leipoldt, *Der soziale Gedanke in der altchristlichen Kirche*, 1952, 229; G. Zuntz, *The Text of the Epistles*, 1953, 17; E. Fascher, *Textgeschichte als hermeneutisches Problem*, 1953, 102 f; E. Schweizer, *Neotestamentica*, 1963, 336 f; G. Fitzer "Das Weib schweige in der Gemeinde," ThE 110, 1963.

[21] P. Gaechter, *Petrus und seine Zeit*, 1958, 311 ff.

[22] U. Wickert, "Einheit und Eintracht der Kirche im Präskript des 1 Kor," ZNW 50, 1959, 73 ff.

formulated characterization of the whole of Christendom.[23] If the comprehensiveness of the formula is to be explained as liturgical in origin, it is still not clear why in this letter the reference to the whole of Christianity is introduced. But our lack of insight is no adequate ground for assuming an interpolation. The commandment "Let a woman keep silent in church . . ." (I Cor 14: 33b-35[36]) does stand in tension with 11:33 ff, and 14:33a leads smoothly into 14:37, while 14:33b-36 is not self-explanatory in its context. Nevertheless λαλεῖν and ἐπερωτᾶν are prohibited in 14:34 f, while in 11:5 prayer and prophecy are the subjects. Why the text 14:33b-36 was inserted here no one has been able to explain, so the assumption of an interpolation is very unlikely here as well.

Although the Pauline origin of I Cor is not disputed, its integrity and the related matter of the integrity of II Cor are contested.[24] Beginning from the fact (1) that in I Cor 5:9 and II Cor 2:4 a letter is mentioned that must be lost, and (2) from the assumption that it is unlikely that "only a part of an apostolic letter would have been preserved or published," [25] the contradictions in I Cor have been noted and the consequence drawn that I Cor is composed of at least two letters of Paul. This thesis, which was formerly proposed in a variety of forms, has recently been propounded in a quite variable way. While some scholars would like to see in II Cor 6:14–7:1 only a fragment of the otherwise lost "prior letter" mentioned in I Cor 5:9,[26] others reconstitute this "prior letter" out of I Cor (e.g., II Cor 6:14–7:1; I Cor 6:12-20; 9:24–10:22; 11:2-34; 15:1-58; 16:13-24) and find in the remainder of I Cor Paul's second letter to the Corinthians (1: 1–6:11; 7:1–9:23; 10:23–11:1; 12:1–14:40; 16:1-12), which is a response to the letter from the Corinthians (cf. 7:1).[27] Other reconstructions reckon with a still more complicated prehistory of I Cor.[28] As the basis for a compilation of I Cor from several letters

[23] See Lietzmann-Kümmel, in loc.
[24] Cf. the surveys in Goguel, Intr. IV, 2, 86 ff; B. Rigaux, Saint Paul et ses lettres, 1962, 153 ff; Hurd, 43 ff (table 45).
[25] Schmithals, Gnosis,[3] 87.
[26] Craig, Héring; R. M. Grant, Fuller, Guthrie, Henshaw; T. W. Manson, Hurd; Buck-Taylor. N. A. Dahl, "Der Eph und der verlorene erste Brief des Paulus an die Korinther," Abr., 64 ff, wants to see as being reproduced in Eph fragments of the Pauline catechism also used in II Cor 6:14–7:1 and in this way to reproduce the "prior letter."
[27] Thus Schmithals, Jewett; similarly Dinkler. Héring divides I Cor differently into two letters.
[28] Cleary; Schenk, who finds four letters combined; according to J. Harrison, I Cor 1:1–4:21 and II Cor 10–13 originally formed one letter.

it is adduced mainly that Paul promises to come quickly to Corinth
(4:19), but 16:3 ff presupposes a long period before the journey
to Macedonia; 10:1-22 forbids any participation in cultic meals,
but 8; 10:23–11:1 prohibits eating food offered to idols only in
consideration of the weak; in 9, Paul defends his apostolate against
attacks, while 1–4 does not imply that Paul's dignity as apostle is
under attack; 11:18 ff implies that Paul has heard of the conflicts
for the first time, but in 1–4 he has more precise information. To
account for the subsequent interweaving of two originally independent letters, it is adduced that in assembling the Pauline letters
into a seven-part corpus—which took place in Corinth at the end
of the first century—it was necessary to combine smaller letters
into larger ones, especially if it was desired to place the letters to
Corinth at the head of the corpus,[29] or to create a comprehensive
complex for use within the community.[30]

In fact 5:9 cannot be used to demonstrate that II Cor 6:14–7:1
is the "prior letter" or part of it and, building on that conjecture,
to tack on pieces of I Cor, since the warning against sexual relations with πόρνοι is not in that hypothetical letter. The "prior
letter" has simply not survived. But the arguments for splitting
up I Cor into two or more letters are not convincing either.[31] The
reference to Paul's intention of coming to Corinth ταχέως (4:19)
is quite compatible with the plans in 16:3 ff. Also, in the course
of composing a letter that need not have been dictated all at once,
Paul could have made his plans more precise. The statements about
the rightness or wrongness of eating food sacrificed to idols (8:1–
11:1) are only contradictory in form, but are unified in content,
since Paul maintains that there is danger for even the "strong"
Christians from the demons, whose existence is not to be denied, if
they think that by their "strength" they can show off before God.[32]
Although Paul does not explicitly defend his apostleship against
attack in 1–4, as he does in 9, he alludes in 4:9 to the contempt

[29] Schmithals (see n. 19) 190 ff; Eng. tr., 253 ff, esp. 258.

[30] J. Müller-Bardorff, "Zur Frage der literarischen Einheit des Phil," *Wissenschaftliche Zeitschrift der Friedrich-Schiller-Universität Jena* 7, 1957/58, Gesell-
schafts- und sprachwissenschaftliche Reihe 4, 601 f. Héring ponders whether
perhaps a portion of a letter has dropped out or a supplement to the letter has
become illegible.

[31] Thus also Barrett, Bruce, Conzelmann; Fuller, Grant, Marxsen, Michaelis
(ErgH, 25 f); Schelkle; Hurd, 47, 141 f; C. J. Bjerkelund, *Parakalô*, 1967,
148, 154.

[32] Cf. H. von Soden, "Sakrament und Ethik bei Paulus," in *Urchristentum
und Geschichte* I, 1951, 254 ff; G. Bornkamm, "Lord's Supper and Church in
Paul," *Early Christian Experience*, 1969, 123 ff.

for his apostolic authority, and in 3:5 ff and 4:1 ff he presupposes a criticism of his activity in establishing the community, while in 9:1 ff the reference to his apostolic rights is explicable on the basis of his taking up in excursus-like fashion the theme of his readiness for renunciation. 11:18 ff is hardly treating the same σχίσματα as in 1:10 ff, and it cannot be inferred from the remark "and I partly believe it also" (11:18) that Paul is (still!) less well informed in 11:18 ff than he was in 1:10 ff.[33] The arguments advanced for the hypothesis of a secondary composition of I Cor are accordingly in no case persuasive. Rather the occasionally jerky transition from one theme to another in I Cor can be explained on the basis of the special nature of this letter, which treats questions and communications one after the other, and which in this way frequently uses the literary device of excurses (2:6-16; 6:1-11; 9:1-27; 10:1-13; 13:1-13). Also it is worth considering that "it is equally possible that St. Paul was great enough to be inconsistent at some points and that he did not have the thoroughness of the German or the lucidity of the French mind." [34]

The chief argument against the hypothesis of a secondary composing of I Cor, however, is that in this case as in that of I Thess (see above, §14.4), the historical probability for such a secondary composition cannot be made evident. It is hardly convincing that the redactor who combined the letters used a "simple way of proceeding," [35] and beyond that, the hypothesis of a secondary assembling of I Cor presupposes that at least an introduction or a conclusion to a letter was trimmed off, for which no plausible motive can be offered. Thus the assumption of a secondary compilation of I Cor is to be rejected as being extremely improbable.

5. Time and Place of Writing

Some time before writing I Cor, Paul had sent Timothy through Macedonia to Corinth (4:17; 16:10; Acts 19:22). He thought that Timothy would arrive there later than a letter sent by a direct route. Meanwhile those sent from Corinth had reached him, and to them he perhaps gave I Cor, in which he answered the questions of the community and spoke also of things that he had heard

---

[33] Cf. Barrett and Conzelmann, in loc.
[34] McNeile-Williams, Intr., 136.
[35] Schenk, 242; similarly Schmithals, Gnosis,[3] 93.

about by other means.[36] The letter was written in Ephesus (16:8). The Sosthenes mentioned in the prescript is perhaps the former official of the Corinthian synagogue (Acts 18:17). Paul conveys greetings from the churches of Asia (16:19), so he must have worked for a long period in that province. He has not been in Corinth for some time (4:18), but is now thinking of a visit there, if possible for an entire winter (16:6). It is spring (16:8)[37] at the time he is writing, and in all probability the spring prior to the end of Paul's stay in Ephesus. I Cor would then be dated in the spring of 54 or 55.[38]

§17. THE SECOND LETTER TO THE CORINTHIANS

Commentaries: see §41. Research: in addition to bibl. in §16: A. Hausrath, *Der Vier-Capitel-Brief des Paulus an die Korinther*, 1870; E. Käsemann, "Die Legitimität des Apostels," ZNW 41, 1942, 33 ff (="Das Paulusbild in der neueren deutschen Forschung," *Wege der Forschung* 24, ed. K. H. Rengstorf, 1964, 475 ff); R. Bultmann, "Exegetische Probleme des zweiten Korintherbriefes," SyBU 9, 1947 (=R. B., *Exegetica*, 1967, 298 ff); L. P. Pherigo, "Paul and the Corinthian Church," JBL 68, 1949, 341 ff; C. H. Dodd, *NT Studies*, 1952, 80 ff; J. Munck, *Paul and the Salvation of Mankind*, 1959, 168 ff; W. Schmithals, "Zwei gnostische Glossen im Zweiten Korintherbrief," EvTh 18, 1958, 552 ff (=W. Sch., *Die Gnosis in Korinth*, ³1969, 286 ff); G. Bornkamm, *Die Vorgeschichte des sog. Zweiten Korintherbriefes*, SAH 1961, 2 (= G. B., *Geschichte und Glaube* II, *Gesammelte Aufsätze* IV, BevTh 53, 1971, 162 ff; expanded); J. A. Fitzmyer, "Qumran and the Interpolated Paragraph in 2 Cor 6:14–7:1," CBQ 23, 1961, 271 ff; J. Gnilka, "2 Kor 6,14–7,1 im Lichte der Qumranschriften und der Zwölf-Patriarchen-Testamente," *Nt. Aufsätze, Festschr. J. Schmid*, 1963, 86 ff; G. Friedrich, "Die Gegner des Paulus im 2 Kor," Abr., 181 ff; A. M. G. Stephenson, "Partition Theories on 2 Corinthians," StEv II, TU 87, 1964, 639 ff;

[36] According to Hurd, Paul originally adopted a "Gnostic" position in Corinth (thus also Freeborn). But in his "prior letter" he tries to foster in Corinth respect for the "Apostolic Decree" which he has taken over in the interim. Paul counters the charge of inconsistency raised by the Corinthians in their letter by the attempt to fashion a compromise between his original preaching in Corinth and his instructions in the "prior letter." But neither this change in Paul's thinking nor his adopting of the Apostolic Decree can be made remotely likely (see Kümmel, ThLZ 1966; Barrett, *Comm.*, 7 f).

[37] The inference from 5:7 f that the letter was written at Passover is unfounded (against Hurd, 139, with n. 3); Feuillet, 172; Buck-Taylor, 28 f; K. H. Rengstorf, *Die Auferstehung Jesu*, ⁴1960, 64; W. Rordorf, *Der Sonntag*, AThANT 43, 1962, 193).

[38] Richards thinks he can prove that I Cor was written soon after the accession of Nero in October, 54 (sheer fantasy!).

idem, "A Defence of the Integrity of 2 Corinthians," in *The Authorship and Integrity of the NT*, Theological Collections 4, 1965, 82 ff; D. Georgi, *Die Gegner des Paulus im 2 Kor*, WMANT 11, 1964; *idem*, *Die Geschichte der Kollekte des Paulus für Jerusalem*, ThF 38, 1965, 54 ff; J. Roloff, *Apostolat—Verkündigung—Kirche*, 1965, 75 ff; W. H. Bates, "The Integrity of II Corinthians," NTS 12, 1965/66, 56 ff; E. Güttgemanns, *Der leidende Apostel*, FRLANT 90, 1966, 282 ff; K. F. Nickle, *The Collection: A Study in Paul's Strategy*, SBT 48, 1966, 16 ff; D. W. Oostendorp, *Another Jesus: A Gospel of Jewish-Christian Superiority in II Corinthians*, diss. Amsterdam, 1967 (on this see Schmithals, ThLZ 93, 1968, 503 f); J. L. Price, "Aspects of Paul's Theology and Their Bearing on Literary Problems of Second Corinthians," *Studies in the History and Text of the NT: Festschr. K. W. Clark*, StD 29, 1967, 95 ff; C. K. Barrett, "Titus," *Neotestamentica et Semitica: Festschr. M. Black*, 1969, 1 ff; *idem*, " 'Ο 'ΑΔΙΚΗΣΑΣ (2 Cor 7,12)," *Verborum Veritas, Festschr. G. Stählin*, 1970, 149 ff; *idem*, "ΨΕΥΔΑΠΟΣΤΟΛΟΙ," *Mélanges Bibliques, Festschr. B. Rigaux*, 1970, 377 ff; *idem*, "Paul's Opponents in II Corinthians," NTS 17, 1970/71, 233 ff.

1. Contents

The letter falls into three parts not clearly connected: 1–7; 8–9; 10–13. The first part opens with the prescript (1:1, 2) and the thanksgiving for Paul's deliverance from danger of death in Asia (1:3-11). Then Paul turns directly to the defense: first against challenges to his stability in light of his changes of travel plans (1:12–2:4), which Paul describes as motivated by forbearance toward the community, as was his letter written to the Corinthians for that reason. This leads to an instruction for settling by milder means an incident of opposition to Paul (2:5-11), and then Paul begins to portray the events which are directly presupposed in the writing of the present letter (2:12-13). This portrayal is interrupted in 2:14 by a thanksgiving, which in turn gives way to an apology for Paul's apostolic office extending to 7:4. The description of the prior history of the letter resumes at 7:5 ff. The apology for the apostolic office, which extends from 2:14 to 7:4, first pictures the apostle's self-confidence, which is based on his divine commission (2:14–4:6), and then the necessity of suffering (4:7–5:10) and the apostolic commission (5:11–6:10), in which as a kind of excursus (5:14–6:2) the content of the commission is described. 6:11-13 returns to the address to the community, but this address is interrupted in 6:14–7:1 by a general warning against relations with unbelievers, and then concludes in 7:2-4. In 7:5-16 Paul pursues to the end the prehistory of the letter. In 8:1-24 there follows without transition the recommendation concerning the collection for Jerusalem and Paul's fellow workers who have been sent to gather it up. 9:1-15 goes into the discussion of the collection question again, mentions again the sending of the co-workers, and concludes with a benediction. Thereupon 10:1 makes a completely new beginning with a sharp warning and defense against charges (10:1-18), which leads on to a "foolish" praise of himself by way of justification (11:1–12:13). In 12:14–13:10 the charge of his robbing the community is denied and travel plans are discussed. Closing wishes and a threefold benediction in 13:11-13.

2. Prehistory and Occasion

The letter presents a very contradictory impression. Not only is there no clear connection between the three parts, 1–7, 8–9, 10–13, not only is the theme of the collection in 8 and 9 dealt with twice with no clear reference to each other, and not only is the community addressed in 10–13 in a completely different tone than in 1–9, but even the first main section (1–7) is itself not a unity. The narrative about the history prior to the writing of the letter is interrupted in 2:13 and then resumed in 7:5; the transition from 6:2 to 6:3 is very rough, and 6:3 would really tie in better with 5:13, so that 5:14–6:2 functions as an excursus. The general warning (6:14–7:1) interrupts the personal address in 6:11-13 and 7:2-4 in a very clumsy manner. Widespread doubts that this letter as a whole originally belonged together are comprehensible.

The assumption that the letter as we have it is not intact is given support by the difficulty one has in determining clearly the prehistory and occasion of the letter. Since Acts mentions only one visit of Paul to Greece after the conclusion of his stay in Ephesus (20:1-3), during which he wrote I Cor, our only knowledge of his relations with the Corinthian church after the writing of I Cor is what we can infer from II Cor. And this information is in part very opaque. Something like the following may be inferred:

1. II Cor is later than I Cor. Not long before the writing of II Cor Paul was delivered from a most severe threat of death in Asia.[1] He then journeyed via Troas to Macedonia, where he was staying at the time of II Cor (1:8 ff; 2:12 f; 7:5; 9:2). The situation obviously corresponds to Acts 20:1 f, according to which

---

[1] Paul cannot here be referring merely to the effect upon himself of bad news from Corinth (thus Dean).

Paul ended his three-year stay in Ephesus probably in early fall of 54 or 55 (see §13) and went to Macedonia. Then II Cor shows the arrangements for the collection for Jerusalem in a more advanced stage than in I Cor. The collection is only briefly alluded to in I Cor 16:1 ff, but in II Cor 8–9 knowledge of it is presupposed and it is dealt with extensively and urgently, since it is to be concluded and sent off (II Cor 8:6, 11, 14). The remark that it has already been in process "since last year" (8:1; 9:2) refers to the earliest beginnings—even before the instructions offered in I Cor 16:1 ff—but is not chronologically useful.

2. II Cor pursues the goal, among others, of settling once and for all the serious conflict between the apostle and the church. According to 12:14; 13:1, Paul will soon come to Corinth for the third time. On his second visit Paul had threatened that, if he returned, he would practice no forbearance (13:2; cf. 12:20 f). Therefore his second visit had aroused signs of tension between him and the community. 2:1 ff goes beyond that, since according to it Paul had once been in a state of grief in Corinth, and indeed he had caused them grief, just as they had to him.

This second visit cannot have taken place before I Cor. In I Cor nothing points to this tension: Paul speaks to the community throughout in the expectation that they will obey him unconditionally. By virtue of his authority as an apostle to whom the community is subject and whose instructions they have asked for, nothing hinders him from reprimanding them and taking them severely to task.

The second visit, therefore, occurs between I Cor and II Cor (the intermediate visit).

To be sure, the information about Paul's travel plans is not wholly unified. While he is clearly planning a third visit to Corinth soon in 2:12, 14; 13:1, 10, he excuses himself in 1:15 f for having had to abandon the plan to come to Corinth a second time, then to journey to Macedonia, and from there to return to Corinth. He explains his abstention from a further visit to Corinth (2:1) on the ground of his intention to be forbearing toward the Corinthians. It is debated whether Paul is speaking here of a plan that he has not even begun, or a plan that has been only half carried out. Neither can it be determined with assurance whether Paul communicated this plan to the Corinthians orally or in writing (cf. 1:13). But even if, according to the most probable interpretation, Paul had *begun* to carry out his plan (δευτέρα χάρις = intermediate visit, 1:15), he in any case states here that he has given up his original plan to visit Macedonia and Corinth after the intermediate visit to Corinth. This alteration of plans is explained (2:1) on the basis of forbearance. That does not accord with the intention to go to Corinth soon, and is therefore adduced as an argument against an original connection between 1–9 and 10–13 (see below, p. 289).

3. The reason for the clouding of the relationship between Paul and the community is difficult to determine exactly. According to 12:21 and 13:2, during his second visit Paul must have felt sad about members of the community who had still not repented of their immoral life. But since 13:2 mentions in addition "all the other [sinners]," other offenses are in the picture as well. The theme is developed in 7:12, where a man is mentioned who has done Paul a personal injustice (ὁ ἀδικήσας), and in 2:5 ff, where someone is referred to who has "grieved," not Paul, but the majority, or basically the whole community. The situation to which both these passages allude can have arisen only at a time when Paul was there (2:1), and therefore must have occurred during his second stay in Corinth (1:15), not during the first stay when he was founding the community.

The evildoer (2:5; 7:12) is not to be identified with the incestuous man of I Cor 5:1 ff. There are weighty reasons against equating the two, an interpretation that was already rejected by Tertullian.[2] The exclusion of the sinner from the congregation demanded in I Cor 5:3 f, his being handed over to Satan, is in no way consistent with the mild attitude of II Cor 2:6 ff ("For him with whom we are concerned this punishment by the majority is sufficient"). It is inconceivable that Paul, who wrote I Cor 6:12 ff; I Thess 4:3 ff; Rom 13:12, should have subsequently taken so lightly a grave case of sexual misbehavior. But the injustice against Paul can also not have lain in the charge (II Cor 12:16 ff) that he was using collection money for himself, since this suspicion is not attributed to any specific malefactor and could not be characterized as aggrieving the whole community (2:5). What kind of wrong was done to Paul remains obscure for us. It is nothing more than a conjecture to link the incident with the agitation that had arisen in Corinth against Paul in the interim. It cannot be determined either whether the evildoer was a mem-

---

[2] Tert., *De pud.* 13. Stephenson, "Integrity," 96, once more considers identifying the ἀδικήσας with the man guilty of incest (I Cor 5).

ber of the community, but it is certain that the community passed judgment on him.[3]

4. Since the sending of I Cor, the polemic against Paul in the Corinthian community seems to have intensified. On the one hand, throughout the letter Paul has to counter attacks against his person: the change in travel plans betrays an instability (1: 15 ff); his letters do not say clearly what he means (1:13 f); he lacks a letter of recommendation (3:1; 4:2); his gospel is not clear (4:3); his behavior is opaque and offensive (5:11 ff; 6:3 f; 10:2); he harms the community and enriches himself (7:2; 12: 16); only at a distance is he courageous (10:1, 10); he cannot support the claim that he belongs to Christ (10:7); his speech is pitiful (10:11; 11:6); he came to Corinth without orders (10: 13 f); he is inferior to those whom he calls "super-apostles" (11: 5; 12:11); he will not risk letting himself be supported by the congregation (11:7 ff; 12:13); he is no apostle at all (12:12); indeed, Christ does not speak through him (13:3). It is fully clear that Paul here, in contrast to I Cor, is polemicizing, not against a Gnostic perversion of the Christian message, but against people in Corinth who disparage the person of Paul as an apostle of Jesus Christ and contest his apostolic office. Thus it can be perceived moreover that Paul in II Cor is polemicizing against specific people who have attacked him within the community. A minority (2:6; 10:2) which accepts pay (2:17; 11:20) and has gained entrance into the community by means of letters of recommendation and self-recommendation (3:1; 10:12, 18) boasts of certain excellences (5:12; 11:12, 18): they experience ecstasies (5:13; 12:1, 7); they know Christ and belong to him (5:16; 10:7; 11: 23), they claim the apostolic office, which they deny to Paul (11:5, 13; 12:11); they know their superiority to Moses (3:4 ff); they are, however, proud of their unassailable Jewish ancestry (11:22). Paul reproaches them with preaching another Christ and another gospel (11:4), with venturing into alien missionary territory (10: 15 f), with debauchery and impenitence (12:21; 13:2), with comparing themselves only with themselves and therefore boasting boundlessly (10:12 f); he calls them servants of Satan (11:13-15). It can probably not be inferred that a specific person is leading them (11:4; cf. 10:2). It is clear that the presence of these people and the agitation they arouse represents a new situation in the community as compared with that in I Cor. And the assumption that

[3] According to Barrett, *Festschr. Stählin,* 153, the ἀδικήσας was a visitor in the Corinthian community, but the community had not taken a sufficiently clear position to suit Paul.

Paul is here too doing battle against Gnostic opponents as in I Cor[4] does not explain the situation. On the other hand there is no trace of a polemic against demands made by his opponents that the Law is to be fulfilled by the Corinthians, and it is therefore unjustified to equate his opponents here more or less with the Judaizers in Galatia (see below, §18.4.a)[5] or to attribute to them a support operation on the part of the original apostles in Jerusalem.[6] Equally inaccurate for the situation is the characterization of the opponents as itinerant Jewish-Christian preachers for whom "respect for the traditional letter of the law and pneumatic self-consciousness" are to be combined and who regard Jesus as a θεῖος ἀνήρ,[7] or as "Stephanus' people," i.e., Hellenistic Jews who would like to be considered θεῖοι ἄνδρες.[8] It is correct that the opponents first came into the community after the writing of I Cor (3:1; 10:15 f; 11:4), pride themselves on the gifts of the Spirit and miracles, can offer letters of recommendation, accept support from the community, and deny Paul's right to these advantages. Especially characteristic of these people is that they claim irrefutable apostolic authority, Palestinian origin ('Εβραῖοι 11:22)[9] and unassailable Jewish ancestry. And possibly they also lay stress on the relationship with the earthly Jesus (4:10 f; 5:16; 11:4).[10] These intruders from Palestine are therefore not "Judaizers," but Palestinian opponents of the Pauline mission and apostolic authority; they have to all appearances joined with the Gnostic opposition to Paul recognizable from I Cor, or even before they reached Corinth

[4] Schmithals, Dinkler (see §16); Bultmann, Güttgemanns.

[5] Thus in various ways Feuillet, DBS VII, 185; Oostendorp (the opponents preached the superiority of Israel over the Gentiles and the reception of the Spirit through the fulfillment of the Law); Barrett, NTS 1970/71 (the intruders were judaizing Jewish-Christians from Jerusalem who adapted themselves to the Gentile Corinthians); II. J. Schneps, Paul, 1961, 80 ff; J. Jervell, Imago Dei, FRLANT 76, 1960, 177 n. 20.

[6] Manson; Käsemann. ὑπερλίαν ἀπόστολοι in 11:5 does not indicate high authorities from Jerusalem (so again Barrett, NTS 1970/71), but the opponents in Corinth (see Roloff, 79; Oostendorp, 11 n. 16).

[7] Chiefly Georgi (cf. Gegner, 251); also Jewett (see §16), 28 ff; Fuller, Intr., 50; Bornkamm, 10 ff; Roloff, 80 ff; Robinson, Trajectories, 59 ff; Köster, ibid. 187 ff; D. Lührmann, Das Offenbarungsverständnis bei Paulus und in den paulinischen Gemeinden, WMANT 16, 1965, 45 f; M. Rissi, Studien zum 2 Kor, AThANT 56, 1969, 9 ff, 42 ff.

[8] Friedrich; H. R. Balz, Methodische Probleme der nt. Christologie, WMANT 25, 1967, 158 ff.

[9] On this meaning cf. Georgi, Gegner, 51 ff, 58; W. Gutbrod, TDNT IV, 388 f; on the other hand, Schmithals, Gnosis, 356.

[10] See Friedrich, 189 f; Georgi, Gegner, 283 ff (it is not demonstrable, however, that Jesus was viewed by the opponents as θεῖος ἀνήρ).

adopted Gnostic-pneumatic features. So Paul is not polemicizing on a "double front"[11] but rather against newly added opponents who promote a Gnostic-Palestinian-Jewish-Christian anti-Pauline opposition, and at the same time against the community,[12] which has not yet completely freed itself from Gnostic conceptions (cf. 12:20 f) and is undecided about Paul's opponents. Against both kinds of opposition he defends throughout the letter the legitimacy[13] of his apostolic office.

5. Paul had written a letter to the community between I and II Cor "in great distress and anxiety of heart, with many tears" (2:3 f), the so-called intermediate letter or tearful letter. This letter had caused great trouble among the Corinthians (7:8 ff; 2:9) in that Paul in this letter ordered the punishment of the ἀδικήσας (7:12). In relation to the conflict between Paul and the community, the letter stands in the period of severest tension. To all appearances, the bearer of this letter was Titus, whom Paul credited with the steadfastness, perspicacity, and tact to bring the community again under his authority. It had taken much effort, in view of the difficulty of the task, to persuade Titus to undertake the mission (7:13 f). He had agreed with Titus precisely on the route and time of the journey back. He expected to meet him in Troas (2:12 f). Titus' delay upset him greatly, so that in spite of great missionary results, he set out from Troas toward Macedonia to meet Titus en route (2:13; 7:5). Here finally the arrival of Titus relieved him of all his cares: he brought good news that the Corinthian community was deeply moved by remorse and by the wish for reconciliation with Paul (7:6 f). Titus had also been able to carry out the instruction that he work on the collection (8:6; 12:17 f).

6. Thus the following picture emerges of the events between I and II Cor: The sending of Timothy to Corinth (I Cor 4:17; 16:10) seems to have brought no complete success; rather, Timothy had brought back bad news from Corinth. Even I Cor had not enduringly established respect for Paul. So then Paul—perhaps soon after I Cor—went over from Ephesus to Corinth in order to establish order, but he experienced a great disappointment. The visit to the community, which stood in nearly open revolt against him, brought him deep sorrow, especially an injustice done him by a

[11] Thus Lietzmann-Kümmel; Wikenhauser; somewhat otherwise, Barrett, NTS 1970/71, 252 f.

[12] Cf. Georgi, *Gegner*, 303 f; G. W. McRae, "Anti-Dualist Polemic in 2 Cor 4:6?" StEv IV, TU 102, 1968, 430 f.

[13] Käsemann.

Corinthian that the community allowed to take place. He did not succeed in becoming master of the situation, but broke off his visit in annoyance and sadness and returned to Ephesus, though he promised to return. Although he had forgone this new visit out of forbearance for the Corinthians, he had procured Titus for the task of restoring order in Corinth, sending him off with the vigorous "tearful letter." [14] In the presence of Titus the shift was accomplished at Corinth: the community as a whole subjugated itself and repented its insubordinate behavior. Full of disquietude, Paul set out to meet Titus on the way, and met him in Macedonia. The good result of the mission filled Paul with joy and satisfaction. He quickly sent Titus back to Corinth in order for him expeditiously to conclude the collection affairs before Paul's own arrival in Corinth. Titus was accompanied by two unnamed brethren (8: 16 ff), among whom was probably the one who according to 12:18 had at an earlier time been his aide in canvassing for the collection. Paul gave Titus II Cor as the precursor of his own visit (12:20; 13:2).

This picture of the events between I and II Cor is of course tenable only if it is presupposed that II Cor represents an original unity in the form in which it has been handed down—which is a much-debated assumption.

3. Authenticity and Unity

The authenticity of II Cor as a whole is uncontested. On the other hand, the Pauline origin of II Cor 6:14–7:1 has long been doubted,[15] while others conjecture that a text taken over by Paul from Jewish Christianity or from Qumran has been mistakenly inserted here.[16] Determinative for this assumption is not so much

---

[14] That Titus was to restore order in Corinth is not excluded by 7:14 f (thus Barrett, "Titus," 9), cf. εἴ τι κεκαύχημαι.

[15] The section is non-Pauline but Christian according to Fuller, Harrington, Jülicher-Fascher, Marxsen; Dinkler (see §16); Bornkamm, Fitzmyer, Gnilka, Georgi; R. Bultmann, *Theology of the NT* I, 205 n; L. Baeck, "Der Glaube des Paulus," in *Paulus, die Pharisäer und das NT*, 1961, 7 f; G. Friedrich, "Christus, Einheit und Norm des Christen. Das Grundmotiv des I Kor," KuD 9, 1963, 235; H. Braun, *Qumran und das NT* I, 1966, 201 ff. An origin at Qumran is proposed by E. Schweizer, "NT und heutige Verkündigung," *Biblische Studien* 56, 1969, 40 n. 5; L. Gaston, *No Stone on Another*, Suppl. NovTest 23, 1970, 177 f.

[16] K. G. Kuhn, "Les rouleaux de cuivre de Qumran," RB 61, 1954, 203 n. 2; L. Cerfaux, *Le chrétien dans la théologie paulinienne*, 1962, 260 ff; O Böcher, *Der joh. Dualismus im Zusammenhang des nachbibl. Judentums*, 1965, 32 n. 82.

the incontestable fact that this section fits poorly in its context—
the text then could be Pauline but wrongly inserted here[17]—as
the relatively large number of words which do not occur in Paul
or in the NT as a whole, the combination of terms not used customarily by Paul, μολυσμὸς σαρκὸς καὶ πνεύματος (7:1) and κοινωνία
πρός (6:14), and the strikingly strong kinship with the concepts
of the Qumran community.[18] But even though it is correct that
the dualism of God and Belial is characteristic of Qumran and
that Paul elsewhere does not speak of μολυσμος σαρκὸς καὶ πνεύματος,
still it is to be noted that Paul has no fixed linguistic usage for
the Devil and that I Cor 7:34 presupposes the possibility of the
desecration of σῶμα καὶ πνεῦμα. It cannot be proved that the section
is Pauline (cf., however, the parallelism of κοινωνία and μετέχειν
in I Cor 10:16 with II Cor 6:14!). But even less can it be proved
that it could not come from Paul or that it must come from
Qumran. In any case, the poor connection with the context requires an explanation. In addition, Schmithals[19] has tried to show
that II Cor 3:17, 18b, and 5:16 are Gnostic glosses which Paul
could not have formulated, but which were written by Gnostic
opponents of Paul in Corinth in the margin of his letter, whence
they "slid into the text" in the process of copying. But the
thoroughgoing Gnostic interpretation of these verses is convincing
only if one were to attribute to the Corinthian Gnostics a thoroughgoing Gnostic Christology, which is certainly highly questionable
for I Cor (see above, p. 274). And it is most improbable that
glosses by Paul's opponents would have passed unnoticed into the
text of the archetype which underlies our manuscripts.

Even though there is no adequate ground for considering small
sections of the text of II Cor to be non-Pauline, the difficulty in
regarding the text of II Cor as transmitted as an original unity
remains so great that this unity has been called into question in a
variety of ways. This is above all the case with regard to whether
10–13 belongs together with 1–9: while in 1–7 Paul expresses his
joy that the conflict with the community has been settled and can
advise against too stiff a punishment for ἀδικήσας in 2:7, he goes
into action once more in 10:1 with "I myself, however, Paul . . ."

---

[17] Goguel; Schmithals; B. Gärtner, *The Temple and the Community in
Qumran and the NT*, SNTSMS 1, 1965, 49 ff. Cf. also n. 16 and the supposition
that 6:14–7:1 belongs to the "prior letter" (see §16 nn. 26, 27).

[18] On the kinship with Qumran, see the details in Fitzmyer, Gnilka, Braun,
Gärtner (see nn. 15, 17); further H. W. Huppenbauer, *Der Mensch zwischen zwei
Welten*, AThANT 34, 1959, 59 n. 222.

[19] Schmithals, "Glossen"; for 5:16 Güttgemanns, 290 ff, agrees.

He attacks "certain people" (10:2), "the persons concerned" (10:11), "people who want to cause trouble" (11:12), "super-apostles" (11:13), "servants of Satan who clothe themselves as servants of righteousness" (11:15), etc. He fears that when he comes he will not find the Corinthians as he would like (12:20). He threatens then "not to spare them yet again" (13:2), and hopes that "on his arrival" he "will not need to act severely" (13:10). Because these features evidence a completely different set of relationships between Paul and the Corinthian church in 1–9 compared with 10–13, the latter section has since the time of J. S. Semler[20] been regarded as an independent letter or a fragment of one, which was written either later than 1–9[21] or between I and II Cor (the intermediate letter; see above, §17.2.5).[22] Many scholars go a step farther and draw attention to the fact that in 2:13 the discussion of the incident is interrupted, to be resumed—after a long defense of Paul's apostleship—only in 7:5, where there are clear linguistic echoes of 2:13. Furthermore, as already noted, the general reminder in 6:14–7:1 functions like an alien insertion into the personal remarks to the community (6:11-13; 7:2-4), and the two reminders about the collection in 8 and 9 seem not to have belonged together originally. As a result, the assumption is declared to be inescapable that not only 10–13, but also 2:14–7:4; 6:14–7:1 and 9, did not originally belong together with 1:1–2:13; 7:5-16. It is assumed either that 2:14–6:13; 7:2-4, together with 10–13, represent the basic substance of the intermediate letter,[23] or that 2:14–6:13; 7:2-4 comprise a letter that preceded the intermediate letter (10–13),[24] in which case 8–9 would be considered a part of this letter or an independent communication.[25] To this reconstruction one cannot object that the difference between the hypotheses proves that they are all untenable, for owing to their hypothetical character even well-grounded hypotheses always leave open other possibilities.

[20] J. S. Semler, *Paraphrasis II. Epistulae ad Corinthos*, 1776.

[21] Thus Semler; Bruce, Windisch; Jülicher-Fascher (hesitantly); Barrett, *Christianity*, 271, 287; Batey (see §16); Pherigo, who relocates the letter to the end of Paul's first stay in Rome.

[22] First proposed by A. Hausrath, *Der Vier-Capitelbrief des Paulus an die Korinther*, 1870. More recently Filson, Héring; Goguel, Klijn, Marxsen, Sparks, de Zwaan; T. W. Manson, Dean, Cleary, Schmithals, Dinkler (see §16), Bultmann, Dodd, Georgi, Nickle; Buck-Taylor, 113.

[23] Dean, Dinkler (see §16); Bultmann.

[24] Wendland; Fuller, Marxsen; Schmithals (see §16); Bornkamm, Georgi; C. L. Mitton, *The Formation of the Pauline Corpus*, 1955.

[25] Cf. Georgi, "Kollekte," 56 ff; Nickle, 17. Other hypotheses in Goguel, *Intr.* IV, 2, 86 ff; Guthrie, *Intr.* II, 62 ff; Schmithals, *Gnosis* (see §16), [3]321.

Rather, in view of these literary-critical hypotheses, the response to two questions is more crucial: (*a*) Does the text as transmitted compel us to assume that material has been combined secondarily? (*b*) Can a convincing motive be perceived for the combining as it has been transmitted?

a. The crucial problem is the question whether 1–9 and 10–13 could have been parts of the same letter, since the difficulty in the relationship between these two sections is not merely a matter of smoothly compatible ideas but of different stances of Paul in his relation to the community. That there are differences cannot be disputed (see above, p. 289), but it cannot be overlooked that Paul in no way assumes in 1–7 that everything in Corinth is in order.[26] Rather, this section of the letter too is shot through with defenses against misinterpretation of Paul's behavior (1:13 ff, 23 ff; 4:2 f; 5:11 ff; 7:2) and with polemic against other missionaries (2:17 f; 3:1), and only a minority of the community has complied with Paul's wishes (2:6). On the other hand, even in 10–13 Paul assumes that only certain people are attacking him (10:2, 7, 11 f; 11:5, 12 f, 18, 20; 12:11, 21; 13:2) and the rest of the community is endangered by these people (11:1b, 4, 16; 12:11, 19; 13:2). Against the assumption that 10–13 is related to the intermediate letter is the further evidence that 12:18 clearly *refers back* to the sending of Titus and a "brother" mentioned in 8:6, 16-18, and that the event dealt with in the intermediate letter according to 2:3–5:9 is in fact not dealt with at all in 10–13, and, conversely, 2:3 ff and 7:8 ff say nothing of the community's reaction to the polemic against the "super-apostles" in 10–13, which would scarcely have been the case if 10–13 were in fact part of the intermediate letter. The assumption that 10–13 belongs to a letter written later than 1–9 is contradicted by the fact that 10–13 contains no allusion to Paul's knowing that the situation in Corinth has deteriorated following the writing of his letter (1–9), which could scarcely fail to be mentioned. Both these hypotheses (that 10–13 is the intermediate letter, or that it is a later letter) require an additional supposition: that the end of the letter 1–9 and the beginning of the letter 10–13 (or of the more extensive letter of which this is a part) were broken off. And for this no plausible explanation can be offered. Although it is only remotely possible that 1–9 and 10–13 were dictated in immediate sequence, it is not inconceivable that Paul, after a certain lapse of time, added a conclusion to his letter, in which he expressed more sharply his present concerns about the

[26] Cf. on this Stephenson, "Integrity," 87 ff; Bates, 63 f; Price, 100.

community. But above all, he discussed his travel plans for the immediate future, which he had not treated in 1–9. The development of more hypotheses to account for this adding on[27] should be renounced, however, since they are all unprovable conjectures.

But can the original unity of 1–9 be upheld? Though there is no doubt that 2:14–7:4 interrupts the report of the community's reaction to the intermediate letter, it is fully comprehensible that Paul, at the mention (2:13) of his meeting Titus, would make it the occasion for a doxology (cf. 8:16; Rom 9:5) and then go on to an apology for his apostolic office, from which point he slowly returns (6:11–7:4) to his original theme. In this way, the formula in 7:5 is understandable as the resumption of the theme, whereas a transition from 2:13 to 7:5 is scarcely tolerable in view of the switch from singular to plural and from πνεῦμα to σάρξ.[28] Though there is no inescapable necessity to regard 2:14–7:4 as a secondary insertion, it is striking that in 9, Paul takes up again the discussion of the arrangements for the collection after he had in 8:24 concluded his admonitions (8:1–23). But 9:1 is not a completely new beginning (cf. γάρ): 9:3, 5 refers back with the simple mention of the "brethren" to 8:18 ff,[29] and the necessity of help for Jerusalem is not discussed again at all, but only the invitation to help more generously. Ch. 9, therefore, could not have formed a letter by itself or even part of a letter, but it is conceivable that Paul, after breaking off the theme, resumed it once more and gave it a new urgency.

A difficulty that really is scarcely to be resolved is presented by 6:14–7:1, which interrupts the good connection between 6:13 and 7:2, and has no thematic link with its context. Although there is no adequate basis for regarding the text as non-Pauline, the most that can be said of the presence of this section at this point is that from 6:3 onward Paul, hesitantly and by fits and starts, resumes his correspondence and carries forward substantively in 6:14–7:1 the warning to rid themselves of sin which he had begun in 6:1. Even so, as the start of this return to his correspondence about personal matters, 6:3-13 interrupts the warning: 6:3 has a very bad connection with 6:2! But this does not offer a

---

[27] 10:1 ff is Paul's conclusion in his own hand, according to Feine-Behm; Bates; M. Dibelius, *A Fresh Approach to the NT*, 157; Paul received new information, according to R. M. Grant, Harrington, Jülicher-Fascher; Price, 102; Munck (see §16); between 1–9 and 10–13 Paul had a sleepless night, according to Lietzmann; Paul suddenly has his doubts about the genuineness of the change of heart in Corinth, according to Guthrie, etc.

[28] Barrett, "Titus," 9 n. 25.

[29] See Stephenson, "Partition Theories," 642.

really illuminating explanation, and the assumption of a secondary insertion of a Pauline fragment is really appealing. But what could be the basis for such an insertion at precisely this point?

b. For the decisive question is whether a convincing motive can be advanced for the conjectured combining of two or three letters or parts of letters into II Cor as we have it preserved. The general objections against such combination hypotheses have already been stated (see above, § 14.4), but the special arguments adduced for the compilation of II Cor are not convincing either. Why should Paul have agreed to someone in Corinth inserting 2:14–7:4 into his conciliatory letter (1–8)? In order to avoid undue emphasis on the conflict with which he was dealing (so Dean)? Bornkamm would like to account for the attachment of 10–13 to the end of the letter on the grounds of the literary convention of placing at the end of a text a warning about heretics in the time of the End. And he wants to explain the insertion of 2:14–7:4 on the basis of the redactor's tendency to interpret the activity of Paul as a divine triumphal procession, even in its failures (cf. 2:12 f). This second motive is not indicated in the text, and the first is convincing only if it could be antecedently explained what possible occasion there might be for coalescing the various Pauline letters into a conglomerate by omitting their prescripts and postscripts. The evidence that II Cor, in contrast to I Cor, is not certainly attested before Marcion[30] tells nothing, since Gal is not attested in Ign. either.[31] Bornkamm is unable to adduce any real basis for the insertion of II Cor 9, either.

Looking at the whole question, the best assumption is that II Cor as handed down in the tradition forms an originally unified letter. Paul dictated the letter with interruptions, so the possibility of unevenness is antecedently present. If II Cor is understood as an actual letter out of a unique complicated historical situation, it is comprehensible as a historical substance. Connecting lines between the different parts are not lacking. In the first chapters Paul deals with what had liberated him from his great concern about the Corinthian church: the settlement of the conflict. But already here through all the joy there sounds again and again the fact that he still has much to wish for for the community: "You

---

[30] Thus Bornkamm, *Vorgeschichte,* 33 f (=187 f), with reference to Ign. and Polyc. The date of Polycarp's letter is of course wholly uncertain, but Polyc 4:1 clearly refers to II Cor 6:7.

[31] Bornkamm's argument (*Gesammelte Aufsätze* IV, 193 f) that the Pauline letters were handed on as scripture for edification and instruction does not explain why they should have been telescoped into one another.

have understood us [at least] in part" (1:14); "punishment by the majority" (2:6), etc. It is the subject matter itself that results in Chs. 8 and 9 having a tone of their own, in contrast to prior and subsequent statements. That Paul canvasses for the collection in tortured arguments and with a certain diffidence is thoroughly understandable in his position with regard to a newly reconciled community. In 10:1 the apostle starts once more to append a final greeting, but once again he expresses concern about the future of the community which is still endangered by his opponents. Briefer parallels to this type of severe concluding remarks are offered in Gal 6:12 ff; I Cor 16:22; Rom 16:17 ff. But a conciliatory wish and greeting (13:11-13) are still the last words of the letter.

4. Time and Place of Writing

If the reconstruction adopted above (§17.2.6) for the events between I and II Cor is accurate, then between the writing of I Cor in the spring of 54 or 55 and the writing of II Cor are to be set Timothy's return from Corinth, Paul's journey there, his return to Ephesus, his sending of Titus to Corinth, the start and the breaking off of Paul's missionary activity in Troas, his journey to Macedonia, and his meeting there with Titus. This journey from Ephesus to Macedonia must correspond to the one mentioned in Acts 20:1 f, and if Acts 20:2-16 is correct, Paul must have journeyed on to Corinth soon after writing II Cor, remaining there three months and at Passover returning again to Philippi. Since it is quite possible to place within a half-year these events which are assumed to have occurred between I and II Cor, and since the journey from Macedonia to Greece, the three-month stay there, and the return to Macedonia must be set after the writing of II Cor, the time of writing of II Cor may be inferred to have been late fall of the year 55 or 56.[32] There is no occasion for assuming that a year and a half passed between the writing of I and II Cor. Without doubt, II Cor was written in Macedonia.

It is probable that II Cor effected the final settlement of the conflict with the Corinthian community, because the Letter to the Romans, presumably written in Corinth, gives no evidence of difficulties with the community.

---

[32] The proposal that only seven weeks lie between I and II Cor and that the connection in II Cor 3 with the account of the giving of the Law (Ex 20) shows that II Cor was written at the time of Pentecost (Buck-Taylor, 20) rests on completely untenable presuppositions.

294   Introduction to the New Testament

§18. The Letter to the Galatians

Commentaries: see §41. Research: W. M. Ramsay, *The Church in the Roman Empire*, [3]1894, 74 ff; W. Lütgert, *Gesetz und Geist. Eine Untersuchung zur Vorgeschichte des Gal*, BFChTh 22, 6, 1919; J. H. Ropes, *The Singular Problem of the Epistle to the Galatians*, HTS 14, 1929; T. W. Manson, "St. Paul in Ephesus: (2) The Problem of the Epistle to the Galatians," BJRL 24, 1940, 59 ff (=Manson, *St.*, 168 ff); B. Orchard, "A New Solution of the Galatians Problem," BJRL 28, 1944, 154 ff; F. C. Crownfield, "The Singular Problem of the Dual Galatians," JBL 64, 1945, 491 ff; C. H. Buck, "The Date of Galatians," JBL 70, 1951, 113 ff; J. Munck, *Paul and the Salvation of Mankind*, 1959, 87 ff; W. Schmithals, "Die Häretiker in Galatien," ZNW 47, 1956, 25 ff (=W. Sch., *Paulus und die Gnostiker*, ThF 35, 1965, 9 ff); G. Stählin, RGG[3] II, 1958, 1187 ff; H. Schlier, LThK IV, 487 f; C. E. Faw, "The Anomaly of Galatians," BR 4, 1960, 25 ff; A. Viard, DBS VII, 1961, 211 ff (bibl.); K. Wegenast, *Das Verständnis der Tradition bei Paulus und in den Deuteropaulinen*, WMANT 8, 1962, 36 ff; W. Foerster, "Abfassungszeit und Ziel des Gal," *Apophoreta, Festschr. E. Haenchen*, Bh. ZNW 30, 1964, 135 ff; D. Lührmann, *Das Offenbarungsverständnis bei Paulus und in den paulinischen Gemeinden*, WMANT 16, 1965, 67 ff; E. Güttgemanns, *Der leidende Apostel und sein Herr*, FRLANT 90, 1966, 170 ff; F. R. McGuire, "Did Paul Write Galatians?" *Hibbert Journal* 65, 1966/67, 52 ff; C. H. Talbert, "Again: Paul's Visits to Jerusalem," NovTest 9, 1967, 26 ff; H. Köster, "Gnomai Diaphoroi: The Origin and Nature of Diversification in the History of Early Christianity," *Trajectories*, 1971, 114 ff; A. E. Harvey, "The Opposition to Paul," StEv IV, TU 102, 1968, 358 ff; R. M. Wilson, "Gnostics—in Galatia?" *ibid.*, 358 ff; J. B. Tyson, "Paul's Opponents in Galatia," NovTest 10, 1968, 241 ff; P. Stuhlmacher, *Das paulinische Evangelium* I, FRLANT 95, 1968, 65 ff; F. F. Bruce, "Galatian Problems: 1. Autobiographical Data," BJRL 51, 1968/69, 292 ff; *idem*, "2. North or South Galatians?" BJRL 52, 1969/70, 243 ff; R. Jewett, "The Agitators and the Galatian Congregation," NTS 17, 1970/71, 198 ff.

1. Contents

After the prescript (which is expanded along apologetic lines; 1:1-5), there follows no giving of thanks for those addressed, contrary to epistolary custom, but Paul begins immediately his references to the situation in the community, in which he censures the readers for their fall from the gospel and pronounces his judgment on their seducers (1:6-10). First comes (Part One: 1:11–2:21) a personal defense by Paul against attacks on his apostolic office: his gospel does not originate with human beings; he has received it directly from God in the revelation of Christ before Damascus, hence his independence in his call to be a missionary from the first day on (1:11-24). Expressly in its own distinctive form, his gospel was approved and recognized by the primitive church in Jerusalem and by the original apostles at the apostolic conference (2:1-10). On the occasion of a visit to Antioch by Peter, Paul had even demonstrated in an encounter with the leading original apostle the latter's dependence on human beings and had defended the truth of the law-free gospel (2:11-21). Part Two (3:1–5:12) demonstrates, by exegetical means and by reference to the experience of the reader, the necessity of freedom from the Law. Faith gains salvation, not works. Justification is linked, not to the fulfillment of the Law, but to the promise. The readers know that out of their own experience (3:1-5); it is attested for them by the example of Abraham (3:6-9); rightly understood, the OT tells them that (3:10-14) by setting Law and faith in mutually exclusive opposition. Through Christ the Law is now disposed of (3:15-24) and the time freely to become children of God has dawned (3:25–4:7). Since by this means their slavery to the world-elements has been abolished, the Galatians dare not at any cost submit themselves to them once more (4:8-11). After a personal appeal to them to bear in mind the love which exists between them and their apostle (4:12-20), there follow a scriptural proof for the freedom of Christians, based on an allegorical interpretation of the narrative of Hagar and Sarah (4:21-31), and a renewed admonition to renounce slavery to the Law (5:1-12). Part Three (5:13–6:10),[1] which ties in with the theme of the freedom of Christians, admonishes them to preserve—in freedom from the Law—the freedom that has been given, and to do so by obedience to the Spirit, and closes with concrete instructions. The final greeting written in his own hand (6.11 18) warns again about self-seeking teachers of error, but contains no personal greeting, only a benediction.

2. The District of Galatia

The Galatians in the narrower sense, who until the middle of the eighteenth century were thought to be the exclusive addressees, were Celts who in the first half of the third century before Christ migrated to central Asia Minor. About 240 B.C. King Attalus of Pergamum reduced their territories to the region of the Halys and

---

[1] O. Merk, in "Der Beginn der Paränese im Gal," ZNW 60, 1969, 83 ff, has shown the likelihood that the paraenesis does not begin until 5:13.

Sangarius rivers, comprising the cities of Ancyra, Pessinus, and
Tavium. In the year 25 B.C., the last of the Galatian kings be-
queathed his realm to the Romans, who made of it a province,
with its capital at Ancyra. This province encompassed, in addition
to Galatia proper, some other districts: among them, Pisidia, Isauria,
parts of Lycaonia, Phrygia, Paphlagonia, and Pontus. The limits
of the districts and cities incorporated in the province of Galatia
changed frequently, and it bore no officially united name. The
abbreviated designation for the province, Galatia, is used at times
by the writers of the imperial period, but is not found in inscrip-
tions. The name Galatians occurs only for the inhabitants of the
Galatian district proper.[2]

3. Recipients of the Letter

At the time of the writing of Gal, there were in Galatia several
congregations in unnamed places (1:2); about the time of their
founding the letter tells nothing. Acts mentions the land of Galatia
twice: in 16:6 the passage of the apostle and his companions
through the Galatian and Phrygian land is mentioned; according
to 18:23 there were disciples in the Galatian and Phrygian land at
the beginning of the so-called third missionary journey, which
means there were churches in this region. Is it to these communities
"in the Galatian land" that Paul is writing?

Two answers stand opposing each other: the falsely named "South
Galatian" and the "North Galatian" theories. The South Galatian
theory, or, better, the province theory, refers to the churches in
Antioch, Lystra, Derbe, and Iconium, among others (Acts 13:14)
founded in Pisidia and Lycaonia on the so-called first missionary
journey and revisited by Paul on the so-called second missionary
journey (Acts 16:1 ff). The North Galatian theory, or, better, the
territory hypothesis, looks for the recipients of the letter in the
actual Galatian land, the district of Galatia. In spite of the silence
in Acts, mention of churches there in Acts 18:23 leads to the
hypothesis that Paul as he passed through this Galatian district
(Acts 16:6) had given the impetus to founding churches.

The province theory first emerged with Joh. Joachim Schmidt
(1748), and since it was vigorously championed by W. Ramsay
and Th. Zahn, it has found many adherents.[3] The main arguments

---

[2] Cf. H. Schlier, Meyer VII, [12]1962, 15 f.

[3] E.g., Cole, Ridderbos, Stamm; Albertz, Fuller, Goodspeed, Guthrie, Heard,
Henshaw, Klijn, McNeile-Williams, Michaelis; T. W. Manson, Orchard, Talbert,
Bruce; earlier representatives in J. C. Hurd, *The Origin of I Cor*, 1965, 304 f.

for the theory are as follows: (1) Paul is accustomed to using the Roman provincial names of the districts he passes through rather than the regional names; Lycaonia and Pisidia, however, belonged to the province of Galatia. (2) In the churches of Galatia there were birthright Jews, which fits only the province of Galatia, for of Jews in the actual land of the Galatians we know as good as nothing. (3) According to Acts 20:4 Paul had designated Christians from the province of Galatia—Gaius from Derbe, Timothy from Lystra—among the bearers of the collection, but no delegates from the land of the Galatians, even though according to I Cor 16:1 money was gathered for the collection in Galatia as well. (4) The activity of those sent from Jerusalem would be more likely in the southern part of the Taurus Mountains than in the nearly inaccessible interior of Asia Minor.

None of these arguments is really effective, however. (1) The claim that Paul used only official names of provinces cannot be maintained.[4] When he speaks of Syria (1:21), it is not in the official sense of the Roman province, to which even Jerusalem belonged, but in describing his journey from Jerusalem he calls the region to which he came first Syria, the Seleucid territory in which Antioch lay. In I Thess 2:14, when he is speaking of the Christian communities in Judea, he is thinking of the region of Judea, just as in II Cor 1:16. And Arabia, to which Paul went after his call (Gal 1:17) was an unofficial name for the Nabataean realm. (2) The texts which might refer to Jewish Christians in the congregations (3:2 f, 13 f, 23 f; 4:2, 5; 5:1) are speaking of Christians in general, but on the basis of 4:8; 5:2 f; 6:12 f it is certain that the Galatians were Gentile Christians. The texts mentioned really attest that as a former Jew Paul is naturally of the opinion that the OT Law is valid for all humanity so that the redemptive death of Christ frees even the Gentiles from the Law. (3) In Acts 20:4 Achaia's representatives in the collection delegation are missing also, though they would be expected according to I Cor 16:1 ff. It is open to question furthermore whether Gaius might not have been a Macedonian.[5] (4) If the opponents in Galatia are actually people sent from Jerusalem (see below, pp. 298 ff), then we know absolutely nothing about their travels, so this argument is useless.

On the other hand, at least two factors support the assumption that Gal was written to Christian communities in the Galatian

[4] Cf. also E. Haenchen, *Acts,* 481 n. 2.

[5] Cf. Acts 19:29 and 20:4; if in 20:4 Δουβ[ε]ριος is to be read on the basis of D *gig,* cf. F. G. Kenyon, *The Text of the Greek Bible,* 1949, 234 n. 1; *contra,* Haenchen, *Acts,* 52 f.

region: (1) If Gal was addressed to churches founded on the so-called first missionary journey, Paul would scarcely have written (2:1), "Then I came into the regions of Syria and Cilicia," but, "Then I came to Syria and Cilicia, and on to you." (2) Paul could not possibly have written to the Lycaonians or the Pisidians, "O you Galatians" (Gal 3:1), since that usage is not attested anywhere. The linguistic usage in Acts and in contemporary writers of the period distinguishes the Galatians clearly from the neighboring tribes; it must also be assumed for Paul as a native of Asia Minor. The most readily justified assumption is that in this letter Paul is addressing the Galatians living in the interior of Asia Minor, whom he visited on the second and third missionary journeys.[6] However, this decision can be certified to some extent only if it can be shown that it corresponds to the historical situation presupposed by Gal.

4. Historical Situation

To determine the historical occasion for the letter, one must first be able to answer two questions, both of which are much-disputed: (a) Who are the opponents whom Paul is attacking in Gal? (b) Which events in the life of Paul does Gal presuppose to have occurred?

a. It is clear that the letter is directed against a disturbance in the Galatian churches which was brought into the churches from outside. People who "distort the gospel" (1:7) and "confuse the churches" (1:7; 5:10, 12) have turned up in the churches of Galatia since Paul's last visit. They are presumably Christians who are inducing the churches to adopt circumcision (5:2; 6:12 f) and obviously demand obedience to the Law (3:2; 5:4). Probably the Galatians are already observing certain festival periods (4:10), but on the whole they do not seem to have bought the intruders' propaganda (4:9; 6:13, 16). Paul turns on the intruders vigorously, curses them "because they proclaim a different gospel, which is really none at all" (1:6), charges them with pursuing insincere objectives (4:17; 6:12), with not obeying the Law themselves (6:13), and sarcastically orders them to castrate themselves (5:12). It is unclear whether a specific leading person is behind

---

[6] Thus Bonnard, Lietzmann, Schlier; Goguel, R. M. Grant, Harrington, Jülicher-Fascher, Mariani, Marxsen, Schelkle. Cf. further J. C. Hurd (see n. 3), 303 f; U. Borse, Die Wundmale und der Todesbescheid," BZ, NF 14, 1970, 97, and R. Jewett, *Paul's Anthropological Terms*, AGaJU 10, 1971, 17 f.

these intruders (5:7, 10).[7] Since the second century—the evidence
is in the Anti-Marcionite Prologues to Gal—*Galatae . . . temptatit
sunt a falsis apostolis, ut in legem et circumcisionem verterentur*
("The Galatians were tempted by false apostles to turn to the Law
and to circumcision")—it has been inferred that radical Jewish-
Christian opponents of Paul from Jerusalem, the so-called Judaizers,
had penetrated the churches of Paul and had attempted to persuade
the Gentile Christians living free from the Law to accept circumcision and thus to adopt the Jewish Law. From various points of
view, questions have in more recent times been raised about this
assumption. On the one hand it is asserted that the opponents in
Galatia can only be Gentile Christians who want to bring other
Gentile Christians to adopt circumcision as they have, and that
only on this basis can the sarcastic exaggeration of the demand for
circumcision (5:12), the present tense of οἱ περιτεμνόμενοι in 6:13,
and the claim that the opponents themselves do not keep the Law
be explained.[8] On the other hand it has been observed that Paul
must defend himself against charges that he has a merely human
commission in his apostolic office (1:1, 11) and at the same time
he combats libertine views, which could not be directed against
the Judaizers (5:13, 16; 6:1, 8). From this the conclusion has been
drawn that Paul is fighting on two fronts: Judaizers and libertine
pneumatics, who are battling within the community (5:15).[9] It is
justly to be objected against this thesis that there is no trace of
a polemic alternating between two fronts. Accordingly the attempt has been made to justify the evidence just mentioned and
the grounds traditionally adduced for referring it to Judaizers, by
describing the Galatian opponents as syncretistic Jews[10] or as Gnostic

---

[7] This cannot possibly be an allusion to Peter (thus H. Lietzmann, "Zwei
Notizen zu Paulus," SAB 1932, 154=*Kleine Schriften* II, TU 68, 1958, 288);
against this theory is the tone in which Peter is mentioned in 1:18; 2:8 ff, and the
lack of any tradition for a ministry of Peter in Asia Minor (even I Peter 1:1
scarcely proves an ancient tradition of this kind, against K. Weiss, DLZ 89,
1968, 299). In view of 4:17; 6:12, it is unlikely that the opponents were
Galatian Jewish Christians (against Tyson, 252).

[8] Beyer, Lietzmann; Munck; E. Hirsch, "Zwei Fragen zu Gal 6," ZNW 29,
1930, 192 ff; E. Haenchen, "Mt 23," ZThK 48, 1951, 47 (=*Gott und Mensch*,
1965, 38); according to Harvey, 324, the ταράσσοντες (1:7; 5:10) are Gentiles
who have recently become proselytes and intend to have themselves circumcised.

[9] Lütgert; Ropes.

[10] Beyer-Althaus, Schlier; Fuller, Marxsen, Schelkle; Crownfield, Stählin,
Lührmann, Talbert, Köster, Stuhlmacher, Jewett; H. R. Balz, *Methodische
Probleme der nt. Christologie*, WMANT 25, 1967, 162.

Jewish Christians.[11] In addition to the arguments that the Judaizers could not cast in Paul's teeth his dependence on the original apostles and that as opponents of the Gentile mission they could not encourage that mission, Schmithals uses to prove this thesis the fact that Paul had first to draw the Galatians' attention to their obligation to keep the whole Law once they were circumcized (5:3), and that the observance of special times in connection with angel worship makes sense only on Gnostic presuppositions (4:9 f).

Now first of all it is incontestable that the Galatian intruders demanded that the Law was to be observed, including circumcision (2:16; 3:2, 21 b; 4:21; 5:4), and that Paul did not try to inform the Galatians with a fact new to them in 5:3 but to remind them again (πάλιν) of a known fact to which they had not paid sufficient notice. In any event the Galatian opponents were representatives of Jewish legalism, and to interpret their demand for circumcision as a means of gaining symbolic release from dominance by the flesh has no basis at all in Gal. Since in 4:3 ff, 8 ff, Paul interprets submission to the Jewish Law as worship of the elemental spirits just as he does with respect to the honoring of the φύσει μὴ ὄντες θεοί, the reason for the Galatians' observance of special times (4:10) is uncertain, but it is sooner to be understood in the context of obedience to the Law.[12] Once the ground for interpreting the opponents as Gnostics is removed, it is also evident that their Gentile origin is highly unlikely: περιτεμνόμενοι in 6:13 together with 5:3 offers no proof that the circumcision has just now been performed;[13] whether it would be intolerable to direct a statement such as 5:12 against Jews is a question of taste. And the reproach that the opponents do not themselves obey the Law (6:13) obviously ties in with the fact that their primary interest is in circumcision, not in having the Galatian Christians observe the Law (cf. 5:2 f, 6, 12, 13b).

The opponents were without doubt Jewish Christians who preached first of all circumcision, but fulfillment of the Law as well. It is not clearly stated that they had ties with Jerusalem, yet it seems that Paul is being faulted not merely in general because his apostolic authority is derived from human sources, but specifically because he is dependent on the Jerusalem apostles and therefore not a real apostle at all—a charge that he tries to show

[11] Schmithals, Wegenast, Güttgemanns.

[12] The assertion is not convincing that the calendar of feasts (4:10) must be syncretistically based (thus Lührmann, 69, and Jewett, 208).

[13] On the interpretation of περιτεμνόμενοι as "those who promote circumcision" see Jewett, 202 f.

is historically incorrect (1:15 ff). There is some likelihood that the Galatian opponents did have a relationship with the primitive community in Jerusalem, though not with the "pillars," as 2:6 ff shows, but with "false brethren" (2:4), who in any case were not still Jews.[14] Gal 2:1 ff precludes any disputing of the fact that the Jerusalem community, in addition to the "pillars," had a radical wing which rejected a law-free Gentile mission—though it did not reject a Gentile mission as such.[15] But 5:13 ff is combating, not an antinomian libertinism, but the conclusion that freedom from the Law leads to licentiousness, a position either really drawn by the Galatian Christians or falsely asserted by Paul's opponents to be the logical consequence of his teaching. Paul combats this by tying in the Christians' guidance by the divine Spirit, from which it can be understood that Paul addresses the *entire* community as οἱ πνευματικοί (6:1). Thus Paul's opponents in Galatia were in any event Jewish Christians who remained true to the Law.[16] That further syncretistic features are to be attributed to them is not certain. This conclusion makes comprehensible the occasion for Gal, but does not permit a more exact determination of the historical setting of the letter.

b. The date of the letter depends on the answer to the question how the narrative of Paul's journeys and of his and Barnabas' meeting with the "pillars" in Jerusalem (Gal 1:18; 2:1 ff) is related to the accounts in Acts of the Jerusalem journeys of Paul and of his meeting with the apostles there (Acts 15:1 ff). Since Paul tells of only two visits to Jerusalem including this meeting (Gal 1:18; 2:1), while Acts mentions three (9:26; 11:30; 12:25; 15:4), the decisive question is whether the two accounts—Gal 2:1 ff and Acts 15:1 ff—relate to the same event, and if that is the case, how the difference in counting the visits to Jerusalem in the two sources is to be explained.[17]

1. The simplest solution is to deny that the two accounts (Gal 2 and Acts 15) are about the same event. In support of this view it can be adduced that the absence of the Apostolic Decree of Acts 15 in Gal 2 is thus understandable, and no error need be attributed to the author of Acts in the number or order of Paul's visits

[14] Thus Schmithals.

[15] Against Munck, Schmithals.

[16] Thus recently, e.g., Bring, Cole; R. M. Grant, Guthrie, Harrison, Klijn, Mariani, Schelkle; Foerster, Harvey, Wilson, Tyson; O. Merk (see n. 1), 95 n. 51, 100 n. 79 (bibl.).

[17] See the listing of the possible combinations in Talbert, 26 n. 3; and the tables in J. C. Hurd (see n. 3), 18.

to Jerusalem. In this case the Jerusalem journey reported in Gal 2:1 ff is simply identified with the visit mentioned in Acts 11:30 and 12:25; the Apostolic Council of Acts 15:1 ff occurred after the writing of Gal. But to be able to place the writing of Acts prior to the Apostolic Council of Acts 15:1 ff, it must be further assumed that ἐνηγγελλισάμην ὑμῖν τὸ πρότερον (Gal 4:13) relates to only one visit of Paul to the churches in the province of Galatia —or at most to his stay while founding the churches (Acts 13:13– 14:20), which is balanced by the return journey (Acts 14:21 ff). In this case Gal would be the oldest preserved letter of Paul, written between the missionary journey of Acts 13–14 and the Apostolic Council of Acts 15.[18] But this attempt at a solution involves too many improbabilities. It is highly unlikely that the two reports, Gal 2:1 ff and Acts 15:1 ff, are not describing the same event, since in both cases the point at issue between Paul and Barnabas and the apostles in Jerusalem concerns circumcision and the obliga-tion to fulfill the Law. Furthermore, the "province hypothesis" must be adopted, in spite of its problems. And finally it must be said against this solution that τὸ πρότερον (4:13) in Hellenistic Greek can mean "the former time" in the sense of "the only earlier time," but in that case the introduction of this expression into Gal 4:13 would be completely superfluous. 4:13 on the basis of the more usual meaning presupposes rather two visits of Paul to Galatia.

2. If the more probable theory is that Gal 2:1 ff and Acts 15: 1 ff are recounting the same events, two possibilities remain for clarifying the situation regarding the Jerusalem visits: (a) either the event in Acts 15:1 ff (=Gal 2:1 ff) is wrongly transposed to after Acts 13–14—though it actually occurred at the time of Acts 11:30 and 12:25—in which case the journey of Acts 15 is a mistaken duplication; or (b) Acts 15:1 ff is in the right place, but errs in mentioning a visit of Paul to Jerusalem in Acts 11:30; 12:25 between the two journeys, Gal 1:18 (=Acts 9:26) and Gal 2:1 (=Acts 15:4). The Acts account is in error in both

[18] Thus recently Cole, Guthrie; Heard, Henshaw; Orchard, Bruce; D. R. Hall, "St Paul and the Famine Relief: A Study in Galatians 2:10," ExpT 82, 1970/71, 309 ff. Talbert defends the even more improbable proposal that Paul wrote Gal shortly after the visit to the province of Galatia recounted in Acts 16:1-4, on which occasion he handed on to this community the Apostolic Decree of Acts 15; Gal 2:1 ff is a report of the journeys to Jerusalem men-tioned in Acts 11:30 and 12:25, while the meeting in Acts 15 is left unmen-tioned.

cases. The first proposal, (*a*), which has found many supporters,[19] must not only place the so-called first missionary journey (Acts 13–14) after the Apostolic Council—for which no other reason can be given—but it must also utilize as a serviceable narrative the unquestionably fragmentary notes in Acts 11:27 ff and 12:25 ff. Both assumptions are most unlikely. The second proposal, (*b*), is more probable. Since 4:13 according to the most probable interpretation presupposes two visits of Paul to Galatia, we may infer that the writing of Gal after the Apostolic Council in Acts 15 fully permits the adoption of the "territory hypothesis."

There would be substantive support for this decision if on other grounds it could be shown as likely that Gal was written after Acts 18:23, and thus after the second visit into the region of the Galatians and at the earliest during the stay in Ephesus (Acts 19:1 ff). This is in fact the case. It has been noted that the terminology and language of Gal have significant contacts with Rom, especially in the extended use of justification terminology in these two letters, but also in other respects as well (cf. Gal 5:13-25 with Rom 8:2-25). It has also been shown that Paul defends himself against the same reproaches in Gal and II Cor (cf. Gal 1:6, 10; 2:4 with II Cor 11:4; 5:11; 11:26).[20] Finally, it has been correctly stressed that Paul's remark "I have wished I were with you now" (4:20) shows that in spite of the threat to the community he finds himself unable to come to them once more.[21] There is no mention of the Galatians in relation to the collection mentioned in 2:10, either because it was already completed or because they had withdrawn from the undertaking.[22] All this shows that the writing of Gal was not chronologically far from that of II Cor and Rom. On the other hand, the further attempt to demonstrate that Rom combines ideas from the chronologically close letters Gal and II Cor,[23] or that Gal stands between II Cor and

[19] See W. G. Kümmel, ThR NF 17, 1948/49, 29 f; further Bonnard; G. Bornkamm, *Paul*, 31 ff.

[20] Thus Bonnard; Goguel, Jülicher-Fascher; Buck, Viard; J. N. Sanders, "Peter and Paul in the Acts," NTS 2, 1955/56, 140 f; J. Dupont, "Pierre et Paul dans les Actes," RB 64, 1957, 46 (=*Études sur les Actes des Apôtres*, 1967, 183); U. Wilckens, "Was heisst bei Paulus: 'Aus Werken des Gesetzes wird kein Mensch gerecht'?" EKK, Vorarbeiten I, 1969, 57; U. Borse (see n. 6), 97 f. According to D. M. Stanley, *Christ's Resurrection in Pauline Soteriology*, 1961, 67 f, Gal is later than II Cor because Paul now knows that the opponents are attacking his teaching as well.

[21] R. W. Funk, "The Apostolic 'Parousia': Form and Significance," *Christian History and Interpretation: Festschr. J. Knox*, 1967, 266.

[22] See U. Wilckens (see n. 20), 57.

[23] Buck; Buck-Tayor, 82 ff.

Rom in its teaching of the Spirit and of the cross and resurrection,[24] has not been brought off. Yet the observations offered are sufficient to show that Gal is chronologically close to II Cor and Rom, so that the territory hypothesis is thereby confirmed.

5. Time and Place of Writing

The time and place of writing of Gal cannot be determined very exactly within the limits indicated above. A date in the later period of Paul's stay in Ephesus[25] is as possible as is the assumption that Gal was written, like II Cor, in Macedonia. It is less likely that Gal was written first in Corinth before Rom (at the time mentioned in Acts 20:2 f),[26] because then the actual differences between Gal and Rom could not be accounted for. The writing of Gal after Rom on the way from Corinth to Jerusalem cannot be based on the interpretation of οἱ σὺν ἐμοὶ πάντες ἀδελφοί (1:2) as though it referred to the delegates of the communities who accompanied Paul on this journey.[27] Accordingly, it is possible to date Gal *ca.* 54 or 55 in Ephesus or Macedonia.

6. Authenticity

Doubts have been expressed occasionally about the authenticity of Gal from the time of Br. Bauer (1850/52) to the present,[28] but have quite rightly not been taken seriously. (Polyc., Phil 3: 3; 5:1 already knows this letter.) The older, frequently represented hypotheses of interpolation or compilation of Gal [29] are nowadays scarcely discussed,[30] and this is no doubt correct. That Gal is a real, genuine letter is indisputable.

[24] Faw, who draws attention to the lack of mention of the co-workers and to the featuring of the apostolic office only in the prescripts of Gal and Rom.

[25] This appears as early as the Marcionite Prologue: *scribens eis ab Epheso.*

[26] Thus Bonnard.

[27] Against Foerster.

[28] On the earlier radical criticism, see J. Gloel, *Die jüngste Kritik des Gal auf ihre Berechtigung geprüft,* 1890. Recently the authenticity has been contested by McGuire.

[29] Cf. C. Clemen, *Die Einheitlichkeit der paulinischen Briefe,* 1894, 100 ff.

[30] The arbitrary assumption of W. Koepp that a midrash on Abraham has been taken over ("Die Abraham-Midraschimkette des Gal als das vorpaulische heidenchristliche Urtheologumenon," *Wissenschaftliche Zeitschrift der Universität Rostock* 2, Gesellschafts- und Sprachwissenschaften 3, 1952/53, 181 ff) was referred to by K. Weiss, DLZ 89, 1968, 299.

§19. THE LETTER TO THE ROMANS

Commentaries: see §41. Research: W. Lütgert, *Der Röm als historisches Problem*, BFChTh 17, 2, 1913; R. Schumacher, *Die beiden letzten Kapitel des Röm*, NTA 14, 4, 1929; R. M. Hawkins, "Romans: A Reinterpretation," JBL 60, 1941, 129 ff; R. Bultmann, "Glossen im Röm," ThLZ 72, 1947, 197 ff (=R. B., *Exegetica*, 1967, 278 ff); J. Dupont, "Pour l'histoire de la doxologie finale de l'Épître aux Romains," RBén 58, 1948, 1 ff (bibl.); idem, "Le problème de la structure littéraire de l'Épître aux Romains," RB 62, 1955, 365 ff; T. M. Taylor, "The Place of Origin of Romans," JBL 67, 1948, 281 ff; T. W. Manson, "St. Paul's Letter to the Romans—and Others," BJRL 31, 1948, 224 ff (=Manson, *St.*, 225 ff); A. Feuillet, "Le plan salvifique de Dieu d'après l'Épître aux Romains," RB 57, 1950, 336 ff, 489 ff; E. J. Goodspeed, "Phoebe's Letter of Introduction," HTR 44, 1951, 55 ff; S. Lyonnet, "Note sur le plan de l'Épître aux Romains," RechSR 39/40, 1951/52, 301 ff; N. A. Dahl, "Two Notes on Romans 5," StTh 5, 1951, 37 ff; H. Preisker, "Das historische Problem des Röm," *Wissenschaftliche Zeitschrift der Friedrich-Schiller-Universität Jena* 1952/53, 25 ff; G. Schrenk, "Der Röm als Missionsdokument," (in G. S., *Studien zu Paulus*, AThANT 26, 1954, 81 ff); J. Munck, *Paul and the Salvation of Mankind*, 1959, 196 ff; J. Knox, "A Note on the Text of Romans," NTS 2, 1955/56, 191 ff; W. Schmithals, "Die Irrlehrer von Röm 16,17-20," StTh 12, 1958, 51 ff (=W. S., *Paulus und die Gnostiker*, ThF 35, 1965, 159 ff); *Paul and the Gnostics*, English translation, 1972, by J. Steely, 219 ff; N. Krieger, "Zum Röm," NovTest 3, 1959, 146 ff; G. Harder, "Der konkrete Anlass des Röm," ThViat 6, 1959, 13 ff; T. Fahy, "St. Paul's Romans Were Jewish Converts," *Irish Theological Quarterly* 26, 1959, 182 ff; E. Trocmé, "L'Épître aux Romains et la méthode missionnaire de l'apôtre Paul," NTS 7, 1960/61, 148 ff; G. Friedrich, RGG[3] V, 1961, 1137 ff; A. Descamps, "La structure de Rom 1–11," *Studiorum Paulinorum Congressus* I, AnBibl 17, 1963, 3 ff; X. Léon-Dufour, "Situation littéraire de Rom V," RechSR 51, 1963, 83 ff; K. H. Rengstorf, "Paulus und die römische Christenheit," StEv II, TU 87, 1964, 447 ff; A. Roosen, "Le genre littéraire de l'Épître aux Romains," StEv II, TU 87, 1964, 465 ff; K. Grayston, " 'Not Ashamed of the Gospel': Romans 1:16a and the Structure of the Epistle," ibid., 569 ff; P. N. Harrison, *Paulines and Pastorals*, 1964, 79 ff; J. Kinoshita, "Romans—Two Writings Combined," NovTest 7, 1964/65, 258 ff; B. Noack, "Current and Backwater in the Epistle to the Romans," StTh 19, 1965, 155 ff; J. R. Richards, "Romans and I Corinthians: Their Chronological Relationship and Comparative Dates," NTS 13, 1966/67, 14 ff; M. J. Suggs, " 'The Word Is Near You': Romans 10:6-10 Within the Purpose of the Letter," *Christian History and Interpretation: Festschr. J. Knox*, 1967, 289 ff; H.-M. Schenke, "Aporien im Röm," ThLZ 92, 1967, 881 ff; H. W. Bartsch, "Die antisemitischen Gegner des Paulus im Röm," *Antijudaismus im NT?* Abhandlungen zum christlich-jüdischen Dialog 2, 1967, 27 ff; idem, "Die his-

torische Situation im Röm," StEv IV, TU 102, 1968, 281 ff; G. Klein,
"Der Abfassungszweck des Röm," (in G. K. *Rekonstruktion und Inter-
pretation*, 1969, 129 ff); U. Luz, "Zum Aufbau von Röm 1–8," ThLZ
25, 1969, 161 ff; J. I. H. Macdonald, "Was Romans XVI a Separate
Letter?" NTS 16, 1969/70, 369 ff; K. P. Donfried, "A Short Note on
Romans 16," JBL 89, 1970, 44 ff; P. S. Minear, *The Obedience of Faith*,
SBT II, 19, 1971; R. Jewett, *Paul's Anthropological Terms*, AGaJU 10,
1971, 41 ff; G. Bornkamm, "Der Röm als Testament des Paulus," (in
G. B., *Geschichte und Glaube* II, *Gesammelte Aufsätze* IV, 1971, 120 ff).

1. Contents

After a prescript expanded to set forth the content of the gospel (1:1-7) and an expression of thanks (1:8-15) which explains
how Paul came to write this letter, the theme of the letter is
stated (1:16-17): "The gospel is a power of God to effect salvation for everyone who believes, since in it God's setting things
right on the ground of faith is revealed for Jews and Greeks." The
development of the theme offers first the positive and negative
evidence of God's saving act in Christ, which alone makes possible
justification by faith (1:18–4:25). On the negative side it is shown
(1:18–3:20) that those outside the gospel stand under the wrath
of God. Then follows the positive evidence (3:21–4:25): the new
justifying act based on grace through faith in Christ (3:21-26);
through God's new revelation of faith all self-pride in excluded
(3:27-30); the objection that the Law is rendered ineffective is
contradicted by reference to Abraham, who was justified on the
basis of faith. Following this evidence of the grounding of redemption in the saving act of God is the portrayal of the reality of
the new being of Christians (5:1-8, 39).[1] Paul shows first that with
justification is given assurance of redemption (5:1-11); Christ as
the Second Adam brings the justification which brings life much
more certainly than Adam brought death to all men (5:12-21). The
objection that the proclamation of justification based on grace alone

---

[1] The second larger section probably does not begin after 5:21 (as asserted
recently, e.g., by Althaus, Gaugler, Kuss; Goguel; Léon-Dufour, Grayston) or
after 5:11 (thus Leenhardt, Zahn; Feuillet, and with some hesitation Luz and
N. A. Dahl, "The Atonement—an Adequate Reward for the Akedah? Rom
8:32," *Neotestamentica et Semitica*, Festschr. M. Black, 1969, 17 n. 15), but
with 5:1 (cf. Dodd, Lietzmann, Michel, Nygren, H. W. Schmidt; Dupont,
Lyonnet; Dahl, StTh 1951; Descamps; H. Balz *Heilsvertrauen und Welterfahrung*,
BevTh 59, 1971, 27; N. Gäumann, "Taufe und Ethik. Studien zu Röm 6,"
BevTh 47, 1967, 24 ff; H. Frankemölle, *Das Taufverständnis des Paulus*, StBSt
47, 1970, 18).

makes sin a matter of no concern is countered by Paul: the new
life is basically freed from sin on the basis of baptism (6:1-14); it
is obedience and service (6:15-23); it is freedom from the Law (7:
1-6), which effects only sin and death in men who are under
it (the Law), but which no longer has power, thanks to the
saving act of Christ (7:7-25); whoever is ruled by the Spirit is
free from sin and death (8:1-11); possession of the Spirit guarantees certainty of redemption (8:12-17); in this way the hope of
eternal salvation is certainly guaranteed (8:18-30), for which Paul
offers joyous thanks (8:31-39).

Paul turns then in 9–11 to the question of the basis of the
Jews' unbelief in the dawning time of salvation. The inconceivable
fact of the present rejection of Israel is contrasted with her redemptive benefits (9:1-5); but in rejecting the Jews God has not gone
back on his promise to Israel, and he has the freedom to reject
(9:6-29); human guilt is the real cause of the rejection (9:30–
10:21); but the rejection of the Jews is only a provisional measure
in the divine redemptive plan (11:1-32); a hymn brings to a
close this line of thought (11:33-36).

With 12:1-2 Paul introduces a string of paraenetic statements:
general admonitions for the behavior of Christians to one another
(12:3-13); basic principles for the position of Christians in relation
to non-Christians (12:14-21); obligations of Christians toward
those who hold the power of the state (13:1-7); love of neighbor
as the highest obligation (13:8-10); the nearness of the End as
motivation for moral seriousness (14:1-12). In 14:1–15:6 the
concrete question of the strong and the weak in the Roman community is discussed: warning to those weak in faith (14:1-12);
admonition to those strong in faith (14:13–15:6); general admonition with reference to the example of Christ (15:7-13). In the
personal conclusion Paul justifies his writing (15:14-21), mentions his travel plans, and announces his visit to Rome (15:22-33).
In 16:1-2 he commends Phoebe; 16:3-16 consists of greetings;
16:17-20 is a warning about false teachers; 16:21-24 brings greetings from Paul's associates; 16:25-27, a doxology.

2. The Beginnings of the Roman Community

The earliest sure attestation of the existence of a Roman community is Rom itself, followed by Acts 28:15 with the report that
Christians from there brought Paul to Rome. In Rom 15:22 f (cf.
1:13) Paul writes that he had for many years intended to come

to the brethren in Rome, which implies that there must have been
Christians in the capital of the *Imperium Romanum* as early as the
fifties. Probably the remark of the Roman writer Suetonius in his
Life of Claudius, 25 (*ca.* 120), leads still farther back: [Claudius]
Judaeos impulsore Chresto assidue tumultuantes Roma expulit
(=Claudius expelled the Jews from Rome since they had been
continually causing disturbances at the instigation of a certain
Chrestos"). Since *Chrestos* can be another way of writing *Christos*,
so that the names are the same, Suetonius is likely concerned, not
with a Jewish insurrectionist in Rome by the name of Chrestos,[2]
but with Jesus Christ, whose gospel had brought great unrest to
the Jewish community in Rome, thus providing the occasion for
the Emperor Claudius to expel the Jews or a segment of them. The
report, which is not quite clear, is based on inexact information
of the Gentile writer. This information does not necessitate the inference that Christianity first reached Rome shortly before the
edict of Claudius, which occurred in the year 49 (see §13), but
it had spread effectively among the Roman Jews by that time to
the extent that fierce struggles arose between those who held to the
old faith and those with faith in Christ.

In any case Peter was neither the founder of the Roman church
nor had he been active in Rome before Paul wrote Rom. Against
the assumption that Peter had conducted a mission in Rome before
Paul[3] is the evidence of Gal 2:7; Rom 15:20; II Cor 10:15 f (Paul
will not intrude on someone else's mission territory); and I Cor
9:5, where the itinerant missionary preaching of Peter is mentioned, but nothing is said of his settling down in a community
founded by him.

Rom nowhere mentions any persons to whom the community
is indebted for the gospel, even at those points where it might be
expected: e.g., 1:8 ff; 15:14 ff. Probably Christianity entered the
capital of the Empire, not through a particular apostle or missionary, but very early on the streams of world commerce through the
instrumentality of the great Jewish Diaspora at Rome. A sign of
the religious ties between the Roman Jews of the Diaspora and
Jerusalem is perhaps the fact that there was in Jerusalem a Synagogue of the Libertines (Acts 6:9) which is understood by many
scholars to represent in the main the descendants of Jews who had

[2] Thus once more St. Benko, "The Edict of Claudius of A.D. 49 and the In-
stigator Chrestus," ThZ 25, 1969, 406 ff.
[3] Thus H. Lietzmann, "Zwei Notizen zu Paulus," SAB 1930, 155 f (=*Kleine
Schriften* II, TU 68, 1958, 290 f); E. Hirsch, "Petrus und Paulus," ZNW 29,
1930, 63 ff.

been dragged off to Rome as prisoners of war by Pompey in 61 B.C. Later they were released and formed a powerful element in the Roman Jewish community.[4] Christianity in Rome had a stretch of history already behind it when Paul wrote his Letter to the Romans.

3. The Composition of the Community at the Time of the Letter

Rom manifests a double character: it is essentially a debate between the Pauline gospel and Judaism, so that the conclusion seems obvious that the readers were Jewish Christians. Yet the letter contains statements which indicate specifically that the community was Gentile-Christian. The suppositions (a) that the Roman community was predominantly Jewish-Christian,[5] or (b) that Paul is trying to win over Jewish Christians to the Gentile mission,[6] or (c) that Paul is combating Jewish Christians who have returned to Rome in order to regain control there,[7] can appeal only to Paul's lively controversy with Jewish arguments (cf. 2:17; 3:1; 4:1; 7:1, 4). But there is no text which depicts the Roman Christians as in the majority former Jews. Nor does anything lead to the related supposition that the Gentile Christians had submitted to circumcision before baptism,[8] or that there were in the Roman church circumcised Jewish Christians and uncircumcised Gentile Christians.[9] In Rom the argument is entirely lacking against Gentile Christians' accepting circumcision, as is the case in Gal. Rather the letter characterizes its readers unambiguously as *Gentile Christians*. In 1:5 Paul represents himself as the bearer of the apostolic office among all Gentile nations, to which the Christians in Rome also belong. In 1:13 he expresses the wish to gain among the Romans "some fruit, just as [I have] among the other Gentile peoples" and similarly in 15:15 ff. In 11:13 he writes, "To you Gentiles I say," and in so doing he addresses the readers as Gentiles, as distinct from the unbelieving Jews. And in 9:3 ff; 10:1 f; 11:23, 28, 31, Paul speaks to non-Jews concerning his own people.

[4] See E. Haenchen, *Acts*, 271 n. 1; otherwise, H. J. Leon, *The Jews of Ancient Rome*, 1960, 156.
[5] Thus still Fahy; W. Manson, *The Epistle to the Hebrews*, 172 ff.
[6] Krieger.
[7] Michel.
[8] Michaelis.
[9] Harder.

Any attempt to gain a picture of the readers of Rom must be made from this established point of view. Even 4:1 and 7:1 ff offer no hindrance to achieving that goal, since in 4:1 Paul presents himself in a debate with a Jewish opponent and identifies himself with him as a Jew. The supposed opponent is not to be sought among the readers of the letter any more than is the Jew addressed in a rhetorical aside in 2:17. In 7:1 he calls his readers "people who know the law." Since Paul undoubtedly means here the Law of Moses, he can simply presuppose this knowledge on the part of the Gentile Christians. The OT was their Bible as well as that of the Jewish Christians, fully authoritative for them by reason of continual use in worship and instruction. Through death both Gentile Christians and Jewish Christians (3:19 f; Gal 4:1 ff, 8 ff; 5:1, 13) are freed from the Law (7:4). The whole of pre-Christian humanity stands under the Law and through Christ is freed from it.

Even so the Roman community is *not purely Gentile-Christian*.[10] The story of the origin of the Christian community in Rome makes likely a Jewish-Christian strain in it, even though after the edict against the Jews under Claudius the Jewish-Christian minority would have been severely decimated. Nevertheless Jewish Christians could have returned after 54. Above all, there would be no point to the appeal for mutual acceptance, with its reference to the effect of the incarnation on Jews and Gentiles (15:7 ff), if both groups were not represented in the church. Furthermore, the repeated reference to Jews and Gentiles having the same responsibility before God (1:16; 2:9 ff, 25 ff; 3:29; 10:12) and the broad discussion of the grounds for the unbelief of the majority of Israel, including the proclamation of God's ongoing redemptive goal for Israel (9–11), would alike be incomprehensible if there were no Jewish Christians in the church at Rome. If Ch. 16 belongs to Rom (see below, §19.5), 16:7, 11 proves the presence of former Jews in the Roman community. It is, to be sure, questionable whether the contrast of "strong" and "weak" on the question of eating meat (14:1 ff) is to be equated with the contrast of Gentile Christians and Jewish Christians, as is supposed again and again.[11] On the one hand, Judaism knows no basic vegetarianism, while it

[10] Against Munck.
[11] Thus recently Michel, H. W. Schmidt; Marxsen; Bartsch, Donfried, Minear, Jewett, Bornkamm. Minear thinks, in fact, that he can show that the whole of Rom is alternately directed at one or the other of these groups (cf. p. 45 n. 8!), which is unconvincing.

is often found in paganism of that time;[12] on the other hand, nothing mentioned about the "weak" in Rome refers to a specifically Jewish abstinence from meat.[13] Accordingly nothing can be deduced from 14:1–15:6 about the matter of the composition of the Christian community in Rome.[14]

4. Time, Place, Occasion, and Aim of Romans

The letter was most probably written in Corinth during Paul's last, three-month stay there (15:25; Acts 20:2 f), about the spring of 55 or 56 (according to Acts 20:6, Paul was again in Philippi at Passover),[15] and before the journey to Jerusalem with the collection. In support of this place of writing is the mention of the recommendation of Phoebe from Cenchreae, the port city of Corinth (16:1 f), but beyond that it suits the personal situation of Paul. He sees his task in the East as fulfilled, and his outlook turns to the West, the other half of the Roman Empire. He wants to have Rome as the point of departure for his mission in the West, to press forward through Rome to Spain (15:24, 28). Prior to that, however, it is important for him to undertake a journey to Jerusalem, rendered dangerous on account of the hatred felt by Jews in Judea toward the apostate, and to carry to conclusion the collection project. This situation corresponds best to the three-month stay of Paul in Corinth, while nothing really speaks in favor of Athens[16] or Philippi.[17] In view of the conceptual priority of Gal, as well as in consideration of the biographical information in Rom 15:19 ff, it is scarcely defensible that Rom was written in Asia Minor before I Cor.[18]

[12] Cf. RAC I, 1950, 730 ff; VII, 1969, 447 ff, 1103 ff.

[13] The supposition that the weak were the Jewish Christians who renounced the use of meat after the edict of Claudius against the Jews because they could no longer obtain cultically pure meat is picked out of thin air (against Bartsch, *Antijudaismus*, 33). The "distinction between days" (14:5) also does not point unambiguously to sabbath observance.

[14] See Klein, 136 f.

[15] Nothing points to the conclusion of K. H. Rengstorf (*Die Auferstehung Jesu*, [4]1960, 64 f) that Paul intended that the letter "should be in the hands of the addressees by Easter."

[16] L. P. Pherigo, "Paul and the Corinthian Church," JBL 68, 1949, 341 ff.

[17] Taylor; H. Binder, "Die historische Situation der Past," *Geschichtswirklichkeit und Glaubensbewährung*, Festschr. Bischof F. Müller, 1967, 74; questioningly, Michaelis; Schmid.

[18] Thus G. S. Duncan, "Were Paul's Imprisonment Epistles written from Ephesus?" ExpT 67, 1965/66, 164, and Richards, who thinks he can prove

The occasion for and aim of Rom are derived from the situation and plans of the apostle. Paul does not know the Christians of Rome personally, but seeks by means of the letter to make contact with them.[19] In view of his intention it is necessary immediately to establish relations with the community in Rome, since he needs them as helpers in his further work.[20] Paul does not come to this community that he did not found in order to work there as a missionary, but as "servant of Jesus Christ for all people" (15:16) he has the understandable "wish to preach the gospel also to you in Rome" (1:15), or as he also expressed it, "to call to your remembrance [the gospel] through the grace which was given to me" (15:15). And Rom already represents the carrying out of such a "remembrance." But only the external occasion and the immediate aim of the letter are accounted for by the announcement of his visit, by the clarification of his objectives, and by the enlisting of the understanding and help of the Christians in Rome for the missionary goals which he is pursuing. The broad theological discussion and the debate with Judaism that pervade the letter must have other, deeper grounds.

The old view that Rom is a carefully planned, doctrinal presentation of the Christian faith (cf. Melanchthon: "a compendium of Christian doctrine")[21] is untenable, since important aspects of Pauline doctrine, such as eschatology and Christology, are not fully treated, and the Lord's Supper and church order are not touched on at all. On the other hand, since Paul is seeking ties with the Roman Christians in the interests of his ongoing missionary activity, it is quite appropriate that he presents himself to them and tells them what is the essence of Christianity and what is the content of the gospel that he preaches as apostle to the Gentiles. The desire to introduce himself to the Christians in Rome and to tell them who he is and what he preaches gives Paul the occasion to express himself at some length about the basic truths of Christianity as he sees and teaches it. Though it arose out of concrete necessity for his missionary work, Rom is the theological

that I Cor develops the theological statements in Rom, and that Rom was written in the situation of Acts 19:21, while I Cor was written after the delay mentioned in Acts 19:22.

[19] Rengstorf is unable to show that the Roman community knew Paul and vice versa. See on the contrary Bornkamm, 127 n. 24.

[20] Thus Schrenk.

[21] Thus once more Roosen: Rom is a "gospel sermon, accompanied by a letter instead of a supplement."

confession of Paul, which has been appropriately characterized as "the testament of Paul."[22]

Yet this "testament" does not by any means give the impression of a monologue;[23] rather, numerous indications lead to the conjecture that Paul is directing his attention against false views that were represented in the Roman community. This is the case not only for the polemic against the criticism of the "weak" by the "strong" and the lack of consideration of the "strong" for the "weak" in 14:1–15:7, not only for the admonition to those who "provoke dissensions and offences against the teaching that you have learned" (16:17 f), but also for the pervasive polemic against Jewish errors and criticisms of the gospel (2:17; 3:1-31; 4:1; 7:13; 9:31 f; 11:11) as well as for the rejection of libertine-antinomian conclusions from the message of Christians' freedom from the Law (3:8, 31; 6:1, 15; 7:7 ff) and of the presumptuousness of Gentile Christians (11:13 ff). The literary character of Rom does not fit the theory that it was written as an encyclical or manifesto intended to be sent around to several churches, which was then reworked into a letter to the Romans by the addition of concrete details in 15:14 ff.[24] On the other hand it is highly questionable whether a fundamentally polemical character is to be attributed to Rom. The numerous attempts to discover such a polemic[25] are as unconvincing as is the supposition that Paul is trying by means of this letter to encourage the development of a unified Christian community in Rome,[26] or to provide for the first time an apostolic basis for the Roman community.[27] There is, of course, no doubt that in Rom Paul controverts the antinomian distortion of his

[22] Thus Bornkamm, 139, who shows how in Rom the motifs of the earlier letters are brought together, but without their concrete links to the circumstances (cf. 130 ff).

[23] Feine-Behm, 173.

[24] T. W. Manson, 241; Suggs, 295 ff; R. W. Funk, "The Apostolic Parousia: Form and Significance," *Christian History and Interpretation: Festschr. J. Knox,* 1967, 267 f.

[25] Rom is an echo of Paul's controversy with Judaists and antinomians (Trocmé; similarly Munck; W. Manson, see n. 5); Paul seeks to mediate between Jewish Christians and Gentile Christians in Rome (Preisker, Bartsch, Minear); or is battling only the Jewish Christians (Marxsen, Harder), or only the Gentile Christians (Bartsch), or antinomianism (Lütgert); he has to defend himself against the circumcised Gentile Christians in Rome (Michaelis), or against a supposed rejection by the Roman community (J. Knox), or against a criticism of his planned journey to Jerusalem (Noack).

[26] Esp. Bartsch and Minear, who refer to the omission of ἐκκλησία from the prescript.

[27] Klein; *contra,* Donfried, 441 f; Bornkamm, 128 f.

message about the gospel's saving power for every believer; and that he joins in the opposition between the vegetarians and their opponents in the Roman community, and in so doing pursues a concrete objective the presuppositions of which we can no longer perceive in detail. It is just as clear, however, that the most weighty part of the letter does not lie in such specific polemics[28] but in the setting forth of the Pauline message of redemption in ongoing debate with Jewish teaching about redemption. Rightly to be recalled is that Paul is writing this redemptive message both in response to the concrete missionary occasion related to the Roman community and also in his situation of anticipating a renewed controversy with his Jewish opponents in Jerusalem.[29] On the basis of this double biographical-historical situation the distinctive character of Rom may be understood in contrast to the other Pauline letters: a "testament," and at the same time a concrete message for the Roman church.

5. Authenticity and Integrity of the Letter

The authenticity and homogeneity of Rom 1–15 are subject to no serious doubt.[30] The supposition that individual verses have been interpolated[31] has found only scattered agreement, especially for 7:25b, but is in no instance convincing. And the hypothesis that Rom is a compilation of a genuine Pauline letter to Gentile Christians and a non-Pauline "Handbook on Jewish Problems"[32] lacks any sort of basis. On the other hand, the conclusion of Rom offers significant text-critical difficulties.

[28] Noack wrongly characterizes Chs. 3–8 as "backwater" and the communication about Paul's travel plans and the defense of his first journeying to Jerusalem as the main stream of the letter.

[29] Suggs, 295; Bornkamm, 137 f.

[30] Hawkins' proposal of extensive interpolations is wholly arbitrary, but even the claim that there are individual interpolated sections is unproved: P. N. Harrison tries to prove by word statistics that 1:9–2:1 is an interpolation of the later second century; L. H. Talbert, "A Non-Pauline Fragment at Romans 3:24-26?" JBL 85, 1966, 287 ff, considers 3:25 f to be a summarizing interpolation; E. Barnikol, "Römer 13. Der nichtpaulinische Ursprung der absoluten Obrigkeitsbejahung von Röm 13:1-7," Studien zum NT und zur Patristik, Festschr. E. Klostermann, TU 77, 1961, 65 ff, interprets 13:1-7 as non-Pauline on the basis of its contents; similarly J. Kallas, "Romans XIII, 1-7: An Interpolation," NTS 11, 1964/65, 365 ff; according to J. Knox, IntB, in loc., the church at Rome added Ch. 16 to Rom.

[31] Cf. Bultmann, Schenke.

[32] Kinoshita, who does not even attempt to explain the compilation.

In Marcion's *Apostolikon* there was a shorter text of Rom. Origen[33] reports concerning it: *Caput hoc* [16:25 ff] *Marcion, a quo scripturae evangelicae et apostolicae interpolatae sunt, de hac penitus abstulit; et no solum hoc, sed et ab eo loco, ubi scriptum est, "omne autem, quod non est ex fide, peccatum est"* [14:23] *usque ad finem cuncta dissecuit* ("Marcion, by whom the scriptures—both Gospels and epistles—were corrupted, completely removed this section [16:25 ff] from this epistle; and not only this, but also from the place where it is written, 'Whatever is not of faith is sin' [14:23], he cut off everything to the end"). That is, Marcion had expunged Chs. 15 and 16, according to Origen (*dissecuit = desecuit*); his Rom ended with 14:23. Marcion's text of Rom, minus Chs. 15 and 16, has affected a few manuscripts of the Western church, which have only the doxology of 16:25 ff following 14:23.[34] That 15:1–16:23 is Pauline is indisputable, but the doxology in 16:25 ff is found in the text tradition not only after 14:23, but also in strikingly different places:[35]

(*a*) 1:1–14:23;	15:1–16:23; 16:25-27	$\mathfrak{P}^{61}$ ℵ B C bo sa D d e f vg sy^p
(*b*) 1:1–14:23; 16:25-27	15:1–16:23; 16:25-27	A P min
(*c*) 1:1–14:23; 16:25-27	15:1–16:24	$\mathfrak{M}$ sy^h
(*d*) 1:1–14:23	15:1–16:24	F G g Archetype of D
(*e*) 1:1–14:23; 16:24–27		vg^{2089} Old Latin according to chapter lists in Cyprian
(*f*) 1:1–15:33; 16:25-27	16:1-23	$\mathfrak{P}^{46}$

The doxology could not have stood after 14:23 *and* 16:23, especially since after 14:23 it destroys the continuity. But if it was originally after 16:23, how did it come to be placed after 14:23? The conjecture that Marcion's text—omitting Chs. 15 and 16— has a role to play obtrudes itself, especially since the text form

---

[33] Origen, *Commentaria in epistolam ad Romanos* (VII, 453, Lommatzsch).

[34] Cf. Dupont, RBén 1948, 6 f; H. J. Frede, *Altlateinische Paulus-Handschriften, Vetus Latina. Aus der Geschichte der lat. Bibel* 4, 1964, 152 ff.

[35] The table offers only a selection of the textual witnesses; on the testimony of the minuscules, see K. Aland, "Glosse, Interpolation, Redaktion und Komposition in der Sicht der nt. Textkritik," *Apophoreta, Festschr. E. Haenchen*, Bh. ZNW 30, 1964, 18 ff (=*Studien zur Überlieferung des NT und seines Textes*, ANTF 2, 1967, 46 ff).

e existed in ecclesiastical circles as well. On the basis of these observations, and independently of each other, P. Corssen and D. de Bruyne[36] advanced the obvious hypothesis that Marcion's shortened text represents the point of origin for the textual tradition that we can now perceive, since it was to this shortened text that the doxology was attached for purposes of liturgical rounding off (text e). This text form was adopted by the main body of the church, but when this *e* text confronted the original Pauline text, as preserved elsewhere, there arose the different forms of the text in which the doxology remained in its original place (text c), or dropped out (text d), was moved to a position after 15:33 or 16:23 (texts f and a), or both remained in position and was attached (text b). The following ancestry of the text forms is implied:

Original text (1:1–16:23)

Marcion's text (1:1–14:23)

Marcion's text expanded by the doxology—text e

Combination of the original text and text e: a, b, c, d, f

The presupposition of the hypothesis, which is affirmed by the great majority of scholars,[37] is that 16:25-27 is either a fragment of another Pauline letter,[38] or a non-Pauline supplement.[39] That so small a Pauline fragment would be preserved is not in itself

[36] D. de Bruyne, "Les deux derniers chapitres de la lettre aux Romains," RBén 25, 1908, 423 ff; P. Corssen, "Zur Überlieferungsgeschichte des Rom," ZNW 10, 1909, 1 ff, 79 ff.

[37] 16:25-27 is still regarded as the Pauline conclusion to Rom by Leenhardt, Murray, Nygren, H. W. Schmidt; Cambier in Robert-Feuillet, Guthrie, Harrison, Höpfl-Gut, Mariani, Meinertz; Roosen; Frede (see n. 34), 156 f; after 15:33, Feuillet.

[38] Feine-Behm, Michaelis, Wikenhauser; Schumacher.

[39] Thus more recently, e.g., Althaus, Barrett, Gaugler, Lietzmann, Michel; Jülicher-Fascher, Klijn, Marxsen, Schelkle; Dupont, RBén, 1948; T. W. Manson, Schenke, Bartsch, Donfried; G. Zuntz, *The Text of the Epistles*, 1953, 227; E. Kamlah, "Traditionsgeschichtliche Untersuchungen zur Schlussdoxologie des Röm" (diss. Tübingen), ThLZ 81, 1956, 492; D. Lührmann, *Das Offenbarungsverständnis bei Paulus und in paulinischen Gemeinden*, WMANT 16, 1965, 122 ff; hesitantly, R. H. Fuller; Minear. F. Renner, " 'An die Hebräer'—ein pseudepigraphischer Brief," 1970, 94 ff, considers 16:25-27 to be a combination of two non-Pauline fragments, a doxology and a paraenetic passage.

likely, but a plausible theory is that in ecclesiastical circles[40] or in Marcionite circles after Marcion[41] a liturgical conclusion was composed for the shortened text. Weighing against Pauline authorship of this section in fact is the unusual style on the whole and expressions such as αἰώνιος θεός, μόνος σοφὸς θεός, γνωρίζειν τὸ μυστήριον, but, above all, the idea that the gospel has been "a secret hidden since eternal ages" which is "now revealed through prophetic writings." These ideas are readily explicable as being of Marcionite origin, but while holding this question open, it should be regarded as certain that the doxology does not originate with Paul and was created originally as a conclusion following 14:23. We do not know how the truncated text form attested by Marcion originated (1:1–14:23); it is just as possible that Marcion found it truncated as that he shortened it himself. In any case it may be concluded that the archetype on which our text tradition is based included only 1:1–16:23.

The denial that the text of this compass represents the original letter of Paul to the Romans makes reference to two sets of facts: (1) Before the oldest preserved MS of Rom was prepared— Papyrus[46] from the end of the second century (see below, §38.1.b) —Rom could have included only Chs. 1–15, since only in this way can the location of the doxology after 15:33 in 𝔓[46] be explained.[42] T. W. Manson[43] has drawn from this the conclusion that Paul wrote Rom 1:1–15:33 for the Romans and sent it off to them, and then sent a copy of this text, expanded by the addition of Ch. 16, to Ephesus. Albertz would like to regard Ch. 16 as a II Rom which Paul appended to I Rom in Puteoli (cf. Acts 28:13). No cogent argument can be adduced for Albertz' hypothesis, and the existence of the doxology in 𝔓[46] following 15:33 in no way proves that there ever was a MS that ended with 15:33, much less that this was the text form that Paul sent to the Romans, especially since 𝔓[46] contains Ch. 16! (2) Manson's hypothesis does accord with earlier observations about Ch. 16. After C. A. Heumann (1755) first posed the question whether Chs. (12–15 and) 16 were Pauline supplements to Rom and J. S. Semler[44] charac-

---

[40] Kamlah (see n. 39) refers to kinship with the Pastorals; Jülicher-Fascher and Klijn propose that there was an addition when the Pauline letters were made into a collection.

[41] Thus Goguel; Lietzmann; T. W. Manson; Zuntz; Lührmann (see n. 29).

[42] Friedrich.

[43] Followed by Munck and P. N. Harrison.

[44] J. S. Semler, 1769; cf. WGK, NT, 67, 416.

terized Chs. 15 and 16 as supplemental Pauline essays, D. Schulz[45] was the first to regard Ch. 16 as a fragment of a Pauline letter to Ephesus. This hypothesis is represented today by numerous scholars[46] with slight variations[47] and rests on the following arguments:

1. The list of greetings in 16:3-16 assumes that Paul is acquainted with a strikingly large number of persons in the community that he does not know. Even when account is taken of the freedom of movement in this period, it is hard to imagine that all these persons would have migrated from the East to Rome. It would scarcely have served the objectives Paul is pursuing in this letter to Rome to extend greetings, not to the leading personalities of the community, but with emphasis on his old friends.

2. One would expect "the first converts in Asia" (16:5) to be in Ephesus, not in Rome, like Prisca and Aquila with their household, who were driven out of Rome (Acts 18:2) and took up residence first in Corinth and then in Ephesus (Acts 18:18 f, 26; I Cor 16:19).

3. The sharp admonition concerning those who provoke the divisions (16:17-20) does not fit in the framework of Rom: it suits neither the situation of the readers nor is its imperious tone compatible with the cautious attempts at rapport (1:10 ff; 15: 14 ff; 12:3 ff). This argument has special validity if the antagonists here as in Gal are Judaizers.

4. 15:33 has the character of a ceremonial epistolary conclusion, as does 16:20. The duplication is wholly atypical for Paul.

5. There is no other place where Paul greets so many individual Christians at the end of a letter.

The arguments presented under points 1–3 provide the ground of the probability that essential parts of Romans 16 were originally addressed *to Ephesus*. But this hypothesis is by no means convincing. (1) Paul does not by any means know personally all the persons greeted. Only nine of the twenty-six must be assumed to have migrated from the East to Rome: Prisca and Aquila,

[45] D. Schulz, review of the Introductions by Eichhorn and De Wette, ThStKr 2, 1829, 609 ff.

[46] According to Feine-Behm and Michaelis, 16:1-2 still belongs to Rom; according to Schenke, 16:1, 2, 21-23; according to D. Georgi, *Die Geschichte der Kollekte des Paulus für Jerusalem,* ThF 38, 1965, 79 f, only 16:21-23.

[47] E.g., Leenhardt; Goodspeed, Heard, Henshaw, Marxsen, McNeile-Williams; T. M. Taylor, T. W. Manson, Feuillet, Munck, Schmithals, Friedrich, P. N. Harrison, Kinoshita, Richards, Suggs, Schenke, Macdonald, Jewett, Bornkamm; R. Bultmann, "Die kirchliche Redaktion des I Joh," *In memoriam E. Lohmeyer,* 1951, 190 (=*Exegetica,* 1967, 382); P. N. Harrison, *Paulines and Pastorals,* 1964, 86 ff.

Epaenetus, Andronicus and Junia, Ampliatus, Stachys, Rufus and his mother. But even if significantly more of those greeted had come to Rome from the East, this involved only a small number of Christians who in the course of several years would have moved to the capital city—which is surely not inconceivable.[48] (2) The first convert in Asia, Epaenetus, can easily be thought of as being now in Rome, and the allusion to his special role in Asia is substantially more natural in a letter to Rome than to Ephesus, where his role would be known. And the conjecture that, following the lifting of Claudius' edict against the Jews at his death in 54, Prisca and Aquila had returned to their home in Rome is not to be dismissed out of hand. (3) Who the target is of the sharp attack in 16:17-20 cannot be determined for sure: nothing indicates "Judaizers" reliant on the Law;[49] Gnostics have been suggested,[50] without any real evidence being presented. But to warn the community about a danger which has not yet become a reality is much less difficult to understand for Rome than for Ephesus. (4) The concluding wish (15:33) is by no means impossible within a Pauline letter (cf. I Thess 3:11-13; Phil 4:9).

(5) Two factors tell decisively against the Ephesus hypothesis, however: (a) The letter consisting of 16:1-23 or 16:3-23, would be a literary impossibility. No one has been able to produce from antiquity a letter that consists mostly of greetings,[51] and certainly Paul could not write a letter so devoid of content to a community he had known over a period of years in Ephesus. (b) Why should anyone have removed the indispensable greetings from a letter that ended at 15:33 and also have cut off the address of the conjectural letter to the Ephesians? Neither the assumption that someone "piously added what was left over from the Pauline material in the archives"[52] as a conclusion to the collected Pauline letters, nor the conjecture that Paul, by means of this supplement, made his letter to the Romans suitable for sending to Ephesus as well, can

---

[48] Lietzmann has indicated as an analogy a Bacchic *thiasos* that according to an inscription (published in AJA 37, 1933, 115 ff) was taken to Rome from the East.

[49] So once more Schenke, 282 n. 1; according to Donfried, 448 f, the admonitions in 14:1-3, 20 f are continued in 16:17-20.

[50] Michel; Preisker, Schmithals.

[51] Not even in a letter of recommendation for a woman, in which that would be necessary according to Goodspeed. The letter mentioned by Macdonald, 370, as a parallel, sent from a student to his father (Oxyrhynchus Papyri X, 1296), is a private note in the style of a modern postcard greeting.

[52] Feine-Behm (see also n. 40); but we know nothing at all about Rom standing at the end of the collection of Pauline letters.

offer a satisfactory answer. The claim that we are dealing with
only a fragment of a letter to the Ephesians makes even the preservation of such a fragment as this inconceivable. On the other
hand, Paul had good reason for exploiting personal connections
with a community that he did not know, as Col 4:10 ff shows.
It has been correctly stressed[53] that the greeting to "all the
churches of Christ" was substantially more appropriate in a letter
to Rome than to Ephesus. The most convincing assumption about
the text tradition is that it originally included 1:1–16:23.[54]

§20. THE LETTER TO THE PHILIPPIANS

Commentaries: see §41. Research: W. Lütgert, "Die Vollkommenen
in Philippi und die Enthusiasten in Thessalonich," BFChTh 13, 6, 1909,
1 ff; P. Feine, "Die Abfassung des Phil in Ephesus," BFChTh 20, 4,
1916; W. Michaelis, *Die Gefangenschaft des Paulus in Ephesus und das
Itinerar des Timotheus* NTF I, 3, 1925; idem, *Die Datierung des Phil*,
NTF I, 8, 1933; G. S. Duncan, *St. Paul's Ephesian Ministry: A Reconstruction with Special Reference to the Ephesian Origin of the
Imprisonment Epistles*, 1929; J. Schmid, *Zeit und Ort der paulinischen
Gefangenschaftsbriefe. Mit einem Anhang über die Datierung der Past*,
1931; T. W. Manson, "St. Paul in Ephesus: The Date of the Epistle to
the Philippians," BJRL 23, 1939, 182 ff (=Manson, *St.*, 149 ff); C. H.
Dodd, *NT Studies*, 1953, 85 ff; G. S. Duncan, "Were Paul's Imprison-
ment Epistles Written from Ephesus?" ExpT 67, 1955/56, 163 ff; idem,
"Paul's Ministry in Asia—the Last Phase," NTS 3, 1956/57, 211 ff;
idem, "Chronological Table to Illustrate Paul's Ministry in Asia," NTS
5, 1958/59, 43 ff; P. N. Harrison, "The Pastoral Epistles and Duncan's
Ephesian Theory," NTS 2, 1955/56, 250 ff; L. Johnson, "The Pauline
Letters from Caesarea," ExpT 68, 1956/57, 24 ff; W. Schmithals, "Die
Irrlehrer des Phil," ZThK 54, 1957, 297 ff (=W. S., *Paulus und die
Gnostiker*, ThF 35, 1965, 47 ff; English translation, *Paul and the
Gnostics*, 1972, 65 ff); J. Müller-Bardorff, "Zur Frage der literarischen
Einheit des Phil," *Wissenschaftliche Zeitschrift der Friedrich-
Schiller-Universität Jena*, 7, 1957/58, Gesellschafts- und sprachwissen-
schaftliche Reihe 4, 591 ff; B. D. Rahtjen, "The Three Letters of Paul
to the Philippians," NTS 6, 1959/60, 167 ff; B. S. Mackay, "Further
Thoughts on Philippians," NTS 7, 1960/61, 161 ff; G. Delling, RGG[3]

[53] K. Holl, "Der Kirchenbegriff des Paulus in seinem Verhältnis zu dem der
Urgemeinde," SAB, 1921, 924 n. 1 (=*Gesammelte Aufsätze* II, 1928, 47 n. 2).
[54] Thus, e.g., Barrett, Gaugler, Huby-Lyonnet, Lietzmann, Michel, Murray,
H. W. Schmidt; Goguel, Guthrie, Harrington, Harrison, Jülicher-Fascher, Klijn;
K. Maly, GANT, 93; Mariani, Wikenhauser; Preisker, Harder, Rengstorf, Don-
fried; E. Lohse, "Die Mitarbeiter des Paulus im Kol," *Verborum Veritas, Festschr.
G. Stählin*, 1970, 190.

V, 1961, 333 ff; G. Bornkamm, "Der Phil als paulinische Briefsammlung," *Neotestamentica et Patristica, Freundesgabe O. Cullmann*, NovTest Suppl. 6, 1962, 192 ff (=G. B., *Geschichte und Glaube* II, *Gesammelte Aufsätze* IV, BevTh 53, 1971, 195 ff); H. Köster, "The Purpose of the Polemic of a Pauline Fragment (Phil. III)," NTS 8, 1961/62, 317 ff; V. Furnish, "The Place and Purpose of Philippians III," NTS 10, 1963/64, 80 ff; A. F. J. Klijn, "Paul's Opponents in Philippians III," NovTest 7, 1964/65, 278 ff; J. Murphy-O'Connor, DBS VII, 1965, 1211 ff (bibl.); T. E. Pollard, "The Integrity of Philippians," NTS 13, 1966/67, 57 ff: R. Jewett, "The Epistolary Thanksgiving and the Integrity of Philippians," NovTest 12, 1970, 40 ff; *idem*, "Conflicting Movements in the Early Church as Reflected in Philippians," NovTest 12, 1970, 362 ff; B. Reicke, "Caesarea, Rome and the Captivity Epistles," AHG, 1970, 277 ff.

1. Contents

Following the prescript (1:1 f) and the introduction to the letter (1:3-11), in which Paul offers thanks for the state of the community and offers intercession for its further growth, there is information about the situation of the apostle (1:12-26): he is imprisoned, though the work of the gospel is not restricted thereby but is actually fostered; his associates have been stimulated by his condition to joyous confession and proclamation of the gospel (1:12-18a); also his personal prospects are favorable: filled with a longing for death, he nevertheless perceives a good outcome of his trial: his release. He knows that he will remain alive, that his churches will be preserved, and that he will see the Philippians again (1:18b-26). Then come the exhortations to the community (1:27–2:18): first the appeal to persevere bravely in the battle for the faith (1:27-30); then the admonition to maintain a right frame of mind, which consists above all in humility and selflessness as members of the body of Christ (2:1-5). This appeal provides the occasion for inserting the Christ psalm (2:6-11), in which Paul praises Jesus Christ as the foundation of a mind that is prepared for self-forgetting renunciation to the utmost. The paraenesis resounds with yet further exhortation to struggle for salvation, from which springs joy for Paul and for the readers themselves (2:12-18). In 2:19-30 there follow communications concerning Timothy and Epaphroditus: Timothy, whose fidelity is praised by Paul, is to come to Philippi soon; Epaphroditus, from Philippi, who was very ill when he visited Paul, is well and is setting out on his journey home. In 3:1a it appears that the conclusion of the letter is beginning. But then the apostle once again begins more extended statements, the tone of which is strikingly altered: in 3:1b-21 there are urgent warnings about people who falsely rely on the flesh, a reliance that Paul has abandoned in order to strive for the upward call, a goal which is based on faith. Paul is set forth as a model over against people who live as enemies of the cross of Christ. Attached to these general exhortations are brief detailed warnings and then more general admonitions (4:1-9). In conclusion Paul thanks the Philippians for a gift which he rejoices in as proof of their deep solidarity with him (4:10-20). General greetings (4:21 f) and the benediction (4:23) constitute the conclusion.

2. Paul and the Community at Philippi

Founding the community was Paul's first act on European soil, when in the year 48/49 he arrived in Macedonia from Asia on his so-called second missionary journey. Philippi, built by Philip of Macedon (father of Alexander the Great) and named for him, had been since 42 B.C. a Roman military colony, *Colonia Augusta Julia Philippensis*, whose inhabitants enjoyed the privileges of the *ius Italicum*.[1] The story of Paul's first mission in Philippi is known from Acts 16:12-40. From I Thess 2:2 and Phil 1:30 it can be inferred that on this occasion Paul experienced struggles and maltreatment. His first stay does not seem to have been for long, nor does it seem to have led to the establishment of a larger community. Acts mentions only the proselyte Lydia, a dealer in purple dye from Thyatira, together with her household (16:14 f), in addition to the family of the jail-keeper (16:33 f). Otherwise we know only those mentioned in Phil, who were perhaps converted later: Epaphroditus (2:25 ff; 4:18), Euodias, Syntyche, Clement, and the unnamed "co-worker" (Σύζυγος is not used as a proper name) in 4:2 f. From these names it can be inferred that this was an essentially Gentile-Christian community, and 3:3 assumes that the readers are not circumcised Jews. In the prescript Paul greets "administrators" and "aides" (ἐπίσκοποι καὶ διάκονοι) especially (1:1): the community has persons with certain specific tasks whose achievements in service are indicated by designations in common use in clubs and cult-fellowships of the culture. For many years Paul had not visited Philippi again, but the tie to the Christians there was close. That is shown by the gift of money with which

---

[1] Cf. P. Lemerle, *Philippes et la Macédoine orientale à l'époque chrétienne et byzantine*, 1945, 7 ff.

they had offered help, both in Thessalonica and later in Corinth as well (4:15 f; II Cor 11:8 f). The mission of Timothy and Erastus to Macedonia (Acts 19:22) had surely included the Philippians as well. Paul himself had probably first returned to Macedonia in late autumn of 54 or 55 (Acts 20:1 f) and at that time must surely have stopped in Philippi. It is possible that he there had his meeting with Titus, who had come from Corinth, and that he wrote II Cor there (see p. 293). He visited the community for the last time in 55 or 56, as he journeyed from Corinth through Macedonia to Jerusalem for the purpose of taking the collection. Probably he celebrated Passover in their midst (Acts 20:3 ff).

3. The Occasion for the Letter

(a) Recently Paul had received another gift of money from Philippi. Epaphroditus had brought it to him as commissioned by the community (4:14, 18; 2:25). In the letter he gives expression to his thankfulness for the evidence of love he had received. Paul sent the letter with Epaphroditus, who had been very ill when he was with Paul, but had now recovered (2:28). (b) Between Epaphroditus' arrival where Paul was and the writing of Phil, a report of Epaphroditus' illness must have reached the Philippians (2:26). It is usually inferred from the statement "He was in distress because you had heard that he was ill" that a report of the Philippians' alarm had already come back to the place where Paul and Epaphroditus were, but it is by no means certain that the statement implies that.[2] In any case Phil seeks to convey to the Philippians that, since the illness which Epaphroditus contracted in the course of Christian service brought him near to death, he should be received back by the Philippians with even greater respect (2:27-30). (c) Paul also wants to tell the community in Philippi how things are going with him (1:12 ff), although as a result of his imprisonment he cannot come to them at the moment, and to announce to them that he will soon send Timothy to Philippi, because he is awaiting news from the community (2:19 ff). (d) Paul wants to help the community, since he himself cannot come for the time being. Actually the condition of the community scarcely provides Paul with occasion for admonitory intervention. 1:3 ff; 2:12; 4:1 present the picture of a community which merits the complete trust of their apostle. Only the em-

[2] See Mackay, 168 f; Reicke, 284.

phatic reminder that harmony is a duty (1:27–2:18) points to
a specific lack in the moral behavior of the members of the community, which in an individual case (4:2) escalated in a crass
manner into a conflict between two women. Yet Paul wants to
warn the community about persons whom he characterizes as "evil-
workers" and "enemies of the cross of Christ" (3:2, 18) who
could make an impression on the Philippians; he does not, however,
regard the community as seriously endangered.

The reasons for writing this very personal letter are so numerous that its origin is readily understandable. But the immediate
historical circumstances for its composition are all the more unclear.

4. Place and Time of the Writing of the Letter

Paul is writing as a prisoner (1:7, 13, 17),[3] but the letter discloses nothing of anxiety about the outcome of the charge against
him. Rather, Paul sees his situation as developing for the further-
ance of the gospel: in the whole Praetorian Guard and beyond it
has become known that he has been seized as a Christian missionary,
not as a common lawbreaker (1:12 f). His trial can end in the
death sentence (1:20; 2:17), but to him it seems more likely that
he will be released. Thus he is in a good mood and hopes to come
to Philippi again as a free man (1:25; 2:24). At the place where
he is imprisoned there is lively evangelistic activity (1:14 ff), and
Timothy is in the same place as well (1:1; 2:19, 23).

When was Paul in the situation that fits this information in
Phil?

From Acts 23:33–26:32 and 28:14–31 we know of two imprisonments of Paul: in Caesarea and in Rome. How long Paul was under
investigation during the trial in Caesarea following his arrest in
Jerusalem (around Pentecost in 56 or 57) we do not know. Acts
24:27 mentions two years, but it cannot be decided for sure
whether the two years relate to the imprisonment of Paul or, as is
less likely, to the term of Felix as procurator.[4] According to Acts
28:30 Paul was under protective custody (*custodia libera*) for
two years in Rome. Does Phil stem from one of these two imprisonments or from an imprisonment to be assumed on hypothetical
grounds in a third location?

[3] Disputed by T. W. Manson without adequate reason.
[4] Cf. E. Haenchen, *Acts*, 67 ff.

1. The traditional view is that Phil was written in Rome.[5] In support are adduced the following arguments:

a. The Praetorian Guard (πραιτώριον 1:13), which was located in Rome. According to Acts 28:16, Paul was under house arrest in his own quarters with a soldier as guard. He was therefore placed under the surveillance of members of the Praetorian Guard, who guarded him by turns.

b. The expression οἱ ἐκ τῆς καίσαρος οἰκίας (4:22), which according to linguistic usage in imperial times (cf. *domus* or *familia Caesaris*) indicated those who belonged to the household of Caesar, the servants of the emperor, slaves and freedmen. In no place was there a better possibility for easy encounter with imperial slaves and for converting them to Christianity than in Rome.

c. The situation of the imprisoned Paul. For a crowd of preachers of the gospel to be active in the place where Paul is staying (1:14 ff) is readily understandable in Rome, where there was a large community of Christians. But the personal circumstances of the apostle (1:7, 12 ff) fit as well: his trial before the imperial court is about to end; Paul sees the alternatives in the judicial decision as the death sentence or release (1:19 ff). A hearing has already taken place (1:7, ἀπολογία, βεβαίωσις), the result of which was that he is being held and brought before the court by the will of Christ solely as a missionary of Christianity. And the freedom to send letters and to carry on activities with his missionary companions fits well the situation of Paul depicted in Acts 28:16, 30 f.

Strong considerations may be advanced against these arguments for the origin of Phil in Rome, however:

a. From Rome Paul wanted to go on to Spain (Rom 15:24, 28). How does this square with the announcement of a visit to Philippi which Paul promises if the outcome of the trial is favorable (2:24; 1:26)?

b. In view of the great distance from Rome to Philippi, how are we to conceive of the lively transactions and exchange of letters between Paul and the community which Phil presupposes? It has been calculated that before Paul wrote his letter there must have been four traversings of the distance between the place of Paul's imprisonment and Philippi: the Philippians hear of Paul's arrest and send Epaphroditus to him; his illness is reported at Philippi, and the community communicates its concern in return. Between

[5] From the Marcionite Prologue of the second century until the eighteenth century, this was not disputed; but see more recently, e.g., Beare, Johnston, Müller; R. M. Grant, Guthrie, E. F. Harrison, Heard, Henshaw, Jülicher-Fascher, Sparks; Schmid, Dodd, P. N. Harrison, Rahtjen, Mackay, Reicke.

the writing of Phil and Paul's planned journey to Philippi the same distance would have had to be bridged three additional times: Epaphroditus returns to Philippi with Phil; Timothy is soon to follow him and take back news of the Philippians. However one reckons the length of time for a journey from Rome to Philippi, these numerous journeys demand in any case several months. Can Paul only after several months thank the Philippians for their gift (4:10 ff); and could he still describe his journey there, planned for some months later, as a "soon coming" (2:24)?

c. Paul has "obviously not been in Philippi again since the founding of the community, according to 1:30; 4:15 f (cf. also 2:12; 1:26 and 2:22)." [6] But that statement is not true for the time of the Roman imprisonment (cf. Acts 20:1 ff).

d. Paul polemicizes in 3:2 ff against Judaizers in a manner similar to Gal and I Cor, but Rom shows that at that time there was no danger from Judaizers either in Corinth or in Rome. This polemic is therefore incomprehensible in the period of the Roman imprisonment.

These arguments for and objections against the writing of Phil in Rome by and large carry no real weight.

a. The allusion to the widespread knowledge of his imprisonment as a Christian ἐν ὅλῳ τῷ πραιτωρίῳ (1:13) and the greeting from the imperial slaves (4:22) fit well for Rome, but they are just as possible elsewhere, since πραιτώριον can also indicate the place of residence of a Roman governor or of other Roman officials, and there were imperial slaves in many places.

b. Nothing certain can be inferred from 1:14 about the size of the Christian community in the place or about the number of missionaries who were active there. The personal situation of Paul with the alternatives of death sentence or release fits best a trial before the emperor in Rome, since there was no higher appeal. But we do not know whether Paul in Caesarea, for example, intended from the outset to appeal the decision (Acts 25:11; 26:32; 28:19).

c. We know nothing about whether Paul during his two years in prison in Rome abandoned his planned journey to Spain or postponed it in order to return to the East following his hoped-for release. But in any case, this factor creates a real difficulty for the theory of a Roman origin for Phil.

d. The journeys presupposed in Phil and planned between Paul's place of residence and Philippi are undoubtedly better understood

---

[6] W. Michaelis, *Einl.*, 207; cf. Gnilka, *Comm.*, 20.

if Paul was nearer to Philippi than Rome or Caesarea. But it must be noted in any case that four movements back and forth are not necessarily to be considered as prior to the writing of Phil,[7] since on the one hand it is nowhere said that the Philippians sent their gift with Epaphroditus after they had heard of Paul's imprisonment. And on the other hand 2:26 does not imply that Epaphroditus learned how the Philippians reacted to the news of his illness. We cannot therefore infer with assurance from Phil anything more than that Paul, following Epaphroditus' recovery from his illness, thanked the Philippians for the gift which was conveyed to him by Epaphroditus. And this chronological period between the receipt of the gift and the writing of the letter of thanks is independent of the length of time for a journey between Philippi and wherever Paul was then staying. Indeed 2:19, 24 assumes that Timothy is to travel to Philippi and back before Paul himself undertakes his journey there soon, as a consequence of the great distances, that is more difficult to understand from Rome or Caesarea than from a place closer to Philippi.

e. No passage in Phil indicates unambiguously that Paul has not been in Philippi since the community was established. This argument therefore does not tell against Rome or Caesarea.

f. The target of the polemic in 3:2 ff, 17 ff is debated. It is extremely unlikely that Paul is here polemicizing against Judaizers who are seeking to convert the community in Philippi to obedience to the Jewish Law,[8] because any polemic is lacking against the adoption of circumcision and the conformity to the Law by Christians in Philippi, as is any defense of Paul's apostolic office. On that basis no convincing objection can be raised against the writing of Phil in Rome. But it cannot be determined with anything like complete certainty whom the polemic is directed against. Those who reject the interpretation that Judaizers are being attacked have often suggested Jewish propagandists[9] whose propaganda in behalf of circumcision ἐν σαρκί is countered by the assertion "We are the circumcision" (3:3). But it is as improbable that Paul would have used the term of insult "mutilation" (3:2) against

---

[7] See n. 2.

[8] Thus (in some cases only for 3:2 ff) Beare, Bonnard, Friedrich, Martin, Müller; Appel, Cerfaux in Robert-Feuillet, Feine-Behm, McNeile-Williams; T. W. Manson, Delling, Jewett; B. Reicke, "Diakonie, Festfreude und Zelos," *Uppsala Universitets Årsskrift* 1951: 5, 298 ff; O. Cullmann, *Peter*, 2d Eng. ed., 1962, 105 ff.

[9] Dibelius, Johnston, Lohmeyer; Albertz, Goguel, Harrington, Jülicher-Fascher, Klijn, Meinertz, Duncan, Pollard; J. Munck, *Paul and the Salvation of Mankind*, 280 n.

Jews as that he would have said to Jews who demand circumcision of the Gentiles, "their glory" consists "in their shame" [tr. note: a euphemism for genitals] (3:19). It is difficult to see in the propagandists for circumcision (3:2 ff) the same people as the proponents of an obviously lax life-style in matters of food and sex (3:17 ff). Accordingly it has long been assumed[10] that in 3:2 ff and 3:17 ff Paul is directing his attention to two different groups that endanger the community: he is opposing either Jews and wretched Christians[11] or Judaizers and libertines[12] or Jewish-Christian missionaries that are only related to the false teachers of Gal and libertine Christians who had left the community.[13] But since Paul nowhere indicates clearly that he is uttering warnings against two different groups in 3:2 and 3:17 ff, recently the opponents have been portrayed in a unified way as Gnostics who propagandized in behalf of circumcision,[14] or as representatives of a nomistic θεῖος ἀνήρ Christology.[15] But there are no unambiguously Gnostic features in the polemic of 3:2 and 3:17 ff, and no christological error can be deduced from the charge "enemies of the cross of Christ" (3:18). Thus it is not possible to form a clear picture of the false teachers on the basis of the few indications from the polemic in Phil 3. What alone is clear is that in Paul's opinion the opponents whom he is attacking only endanger or could endanger (3:2 βλέπετε; 3:17 σκοπεῖτε) the enthusiasm-prone community (cf. 2:3 f; 3:15 f; 4:9)[16] without actually belonging to it. In any case the character of the opponents in Phil 3 is of no use in determining the place of writing of the letter.

2. Since there are no unambiguous arguments for the writing of Phil in Rome, and some evidence against it, it is easy to understand why since H. E. G. Paulus (1799) numerous scholars[17] have spoken out in behalf of Paul's having written the letter in the other place where Acts informs us he was imprisoned: Caesarea. Of course, the same difficulties arise for Caesarea as for Rome in connection with the journeys backwards and forwards from Phi-

[10] See lit. in Jewett, 363 n. 1.
[11] Dibelius; O. Michel, CBL, 1033.
[12] Beare, Martin; Appel; Lütgert, Delling.
[13] Jewett; similarly L. Mattern, *Das Verständnis des Gerichtes bei Paulus*, AThANT 47, 1966, 112 f.
[14] Marxsen; Schmithals. Bornkamm suggests "Jewish-Christian Gnostics, or gnosticizing Judaizers"; Köster mentions "typical early Christian gnosis."
[15] Gnilka; somewhat otherwise Fuller: syncretists who link circumcision with Hellenistic sacramental ideas.
[16] Cf. Jewett, 373 ff.
[17] See the list in J. Schmid, 2 n. 1; more recently Lohmeyer; L. Johnson.

lippi, even though the sea route from Caesarea to Philippi is somewhat shorter than that from Rome to Philippi. In support of
Caesarea would be the fact that the church in the place where
Paul is imprisoned does not seem to have been founded by him
(cf. 1:13-17). Also the plan mentioned in Phil for another journey
to Philippi can be harmonized with the plan announced in Rom
for missionary activity in Spain, if it is supposed that in the
period before Acts 25:11 Paul is counting on the probability that
he will be released and therefore could plan a journey through
Philippi to Rome. There are no really cogent objections to Caesarea
as the place of writing for Phil,[18] but neither is there in Phil any
special evidence pointing to Caesarea as the place of writing. Today
this location is almost universally abandoned, although in some
cases much too quickly.[19]

3. The setting for the writing of Phil is not necessarily limited
to the alternatives of Caesarea or Rome. Years before the trial reported in Acts 23 ff, Paul on his own testimony had been in prison
more than once (II Cor 11:23; 6:5). And according to I Clem
5:6, Paul "bore chains seven times." From this arises the possibility
that Phil comes from a period of imprisonment of which the NT
gives no direct account, but for which there are indications in the
sources. In the view of many scholars, a question must be raised
about an imprisonment in *Ephesus*.

The Ephesus hypothesis was first advanced by A. Deissmann
(1897)[20] and today has many supporters.[21] The most important
arguments for it are as follows:

a. Judged by language, literary style, and concepts, Phil fits
better with the earlier letters than with the other prison letters
that can be assigned to Rome or Caesarea. But the observations
concerning linguistic kinship of Phil with I and II Cor and Rom[22]

[18] Marxsen, *Intr.* 64, offers as proof only that, apart from the great distance
to Philippi, there is no evidence of a church in Caesarea—which is contradicted
by Acts 21:16.

[19] "In my opinion . . . Caesarea should be excluded from the discussion,"
Bornkamm, *Aufsätze* IV, 204.

[20] See A. Deissmann, *Paul,* 17 n. 1.

[21] Detailed support is offered by Feine, Michaelis, Duncan; more recently,
cf., e.g., P. Benoit, JB, 499; Bonnard, Friedrich, Gnilka (for Chs. 1, 2, 4);
Johnston (for Ch. 3); Albertz, Appel, Feine-Behm, Fuller, Goguel, Harrington,
Klijn, Marxsen, McNeile-Williams, Riddle-Hutson, de Zwaan; Schmithals, Müller-
Bardorff, Delling, Bornkamm, Murphy-O'Connor, Jewett; Lemerle (see n. 1),
49; Buck-Taylor, 80; D. M. Stanley, *Christ's Resurrection in Pauline Soteriology,* 1961, 66; P. Hoffmann, *Die Toten in Christus,* NTA, NF 2, 1966,
326 ff. Duncan attributes Phil to the first of several imprisonments in Ephesus.

[22] See Feine, 43 ff.

can be matched by observations of linguistic kinship with Col
(and Eph),[23] which shows that Phil does not have a unilateral
association linguistically with one or the other group of Pauline
letters. A list of parallels between Phil and the other Pauline
letters[24] shows clearly that Phil has contacts with almost all the
letters of Paul.

b. Phil 3 fits only in the period of the struggle of Paul with
Judaizers (or Gnostics), the literary monuments of which conflict are Gal and II Cor. But even if Paul should issue admonitions
about judaizing or Gnostic danger, as in Gal and II Cor, that does
not say that at a later time and on the basis of new experiences
Paul could not have been anxious about an analogous danger.

c. The trial of Paul in Phil 1–2 cannot be the same as that described in Acts 23 ff. Phil 1:7, 12 f, 16 f; 2:17 show that in some
way Paul's preaching of the gospel had become the occasion for his
legal prosecution, but according to Acts 21:28; 25:7 ff; 28:17 ff
the issue was that of alleged offenses by Paul against the Jewish
Law in connection with the desecration of the temple. If in Phil
Paul was standing at the last stage in the trial which had begun
in Jerusalem and Caesarea and then been shifted to Rome, his
allusions to the object of that trial should have run quite differently.
"Defense and strengthening of the gospel" (1:7; cf. 1:16) lie
on quite a different plane from defense against Jewish accusations
in Acts. Yet this argument is reasonable only if the charge mentioned in Phil against preaching the gospel is regarded as something
different from the accusation of hostility toward the Law as
mentioned in Acts. But that is scarcely the case, since the information about Paul's trial in Acts is ambiguous.

d. Both the "Praetorian Guard" (1:13) and the "imperial slaves"
(4:22) can be claimed for Ephesus, since it was the seat of a
praetorian garrison, and imperial slaves or freedmen were all over
the Empire wherever imperial property was administered, and thus
in Ephesus. This is the case for Caesarea as well, so it proves
nothing.

e. The journeys between Paul's place of residence and Philippi
which Phil presupposes (see p. 325) are more readily conceivable
from Ephesus than from Caesarea or Rome. Paul's plan to come
to Philippi after his release and to send Timothy on ahead to wait
there for his return fits Acts 19:22; 20:1; I Cor 4:17; 16:5, 10.
Though this argument is apt, it must be noted that Paul himself
(I Cor 4:17; 16:10) does not indicate that he is sending Timothy

---

[23] Thus Schmid, 122 ff.
[24] C. L. Mitton, *The Epistle to the Ephesians,* 1951, 322 ff.

to Corinth by way of Macedonia, and Acts 19:22 does not mention that Paul expects Timothy back before his own departure. Concerning the fate of Timothy after Acts 20:6—i.e., after departing from Philippi following Paul's last visit there—we know nothing, so that the supposition is thoroughly possible that Paul would want to send him to Philippi again from Caesarea or Rome. Therefore even this argument is not convincing.

f. In 1:30 Paul compares his conflict with the officials in Philippi (Acts 16:19 ff) with a similar experience of which the Philippians are *now* hearing. That points to an event from the recent past, not to detainment in Rome or Caesarea over a period of years. But 1:30 assumes that the Philippians are hearing for the first time details about the recent ἀγών of Paul; that shows nothing concerning the duration of his imprisonment up to the time of writing.

Then comes the undubitable difficulty that the facts of an imprisonment in Ephesus cannot be directly confirmed from the sources. All that is sure is that Paul underwent severe suffering there. In I Cor 15:30 ff he writes from Ephesus: "Why do we run the risk of danger from hour to hour? Day by day I die, brothers—as sure as I am boasting of you in Christ Jesus my Lord. If in Ephesus I have fought wild beasts by human means, what is the use of that?" Perhaps the reference to animals is to be understood figuratively[25] and cannot be used as evidence for a longer period of detention. And in II Cor 1:8 ff Paul says in retrospect concerning the time which lies just behind him in Ephesus: "You must know, brothers that in Asia the need was so overpowering, so unbearably loaded upon us that we already despaired of life itself. Yes, we had already pronounced upon ourselves the sentence of death, so that we no longer trusted in ourselves, but only in God who raises the dead. And he has indeed saved us from such a death, and delivers us again and again" (cf. also 4:8 ff; 6:9 f). But the text does not imply that this peril was connected with an imprisonment. There is still today in Ephesus a ruin, "the prison of Paul," but the age of this local tradition is unclear and can be traced no farther back than the seventeenth century.

There is no convincing attestation of a longer imprisonment of Paul in Ephesus—note the journeys back and forth to Philippi!—and the difficulty remains that Acts is silent about the harsh experiences of the apostle in Ephesus, which probably did indeed include an imprisonment. But this difficulty exists even without mixing up the question of the place of origin of Phil with the

[25] Cf. Schmid, 39 ff; H. Conzelmann, *I Cor*, Meyer V, [11]1969, 329 f.

fate of Paul in Ephesus, yet it cannot be dismissed with the unfounded hypothesis that the author of Acts "intentionally said nothing about an imprisonment in Ephesus." [26]

So the question where Phil was written cannot be answered with any certainty.[27] If the problem of the journeys to Philippi and the kinship of the polemic in Phil 3 with that of Gal and Rom (cf. Phil 3:19 with Rom 16:18) are regarded as sufficient grounds for a case, then Ephesus will be presumed to be the place of origin. But if the hypothesis of a more extended imprisonment in Ephesus is considered to be inadequately grounded, then Caesarea will be taken more seriously into consideration. In any case, the Roman hypothesis offers the least probability. The most likely time of writing is either 53–55 (Ephesus) or 56–58 (Caesarea).

5. Authenticity and Unity

The doubts of the Baur school about the authenticity—already attested in Polyc., Phil 3:2—are not advanced today, and attempts to exclude from Phil certain sections as being inauthentic[28] have also failed. On the other hand, the view developed in the seventeenth century and often advocated since then[29] has recently been offered in various forms: Phil as handed down in the tradition is a later compilation of two or three originally independent letters or fragments of letters. Adduced as evidence is the fact that in Phil Paul "offers a perfect model of a clear and specific letter up to 3:1," [30] but at 3:1 a concluding section begins, which at 3:2 is interrupted by a warning against opponents that in tone and content differs completely from what precedes it, while 4:4 ties in excellently with 3:1. On this basis it has been inferred that 3:2–4:3 (or 3:2–4:9) is an interpolation. It is further thought that the thanks for the gift from the Philippians to Paul at the end of the letter (4:10-20) is not in its proper place, particularly because the interval since the gift was brought to Paul from the Philippians must have been long (2:25 ff); this section is separated out as an earlier letter of thanks. In addition, 3:2–4:3 is said not to pre-

[26] W. Michaelis, *Einl.*, 207.

[27] Thus Dibelius, Martin; Wikenhauser.

[28] According to E. Barnikol, *Phil 2. Der marcionitische Ursprung des Mythos-Satzes Phil 2:6-7*, 1932, 2:6 f is a Marcionite interpolation. According to Riddle-Hutson, *NT Life and Literature*, 1946, 123, 1:1b is interpolated, since Paul never mentions ἐπίσκοποι.

[29] Cf. Goguel, *Intr.* IV, 1, 404 f.

[30] Schmithals, 72 ff.

suppose an imprisonment but to polemicize against Christian opponents, while 1:28 warns against Jewish and pagan antagonists. Thus there follows in slightly differing forms the supposition that Phil was compiled from three chronologically successive letters of Paul to the Philippians: of these the letter of thanks (4:10-20, or 23) was written soon after the arrival of Epaphroditus, the second (1:1–3:1 or the like) after his recovery, and the third (3:1–4:3, or 9) later after the receipt of new information.[31] As confirmation of this proposal it is pointed out that Polycarp (Phil 3:2) says concerning Paul: ὃς καὶ ἀπὼν ὑμῖν ἔγραψεν ἐπιστολὰς εἰς ἃς ἐὰν ἐγκύπτητε . . . ("who, when he was not with you, wrote you letters in which, if you examine carefully . . ."); thus he must have known of several letters of Paul to the Philippians. The two or three letters were combined into a single letter because in this way the letters could develop from community-oriented and situation-conditioned communications into epistles for the whole church. The authority of Paul was such that the exact wording of his letters was preserved and out of them was created only a larger whole.[32]

But this whole line of argument is totally unconvincing.[33] The new insertion in 3:2 is striking and the sharpness of the warning in 3:2 ff, 18 f is unexpected. But on the one hand 1:28 already includes a warning against the ἀντικείμενοι, and it cannot be proved that Paul in 1:28 does not have in mind the same adversaries as in 3:17 ff. On the other hand, Paul does exhibit abrupt shifts in style elsewhere as well (Rom 16:17 ff; I Thess 2:15 f; I Cor 15:58). And the invective in 3:2 ff serves Paul well for resuming the ethical admonitions of 2:12 ff in 3:15 f, just as 1:30 links up with 3:17. Only when the text of 3:2–4:3 has been wrested from its context can one assume that it does not presuppose the

[31] Three letters of about the same compass, though not always in the same sequence, are proposed by Beare; Benoit, JB; Marxsen; Schmithals, Rahtjen, Bornkamm, Köster, Murphy-O'Connor; see the list in Gnilka, 6 f; Schmauch, *ErgH to Lohmeyer,* 14; Murphy-O'Connor, 1211 f. Only the "fighting letter" (3:2–4:1, or similarly) is excluded by Friedrich, Gnilka, Johnston; Goodspeed, Harrington, McNeile-Williams; J. Weiss, *Early Christianity,* 1959, I, 387. According to Müller-Bardorff, the middle letter had originally the following sequence: 1:1-26; 2:17 f; 1:27–2:16; 4:1-3; 2:19-30; 3:1a; 4:4-7, 21-23. Without determining the details, Riddle-Hutson and Wikenhauser advocate that Phil was compiled from several letters.

[32] On the motives for the redaction, see esp. Gnilka, 14 ff; Marxsen, 63 ff; Müller-Bardorff, 601 f.

[33] The unity of Phil is supported by Schmauch, *ErgH to Lohmeyer,* 15 f; R. M. Grant, Guthrie, E. F. Harrison, Klijn, Mariani; Michaelis, ErgH; Schelkle; Mackay, Delling; Furnish, 88; Pollard; Jewett, 53; Buck-Taylor, 76 ff.

imprisonment of Paul. Why Paul should not get around to thanks until 4:10 ff, in the midst of a disjointed personal concluding section, cannot be discerned, the more so since 1:7 and 2:25 contain clear allusions to help extended by the Philippians. What tells decisively against all such compilation theories is the fact that they presuppose not only arbitrary juxtapositions but also at the very least the elimination of prescripts and postscripts and perhaps a redactor's composing a connective sentence (3:1b).[34] How a redactor who is supposed to have recognized the authority of Paul is to be credited with such arbitrariness is incomprehensible. And there is no evidence of "a method that can be demonstrated elsewhere."[35]

The remark of Polycarp is indeed striking, and a mistake or a mix-up by Polycarp may be considered by no means "erroneous,"[36] even though it is no more than a possibility. But in no event does Polycarp's formulation prove—even if it reproduces his information accurately—that the Pauline letters to the Philippians that he knows have then been combined to form our Phil. There is no adequate ground, therefore, to doubt the unity of Phil as we have it. Yet we cannot prove this unity, even if we draw attention to motifs that pervade all parts of the letter.[37] Apart from the discovery of new sources it would scarcely be possible to gain full insight into the origin of an epistolary document so conditioned by its circumstances and so personal as Phil.

Finally, the unity of Phil as transmitted in the tradition is not called into question by the widespread assumption that in 2:6-11 a pre-Pauline hymn has been incorporated into the letter. The numerous strophic arrangements of the text that have been proposed since Lohmeyer (1928)[38] proceed almost without exception on the

[34] Thus Beare; Müller-Bardorff.

[35] Thus Bornkamm, *Aufsätze* IV, 205.

[36] Against Gnilka, 11. On possible explanations for the passage, see W. Bauer, *Die Briefe des Ignatius von Antiochia und der Polykarpbrief*, HNT, suppl. vol., 1920, 287.

[37] According to Mackay these motifs include the ideas of joy and confidence in the community; according to Pollard they are the ideas of self-abasement of Jesus and of the Christians; according to Jewett the motif is the idea of the messianic sufferings of the apostle and the community. The attempt to explain the difficult transitions in Phil on psychological grounds is also unconvincing (Buck-Taylor, 76 ff).

[38] Cf. the surveys and bibl. in Gnilka, 131 ff; Schmauch, *ErgH to Lohmeyer*, 19 ff; R. P. Martin, *Carmen Christi: Phil 2:5-11 in Recent Interpretation and in the Setting of Early Christian Worship*, SNTSMS 4, 1967; Deichgräber, *Gotteshymnus und Christushymnus in der frühen Christenheit*, StUNT 5, 1967, 118 ff, 219 ff; K. Wengst, *Christologische Formeln und Lieder des Urchristentums*, diss.

twofold assumption (*a*) that a more or less symmetrical hymn structure, with or without Pauline additions, can be perceived, and (*b*) that these additions as well as the linguistic form and the conceptual content of the hymn show that Paul has taken over a pre-Pauline text and has to some slight extent expanded it. Of course, it is not clear up to the present moment by what formal standards we are to reconstruct an early Christian hymn, so that the separating out of the Pauline additions from the traditional text on the basis of formal criteria is extremely uncertain. Even if the hymn (2:6-11) was composed by Paul as he dictated, which seems improbable, but employs traditional formulaic details or even a traditional hymnic text, nothing compels the conclusion that Paul himself could not have formulated this hymn on the basis of such tradition.[39] But even if Paul did incorporate an older hymn in 2:6-11, he has by this means expressed his own proclamation of Christ, and the Pauline origin of the traditional text is not called into question on this account.

§21. THE LETTER TO THE COLOSSIANS

Commentaries: see §41. Research: Duncan, Schmid, Dodd, Johnson, Reicke see under §20; H. J. Holtzmann, *Kritik der Epheser- und Kolosserbriefe*, 1872; M. Dibelius, *Die Geisterwelt im Glauben des Paulus*, 1909, 125 ff; J. Knox, "Philemon and the Authenticity of Colossians," JR 18, 1938, 144 ff; E. Percy, *Die Probleme der Kolosser- und Epheserbriefe*, Skrifter utgivna av Kungl. Humanistika Vetensskapssamfundet i Lund XXXIX, 1946 (on this see E. Käsemann, Gn 21, 1949, 342 ff); G. Bornkamm, "Die Häresie des Kol," ThLZ 73, 1948, 11 ff (=G. B., *Das Ende des Gesetzes*, BevTh 16, [2]1958, 139 ff); *idem*, "Die Hoffnung im Kol. Zugleich ein Beitrag zur Frage der Echtheit des Briefes," *Studien*

Bonn, 1967, 137 ff, 201 ff; A. Stecker, *Formen und Formeln in den paulinischen Hauptbriefen und den Past*, diss. Münster, 1968, 53 ff, 197 ff; further, H. W. Boers, *The Diversity of NT Christological Concepts and the Confession of Faith*, diss. Bonn, 1962, 114 ff; W. Böld, "Gott-Sklave-Weltenherr," in W. B., *Beiträge zur hermeneutischen Diskussion*, 1968, 30 ff; C.-H. Hunzinger, "Zur Struktur der Christus-Hymnen in Phil 2 und I Pet 3," in *Der Ruf Jesu und die Antwort der Gemeinde, Festschr. J. Jeremias*, 1970, 142 ff; K. Gamber, "Der Christus-Hymnus im Phil in liturgiegeschichtlicher Sicht," Bb 51, 1970, 369 ff; J. T. Sanders, *The NT Christological Hymns: Their Historical Religious Background*, SNTSMS 15, 1971, 9 ff, 58 ff.

[39] Isolated examples of defenders of this viewpoint are mentioned by Martin (see n. 38), 55 n. 1; and Deichgräber (see n. 38), 120 n. 2; cf. R. M. Grant, *Intr.*, 194; J. M. Furness, "The Authorship of Phil 2:6-11," ExpT 70, 1958/59, 240 ff; Martin, 55 ff. According to Beare, Paul adopted a hymn of one of his companions.

zum NT und zur Patristik, Festschr. E. Klostermann, TU 77, 1962, 56 ff (=G. B., *Geschichte und Glaube* II, *Gesammelte Aufsätze* IV, BevTh 53, 1971, 206 ff); P. N. Harrison, "Onesimus and Philemon," ATR 32, 1950, 268 ff; *idem, Paulines and Pastorals,* 1964, 65 ff; W. Bieder, "Die kolossische Irrlehre und die Kirche von heute," ThSt 33, 1952; J. Coutts, "The Relationship of Ephesians and Colossians," NTS 4, 1957/58, 201 ff; E. Käsemann, RGG³ III, 1959, 1727 f; P. Benoit, DBS VII, 1961, 156 ff (bibl.); H.-M. Schenke, "Der Widerstreit gnostischer und kirchlicher Christologie im Spiegel des Kol," ZThK 61, 1964, 391 ff; E. P. Sanders, "Literary Dependence in Colossians," JBL 85, 1966, 28 ff; C. P. Anderson, "Who Wrote 'the Epistle from Laodicea'?" JBL 85, 1966, 436 ff; F. F. Bruce, "St. Paul in Rome, III. Epistle to the Colossians," BJRL 48, 1966, 268 ff; W. Foerster, "Die Irrlehrer des Kol," *Studia Biblica et Semitica, Festschr. Th. Ch. Vriezen,* 1966, 71 ff; E. Grässer, "Kol 3,1-4 als Interpretation secundum homines recipientes," ZThK 64, 1967, 139 ff; E. W. Saunders, "The Colossian Heresy and Qumran Theology," *Studies in the History and the Text of the NT: Festschr. K. W. Clark,* StD 29, 1967, 133 ff; P. Stuhlmacher, "Christliche Verantwortung bei Paulus und seinen Schülern," EvTh 28, 1968, 174 ff; N. Kehl, "Erniedrigung und Erhöhung in Qumran und Kolossä," ZKTh 91, 1969, 364 ff; F.-J. Steinmetz, *Protologische Heilszuversicht. Die Strukturen des soteriologischen und christlichen Denkens im Kol und Eph,* Frankfurter Theologische Studien 2, 1969; J. Lähnemann, *Der Kolosserbrief: Komposition, Situation und Argumentation,* StNT 3, 1971.

1. Contents

Following the prescript (1:1 f)[1] the first, introductory part (1:1–2:5) begins with thanks to God for the good, faithful condition of the community founded by Epaphras (1:3-8) and an intercession for the continued growth of their knowledge (1:9-12). To this is attached somewhat loosely a hymnic description of the significance of Christ: he is the agent of creation, redeemer of the world, head of the church (1:13-20); also, the Colossians have experienced salvation in Christ (1:21-23). As servant of the church, the imprisoned apostle is charged to preach the divine mysteries, even to those like the Colossians who are personally unknown to him (1:24–2:5). The second part ((2:6-23) is devoted to the situation of the community, which is threatened by false teaching: they should not allow themselves to become deluded by a philosophy that will subject them to angelic powers, over whom Christ is highly exalted; in Christ dwells the fulness of the Godhead bodily; he is the head of all angelic and spiritual

[1] On the analysis cf. Lähnemann, 29 ff, esp. 61 f.

powers; dependence on Christ makes one free from ties with the world elements and does not tolerate any ascetic ritual piety. Following the polemic, in the third part (3:1–4:6) is the paraenesis, first basic principles (3:1-4), then detailed admonitions which place one in relation to Christ (3:5-17), and finally advice to individual groups within the community: women, men, children, fathers, slaves, masters ([= *Haustafel*] 3:18–4:1). The letter draws to a close with exhortations to pray, even for the apostle (4:2-4), to behave intelligently toward the non-Christians (4:5 f). The conclusion of the letter (4:7-18): commendation of Tychicus (4: 7-9), the bearer of the letter, who is a Christian from Colossae; (4:10-17) greetings and instructions; (4:18) greeting in Paul's own hand, and benediction.

2. The Origin of the Community

The Phrygian city of Colossae, situated on the upper Lycus, a tributary of the Maeander, and on the great highway that led eastward from Ephesus, was at the time of Paul an insignificant market town, in contrast to the larger and more flourishing neighboring cities of Hierapolis and Laodicea. In these three adjacent places there were, according to Col, Christian communities with close relationships to one another (4:13, 15). Paul did not found the church in Colossae, and had not even visited it prior to Col (2:1; cf. 1:4, 7 ff). On his journeys through Phrygia (Acts 16: 6; 18:23) the apostle probably did not reach the southwestern part of the region, which is where Colossae lay. Like the communities in Laodicea and Hierapolis, that in Colossae had been founded by Epaphras (4:13; 1:7; 4:12). It is implied in 1:7 (reading, ὑπὲρ ἡμῶν) that Epaphras' ministry in Colossae was commissioned by Paul, and in any event Paul regarded the communities as belonging to his missionary territory in Asia and acknowledged Epaphras as "a trustworthy servant of Christ in our stead" who had preached "the word of truth of the gospel" (1:5 ff; 2:6).

The community, from among which two house-churches are mentioned (4:15, 17; cf. Phlm 2), consisted predominantly of Gentile Christians (2:13; 1:21, 27). There is no sign of a Jewish-Christian element in the church there. Paul writes the letter as a prisoner (4:3, 10, 18; 1:24). From scattered remarks about Epaphras—he is called a fellow prisoner of Paul (Phlm 23); he has told the apostle of the community's love (Col 1:8); he sends greetings (Col 4:12)—it may be inferred that he sought out Paul because of the situation in Colossae and willingly shared his imprisonment. Impressed by his report, Paul wrote to the Colossians; Tychicus delivered the letter, while Epaphras remained with Paul (4:7 f, 12 f). Ἐπαφρᾶς is a shortened form of the very common name Ἐπαφρόδιτος, but in spite of the similarity, the Epaphras of Col and Phlm is not to be identified with the Epaphroditus of Phil 4:18.

3. Occasion for the Letter

The Christians of Colossae are being threatened by the danger of false teachers. Though they have not yet achieved complete success (2:4, 8, 20),[2] they have obviously made a strong impression on the community.[3] Paul is accordingly grateful for the condition of the Colossians as Christians and is joyful for the order within their ranks and for their fidelity to faith in Christ (1:3 ff; 2:5). He considers necessary, however, the perfecting and strengthening of the community's Christian confession (1:9 ff; 2:6 f). The false teachers are demanding observance of feasts, new moon, and sabbath (2:16), are giving dietary prescriptions (2:16, 21) the intent of which is strongly ascetic (2:20 ff) and serves to mortify the body (2:23).[4] If the ascetic dimension in the cultic statements sounds Hellenistic, the religiocultic doctrine of angels taught by the false teachers is unmistakably so. They demand the "veneration of angels" (θρησκεία τῶν ἀγγέλων; 2:18), "of the elemental spirits of the world" (τὰ στοιχεῖα τοῦ κόσμου; 2:8; cf. Gal 4:9), the spirit-beings which fill the world and have power over humankind, perhaps also star-spirits (2:16, so Bornkamm). The asceticism and the cult of "humility" (2:18, 23) are supposed to prepare one for direct encounter with the angelic powers which is fulfilled in visions (2:18). Paul condemns the ritual demands of the false teachers because they treat things as being of primary importance that are only "shadows of things to come," and thus religiously irrelevant (2:17 f). The Gnostic secret wisdom, which is indicated by the

---

[2] On δογματίζεσθε="you are burdened with demands," cf. Masson, in loc.; Foerster, 72.

[3] The false teachers are hardly an external threat only (contrary to Foerster, 72 f; cf. Lähnemann, 43, 107).

[4] It is widely assumed that the description of baptism as a "circumcision not made with hands" (2:11) shows that the heretics are demanding that the Colossians be circumcised (thus, e.g., Schenke, 392; Saunders, 134, 140; Lähnemann, 51, 78, 120 ff), but that is unlikely, because there is no admonition against the rite.

Gnostic concept of "philosophy" as revelatory instruction, is in his opinion only an illusory wisdom, in truth an "empty lie based on human tradition" (2:18, 22 f). The "arbitrarily contrived cult," the "humility," the "castigation of the body" (2:23) arise from a fleshly mind and from a foolish imagination (2:18, 22 f). Possibly this veneration of angels took the form of a mystery cult (cf. ἐμβατεύων 2:18; ἐθελοθρησκεία 2:23; the depiction of Christ as μυστήριον 2:2); it was in any event bound up with the Christian faith. In opposition to the false redemptive doctrine of the false teachers, Paul holds out the true one: Christ is the origin and the head of the universe, of all creatures, also of all angelic beings, the bearer of reconciliation for them as well as for mankind; his cross is the triumph over the spiritual powers. In him lives all the fulness of the Godhead bodily. In him the whole world has all the fulness of its being, of redemption, of wisdom, and of knowledge (1:16; 2:10; 1:20-22; 2:14 f; 2:9, 3).

No complete agreement has been achieved concerning the nature of the Colossian heresy,[5] though it is scarcely a matter of Jewish nomism related to Qumran.[6] With obvious justice Paul sees in the heretical teaching secret wisdom of a syncretistic type (2:8, 18) which combines the ascetic-ritualistic veneration of the elements with Jewish ritualism and Jewish speculation about angels. Influences of a particularly Gentile-Eastern cult cannot be demonstrated for sure, and gnosis in the strict sense of the term is scarcely in the picture, since the cult of elements is not comprehensible on that basis.[7] Thus the broad designation of the Colossian error as an early form of gnosis or as gnosticizing Judaism[8] is not really helpful, although we do know that in Asia Minor there was some form or other of syncretistic Judaism, and the Colossian heresy seems to have involved some form of syncretism strongly influ-

---

[5] On the earlier discussion see H. J. Holtzmann, *Einl.*,[3] 250; on the more recent bibl., see Lohse, *Comm.*, 127 ff; Guthrie, *Intr.*, 162 ff; further Saunders; Lähnemann, 63 ff.

[6] Thus Johnston; Mariani; Foerster, 79 f; Saunders, 141; Kehl, 374, 388; on the other hand H. Braun, *Qumran und das NT*, I, 1966, 228 ff.

[7] Schenke, 397 f, considers the false teachers to be "real Gnostics," but must then explain the cult of the elements as a "camouflage." The denial of any cult of the elements in Colossae (thus recently Masson; Klijn; Percy; Bieder; Kehl, 389 ff; G. Delling, TDNT VII, 685; E. Schweizer, "Die 'Elemente der Welt' Gal 4:3-9; Kol 2:8-20," *Verborum Veritas, Festschr G. Stählin*, 1970, 245 ff) is scarcely tenable.

[8] Thus, e.g., Conzelmann, Dibelius-Greeven, Lohse; Fuller, Harrison, Klijn, Marxsen; Bornkamm, Bruce, Saunders; G. Dautzenberg and G. Ziener, GANT, 109-301.

enced by Judaism and tied in with Christianity.[9] It is because the
Colossian false teachers raise doubts about Christ's having overcome
the spirit world and seek to ingratiate themselves with these powers
by cultic and ascetic measures—which efforts have impressed a
segment of the community—that Paul stresses the cosmic role
of Christ and the overcoming of the spiritual powers by him (1:
15-17, 19; 2:9 f, 15).

4. Authenticity and Integrity

The Pauline authorship of Col [10] was first disputed by Mayer-
hoff (1838), who found in the letter a dependence on Eph, un-
Pauline ideas, and a controversy with Cerinthus. Accordingly, F. C.
Baur and his pupils traced the letter to Gnostic circles of the
second century. Holtzmann assumed that there was a shorter, genuine Col, which was worked over by the author of Eph for anti-
Gnostic ends in order to gain a place for Col as a canonical companion piece for Eph. Independently of Holtzmann, Masson came to
a similar hypothesis. In addition, various interpolation hypotheses
have been offered.[11] Against the oft-repeated assumption of the
Pauline origin of Col,[12] especially since the work of Dibelius, Lohmeyer, and Percy, doubt has been expressed again recently and in
increasing measure.[13]

Grounds for careful testing of the authenticity are: (1) lan-

[9] Cf. Lähnemann, 63 ff, esp. 102 ff.

[10] On the history of the problem, see Percy, 5 ff; Lähnemann, 12 ff.

[11] Without specification, this assumption is represented by Steinmetz,
13 n. 74; J. Weiss, *Earliest Christianity* I, 150 ff; J. Knox, *Jesus, Lord and
Christ*, 1958, 158 n. 20. P. N. Harrison seeks to prove by word statistics that
1:6b; 1:9b-25; 2:2b-4, 7; 2:8-23; 3:14-16 are interpolations.

[12] Recently, e.g., Bruce, Dibelius-Greeven, Johnston, Moule; Fuller, Grant,
Guthrie, Harrington, Harrison, Mariani, Michaelis, Schelkle; Anderson, 436 n. 6;
Saunders, 142 n. 1; Steinmetz, 139; N. Kehl, *Der Christushymnus im Kol*, StBM
1, 1967, 164; O. Merk, *Handeln aus Glauben*, MbThSt 5, 1968, 201 ff; O. Kuss,
Paulus, 1971, 218 ff.

[13] Thus recently, e.g., Conzelmann, Lohse; Marxsen; Bornkamm, Käsemann,
Schenke, Saunders, Grässer, Stuhlmacher; E. Fuchs, *Die Freiheit des Glaubens*,
BevTh 14, 1949, 30; E. Schweizer, "Zur Frage der Echtheit des Kol und Eph,"
ZNW 47, 1956, 287 (=*Neotestamentica*, 1963, 429); R. Bultmann, *Theology*,
133 ff; H. J. Schoeps, *Paul*, 20 f; K.-G. Eckart, "Exegetische Beobachtungen zu
Kol 1,9-20," ThViat 7, 1960, 95 ff; P. Pokorný, *Der Eph und die Gnosis*, 1965,
14 f; N. Gäumann, *Taufe und Ethik. Studien zu Röm 6*, BevTh 47, 1967, 64;
A. Grabner-Haider, *Paraklese und Eschatologie bei Paulus*, NTA, NF 4, 1968,
98 f; G. Dautzenberg, GANT, 105 ff; R. Schnackenburg, "Die Aufnahme des
Christushymnus durch den Verf. des Kol," EKK Vorarbeiten 1, 1969, 33 ff;
Beare and Lähnemann leave the question open.

guage and style; (2) theology, especially the Christology of the letter; (3) the relationship of Col to Eph.

1. Col has some distinctive features in *vocabulary* and *sentence structure*.[14] In addition to some *hapax legomena* there are thirty-six words which occur elsewhere in the NT but not in the letters of Paul (omitting Eph and the Pastorals). Still more striking is the frequency of synonyms—such as "praying and asking," "in all wisdom and spiritual understanding" (1:9); "holy and blameless and unimpeachable" (1:22)—and linking of genitives—πᾶν πλοῦτος τῆς πληροφορίας τῆς συνέσεως (2:2); τῆς πίστεως τῆς ἐνεργείας τοῦ θεοῦ (2:12).[15] Noteworthy also is the sparse use of δέ and the lack of μὲν—δέ.[16] The style is cumbersome, wordy, overloaded almost to opaqueness with dependent clauses, participial and infinitive constructions, or substantives with ἐν. For example, 1:9-20 is one sentence (cf. 2:9-15)! Some known Pauline concepts are missing, such as justification, righteousness, law, salvation, revelation, glory. But the different mode of expression is in part explicable by reason of the strong use of liturgical-hymnic style in which thanksgiving and prayers are offered in the letters acknowledged as genuine,[17] and in part by reason of the polemical aim of the letter. The peculiarities of speech and mode of expression are most evident in those sections of Col in which Paul is polemicizing against the false teaching, or when, with it in view, he sets forth his own ideas in hymnic form (1:10-20; 2:16-23). The lack of familiar Pauline concepts proves nothing, because analogous observations could be made with respect to other Pauline letters.[18] Even the fact that ἀδελφοί or ἀδελφέ, which appears in all the other Pauline letters, is missing in Col [19] scarcely proves anything, since there are other long stretches of Pauline text where this expression does not appear (Rom 1·14–6:23; II Cor 1:1-7:16).

On the other hand, Col does display stylistic idiosyncrasies of Paul: pleonastic καί after διὰ τοῦτο (1:9) is found elsewhere in the NT only in Paul (I Thess 2:13; 3:5; Rom 13:6; cf. also Rom 9:24 [and in Eph 1:15, in dependence on Col 1:9]); χαρίζεσθαι = "forgive" in 2:13; 3:13, and only in II Cor 2:7, 10; 12:13 (and Eph 4:32 = Col 3:13) elsewhere in the NT; ἐν μέρει (2:16) = "with

---

[14] Cf. Lohse, *Comm.*, 84 ff (bibl.).

[15] See Lohse, *Comm.*, 88; Percy, 20 f, 26 f.

[16] Cf. Sanders, 40 f.

[17] Percy, 38. There is no more of a ready answer to why Paul should use this form more extensively in Col than there is to why he should have used it at all in Phil 2:5 ff (against Lähnemann, 20).

[18] Cf. Lohmeyer, *Comm.*, 12 f.

[19] See E. Schweizer (see n. 13).

regard to" and only in II Cor 3:10; 9:3 elsewhere in the NT; πᾶν ἔργον ἀγαθόν (Col 1:10) is found in Paul in II Cor 9:8; II Thess 2:17, as well as in the singular alone in Rom 2:7; 13:3; Phil 1:6, while the plural is found in the NT only in Eph 2:10; I Tim 2:10; Acts 9:36.[20]

On the basis of language and style, therefore, there is no reason to doubt the Pauline authorship of the letter.[21]

2. So long as it was assumed that the false teachers of Col were Gnostics, and that gnosis was first encountered in the form of the Christian gnosis of the second century, the combating of such false teaching in Col made Paul's authorship of Col seem unlikely. But if already in I Cor Paul was debating enthusiastic-Gnostic views, and if it is furthermore questionable that the Colossian false teachings are to be characterized as Gnostic (see above, pp. 339f), these false teachings are not sufficient reason to deny that Paul wrote Col. Some have thought, however, that the manner in which the false teaching is combated is un-Pauline: the terminology of the false teachers, "unlike in Gal, is not repudiated but is simply christianized"; "the gnostic christology of the heretics is countered by a radicalized gnostic christology"; "the gnostic soteriology of the heretics is countered by a radicalized gnostic soteriology"; "a profound change in Pauline theology has taken place which has led . . . to new formulations in christology, ecclesiology, the image of the apostle, in eschatology, and in the understanding of baptism." [22] In this connection reference is made above all to the cosmic character of the Christology (1:16-19; 2:9 f, 19) in the representation of Christ as the "head of the body, the church" (1:18; cf. 2:19), but also more generally to the moralism, the declamatory mode of argumentation, the replacement of temporal by spatial redemptive concepts. The attempt has been made to show that in 1:15-20 a pre-Christian or a Hellenistic-Christian hymn has been adopted, which the author of the letter has "paulinized," and in so doing has expanded Pauline Christology cosmically while transforming the cosmic statements of the hymn along churchly lines. To begin with this last supposition, it certainly cannot be denied that 1:15-20 bears a hymnic character,

[20] On the singular ἔργον ἀγαθόν cf. W. Schrage, Die konkreten Einzelgebote in der paulinischen Paränese, 1961, 54 ff. That there is Jewish precedent for this means nothing (Lohse, Comm., 29), since in Jewish linguistic usage the plural is dominant.

[21] Sanders has scarcely made evident the literary dependence of Col on the letters of Paul "in a relatively few verses" (p. 45).

[22] Marxsen, Intr., 179; Schenke, 403; Grässer, 152; Lohse, Comm., 180.

but the numerous reconstructions of the hymn expanded by the author that have been undertaken since Lohmeyer's analysis[23] have scarcely led to a really convincing result. Indeed, the assumption is not yet proved that a *hymn constructed according to a strict scheme* has been used and that accordingly every fragment of a sentence beyond the scheme must stem from the author of Col. What is far more likely is that the author of Col himself has formed the hymn, utilizing traditional material;[24] by this line of reasoning, the oft-repeated assumption that the cosmic statements of the hymn have by the addition of τῆς ἐκκλησίας (1:18) been transmuted into churchly statements is completely unproved. Rather, in antithesis to the teachings of the false teachers, the author assigns to Christ the cosmos-encompassing role of mediator of creation and victor over the cosmic powers by his death and resurrection (1:15-17, 20a; 2:10, 15), in addition to the Christ who encompasses in himself the church as his body (1:18, 19, 20b; 2:19).[25] The cosmic Christology which is thus evident has its antecedents in the acknowledged Pauline letters: I Cor 2:8; 8:6; II Cor 4:4; Gal 4:3, 9; Phil 2:10. Although in comparison with the recognized Pauline letters the idea of Christ as "the head of the body, the church" (1:18; 2:19) is new, it is really not surprising in the framework of Pauline ecclesiology if one notes that in the acknowledged letters—in addition to the *comparison* of the church with a σῶμα (Rom 12:4 f; I Cor 12:12, 14 ff; cf.

[23] Cf. bibl. in W. Schmauch, *ErgH to Lohmeyer*, 47 ff; H. J. Gabathuler, *Jesus Christus, Haupt der Kirche—Haupt der Welt. Der Christushymnus Colosser 1,15-20 in der theologischen Forschung der letzten 130 Jahre*, AThANT 45, 1965; N. Kehl (see n. 12), 167 ff. Also H. W. Boers, *The Diversity of NT Christological Concepts and the Confession of Faith*, diss. Bonn, 1962, 149 ff; R. H. Fuller, *The Foundations of NT Christology*, 1966, 214 ff; A. Feuillet, *Le Christ, Sagesse de Dieu d'après les épîtres Pauliniennes*, Ét. bibl., 1966, 163 ff; R. Deichgräber, *Gotteshymnus und Christushymnus in der frühen Christenheit*, StUNT 5, 1967, 143 ff; K. Wengst, *Christologische Formeln und Lieder des Urchristentums*, diss. Bonn, 1967, 163 ff; E. Schweizer, "Kol 1,15-20," EKK Vorarbeiten I, 1969, 7 ff; R. Schnackenburg (see n. 13), 33 ff; A. Vögtle, *Das NT und die Zukunft des Kosmos*, 1970, 208 ff; J. Reumann, "Herrschaft Christi nach dem NT," in *Humanität und Herrschaft Christi*, ed. I. Asheim, 1970, 162 ff; J. T. Sanders, *The NT Christological Hymns*, SNTSMS 15, 1971, 12 ff, 75 ff; B. Vawter, "The Colossians Hymn and the Principle of Redaction," CBQ 33, 1971, 67 ff.

[24] Thus, e.g., Dibelius-Greeven, Moule; C. Maurer, "Die Begründung der Herrschaft Christi über die Mächte nach Col 1,15-20," WuD, NF 4, 1955, 79 ff; A. Feuillet (see n. 23).

[25] Christ is the head of the powers, but the powers are not his body (2:10, 19); cf. Lähnemann, 119 n. 41; 140 f.

also Col 3:15)—Paul knows the concept of Christ's identity with the ἐκκλησία as his "body" (I Cor 1:13; 12:12c, 13; Gal 3:28). And the representation of Christ as the *makroanthropos* lies at its root, wherever it may ultimately derive from. Viewed in this way, there is no break between understanding Christ as master (κεφαλή, 2:10; cf. 2:15) and as head of his body, the church (1:18, 24; 2:19), whether this is regarded as the development of an existing concept or viewed as first originating as a part of the polemic against the false teachers.[26]

If the concept of Christ as head of the church does not tell against Paul's having written the letter, then neither does the letter's eschatology. It is alleged that in Col 1:5, 23, 27 hope is no longer chronologically conceived, but that it has become an otherworldly quality of hope. The few remaining traces of futuristic eschatology (3:4, 24; 4:11), it is said, ought not to mislead anyone from the fact that in 1:26 f; 3:3 f the notion of spheres is present and that none of the eschatological Pauline ideas— parousia, resurrection of the dead, judgment of the world—is encountered in Col.[27] But in Rom 8:24 ἐλπίς does appear as a quality of hopefulness too, and so it is used of a hopeful way of life in Col 1:23. Nor does 3:3 f present a spatial concept, since the now revealed mystery (1:26) and the exaltation of Christ which has already occurred (2:12; 3:1; cf. I Cor 2:7, 10; Phil 3:20) are placed in balance with the expectation of Christ at the parousia (cf. I Thess 4:16; Phil 3:20). Similarly, the statement about being raised with Christ (Col 2:9; 3:1) is not in opposition to Paul (Rom 6:8 συζήσομεν), because the co-resurrection is effective only διὰ τῆς πίστεως and "the life with Christ is hidden in God" (2:12; 3:3).[28] Although there is no clear mention of the near expectation, yet the genuine eschatological tension as in Paul is present in Col as well.

Finally it is also not true that in Col the community is bound to the apostolic office and that, in contrast to Paul, the epistle argues

[26] Cf. Bruce, 283; Lähnemann, 140 f; E. Best, *One Body in Christ*, 1955, 115 ff.

[27] Thus Lohse, *Comm.*, 180; Bornkamm; Grässer, 159 ff; Stuhlmacher, 180; Steinmetz, 29 ff, 59, 132 ff.

[28] Lähnemann, 174 n. 61; H.-W. Kuhn, *Enderwartung und gegenwärtiges Heil*, StUNT 4, 1966, 186. It is a false leveling of Col when Steinmetz asserts, 59 ff, 122 ff, that in Col as in Eph the eschatological tension has been appropriately replaced by the terms of growth and fulfillment, which would imply no "substantive difference of expression" (p. 139) from the older Pauline letters.

with rigidly formulated concepts.[29] Lähnemann[30] has shown rather that the traditional formulations are critically employed in Col and that the views of the false teachers are not christianized, but that in contrast with Eph the community is made to participate in the critical and ongoing debate with the false teaching and is led to the recognition "that life in obedience to Christ lays hold of the faithful in their totality" (p. 175). But that of course corresponds to Pauline theological argumentation.

If the substantive differences of Col can be understood on the basis of the concrete polemical argument of the letter, then there are other substantive matters which support the assumption of Pauline authorship as well. (*a*) The assumed relationship of the writer to the readers corresponds in several points to Phlm: in both letters there are greetings from Epaphras, Aristarchus, Mark, Luke, Demas (Col 4:10 ff; Phlm 23 f); both letters mention the sending of Onesimus (Col 4:9; Phlm 12) and have special words for Archippus (Col 4:17; Phlm 2). These agreements do not occur in the same relationships and formulations, however, so that the thesis is unconvincing that the indubitably Pauline Phlm has been imitated by a non-Pauline writer only in these personal remarks.[31] (*b*) The household admonitions in Col 3:18–4:1 show a remarkably small christianizing, especially in comparison with Eph 5:22–6:9, which is much less easily understood for a non-Pauline writer than for Paul himself.[32] (*c*) In contrast to Eph, the use of the formulas ἐν χριστῷ and ἐν κυρίῳ in Col correspond completely to Paul's usage.[33] (*d*) J. Knox has pointed out that the letter, which was also intended for Laodicea (4:16a) was probably addressed to the smaller city Colossae because Onesimus was from Colossae and Paul sought contact with the community in which Onesimus' master lived, since it was he to whom Phlm brought so grave a request. Besides, the unusually comprehensive rule for slaves is best understood (3:22-25) if the business with the slave Onesimus were to be settled at the same time. Even though all these argu-

---

[29] Above all, Marxsen, *Intr.*, 180 ff; Bornkamm, 212; Dautzenberg, GANT, 106.

[30] Lähnemann, 35, 42 f, 112, 105 f, 175 ff. Cf. also H. Chadwick, "'All things to all men' (I Cor 9:22)," NTS 1, 1954/55, 270 ff.

[31] Contrary to Lohse (*Comm.*, 175 ff), there is no indication that Col is literarily dependent on and has expanded the list of greetings from Phlm, and nothing in the list of greetings indicates that it was written soon after Paul's death (thus Lohse, *Festschr. Stählin*, 193).

[32] Cf. Dibelius-Greeven on Col 3:18–4:1; O. Merk (see n. 12), 214 ff, against Stuhlmacher, 177 ff, who interprets this from the standpoint of Eph.

[33] See F. Neugebauer, *In Christus*, 1971, 175 ff, against whom Steinmetz is unable to bring convincing objections (p. 96 f).

ments may not be of equal weight, together they strengthen the supposition the Col originated with Paul.

3. The supposition that Col was worked over by the author of Eph rests on the undoubtedly close relationship of Col and Eph. But the arguments for the dependence of only the major part of Col on Eph is by no means convincing, because the notion of the Pauline origin of a very brief letter that can be separated out as original is purely negative in that it is based solely on the lack of contacts with Eph—quite apart from the improbability of such a revision—and because the flow of the development of ideas clearly runs from Col to Eph and not the reverse (see below, §23.3). Jülicher has correctly declared that "the suspicion concerning such an interpolating revision would never have been raised in view of the smooth flow of Col, free of awkwardnesses and gaps, if Eph were not there as well." [34] The opposite assumption—that Col is as a whole dependent on Eph[35]—rests on the unprovable assumptions that the smoother flow of words in Eph (in contrast to the greater difficulties in Col) is primary and that any overlap in wording in scattered passages in the other letter can only be explained as literary dependence.

All the evidence points to the conclusion that Col, probably used as early as Justin (*Dial.* 85. 2; 138. 2) and listed in Marcion's canon, is to be regarded as Pauline.[36]

5. Place and Time of Writing

Paul is in prison (4:3, 10, 18) in Ephesus, Caesarea, or Rome (see §20). Often proposed recently as the place of writing of Col is Ephesus,[37] which is indicated as early as the Marcionite prologue for Col: *ergo apostolus iam ligatus scribit eis ab Epheso.*[38] This is an obvious inference, since Ephesus was the capital of the province of Asia, to which the cities of the Lycus valley belonged,

---

[34] Jülicher-Fascher, *Einl.*, 134. With Masson cf. also W. Bieder, ThZ 8, 1952, 139 ff.

[35] Thus Coutts.

[36] The conjecture that Epaphras is the author of Col (thus A. Suhl in Lähnemann, 181 n. 82) is as arbitrary (cf. 1:7) as the hypothesis of Anderson that Epaphras wrote the letter to Laodicea (4:16).

[37] Cf. Preuschen, *Analecta*, 87.

[38] Masson; Appel, Klijn, Michaelis, Riddle-Hutson; P. N. Harrison, Foerster; Duncan, see bibl. in §20; Buck-Taylor, 121. Schenke, 399, proposes Asia Minor as the place of writing; according to Lohse, *Comm.*, 181, the school tradition of Paul used in the letter is at home in Ephesus.

and since Epaphras would have only a brief journey in order to reach Paul, and Paul would be surrounded by a larger number of helpers in his missionary work, as 4:10 ff presupposes. Also the request in Phlm, written at the same time and in the same place, for quarters to be prepared (Phlm 22) fits best if Paul is such a short distance from Colossae, i.e., in Ephesus. But the list of names includes Luke and Mark, yet Luke was not in any event with Paul in Ephesus (if significance is attached to the "we" passages as indicating Luke's participation in the events narrated; see §9.4), and we learn from Acts 15:37-39 that Mark had not accompanied Paul since the so-called second missionary journey. If we are to include in our understanding of Col a development in Paul's thought,[39] then the indications are against a chronological proximity of Col to Gal, I and II Cor, quite apart from the general problem of Paul's having been imprisoned in Ephesus (see §20.4).

Accordingly some scholars assume that Col was written during Paul's imprisonment in Caesarea.[40] That Aristarchus shared Paul's imprisonment (4:10) can be harmonized with Acts 20:4; 24:23, and Tychichus too, who according to Acts 20:4 had traveled with Paul to Jerusalem, might well have gone on with him to Caesarea. Mark and Luke in as well in Caesarea as in Rome. Where the runaway slave, Onesimus, is most likely to have wandered, is an unanswerable question, though a slave on foot could have reached Caesarea but not Rome. The request for accommodation (Phlm 22) is possible from Caesarea if Paul has not yet counted on an appeal to the emperor, or if he supposes that he will be escorted through Asia Minor as Ignatius later was. It can be objected against Caesarea that this little city was scarcely the place for the missionary activity of Paul's many companions, among whom only a few were Jewish Christians (4:11).[41]

Accordingly the old view (John Chrysostom) still is dominant today that Col comes from Rome. The imprisonment in Rome with its mild restrictions (Acts 28:16, 30) offered the apostle the possibility for doing his own preaching and for vigorous interchange with an imposing staff of co-workers appropriate to a metropolis. Also his joy over the triumph of the gospel throughout the whole world fits well in Rome (1:6, 23). Epaphras' visit to

---

[39] See on this Lähnemann, 164 ff.

[40] Dibelius-Greeven, Lohmeyer; Goguel, de Zwaan. Johnson, Reicke, see §20.

[41] The absence of the names of those extending greeting in Col from the Acts account (23:23–26:32) of Paul's imprisonment in Caesarea cannot be used against the hypothesis of Caesarea as the place where Col was written (contrary to Lohse, *Comm.*, 166).

Paul is more difficult to conceive as occurring in Rome than in Caesarea, and the request for accommodation (Phlm 22) implies the abandonment of the plans to go to Spain. Thus there is some evidence for Col's having been written in Caesarea, but Rome is not excluded either. The time of writing would be either 56–58 or 58–60.

§22. THE LETTER TO PHILEMON

Commentaries: see §41. Research: see J. Knox and P. N. Harrison under §21; further J. Knox, *Philemon Among the Letters of Paul* (1935), [2]1959; Th. Preiss, "Life in Christ and Social Ethics in the Epistle to Philemon," in Th.P., *Life in Christ*, Eng. tr., 1954, 65 ff; H. Greeven, "Prüfung der Thesen von J. Knox zum Phlm," ThLZ 79, 1954, 373 ff; U. Wickert, "Der Philemonbrief—Privatbrief oder Apostolisches Schreiben?" ZNW 52, 1961, 230 ff; P. Benoit, DBS VII, 1966, 1204 ff; F. F. Bruce, "St. Paul in Rome, II. The Epistle to Philemon," BJRL 48, 1966, 81 ff.

1. Contents

Prescript (1-3). Thanks to Philemon for his love and his faith (4-7). Request to Philemon concerning the slave Onesimus, who has run away and meanwhile has been converted to Christianity, that he be forgiven and that he be accepted as a Christian brother and helper of Paul, who himself hopes to come soon as a guest at the home of Philemon (8-22). Greetings (23 f) and benediction (25).

2. Occasion, Time, and Place

Phlm is a letter to an individual person, to Philemon, a well-to-do Christian probably unknown to Paul personally (5; cf. Col 1:4). A slave of his, Onesimus, had run away (15 f), apparently following a theft (18). Philemon lived with his sister, Apphia, and Archippus (who without adequate ground have often been identified as the wife and son of Philemon) and the community that met in his house (2), obviously in Colossae. Onesimus came from there (Col 4:9 "your countryman") and Archippus, who is named in Phlm 2, together with Philemon, was also from Colossae (Col 4:17). The fugitive, Onesimus, encountered the imprisoned Paul for reasons which we do not know. Perhaps he had become acquainted with Paul through Philemon and fled to him, or perhaps he was accidentally placed in the same prison. He was converted by Paul (10) and developed a close personal relationship with him (12 f, 16 f). The apostle would have preferred to keep Onesimus with him in the service of the gospel, but he observed the legal right which Philemon had over his slave and sent him back to his master. He makes a plea to Philemon in behalf of the fugitive, who otherwise would have suffered a severe penalty. Paul does not command, although he could have done so on the ground of his apostolic authority (8 f, 14, 21).[1] That Paul, in saying that he hopes Philemon will "do beyond what I say," expects the manumission of Onesimus,[2] is unlikely.[3] It is only clear that Paul requests that Onesimus be received again into the household of his master, Philemon (17). The thesis that the master of Onesimus is Archippus, who in Col 4:17 was advised to set Onesimus free, and that the letter mentioned "from Laodicea" in Col 4:16 is indeed Phlm,[4] is controverted by the natural exegesis of Phlm 1, 2, and Col 4:17, as well as by the fact that Marcion knows both a letter to Philemon and a letter to the Laodiceans.[5] The frequently proposed conjecture[6] that Onesimus is identical with the Bishop of Ephesus mentioned by Ignatius (Eph 1:3; 2:1; 6:1) is no more than a possibility.

Since Onesimus returned to Colossae with Tychicus, the bearer of Col (Col 4:7 ff), and is mentioned by Paul in Phlm and Col in association with the same persons (see above, p. 345), it is clear that Phlm is to be dated at the same time as Col.[7] (See above, §21.5).

3. Authenticity

Only tendenz-criticism could doubt the authenticity of this letter, which was already included in the canon of Marcion.[8] The letter,

[1] Cf. Wickert, who correctly interprets πρεσβύτης (v. 9) as meaning "one who bears a commission" (so also Johnston, Lohmeyer, Moule, Preiss); opposed to this are Lohse; G. Bornkamm, TDNT VI, 683.

[2] Johnston, Knox.

[3] Cf. Preiss.

[4] Knox, in partial agreement with Greeven and W. Schmauch, EKL III, 183.

[5] Against Knox: Lohse, Moule; Guthrie; Benoit, Bruce.

[6] Moule, Goodspeed; Harrison, Knox.

[7] Phlm is dated from the Ephesian imprisonment by Lohse; Klijn, Marxsen, Michaelis.

[8] Thus, e.g., F. C. Baur; but also C. Weizsäcker, *Das Apostolische Zeitalter der christlichen Kirche*, [3]1902, 545.

which of all Paul's letters stands closest in form to ancient private letters, displays in its personal features the signs of a genuine true-to-life quality. Phlm is the test case for the views on slavery which are expressed in I Cor 7:20 ff; Col 3:22 ff. Paul has not overturned the social and judicial orders. There is no word in Phlm of the liberation of Onesimus, but Paul knows that the Christian faith joins men as brothers across the barriers created by status, and he therefore expects that the runaway slave will return to his master and that his master will receive him in forgiveness as a "beloved brother" (16).

§23. The Letter to the Ephesians

Commentaries: see §41. Research: Holtzmann, Percy, Coutts, Steinmetz, see under §21; further A. Harnack, "Die Adresse des Eph des Paulus," SAB 1910, 696 ff; J. Schmid, *Der Eph des Apostels Paulus*, BSt 22, 3/4, 1928 (bibl.); E. J. Goodspeed, *The Meaning of Ephesians*, 1933; *idem*, *The Key to Ephesians*, 1956; W. Ochel, *Die Annahme einer Bearbeitung des Kol im Eph in einer Analyse des Eph untersucht*, diss. Marburg, 1934; M. Goguel, "Esquisse d'une solution nouvelle du problème de l'épître aux Ephésiens," RHR 111, 1935, 254 ff; 112, 1936, 73 ff; P. Benoit, "L'horizon Paulinien de l'Épître aux Ephésiens," RB 46, 1937, 342 ff, 560 ff (=P. B., *Exégèse et théologie* II, 1961, 53 ff); *idem*, "Rapports littéraires entre les épîtres aux Colossiens et aux Ephésiens," *Nt. Aufsätze, Festschr. J. Schmid*, 1963, 11 ff (=P. B., *Exégèse et théologie* III, 1968, 318 ff); *idem*, DBS VII, 1966, 195 ff (bibl.); N. A. Dahl, "Adresse und Prooemium des Eph," ThZ 7, 1951, 24 ff; *idem*, "Der Eph und der verlorene erste Brief des Paulus an die Korinther," Abr., 65 ff; C. L. Mitton, *The Epistle to the Ephesians*, 1951; C. Maurer, "Der Hymnus von Eph 1 als Schlüssel zum ganzen Brief," EvTh 11, 1951/52, 151 ff; W. Nauck, "Eph 2,19-22 ein Tauflied?" EvTh 13, 1953, 362 ff; F. Cornelius, "Die geschichtliche Stellung des Eph," ZRGG 7, 1955, 74 ff; *Studies in Ephesians*, ed. F. L. Cross, 1956; J. Coutts, "Ephesians 1:3-14 and I Peter 1:3-12," NTS 3, 1956/57, 115 ff; J. A. Allan, "The 'In Christ' Formula in Ephesians," NTS 5, 1958/59, 54 ff; E. Käsemann, RGG[3] II, 1958, 517 ff; *idem*, "Das Interpretationsproblem des Eph," ThLZ 86, 1961, 1 ff (=E. K., *Exegetische Versuche und Besinnungen* II, 1964, 253 ff); *idem*, "Ephesians and Acts," StLA, 288 ff; H. J. Cadbury, "The Dilemma of Ephesians," NTS 5, 1958/59, 91 ff; H. Schlier, LThK III, 1959, 916 ff; L. Cerfaux, "En faveur de l'authenticité des Épîtres de la Captivité," *Littérature et théologie Pauliniennes*, RechB V, 1960, 60 ff (=*Recueil L. C.* III, 1962, 266 ff); H. Chadwick, "Die Absicht des Eph," ZNW 51, 1960, 145 ff; K. G. Kuhn, "Der Eph im Lichte der Qumrantexte," NTS 7, 1960/61, 334 ff; P. Pokorný, "Eph und gnostische Mysterien," ZNW 53, 1962, 160 ff; *idem, Der Eph und die Gnosis*.

Die Bedeutung des Haupt-Glieder-Gedankens in der entstehenden Kirche,
1965; R. Batey, "The Destination of Ephesians," JBL 82, 1963, 101;
F. Mussner, "Beiträge aus Qumran zum Verständnis des Eph," *Nt.
Aufsätze, Festschr. J. Schmid,* 1963, 185 ff (=F. M., *Praesentia Salutis,*
1967, 197 ff); P. N. Harrison, *Paulines and Pastorals,* 1964, 31 ff; *idem,*
"The Author of Ephesians," StEv II, TU 87, 1964, 595 ff; A. R. Wilson,
" 'We' and 'You' in the Epistle to the Ephesians," StEv II, TU 87, 1964,
676 ff; W. Bieder, *Die Verheissung der Taufe im NT,* 1966, 221 ff; F. F.
Bruce, "St. Paul in Rome, IV. The Epistle to the Ephesians," BJRL 49,
1967, 303 ff; R. P. Martin, "An Epistle in Search of a Life-Setting,"
ExpT 79, 1967/68, 296 ff; J. C. Kirby, *Ephesians, Baptism and Pentecost:
An Inquiry into the Structure and Purpose of the Epistle to the Ephesians,*
1968 (on this see E. Lohse, ThLZ 94, 1969, 434); M. Santer, "The
Text of Ephesians 1:1," NTS 15, 1968/69, 247 f; J. Gnilka, "Paräne-
tische Tradition im Eph," *Mélanges Bibliques, Festschr. B. Rigaux,* 1970,
397 ff.

1. Contents

Apart from the prescript and conclusion the letter is divided
into two parts. 1:3–3:21 deals with the mystery of the call of the
Gentiles within the framework of the introductory petitions, and
4:1–6:20 moves abruptly into the concluding admonitions; thus
the otherwise customary middle section of the Pauline letter is
lacking (there is also a similarity in form to I Thess). Following
the prescript (1:1 f) there is a hymnic doxology to God (1:3-14),
who placed in his cosmic redemptive plan "us" and "you" (probably meaning the author with all Christians as distinct from the
addressees).[1] Then there is attached to the giving of thanks (which
is characteristic for the introduction to a letter) a petition for
the readers to perceive properly the worldwide redemption which
is given to us in Christ (1:15-23). The readers as former pagans
were like "us"—here probably the Jewish Christians—at one time
lost, but all now are saved through Christ (2:1-10), so the
readers are to contemplate the removal of the separation between
Israel and the Gentiles through the reconciling act of Christ (2:11-
22). The apparent resumption of the petition in 3:1 leads to a
description of the office which Paul bears for summoning the
pagans to faith (3:2-13). Finally in 3:14-19 the petition concern-

---

[1] Wilson's assumption that the "we" in Eph always means all Christians
while "you" addresses the newly baptized is refuted by the fact that "you"=
Gentile Christians in 2:11 and 3:1 is in 2:17 f clearly contrasted to the "we"
referring to the Jewish Christians.

ing the readers' insight into the breadth of the mystery of Christ comes to an end so that a doxology (3:20 f) can conclude the introduction of the letter. The paraenesis begins with a summons to unity in love and faith with all the riches of the gifts of grace which are active in the community (4:1-16), and then urgently warns the readers to turn aside from a pagan mode of life (4:17-24) and to demonstrate the Christian mode of life in all areas (4:25–5:21) and all social strata (5:22–6:9) ("household admonitions," of which 5:22 ff enlarges in an especially broad way on marriage as the image of the relationship between Christ and the church). Finally there is an admonition to struggle against the Devil and the powers of darkness by means of the armor of God and by means of prayer, which should also include the imprisoned apostle (6:10-20). With a recommendation of the bearer of the letter, Tychicus (6:21 f), and a benediction (6:23 f) the letter closes.

2. The Literary Problem

The letter, which according to the superscription πρὸς Ἐφεσίους (thus all the manuscripts since the end of the second century) and the text of 1:1 in the great majority of the manuscripts since the end of the fourth century,[2] was sent by the apostle Paul to the community in Ephesus. Compared to the other Pauline letters it is remarkable for the almost complete lack of any concrete details. The imprisonment of Paul is in fact mentioned (3:1; 4:1; 6:20; cf. 3:13), but the author seems to lack any sort of relationship with the readers. He has heard of their faith and their love (1:15) and addresses them as Gentile Christians (2:1 ff, 11 ff; 3:1 f; 4:17) who are threatening to sever their relationship with Jewish Christianity (2:11 ff), but he does not address himself to concrete problems within the community. All personal greetings are lacking, which phenomenon has a parallel only in the polemical Letter to the Galatians. On the other hand the author must present himself first to the readers as a missionary to the Gentiles commissioned by God (3:2 ff) and can allude to the preaching which the community has heard as something which is strange to him (4:21 f).

Since, however, Paul had been active in Ephesus for more than three years and, based on its contents, could in no case have written the letter before this time, it is inconceivable that Paul

---

[2] See Schmid, 66 f.

could have written this letter to the Christian community in
Ephesus. That is not, however, assumed by the oldest attainable
text of Eph, since whom the letter is addressed to cannot be inferred with any degree of certainty either from the superscription
(πρὸς Ἐφεσίους) or from the prescript (1:1). The superscription
comes first from the time of the collecting of the Pauline letters,
and therefore merely passes on an early Christian interpretation of
those to whom it was addressed (taken over by the oldest codices
since $\mathfrak{P}$ 46), and in the text of 1:1 the words ἐν Ἐφέσῳ are not
original.

These two words are not offered in B ℵ Codex 1793 (which
goes back to a very old prototype) or by a corrector of Minuscule
424 who has used a good text, and Origen did not find them in his
text.[3] $\mathfrak{P}$46, the oldest manuscript of Paul (beginning of the third
century) reads τοῖς ἁγίοις καὶ πιστοῖς. Marcion (ca. 140) did not
have "in Ephesus" in his text of Eph 1:1, as is pointed out against
him by Tertullian, who seems to have had before him the same
text as Marcion.[4] According to Tertullian, Marcion had the
audacity to insert an interpolation in the titulus of the letter. By
titulus, however, Tertullian means not the prescript 1:1 f, but the
superscription. Since he speaks of the letter "which we have with
the superscription as Ephesians [ad Ephesios praescriptam habemus],
but which the heretics [i.e., Marcion] have as the letter to the
Laodiceans [ad Laodicenos]." If "in Ephesus" had already been
present in 1:1, Tertullian would certainly have revealed the contradiction in which Marcion was involved. He presupposes therefore
that Marcion had the text of 1:1 without these two words. We
do not know how Marcion came to assign to the letter the superscription "to the Laodiceans." Marcion could as well have found
this conjecture deduced from Col 4:16 as assigned it himself, but
that he found a text of 1:1 with ἐν Λαοδικείᾳ instead of ἐν Ἐφέσῳ
is contradicted not only by the witness of Tertullian but also
by the lack of any trace of such a text in the tradition. Probably
Marcion knew as little about the original destination of the letter
as did the creator of the superscription "to the Ephesians," whose
interpretation concerning the address the church tradition has
adopted as its own since the end of the second century.[5] On the
ground of this tradition, the phrase ἐν Ἐφέσῳ made its way into
the text of the prescript before the end of the fourth century.

Since ἐν Ἐφέσῳ was doubtless lacking in the archetype which

[3] J. A. F. Gregg, JTS 3, 1902, 235.
[4] Tert., Adv. Marc. V. 11, 17.
[5] Muratorian Canon, Irenaeus, Clement of Alexandria, Tertullian, among others.

lies at the base of our textual tradition, the question is raised whether instead of this place name there was originally another. Laodicea comes into the picture solely on the ground of the super-scription of Marcion and the reference to Col 4:16. This pro-posal[6] has against it only the lack of any other attestation of such an address for the letter. In the letter itself there is nothing that especially indicates Laodicea, and it would be senseless for Paul when he was sending Col and Eph (= the letter to the Laodi-ceans) at the same time (see Col 4:16) not to have included in his letter special communications for the Laodiceans but to have relayed them through Colossae (Col 4:15 f). Furthermore it is inexplicable why then the name Laodicea would have been elimi-nated from the prescript. Harnack tried to explain the elimination of the original address of the letter on the ground that the church of Laodicea had at the time all but disappeared as a consequence of inner neglect (Rev 3:14 ff) so no one would want to read a letter of Paul addressed to them. But where in primitive Christianity was there the inclination toward literary proscription, and what would have been the agency to carry it out? Another proposal[7] which is based on modern points of view is that when the letter was circulated from Ephesus, "in Laodicea" (or some other name) was crossed out because the letter was not in fact aimed at any one par-ticular community. Not only arbitrary, but incapable of explain-ing the lack of any place name in the oldest text tradition, is the thesis[8] that ἐν Κολοσσαῖς originally stood in the prescript of Eph which was intended as a substitute for the Pauline Col but that in the process of canonization the phrase was replaced by ἐν Ἐφέσῳ. Accordingly, it is very improbable that any name whatsoever originally stood in the prescript of Eph.

As a result the hypothesis has found many supporters that Eph was not written as a letter to a particular community but as an encyclical for several communities, and that either there was a gap in the prescript in which the name of a particular community to which it was being sent could be added[9] or, as in the oldest manu-

---

[6] Thus Masson; Meinertz, Schäfer; Harnack; O. Roller, *Das Formular der paulinischen Briefe*, BWANT 4, Series 6, 1933, 193 ff, 520 ff.

[7] Masson; similarly Wikenhauser; Dahl.

[8] Ochel.

[9] The conjecture first expressed by Beza and Grotius and then established by James Ussher (1654) is represented today by Schlier; Albertz, Cerfaux in Robert-Feuillet, Harrington, Henshaw, Klijn; Percy; H. Zimmermann, *Nt. Methodenlehre*, 1967, 63 f.

scripts, it contained no name other than the general address.[10] But even if it could be explained why a letter intended for several communities did not contain a general address of the sort found in Gal, II Cor, or I Pet (e.g., Paul could have given Tychicus the authority to supply the name of a place on any occasion of the reading of the letter, 6:21),[11] the supposition of a letter with a gap in the prescript for a subsequent insertion of the address is without any parallel in antiquity[12] quite apart from the fact that then our manuscripts must have come from the Pauline original, which was surely not intended for distribution without any name. Beyond this, the position of the inserted place name in the prescript of Eph before καὶ πιστοῖς, in comparison with Col 1:2, would be completely inexplicable. But if the text of the archetype of our manuscripts τοῖς ἁγίοις τοῖς οὖσιν καὶ πιστοῖς is considered to be the Pauline original text, it is inconceivable what τοῖς οὖσιν καὶ πιστοῖς as a more precise designation for τοῖς ἁγίοις could have meant in the mind of Paul.[13] So then if the oldest text attainable by text-critical methods for the prescript is impossible for Paul,[14] it is not impossible for an unknown author who could have understood οἱ ἅγιοι (2:19) in the sense of the old people of God, in which case πιστοί would represent a really specific designation of the "faithful." [15] All this implies that the question concerning the original text of the prescript cannot be answered by assuming the letter's authenticity, but on the contrary, by assuming that it was written under a pseudonym, the text of the oldest manuscripts can be seen as possibly the original text.

So if the prescript of Eph provides no certain information about the literary character of the writing, the circumstances mentioned on p. 352 above show that in Eph we are not dealing with a letter to a particular community, nor with a circular letter for several specific communities. Only 1:15 mentions—and in a completely general way at that—the faith and love of the readers, while in

[10] Thus Feine-Behm, Guthrie, Michaelis; J. N. Sanders in F. Cross, *Studies,* Cadbury. According to Goguel and Schmid, τοῖς οὖσιν is a later addition; according to Benoit, the reading of 𝔓⁴⁶ is possibly the original text.

[11] Albertz.

[12] G. Zuntz, *The Text of the Epistles,* 1953, 288 n., is no further help either.

[13] See the evidence in Schmid, 110 ff; Percy, 450 f. The lack of an article before οὖσιν in 𝔓⁴⁶ alters nothing; and the assumption that τοῖς οὖσιν has been added does not explain how these words came into the text without placenames.

[14] Batey conjectures that the original text was τοῖς ἁγίοις τοῖς 'Ασίας καὶ πιστοῖς; Santer, that it was τοῖς ἁγίοις καὶ πιστοῖς τοῖς οὖσιν ἐν Χριστῷ Ἰησοῦ; but both are improbable.

[15] Thus Beare; similarly Pokorny, *Gnosis,* 17; Kirby, 170.

other places where a "you" is distinguished from the totality of
Christians or of Jewish Christians, there is no locally limited
readership discernible. The only exception to this fact is the communication concerning the sending of Tychicus to the readers (6:
21 f) which is almost word for word identical with Col 4:7. On
the ground of this concluding sentence it has been assumed again
and again that Eph was intended for Christian communities which
lay on the travel route of Tychicus as he journeyed toward Colossae,[16] but even then it is totally incomprehensible why in contrast to Rom and Col Paul establishes no sort of personal connection with these readers, and the completely nonepistolary character
of the rest of the writing stands clearly in tension with 6:21 f.
But if nothing indicates a real circular letter, the question concerning specific addressees is not settled by the thesis that Eph was
written to recently baptized Christians in order to call to their
remembrance their baptism (and that therefore in 1:3-14; 2:19-
22 and elsewhere parts of a baptismal liturgy were taken up, so
that we are dealing here with a "postbaptismal mystery address").[17]
For even if 1:3 ff and 2:19 ff were based on originally baptismal
hymns and in 5:14 an eschatological hymn were interpreted as
a baptismal hymn,[18] only scattered references to baptism are found
(1:13; 4:5; 4:30; 5:26), and the "quite lofty level of the letter
itself" tells against its being addressed to recently baptized Christians.[19] What seems indicated, rather, is that in Eph, apart from the
form of the letter and the specifics in 6:21 f, we are not dealing
with a writing that has specific readers in view. On this, Eph is
distinguished from all the letters of Paul which we have considered
up till now, and accordingly, in recognition of this non-letter
quality of Eph, the writing has been characterized as "the spiritual
testament of Paul to the church," [20] or as "a meditation on great
Christian themes," [21] or as "a letter directed to no specific address." [22] That would be in fact the single possible designation of
this letter if there did not exist serious considerations against Eph's
having been written by Paul.

[16] Schlier; Michaelis; Dahl, ThZ.

[17] Schlier; Dahl, ThZ; Nauck, Coutts, Kirby; S. Lyonnet, "La bénédiction
de Éph 1,3-14 et son arrière-plan judaïque," *Mémorial A. Gelin*, 1961, 341 ff.

[18] B. Noack, "Das Zitat in Eph 5,14," StTh 5, 1952, 52 ff.

[19] Michaelis, *Einl.*, 195. Against the newly baptized as those addressed are
also Johnston, 6; Gnilka, 405.

[20] J. N. Sanders, in F. Cross, *Studies*.

[21] Guthrie.

[22] H. Rendtorff, NTD 8, 1933, 44.

3. Authenticity

Eph is extraordinarily well attested in the early church.[23] Ign., Polyc 5:1; and Polyc, Phil 1:13; 12:1 clearly have echoes of Eph. Since Marcion, Eph has been an uncontested part of the canon of Pauline letters, and since Irenaeus and Clement of Alexandria the letter has been accepted without challenge as being by Paul. Erasmus[24] was the first to show that the style of Eph differs so sharply from that of Paul *ut alterius videri possit* ("that it must be seen to be by someone else"), without drawing the consequences from this. Then later, in 1792, Edward Evanson on the basis of the contradictions between the address and the content of Eph described it as a forgery. In 1826 De Wette was the first to deny Eph to Paul on the ground of the address, the style, the relationship to Col, and individual statements. F. C. Baur and his pupils shifted the letter to the second century as being "typical of early Catholicism," while Holtzmann sought to show that it was a revision of the not yet interpolated Col (see §21.4) by means of the use of other Pauline letters. Today Eph is still defended as Pauline, by many scholars,[25] while the number of those who contest its authenticity is equally high.[26] How difficult a decision is in this case is evident from the fact that Goguel thinks that he can defend the Pauline origin of Eph only by the wholly undemonstrable assumption of extensive new interpolations, while many scholars leave the question undecided[27] or link the assumption of its authenticity with the limitation that Paul must have

[23] Cf. Schmid, 16 ff; Mitton, 160 ff.

[24] On the history of criticism, cf. Schmid, 1 ff; Percy, 1 ff.

[25] Among others, Gaugler, Rendtorff, Schlier, Simpson; Albertz, Appel, Grant, Guthrie, Harrington, E. F. Harrison, Henshaw, Klijn, Lo Duc, Mariani, Meinertz, Michaelis, Schelkle, Wikenhauser; Schmid, Benoit, Percy; Dahl, ThZ; Cornelius, J. N. Sanders, in F. Cross, *Studies;* Cerfaux, Bieder; Buck-Taylor, 124 ff.

[26] E.g., Beare, Conzelmann, Dibelius-Greeven, Johnston, Masson; G. Dautzenberg, GANT, 118; Fuller, Heard, Lake, Marxsen, Riddle-Hutson, Sparks; Goodspeed, Mitton, Maurer, D. E. Nineham in F. Cross, *Studies;* Allan; Dahl (1963); Käsemann, Pokorný, P. N. Harrison, Kirby, Gnilka; J. Knox, *Philemon Among the Letters of Paul,* 1935; W. L. Knox, *St. Paul and the Church of the Gentiles,* 1939, 182 ff; S. G. F. Brandon, *The Fall of Jerusalem and the Christian Church,* 1951, 215 f; C. K. Barrett, *Studia Paulina, Festschr J. de Zwaan,* 1953, 13; F. Lang, CBL, 266 ff; J. Blank, *Paulus und Jesus,* StANT 16, 1968, 20 f; G. Bornkamm, *Paul,* 242; R. Schnackenburg, EKK Vorarbeiten I, 1969, 41; H. Hegermann (see below, n. 47), 54.

[27] Among others, Jülicher-Fascher, McNeile-Williams; Cadbury; B. Rigaux, *Saint Paul et ses lettres,* StN Subsidia 2, 1962, 148; O. Kuss, *Paulus,* 1971, 28 ff.

assigned to one of his pupils the actual working out of the letter.[28] At most this totally baseless "secretary hypothesis" could explain the matters of language and style of the letter, but it contributes nothing to the decisive questions concerning the relationships to Col and the theology of Eph.

1. Language and style.[29] The presence of numerous terms which are not found in Paul but are encountered in the later writings of the NT and in the apostolic fathers (e.g., ἀσωτία, εὔσπλαγχνος, κλυδωνίζομαι, ὁσιότης, πολιτεία)[30] is only striking when it is joined with the fact that Eph uses other words than Paul does for important concepts: 'εν τοῖς 'επουρανίοις 1:3, 20; 2:6; 3:10; 6:12 appears in addition to οἱ οὐρανοί which is the only term met in Paul; ὁ ἠγαπημένος 1:6 as a christological predicate; the sequence αἷμα καὶ σάρκα 6:12; χαριτόω 1:6 instead of the Pauline χάριν δίδωμι. Still more important is the fact that the piling up of synonyms and genitival links which we have already observed in Col is found to a far greater extent[31] in Eph. E.g., 'ενέργεια τοῦ κράτους τῆς ἰσχύος 1:19; κατὰ τὸν αἰῶνα τοῦ κόσμου τούτου 2:2; διὰ πάσης προσευχῆς καὶ δεήσεως . . . 'εν πάσῃ προσκαρτερήσει καὶ δεήσει in 6:18 among others. This goes along with the love of complex sentences that are overlong and scarcely to be parsed (1:15-23; 4:11-16, etc.). This language, which recalls the conceptual world of the Qumran texts, manifests "such appearances of Semitic syntax four times more frequently than all the other letters of the Pauline corpus."[32] Although these and related linguistic and stylistic differences alone could not prove the Pauline authorship of Eph to be impossible, they make extremely difficult the supposition that Paul could have written Eph in the form in which it has been handed down.

2. More essential for deciding the authorship question is the relationship of Eph to Col.[33] The kinship of Eph with Col is undoubtedly far greater than the kinship of any other letter of Paul with the rest of the Pauline corpus: about a third of the words in

[28] Albertz, Appel, Harrington, Schelkle; Benoit. Rigaux and Kuss (see n. 27) consider this possibility.

[29] Cf. Schmid, 131 ff; Percy, 179 ff; Mitton, 8 ff, 29 ff; Harrison, *Paulines*, 48 ff.

[30] Harrison (see n. 29) mentions words which are nowhere attested before the end of the first century.

[31] See Percy, 186 ff. Cf. also the fact that, completely unlike Paul, Eph has only a single interrogative sentence (4:9; see Harrison, StEv II, 597).

[32] K. G. Kuhn, 334 f. This holds true also for the relationship of Semitic and Greek influence on the syntax of the conditional sentences; cf. K. Beyer, *Semitische Syntax im NT*, I, 1, 1962, 298.

[33] Percy, 360 ff; Benoit, *Festschr. Schmid;* Mitton, 55 ff; 279 ff.

Col are found again in Eph (Mitton), and these verbal contacts are spread throughout the whole of Eph. Only brief portions of Eph (e.g., 2:6-9; 4:5-13; 5:29-33) have no verbal parallels in Col,[34] but in spite of the pervasive agreements only the information concerning Tychicus in Eph 6:21 f agrees so exactly with Col 4:7 that a written prototype must have been used directly in the event that the same author did not dictate the two letters at the same time himself. But that assumption is seriously called into question by the fact that Eph to a far greater extent than all the other letters of Paul manifests verbal contacts with the totality of the Pauline corpus (with the exception of II Thess).[35] These contacts are found frequently in connected sections of the other letters (cf., for example, Rom 3:20-27; 11:32–12:5 with Eph 1:19; 2:5, 8; 1:7; 3:8, 21; 4:1; 5:10, 17; 3:7; 4:7, 4, 25). Both these things would be extremely remarkable if the writings were by the same author.

Decisive against assuming that the same author wrote Col and Eph very quickly one after the other are those instances where Eph manifests clearly (a) literary dependence or (b) at the same time a really substantive difference from Col. (a) Thus Col 3:7 reads, following a catalogue of vices, quite naturally ἐν οἷς (vices) καὶ ὑμεῖς περιεπατήσατέ ποτε while Eph 2:2 f first appends to ἁμαρτίαι the quite natural relative clause ἐν αἷς ποτε περιπατήσατε but then with reference to the activity of the adversary ἐν τοῖς υἱοῖς τῆς ἀπειθείας in a clear echo of Col 3:7 clumsily appends the relative clause ἐν οἷς καὶ ἡμεῖς πάντες ἀνεστράφημέν ποτε. And the household admonition of Eph 5:22 ff is not only a strongly christianized version of the same sequence and offers the same wording of the household admonitions as in Col 3:18 ff, but the command to the women to obey their husbands ὡς ἀνῆκεν ἐν κυρίῳ (Col 3:18) is in Eph 5:22 escalated to the subordination ὡς τῷ κυρίῳ. (b) In Col 1:26 f Paul characterizes as μυστήριον the eschatological redemptive act of God in Christ (just as in 2:2; 4:3) in agreement with I Cor 2:1, 7. But in Eph 3:3 ff μυστήριον, in clear linguistic echo of Col 1:26, characterizes the participation of the Gentiles with the Jews in salvation. Furthermore in Eph 1:9 μυστήριον serves to describe the joining together of the universe in Christ, but in 5:32 it is a designation for the secret analogy

---

[34] Of 155 verses in Eph, 73 have verbal parallels in Col; see the list in Goguel. *Intr.* IV, 2, 460 f.

[35] Mitton, 98 ff, based on the example of Phil, has proved this persuasively. Cf. also the tables in Harrison, *Paulines*, 40 f, and the lists in Mitton, 120 ff, 333 ff.

between marriage and the relationship of Christ to his church. These three meanings for μυστήριον are completely alien to Paul. The case is similar in the use of οἰκονομία. In Col 1:25 as in I Cor 4:1; 9:17, Paul indicates by this word his having been commissioned to preach the mystery of Christ. In Eph 3:2, on the other hand, in spite of a clear echo of Col 1:25, οἰκονομία means the redemptive plan of God and has the same meaning in Eph 1:10 and 3:9, where the redemptive plan has as its content the mysteries which were mentioned in Eph 1:9; 3:3 ff.[36] It may be regarded as out of the question, therefore, that Paul could have given completely new meanings to these words μυστήριον and οἰκονομία in a letter that was written at almost exactly the same time as Col.

3. These two complexes of factors therefore weigh most heavily against the Pauline authorship of Eph, but the theology of Eph makes the Pauline composition of the letter completely impossible. This is shown first of all in comparing Eph with Col. While in Col 2:7 it is said that Christians "are rooted and grounded in Christ," in Eph 2:20 f they are "built on the foundation of the apostles and prophets in which Jesus Christ is the cornerstone," which represents a clear shift from the exclusive statement in I Cor 3:11. When, however, in a related passage, Eph 3:5, there is mention of the revelation of the mystery to "the holy apostles and prophets"—while Col 1:26 speaks of the revelation "to his saints"—the evaluation of the apostles as the foundation of the church is as impossible for Paul as is his characterization of the apostles in some special sense as "holy." Linked with this is the fact that in Eph ἐκκλησία is used exclusively of the universal church (1:22; 3:10, 21; 5:23-25, 27, 29, 32), while in all the letters of Paul, including Col, ἐκκλησία could as well indicate the church as a whole as the individual community.[37] Still further connected with this is the fact that the μυστήριον τοῦ χριστοῦ (Eph 3:4 f) which has now been revealed is not Christ as in Col 2:2, but is the unity of the Gentiles and the Jews in the body of Christ. As a result "now Christology is almost exclusively interpreted from the standpoint of ecclesiology."[38] But there is further evidence of the development in Eph of Christology beyond Paul. In the two texts where the word ἀποκαταλλάσσειν appears, Eph

---

[36] J. Reumann, "OIKONOMIA-Terms in Paul in Comparison with Lucan Heilsgeschichte," NTS 13, 1966/67, 163 ff, disputes the meaning of οἰκονομία= "redemptive plan" in Eph, though not convincingly.

[37] Cf. also Pokorný, Gnosis, 65.

[38] Käsemann, Interpretationsprobleme, 3; cf. also 255.

2:16 presents Christ as the agent of reconciliation, while in Paul, Col 1:20, God effects a reconciliation. Similarly in Eph 4:11 it is Christ who establishes the apostles and prophets, not God as in I Cor 12:28.

If these developments beyond Paul are in any case completely inconceivable in a letter of Paul written at almost exactly the same time as Col, other ideas and formulations in Eph stand in any case in irreconcilable opposition to Paul. In characteristic fashion, Eph 2:10 in reworking Col 1:10 employs the plural ἔργα ᾿αγαθά which Paul always avoids (see §21.4.1).[39] Equally characteristic is the fact that Eph in contrast with Col uses several ἐν-formulae that Paul does not have: ἐν τῷ χριστῷ Ιησοῦ (3:11), ἐν τῷ ᾿Ιησοῦ (4:21), ἐν τῷ κυρίῳ ᾿Ιησοῦ (1:15). And in 1:15 πίστις is linked with κύριος, while in Paul it is linked only with χριστός.[40] Also it cannot be an accident that only in Eph 1:17; 3:14 (in contrast to all the Pauline letters) do we hear God addressed as Father in petition.[41] Still more essential than these divergences, however, are three other factors which cannot be reconciled with Pauline authorship. First, in contrast to all the Pauline letters including Col 3:4, there is lacking in Eph any mention of the expectation of the parousia. With its formulation εἰς πάσας τὰς γενεὰς τοῦ αἰῶνος τῶν αἰώνων, Eph 3:21 is scarcely counting on a near eschaton.[42] The valuing of marriage as the image of the heavenly union of Christ and his church (5:25 ff) is scarcely open to the same Paul who wrote I Cor 7. Finally, the statement that Paul's commissioned office was to proclaim the unity of Jews and Gentiles in the promise of Christ (3:2 ff) is contradicted by his own statements including Col 1:25 ff, and the self-designation of Paul as ᾿ελαχιστότερος πάντων ἁγίων (3:8) is a scarcely conceivable overstatement of ᾿ελάχιστος τῶν ἀποστόλων (I Cor 15:9).

In view of this linguistic, literary, and theological state of affairs, it cannot seriously be doubted that Eph does not come from Paul and is therefore a pseudonymous writing.[43] Since the theology of Eph is not simply an extension of Paul, but in part clearly in

[39] Bieder, 226, thinks he can resolve the difficulty: Paul has "become free with respect to his own battle position."
[40] Cf. Steinmetz, 96 ff; Allan; F. Neugebauer, In Christus, 1961, 176, 179 ff.
[41] G. Harder, Paulus und das Gebet, NTF I, 10, 1936, 186. Steinmetz, 84, speaks of a "certain 'blending' of the picture of Christ with the picture of God."
[42] Steinmetz, 34 ff, with reference to 1:14; 4:30; 5:5; 6:13, speaks of "traces" of futuristic eschatology; according to Kirby, 163, past and future meet in the "liturgical eschatology" of the present.
[43] The identification of the writer as Onesimus (Col 4:9; Phlm 10 ff: thus Goodspeed, P. N. Harrison; J. Knox, see n. 26) is fantasy.

contradiction to Paul, the difference from Paul cannot be explained simply on the ground that this letter is not to be regarded as "kerygma in the strict sense" but as "Sophia, Sophia of the Mystery, . . . meditation of wisdom on the mystery of Christ himself," [44] or by showing that "the symphony of the Pauline doctrine has been transposed as a whole from a lower manual to a higher one: the gospel has become the mystery." [45] Such formulations create a fog, not a clear historical result, and it remains only to ask what purpose this pseudonymous writing served and in what historical connection it is to be set.

Against the assumption that in Eph we are dealing with a pseudonymous writing, an objection has been raised which is also of importance for the remaining NT letters which we have yet to consider: that the practice of writing pseudonymous letters scarcely existed in the setting of early Christianity, and in religious writings which explicitly underscore their obligation to truth (cf. 4:15, 25; 6:14) such deception would scarcely be conceivable.[46] Now it really cannot be denied that not only were there numerous pseudonymous writings in the ancient world in general, but that precisely in the time of Hellenism the literary practice of pseudonymous writings was very widespread and evidence for it also exists in Judaism as well as in early Christianity: the Letter of Jeremiah, the Letter of Aristeas, Acts 23:26 ff, the exchange of letters between Paul and Corinth = III Cor (compare also the possibility presupposed by Paul in II Thess 2:2; 3:17 of a spurious letter of Paul). Indeed, no adequate way has yet been found to clarify the problem of pseudonymity in antiquity, especially the question of intentional or unintentional deception of the reader by the writer of a pseudonymous religious document.[47] As the discussion has

[44] Schlier, Comm., 21 f.

[45] Cerfaux, RechB V, 68 = Recueil L.C. III, 275.

[46] Guthrie, 282 ff; Michaelis, 2 f.

[47] Cf. on this F. Torm, Die Psychologie der Pseudonymität im Hinblick auf die Literatur des Urchristentums, 1932; A. Meyer, "Religiöse Pseudepigraphie als ethisch-psychologisches Problem," ZNW 35, 1936, 262 ff; E. J. Goodspeed, "Pseudonymity and Pseudepigraphy in Early Christian Literature," in E. J. G., New Chapters in NT Study, 1937, 169 ff; J. Schneider, art. "Brief," RAC II, 1954, 574 f; J. C. Fenton, "Pseudonymity in the NT," Theology 58, 1955, 51 ff; J. A. Sint, "Pseudonymität im Altertum," Commentationes Aenipontanae 15, 1960 (criticism in M. Foderer, Gn 33, 1961, 440 ff); D. Guthrie, "The Development of the Idea of Canonical Pseudepigrapha in NT Criticism," VE 1, 1962, 43 ff; W. Schneemelcher, in Hennecke-Schneemelcher-Wilson, NT Apocrypha II, 1965, 31 ff; K. Aland, "Das Problem der Anonymität und

shown, there were many different kinds of pseudonymous literature
and motives for it in Hellenism, Judaism, and Christianity, and
actual forgeries, i.e., writings with the intent to deceive, were
criticized very early in all quarters. But it is really impossible to
prove either the assertion that the fictitious information about the
author in Eph "was not meant to deceive anyone," [48] or the contradictory hypotheses that in earliest Christianity "the writing of
a pseudonymous letter in good faith is rather unlikely" [49] or that
the pseudepigraphic statement of an apostle as author was "only
the logical consequence of the presupposition that the Spirit itself
is the author." [50] The only thing that is clear in relation to the
pseudepigraphic material we encounter in the NT is that "the
decisive presupposition for pseudepigraphic writing in the NT [is
represented by] the establishment of the apostolic as the norm"
(cf. Eph 2:20), so that literary fiction "brings into play the
authority" of an apostle.[51] But even if the *Sitz im Leben* of religious pseudepigraphic writings in early Christianity has not yet
been adequately explained, there still exists in any event no ground
for declaring that pseudepigraphic writing is impossible for early
Christian epistolary literature, or that it precludes truthfulness.
Even if it could be proved that in Judaism and early Christianity
there was no pseudonymous epistolary literature—as Guthrie insists without justification (see above)—in view of the existence
of other types of pseudonymous writing in Judaism and later primitive Christianity (cf., e.g., Wisdom and Did) this fact would
mean nothing in the event that the supposition of an anonymous
authorship for an early Christian letter emerges as unavoidable.
But then if the assumption of pseudepigraphic authorship appears
to be necessary, we must still clarify the question what sort of
pseudonymous writing is before us, and what end is served by the
piece of writing with which we are dealing.

Pseudonymität in der christlichen Literatur der ersten beiden Jh," in K. A.,
Studien zur Überlieferung des NT und seines Textes, ANTF 2, 1967, 24 ff;
W. Speyer, "Religiöse Pseudepigraphie und literarische Fälschung im Altertum,"
JbAC 8/9, 1965/66, 88 ff; *idem,* art. "Fälschung, literarische," RAC VII, 1969,
236 ff (bibl.); *idem, Die literarische Fälschung im Altertum. Ein Versuch ihrer
Deutung,* in Handbuch der Altertumswissenschaft I, 2, 1971; N. Brox, "Die
Past," RNT VII, 2, [4]1969, 60 ff; H. Hegermann, "Der geschichtliche Ort der
Past," *Theologische Versuche* II, ed. J. Rogge and G. Schille, 1970, 48 ff; R. Balz,
"Anonymität und Pseudepigraphie im Urchristentum," ZThK 66, 1970, 403 ff.

[48] Harrison, StEv II, 604.
[49] W. Speyer, JbAC 8/9, 123 (see n. 47).
[50] Aland (see n. 47), 30.
[51] Balz (see n. 47), 420, 431; similarly Hegermann (see n. 47), 54.

4. Aim, Historical Situation, and Time of the Letter

The links between Eph and Paul are made known in 1:1; 3:1; 4:1; 6:19-22 by clear agreement with the language and situation which are evident in Col, even though this historical situation is in no way exactly characterized. Even less is made known about the position of the readers, other than that they are Gentile Christians (2:1 ff, 11 ff; 3:1, 13; 4:17), and concrete insight into false teaching or abuses among the readers is completely lacking. Only one point is stressed by the letter, with regard both to the commission of the "Paul" who is writing and to the readers: that the Gentiles now belong in Christ among the people of God and that through the death of Christ the wall between the two has been broken down and through him "the two have access in one spirit to the Father" (2:11 ff; 3:1 ff; 4:3). In order to set forth comprehensively the significance of Christ, the letter depicts the all-penetrating action of God's work in Christ (1:10, 20 ff; 3:10, 18; 4:10), and thereby emphasizes the eternal relationship between Christ, the head, and his body, the church (1:4 f, 22 f; 2:15 f, 21 f; 4:13, 15 f; 5:23 f, 29, 32), and the necessity to consider the importance of belonging to this body and to show oneself worthy of it (1:18 f; 2:11; 4:1 ff, 20 ff, 25; 5:22 ff). But what the concrete occasion was for this reworking of the Pauline message by emphasizing the unity of the church comprised of Gentiles and Jews cannot now be perceived.[52] It is not enough, however, to see in Eph only a "comprehensive presentation of Pauline doctrine"[53] or a "commendation of the theology of Paul to the church of another generation."[54] Rather Eph is addressed to a general spiritual crisis in post-Pauline Gentile Christianity in which it must be stressed that the church of the Gentiles includes also the Jewish past of the church because it is in every sense a universal church which is in the process of attaining "the fully grown measure of the fulness of Christ" (4:13). In this context the Gentile Christians are warned against falling back into their pre-Christian moral state (4:17 ff; 5:6 ff).[55]

[52] Contrary to W. Grundmann ("Die NHΠIOI in der urchristlichen Paränese," NTS 5, 1958/59, 194 n. 1), there is no trace of tensions between Gentile Christians of Asia Minor and Jewish Christians who left Palestine after the Jewish war. And the hypothesizing of connections between Eph and a covenant renewal ceremony linked with Pentecost in the Christian community of Ephesus (Kirby) is completely arbitrary (cf. Lohse).

[53] Mitton.

[54] Beare.

[55] See Chadwick, Martin.

In this "letter" which speaks to a concrete post-Pauline situation Gentile Christianity, the author shows that he is thoroughly familiar with Col especially but also with the other Pauline letters, although he seems to have had the wording of Col before him only for 6:21 f. Moreover it is clear that the author is writing in a twofold religious situation. On the one hand, his religious terminology and his paraenetic material show a striking contact with the literature of the Qumran sect.[56] On the other hand, not only do the household admonitions (which are taken over from Col) come from Hellenistic-Jewish tradition; but in addition, the development of Christology and ecclesiology—especially the representations of Christ as the primal man, of the syzygy between Christ and the church, and of the church as the body of Christ—can only be understood against the background of a christianized mythological gnosis.[57] In view of these facts and the strongly Semitic language of Eph, it is likely that the author was a Jewish Christian as he himself seems to indicate (2:3, 11, 17).[58] The only thing certain is that he had some relationship with a Gentile Christianity that had adopted certain strong influences of Gnostic mythology and perhaps also of a strongly hellenized Judaism.[59] He recognizes the danger of dissolving the redemptive-historical connection with the ancient people of God and regards this as a threat. Thus, in spite of strong dependence on Pauline ideas and formulations, there arises a development of Pauline theology which is characterized by a relaxing of the eschatological tension and a stronger mythologizing of Christology and ecclesiology, as well as by moralizing (3:10!)—all of which demonstrates clear traces of "early Catholicism"[60] that is difficult to define in detail.

All this goes to show that the widely held thesis among English-speaking scholars[61] that Eph was written as an accompanying letter to go with the first collection of the Pauline letters must be regarded as improbable. Against it is not only the fact that according to our information Eph never stood at the beginning of the

[56] Käsemann, Kuhn, Mussner; D. Flusser, in *Scripta Hierosolymitana* 4, 1958, 263 n. 163 f; J. Murphy-O'Connor, "La 'vérité' chez Saint Paul et à Qumrân," RB 72, 1965, 51 ff; H. Braun, *Qumran und das NT* I, 1966, 215 ff.

[57] Cf. Schlier; Käsemann, Pokorny.

[58] Beare; Kirby, 165.

[59] Thus C. Colpe, "Zur Leib-Christi-Vorstellung im Eph," *Judentum-Urchristentum-Kirche, Festschr. J. Jeremias*, Bh. ZNW 26, 1960, 172 ff.

[60] See above, p. 146, with n. 80. Käsemann and Martin stress the theological kinship between Eph and Acts. Martin's conclusion that Luke could have written Eph under Paul's guidance is, however, completely inadequate in its grounding.

[61] See esp. Goodspeed, Mitton.

Pauline collection (see §35.2), but, above all, that the special aims of Eph are not clarified on the basis of such an assumption.[62]

If, then, it is determined that Eph was written in the post-Pauline period, the fact that Ignatius knows it (see §35.2) implies a date no later than the first decade of the second century. A more exact date might be determined if we could prove a literary dependence of I Peter on Eph,[63] but in view of the common paraenetic tradition this is not convincing. And since Eph seems to know the collected Pauline letters, an earlier date is not likely. The date of writing cannot be determined more closely than sometime between 80 and 100. The special familiarity with Col might suggest Asia Minor as the place of writing, but that is no more than a conjecture.

§24. THE PASTORAL LETTERS: I AND II TIMOTHY, TITUS

Commentaries: see §41. Research: H. J. Holtzmann, *Die Past, kritisch und exegetisch bearbeitet*, 1880; W. Lütgert, *Die Irrlehrer der Past*, BFChTh 13, 3, 1909; P. N. Harrison, *The Problem of the Pastoral Epistles*, 1921; *idem*, "The Authorship of the Pastoral Epistles," ExpT 67, 1955/56, 77 ff; *idem*, "The Pastoral Epistles and Duncan's Ephesian Theory," NTS 2, 1955/56, 250 ff; *idem*, *Paulines and Pastorals*, 1964; W. Michaelis, "Past and Wortstatistik," ZNW 28, 1929, 69 ff; *idem*, *Past und Gefangenschaftsbriefe*, NTF I, 6, 1930; W. Bauer, *Orthodoxy and Heresy in Earliest Christianity*, 1971, 88 ff, 222 ff; R. Falconer, *The Pastoral Epistles*, 1937; C. Maurer, "Eine Textvariante klärt die Entstehung der Past auf," ThZ 3, 1947, 321 ff; H. Schlier, "Die Ordnung der Kirche nach den Past," in *Festschr. F. Gogarten*, 1948, 38 ff (=H. S., *Die Zeit der Kirche*, 1956, 129 ff); O. Michel, "Grundfragen de Past," in *Festgabe für Th. Wurm*, 1948, 83 ff; *idem*, CBL, 992 ff; H. von Campenhausen, "Polyk und die Past," SAH 1951, 2 (=H. v. C., *Aus der Frühzeit des Christentums*, 1963, 197 ff); *idem*, *Kirchliches Amt und geistliche Vollmacht in den ersten drei Jahrhunderten*, BHTh 14, 1953, 116 ff; W. Nauck, "Die Theologie der Past I," ThLZ 79, 1954, 124 f (diss. Göttingen); R. Bultmann, *Theology of the NT*, 1955, 183 ff; B. M. Metzger, "A Reconsideration of Certain Arguments Against the Pauline Authorship of the Pastoral Epistles," ExpT 70, 1958/59, 91 ff; E. Schweizer, *Church Order in the NT*, SBT 32, 1961, 77 ff; W. Kasch, EKL III, 1959, 78 f; J. Müller-Bardorff, "Zur Exegese von I Tim 5,3-16," in *Festgabe für E. Fascher*, 1959, 113 ff; K. Grayston and G. Herdan, "The Authorship of the Pastorals in the Light of Statistical Linguistics," NTS 6, 1959/60,

---

[62] For criticism of this thesis, cf. Schlier, 26 f; Guthrie, 132 f.

[63] Thus, e.g., Gaugler; Mitton, Cornelius (who thinks that Eph was written at the time Peter was in Rome!), Pokorný.

1 ff; E. E. Ellis, *Paul and His Recent Interpreters*, 1961, 49 ff; J. Jeremias, "Zur Datierung der Past," ZNW 52, 1961, 101 ff (=J. J., Abba, 1966, 314 ff); W. Schmithals, RGG³ V, 1961, 144 ff; C. Spicq, DBS VII, 1966, 1 ff (bibl.); K. Wegenast, *Das Verständnis der Tradition bei Paulus und in den Deuteropaulinen*, WMANT 8, 1962, 132 ff; J. A. Allan, "The 'in Christ' Formula in the Pastoral Epistles," NTS 10, 1963/64, 115 ff; J. Schmid, LThK VIII, 1963, 155 ff; C. F. D. Moule, "The Problem of the Pastoral Epistles," BJRL 47, 1964/65, 430 ff; A. T. Hanson, *Studies in the Pastoral Epistles*, 1968; A. Strobel, "Schreiben des Lukas? Zum sprachlichen Problem der Past," NTS 15, 1968/69, 191 ff; N. Brox, "Zu den persönlichen Notizen der Past," BZ, NF 13, 1969, 76 ff; *idem*, "Historische und theologische Probleme der Past," Kairos, NF 11, 1969, 81 ff; H. Hegermann, *Der geschichtliche Ort der Past*, Theologische Versuche 2, 1970, 47 ff; J. M. Ford, "A Note on Proto-Montanism in the Pastoral Epistles," NTS 17, 1970/71, 338 ff.

The name Pastoral or Shepherd letters for these writings first appeared in the eighteenth century.[1] They contain instructions and admonitions for the fulfillment of the pastoral office in the Christian communities. These instructions are addressed in the form of letters to Paul's closest workers and companions, but they do not give the impression of private letters; rather, they are official communications "for ordering church discipline" (Muratorian Canon). In terms of content the three letters, of which I Tim and Titus are most closely related, form a group within themselves among the traditional letters of Paul. They presuppose the same false teachers, the same organization, and entirely similar conditions in the community. They move within the same relative theological concepts and have the same peculiarities of language and style.

1. Contents

I Timothy. Following the prescript (1:1) is an appeal to Timothy to do battle against the false teachers who lose themselves in mythical speculations about genealogies and want to be teachers of the Law without knowing the true meaning of the Law (1:3-11). Paul, who was once a persecutor, has by the mercy of God been entrusted with the gospel that saves sinners (1:12-17). Accordingly Timothy is to guard in trust the Christian tradition (1:18-20). Then follow prescriptions concerning the com-

---

[1] First used for Titus in D. N. Bardot (1703); used for all three Pastorals in P. Anton, *Exegetische Abhandlungen der Past. Pauli* (1753/55).

munity prayer (2:1-7) and the deportment of men and women
in the service of worship (2:8-15), concerning the prerequisites
for those who fulfill the office of bishop (3:1-7) and the male
and female offices of deacon (3:8-13). At the conclusion is a
word to Timothy concerning the significance of such prescriptions.
They are concerned with the house of God, the church, the
guardian of the great mystery of God (3:14-16). Ch. 4 predicts
the appearance of false teachers and gives counsel for combating
them (4:1-10), and reminds Timothy of the obligations which
were laid upon him through the charisma which he received
through the laying on of hands (4:11-16). The section 5:1–6:2
gives advice concerning the conduct of various age groups and the
sexes (5:1-3), regulations for the ranks of widows (5:4-16) and
the aged (5:17-22), including in part a personal word for Timothy;
a personal counsel to Timothy (5:23), a reference to the coming
revelation of sins and good works (5:24 f), and finally rules of life
for Christian slaves (6:1 f). A group of general admonitions fills
the last section (6:3-21a): warning concerning false teaching
and greed (6:3-10), warnings to Timothy to hold fast to the
faith (6:11-16), counsel concerning pastoral care of the rich
(6:17-19), final warning to Timothy concerning false Gnosticism
(6:20-21a), benediction upon the majority of the congregation
(6:21b).

II Timothy. Joined to the prescript (1:1 f) is a petition for
Timothy (1:3-5), an admonition to him to hold fast to the
charisma which was transmitted by the laying on of hands (1:6-
14), and references to the experiences of Paul in his immediate
circumstances (1:15-18). Ch. 2 admonishes Timothy to endure
suffering unswervingly like Paul in the faithful guarding of the
tradition (2:1-13), and properly to present the truth while avoid-
ing foolish controversy with those who have fallen into ways of
error (2:14-26). There follows a prediction of the appearance of
false teachers in the last days, who will lead astray the "women"
especially (3:1-9). It is the more urgent therefore for Timothy to
remain true to what he has learned from Paul and from the Holy
Scripture (3:10-17) and to proclaim the sound doctrine (4:1-5).
Finally Paul portrays his own situation: he sees himself confronting
death as a martyr (4:6-8), gives communications concerning his
fellow workers (4:9-12), commissions for Timothy (4:13-15),
final information concerning the seriousness of his condition (4:16-
18), conveys greetings (4:19-21) and a benediction to the majority
of the congregation (4:22).

Titus. The wordy prescript also presents the content of the message of Paul (1:1-4). In 1:5-16 are given the rules for the installation and the character of the elders or bishops in Crete (1: 5-9), in view of the false teachers who have appeared there, spreading abroad Jewish myths and making ascetic requirements, all of them motivated by greed (1:10-16). Ch. 2 offers instruction for all the groups within the community (the household admonitions) (2:1-10). The instructions correspond to the grace of God, which brings salvation that has been revealed in Christ (2:11-15). In 3:1 f there are admonitions to obey the established authorities and to behave in friendly fashion toward every man. These commandments are once more grounded by reference to the kindness which has appeared in Christ and on the friendliness of God (3:3-7) which leads to good works (3:8 f). Finally there is once more a warning about the false teachers (3:10 f), instructions and greetings (3:12-15a), and a benediction for "you all" (3:15b).

2. The Addressees

The Pastorals present as addressees Timothy in Ephesus (I Tim 1:3; II Tim 1:15) and Titus in Crete (Tit 1:5). Both men are known co-workers of Paul in his great mission over a period of years. Timothy was from Lystra in Lycaonia, the son of a pagan father and a Jewish-Christian mother (Acts 16:1). According to II Tim 1:5 his mother's name was Eunice. Perhaps already converted during Paul's first mission in his native city (Acts 14:6 ff), he was commissioned by the apostle to travel with him on his mission on the occasion of Paul's second visit in Lystra and was circumcised (Acts 16:3). From that time on he was the regular companion of Paul (Acts 17:14 f; 18:5; 19:22; 20:4; I Thess 1:1; II Thess 1:1; II Cor 1:1, 19; Phil 1:1). On occasion during this period he was sent to individual communities with special responsibilities (I Thess 3:2, 6; I Cor 4:17; 16:10; Phil 2:19, 23): on the collection journey to Jerusalem in the company of Paul (Acts 20:4) and according to Col 1:1 and Phlm 1, he was with Paul in the place of his imprisonment. Phil 2:20 ff shows the apostle's high esteem for the person and the service of Timothy. What the historical circumstances of Heb 13:23 may be—this is the last place in the NT where Timothy is mentioned—lies in the dark.

Titus, a Gentile Christian concerning whom Acts is remarkably silent, is first named by Paul in Gal 2:1, 3, as one of his companions on the journey to the Apostolic Council, on which occasion the apostle successfully resisted the demand that Titus be circumcised. According to II Cor, Titus carried the intermediate letter to the Corinthian community, resolved the tension which existed between them and Paul, and effectively fostered the matter of the collection (2:13; 7:6 ff, 13 ff). Following the completion of this mission he came once again from Macedonia to Corinth with the second Corinthian letter as a forerunner of Paul (8:6, 16 ff; 12:18). II Tim 4:10 mentions yet another journey of Titus, from Rome, where he was with Paul, to Dalmatia.

3. The Historical Problem

The historical and theological problem of the Pastorals is indissolubly linked with the question whether or not these letters originated with Paul.

External attestation for them in the early church is less satisfactory than for the other Pauline letters. The Pastorals are lacking in the canon of Marcion, but, in spite of the statement by Tertullian,[2] the view that Marcion knew these letters but rejected them[3] is no more demonstrable than the opinion that the letters could not have been in existence at the time Marcion formulated his canon.[4] From the end of the second century on, however,[5] the Pastorals are considered without question to be letters of Paul. The fact that in $\mathfrak{P}$[46] (see §38.b) there would not have been room for the Pastorals in the space presumably available in the now missing sheets at the end of the papyrus can be interpreted otherwise than by the scribe's not wanting to include the Pastorals. Linguistic similarities to the Pastorals in Ignatius and Polycarp do not in any way prove dependence on these letters[6] but only that they all stand in the same ecclesiastical and cultural tradition. We have, then, no cer-

---

[2] Miror . . . quod ad Timotheum duas et unum ad Titum de ecclesiastico statu compositas recusaverit ("I am surprised . . . that he rejects the two [letters] to Timothy and the one to Titus written about ecclesiastical status") (Tert., Adv. Marc. V. 21).

[3] Spicq, Comm., 168; Michaelis.

[4] Von Campenhausen, 179; W. Bauer. On the basis of Jerome's account, Tatianus . . . qui et ipse nonnullas Pauli epistulas repudiavit, hanc vel maxime, hoc est ad Titum, apostoli pronuntiandam credidit ("Tatian . . . who himself rejected several letters of Paul, thought that this one to Titus ought to be credited to Paul"; from the Preface to the Commentary on Titus), the only sure inference is that Tatian knew Titus.

[5] Muratorian Canon, Athenagoras, Irenaeus, Tertullian.

[6] Thus, e.g., Brox Comm., 26 ff; also Kairos, 77 ff; von Campenhausen, Polycarp, 28 f=224 f, against Spicq, Comm., 160 ff; Binder, 70.

tain evidence of familiarity with the Pastorals before the third quarter of the second century, but that in itself is no unambiguous indication of their age.

The Pauline origin of the Pastorals was not contested from the time of their recognition as canonical scripture toward the end of the second century until the beginning of the nineteenth century. But after J. E. C. Schmidt (1804) had expressed doubt about the authenticity of I Tim, F. Schleiermacher in his *Sendschreiben an J. C. Gess* (1807) disputed the Pauline authorship of I Tim on the ground of language and biographical information. A few years later J. G. Eichhorn (1812), referring to the different religious language, extended this judgment against all three Pastorals. In 1835, F. C. Baur closed the circle by his demonstration of the links between the polemic in the Pastorals and gnosis of the second century.[7] H. J. Holtzmann collected all the objections; since then the view has become widespread that Pauline authorship of the Pastorals is impossible.[8] Numerous scholars have discussed the Pauline authorship of the letters but have, with more or less confidence, assumed the position that they include genuine Pauline fragments.[9] Even so, the conviction that the Pastorals go back to Paul directly or indirectly still, has many champions.[10]

The objections against the Pauline authorship of the Pastorals depend chiefly on (1) language and style, (2) the presumed historical situation, (3) the struggle against the false teachers, (4) the relationships within the community, and (5) the theology of the Pastorals.

1. *Language and style.* The first doubts about the authenticity of the Pastorals were based on the language. H. J. Holtzmann demonstrated thoroughly the great difference between the language of

[7] Cf. WGK, NT, 84 f; 130 f.

[8] Thus Brox, Dibelius-Conzelmann, Gealy; Fuller, Goodspeed, Jülicher-Fascher, Klijn, Marxsen, Schelkle; Bauer, Maurer, von Campenhausen, Bultmann, Schweizer, Kasch, Müller-Bardorff, Wegenast, Allan, Hanson, Strobel, Hegermann; J. Blank, *Paulus und Jesus*, StANT 18, 1968, 16 f; O. Kuss, *Paulus*, 1971, 30 f, 77.

[9] Cf. Easton, E. F. Scott; Appel, Goguel, Heard, Henshaw, McNeile-Williams, Sparks; P. N. Harrison, Falconer, Michel, Schmithals.

[10] E.g., Holtz, Jeremias, Kelly, Schlatter, Spicq; Albertz, Cerfaux in Robert-Feuillet, Feine-Behm, Guthrie, Harrington, E. F. Harrison, Meinertz, Michaelis, Wikenhauser, de Zwaan; Metzger; Binder (assumes there were extensive secondary expansions); O. Roller, *Das Formular der paulinischen Briefe*, BWANT 4th Series 6, 1933; E. E. Ellis, *Paul and His Interpreters*, 1961, 56 ff; L. Goppelt, "Die apostolische und nachapostolische Zeit," *Die Kirche in ihrer Geschichte* I A, 1962, 71. The question is left undecided by R. M. Grant; Schmid; B. Rigaux, *Saint Paul et ses lettres*, StN Subsidia 2, 1962, 149 ff.

the Pastorals and that of the rest of the Pauline letters. By statistical means, Harrison (1921) sought to show that the Pastorals
diverge from the language of Paul in the limited use of particles,
the number of words which are not encountered elsewhere in Paul,
and the kinship of the language with that of the second century.[11]
To be sure, Harrison's methods have been called into question[12]
because he compared the vocabulary of individual pages rather than
that of whole letters; Metzger has objected that, in view of the
brevity of the text of the Pastorals, word statistics cannot be employed at all. On the basis of word statistics, of course, one can
prove nothing more than that the language of certain writings
differs from that of other comparable writings in striking ways.[13]
But that is indeed the case beyond dispute in the comparison of the
Pastorals with the other Pauline letters. Morgenthaler[14] has shown
that the Pastorals, with 335 words in their special vocabulary, use
such words two and a half times more frequently than is the case
in a cross section of the Pauline letters. The mathematically refined
statistics of Grayston and Herdan have confirmed this result and,
further, have shown that the relationship between the logarithms
of vocabulary and of length of text in the Pastorals varies markedly from this same relationship in the letters of Paul as a whole,
including Col, Eph, and II Thess. Furthermore, the statistics on
the relationship of Greek as contrasted with semitizing conditional
sentences in the NT writings show[15] that the Pastorals exhibit ten
to twenty times as many "Grecisms" as the other Pauline letters.
The conclusion to which these observations lead—that the language
and style of the Pastorals do not permit us to assume that Paul
wrote the Pastorals—cannot be avoided by the claim that during
the five- or six-year interval between the writing of the older

[11] Harrison, *Paulines,* 16 f, 22 f, expanded his earlier evidence by showing
that (*a*) of the *hapax legomena* of the Pastorals which are not encountered in
the rest of the NT, a larger percentage are *not* found in the LXX than is the
case with Paul; (*b*) a significant number of the hapax legomena of the Pastorals
are not attested before the end of the first century.

[12] Cf. Spicq, *Comm.,* 183 ff; Michaelis. Further bibl. in Guthrie, *Intr.* II,
221 f.

[13] G. D. Kilpatrick, "What John Tells Us About John," in *Studies in John:
Festschrift for J. N. Sevenster,* Suppl. NovTest 24, 1970, 80 f, has shown
that the Pastorals simply do not have a whole series of stylistic refinements
frequently found in Paul. And M. P. Brown, *The Authentic Writings of Ignatius,*
1963, has demonstrated that word statistics and comparison of style confirm
clearly the acknowledged fact that the letters in the so-called longer recension
of the Ignatian correspondence are linguistically later than the genuine letters
of Ignatius.

[14] R. Morgenthaler, *Statistik des nt. Wortschatzes,* 1958, 28, 38.

[15] K. Beyer, *Semitische Syntax im NT,* I, 1, 1962, 232, 295, 298.

Pauline letters (assuming the prison letters were written in Ephesus) and the Pastorals, a marked change occurred in the language of Paul, or that the change occurred under the influence of Latin during his second imprisonment in Rome, or even that it is the result of the advanced age of the writer.[16] Even if these wholly questionable influences could have effected a change in his vocabulary, it would still be completely inconceivable that the relationship between the logarithms of vocabulary and of length of text should also have changed so decisively.

In addition to these statistical observations about the language and style of the Pastorals, there are broader, more clearly weighty linguistic phenomena. For one thing, the Pastorals lack many shorter words that are used with great frequency by Paul, such as ἄν, ἄρα, διό, εἴτε, ἕκαστος, ἔτι, νυνί, οὐκέτι, πάλιν, σύν, ὥσπερ, ὥστε,[17] and the use of just such words as these occurs unconsciously as a rule. Still more remarkable is the use of different words for the same thing: κύριοι for the possessor of slaves (Col 3:22; 4:1), δεσπόται in the Pastorals; 'αρχαί used in Paul for the spiritual powers, but in Tit 3:1 for the earthly authorities; in Pauline introductions 'ευχαριστεῖν is used with reference to God, but in I Tim 1:12; II Tim 1:3 χάριν ἔχειν is used, a phrase which in II Cor 1:15 means "to receive grace." Setting aside for a moment the problem of the theological concepts, we must add the repeated use of phrases which are not found elsewhere in Paul: e.g., διαβεβαιοῦσθαι περί τινος (I Tim 1:7; Tit 3:8); διαμαρτύρεσθαι ἐνώπιον τοῦ θεοῦ (I Tim 5:21; II Tim 2:14; 4:1); πιστὸς ὁ λόγος five times; δι' ἣν αἰτίαν three times. On the other hand, there is the infrequent use of 'εν χριστῷ in the Pastorals, which, besides, is almost wholly restricted to combination with abstract nouns in a way that is never encountered in Paul.[18] If one takes all these observations into account, it cannot be denied that the language and the style speak decisively against the Pauline origin of the Pastorals.

In line with a conjecture expressed by H. A. Schott in 1830, O. Roller[19] has sought to show that Paul himself did not dictate the Pastorals, but had them written by an amanuensis on the basis of his own notes and then only corrected the text and signed it with his own hand. That not only corresponds, it is argued, to the situation which is presupposed in almost all the Pauline letters,

---

[16] Kelly, 25; Spicq, 147 ff, 189 ff; Michaelis, *Einl.*, 239 f.
[17] Cf. the list in Harrison (1921), 37.
[18] See the evidence in Allan.
[19] O. Roller (see n. 10), 20 ff.

but may be inferred as a necessity in the situation depicted in II Tim 1:8, 16; 2:9, where Paul is a fettered prisoner. To many scholars, this thesis appears to offer adequate explanation for the presence of Pauline and non-Pauline features side by side in the language of the Pastorals.[20] But Roller's denial of the fact that Paul dictated his letters verbally is untenable (see p. 251), and there is not a trace of evidence for assuming that the writing was assigned to a secretary—and judging by the uniformity of the language always to the same one! Moreover, even though the secretary theory could perhaps explain the linguistic and stylistic variations from the rest of the letters of Paul, it can do nothing to resolve the difficulties yet to be described.[21] When Jeremias, following Roller, mentions as a formal sign of authenticity the fact that the letter formula of the Pastorals in its development corresponds exactly to the formula in the last of the Pauline letters, Col, this is not entirely accurate, since the introductory greeting (χάρις, etc.) of all three Pastorals differs from that of all the other Pauline letters,[22] and furthermore an imitator could just as well copy one of the latest as one of the earliest Pauline letters. The attempts to determine the identity of the amanuensis commissioned by Paul are all failures: nothing points to Tychicus,[23] who, according to II Tim 4:12; Tit 3:12 was with Paul. And in spite of certain linguistic parallels between Lk-Acts and the Pastorals, Luke,[24] who according to II Tim 4:11 was "the only one with me" (i.e., Paul), is simply out of the question because of the large theological differences between the two groups of writings. As a result even the secretary hypothesis cannot really refute the linguistic objections against even an indirect Pauline origin for the Pastorals.

[20] Benoit, JB; Holtz, Jeremias, Kelly, Spicq, Albertz, Feine-Behm; E. F. Harrison, Falconer, Moule.

[21] See also Michaelis, *Einl.*, 242 ff.

[22] Cf. Table 3 in Roller (see n. 10).

[23] Thus Jeremias; Albertz, 217.

[24] On Luke as amanuensis, see E. F. Harrison; Falconer; Moule; G. W. Knight, *The Faithful Sayings in the Pastorals*, 1968, 150 f. Without employing that concept, Strobel would like to show that the Pastorals are the work of Luke during the lifetime of Paul, and that later in Acts Luke refers back to them. But the lists—which must be critically reduced!—of word usage show only a strong commonality between Lk-Acts and the Pastorals, while a dependence on Lukan tradition in the Pastorals cannot be proved. And the alleged agreement in theology on the one hand reveals that both belong to a strongly hellenized Christianity, and, on the other hand, distorts the eschatology and the community situation in the Pastorals. The problem of the setting of the Pastorals is explicitly left out of consideration, although the author of Acts is supposed to be proved as their author!

2. *The historical situation presupposed.* I Tim presupposes that until a short time previously Paul and Timothy worked together in Ephesus, then Paul journeyed to Macedonia and left Timothy behind to carry on the struggle against the false teachers in Ephesus (1:3). The letter is an instruction to Timothy on how he is to carry on Paul's office during the latter's temporary absence (3:14; 4:13). But this instruction is not primarily aimed at Timothy. He did not require detailed repetition in written form, since he had been commissioned orally as the tested helper of the apostle (1:3 ff). Furthermore, Paul himself was to return soon. It is intended above all for the congregations in which Timothy is to carry out his official commission.

According to Titus, Paul had been in Crete and had left Titus behind there to carry on the organization of the communities which had begun in the cities of the island (1:5 ff). The aim of the letter is to offer instructions and to designate Titus in the eyes of his communities as the one formally commissioned by Paul, just as Timothy is designated in I Tim. Perhaps Zenas the lawyer and Apollos are the bearers of the letter (3:13). Paul will soon replace Titus with Artemas or Tychicus. Then Titus is to come as quickly as possible to Nicopolis, where he will spend the winter (3:12). Of the many cities with the name Nicopolis, only the one in Epirus comes seriously into consideration.

According to II Tim, in which the personal and the official are more closely interwined than in I Tim and Titus, Paul is in prison in Rome (1:8, 16 f; 2:9). He has already had a hearing once before the court; all his friends have abandoned him, but he has been saved from the jaws of the lion (4:16 f). Onesiphorus has visited him (1:17); now only Luke is with him (4:11). Crescens has gone to Gaul (or Galatia?), and Titus has gone to Dalmatia. Tychicus has been sent by Paul to Ephesus, Demas has abandoned him (4:10 ff), as have the brothers from Asia, among whom are Phygellus and Hermogenes (1:15). Alexander the coppersmith has proved to be a bitter enemy of Paul, and Timothy is being warned about him (4:14 f). Paul thinks that he is near death (4:6 ff, 18); Timothy should hurry to come to him (1:4; 4:9) before the coming of winter (4:21) and bring Mark with him (4:11). Paul was not long ago in Troas, where he left behind his cloak and his books with Carpus, which Timothy should bring with him (4:13), and in Miletus, where he had had to leave Trophimus behind because of illness (4:20). Obviously Timothy does not yet know all these things. Where Timothy is staying is not directly stated, but 4:13 suggests Asia, while in 4:19 the greeting to Priscilla and

Aquila suggests Ephesus, where according to I Tim Timothy had the center of his activities.

None of the situations here indicated fits into the life of Paul from Damascus to Rome as we know it from the remaining letters of Paul and Acts.[25]

I Timothy. After a three-year period of activity in Ephesus, Paul traveled from there to Macedonia (Acts 20:1 f; cf. 19:21). But on that occasion he did not leave Timothy behind in Ephesus but sent him ahead to Macedonia (Acts 19:22). Beyond that he planned to journey to Corinth and Jerusalem (Acts 20:2 ff) and did not return again to Ephesus (Acts 20:16 ff). And Timothy, who must already have met Paul again in Macedonia (II Cor 1:1), was among his companions on the journey to Jerusalem (Acts 20:4 ff). *Titus.* So far as we know, Paul in the course of his great mission had never been in Crete or in Nicopolis. The voyage of Paul the captive had passed along the shore of Crete (Acts 27:7 ff), but even while anchored in Fair Havens there was no opportunity for missionary activity. Whether Titus was with Paul at that time we do not know. The following winter Paul spent in Malta (Acts 28:1 ff) not in Nicopolis. *II Timothy.* Corinth, Troas, and Miletus were visited by Paul on the journey described in Acts 20:2 f, 5 f, 15 ff, but in II Tim (especially 4:9 ff) the reference is not to this journey which Timothy made as a companion of Paul, since he would have had no need to be informed about it in a letter. If Timothy at this time was journeying with Paul to Jerusalem (Acts 20:4 ff) he could not be commissioned to bring with him to Rome the things which had been left behind in Troas many years before (4:13). In Acts 21:29, Trophimus went with Paul to Jerusalem, whereas here (4:20) he is remaining behind ill in Miletus and Paul would have to wait several years to convey to Timothy information concerning this illness. During the imprisonment when Col was written, Paul had Timothy with him according to Col 1:1. If that took place in Rome (see §21.5), it would contradict his appeal to Timothy to come from Ephesus to Rome (4:9, 21).

The situations presupposed in the Pastorals, if they are historical,

---

[25] Binder's attempt to show that Titus was written in Nicopolis before the writing of Rom, that II Tim 4:9-22 and I Tim were written during the imprisonment of Paul in Caesarea, and that the rest of II Tim was written during the first imprisonment of Paul in Rome, is based on impossible exegesis of several texts and the unproved assertion that there was a later ecclesiastical editing of the Pastorals.

must belong to the time after Paul's imprisonment in Rome (Acts 28).

But is there historical information concerning the life of Paul beyond the end of Acts?

a. The conclusion of Acts 28:30 f does not clearly indicate what happened to Paul after his two-year imprisonment and his unhindered preaching in Rome. The assertions that Paul must have been set free because Acts 25:20 and 26:32 assume Paul's innocence to be the opinion of Festus and Agrippa,[26] and because the author of Acts would have had to mention the death of Paul if it had followed immediately on the events of Acts 28:30 f,[27] overlook the fact that we know absolutely nothing about the propriety of a decision in an appeal case in Rome. Further, the apologetic goal of Acts was obviously reached by 28:30 f and we cannot postulate what its author had to write or omit. In addition, Acts 20:25, 38 indicate clearly that in the understanding of the author of Acts Paul was no longer able to return to his churches in the East. Thus the conclusion of Acts leaves open the possibilities that, after two years of Roman imprisonment, Paul was either released or executed, but excludes the possibility of another journey to the East.

b. If Paul were released, then both the old reports could be correct that Paul carried on missionary activity in Spain as he had planned in Rom 15:24, 28. At the end of the first century, I Clem 5:7 concludes its praise of Paul the warrior of the faith with the words "he has taught justification to the whole world and has pressed on to the outer limits of the West [ἐπὶ τὸ τέρμα τῆς δύσεως ἐλθών], and has presented his witness before the authorities. So was he then taken out of the world." That was written from Rome, from which standpoint τὸ τέρμα τῆς δύσεως can only mean Spain. The Muratorian canon (see §35.3) says of Acts that Luke has written it as an eyewitness of the particular events "which he also demonstrates clearly in that he omits both the passion of Peter and the journey of Paul from Rome to Spain." In this are presupposed both the journey of Paul to Spain as a known fact and the martyrdom of Peter. Of course, the journey to Spain by Paul could be inferred by the author of the Muratorian Canon on the basis of Romans, which he knew, but this would not be true of the passion of Peter, and so there must in fact be a tradition behind this, which at the end of the second century could of course be legendary. Less likely is the theory that the Roman author of I Clem at the end of the first century no

---

[26] Guthrie.
[27] Michaelis.

longer had any independent tradition about the end of Paul's life; and since in Chs. 5 and 6 he clearly wants to discuss *Roman* martyrs, there is a real possibility that he knew on reliable grounds that Paul had carried on missionary activity in Spain and then died in Rome as a martyr.[28] Therefore there does exist the possibility or probability that Paul was set free in Rome and later became a martyr in Rome, but the situations presupposed by the Pastorals for journey to the East are not indicated in these witnesses any more than is a second Roman imprisonment during which Paul, following his first defense, expected to be detained so long that he could ask Timothy to come quickly to him before "the time of my departure has arrived" (II Tim 4:6 ff, 16, 18, 21).[29]

The report first mentioned by Eus. HE II. 22. 2, concerning a second Roman imprisonment of Paul during which II Tim was supposedly written and the related assumption of a journey of Paul to the East (which is defended by almost all modern representatives of the Pauline authorship of the Pastorals) is by no means adequately attested and must be characterized as an ungrounded construct.

3. *The struggle against the false teachers.* If the false teaching against which the Pastorals are directed is to be regarded as a uniform,[30] two indissolubly linked phenomena come into view: Judaism (or Jewish Christianity) and gnosis.

The opponents belong mostly to the περιτομή (Tit 1:10), want to be teachers of the Law (I Tim 1:7), start fights concerning the Law (Tit 3:9), and take money for their instructional lectures (Tit 1:11, I Tim 6:5). They place weight on "Jewish myths and human commandments" (Tit 1:14); they provoke "struggles and battles over the [Mosaic] Law" (Tit 3:9); their clinging to ritual commandments concerning clean and unclean (Tit 1:14 f) shows a Jewish root to this heresy. But what is said concerning Crete explicitly—that not only Jewish Christians are the perpetrators of this false teaching (Tit 1:10 ff)—is true also for I and II Tim. The false teachers pride themselves on their superior "knowledge" (I Tim 6:20), they engage in speculation about the order of the ages (I Tim 1:4; 4:7; Tit 3:9), and they practice asceticism through the prohibition of marriage and prohibitions concerning food (I Tim 4:3; Tit 1:14 f). Thus they represent a Gnostic

---

[28] See E. Dinkler, ThR, NF 25, 1959, 209 f.

[29] Marxsen, *Intr.,* 210 ff, shows that a second Roman imprisonment cannot be inferred from the Pastorals.

[30] In spite of Michaelis, *Past und Gefangenschaftsbriefe,* 102 ff.

standpoint: redemption by means of access into the mysteries of the upper world and through ascetic achievement. It is from that perspective that we are to understand the explicitly Gnostic idea "the resurrection of the dead has already occurred," a teaching recommended by two of the errant members of the community (II Tim 2:18). The false teachers make an impression on credulous minds, above all on highly excitable women (II Tim 3:6; Tit 1:11). This error is the forerunner of a fearful eschatological perversion which will come on all areas of life (I Tim 4:1 ff; II Tim 3:1 ff; 4:3 f).

If the concern in the Pastorals is over a Gnosticism more or less influenced by Jewish Christianity, this corresponds well to what we have already observed as the danger to the community in Colossae (see p. 339), and there is then not the slightest occasion, just because the false teachers who are being opposed are Gnostics, to link them up with the great Gnostic systems of the second century. It has repeatedly been proposed that the polemic against heresy in the Pastorals is directed against Marcion, and that in the ἀντιθέσεις τῆς ψευδωνύμου γνώσεως of I Tim 6:20 the author is countering the 'Αντιθέσεις of Marcion, that great work in which the words and deeds of the creator of the world and of the good god are set in opposition one to another.[31] This theory is disproved, however, by the dominant sharp antithesis in Marcion between the OT and Judaism, not to mention the fact that any polemic against specific Marcionite views is completely missing.

The Jewish-Christian-Gnostic false teaching which is being combated in the Pastorals is therefore thoroughly comprehensible in the life span of Paul, but it is already striking that, in addition to the predictions concerning the appearance of the false teachers "in the last days" (I Tim 4:1 ff; II Tim 3:1 ff, 13; 4:3 f), there are references to the present activity of the false teachers and instructions about combating them (I Tim 1:3 ff, 19 f; 6:20 f; II Tim 2:16 ff; 3:8; Tit 1:10 ff; 3:9 ff), so that there is no perceptible distinction between the teaching of the predicted false teachers and the present ones. But since nowhere in the Pastorals is there to be found any consciousness of living "in the last days," in the prediction of the End-time which evidently describes present phenomena it is clear that we are dealing only with a traditional literary motif (*vaticinium ex eventu*) which is now being employed by

---

[31] Thus Gealy; Goodspeed, Riddle-Hutson; von Campenhausen; J. Knox, *Philemon Among the Letters of Paul*, [2]1959, 74. Bauer is uncertain. Completely drawn out of thin air is the conjecture of Ford that the Pastorals' opponents are Proto-Montanists before the time of Montanus.

"Paul." Still more striking, however, is the matter of *how* the false teachers are opposed. Completely otherwise than in Col, the viewpoints of the false teachers are not contradicted by being confronted with the preaching about Christ, but they are countered simply by reference to the traditional teaching, from which the false teachers have erred and which is to be held fast (I Tim 4:1; 6:20; II Tim 1:14; 2:2; Tit 3:10 f). The lack of any substantive debate cannot be explained on the ground that Paul did not regard the prattle of the false teachers as being worth contradicting and assumed that Timothy and Titus themselves knew what should be said in refutation of the false teachers.[32] In that case there would be no necessity to make those addressed aware of the dangers of the false teaching in detail. This lack is much more readily explained by the fact that Paul is not writing these letters.

4. *The community situation.* In the instructions which Timothy and Titus receive for the strengthening of the churches, there stand in the foreground the officials: presbyters, bishops (I Tim 3:1 ff; 5:17 ff; Tit 1:5 ff) as the leaders of the community, ordained through the laying on of hands (I Tim 5:22), supported by the community (5:17 ff). In addition the deacons (3:8 ff) and the widows (5:9 ff). The chosen bearers of office are the guardians of order in individual communities. Accordingly full weight is attached to those requirements which they must meet. Concerning prophets, the bearers of the spirit, there is mention only in passing (I Tim 1:18; 4:14). The presbyters and bishops do not all have to be preachers and teachers (I Tim 5:17); but overseers capable of preaching the word are mentioned with extraordinary frequency in the letters, since they have to assume the lead in the struggle against the false teachers (I Tim 3:2; II Tim 2:2; Tit 1:9).

It cannot be determined exactly whether in the Pastorals in addition to a single ἐπίσκοπος (I Tim 3:2; Tit 1:7) there are a number of πρεσβύτεροι (I Tim 5:17, 19; Tit 1:5); that is, whether a monarchic episcopacy is presupposed,[33] or whether the bishop, though their head, is at least on a par with the presbyters,[34] or whether the ἐπίσκοπος is only another designation for the πρεσβύτεροι.[35] The question would be inconsequential if πρεσβύτεροι in the Pastorals were always (as it is in I Tim 5:1) an indication

[32] Guthrie.
[33] Von Campenhausen.
[34] Spicq.
[35] Schweizer, Brox (who considers the bishops to have been a narrower circle of elders, *Kairos*, 91 f); H. W. Bartsch, *Die Anfänge urchristlicher Rechtsbildungen, Studien zu den Past, ThF* 34, 1965, 107.

of age, and if ἐπίθεσις τῶν χειρῶν τοῦ πρεσβυτερίου (I Tim 4:14)
were to be translated as "the laying on of hands which makes
[one] a presbyter." [36] But this interpretation is contradicted not
only by the fact that this translation, which builds on a technical
rabbinical term, would be incomprehensible to a Greek reader and
contradicts the use of πρεσβυτέριον elsewhere in the NT,[37] but also
because in Tit 1:5 πρεσβύτεροι clearly indicates an office. Since,
however, in Tit 1:5, 7 πρεσβυτέρους shifts over into τὸν 'ἐπίσκοπον,
and since the superintendent role in I Tim 3:4 f and 5:17 is expressed in a similar manner for both the bishop and the elder,
the Pastorals apparently mean by ἐπίσκοπος and πρεσβύτερος the
same office, which is not yet monarchic, so that the change to the
singular τὸν ἐπίσκοπον in Tit 1:7 is explained on the basis of assuming a bishop's rule.[38] Since, therefore, the Pastorals know only
presbyter-bishops and in addition deacons (I Tim 3:8, 12), the
office of presbyter-bishop is a matter of a civic post which has
its claim to pay (I Tim 3:1; 5:17). According to I Tim 5:22,
installation in this office takes place through ordination by the laying on of hands on the part of Timothy, who was himself ordained
by the presbyters (I Tim 4:14), which in turn corresponds to the
installation of the presbyters by Titus (Tit 1:5). The attempt
has been made to see the office of Timothy and Titus as the real
bishop's or metropolitan's office to which individual churches are
subordinated,[39] or to perceive these disciples of the apostles as
apostolic delegates.[40] But "the presumed relationships remain much
too indefinite" [41] to establish a connection between the position of
both these disciples of apostles and a later church office. The "office
that Timothy and Titus embody according to the statements in
this letter never existed in the constitution of the church" and
can be explained only on the basis of the fictional address of the
Pastorals.[42] The actual task of Timothy and Titus consists rather
in preserving the correct teaching which they received from Paul
and passing it on to their pupils (I Tim 1:11; 6:20; II Tim 1:
14; 2:2). Though there is no chain of *succession* constructed from
Paul via his apostolic disciples to the holders of office in the congre-

[36] Jeremias and those cited by Spicq, *Comm.*, 728 n. 3; but even as early as
Calvin (see O. Hofius, ZNW 62, 1971, 128 f).
[37] P. Katz, ZNW 51, 1960, 27 ff, shows that there is no documentation in
Greek for πρεσβυτέριον=office of elders. Cf. also Spicq (see n. 36).
[38] Dibelius-Conzelmann.
[39] Easton, Gealy.
[40] Guthrie.
[41] Von Campenhausen, *Kirchliches Amt*, 117.
[42] Brox, *Kairos*, 87 f.

gations—not even in II Tim 2:2,[43] the chain of *tradition* is strongly stressed, whose beginning lies with the apostle (II Tim 2:2, 8). The presupposition of this central role of the tradition is a community which, in contrast to Paul's expectation of a near end of the age, is already making provision for the time after the death of the bearers of tradition appointed by the apostolic disciples (II Tim 2:1 f). Although Paul certainly did not know of the task of preserving the tradition through ordained presbyters (πρεσβύτερος is not meant in Paul as an indication of an office), the ecclesiastical office of the widows (I Tim 5:3 ff) whose essential task is continual prayer in connection with sexual abstinence[44] is totally foreign to Paul. Though it is questionable whether the Pastorals presuppose a distinction between clergy and laity,[45] still there is no longer any indication of active cooperation and responsibility on the part of the community.[46] In short, the Pastorals are a document "of an already rather far developed church law" [47] in a community which is establishing itself in the world as Paul never knew it.

5. *The theology of the Pastorals.* Consonant with these results is the whole compass of the theological realm of concepts and images of the Pastorals. Indeed, the Pastorals contain a string of statements which do correspond to the central ideas of Paul: the salvation of sinners through Christ (I Tim 15 f), revelation of the grace of God now through the appearance of Christ (II Tim 1:9 f), justification not by works (Tit 3:5), faith as a way to eternal life (I Tim 1:16). But along with them appears Hellenistic terminology which is totally foreign to Paul for describing the redemptive event: 'επεφάνη ἡ χάρις . . . σωτήριος . . . παιδεύουσα 'ημᾶς (Tit 2:10 f), ὅτε . . . ἡ φιλανθρωπία 'επεφάνη τοῦ σωτῆρος 'ημῶν θεοῦ (Tit 3:4), and the gift of redemption: προσδεχόμενοι τὴν μακαρίαν 'ελπίδα καὶ ἐπιφάνειαν τῆς δόξης τοῦ μεγάλου θεοῦ καὶ σωτῆρος ἡμῶν Ἰησοῦ Χριστοῦ (Tit 2:13), for God ὁ μόνος ἔχων ἀθανασίαν, φῶς οἰκῶν ἀπρόσιτον (I Tim 6:16), ὁ μακάριος καὶ μόνος δυνάστης (I Tim 6:15), and Christ ἐπιφάνεια, and σωτήρ for the earthly appearance

---

[43] Against Schlier; Schmithals; Brox, *Kairos,* 86. Correctly Dibelius-Conzelmann, 8; Strobel, 207.

[44] Müller-Bardorff. Bartsch (see n. 35), 129 f, stresses that no ascetic motive is behind this. The argument against an office of widows by A. Sand, "Witwenstand und Ämterstrukturen in den urchristlichen Gemeinden," *Bibel und Leben* 12, 1971, 186 ff, is not persuasive.

[45] Schlier, Spicq.

[46] "The statements about the theology of the church are missing" (Brox, *Kairos,* 83).

[47] Von Campenhausen, *Kirchliches Amt,* 129.

of Christ (II Tim 1:10; Tit 3:6), εἰς μεσίτης θεοῦ καὶ ἀνθρώπων (I Tim 2:5). And yet in spite of this terminology of glory, the Christology of the Pastorals in many of its expressions falls short of the Pauline Christology of preexistence.[48] So there is evident here a completely different christological stance than in Paul, and the assumption that Paul has enlarged the range of his ideas since the beginning of his first Roman imprisonment "in an entirely new situation" which has "left its impress" "in the introduction into his vocabulary of words which up to this time were alien to him,"[49] especially from the terminology of the imperial cult, makes Paul into a syncretist.

Still more striking than the divergent formulation of soteriological expressions is the description of Christian existence which one finds in the Pastorals. Frequently the proper behavior of Christians is called εὐσέβεια (I Tim 2:2; 4:7 f, 6:3, 5 f, 11; II Tim 3:5; Tit 1:1); also frequently πίστις continues to indicate the maintenance of the faith (e.g., I Tim 1:5) as well as the rule of faith (I Tim 3:9; 6:10; II Tim 4:7, and elsewhere), so that often the formula ἐν πίστει appears (I Tim 1:2; 2:7, and elsewhere). In parallel with πίστις in this sense stands also καλὴ διδασκαλία (I Tim 4:6), ἡ κατ' εὐσέβειαν διδασκαλία (I Tim 6:3), and especially ὑγιαίνουσα διδασκαλία (I Tim 1:10; II Tim 4:3; Tit 1:9; 2:1) or ὑγιαίνοντες λόγοι (I Tim 6:3; II Tim 1:13). What is required of Christians is ὑγιαίνειν ἐν τῇ πίστει (Tit 1:13; 2:2), σωφρόνως καὶ δικαίως καὶ εὐσεβῶς ζῆν (Tit 2:12), ἤρεμον καὶ ἡσύχιον βίον διάγειν ἐν πάσῃ εὐσεβείᾳ καὶ σεμνότητι (I Tim 2:2). This rationalistic ethical description of Christian existence and the Christian obligation corresponds to the use of the plural ἔργα ἀγαθά (as in Eph 2:10) which is stressed in the same way (I Tim 2:10; Tit 2:14) as ἀγαθή or καθαρὰ συνείδησις is in I Tim 1:5; 3:9, etc., and ἐν Χριστῷ Ἰησοῦ appears linked only with concepts of redemption, not with persons (e.g., II Tim 1:1; 1 Tim 3:13; see above, p. 373), πνεῦμα is used only twice as the designation for the spirit of God which is given to Christians (II Tim 1:14; Tit 3:5), and in the second passage is limited to salvation by λουτρὸν παλιγγενεσίας; σῶμα is not used at all. In addition to all this, although there is a maintenance of belief in a coming consummation (I Tim 6:14; Tit 2:13, etc.), there is no longer a living expectation of the End, as the careful preparation for coming generations shows.[50] In I Tim 1:15 the

[48] Cf. Brox, Comm., 51, 161 ff.
[49] Michaelis, Einl., 241; similarly Kelly, 45.
[50] See Bultmann, 468, 535; Schweizer, 67 f. Against Strobel, 207, one can scarcely speak of a "vigorously living expectation.."

same crude version of the Pauline self-judgment as is found in Eph 3:8 appears, so there can be no doubt that in these letters it is not Paul who speaks, but a Christian of later primitive Christianity. M. Dibelius has described as bourgeois this strongly Hellenistic-speaking Christianity which is establishing itself in the world,[51] and in so doing he has without doubt hit on an essential feature of this "piety," but it is also "a somewhat pallid Paulinism," [52] for the grace which has appeared equips the Christians first of all "for a pious life in this age" (Tit 2:11 f). If the Pastorals are incorporated in the presentation of Pauline thought,[53] the result is in any case an adulteration of Pauline theology. Even if the Pastorals do not reproduce the theology of Paul, it cannot by any means be said that their "bourgeois Christianity" did not in many ways represent a necessary new interpretation of the early Christian message on the assumption that the near expectation of the End was to be abandoned. Not the literary judgment concerning their authorship, but only critical-theological testing, can decide whether the Pastorals are an appropriate and necessary development of the Pauline message, or whether they represent a complete or partial adulteration.

4. Aim, Time, and Place of Writing

As literary entities the Pastorals are not of similar type. While I Tim and Titus contain instructions for the organization of the community, the instruction of the ranks of membership, and the combating of the false teachers, and thus constitute essentially books of church order, II Tim consists of a warning from Paul, who is about to go to his death, to his pupils to stand fast and to fight against the false teaching. That is, the letter has the form of a literary testament.[54] While in all three letters Paul clearly appears as the author, only in II Tim is there in any considerable compass personal correspondence. Since, on the basis of the numerous matters discussed, the Pastorals cannot be Pauline letters and therefore are

---

[51] See Dibelius-Conzelmann, Excursus on I Tim 1,10; 2,2.

[52] Bultmann, 536.

[53] Cerfaux in Robert-Feuillet, 481, in spite of assuming that the Pauline origin of the Pastorals is probably correct, maintains that the Pastorals "in purely scholarly work on Pauline theology or on the history of primitive Christianity ought to be used only with the requisite caution" (in agreement with Rigaux [see n. 10], 152)!

[54] "In I Tim and Tit, 'Paul' expounds church order; in II Tim, he expounds 'himself,' " Marxsen, *Intr.*, 201.

pseudonymous writings, it remains to be asked what is the character of this pseudonymity, i.e., how are the personal items in the letter to be evaluated, because many of these notes sound as though they were personal accounts free of any special pleading (especially II Tim 4:9-21; Tit 3:12 f). Since 1836 the thesis has been represented in various forms[55] that the Pastorals contain a series of fragments of genuine Pauline letters which the author of the Pastorals has integrated into his own literary structure. Harrison, especially, has been eager to put together from individual verses at first five and later three pieces which originally belonged together, and to show their place within the history of Paul up to the time of his imprisonment in Rome.[56] But two factors speak decisively against this assumption.[57] (*a*) It is inexplicable how such small letters or fragments of letters of Paul could have survived and why the author of the Pastorals would have inserted them into his letters in so splintered a fashion. (*b*) The ordering of these fragments, which only hint at their situation, within the life of Paul as it is known to us is at best only hypothetically possible. No certainty is to be gained as to whether a section really could be a genuine fragment because it fits into a situation which we know, and there simply is no other criterion of authenticity in this case. In any event, however, it is to be acknowledged that this theory, if it does possess any probability, presupposes the strange state of affairs that the author of the Pastorals writes in the name of Paul and then thinks he can give pseudonymous literature the appearance of authenticity by the insertion of genuine fragments.

One must, rather, recognize the fact that the three Pastorals, which presumably come from the same author, claim to be letters of Paul not only in their prescripts but also in the personal remarks and the mention of various persons and in the greetings.[58] It is extremely unlikely that the author intended only to express in the known form of a Pauline letter what according to his and his readers' opinion "the apostle would have said were he still alive," and that the readers should not assume that this really was a letter

[55] See the enumeration in Goguel, *Intr.*, IV, 2, 500 n. 1; and Spicq, *Comm.*, 200, nn. 1, 2.

[56] Cf. recently, e.g., Scott; Appel, Goguel, Heard, Henshaw, McNeile-Williams, Sparks; Falconer, Schmithals. Uncertain are Easton; Fuller; Michel.

[57] Cf. also Brox, Kelly; Guthrie, 224 ff; Marxsen; Schmid; Moule, 433 f, 448.

[58] Brox, BZ 1969, has proved that the feigned personal remarks belong to the literary level of the Pastorals, and has shown that the theological objective linked up with the insertion of such personal information may still frequently be perceived.

of Paul,[59] since nothing indicates that the letters were intended to have only the appearance of Pauline writing. Rather one must assume that the author is really writing in the role of Paul and that the pseudonymity in contrast with Eph is carried through emphatically,[60] but then it is questionable whether the biographical situation of any particular letter is thought through in such a way that the author made clear to himself in which of the periods of Paul's activity known to us or supposed by him this particular letter is to be placed.[61] Neither the presupposed situation of the individual letter nor the sequence of their composition can be determined therefore. The only thing that is clear is that the living authority of Paul[62] in the churches which are threatened by false teaching and which must adjust to the world in view of the delay of the parousia has led a representative of these communities, as guarantor of the Pauline legacy,[63] to employ the fiction of an apostolic writing to a recognized disciple of Paul in order to give his community information on how, through the correct ordering of the community, through sound teaching, and through a pious life, the false teachers may be rebuffed and the Christians "may become heirs . . . of the hope of eternal life" (Tit 3:7).

We know nothing concrete concerning the author. Against the hypothesis that it is Polycarp of Smyrna[64] is the striking literary difference between the Pastorals and Polycarp's Letter to the Philippians, to say nothing of the improbability (see above, p. 379) of setting the Pastorals after the time of Marcion. That the author possessed rabbinic training[65] is, in view of his strongly Hellenistic culture, extremely unlikely. Their origin in Asia Minor which is often conjectured is not demonstrable. The fact that the Pauline

[59] Harrison, ExpT 1955/56, 77.

[60] Von Campenhausen, *Kirchliches Amt,* 121 f, rightly makes a comparison with II Pet.

[61] Maurer's attempt to reconstruct the situation presupposed by the author, based on the assumption that the (undoubtedly secondary) reading προσελθόντες was in the author's text of Acts 20:5, cannot be brought off. See on the contrary Michaelis, *Einl.,* 250 ff.

[62] The vitality of the Pauline tradition in the circle of the author is shown by the numerous echoes of specific texts of the Pauline letters in the Pastorals (see A. E. Barnett, *Paul Becomes a Literary Influence,* 1941, 251 ff), as well as by the general points of linguistic contact between the Pastorals and Paul (cf. Spicq, *Comm.,* 180 f; Harrison, *Problem,* 87 ff).

[63] See Hegermann, 59.

[64] Thus von Campenhausen, *Polykarp; idem, The Formation of the Christian Bible,* 1972, 181 f. On the other hand, see Brox, *Comm.,* 57; Bartsch (see n. 35), 10 f, 140 n. 5; E. Käsemann, VF 1949/50, 1951/52, 215.

[65] Michel, Nauck; opposed is Hanson, 113.

heritage obviously comes "from a living community tradition" [66] tells as much against too late a date as does the rudimentary character of the gnosis which is being combated (see §24.3). As a time of writing, the most likely assumption is the very beginning of the second century.

II. The Letter to the Hebrews and the Catholic Letters

§25. GENERAL BACKGROUND

E. Fascher, "Katholische Briefe," RGG[3] III, 1959, 1198 f; A. Strobel, "Die Kirchenbriefe in der neueren Auslegung," *Lutherische Monatshefte* 3, 1963, Literaturheft, 1 ff.

In addition to the thirteen letters already discussed whose prescript names Paul as sender, the NT contains eight other letters which do not indicate Paul as sender. These eight letters are, of course, not all of the same type. In all the manuscripts known to us, one of them has as its superscription "to the Hebrews" and thus is identified in the church's collection by the name of those to whom it is addressed, as are the thirteen Pauline letters. Accordingly Heb was handed down in the tradition exclusively in association with the Pauline letters and owes to that fact its reception into the NT canon. It was regarded as a Pauline letter even though the name of Paul is not mentioned. Yet today, there can be no doubt that Heb did not originate with Paul, and so it is not being treated here in connection with the Pauline letters.

The situation is completely different, however, with regard to the so-called Catholic letters which in the manuscripts from the very beginning (cf. already $\mathfrak{P}$[72], see §38.b) are identified in the superscription by the name of the author, not of those to whom they are addressed (as in the case of the Pauline letters and Heb): James, I and II Pet, Jude, I, II, III John. The fact that there are seven of these letters and in addition twice seven Pauline letters (including Heb, cf. also the seven so-called Letters of the Apocalypse) is not the result of conscious intent but developed in a slow-changing historical evolution (see §36). Eusebius (HE II. 23. 24 f) was the first to speak of James, Pet, John, and Jude as the "seven Catholic letters." Some of them already bore the designation *Catholic* earlier, as in Dionysius of Alexandria (I John)[1]

---

[66] Käsemann.
[1] Eus., HE VII. 25. 7.

and in Origen (I John, I Pet, Jude, but also Barn). At the close of the second century, the anti-Montanist Apollonius of Rome attacked the Montanist Themison for fashioning a Catholic letter in imitation of the apostle (probably John).[2] Apparently I John was the first to bear the designation "Catholic epistle," which was a way of characterizing the indefiniteness and breadth of its address as contrasted with the specific address of II and III John. This designation was then transferred to the entire group of letters within which I John was classified. In any case among the earliest writers of the Greek church "Catholic" when used in relation to the non-Pauline letters of the NT does not mean recognized by the church as a whole, but "intended for general readership." But the designation preferred in the West, "Canonical letters," shows that the original meaning of the name was not strictly maintained.

Of the Catholic letters, it is clear that II and III John are not intended for general readership. Of the remaining five letters, only I Pet has a geographically specific address, while those addressed in James are not geographically localized and Jude and II Pet are addressed to all Christians. In I John it is not possible to determine who the readers are. Whether the individual writings were actually intended for general readership can be determined only by detailed research.

The Catholic letters stand in the canon of the Greek church after Acts and before the Pauline letters, but in the canon of the Latin church the Pauline letters precede the Catholic letters. As a result the position of the Catholic letters in modern textual editions varies. The sequence of the seven letters also changed considerably,[3] and the sequence of almost all the Greek manuscripts —James, Pet, John, Jude—was altered by Luther on the basis of critical views concerning the canon: Pet, John, Heb, James, Jude.[4]

§26. THE LETTER TO THE HEBREWS

Commentaries: see §41. Surveys of research: B. Rigaux, *Paul et ses lettres*, StN Subsidia 2, 1962, 201 ff; E. Grässer, "Der Hb. 1938–1963," ThR 30, 1964, 138 ff; F. F. Bruce, "Recent Contributions to the Understanding of Hebrews," ExpT 80, 1968/69, 260 ff. Research: W. Wrede, *Das literarische Rätsel des Hb*, 1906; R. Perdelwitz, "Das literarische Problem des Hb," ZNW 11, 1910, 59 ff, 105 ff; Th. Haering, "Gedankengang und Grundgedanken des Hb," ZNW 18, 1917, 145 ff; A. C.

---

[2] Cf. Eus., HE V. 18. 5.
[3] See C. R. Gregory, *Textkritik des NT* II, 1902, 856 f.
[4] See below, §37.

Purdy, "The Purpose of the Epistle to the Hebrews," in *Amicitiae Corolla: Festschr. R. Harris*, 1933, 253 ff; E. Käsemann, *Das wandernde Gottesvolk* FRLANT, NF 37, 1938; T. W. Manson, "The Problem of the Epistle to the Hebrews," BJRL 32, 1949/50, 1 ff (=Manson, *St.*, 242 ff); A. Oepke, *Das neue Gottesvolk*, 1950, 17 ff, 57 ff; W. F. Howard, "The Epistle to the Hebrews," Int 5, 1951, 80 ff; W. Manson, *The Epistle to the Hebrews*, 1953; G. Schille, "Erwägungen zur Hohepriesterlehre des Hb," ZNW 46, 1955, 81 ff; *idem*, "Erwägungen zu Hb 11," ZNW 51, 1960, 112 ff; F. Lo Bue, "The Historical Background of the Epistle to the Hebrews," JBL 75, 1956, 52 ff; C. P. M. Jones, "The Epistle to the Hebrews, and the Lucan Writings," StG, 1957, 113 ff; H. Thyen, *Der Stil der Jüdisch-Hellenistischen Homilie*, FRLANT, NF 47, 1956, 16 ff; Y. Yadin, "The Dead Sea Scrolls and the Epistle to the Hebrews," *Scripta Hierosolymitana* IV, 1958, 36 ff; J. Daniélou, *Qumran und der Ursprung des Christentums*, 1958, 148 ff; C. Spicq, "L'Épître aux Hébreux, Apollos, Jean-Baptiste, les Hellénistes et Qumran," RdQ 1, 1958/59, 365 ff; *idem*, DBS VII, 1966, 226 ff; H. Kosmala, *Hebräer—Essener—Christen*, StPB I, 1959, 1 ff; J. Schneider, RGG³ III, 1959, 106 ff; F. C. Synge, *Hebrews and the Scriptures*, 1959; W. Nauck, "Zum Aufbau des Hb," *Judentum, Urchristentum, Kirche, Festschr. J. Jeremias*, Bh. ZNW 26, 1960, 199 ff; F. J. Schierse, LThk V, 1960, 45 ff; R. Schnackenburg, *Die Kirche im NT*, 1961, 81 ff; J. Betz, *Die Eucharistie in der Zeit der griech. Väter* II, 1, 1961, 144 ff; W. L. Dulière, "Antioche et la lettre aux Hébreux," ZRGG, 13, 1961, 216 ff; J. Coppens, "Les affinités qumrâniennes de l'Épître aux Hébreux," NRTh 94, 1962, 128 ff, 257 ff; C. F. D. Moule, *The Birth of the NT*, HNTC, Companion Volume 1, 1962, 44 f, 53, 75 ff; H. Köster, " 'Outside the Camp' Hebr. 13:9-14," HTR 55, 1962, 299 ff; F. F. Bruce, " 'To the Hebrews' or 'To the Essenes,' " NTS 9, 1962/63, 217 ff; A. Vanhoye, "La structure littéraire de l'Épître aux Hébreux," StN, Studia 1, 1963 (on this see E. Haenchen, Gn 36, 1964, 36 ff); *idem*, *Der Brief an die Hebräer. Griechischer Text mit Gliederung*, 1966; F. V. Filson *"Yesterday"*: A Study of Hebrews in the Light of Chapter 13, SBT, 2nd Series 4, 1967; F. Schröger, *Der Verf. des Hb als Schriftausleger*, BU 4, 1968; G. Theissen, *Untersuchungen zum Hb*, StNT 2, 1969; E. Fiorenza, GANT, 262 ff; O. Hofius, *Katapausis*, WUNT 11, 1970; F. Renner, " 'An die Hebräer'—ein pseudepigraphischer Brief," *Münsterschwarzacher Studien* 14, 1970; E. Grässer, "Hb 1,1-4. Ein exegetischer Versuch," EKK Vorarbeiten III, 1971, 55 ff.

1. Contents

The structure of Heb is characterized by the fact that the exposition begins without any kind of epistolary introduction and is followed by a hortatory section which does not come at the end of the "letter" as in most of the letters of Paul. Rather, the exposition is interrupted again and again by paraenetic passages (2: 1-4; 3:7–4:11; 4:14-16; 5:11–6:12; 10:19-39; 12:1–13:17), and these are actually the real goal of the entire exposition.[1] Although the author has without doubt carefully planned the structure of his writing, the arrangement that he had in mind is not readily to be perceived, and as a result there are a multitude of proposed outlines for the writing.[2] The various attempts to differentiate between dogmatic and paraenetic parts,[3] or to demonstrate the structure based on christological ideas of the letter,[4] are no more convincing than the supposition that Heb is arranged according to the scheme of Greek hortatory addresses with a prologue 1:1–4:13), two expositions concerning Jesus as high priest (4:14–6:20; 7:1–10:18), and epilogue (10:19–13:25).[5] But the organization of the letter into five concentrically arranged sections with subdivisions framed by an introduction (1:1-4), a conclusion (13:20 f), and the secondary insertion of an accompanying letter (13:19, 22-25)—the outlines of which may be perceived by means of catchwords, inclusions, and announcements of the themes[6]— proves to be contrived. Against this, Nauck has shown that Heb is structured by means of the paraenetic passages, which in each case stand in parallel form at the beginning and the end of each large section,[7] and on the ground of this insight the following three main sections in the development of the ideas may be inferred:

1. 1:1–4:13. *Hear the word of God in the son, Jesus Christ, who is higher than the angels and Moses.* Following the stress in 1:1-4a on the eschatological superiority of the Son of God, bearer of the word of God, redeemer from sin, to the prophets and the angels, Jesus' superiority to the angels is indicated by scriptural proof: he has the superior name of Son (1:4b-14), so it is important to obey his word (2:1-4). He was made lower than the angels in that he became man and suffered death in order that according to the will of God he might become the perfect leader

---

[1] Kuss, Michel; Nauck.

[2] Cf. Grässer, ThR, 160 ff; Vanhoye, *La structure*, 11 ff.

[3] Héring; Thyen, Coppens.

[4] Cf. survey in Spicq, *Comm.*, I, 27 ff; Rigaux, 215 ff.

[5] Windisch; Haering.

[6] Vanhoye, in agreement with Montefiore: (1) a name higher than the angels (1:5–2:18); (2) Jesus the trustworthy and merciful high priest (3:1–5:10); (3) Jesus, high priest according to the order of Melchizedek, source of eternal salvation (5:11–10:39); (4) faith and endurance (11:1–12:13); (5) the peaceful fruit of righteousness (12:14–13:19). For criticism see Fiorenza, 268 f.

[7] Similarly Kuss, Michel; Grässer, Schierse, Fiorenza.

of his brethren to salvation (2:5-18). Jesus is also exalted above Moses, since he was only a servant in the house of God, but Jesus as Son is lord over the house of God (3:1-6). Christians therefore must guard themselves against forfeiting by their unbelief and disobedience the rest which God has promised them, as happened to the contemporaries of Moses (3:7-19). They must devote all their efforts to gaining a share in the promise which is theirs as the people of God (4:1-11), since the word of God is pressing them to a decision (4:12 f).

2. 4:14–10:31. *Let us approach the high priest of the heavenly sanctuary and hold fast our confession.* It is fitting to remain true to Jesus, the heavenly high priest (4:14-16). He demonstrates his high-priestly office by the fact that he has a share in human weakness, was ordained by God, and has completed his vocation through his obedience to suffering (5:1-10). A paraenetic intermediate section follows, which aims to stir up the reader to an awareness of the basic truths of the Christian faith which are here developed (5:11–6:20): they must overcome their lethargy, which actually seems to require a repetition of elementary Christian instruction (5:11–6:8); they must cling to the assurance of hope, since by an oath God has guaranteed to them the fulfillment of their hope (6:9-20). Then the portrayal of Jesus' high-priesthood is resumed: he is the perfect, eternal high priest according to the order of Melchizedek—holy, sinless, guarantor of a superior divine order whose everlasting priesthood has accomplished full redemption (Ch. 7). He is the heavenly high priest on the basis of his once-for-all, fully achieved offering of himself (8:1–10:18): as priest in the heavenly sanctuary he serves the new divine order, which is superior to that of the OT (Ch. 8). In place of the inadequate sacrifices in the earthly sanctuary he has offered himself, and through his own blood has achieved an eternally valid redemption (9:1-15). This once-for-all self-offering of Christ was necessary, however (9:16-28), and achieves a complete forgiveness of sins which was not possible by the offering of animals in the OT cultus (10:1-18). Now it is fitting to stand fast in confession of this high priest and not to fall back again into sin (10:19-31).

3. 10:32–13:17. *Hold fast to Jesus Christ, who is the initiator and the perfector of faith.* Since the readers earlier on remained faithful in suffering, they should now await the coming Lord in steady patience (10:32-39). There is a cloud of witnesses, from Abel to Jesus, the inaugurator and accomplisher of faith, to the strength of such faith which hopes for future blessings and is sure of invisible things (11:1–12:3). In the sufferings which are

the means of divine discipline it is appropriate to look to Jesus and thus to endure faithfully (12:4-17). No one should dare to neglect the unique revelation of God in Christ, or else he is subject to the fearful court of divine punishment (12:18-29). This implies the obligation of love to brother, of a modest and contented mode of life, of patient endurance and obedience to the leading powers (13:1-17). There follows the epistolary conclusion (13:18-25), personal greetings, and benediction.

2. The Tradition Concerning the Letter

The strong points of contact between I Clem (17:1; 36:2-5) and Heb can scarcely be explained on any other basis than that of a literary acquaintance of I Clem with Heb,[7a] even though neither the address nor the author of Heb is referred to. The superscription to the Hebrews ($\pi\rho\grave{o}s$ 'E$\beta\rho\alpha\acute{\iota}ous$) is first attested in Pantaenus,[8] then by Clement of Alexandria and Tertullian. It already appears in the earliest manuscript ($\mathfrak{P}^{46}$). This superscription obviously originates from the time of the collection of the early Christian letters and gives expression to the belief that Heb was written to Jewish Christians.[9] Marcion did not have the letter in his *Apostolikon*. According to the old Alexandria tradition, Heb is regarded as a letter of Paul, as is shown by Pantaenus' remarks concerning the lack of a prescript and the conjectures by Clement of Alexandria concerning Luke as the translator of a Pauline letter written in Hebrew,[10] as well as by the inclusion of the letter to the Hebrews in the Corpus Paulinum in $\mathfrak{P}^{46}$ (following Rom). Origen[11] believes it is Pauline but not directly so: a disciple (according to him, the tradition mentions Clement of Rome and Luke) has written down the ideas of the apostle, explaining them in his own way: $\tau\acute{\iota}s$ $\acute{o}$ $\gamma\rho\acute{a}\psi\alpha s$ $\tau\grave{\eta}v$ $\acute{\epsilon}\pi\iota\sigma\tauo\lambda\acute{\eta}v$, $\tau\grave{o}$ $\mu\grave{\epsilon}v$ $\grave{a}\lambda\eta\theta\grave{\epsilon}s$ $\theta\epsilon\grave{o}s$ $o\acute{\iota}\delta\epsilon v$.

In the whole of the Greek and Syrian churches, however, Heb

[7a] Against the denial of literary connection by Theissen, 34 ff; K. Beyschlag, *Clemens Romanus und der Frühkatholizismus*, BHTh 35, 1966, 351, see Grässer, EKK, 64 n. 74; Renner, 29 ff; O Knoch, "Eigenart und Bedeutung der Eschatologie im theologischen Aufriss des ersten Clemensbriefes," *Theophaneia* 17, 1964, 89 ff.

[8] In Eus., HE VI. 14. 4.

[9] Synge's contention that $\pi\rho\grave{o}s$ 'E$\beta\rho\alpha\acute{\iota}ous$ means "against the Jews" is not even tenable solely on the basis of the relationship to the polemical part of Heb.

[10] Eus., HE VI. 14. 2.

[11] In Eus., HE VII. 25. 11 ff; see WGK, NT, 15.

has been regarded consistently since the third century as canonical and Pauline. In most of the manuscripts it stands after the letters to the churches (after II Thess) and before the private letters (I Tim, etc.), but in the Western tradition it appears at the conclusion of the Pauline letters after Phlm. In the older manuscript tradition, its place in $\mathfrak{P}^{46}$ is unique: between Rom and Cor, although this order is also found later occasionally.[12]

In the West, Heb was not regarded as Pauline until the fourth century. It is missing from the Muratorian Canon as well as from the Canonical Index from Africa (*ca.* 360).[13] The anti-Montanist Gaius from Rome (*ca.* 200) does not consider it to be among the Pauline letters, and still at the time of Eusebius it is so regarded in the Roman church.[14] Cyprian does not mention it; Ambrosiaster knows it but does not attribute it to Paul;[15] Irenaeus and Hippolytus, who know Hebrew, dispute that it was written by Paul.[16] We first encounter a tradition concerning Barnabas as the author of the letter in Tertullian, who in *De pud.* 20 cites Heb as a noncanonical but widely known writing in the church: *extat enim et Barnabae titulus ad Hebraeos, a deo satis auctoritati viri* ("There exists [an epistle] to the Hebrews [with the] superscription of Barnabas, a man with adequate authority from God). The source of this tradition is unknown. It is only from the second half of the fourth century on, through the influence of interchange between Western and Eastern theologians, that the Western canon became equivalent to the Eastern, and Heb was recognized as the fourteenth Pauline letter (see §36.2).

In the time of the Reformation doubts again emerged, first in Erasmus and Cajetan in connection with Jerome's reports concerning the doubts in the early church.[17] Luther separated Heb from the Pauline letters and placed it with James, Jude, and the Apocalypse after the "really certain chief books of the NT." He did so chiefly because the letter asserts the impossibility of a second repentance after one has fallen away from the faith.[18] Melanchthon, Calvin, and Beza regard it as non-Pauline. The Council of Trent decreed the existence of fourteen Pauline letters in the NT,

---

[12] See W. H. P. Hatch, "The Position of Hebrews in the Canon of the NT," HTR 29, 1936, 133 ff.

[13] In Preuschen, *Analecta,* 37 (see below, §36.2).

[14] See Eus., HE VI. 20. 3; VI. 13. 6.

[15] I am indebted to A. Vanhoye's kind communication for this item concerning Ambrosiaster.

[16] See Th. Zahn, *Geschichte des Nt. Kanons* I, 1, 1888, 296 n. 2.

[17] See WGK, NT, 19 f.

[18] WGK, NT, 24.

thereby implying that Heb was written by Paul.[19] And from the end of the sixteenth century on, almost all Protestants reverted to the assumption of Pauline origin. Later, however, in the Enlightenment, a doubt was awakened anew.[20] In 1828, Bleek advanced conclusive evidence for the non-Pauline origin of the book.

The Pontifical Biblical Commission decided in 1914 that Heb should be reckoned among the genuine Pauline letters even though Paul may not have produced Hebrews *ea forma qua prostat* ("in the form in which it now stands").[21] Since then, however, almost without exception Catholic scholars as well have come to the conclusion that Heb does not come from Paul even indirectly but is the work of an independent pupil of Paul, and it has been declared explicitly that Catholic scholars are completely free with regard to the decisions of the Pontifical Biblical Commission insofar as what is at stake is not *veritas fidei et morum* ("truth concerning faith and morals"), and this, of course, applies to the question of authorship too.[22]

3. Literary Character

The structure of Heb is not the same as that of the letters of Paul. As a rule Paul has a main section dealing with questions of doctrine and controversial matters, which are followed by a hortatory concluding section. In Heb, on the other hand, the instructional presentations are interrupted again and again by shorter or longer exhortations (see §25.1). The style, language, and mode of expression too are very different from those of Paul. Only the conclusion of the letter in 13:18 ff is reminiscent of Paul and could be interpreted as having connections with Paul. But Heb has its own vocabulary and betrays a writer who, to a much greater extent than Paul, reveals dependence on the modes of expression of Greek

[19] J. Schmid, ThRv 62, 1966, 306, on the other hand, takes the position, "The dominant understanding of the Catholic exegetes assumes that the council has decided only the canonicity of the biblical books, not the question of their authorship." I take note of this, but cannot find that this interpretation accords with the wording of the Fourth Decree of Trent on 8 April 1546: *quatuordecim epistolae Pauli apostoli, ad Romanos . . . . , ad Hebraeos* ("fourteen epistles of Paul the apostle: to the Romans . . . to the Hebrews"), EnchB §60.

[20] J. D. Michaelis, see WGK, NT, 72.

[21] EnchB, §411–413.

[22] Cf. E. Vogt, Bb 36, 1955, 564 f; J. Dupont, RB 62, 1955, 414 ff; J. de Fraine, *Bibel-Lexikon*, ed. H. Haag, [2]1968, 226 f; R. E. Brown, "Rome and the Freedom of Catholic Biblical Studies," *Festschr. R. T. Stamm, Gettysburg Theological Studies* 3, 1969, 129 ff.

rhetoric.[23] The letter is among those written in the best Greek in the NT.

The theology of Heb is not Pauline either. At some points it recalls Paul: e.g., Christ the Son, the preexistent agent of creation; the redemptive death of Christ as the central message of salvation; the idea of the New Covenant of God (καινὴ διαθήκη), cf. I Cor 11:25; II Cor 3:6, 14; Gal 4:24; the decisive importance of faith; the use of the same quotations in scriptural proofs: 10:38 and Rom 1:17; Gal 3:11: Hab 2:4–2:6 ff and I Cor 15:27: Ps 8; echoes of Pauline exposition (cf. 5:12 ff with I Cor 3:1 ff). At some points the thought world of Heb must have been touched by the spirit of Paul, but in its developed form it is definitely differentiated from that of the apostle. None of the features mentioned was expounded in the same manner by Paul. Where Paul speaks of the resurrection of Christ, Heb mentions his exaltation to heaven. The consequence of Christ's saving act, which Paul comprehends in the reconciliation with God, Heb prefers to interpret as cleansing, sanctification, perfection (καθαρίζειν, ἁγιάζειν, τελειοῦν). The dominant major idea in the Christology of Heb—the high-priesthood of Christ—is completely lacking in Paul. The idea of the New Covenant is developed quite independently in Heb and is moved into the central place. Heb has nothing more to say about justification by faith rather than by the works of the Law than it does of the division between flesh and spirit or of being σὺν Χριστῷ. The concepts of Jew and Gentile play no role in the theological views of Heb. Quite differently from in Paul, the Law is seen by Heb essentially from its cultic side as an agency of expiation which is supposed to do away with the sins of weakness. It does not stand in opposition to the NT revelation of redemption, but is an incomplete preparation for it. Paul nowhere insists on the impossibility of a second repentance (6:4 ff; 10:26; 12:17).[24]

The setting of Heb in the history of religions is also quite different than for Paul. There is an obvious contact between Heb and the spirit of Alexandrian Judaism, especially with Philo. Heb uses and interprets the OT in the same way as the Alexandrians, who, unconcerned about the historical sense of the words of Scripture, devoted their attention to uncovering the deeper true meaning. This takes place through the artificial introduction of the author's own ideas (4:3), through the interpretation of proper names (7:2), through relating as many scriptures as possible to Christ (1:5 ff;

[23] Cf. Spicq, *Comm.* I, 351 ff.
[24] On the differences between Heb and Paul, see Spicq, *Comm.* I, 145 ff; E. Grässer, "Der Glaube im Hb," MbThSt 2, 1965, 64 ff.

2:6 ff, 12 f; 10:5 ff), through allegorical exposition which attributes to the word of Scripture a secret meaning which is related to the present (11:13 ff; 13:11 ff); but, above all, it is accomplished by setting over against each other OT persons and institutions and those in the NT in which they find their corresponding fulfillment, i.e., by typological exegesis. Melchizedek is the type of the true NT high priest (Ch. 7), the earthly tabernacle is but the shadowy form of the heavenly tabernacle (8:2, 5), the Law contains only the shadow form of the future realities, not the form of the things themselves (10:1). Heb refers constantly in new ways to the opposition between shadow and reality, earthly and heavenly (9:23 f; 8:1 ff), between created and uncreated (9:11), between present and future (9:1 ff; 13:14; 2:5), between transitory and enduring (7:3, 24; 10:34; 12:27; 13:14). The author wants to convince his readers that only the invisible, heavenly, future things constitute reality (11:1; 6:4 f; 11:16; 12:22; 10:1). Although a direct acquaintanceship of Heb with Philo is not likely,[25] there is clearly a strong influence from the spirit and modes of expression of the Hellenistic synagogues.[26] On the basis of form and content Heb stands closer to the Hellenistic literature and its cultural world than do the letters of Paul.

In addition, however, Heb, both in its Christology and in the prominent idea of "the wandering people of God," shows a clear connection with Gnostic conceptions,[27] and in each case this goes beyond what is to be observed in Paul. Although recently the attempt has been made in various ways to show the influence on Heb of the conceptual world of Qumran,[28] or at least a polemic attack against the Qumranian inclinations of the readers,[29] it has been shown to the contrary that there are no specific contacts between Heb and the Qumranian conceptual world, and that indeed the specific language of Qumran has no analogy in Heb.[30] Heb belongs completely, therefore, in the realm of influence of Hel-

---

[25] Against Montefiore, Spicq; Purdy, cf. Grässer, ThR, 177 f.

[26] Michel; Thyen, Coppens; Grässer (see n. 24), 95 ff.

[27] Albertz, Michaelis; Grässer, ThR, 179 ff; Theissen, 115 ff. Hofius, 153, on the other hand, characterizes "the interpretation of Heb on the basis of Gnostic traditions as a failure."

[28] Spicq, RdQ; Schnackenburg, Betz; and those mentioned in H. Braun, *Qumran und das NT* I, 1966, 240 ff (esp. 275).

[29] Yadin, Kosmala.

[30] Kuss, Montefiore; Vanhoye, *Situation du Christ*, 42; Grässer, ThR, 176; Coppens; Bruce, NTS; Braun (see n. 28), 278; M. de Jonge and A. S. van der Woude, "11 Q Melchizedek and the NT," NTS 12, 1965/66, 318; A. J. B. Higgins, "The Priestly Messiah," NTS 13, 1966/67, 231 ff.

lenistic Judaism and of the primitive Gnosticism which was originally associated with certain segments of Hellenistic Judaism.

In spite of some contacts, Heb diverges decisively on literary,
theological, and history-of-religions grounds from Paul and from
the Pauline letters; so the question concerning its literary character
is the more pressing, since Heb has no epistolary introduction, even
though it has a conclusion which is reminiscent of the letter style
of Paul. The attempt has been made to trace back the lack of any
introduction in the letter to accidental or intentional destruction[31]
or to the literary objective of the writer of the document,[32] and
on the ground of this supposition to regard Heb as indeed being
a real letter.

These proposals are of little use, however, since Heb shows no
epistolary character at all. Furthermore, 1:1 ff is without doubt
stylistically a real introduction which would not tolerate any prescript preceding it.[33] Others have sought to account for the presence of merely an epistolary conclusion by the conjectures that the
author, by adding this conclusion to the letter, has tried to give
to the whole the character of a Pauline letter,[34] or that the conclusion of the letter was added by another hand in order to send
on the nonepistolary text to another community.[35] But the mention of Timothy in 13:23 would scarcely have succeeded in arous-
ing in the minds of the original readers the impression of a Pauline
letter, and nothing suggests the addition of a conclusion by
another hand. Filson has shown to the contrary that the style and
tone of Heb already change at 13:1 and that Ch. 13 contains one
different admonition and communication after the other (13:1-19),
a solemn benediction in 13:20, concluding personal communications and greetings (13:22-24), and a short benediction (13:25),
as one finds similarly following each other in other NT letters.[36]
There is therefore no reason to doubt that 1:1–13:25 originally
belonged together.

---

[31] Feine, *Einl.*[6]; Jülicher; T. W. Manson. That Rom 16:25c, 26, 25b is the
remainder of an original protocol of Heb—truncated today, but actually pseudepigraphic (so Renner, 106)—is a fantastic hypothesis.

[32] Spicq, Windisch; Feine-Behm.

[33] Cf. Vanhoye, *Situation du Christ*, 14 f; Grässer, EKK, 70.

[34] Dibelius, Goodspeed; Wrede, Renner.

[35] Perdelwitz, Thyen. According to Vanhoye, "La structure," 219 ff, 13:19,
22-25 is an accompanying letter which contrasts with the first person singular
of 13:18, 21, although it cannot be determined whether the accompanying
letter comes from the same author as 1:1–13:18, 20 f; the peculiar position of
13:19 is not explained, however.

[36] Filson, 13 f, 22 ff.

It is extremely unlikely, however, that the entire writing was originally written as a real or alleged letter. Rather, everything leads to the conclusion that here we are dealing with a discourse. This is indicated not so much by the expression ὁ λόγος τῆς παρακλήσεως (13:22), with which is juxtaposed ἐπέστειλα ὑμῖν, as by the frequent allusions to the speech of the author (2:5; 5:11; 6:9; 8:1; 9:5), and, above all, the mention of the fact that time is lacking for the speech (11:32). On the other hand this speech obviously presupposes certain specific Christians as hearers whose special situation the author discusses (5:11 ff; 6:9 f; 10:25, 32 ff; 12:4 f), and the promise that he will soon come (13:19, 23) as well as the greeting (13:24) could make sense only to specific readers. The proposal offered by J. Berger (1797) that Heb was a sermon sent to another community has rightly gained widespread recognition, though in the altered form that the author sent on a sermon written down for a particular community together with an epistolary conclusion.[37] It cannot be proved that this sermon was based on a specific scriptural passage, and it is unnecessary to suppose that the sermon rests on earlier individual studies by the author.[38] Completely arbitrary are the proposals that exegetical and paraenetic sections have been compiled by a later redactor,[39] or that there is an interpolation in 5:11b-14; 6:5, 6b.[40] It is quite probable that the author used set traditions,[41] even if the reconstruction of the elements of the tradition by Schille is not convincing. What the objective of the author was in writing and sending on to a community known to him this unusually long sermon we can perceive only if we inquire who the readers are who are addressed.

4. Readers

Quite apart from its superscription, Heb was for a long time generally regarded as a letter written to Jewish Christians. In support of this, attention was called (1) to the manner of scriptural proof, which moves entirely within the realm of OT ideas and which presupposes precise knowledge of Jewish views and concepts,

---

[37] Cf., e.g., Kuss, Michel, Spicq, Strathmann, Windisch; Albertz, Klijn, Mc-Neile-Williams, Wikenhauser; Grässer, ThR; Oepke, Nauck, Schierse, Fiorenza.
[38] Michel, Spicq; Schneider.
[39] Synge.
[40] Kosmala.
[41] As in 1:3; 11:1-38; 13:14; cf. Michel in loc.; Grässer, EKK, 64 f.

above all of the OT sacrificial system; (2) to the extent of the OT citations and the breadth of the scriptural proof; and (3) to the theological arguments aimed at Jews concerning the superiority of the New Covenant over the old, concerning the high-priesthood of Jesus and his sacrifice, and especially concerning the superiority of Jesus to Moses (3:1 ff). Thus the readers were sought in the original home of Jewish Christianity, Palestine or Jerusalem.[42] More recently this thesis has been presented in a different form: namely, that the readers addressed were Essene priests or former members of the Qumran community[43] who had not yet accepted Jesus as Messiah.[44]

But neither the priestly nor the Qumranian origins of the readers can be demonstrated with any probability,[45] and the clear indication is that they were Christians (3:1f, 4; 6:4-6, 9; 10:23, 26; 12:22-24). Furthermore it is certain that the letter was not addressed to Jerusalem. The primitive church was poor and required support from outside communities (cf. the collections for them in Antioch and in the mission territory of Paul). The recipients of Heb, however, have themselves on several occasions supported others (6:10). 2:3 f and 13:7 do not fit for the members of the primitive church, and the one persecution to which the readers were subjected soon after their conversion (10:32 ff) does not coincide with what is known from Acts concerning the periods of suffering of the Christians in Jerusalem.

The hypothesis of Jewish-Christian readers outside Palestine, whether they are thought of in general terms[46] or limited to a Jewish-Christian minority,[47] is utterly improbable in view of the reference to the necessity of faith in God (6:1; 11:6). And that the readers evidenced an inclination to Judaism[48] is nowhere to be perceived.

Much more probable is the proposal, first advanced in 1836 by E. M. Roeth, that the readers were predominantly Gentile Christians or simply Christians.[49] Very early the Gentile Christians were

---

[42] Recently, e.g., Harrington; A. Ehrhardt, *The Framework of the NT Stories*, 1964, 109.

[43] Daniélou; Spicq, RdQ, DBS.

[44] Yadin, Betz; cf. also Kosmala.

[45] See de Jonge–van der Woude (see n. 30), 318.

[46] E.g., Benoit, JB; Bruce, Strathmann; Appel, Cambier in Robert-Feuillet, Harrington, Harrison, Mariani, Meinertz, Schäfer; Coppens; Bruce, NTS; Filson.

[47] Bruce, W. Manson, Spicq; Guthrie, Lo Bue; Howard.

[48] W. Manson; Appel; Moule, 76; Bruce, NTS, 232, and those mentioned by Grässer, ThR, 148.

[49] Cf. Kuss, Michel, Windisch; Albertz, Feine-Behm, Henshaw, Jülicher-Fascher, Marxsen, Michaelis, Schelkle; Wrede, Käsemann, Oepke, Schierse.

regarded as heirs of the blessings and the promises of the OT
people of God. As Christians they are the true Israel, the chosen
people of God (Gal 6:16; I Cor 10:1 ["our fathers"]; I Pet
2:9) for whom the OT was written (Rom 15:4; I Cor 10:11; I
Pet 1:12). The missionary activity of early Christianity had made
the OT into the Bible of the new community everywhere, and
accordingly it had for them unassailable authority and effective-
ness as a source of proofs. Since Paul offered in Gal difficult scriptural proofs to simple Gentile Christians, how much more readily
could this occur among readers who, judging by the elegant style
of such a letter as Heb, must have stood on a considerably higher
cultural level. If the author had wanted to inculcate Jewish Christians once again with basic Christian teachings (5:12 ff), he would
not have had to mention "conversion from dead works and faith
in God, teaching concerning baptism, the laying on of hands, the
resurrection of the dead and eternal judgment" (6:1 f), but rather
the personal work of Christ and the presence of God in the spirit.
What he enumerates are the fundamental articles of the Gentile
missionary preaching,[50] and also the warning against "falling away
from the living God" (3:12) points more readily to Gentile than
to Jewish-Christian readers. Heb knows nothing of any hostility
between Jews and Gentiles, has not once the words "Jew" and
"Gentile," and the author writes to Christians as Christians.

These Christians are not threatened by a specific false teaching,
and the letter has no polemical character.[51] What is referred to
in the isolated warning against "variegated and strange teachings"
and against "foods" which "do [not] strengthen the heart" cannot be clearly determined. Perhaps the Jewish cult (cf. 9:10) is
understood as the type of all human cultic endeavors in favor of
the suffering and doing of good "outside the camp" which is made
possible through grace (13:13, 16).[52] In any case, the Christians
addressed are not seriously endangered by the false evaluation of
foods mentioned in 13:9, but by lethargy of faith, by fear of
suffering, by a want of trust in the community (5:11 f; 10:25,
35; 12:3, 12 f; 13:17) in spite of its praiseworthy Christian past
(6:10; 10:32 ff). By portraying the greatness of the redemption
that is at stake and referring to the eschatological urgency of an attitude of renewed seriousness toward the enlightenment which was
at one time received (6:4), the author of Heb warns his readers

---

[50] See Michel, Windisch on 6:1 ff.

[51] Against Theissen, 79.

[52] Thus Köster, as well as Fiorenza, 280; cf. also Kuss, *Comm.*, 218 f. Opposing are Theissen, 76 n. 2; Grässer (see n. 24), 30 n. 94.

concerning this "general lassitude." [53] Thus it is clear that we are in the midst of a later period of early Christian development.

Where the readers are to be located is a question which has been answered in many different ways as a result of the lack of concrete information in Heb. Corinth,[54] Ephesus,[55] the Lycus valley,[56] Antioch,[57] Cyprus,[58] have been proposed. Recently it has often been suggested that the letter was written to Rome[59] or more generally to Italy.[60] For Rome, the following can be adduced: (1) Heb is first attested in Rome in I Clem 2. (2) The designation of the leaders of the community as οἱ ἡγούμενοι (13:7, 17, 24) is the same as in I Clem 1:3; cf. 21:6; Herm, Vis II. 2. 6 and III. 9. 7 (προηγούμενοι). (3) In 13:24 "those from Italy greet you" οἱ ἀπὸ τῆς Ἰταλίας is most naturally understood if the author is writing from outside Italy and the Italians who are in his vicinity send greetings to their countrymen. But the expression can also be understood as a greeting from Italy,[61] and so Rome or some other Italian community as the destination of Hebrews remains only one possibility.

5. Author

Since the author of Heb keeps his identity completely in the background—only the close connection with Timothy (13:23) points to the Pauline circle, if indeed the well-known companion of Paul is intended—the most diverse possibilities have been proposed, of which the following may be mentioned:

1. Paul. This proposal is represented nowadays even from the Catholic standpoint only very rarely[62] and has proved to be untenable (§26.3).

2. Luke. Clement of Alexandria (see §26.2) on the basis of the kinship of style with Acts held that Luke was the translator of a letter written by Paul in Hebrew. But Heb is not a translation

---

[53] Kuss; see also Fiorenza, 198 f; Grässer (see n. 24), 202 f.

[54] Lo Bue.

[55] Howard.

[56] T. W. Manson.

[57] Spicq.

[58] Riggenbach.

[59] E.g., W. Manson, Strathmann; Feine-Behm, Goodspeed, Grant, McNeile-Williams, Michaelis; Bruce, NTS, 232.

[60] E.g., Michel; Albertz, Fuller.

[61] See Spicq, Comm. I, 261 ff.

[62] Mariani, 416 f, describes the hypothesis of a secretary as worth considering.

and varies so sharply in style and theological distinctiveness that the author of Acts as the author of Heb is not really to be considered.

3. Clement of Rome. The old hypothesis which was already known by Origen (see §26.2) founders on the impossibility of conceiving that Heb and I Clem are the work of the same man, as well as on the assumption of literary dependence of I Clem upon Heb.

4. Apollos. Considered by Luther and represented with vigor by Bleek, this hypothesis has found many adherents.[63] This Jewish-Christian biblical scholar from Alexandria, who was also instructed in Greek rhetoric (Acts 18:24 ff) and who carried on a mission alongside Paul but independently of him (I Cor 1:12; 3:4 ff; 16:12), could be conceived of as the author of Heb. But we do not know whether Apollos was active as a writer, and it cannot be proved that he was the only one among the Christian διδάσκαλοι of the apostolic times who could have written the letter to the Hebrews.

5. Barnabas. In accordance with the tradition attested by Tertullian, Barnabas has frequently been proposed as the author of Heb.[64] But could Barnabas, a Levite from Cyprus (Acts 4:36) who later took up residence in Jerusalem and was a highly regarded member of the community there (Acts 9:27; 11:22) have so completely abandoned the position of the primitive community with regard to the law and the cultus? Could he have been so rhetorically trained and so Hellenistically oriented as to become the author of Heb?

It is in reality no longer possible to determine the identity of the author. This conclusion was reached by Origen and has been adopted from the time of Eichhorn and De Wette down to and including most more recent scholars. W. Manson would like to see the author in direct succession to the teaching of Stephen, but there is not even a more than occasional contact with the speech of Stephen in Acts 7,[65] and the indubitably Hellenistic-Jewish- and Gnostic-influenced character of Heb speaks against the origin of the author of Heb in Palestine.[66] The thesis of Jones that Heb is related most closely within the NT with Lk-Acts linguistically

---

[63] Recently Montefiore, Spicq; Appel, Zahn; T. W. Manson, Howard, Lo Bue; the hypothesis is considered by R. M. Grant, Harrison, Harrington.

[64] Recently Riggenbach, Strathmann.

[65] See Grässer, ThR, 191.

[66] The author of Heb manifests no "Jewish-rabbinic attitude" (against Schröger, 287; Renner, 126; correctly Vanhoye, Situation, 16).

and conceptually is appropriate for the conceptions only in a very limited sense, and proves only that Heb, like the author of Lk-Acts, is influenced by the thought world of later Gentile Christianity.[67] Accordingly the place of writing of the book cannot be determined exactly, although a variety of conjectures have been offered: Rome, Egypt, Ephesus, Antioch.

6. Time of Writing

To the obvious question whether Jerusalem is still standing (13:13 f) and the temple cultus is still in process (9:9 f) Heb gives no answer. In its timeless scholarly movement of ideas only the OT sanctuary plays a role, not the Herodian temple; an origin before 70 cannot be inferred either from the silence concerning the catastrophe of the year 70 or from the expression in 8:13 that the Old Covenant is "in the course of passing away." [68] On the contrary, the persecutions which the community has experienced (10:32-34) and the spiritual proximity to Lk-Acts point in all probability to the post-Pauline period. Heb was, however, written before 96 (I Clem);[69] Timothy, who as a young man had been a mission aide of Paul, is still living (13:23), writer and readers belong to the second Christian generation (2:3), the new suffering which threatens the readers (12:4) may point to the time of Domitian (81–96). Accordingly the letter was probably written between 80 and 90.

§27. THE LETTER OF JAMES

Commentaries: see §41. Research: A. Meyer, *Das Rätsel des Jk*, Bh. ZNW 10, 1930 (on this see M. Dibelius, ThR, NF 3, 1931, 216 ff, and G. Kittel, DLZ 3, Folge 3, 1932, 50 ff); H. Schammberger, *Die Einheitlichkeit des Jk im antignostischen Kampf*, 1936; G. Kittel, "Der geschichtliche Ort des Jk," ZNW 41, 1942, 71 ff (on this see K. Aland, ThLZ 69, 1944, 97 ff); G. Kittel, "Der Jk und die Apostolischen Väter," ZNW 43, 1950/51, 54 ff; W. L. Knox, "The Epistle of St. James," JTS 46, 1945, 10 ff; J. Bonsirven, DBS 4, 1949, 783 ff (bibl.); H. J. Schoeps, *Theologie und Geschichte des Judenchristentums*, 1949, 343 ff; W. Bieder, "Christliche Existenz nach dem Zeugnis des Jk," ThZ 5, 1949,

---

[67] Cf. Ph. Vielhauer, ThR, NF 31, 1965/66, 131.

[68] Thus, e.g., Bruce, Vanhoye, *Situation*, 50; Grant, Guthrie, Harrington, Harrison, Mariani; Moule.

[69] Dulière's dating of 115/17 is arbitrary.

93 ff; M. Lackmann, *Sola fide*, BFChTh II, 50, 1949; D. Y. Hadidian, "Palestinian Pictures in the Epistle of James," ExpT 63, 1951/52, 227 f; G. Eichholz, *Jakobus und Paulus. Ein Beitrag zum Problem des Kanons*, ThE, NF 39, 1953; *idem*, EKL II, 1958, 234 f; *idem, Glaube und Werke bei Paulus und Jakobus*, ThE, NF 88, 1961; J. Jeremias, "Paul and James," ExpT 63, 1954/55, 368 ff; H. Thyen, *Der Stil der Jüdisch-Hellenistischen Homilie*, FRLANT, NF 47, 1956, 14 ff; L. E. Elliott-Binns, *Galilean Christianity*, SBT 16, 1956, 45 ff; M. H. Shepherd, "The Epistle of James and the Gospel of Matthew," JBL 75, 1956, 40 ff; E. Lohse, "Glaube und Werke—zur Theologie des Jk," ZNW 48, 1957, 1 ff; J. B. Souček, "Zu den Problemen des Jk," EvTh 18, 1958, 460 ff; W. Marxsen, *Der "Frühkatholizismus" im NT*, 1958, 22 ff; O. Michel, CBL, 586 f; K. Aland, RGG³ III, 1959, 526 ff; J. Blinzler, LThK V, 1960, 861 ff; G. Braumann, "Der theologische Hintergrund des Jk," ThZ 18, 1962, 401 ff; M. Gertner, "Midrashim in the NT," *Journal of Semitic Studies* 7, 1962, 283 ff; O. F. Seitz, "James and the Law," StEv II, TU 87, 1964, 472 ff; E. Trocmé, "Les Églises pauliniennes vues du dehors: Jacques 2, 1 à 3, 13," StEv II, TU 87, 1964, 660 ff; P. Stuhlmacher, *Gerechtigkeit Gottes bei Paulus*, FRLANT 87, 1965, 191 ff, 229; R. R. Halson, "The Epistle of James: 'Christian Wisdom'?" StEv IV, TU 102, 1968, 308 ff; J. N. Sevenster, *Do You Know Greek?*, Suppl. NovTest 19, 1968; F. O. Francis, "The Form and Function of the Opening and Closing Paragraphs of James and I John," ZNW 61, 1970, 110 ff; U. Luck, "Der Jk und die Theologie des Paulus," *Theologie und Glaube* 61, 1971, 161 ff.

1. Contents

James begins (1:1) with the prescript "James, a slave of God and of the Lord Jesus Christ to the twelve tribes in the Diaspora, greeting." The content of the letter (1:2–5:20) does not disclose any orderly sequence of ideas. It represents, rather, a chain of individual admonitions of larger and smaller compass, of groups of sayings and short sayings which more or less randomly follow one another. The catch-phrases of the admonitions are: Rejoice in the testings, which are a school of probation before God, from whom come only good gifts (1:2-18); hear the word of God, but also act according to it (1:19-27); guard yourself from partiality toward the rich against the poor; rather fulfill the law of love (2: 1-12); then in catchword fashion (2:13) there is appended a reference to the necessity of showing mercy; simple faith is worthless and right action is what is important, as the examples of Abraham and Rahab show (2:14-16); guard your tongues (3:1-12); abandon earthly wisdom, seek the heavenly wisdom (3:13-

18); do not be contentious, but have peace, which comes from being humble before God (4:1-10); do not speak slander (4:11-12); you merchants, do not forget as you formulate your plans that you stand before God (4:13-16); to this is appended in catchword fashion the assertion that man must do good (4:17); you rich, acknowledge your guilt and your deserved punishment (5:1-6); you brothers, be patient in view of the near judgment of God (5:7-11); do not swear (5:12); reference to the efficacy of prayer (5:13-18); save your erring brother (5:19-20). With this writing breaks off without any concluding greeting.

2. The Fate of the Letter

From ancient times to the present, the opinions concerning the origin and character, time and value of James diverge widely from another.[1] As early as I Clem and Hermas there are echoes of James, but they are not so clear that they cannot be understood as originating in common dependence on a paraenetic tradition.[2] The letter is missing in the Muratorian Canon, and in the chief witnesses of the Vetus Latina. It is never quoted by Tertullian, Cyprian, Irenaeus, or Hippolytus. The first certain traces of James to appear come 200 years later in Palestine and Egypt, in the spurious letter of Clement of Alexandria, *De virginitate*, in the papyrus fragment $\mathfrak{P}^{20}$, and in Origen, who cites it chiefly as "scripture," but once as ἡ φερομένη Ἰακώβου ἐπιστολή,[3] and thus gives the impression that it is disputed. Eusebius[4] still declares James to be among the antilegomena (see below, §36.1) but for the first time mentions the Lord's brother as the one acknowledged by many to be the author. In the Syrian church reservations about James were not silenced even after the acceptance of James into the Peshitta; Theodore of Mopsuestia rejects it. In the Greek church, however, James has been generally recognized since the time of the synods of Laodicea (360) and Athanasius. In the West the oldest attestation is the Codex Corbeiensis (ff), which reproduces an Old Latin translation from the fourth century. Under the influence of Hilary, Jerome, and Augustine, James was recognized as canonical by the synods of Rome (382) and Carthage (397). Yet

[1] Cf. Dibelius-Greeven, 74 ff; Meyer, 8 ff.
[2] Thus Mitton, 220; Dibelius-Greeven, 43 ff. Mussner, 35 f, assumes the dependence of I Clem on Jas.
[3] Origen, *Comm. on Jn.* 8. 24 (ed. Preuschen), 325.
[4] Eus., HE II. 23. 25; II. 25. 3.

Jerome's doubts[5] about the authenticity of James were reported in the Middle Ages, and on them were grounded the cautious doubt of Erasmus and the sharp polemic of Luther.

Luther's disparaging judgment on the letter is known:[6] it teaches justification by works in contradiction to Paul, does not preach Christ but the Law and a generalized faith in God, James does not belong in the Bible among the proper chief books of the NT ("compared to them it is simply an epistle of straw, since it has in it no quality of the gospel"). It is disorganized and Jewish and thus not an apostolic writing, even though some good statements may be contained within it. Luther would have preferred to omit it from his Bible, and still in 1543 he rejected the letter as a basis for dogmatic proof.

The opposition to James on dogmatic grounds in the ancient church (not apostolic and so not canonical), and in Luther (incompatible with the Pauline gospel), was replaced in the nineteenth century by doubts about its authenticity on historical-critical grounds. De Wette demonstrated that the letter was not authentic chiefly on the ground of its language: the fluent Greek is hardly to be attributed to James the brother of the Lord. The tendenz-criticism of the Tübingen school proved that the letter did indeed combat Paul's doctrine of justification by faith, but no longer stood in the position of earliest Jewish Christianity with its stress on the Law. Accordingly it regarded the book as a pseudepigraphic work of the second century, representing a Catholicism that was approximating Jewish Christianity. Even after Baur's scheme of the history of Christianity was discredited, the view was widely held that James belonged in the postapostolic period.[7] A new turn was given to research concerning James by the thesis of Spitta and Massebieau (1895/96) that James was a Jewish writing which had been transformed into a Christian writing by the introduction of the name of Christ in two places (1:1 καὶ κυρίου Ἰησοῦ Χριστοῦ; 2:1 τοῦ κυρίου ἡμῶν Ἰησοῦ Χρίστου). A. Meyer went farther in this direction in that he explained James to be a Christian revision of a Jewish basic writing, which went into an extensive allegory concerning Jacob (James) and his twelve sons. The underlying Jewish writing, which is reminiscent of the

---

[5] Jerome, *Vir. ill.*, 2.

[6] Luther, Preface to the NT; Preface to the Epistles of James and Jude (1522) and elsewhere; see Mussner, 42 ff; Meyer, 4 ff; WGK, NT, 24 ff.

[7] Recently Dibelius-Greeven, Easton, Kuss, Michl, Reicke, Ropes, Windisch-Preisker; Fuller, Goodspeed, Henshaw, Jülicher-Fascher, Marxsen; Aland, Eichholz, Thyen, Shepherd, Lohse, Souček, Seitz, Trocmé.

Testaments of the Twelve, skillfully developed artificial interpretation of the names of the family of Jacob. Some scholars have been attracted to this clever hypothesis of A. Meyer,[8] but most reject it as too artificial, since there is no example of an allegory of names which stands only in the background of the text without any reference to it in the foreground. Dibelius classifies James under the category of early Christian paraenesis and considers it to be a writing without any perceptible historical connection: James offers a collection of material from the paraenetic tradition, a succession of admonitions of general ethical content. Nevertheless there has been up to the present no lack of scholarly theologians who understand James in the first instance on the basis of the sayings of Jesus, specifically the sermon on the mount, and who therefore consider the letter to be the work of a man of the first generation.[9] But even within this circle there is no unity on whether James knew Paul and his theology, whether he was writing before the time of Paul as the oldest primitive Christian writer known to us,[10] or whether in the polemic of his letter he attacks Paul or a misunderstood Paul and thus belongs in the later apostolic time. In order to avoid the doubts that have been raised about James the Lord's brother as author, an unknown Christian with the common name of James has also been brought into consideration.[11]

3. The Literary Distinctiveness of James

According to 1:1 this letter is a writing of a Christian named James "to the twelve tribes in the Dispersion." This designation of the recipients is ambiguous. It could indicate Jews outside Palestine,[12] but the content of the letter in no way indicates that a Christian is speaking to Jews. Indeed any sign of a missionary writing is lacking. If Christians are the intended readers, then one might suppose that Jewish Christians of the Dispersion are in-

[8] Easton, Windisch-Preisker; Jülicher-Fascher; Marxsen (for an earlier stage of the tradition); Thyen; A. M. Farrer, *A Study in Mark,* 1951, 320.

[9] E.g., Mitton, Mussner, Ross, Schlatter, Tasker, Feine-Behm, Grant, Guthrie, Harrington, Harrison, Heard, Klijn, Mariani, Michaelis, Sparks, Wikenhauser; Kittel, Lackmann, Elliott-Binns, Michel. Sidebottom; Schelkle; Blinzler consider it possible that it was written by a later Jewish Christian.

[10] Thus Michaelis; Kittel. Guthrie even assumes that Paul is polemicizing against a misunderstood James!

[11] See Hauck, Marty, Appel, Henshaw, de Zwaan.

[12] Cf. Schlatter.

tended.[13] But that is also unlikely, because one would hardly designate Jewish Christians as "the twelve tribes." The only remaining possibility is that James—in the same sense as Gal 6:16; Phil 3:3; I Pet 1:1, 17; 2:11; Rev 7:4; 14:1; Herm., Sim. IX. 17. 1—is addressing Christians as the true Israel that lives on the earth in a foreign country and has its home in heaven. And yet that is not expressed clearly. The obscurity of the destination, the impersonal standpoint of the content, the lack of any conclusion to the letter make it doubtful that James is a letter at all. The supposition that the epistolary address in James was tacked on only later[14] is improbable in view of the play on words χαίρειν (1:1) and χαράν (1:2), but the whole writing arouses the impression of being an essay in the form of a letter[15] which is aimed at a broad circle of readers that cannot be sharply defined. The supposition that 2:2 f; 3:1 f; 4:13 ff; 5:1 ff reflect concrete incidents in a particular community[16] overlooks the typical character of the admonitions which castigate so severely contemporary phenomena such as these. Regarded from the form-critical standpoint James gives rather the impression in its entirety that it is a paraenetic instructional writing composed from strings of sayings and small essays. Consonant with this literary character is its incohesiveness: outside of the three longer statements 2:1 ff, 14 ff; 3:1 ff, there are only small groups of sayings or indeed individual sayings which occasionally are bound together by catchwords. Often, however, they show no perceptible connection of any kind.[17] This fact which was already observed by Luther ("he jumps in such disorderly fashion from one thing to another")[18] suits well the character of the paraenesis and should guard us from creating artificial connections. Quite properly, references have been made to the kinship of the book with the paraenetic parts of the Pauline letters and of other Christian writings such as Heb, I Clem, Barn, Did, Herm. Dibelius has broadened the framework of the perspective and sets James in the history of the paraenetic tradition not only of Judaism

[13] Mussner; Guthrie, Harrison, Mariani, Michaelis, Schelkle, Wikenhauser; Michel.

[14] Albertz, Goodspeed; Elliott-Binns.

[15] Francis is not able to show the likelihood that Ch. 1 contains a typical opening of a letter or that 5:12 introduces a conclusion to a letter.

[16] Feine-Behm, Michaelis; Kittel.

[17] The structuring proposed by Reicke, Comm., 8, and Francis, 120 f, is as artificial as the hypothesis that Jas is a midrash based on the text of Ps 12:1-5 (Gertner).

[18] Preface to the Epistles of Saints James and Jude (1522). (See WA, Deutsche Bibel VII, 384.)

but also of the Greek world and of Hellenism. Quite appropriate is the recent stress on the connection of James with Jewish wisdom literature.[19]

In addition to this disconnected quality there is another—the striking fact of the Jewish character of James, also already noted by Luther: "I believe that some Jew or other did it, who had heard something about Christians, but not in any coherent way." [20] The name of Christ appears only in 1:1; 2:1 and could be removed from both these passages without any difficulty, though of course nothing requires that that be done.[21] There is no mention of the life, death, and resurrection of Jesus; the paraenesis does not point to Jesus as an example, but rather to the OT prophets Job and Elijah (5:10 f, 17). The thesis of an originally Jewish origin of James (see p. 406) is therefore thoroughly understandable, but against it is the fact that in addition to the name of Christ in 1:1; 2:1 there is a series of features which are comprehensible only in view of a Christian origin: in 1:18, "according to his own will he begot us by the word of truth in order that we might be a kind of first fruits of his creation" is impossible as a Jewish statement about God, but is on the other hand thoroughly understandable as a description of the efficacy of baptism.[22] In 1:21, "the implanted word which is able to save your souls" cannot be a characterization of the Law. In 1:25, "the complete law of freedom" is without parallel as a Jewish expression.[23] In 2:7, "the beautiful name which is named over you" is a very unusual designation for the name of YHWH. "The arrival of the Lord is near" (5:8) is not attested within Judaism in this formulation. The prohibition against taking oaths (5:12) can only be understood as an original form of the saying of Jesus in Mt 5:37. ἐκκλησία as a designation for an individual congregation (5:14) is un-Jewish. Furthermore there are in James numerous points of contact with the sayings of Jesus. Compare, for example, ask for good gifts (1:5, 17=Mt 7:7 ff), hearers and doers of the word (1:22=Mt 7:24 ff), do not judge (4:12=Mt 7:1), pray without doubting (1:6=Mk 11:23 f).[24]

---

[19] Thus esp. Halson and Luck.

[20] *Table Talk* (WA, V, No. 5443).

[21] On 2:1 cf. Mussner and J. Brinktrine, Bb 35, 1954, 40 ff.

[22]Cf. Braumann; W. Nauck, *Die Tradition und der Charakter des 1 Joh*, WUNT 3, 1957, 90 ff.

[23] "Law of freedom" is not attested at Qumran either; see W. Nauck, "Lex insculpta . . . in der Sektenschrift," ZNW 46, 1955, 138 ff; H. Braun, *Qumran und das NT* I, 1966, 279 f.

[24] See the lists in Mussner, 48 ff; Kittel, ZNW 41, 84 ff.

These points of contact are a result of literary dependence, not on Mt,[25] but on the paraenetic handing down of the sayings of Jesus which was especially widespread in the postapostolic times.[26]

Thus far all these facts show clearly that James is conceived as a Christian writing, but that is shown even more completely on the basis of the relationship of 2:14-26 to Paul. This relationship is much debated, of course, although the contesting of the statement that man is "justified by faith alone" (2:24) sounds like a polemic against Rom 3:28. The assertion is often made that the theology of Paul is by no means presupposed by James, but that rather "James and Paul come out of the same Jewish school." [27] This assertion is opposed by those scholars too who maintain that James is a writing of the Lord's brother from the beginning of the sixties and assume as a presupposition of the polemic "a misinterpretation and distortion of the Pauline thesis." [28] There can in fact be no doubt that James 2:14 ff is simply inconceivable without the activity of Paul preceding it.[29] In this section not only there is a polemic against the lack of works, but at the same time it is asserted that Gen 15:6 proves that for Abraham faith and works were a joint activity which is by no means indicated in the Genesis text itself; and James further declares it to be untenable that "faith alone" can justify a position which no one had ever expressed before Paul. There can be no question but that James stands in a situation of debate with the view which goes back ultimately to Paul, but in view of the complete misunderstanding of the Pauline formulations (James no longer speaks of ἔργα νόμου in opposition to πίστις) a knowledge of the Pauline letters is very unlikely. James is fighting against a "Paul who has become formalized" [30] and so represents a debate within Christianity which no longer has Paul as a direct opponent.

No clearly perceptible literary connection with other early Christian writings exists. The nearest parallels are with I Pet (cf. James 1:2 f with I Pet 1:6 f; James 4:1 f with I Pet 2:11).[31] But in no instance does the parallel arise from a common dependence on paraenetic tradition which in James is less christianized and specific

[25] Thus Shepherd; on the other hand, Mussner, 51.

[26] See Lohse.

[27] Thyen, 15 n. 55; similarly Schlatter; Meyer, Bieder, Michel.

[28] Mitton, Mussner, Sidebottom, Tasker; Feine-Behm, Harrison, Klijn, Mariani.

[29] Cf. most recently Mussner, 18 f; Eichholz, Lohse, Souček; Stuhlmacher, 193 n. 1. In Jas 2:24 is the first appearance of the μόνον that is presupposed in Rom 3:28.

[30] Eichholz, ThE 39, 38.

[31] Cf. Mussner, 34 f; Meyer, 75 ff.

than in I Pet.[32] Although the paraenesis receives its vitality from the Jewish tradition, it is expressed in very cultivated Greek. In vocabulary, James utilizes the terminology of an elevated Koine, such as κατήφεια (4:9), ἀποκύεω (1:15, 18), δελεάζομαι (1:14), τὰ ἐπιτήδεια τοῦ σώματος (2:16). He uses rhetorical means effectively: play on words (4:14, φαινομένη—ἀφανιζομένη; 2:4, διεκρίθητε—κριτάι; 3:17, ἀδιάκριτος—ἀνυπόκριτος; 1:1 f, χαίρειν—χαράν; 2:20, ἔργων—ἀργή); alliteration (1:2, πειρασμοῖς περιπέσητε ποικίλοις; 3:5, μικρὸν μέλος—μεγάλα). Reminiscent of the Hellenistic diatribe is the presentation of ideas in address and response, question and answer (2:18 f; 5:13 f); the hexameter of 1:17 also is evidence of the literary skill of the author. At the same time there are non-Greek elements in language and sentence formation: e.g., (3:3) τῶν ἵππων τοὺς χαλινοὺς εἰς τὰ στόματα βάλλομεν; (3: 12) οὔτε ἀλυκὸν γλυκὺ ποιῆσαι ὕδωρ; 4:13 ff. Occasionally the translation Greek of the LXX may be observed, e.g., 2:1, 9; 2:13; 2:16; 5:17; but on the whole the Greek is that of an educated Hellenist for whom the purely Greek prescript (1:1) is characteristic (elsewhere in the NT only in Acts 15:23; 23:26).

In determining the literary character, the history-of-religions setting, and the language of James, however, the problem of the author and the time of writing is posed.

4. Author and Time

Who is this James who introduces himself with the simple designation "servant of God and of the Lord Jesus Christ"? In the NT, five men are given this name:

1. James the son of Zebedee (Mk 1:19; 3:17 par.; Acts 12:2).
2. James the son of Alphaeus (Mk 3:18 par.).
3. James the brother of Jesus, son of Joseph and Mary (Mk 6:3 par.; I Cor 15:7; Gal 1:19; 2:9, 12; Acts 12:17; 15:13; 21: 18; Jud 1).
4. James the younger (Mk 15:40 par., son of a Mary, cf. Mk 16:1).
5. James the father of the apostle Jude (Lk 6:16; Acts 1:13).

The author of James, who with no ceremony lays claim to authority for his word, cannot be an unknown man. Of those who bear the name James in the NT, we know nothing but the name for numbers 2, 4, and 5, so that they do not come into considera-

---

[32] See Lohse, 13 ff.

tion. Number 1 is excluded as well, since he became a martyr in A.D. 44, at a time which undoubtedly lies before the date of the writing of James. Thus there remains only number 3. In fact in primitive Christianity there was only one James who was well known and who occupied so significant a position that he is designated by the simple name James the Lord's brother. Without doubt James claims to be written by him, and even if the letter is not authentic, it appeals to this famous James and the weight of his person as authority for its content.

After remaining in the background during the lifetime of Jesus, this James was obviously converted soon after Easter by an appearance of the Risen One (I Cor 15:7).[33] As the Lord's brother, he became the head of the early church (Acts 12:17; Gal 1:19; Acts 21:18). Paul mentions him in his account of the Apostolic Council as being in first place among the authorities—even before Peter—(Gal 2:9), and according to Acts 15:13 ff he was the one who spoke the decisive word. It can only be conjectured on the basis of I Cor 9:5 that he carried on mission activity outside of Jerusalem. James' place in the primitive Christian struggle concerning the question of the Law is debated. According to Gal 2:12 he seems to have belonged to the group within the primitive community that was strict in its interpretation of the Law, but not to the wing which was antagonistic toward Paul (cf. Gal 2:9). The picture of the Jewish saints[34] sketched by Hegesippus is without doubt legendary. James died as a martyr in 62.[35]

In support of the Lord's brother as the author of the letter there are fundamentally only two considerations: (1) the simple self-designation (1:1) in which an obviously well-known man is identified not by his name and his task but as "slave of God and of the Lord Jesus Christ"; (2) the close but probably not literary contacts with important parts of the gospel tradition.

But these not very weighty arguments are opposed by very serious difficulties:

1. The cultured language of James is not that of a simple Palestinian. Sevenster's evidence that the Greek language was much used in Palestine at that time and could be learned does not prove that a Jew whose mother tongue was Aramaic could normally write in literary Greek. Most of those who defend the thesis that James was written by the Lord's brother must assume that it

[33] Cf. also the legendary account of the Gospel of the Hebrews in Hennecke-Schneemelcher-Wilson, NT Apocrypha I, 165.

[34] In Eus., HE II. 23. 4 ff.

[35] Thus Jos., *Ant.* XX. 200.

achieved its linguistic form through the help of a Hellenistic Jew, but there is no evidence in the text that the assistance of a secretary gave shape to the present linguistic state of the document, and even if this were the case the question would still remain completely unanswered which part of the whole comes from the real author and which part from the "secretary."

2. It is scarcely conceivable that the Lord's brother, who remained faithful to the Law, could have spoken of "the perfect law of freedom" (1:25) or that he could have given concrete expression to the Law in ethical commands (2:11 f) without mentioning even implicitly any cultic-ritual requirements.[36]

3. Would the brother of the Lord really omit any reference to Jesus and his relationship to him, even though the author of James emphatically presents himself in an authoritative role?

4. The debate in 2:14 ff with a misunderstood secondary stage of Pauline theology not only presupposes a considerable chronological distance from Paul—whereas James died in the year 62—but also betrays a complete ignorance of the polemical intent of Pauline theology, which lapse can scarcely be attributed to James, who as late as 55/56 met with Paul in Jerusalem (Acts 21:18 ff).

5. As the history of the canon shows (see §27.2), it was only very slowly and against opposition that James became recognized as the work of the Lord's brother, therefore as apostolic and canonical. Thus there does not seem to have been any old tradition that it originated with the brother of the Lord.

Although there can be no doubt that an unknown Christian placed his hortatory writing under the authority of the former leader of the church in Jerusalem,[37] the exact determination of the circumstances from which it originated is difficult. In view of the fact that the author's mode of life was in the Jewish tradition, it is very probable that he was a Jewish Christian, but he did not belong to the Ebionite circles which separated themselves from Gentile Christianity,[38] even though he was committed to the Jewish "piety of the poor," which is also encountered at Qumran.[39]

[36] Seitz points out that the Jewish cultic commands are the concern not of the author of James but of the brother of the Lord.

[37] See H. Hegermann, "Der geschichtliche Ort der Past," *Theologische Versuche* II, ed. J. Rogge and G. Schille, 1970, 55.

[38] Schoeps, 345 ff.

[39] See on this Dibelius-Greeven, 58 ff; Mussner, 76 ff; J. Maier, *Die Texte vom Toten Meer* II, 1960, 83 ff; A. Burgsmüller, *Der 'am ha- 'ares zur Zeit Jesu,* diss. Marburg, 1964; L. E. Keck, "The Poor Among the Saints in Jewish Christianity and Qumran," ZNW 57, 1966, 66 ff; J. Dupont, *Les béatitudes* II, 1969, 19 ff.

But in spite of this, his dependence on the LXX, his literary language, and his designation of Christians as the people of the Diaspora (1:1) tell against the assumption that the author was a Palestinian.[40] Nothing supports Galilee as the home of the author.[41] For its having been written in Syria one can at least adduce that the oldest attestation of James in the third century is found in works which originated in Syria.[42] Any place in Eastern Jewish Christianity is conceivable, while Rome is thoroughly improbable.[43]

The date of writing of James cannot be determined more exactly than toward the end of the first century. There is no basis for dating it later, since the assertion that James shows signs of anti-Gnostic struggle[44] rests on an overinterpretation of some Hellenistic formulations. But in view of the conceptual distance from Paul, James can hardly be located at an earlier date.

5. The Theological Problem

A theological problem with respect to James has existed since Luther (1522) determined that there was an irreconcilable conflict between James and Paul. More recently an awareness that James originated at the end of the first century and an exact exegesis of James 2:14 ff have shown that a pre-Pauline writing of James cannot be assumed, nor can a direct refutation of Paul by James. But if it is the case that there is "no real encounter between James and Paul in James 2," [45] then it is also true that "the statements of James cannot be brought into harmony with the authentic Paul and what we confront is not only a tension but an antithesis." [46] This conclusion points to a real theological problem, because Paul and James are both in the canon of the NT and therefore are both witnesses of revelation, however one may define the normative character of the canon (see §37). Repeated attempts have been made to smooth over the antithesis and to interpret the statement about justification by works (James 2:24) as referring to the believer "who bases his claim upon the guilt offering and reconciliation of Christ which sanctifies him for the

[40] Mitton; Michaelis; Hadidian. On the other hand, Easton; Eichholz.
[41] Elliott-Binns.
[42] Shepherd.
[43] Henshaw.
[44] Schammberger; Schoeps.
[45] Eichholz, ThE 39, 41.
[46] Souček, 467. Similarly recently Stuhlmacher, 194; G. Bornkamm, *Paul*, 153 f; G. Klein, "Bibel und Heilsgeschichte," ZNW 62, 1971, 18.

obedience of faith," [47] or to see the believer in the understanding
of James as caught up in "a movement which the Lord at his
parousia wants to enkindle in those poor persons who have been
chosen by him." [48] And so it has been asserted that Paul did not
indeed use the expression "faith without works is dead" (2:26),
"but he would not have disagreed with it," [49] and against Luther's
opinion it allegedly must be asserted that "the letter to a high
degree is concerned with Christ" which is what the "separated
brethren" too are to see.[50] Here, however, undoubtedly we are
dealing not with a confessional problem but with the interpretation of James by the aid of Pauline theology when it is asserted
that in James 2:14-26 "the understanding of the relationship of
faith to works is, as it seems, not one of simple addition," [51] or
that James like Paul repeats what Jesus said. Only James' quotations would correspond to the beginning of the sermon on the
mount, and Paul's to the end.[52] If the distinctions in the terminology and the divergent polemical aims of Paul and James are
taken into account appropriately, and if accordingly, between the
two forms of theological statement a considerably larger area of
commonality can be established than Luther saw, even then it is
unjustifiable to say that, in contrast to Paul, James presents an
"additive understanding of faith and works," just as it is unjustified
to say that for James "the imperative does not appear without an
indicative on which it is grounded." [53]

If the problem which is created by the juxtaposition within
the canon of James and Paul is to be resolved more fittingly, two
points of view must be sharply differentiated from one another:
(1) Schlatter was undoubtedly right in saying that the churches
"have done serious injury to themselves in that they have given
James only a superficial hearing." [54] James may be regarded as
thoroughly indispensable for Christianity, because in face of the
danger of a bland inwardness he seeks to affirm "the life solidarity
of the community." [55] That is a positive answer which is to be
given to the question whether James, especially when he is interpreted on the basis of his own concrete aims, does not have some-

[47] Lackmann.
[48] Bieder, 100.
[49] R. M. Grant, *Intr.*, 223; similarly Mitton, 8.
[50] Mussner, v, 46 f, 52 f, 234 ff.
[51] Eichholz, ThE 39, 44.
[52] Jeremias, 371; cf. on the contrary Stuhlmacher, 229 n. 3.
[53] Eichholz, ThE 88, 38. Correctly Marxsen, 229 f.
[54] Schlatter, *Comm.*, 7.
[55] Souček, 466.

thing decisive to say for a Christianity that to some extent is manifesting the degenerate "faith" which is being attacked by James. (2) But it must also be said immediately that in view of the lack of any distinctive Christian message in James, and in view of this contradiction of the central Pauline proclamation, "we are summoned to a criticism of James from the perspective of the gospel, not concerning his practical word but his theological form." [56] Wherever "James is understood not as a correction but as a basis" [57] there is a theological misuse of the scripture. His indispensable task in the canon can only be achieved where someone as a Christian has already heard the message of Jesus or of Paul, and through James has his vision sharpened for the exhortation to the work which grows out of faith—a message which is contained in James but which is not so exclusively formulated.

§28. The First Letter of Peter

Commentaries: see §41. Research: R. Perdelwitz, "Die Mysterienreligionen und das Problem des 1 Pt," RVV II, 3, 1911; W. Bornemann, "Der I Pt—eine Taufrede des Silvanus?" ZNW 19, 1919/20, 143 ff; L. Radermacher, "Der I Pt und Silvanus," ZNW 27, 1926, 287 ff; B. H. Streeter, The Primitive Church, 1929, 115 ff; W. C. van Unnik, "De verlossing I Petrus I:18-19 en het probleem van den eersten Petrusbrief," Mededeelingen der Nederlandsche Akademie van Wetenschappen, Afdeeling Letterkunde, Nieuwe Reeks, Deel 5, Nr. I, 1942; idem, "Christianity According to I Peter," ExpT 68, 1956/57, 79 ff; R. Bultmann, "Bekenntis- und Liedfragmente im I Pt," Conjectanea Neotestamentica XI in honorem A. Fridrichsen, 1947, 1 ff (=R. B., Exegetica, 1967, 285 ff); E. G. Selwyn, "The Persecutions in I Peter," SNTS 1950, 39 ff; J. Daniélou, Sacramentum Futuri, 1950, 140 f; C. L. Mitton, "The Relationship Between I Peter and Ephesians," JTS, NS I, 1950, 67 ff; P. Carrington, "Saint Peter's Epistle," in The Joy of Studies: Festschr. F. C. Grant, 1951, 57 ff; J. Knox, "Pliny and I Peter," JBL 72, 1953, 187 ff; F. L. Cross, I Peter: A Paschal Liturgy, 1954; E. Lohse, "Paränese und Kerygma im I Pt," ZNW 45, 1954, 68 ff; W. Nauck, "Freude im Leiden," ZNW 46, 1955, 68 ff; C. F. D. Moule, "The Nature and Purpose of I Peter," NTS 3, 1956/57, 1 ff; M.-E. Boismard, "Une liturgie baptismale dans la Prima Petri," RB 63, 1956, 182 ff; 64, 1957, 161 ff; idem, DBS VII, 1966, 1415 ff; S. I. Buse, in Christian Baptism, ed. A. Gilmore, 1960, 170 ff; S. E. Johnson, "The Preaching to the Dead," JBL 79, 1960, 48 ff; T. C. G. Thornton, "I Peter, a Paschal Liturgy?" JTS, NS 12, 1961, 14 ff; E. Fascher, RGG³ V, 1961, 257 ff;

[56] P. Althaus, in Das Menschenbild im Lichte des Ev., Festschrift E. Brunner, 1950, 48.

[57] Marxsen, "Frühkatholizismus," 37.

R. P. Martin, "The Composition of I Peter in Recent Study," VE 1, 1962, 29 ff; A. R. C. Leaney, "I Peter and the Passover: An Interpretation," NTS 10, 1963/64, 238 ff; C.-H. Hunzinger, "Babylon als Deckname für Rom und die Datierung des I Pt," *Gottes Wort und Gottes Land, Festschrift W. Hertzberg,* 1965, 67 ff; C. Spicq, "La Iª Petri et le témoignage évangélique de saint Pierre," StTh 20, 1966, 37 ff; R. H. Gundry, " 'Verba Christi' in I Peter: Their Implications Concerning the Authorship of I Peter and the Authenticity of the Gospel Tradition," NTS 13, 1966/67, 336 ff; F. W. Danker, "I Peter 1,24–2,17—A Consolatory Pericope," ZNW 58, 1967, 93 ff; E. Best, "I Peter and the Gospel Tradition," NTS 16, 1969/70, 95 ff; M.-A. Chevallier, "I Pierre 1/1 à 2/10. Structure littéraire et conséquences exégétiques," RHPhR 51, 1971, 129 ff.

1. Contents

Because of its paraenetic character, a clear outline of I Pet cannot be given. No delimiting of the sections can be regarded as definitive.[1] The prescript (1:1 f) is followed by praise to God that the reader has been born again to a hope of future salvation which in spite of present suffering is sure and even now the prediction of the prophets is being fulfilled (1:3-12). From this there follow admonitions to hold fast to this hope with confidence in the blood of Christ, to live as those who have been born again, and to be incorporated into the spiritual temple of Christ (1:13–2:10). A second group of warnings is concerned with behavior with reference to the world (2:11–4:6: conduct toward the outsiders, 2:11 f; obedience to the authorities, 2:13-17; responsibilities within the household, 2:18–3:12; preparedness for suffering, for responsibility toward non-Christians, and for laying aside sins, 3:13–4:6). General exhortations and a doxology form a conclusion (4:7-11). Then an exhortation to endure suffering properly begins again (4:12-19), followed by exhortations to older and younger people (5:1-5), again concluding with general exhortations (5:6-11). The letter ends with concluding salutations (5:12-14).

2. Readers

According to the prescript, the apostle Peter is writing "to the elect exiles of the Dispersion in Pontus, Galatia, Cappadocia, Asia,

---

[1] Chevallier seeks to prove that 1:1–2:20 and 4:12–5:14 are carefully structured on the basis of catchwords and verbal correspondences, etc., but this can be largely explained on a thematic basis.

and Bithynia." If these names are intended to indicate Roman provinces,[1a] then the letter was addressed to Christians in Asia Minor as a whole, even though mention is lacking of Lycia, Pamphylia, and Cilicia in the south. But the names could also refer to the old ethnic regions, and in support of that, attention has been drawn to the fact[2] that according to 1:14, 18; 2:9 f; 4:3 f the readers are clearly Gentile Christians; however, in the southern part of the province of Galatia (Iconium, Lystra, and Derbe) there were some Jewish Christians (Acts 13 and 14). Furthermore if it is addressed to ethnic regions I Pet is not addressed to regions within the mission territory of Paul. But these arguments are scarcely adequate for deciding this or any other point of view, so the choice of the geographical names remains inexplicable. To say that the southern regions are omitted because no "ecclesiastically" colored Christianity existed there[3] is an inadequately grounded conjecture.[4] Since the letter is addressed to Gentile Christians, their designation as "the elect exiles of the Dispersion" in the regions mentioned is not to be understood literally. What is in view is Christians as members of the true people of God, who live scattered throughout the earth as strangers, since their true home is in heaven (cf. Gal 6:16; Phil 3:20; Heb 13:14; also I Pet 1:17; 2:11). That these Gentile Christians had previously attached themselves to synagogue communities as "God fearers" [5] is an arbitrary assumption.

3. Aim and Literary Character

The letter is presented (5:12) as a message of comfort and admonition. In the face of persecution, hate, suffering, abusive slander, the readers are to stand fast in their Christianity in the "true grace of God" in view of the heavenly hope which is their goal, which is in store for all who hold fast to the Christian faith and by proper behavior do not allow themselves to wander into error. What was the nature of the persecution besetting those addressed? It has often been suggested that obviously slanders on the part of their Gentile fellow countrymen (2:12, 15; 3:14 ff;

[1a] Kelly; Schelkle.

[2] Michaelis, Wikenhauser.

[3] W. Bauer, *Orthodoxy and Heresy in Earliest Christianity* (tr. R. A. Kraft *et al.*), 81 f.

[4] In spite of Ph. Vielhauer, ThR, NF 31, 1965/66, 132.

[5] Klijn; van Unnik.

4:3 f, 14 f) led to unjust accusations of the Christians before the courts and that this caused surprise among the Christians (1:6; 4:12). This interpretation assumes that there could not have been any civil persecution, since it is inconceivable in light of the positive attitude toward the state (2:13 ff).[6] But while it is true that personal animosity on the part of Gentile fellow countrymen gave rise to this initiative against the Christians, it is also clear that they were brought before the court ὡς χριστιανός (4:16) and not on the ground of charges concerning moral misdeeds (2:20; 4:15). Furthermore these accusations are not locally limited but concern Christianity as a whole (5:9) and therefore are to be interpreted as the beginning of the last judgment (4:7, 17). In view of the resulting danger of apostasy (5:8 ff) the author seeks to convince the readers that suffering of this sort must be regarded as the divine means of testing before the appearance of Christ soon (1:6 f; 4:12 f, 19), so there is no tension between this and the traditional exhortation to obedience (2:20!).

To be sure, it has been observed that the situation of those addressed does not seem to be the same throughout the whole letter. While in 4:12, 14, 19; 5:6, 8 the suffering is described as a present fact, 1:6; 2:20; 3:14, 17 reckon only with the possibility of suffering. Furthermore, since 1:3–4:11 does not display the character of a letter, and since 4:11 concludes with a doxology, while 4:12 ff addresses Christians in a concrete situation of suffering, and elders and novices, this has been interpreted as wider evidence for a different origin of 1:3-4, 11 and 4:12 ff. And finally it has been noted that in 1:3, 12, 23; 2:2, 10, 25; 3:21—thus only in the section 1:3–4:11—are there to be found clear indications that the Christians addressed are newly baptized. From all these observations a series of various conclusions has been drawn. Some claim that the differences between 1:3–4:11 and 4:12 ff are insignificant, and interpret 1:3–5:11 as a baptismal sermon which is later placed in the framework of a letter.[7] Others assume that into a single writing have been combined a baptismal sermon (1:3–4:11) and a hortatory writing by the same author,[8] or that two baptismal sermons have been joined to form a letter, one before and one after bap-

---

[6] E.g., Kelly, Reicke, Schelkle, Selwyn; Albertz, Feine-Behm, Guthrie, Höpfl-Gut, Mariani, Meinertz, Wikenhauser; van Unnik, Moule, Fascher.

[7] Albertz; Bornemann; questioningly Fascher. J. Daniélou, *Sacramentum Futuri*, 1950, 141, and A. Adam, *Das Sintflutgebet in der Taufliturgie*, WuD 1952, 20, suggest a baptismal sermon during passion week.

[8] Reike, Schneider, Windisch; Fuller, Marxsen; Perdelwitz, Streeter; W. Nauck (see §27 n. 22), 48 n. 9.

tism,[9] or two letters, one to those not yet persecuted and the other to the persecuted.[10] Preisker would like to see in I Pet a juxtaposition of portions of a baptismal service of worship in which the baptism is thought of as taking place between 1:21 and 1:22 but which as a consequence of the secrecy of the instruction[11] is not mentioned. On the basis of the repeated stress on πάσχειν and πάθος and of the points of contact with Hippolytus' *Apostolic Tradition*, Cross concludes that I Pet consists basically of instructions for the baptism by the bishop at Passover time.[12] A. Strobel [13] speaks of a "Passover encyclical" and "Passover baptismal ritual." With reason Thornton has objected against the last-mentioned thesis that the linking of πάσχα and πάσχειν is first attested in the later second century and is still unknown in the first century. Furthermore nothing else in I Pet points to the Passover festival,[14] and, apart from all other difficulties, what tells decisively against the supposition of a liturgy is that one cannot conceive how "a liturgy-homily, shorn of its 'rubrics' but with its changing tenses and broken sequences all retained, could have been hastily dressed up as a letter and sent off without a word of explanation to Christians who had not witnessed its original setting." [15] It is scarcely the case, either, that 1:3–4:11 and 4:12 ff presuppose an entirely different situation for the reader with respect to suffering. The first section does indeed already presuppose that the readers are experiencing suffering (1:6 λυπηθέντες, 2:12; 3:16; 4:4),[16] and Nauck[17] has shown that the ideas in I Pet of "the joy in suffering" arise from a "Jewish–primitive Christian persecution tradition" in which the experience of suffering is interpreted as eschatologically necessary and to be expected. Thus the proposal that I Pet consists of the juxtaposition of two parts is unnecessary and improbable.[18] The supposition that the epistolary framework (1:1 f; 5:12-14)

[9] Buse, Martin.

[10] Moule.

[11] Similarly Boismard, though with different divisions.

[12] Leaney speaks of a paschal liturgy.

[13] A. Strobel, "Zum Verständnis von Mt 21:1-13," NovTest 2, 1958, 210, 212, 219. According to Strobel, *Lutherische Monatshefte* 3, 1963, Bibliographical Number, 2, the baptismal act is to be considered as following the reading.

[14] Cf. also Grant, *Intr.*, 225; Harrison, *Intr.*, 377.

[15] Moule, 4.

[16] Kelly; Chevallier, 142. Danker shows that 1:24–2:17 comforts the reader in the face of suffering, and that the optatives in 3:14, 17 ought not to be pressed.

[17] Nauck, ZNW 1955, 79 ff.

[18] Cf. Beare, Selwyn; Guthrie, Harrison, Michaelis; van Unnik, Lohse, Nauck, Thornton, Martin.

has been added subsequently to 1:3–5:11 is contradicted by the evidence that this framework manifests clear points of connection with the letter corpus itself (cf. παρεπίδημοι 1:1 with 1:17; 2:11, and 5:12 with 4:12). The eulogy in the introduction to the letter (1:3 ff) and the household instructions (2:18 ff) suggest as well that I Peter was indeed conceived as a "letter."

But now the unmistakable references to baptism in I Pet must be explained. The theory that a complete baptismal sermon was sent as a letter need not be taken seriously, because the household instructions (2:18 ff) and the paraenesis (3:8 ff; 4:7 ff) are not appropriate in a baptismal sermon. Lohse also has rightly stressed the fact that the actual theme of the letter is the strengthening of Christians for suffering and that references to baptism are found almost entirely in 1:3–2:10. Furthermore it is possible that several hymns may have been worked into I Pet;[19] even though the reconstruction of them remains uncertain, the very fact that they were assimilated speaks against the theory of a self-contained baptismal sermon. Finally it must be considered that the situation of suffering of the readers without doubt presupposes that those Christians addressed had not been recently baptized.[20] Taking all these facts together into consideration, I Pet is to be regarded as a hortatory writing formed from traditional paraenetic and possibly liturgical material, which by recalling the gift of baptism and the eschatologically grounded universality of these sufferings serves to present to the consciousness of these Christians in a convincing way the necessity of enduring suffering and the strength to do so.

4. Author

In the prescript the author calls himself "Peter, apostle of Jesus Christ," and in 5:1 characterizes himself as συμπρεσβύτερος καὶ μάρτυς τῶν τοῦ χριστοῦ παθημάτων; he is writing διὰ Σιλουανοῦ (5:12) and from "Babylon" (5:13). Although the prescript points clearly to Peter as author, "witness of suffering" can scarcely indicate the eyewitness of the sufferings of Christ,[21] but rather a Christian who, like the Christians addressed, has experienced and

---

[19] Attempts to link passages to a hymn include the following: Selwyn: 2:6-8; Lohse: 2:21-25; Lohse, Johnson: 3:18-22; Bultmann wants to combine 1:20; 3:18 f, 22 into *one* confession. For criticism cf. Martin. 31 ff.

[20] Michaelis; Danker, 101 f.

[21] Michl, Reicke, Schlatter, Selwyn; Feine-Behm; Spicq, 39; Gundry, 347.

can bear witness to the sufferings of Christ,[22] or like them is "witness for the sufferings of Christ."[23] This interpretation receives support in 5:1 from the appositional phrase "who also has shared in the glory which is to be revealed"—that sets as parallels the role as witness and the future participation in the glory. The self-designation of the author in 5:1, therefore, is no special indication of an apostle or an eyewitness of Jesus. The Silvanus mentioned in 5:12 is in all probability identical with the Pauline pupil Silvanus who is mentioned in I Thess 1:1; II Thess 1:1; II Cor 1:19, as well as with the companion of Paul, Silas, who appears in Acts 15:22-32; 15:40–18:5. Other than here we hear nothing of a connection between Silvanus-Silas and Peter. Also Μᾶρκος ὁ υἱός μου mentioned in 5:13 was probably a man from Jerusalem (Acts 12:12) who appears elsewhere only as a fellow worker of Paul or Barnabas (Acts 13:5, 13; 15:37, 39; Col 4:10; Phlm 24) but again never in connection with Peter. Accordingly this information from I Pet cannot serve to support the claim in 1:1 that Peter is the author of I Pet. 1:3 ff does not point to an eyewitness of the resurrection[24] nor does the allusion to the example of the suffering of Christ (2:21-24) point to a personal disciple of Jesus.[25] At most the mention of "Babylon" (5:13) as the place of writing of I Pet could support or is intended to support the claim of 1:1. It is very unlikely that by this is meant the Mesopotamian Babylon[26] or an Egyptian city of this name,[27] because there is no known tradition that Peter was active in these areas. On the other hand, in Jewish apocalyptic of the first century after Christ and in Rev 14:8; 16:19; 17:5; 18:2, 10, 21, "Babylon" is a cipher for Rome,[28] and "Babylon" probably has this significance in I Pet 5:13 as well. Thus the place of writing of I Pet is presumably Rome, since the idea

[22] Kelly; H. von Campenhausen, *Die Idee des Martyriums in der alten Kirche,* 1936, 64 f; H. Strathmann, art. "Μάρτυς," TDNT IV, 1967, 494 f; W. Michaelis, art. "πάθημα," TDNT V, 1967, 921 f.

[23] Schneider; Bauer, *Lex.,* 495. It is highly unlikely that μάρτυς represents a play on the martyrdom of Peter (Marxsen, *Intr.,* 237) in view of the late development of this term.

[24] Feine-Behm.

[25] Wikenhauser. The attempt to prove that the author cites many sayings of Jesus and that he chooses them only from those passages where Peter is present does not come off (see Best, NTS).

[26] Schlatter; Heard; J. Munck, *Paul and the Salvation of Mankind,* 1959, 275.

[27] Klijn, de Zwaan.

[28] Evidence in Hunzinger.

that Peter stayed in Rome for some time is attested from the end of the first century on.[29]

But the following decisive arguments tell against the Petrine authorship of I Pet which is implied in the epistolary framework though not in the rest of the writing:

a. The language of I Pet is cultivated Greek which employs many rhetorical devices: word order (1:23; 3:16), parallel sentences (4: 11), a series of similar constructions (1:4, etc.).[30] The numerous OT quotations and allusions originate without exception from the LXX. For a Galilean fisherman, Peter, none of these is conceivable.

b. I Pet presupposes the Pauline theology. This is true not only in the general sense that the Jewish-Christian readers, the "people of God" (2:10), are no longer concerned about the problem of the fulfillment of the Law, but also in the special sense that, as in Paul, the death of Jesus has atoned for the sins of Christians and has accomplished justification (1:18 f; 2:24). Christians are to suffer with Christ (4:13; 5:1), obedience to the civil authorities is demanded (2:14 f), and the Pauline formula ἐν χριστῷ is encountered (3:16; 5:10, 14). The frequently advanced proposal that I Pet is literarily dependent on Rom (and Eph)[31] is improbable because the linguistic contacts can be explained on the basis of a common catechetical tradition.[32] But there can be no doubt that the author of I Pet stands in the line of succession of Pauline theology,[33] and that is scarcely conceivable for Peter, who at the time of Gal 2:11 was able in only a very unsure way to follow the Pauline basic principle of freedom from the Law for Gentile Christians.

Many scholars[34] have sought to weaken both these arguments on the ground that 5:12 διὰ Σιλουανοῦ ὑμῖν . . . ἔγραψα assumes that Silvanus is the real author to whom Peter gave the responsibility for the actual writing. Some[35] think that they can prove

[29] See E. Dinkler, ThR, NF 25, 1959, 211 ff; 1960, 37 f.

[30] Cf. Schelkle, 13; Selwyn, 26; Radermacher, 287 f.

[31] Beare; Feine-Behm, McNeile-Williams; Mitton.

[32] See the evidence in Selwyn, Comm., 365 ff. Boismard, DBS, 1429 f, suggests a common liturgical-hortatory schema.

[33] Otherwise Kelly; Guthrie (who, indeed, thinks Peter heard Paul preach in Rome!). Rightly Fuller, Intr., 157: I Pet "is much more Pauline than the Pastorals."

[34] E.g., Hunter, Reicke, Schelkle, Schneider, Selwyn, Stibbs-Walls; Feine-Behm, Guthrie (as a possible alternative to a direct authorship), Harrington, Harrison, Heard, Henshaw, Klijn, Lo Bue, Mariani, McNeile-Williams, Wikenhauser, de Zwaan; van Unnik, Carrington; L. Goppelt, Apostolic und Post-Apostolic Times, Eng. tr. by R. Guelich, London, 1970, 110.

[35] Selwyn; Harrison.

that clearly common elements in language exist between I and II Thess, I Pet, and Acts 15:29, which indicates a common authorship by Silvanus. But these linguistic contacts are much too insignificant for much weight to be attached to them, and furthermore the distinction in style between I and II Thess and I Pet is important. No one has yet proved that γράφω διά τινος can mean to authorize someone else to compose a piece of writing. Furthermore, if this were the case, then Peter would not be the real author of I Pet in any sense.[36]

But even if the attempt is made to counter the arguments given under *a* and *b* by referring to the authorship of I Pet by Silvanus under commission from Peter, still there are two further incontestable arguments against tracing the letter back to Peter.

c. I Pet contains no evidence at all of familiarity with the earthly Jesus, his life, his teaching, and his death, but makes reference only in a general way to the "sufferings" of Christ. It is scarcely conceivable that Peter would neither have sought to strengthen his authority by referring to his personal connections with Jesus nor have referred to the example of Jesus in some way.

d. The situation of persecution of those addressed can be understood only as occurring at the beginning stages of civil persecution (see pp. 418 f). According to the unanimous tradition of the early church, the first persecution of Christians on more than a merely local basis (cf. 5:9) took place under Domitian.[37] But that, of course, takes us beyond the life-span of Peter.

I Pet is therefore undoubtedly a pseudonymous writing.[38] The pseudonymity is carried out within the framework of a letter, and even there it is done with extreme caution. The uncertainty of the behavior of the churches of Asia Minor at the beginning of the persecution clearly provided the author with the occasion for his writing. He lays claim to the authority of Peter for his exhortation, which builds firmly on the traditional paraenetic material. It cannot be determined why this Gentile Christian seized precisely upon the authority of Peter unless the place of writing provided the occasion for him to do so. The fact of pseudonymity is not contradicted by our inability to perceive the motive for it.[39]

[36] Cf. against the secretary hypothesis, Beare, 188 ff.

[37] Melito, in Eus., HE IV. 26. 9.

[38] First in H. H. Cludius (1808); recently among others Beare, Windisch-Preisker; Albertz, Fuller, Goodspeed, Jülicher-Fascher, Marxsen, Riddle-Hutson; Danker, Best. The question remains open for Kelly, Michl; Cross, Moule.

[39] Against Guthrie.

5. Place and Time of Writing

If by "Babylon" (5:13) is meant Rome (see p. 422), then I Pet could well have been written in Rome, where presumably Peter died, and where early on an appeal was made to his authority (I Clem 5:3 f). The fact that I Pet was known in the East as early as the time of Polycarp (Phil 1:3; 8:1; 10:2) and Papias,[40] whereas in the West it is missing from the Muratorian Canon[41] (though cited by Irenaeus and Tertullian), shows only that it was from the churches in the East that I Pet became known but proves nothing concerning its place of writing.[42] The reign of Domitian should probably be taken as the time of writing, since the mention of the persecution "as Christians" (4:16) is not sufficient ground for going down as late as the beginning of the second century[43] or even to the time of the persecution under Trajan.[44] 90–95 is therefore the most probable time of writing.

§29. THE LETTER OF JUDE

Commentaries: see §41. Research: B. H. Streeter, *The Primitive Church*, 1929, 178 ff; A. Meyer, "Das Rätsel des Jk," Bh. ZNW 10, 1930, 82 ff; R. Leconte, DBS IV, 1949, 1285 ff; E. Fascher, RGG³ III, 1959, 966 f; J. Blinzler, LThK V, 1960, 1155 f.

1. Contents

After the prescript (1 f) the author gives the reason for his writing: the appearance of false teachers who deny God and Christ. In the face of such an outrage it is fitting to do battle for the traditional faith (3 f). The same punishment threatens them as befell Israel in the desert, the fallen angels, and Sodom and Gomorrah (5-7). The portrait of the false teachers (8-16) manifests libertinism; like Cain, Balaam, and Korah they devote themselves to the destruction of the life of the community ("love feasts"), but as Enoch has predicted, they will themselves come to

[40] According to Eus., HE III. 39. 17.
[41] The reason is unknown; the assumption of a gap (Grant, Guthrie) is arbitrary.
[42] According to Hunzinger, the use of "Babylon" as a cipher indicates the East.
[43] Beare.
[44] Lake, Riddle-Hutson; Knox.

a fearful judgment. The readers are to recall the preaching of the apostles who predicted the appearance of such scoffers before the End-time (17-19); they are themselves to hold fast to faith, prayer, love, and hope for the final salvation (20 f), and in contrast to those who have gone astray, they are to combine a horror of sin with loving compassion (22 f). Conclusion: doxology (24 f).

2. Aim and Literary Character

The letter is combating libertine-Gnostic false teachers. They have penetrated the community, created splits (19) and defiled the love feasts (12). They speak in high-handed fashion (16); they claim to be pneumatics, but this designation is to be denied to them. They are really "psychics" (19) and dreamers (8), i.e., visionaries. They have turned aside from the grace of God and deny the only Leader and Lord, Jesus Christ (4). They set themselves above all the God-ordained superterrestrial powers (8). Scorn of God and Christ and the good heavenly angelic powers is their religious act of wantonness, just like Korah, who revolted against the divine order (11). These fanatical pneumatics combine with their pride a mode of life which evokes scandal. They convert the grace of God into debauchery (4), they pervert their own flesh following their sensual desires like unreasoning wild animals (7 f, 10, 18), like waves of the wild sea they foam up their own shame (13). They are therefore representatives of a Gnostic tendency which holds that a real pneumatic existence is not affected in any way by what the flesh does. This characteristic does not fit any particular Gnostic system of the second century.

Libertine Gnosticism of a similar sort is combated in Rev 2:6, 14 f, 20 ff, and in the Pastorals, and in part also in I Cor. It is not possible, however, to draw lines of connection between the related manifestations from point to point, since in this age of syncretism similar phenomena could emerge at any time and in any place.

It is significant that the views of the Gnostics are not really answered in detail; rather the false teachers are scolded and threatened with God's judgment (5-7, 12 f, 15), while those addressed are admonished to hold fast to the "faith once for all delivered to the saints" (3, 20). This mode of polemic against heretics runs counter to the combating of false teachers elsewhere in the NT, but that is in keeping with the fact that the letter does not contain any real message of Christ at all, and with its "early Catholic" concept of faith[1] stands in unrelieved tension with the understanding of faith in the chief witnesses of the NT.

The form of Jude does no more than give the appearance of a letter: it is addressed to "those who are called, beloved of God the Father and preserved for Jesus Christ" (1) and ends with a liturgical conclusion (24 f). Even the reference to the appearance of Gnostics within the community (4, 12) does not suggest that the letter was addressed to specific individual communities.[2] It cannot be clearly perceived whether the Christians addressed were former Jews or Gentiles, although the debauchery which is criticized is more plausible for Gentile Christians.

3. Author and Time of Writing

The author calls himself Jude, servant of Jesus Christ, brother of James (1). Of the different bearers of the name Jude who are known from the NT there is no doubt which is intended: he is clearly designated as "the brother of James." This could only be the one great well-known James, the brother of the Lord (James 1:1; Gal 1:19; 2:9; I Cor 15:7). Jude is mentioned among the brothers of Jesus: in Mk 6:3 he is mentioned in the third place; in Mt 13:55 he is in the fourth place. Concerning this Jude, however, we know nothing further. At the end of the reign of Domitian (therefore *ca.* 95), as Hegesippus reports,[3] two descendants of Jude the brother of the Lord were suspected of being in the Davidic line, were examined by the emperor personally, but were let go by him as harmless. They are said to have been leaders of the church ($\dot{\eta}\gamma\dot{\eta}\sigma\alpha\sigma\theta\alpha\iota$ $\tau\hat{\omega}\nu$ $\dot{\epsilon}\kappa\kappa\lambda\eta\sigma\iota\hat{\omega}\nu$) later on and to have lived until the time of Trajan (98–117). But all that can be inferred is that the name of this brother of Jesus was still known at the end of the first century.

Obviously Jude wants to appear as having been written by this brother of Jesus.[4] The supposition that the author was an unknown

---

[1] See K. H. Schelkle, "Spätapostolische Briefe als frühkatholisches Zeugnis," *Nt. Aufsätze, Festschr. J. Schmid,* 1963, 226; *contra,* A. Strobel (*Monatshefte;* see §28 n. 13), 5.

[2] Thus Kelly, Schelkle, Schneider; Harrington, Lo Bue, Michaelis, Wikenhauser.

[3] In Eus., HE II. 20. 1 ff.

[4] The claim is guesswork that in the introduction to Jude the designation "brother of the Lord" is avoided in favor of "brother of James" in order to conceal his identity (contrary to H. Köster in *Trajectories,* 114 ff, esp. 134).

Jude who had a brother named James[5] is extremely unlikely because of the linguistic similarity of Jude 1 and James 1:1. The theory which equates the author of Jude with the Bishop Jude who is mentioned in the old list of Jerusalem bishops[6] founders on the fact that we know nothing about his having had a brother James. Can Jude have been written by Jude the brother of Jesus?

The author was presumably a Jewish Christian, since he knows such Jewish-apocalyptic writings as the Ascension of Moses (9) and the Enoch Apocalypse (14), and the Jewish legends (9, 11). But the author "speaks of the apostles like a pupil from a time long afterward" (17).[7] Not only does he assume a concept of "a faith once for all delivered to the saints" (3), but against the statements of the false teachers of the End-time, he adduces in similar manner Jewish and early Christian predictions (14 f, 17). All this points to a late phase of primitive Christianity, and the cultivated Greek language as well as the citations from a Greek translation of the Enoch Apocalypse do not well suit a Galilean. The supposition repeatedly presented that Jude really does come from a brother of the Lord[8] is accordingly extremely improbable, and Jude must be considered a pseudonymous writing.[9] That is all the more fitting if Jude 1 contains a reference to a pseudonymous James (see §27.4).

The attestation in the early church is at first good but later becomes uncertain. II Pet used Jude (see §30); the Muratorian Canon, Tertullian, and Clement of Alexandria regard it as canonical. Origen, on the other hand, refers to it occasionally with the observation "If anyone would allow the letter of Jude . . ."[10] Both Eusebius[11] and Jerome include Jude among the "contested" writings. Yet this doubt about canonicity obviously does not rest on an independent tradition but on Jude's offense of using the Apocrypha. In the canonical list of the Western church from the fourth century on, it stands unchallenged. Luther regarded Jude

[5] Appel, Henshaw.

[6] Thus as early as Hugo Grotius; more recently Streeter; similarly A. Adam, "Erwägungen zur Herkunft der Did," ZKG 68, 1957, 46; G. Klein, Die zwölf Apostel, FRLANT, NF 59, 1961, 100.

[7] Luther, Preface to the Epistles of Saints James and Jude (see §27 n. 18).

[8] E.g., Schelkle (questioningly); Green, Schneider; Feine-Behm, Guthrie, Harrington, Harrison, Heard, Klijn, Mariani, Sparks, Wikenhauser.

[9] E.g., Barnett, Kelly, Knopf, Sidebottom, Windisch-Preisker; Dibelius, Fuller, Goodspeed, Henshaw, Jülicher-Fascher, Marxsen, Michaelis; Meyer. According to Michl and Reicke, a disciple of Jude wrote the letter in the spirit of the Lord's brother.

[10] Origen, Tomoi in Mt, 17:30. See below, §36.1.

[11] Eus., HE II. 23. 25; III. 25. 3.

as dependent on II Pet and as postapostolic and did not include it among the "true, certain chief books of the NT," [12] though in this he found few followers until J. D. Michaelis.

Since Jude without doubt belongs to a later period of Christianity, there is no evidence for determining its time of origin exactly. The dependence on James points to the end of the first century as a *terminus a quo,* but there is no adequate basis for assuming that it was written as late as 125.[13] The most likely date is about the turn of the second century. Concerning the place of writing we know nothing.

§30. THE SECOND LETTER OF PETER

Commentaries: see §41. Research: U. Holzmeister, "Vocabularium secundae epistolae S. Petri erroresque quidam de eo divulgati," Bb 30, 1949, 339 ff; E. Käsemann, "Eine Apologie der urchristlichen Eschatologie," ZThK 49, 1952, 272 ff (=E. K., "An Apologia for Primitive Christian Eschatology," in *Essays on NT Themes,* SBT 41, 1964, 169 ff) ; W. Marxsen, *Der "Frühkatholizismus" im NT,* 1958, 7 ff; G. H. Boobyer, "The Indebtedness of 2 Peter to 1 Peter," *NT Essays in Memory of T. W. Manson,* 1959, 34 ff; E. Fascher, RGG[3] V, 1961, 259 f; E. M. B. Green, *2 Peter Reconsidered* (The Tyndale NT Lecture 1960), 1962; J. Schmitt, DBS VII, 1966, 1455 ff; D. von Allmen, "L'apocalyptique Juive et le retard de la parousie en II Pierre 3:1-13," RThPh 99, 1966, 255 ff; C. H. Talbert, "II Peter and the Delay of the Parousia," VigChr 20, 1966, 137 ff.

1. Contents

Following the prescript (1:1 f) by way of introduction the readers are reminded of all the good things which divine power has given them and are admonished to devote themselves with the utmost zeal to fleeing from worldly corruption, to gaining knowledge, and to winning access to the eternal kingdom of Christ (1:3-11). In the face of death Peter wants to instruct his readers once more about the transfiguration of the Lord, of which he was a witness, and which serves as a predicted representation of the coming parousia and the dependability of the prophetic OT word (1:12-21). An important aim of the letter is an urgent warning against false prophets (Ch. 2) who will seek to establish destruc-

---

[12] Preface to the Epistle to the Hebrews (1522). In WA, Deutsche Bibel VII, 344.

[13] Barnett, Sidebottom; Fuller, Goodspeed.

tive factions, who do not recognize Christ as Lord, who promote sensual lust, voluptuous living, and vile covetousness, and who by reason of their seductive stratagems constitute a danger for the recently converted. These false teachers are both predicted (2:1-3) and described as present (2:9-12). Ch. 3:1-13 returns to the theme of Ch. 1 and warns about the scoffers who say that the parousia will not take place at all. Just as there was once a world-wide catastrophe, the flood, so on the day of the Lord which is at hand the world will be destroyed through fire. This will be a day of judgment. Concluding admonition (3:14-18): it is important, therefore, that we prepare ourselves for the parousia as Paul himself has ordered, and that we grow in the grace and knowledge of Christ.

2. Author and Authenticity

The letter clearly and unambiguously makes the claim that it was written by the apostle Peter. It begins (1:1) with the self-designation of the author: "Simeon Peter, servant and apostle of Jesus Christ." In 1:16 ff, the author speaks as an eyewitness of the transfiguration of Jesus.[1] In 1:14 he makes reference to the saying of Jesus concerning the martyrdom of Peter. In 3:15 f, reference to "the beloved brother Paul" places the author on the same level of apostolic authority as Paul. In 3:1, there is clearly a reference to I Pet: "This is already the second letter that I am writing to you." Since Peter regards his death as near (1:13 ff), II Pet is written in the form of a testament of Peter.

But this letter cannot have been written by Peter.

1. The literary dependence on Jude rules this out. II Pet 1 and 3 already have a number of contacts with Jude: cf. II Pet 1:5 with Jude 3; II Pet 1:12 with Jude 5; II Pet 3:2 f with Jude 17 f; II Pet 3:14 with Jude 24; II Pet 3:18 with Jude 25. The most striking agreements with Jude are shown in the portrayal of the false teachers in II Pet 2 and also in the illustrations based on the OT and the pictures drawn from nature, agreements in the exact wording and extensive agreements in sequence. The false teachers deny the Lord Christ and lead a dissolute life (II Pet 2:1 f = Jude 4), they despise and blaspheme the good angelic powers (II Pet 2: 10 f = Jude 8 f), they speak in high-handed fashion (ὑπέρογκα;

---

[1] 1:16 cannot be proved to be an eyewitness account independent of the synoptic tradition (contrary to Green, *II Pet reconsidered,* 27).

II Pet 2:18 = Jude 16), they are blotches on the communal meal (σπίλοι συνευωχώμενοι; II Pet 2:13 = Jude 12), they are clouds tossed about by the wind, devoid of water, for whom the gloom of darkness is reserved (II Pet 2:17 = Jude 12 f), they are denounced for their fleshly corruption and their unrestrained mode of life (II Pet 2:10, 12 ff, 18 = Jude 7 f, 10, 12, 16). The sequence of examples of punishment from the OT in Jude 5 ff (Israel in the desert, fallen angels, Sodom and Gomorrah) is arranged in historical order in II Pet 2:4 ff and modified (fallen angels, Flood, Sodom and Gomorrah) because the author of II Pet needs the example of the Flood to combat the deniers of the parousia. The general statement in II Pet 2:11 makes sense only if note has been made of the concrete example mentioned in Jude 9. The image in Jude 12 f is more genuine and more plastic than the parallel in II Pet 2:17.

This material shows, therefore, that it is II Pet which is the dependent factor. It is further to be observed that the quotation from a noncanonical writing (Jude 14 f = the Apocalypse of Enoch 1:9; 60:8) is lacking in II Pet, and that by omitting certain essential features the allusions to the apocryphal writings have been somewhat obscured in Jude 6 (fallen angels) and 9 (the struggle between the archangel Michael and the Devil). From this it may be concluded that II Pet is already reluctant to use this literature whereas Jude has a naïve attitude toward it. II Pet betrays a literary stratagem in that the false teachers who are characterized by Jude as being in the present are depicted in II Pet as future and indeed predicted by Peter (2:1 ff, in the future; 3:3, 17 προγινώσκοντες). But in spite of this they are also described in the present tense (2:10, 12 ff, 20), and indeed the past tense is used (2:15, 22). Consequently it is almost universally recognized today that II Pet is dependent on Jude and not the reverse.[2] Then II Pet 3:3 ff portrays the libertines as the deniers of the parousia. In this way he represents a more developed stage, while a less developed stage is evident in Jude, who does not yet know that the false teachers against whom he directs his attention might have denied the parousia. Since Jude belongs in the postapostolic age, Peter cannot have written II Pet.

2. The conceptual world and the rhetorical language are so strongly influenced by Hellenism as to rule out Peter definitely, nor could it have been written by one of his helpers or pupils

---

[2] Guthrie still assumes that Jude is dependent on II Pet, and Green, *Comm.*, 53 f; Reicke, 190; A. Strobel (see §28 n. 13), 4, think they can find a common tradition behind II Pet and Jude.

under instructions from Peter. Not even at some time after the death of the apostle.[3]

The Hellenistic concepts include: the ἀρετή of God (1:3); *virtue* in addition to *faith* (1:5); *knowledge* (1:2, 3, 6, 8; 2:20; 3:18); participation in the divine nature (θείας κοινωνοὶ φύσεως) "in order that one might escape the corruption that is present in the world because of lust" (1:4); the term ἐπόπται comes from the language of the mysteries (1:16);[4] placed side by side are a quotation from Proverbs and a trite saying from the Hellenistic tradition (2:22).

3. The letter has a keen interest in opposing the denial of the Christians' expectation of the parousia. 1:12 ff already deals with the hope of the parousia, which is based on the fact of the transfiguration of Jesus and the OT prophecy. In 3:3 ff there is a direct polemic against those who deny the parousia. These ask scornfully, "Where is the promise of the parousia of Christ?" and draw attention to the fact that since the fathers have fallen asleep everything remains as it has been from the beginning of creation (3:4). In I Clem 23:3 f and II Clem 11:2 ff too, there is adduced a writing which was obviously read in Christian circles, in which is laid down the challenge "We have already heard that in the days of our fathers, but look, we are become old and nothing of that has happened to us." I Clem was written *ca.* 95, and II Clem can hardly have been written earlier than 150. We have, therefore, historical evidence from the end of the first century onward for this disdainful skepticism which is expressed in II Pet 3:3 ff. But it is the Gnostics of the second century who have opposed the parousia and reinterpreted it along spiritualistic lines. It is probably also they who are meant by the proclaimers of the "clever myths" (1:16) and of "knowledge" (see point 2). Characteristic of them are the libertinism and the insolent disrespect for spirit powers (see point 1). II Pet is therefore aimed against a movement which bears the essential features of second-century gnosis. A more exact determination is not possible, however.

4. Also indicative of the second century is the appeal to a collection of Pauline letters from which "statements that are hard to understand" have been misinterpreted by the false teachers, and to further normative writings which include not only the OT but also the developing NT (3:16). In view of the difficulty in understanding "scripture," and its ambiguity, II Pet offers the thesis that "no prophetic scripture allows an individual interpreta-

---

[3] Reicke; de Zwaan; Schmitt still consider that to be likely.

[4] In view of the whole context, it is not possible to explain these concepts as mere accommodation (contrary to Green, *II Pet Reconsidered*, 23 f).

tion" because men have spoken under the power of the Holy Spirit (1:20 f). Since not every Christian has the Spirit, the explanation of Scripture is reserved for the ecclesiastical teaching office.[5] Accordingly we find ourselves without doubt far beyond the time of Peter and into the epoch of "early Catholicism."

It is certain, therefore, that II Pet does not originate with Peter, and this is today widely acknowledged.[6] This point of view can be confirmed through two further facts.

5. As in the case of the Pastorals, the pseudonymity in II Pet is carried through consistently by means of heavy stress on the Petrine authorship (see above, p. 430). The author adduces his authority not only on the basis of the fiction of a "testament of Peter" but also by reference back to I Pet in 3:1 f, intending II Pet only to "recall" (1:12, 15; 3:1 f) what was said in I Pet to the extent that it corresponds to the interpretation which the author of II Pet wants to give to I Pet.[7] This appeal to the apostolic authority of Peter and his letter is obviously occasioned by the sharpening of the Gnostic false teaching which is being combated in Jude, as a result of a consistent denial of the parousia on the part of the false teachers. In this way, the apostle has become the "guarantor of the tradition" (1:12 f), and as a consequence of the abandonment of the near expectation (3:8) the parousia is stripped of its christological character and functions as an anthropologically oriented doctrine of rewards.[8] In its consistent quality the pseudonymity betrays the late origin of II Pet.

6. In spite of its heavy stress on Petrine authorship, II Pet is nowhere mentioned in the second century. The apologists, Irenaeus, Tertullian, Cyprian, Clement of Alexandria,[9] and the Muratorian Canon are completely silent about it. Its first attestation is in Origen, but according to him the letter is contested (ἀμφιβάλλεται). Eusebius lists it among the antilegomena. Hippolytus knows II Pet, as does Firmilian, Bishop of Caesarea in Cappadocia (d. 268).[10] The papyrus codex $\mathfrak{P}^{72}$, written in the third century (see §38.1.b), contains I and II Pet and Jude, but they are included along with

---

[5] Cf. Schelkle, in loc.; Käsemann, 291, cf. Eng. tr., 169 ff; Marxsen, "Frühkatholizismus," 16 f.

[6] Green, Guthrie, Höpfl-Gut, Mariani, Meinertz; Holzmeister still consider Peter to be the author. Harrison and Wikenhauser are undecided.

[7] See Boobyer.

[8] Käsemann, 283; Eng. tr., 183 ff.

[9] Since Clement nowhere indicates any knowledge of II Pet, Eusebius' information that Clement expounded all the canonical scriptures (HE VI. 14. 1) is scarcely accurate (cf. J. Leipoldt, Geschichte des nt. Kanons I, 1907, 233).

[10] According to Cyprian, Ep. 75. 6.

other non-NT writings, so that no decision can be made on this basis concerning the canonical recognition of II Pet. Even down to the fourth century II Pet was largely unknown or not recognized as canonical.[11] Then gradually it gained recognition. The canonical lists of Athanasius, Cyril of Jerusalem, and Gregory Nazianzus, among others, contain it, and under the influence of Hilary, Ambrose, and Augustine it was finally accepted into the canon of the West. The Peshitta does not have II Pet, and it never achieved full canonical authority among the Syrians.

3. Time and Place of Writing

Any fixed point for exact dating of II Pet is lacking. The time of writing of Jude is a *terminus a quo,* and the discernible development of gnosis in II Pet suggests the second quarter of the second century, while the lack of any christological heresy advises against coming down as late as 150.[12] About the place of composition we know nothing; Rome[13] is only a guess.

The "early Catholic" features which have already been mentioned, as well as the Hellenistic anthropology and the Hellenistic understanding of redemption (1:3 f) and also the abandonment of the primitive Christian christologically based eschatology and its replacement by "an apocalyptic which Jews and Gentiles both treasure and preach," [14] show that II Pet is probably the latest writing of the NT canon. But this raises in especially sharp form the problem of "the inner limits of the canon" and demands reflection on the normative character of this theology (see §37).

§31. The First Letter of John

Commentaries: see §41. Research: E. von Dobschütz, "Johanneische Studien," ZNW 8, 1907, 1 ff; R. Bultmann, "Analyse des I Joh," *Festgabe für A. Jülicher,* 1927, 138 ff (=R. B., *Exegetica,* 1967, 105 ff); *idem,* "Die kirchliche Redaktion des I Joh," *In memoriam E. Lohmeyer,*

---

[11] Jerome, *Vir. ill.* 1, says of II Pet: *a plerisque eius* [i.e., Peter] *negatur propter stili cum priore dissonantium* ("It is rejected by the majority because in style it is incompatible with the former [letter]).

[12] Barnett; Käsemann, Fascher. The date at the end of the first century (e.g., Reicke, Schelkle; Harrington, Klijn) is in any case too early.

[13] Barnett, Green, Michl; Goodspeed.

[14] Käsemann, *Essays,* "Apologia," 183; von Allmen indicates it as probable that in Ch. 3 II Pet makes use of Jewish apocalyptic tradition in uncritical fashion.

1951, 181 ff (=R. B., *Exegetica*, 1967, 381 ff); *idem*, RGG³ III, 1959, 836 ff; E. Lohmeyer, "Über Gliederung und Aufbau des I Joh," ZNW 27, 1928, 225 ff; F. Büchsel, "Zu den Johbr.," ZNW 28, 1929, 235 ff; C. H. Dodd, "The First Epistle of John and the Fourth Gospel," BJRL 21, 1937, 129 ff; O. A. Piper, "I John and the Didache of the Primitive Church," JBL 66, 1947, 437 ff; W. F. Howard, "The Common Authorship of the Johannine Gospel and Epistles," JTS 48, 1947, 12 ff; W. G. Wilson, "An Examination of the Linguistic Evidence Adduced Against the Unity of Authorship of the First Epistle of John and the Fourth Gospel," JTS 49, 1948, 147 ff; R. Leconte, DBS IV, 1949, 797 ff; E. Käsemann, "Ketzer und Zeuge," ZThK 48, 1951, 262 ff (=E. K., *Exegetische Versuche und Besinnungen* I, 1960, 168 ff); H. Braun, "Literar-Analyse und theologische Schichtung im I Joh," ZThK 48, 1951, 262 ff (=H. B., *Gesammelte Studien zum NT und seiner Umwelt*, 1962, 210 ff); H. Conzelmann, " 'Was von Anfang war,' " *Nt. Studien für R. Bultmann*, Bh. ZNW 21, 1954, 194 ff; A. P. Salom, "Some Aspects of the Grammatical Style of I John," JBL 74, 1955, 96 ff; J. Héring, "Y a-t-il des aramaïsmes dans la Première Épître Johannique?" RHPhR 36, 1956, 113 ff; W. Nauck, *Die Tradition und der Charakter des I Joh*, WUNT 3, 1957; H. Strathmann, EKL II, 1958, 363 f; O. Michel, CBL, 655 ff; E. Haenchen, "Neuere Literatur zu den Johbr.," ThR, NF 26, 1960, 1 ff, 267 ff (=E. H., *Die Bibel und wir*, 1968, 235 ff); J. A. T. Robinson, "The Destination and Purpose of the Johannine Epistles," NTS 7, 1960/61, 56 ff (=J. A. T. R., *Twelve NT Studies*, SBT 34, 1962, 126 ff); H.-M. Schenke, "Determination und Ethik im I Joh," ZThK 60, 1963, 203 ff; J. C. O'Neill, *The Puzzle of I John: A New Examination of Origins*, 1966, (on this see I. de la Potterie, Bb 49, 1968, 139 ff); K. Weiss, "Orthodoxie und Heterodoxie im I Joh," ZNW 58, 1967, 247 ff; W. Thüsing, GANT, 282 ff; F. O. Francis, "The Form and Function of the Opening and Closing Paragraphs of James and I John," ZNW 61, 1970, 121 ff; J. Smit Sibinga, "A Study in I John," *Studies in John: Festschr. J. N. Sevenster*, Suppl. NovTest 24, 1970, 194 ff; H. Klos, "Die Sakramente im Joh," SBS 46, 1970, 53 ff; L. Schottroff, *Der Glaubende und die feindliche Welt*, WMANT 37, 1970, 286 ff; G. Klein, " 'Das wahre Licht scheint schon'. Beobachtungen zur Zeit- und Geschichtserfahrung einer urchristlichen Schule," ZThK 68, 1971, 261 ff.

1. Contents

The letter has no clearly discernible structure, but shifts back and forth by way of frequent repetition between the two themes: proper faith in Christ, and the necessary connection between faith and right behavior. Attempts to demonstrate an ingenious structure of sevenfold grouping[1] are no more convincing than the other attempts to show a systematic arrangement.[2] The unprovable hypotheses that the author or his pupils added to the original writing (1:1–2:27) various independent sketches and meditations without any unified plan[3] or that the letter was composed by bringing together twelve admonitions originally independent of each other[4] show only that no sure sequence of ideas can be discerned. Even the following proposal for an outline[5] is to be seen as nothing more than an attempt, as was the case with I Pet (see above, §28.1).

In the opening section the author attests to the reality of the life which is revealed through the Logos become flesh which also bestows on the readers fellowship with God. In the first cycle of ideas (1:5–2:27)—walking in the light and confession of Jesus as the Christ—two theses are discussed in detail: (a) "Walking in the light": walking in the light does not involve absolute sinlessness (1:5-10); warning and reassurance concerning the reality of sin in the lives of Christians (2:1 f); keeping the commandments as a sign of the confession of God and Christ (2:3-6); love of brother as proof of walking in the light (2:7-11); reminder to the reader of the salvation which he possesses and an urgent warning against love of the world (2:12-17). Then briefly and with sharp blows against false teachers, there follows the christological thesis (b): Confession of Jesus as the Christ (2:18-27).

The theme is repeated in another form in the second cycle of ideas (2:28–4:6)—doing righteousness and confessing Jesus as the Christ as signs of the kingdom of God. Here again the ethical thesis is developed: "doing righteousness" (above all, active love of brother, 2:28–3:24) receives even fuller development. Doing righteousness and purifying oneself characterize the children of God and permit them to stand before him in the judgment (2:28–3:6); committing sins characterizes the children of the Devil, while those who do not sin (who practice love) are the children of God (3:7-17); active brotherly love and faith in Christ and love of the brethren are in their interaction the guarantee of fellowship with God (3:18-24). The christological thesis is: "The

[1] Albertz; Lohmeyer.
[2] See the enumeration in Robert-Feuillet, 617 f.
[3] Bultmann, Comm., 11, 47 f.
[4] O'Neill, 6.
[5] Similar division is proposed by Smit Sibinga, who thinks he can prove that the sections 1:1–2:16 and 4:27–5:21 evidence the same number of syllables. Francis, 123 f, wants to show that there are two main sections, 1:5–2:29 and 3:1–5:12, framed by the introduction and conclusion to the letter.

confession 'Jesus Christ has come in the flesh' is the sign of one's being born of God" (4:1-6), which is once more presented in sharply antiheretical formulation. In the third cycle of ideas (4: 7-5:13) love and faith are united in a single perspective in that love based on faith (4:7-21) and faith which is based on love (5:1-13) are seen together as the signs of having been born of God. Concluding ideas (5:14-21): the certainty of possessing life gives joy in prayer (14 f) and intercession except in connection with mortal sin, (16 f); the basic truths stand sure: not sinning is the result of being born of God and holding fast to the confession of God in Jesus Christ (18-20); final warning: stay away from idols (21).

2. Literary Character

The ordinary features of a letter are missing from I John: prescript and conclusion with greetings and a benediction. It contains no names (except the name of Cain in 3:12) and no concrete personal associations. Therefore it gives the impression that it is not a letter at all. Remarks addressed to the readers (2:1, 7; 4:4 among others) do not prove that specific persons are being addressed[6] any more than the beginning and end of the work can be explained as corresponding to a letter form.[7] I John seems rather to be a tractate intended for the whole of Christianity, a kind of manifesto.[8] The polemic against heresy does not in any way reflect concrete situations. The fact that the readers are familiar with Cain (3:12) does not prove that they were formerly Jews of the Dispersion,[9] nor can that be inferred either from the moralistic standard which is presumably represented among them or from the "judaizing" character of the false teachers who are being combated. But neither is the Gentile origin of the readers stressed, because in light of a peculiar situation the entirety of Christianity is being addressed. I John is not to be understood as being in any way a writing intended for specific readers.

[6] Against Gaugler, Michl, Schnackenburg; Fuller, Harrington, Mariani; Thüsing. According to Marxsen, the writer is always seeking to approximate the form of a letter.

[7] According to Francis, 122 f, 126, 1:1-3; 5:13-21 have a "strictly epistolary function"; and A. Strobel (Monatshefte; see §28 n. 13), 6, thinks that as a result of liturgical-homiletical use, an original catachetical writing for the baptized has lost its epistolary form.

[8] Thus Boismard, JB; Knopf, Windisch-Preisker; Jülicher-Fascher, Klijn, Riddle-Hutson, Schelkle; Bultmann, Lohmeyer.

[9] Robinson.

Attempts have been made to explain the special literary character of I John in various ways on the basis of secondary compilation.[10] From 2:28–3:17 von Dobschütz separated out four antithetical statements (3:9aa and 3:10ba) which the author of the letter revised and commented upon. Following this lead, Bultmann, utilizing stylistic and conceptual criteria, has distilled from the letter as a whole twenty-six antithetical couplets which constituted the *Vorlage*. He distinguishes them from the homiletical revisions and designates the *Vorlage* as part of the Gnostic source of the revelatory speeches which according to Bultmann was also used in John (see §10.3). Later Bultmann expanded this analysis with the hypothesis that an ecclesiastical editor has not only added a supplement (5:14-21) which betrays itself as a foreign body by reason of its ideas, but has also made interpolations in 1:7c; 2:2, 28; 3:2 (ἐὰν φανερωθῇ); 4:10b, 17b; 5:7-9 which introduce the eschatology of the church and the idea of atonement through the blood of Christ. Bultmann received some support for his source analysis,[11] but firm rejection as well.[12] Braun, who is in basic agreement with Bultmann's method, tries to extend the compass of the source which underlies I John but rejects the idea of a pre-Christian origin of this source and distinguishes the point of view of the source ("authentic Christian") and the editing ("early Catholic"). Nauck maintains the distinction between *Vorlage* and editing but traces both back to the same author: by means of his antithetically formulated *Vorlage*, the author intervenes in the situation of a community which is endangered by false teaching and seeks to lead them ultimately to a sure position by his editorial comments. More recently, O'Neill has separated out from I John twelve Jewish heterodox hortatory texts which following his conversion the author has expanded in Christian form, in order to convince those members of his sect who still remain in Judaism of the truth of the Christian faith.

This observation of a stylistic distinction between short sententious statements (i.e., 2:9) and the broader homiletical developments (i.e., 2:1 f) is absolutely correct. But the boundaries be-

---

[10] Cf. the survey in Nauck, 1 ff.

[11] Windisch; Wilder; somewhat more cautiously Klein, 280 n. 92; Ph. Vielhauer, ThR 31, 1965/66, 133. Preisker (in the new edition of the Windisch Comm.) assumes that instead of an editing process there was a second *Vorlage* (prototype) which developed its argument eschatologically in the traditional sense. According to J. Heise, *Bleiben. Menein in den Joh. Schriften*, Hermeneutische Untersuchungen zur Theologie 8, 1967, 108 f, 174 ff, the source is dependent upon the Fourth Gospel as a whole.

[12] Cf. the authors cited by Klein, 280 n. 92; further Grant, *Intr.*, 232.

tween the two stylistic forms cannot be drawn very sharply, and
therefore the analysis leads again and again to the necessity either
of assuming that the *Vorlage* and the editorial process have influenced each other or of conceding the impossibility of making a
decision.[13] This shows that the distinction on the ground of
stylistic peculiarities cannot be convincingly presented. On the
other hand, if it can be shown that the *Vorlage* too must be of
Christian origin (Braun) but that there is no clear distinction between the *Vorlage* and the editorial process,[14] then this criterion
for making a differentiation of the sources as intended by Bultmann
and Braun is useless. Contrary to Nauck's assumption that the
Vorlage and the editorial reworking were done by the same author
is the fact that it would be inconceivable for a writer to have so
thoroughly fragmented his own artistic work subsequently that it
would no longer be possible to discover what the original had been.
Finally to O'Neill's source theory it may be objected that the
sections of the source as reconstructed cannot by any means be
shown to have been Jewish,[15] nor could the ostensibly missionary
aim have been achieved by the unmistakable christianizing of a
text which was already known to the intended readers. The supposition that there was a *Vorlage* and that it was edited is therefore unproved and improbable. The differences of style are to be
traced back to the use of traditional material and to the changing
content of what is being said.[16]

But what of Bultmann's assumption that I John has undergone
an ecclesiastical redaction?[17] Exclusion of references to futuristic
eschatology and to the redeeming function of the blood of Jesus
can be established persuasively only by the assertion of a counter
position over against Johannine theology. The allegedly offending
features in the context do not loom especially large, so that this
assertion can be maintained only on the unlikely assumption of

[13] See Braun, 267, cf. also 215; Nauck, 74 ff, 123.

[14] Käsemann, 307 f, cf. also 182 f n. 47; Haenchen, 18 ff, cf. also 254 f; Klein, 281 f n. 92, thinks that he can demonstrate such a distinction; but this is dependent on his analysis of I John (see below, p. 444 f).

[15] Cf. the observations of de la Potterie and, e.g., 2:5, "by this we know that we are in him."

[16] Cf. Schnackenburg, 12; Piper; Schenke, 205.

[17] Schenke, 204; Schottroff, 287, agree with Bultmann; critical are Schnacken-burg, 14 f; Nauck, 128 ff; Francis, 124 ff; Klein, 320 ff. O'Neill, 66, assumes secondary glosses in 1:7; 2:8, 17, 24; 3:20; 4:13; 5:4b, 6-8. Feuillet, in Robert-Feuillet, 622 ff, thinks it possible that 5:14 ff has been added; Heise (see n. 11), 132 ff, considers 2:15-17 to be an ascetic interpolation.

interpolations in Jn (see §10.3) and accordingly is not justified.[18] There are more grounds for assuming that 5:14 ff has been added secondarily: the distinction between two classes of sinners (5:16 ff) is lacking elsewhere in John and stands in tension with 1:5 ff; in 5:20 ἥκει for the coming of the Son of God is unique, and 5:21 is linguistically non-Johannine. But these deviations or singularities are not real contradictions to the rest of I John, and so it is thoroughly understandable that 5:14 ff belonged to the original I John, even though naturally it cannot be proved. It must be regarded as probable, therefore, that I John in the form in which we have it is the work of a single author.

This judgment does not apply, however, to the trinitarian addition in 5:7 f, the so-called *Comma Johanneum*.[19] Except for three minuscules from the fourteenth to sixteenth centuries, the text of which is translated from the Vulgate, this section is missing in all Greek manuscripts, as it is in the original Vulgate and the Eastern translations. It was first adopted by Erasmus in the third edition of his text, and from there was taken over into the *textus receptus* (see below, §39). Without exception it is regarded today as a later addition. The oldest sure witness is Priscillian (at the end of the fourth century), but whether the addition is somewhat older or not is debated.[20]

3. Aim

I John is seeking to warn against false teachers who have arisen in the Christian communities (2:18 f, 26; 3:7). Many false prophets have gone out into the world (4:1); I John calls them Antichrists (2:18, cf. 4:3). From their coming it may be inferred (cf. Mk 13:22 par.) that the parousia of Christ stands close at hand (2:18). The seriousness of the age which is breaking in upon them demands that Christians differentiate the spirit of error from the spirit of truth (4:6). The Christians to whom this letter is addressed have already vigorously opposed the false leaders (4:4). The false spirits have been excluded from the community (2:19), but their dangerous influence has not yet been destroyed (4:1 ff). The features which John highlights show what they desire and

---

[18] Klein, 320 ff, presupposing interpolations in Jn, considers on the contrary that interpolations in the theologically deviant I Jn are unnecessary.

[19] See on this Schnackenburg, 44 ff.

[20] That the insert was already introduced into the Greek text is most improbable (against W. Thiele, "Beobachtungen zum Comma Johanneum," ZNW 50, 1959, 61 ff).

what they undertake: they boast of their perception of God (2:4; 4:8), their love of God (4:20), and their fellowship with God (1:6; 2:6, 9); they lay claim to unique pneumatic experiences (4:1 ff); and they think that they are above sinning (1:8, 10). They deny that Jesus is the Christ (2:22 f), the Son of God, as that is understood in the primitive Christian faith (4:15; 5:5, 10 ff). They reject the confession that Jesus has come in full historical humanity, that he has "come in the flesh" (4:2), and that his work on earth began with his baptism and ended with his death (5:6). It must therefore have been a Gnostic-enthusiastic movement which offered a Docetic Christology[21] against which is asserted the identity of the man Jesus with the Son of God and the Christ (4:15; 5:1, 5), and the redeeming power of his death (5:6; 1:7; 2:1 f; 3:16; 4:10), as the indispensable essential parts of the certainty of Christian faith. Combined with this hostility toward the Christian confession of faith was an ethical point of view which saw the strong bond between Christian faith and Christian life as being of no value. Obedience to the commandments of Jesus does not seem to them a basic demand (2:4); they attach no importance to doing righteousness (3:7, 10), to active love of brother (2:9, 11; 3:10 ff; 4:20), to help for the poor (3: 17). They make concessions to the world instead of separating themselves from it (4:5; 2:15 ff), and in this way they are conscious of their own moral perfection (1:8, 10). With great emphasis, I John stresses against this point of view that confession of God and walking in the light are inseparably related, and that only Jesus Christ, the Word made flesh, has brought the love of God which is able to blot out sin.

The variety within the early Christian gnosis which John is combating cannot be linked with names from the history of heresy. It has repeatedly been assumed that in I John the false teacher who is being combated is Cerinthus, who lived in Asia Minor at the end of the first century.[22] But I John shows no trace

---

[21] In view of 2:19, 24; 4:2 f, there cannot be said to be an "overwhelming weight" of proof for the thesis that I John defends the confession of Jesus as Messiah against the Jews (thus O'Neill, 60, 65); in actuality these texts show the opponents to be former Christians who do not acknowledge the σάρξ of Jesus.

[22] Thus, e.g., Chaine, Ross; Feine-Behm, Feuillet in Robert-Feuillet, Harrison, Wikenhauser, de Zwaan; Bultmann, Robinson. *Contra,* see above all Schnackenburg, 19 f. The attempt to trace back the false teaching to Menander of Antioch is simply unfounded (Grant, *Intr.,* 233), as is the assertion that the author is seeking to gain the position of right belief only in the reflection which is taking place (thus Weiss).

of the point of view that was characteristic of Cerinthus: that Christ was only temporarily united with the man Jesus. Furthermore I John does not polemicize against the distinction between an upper and a lower god. The ethical danger against which I John warns cannot be demonstrated in Cerinthus. Although the Gnostic false teaching cannot be determined with historical exactitude, it is nonetheless significant that here—unlike the situation in Col, the Pastorals, Jude, and II Pet—enthusiastic Gnosticism has christological implications, so that here we have to do with a developed form of Gnosticism. The opposition to this Gnostic false teaching appears, however, in a kind of language which is strongly influenced by gnosis and which has close connections with the conceptual world of Jn (see §10.4). The attempt to prove that from the standpoint of tradition history I John is associated with Qumran and with Christian baptismal ritual[23] is scarcely successful, since similarities in detailed motifs do not prove any links in the history of tradition.[24]

4. Author and Relationship to the Fourth Gospel

As was already recognized by Dionysius of Alexandria,[25] the relationship of I John with Jn is the most striking fact in the historical evaluation of I John. On the basis of agreement of language and conceptual world, Dionysius inferred that both works were by the same author. This view remained uncontested until the beginning of the nineteenth century and is shared today by many scholars independently of the question as to who the author is. But especially since the Tübingen school drew attention to the differences which might imply different authors, this opinion has had repeated support.[26] On the basis of language and content evidence can be adduced for both points of view.

a. It is undisputed [27] that I John and Jn are strikingly closely

[23] Nauck (in agreement with M.-E. Boismard, RB 66, 1959, 146); O'Neill attempts to demonstrate that the supposed Jewish basic document was of heretical-Jewish origin.

[24] See Haenchen, 21 ff, 41 f, cf. also 257 ff, 280 ff; H. Braun (see §27 n. 23), 290 ff, esp. 304 ff.

[25] In Eus., HE VII. 25. 18 ff.

[26] Cf., e.g., Bultmann, Dodd, Wilder, Windisch-Preisker; Dibelius, Goguel, McNeile-Williams, Moffatt, Schelkle; Conzelmann, Haenchen, O'Neill, Thüsing, Schottroff, Klein; E. Lohse, "Wort und Sakrament im Joh," NTS 6, 1959/60, 115; P. Stuhlmacher, *Gerechtigkeit Gottes bei Paulus*, FRLANT 87, 1965, 199; J. Heise (see n. 11), 105.

[27] Cf. Brooke, i ff; Chaine, 104 ff.

related in vocabulary and style, which would seem to indicate the same author. C. H. Dodd has pointed out, however, that I John uses significantly fewer prepositions, particles, and compound verbs than Jn and that numerous expressions and words of Jn are completely missing in I John. Especially striking is the lack of οὖν (194 times in Jn), δόξα (18 times), κρίνειν (19); and γάρ appears 63 times in Jn but only 3 times in I John. The significance of this evidence has been called into question[28] by noting that the frequency of the use of particles, etc., and the presence of favorite particles change in the same writer, corresponding to the length of the writings and the subject in question, so that on this basis no conclusions can be drawn. Salom has shown further that both writings are strikingly similar in the frequency of the sequence of sentence parts and in detailed stylistic peculiarities (e.g., ἐν τούτῳ . . . ὅτι or ἐάν). Haenchen on the other hand has taken up Dodd's observations and has stressed that a distinction in the use of prepositions (Jn has, for example, παρά with the genitive 25 times; I John has instead ἀπό) does indeed suggest a different author. These are indeed striking phenomena (i.e., in connection with the verbs αἰτεῖν and ἀκούειν), but pointing in the opposite direction is such evidence as the fact that I John 4:13 and Jn 6:11 agree in the rare linking of διδόναι (or διαδιδόναι ἔκ τινος). Even though a certain linguistic difference between Jn and I John cannot be denied, one cannot go to the opposite extreme and say that it is inconceivable that they may both have been written by the same writer with a considerable passage of time in between.[29]

b. Decisive, however, is the question whether I John really differs substantively from Jn. Here too that both writings represent pretty much the same ideas is uncontested.[30] Yet without doubt there are clear distinctions: in I John there are no quotations from the OT; futuristic eschatology is stressed (2:28, parousia; 3:2; 4:17); the false teachers are characterized as present-day ἀντίχριστοι (2:18, 22; 4:3); παράκλητος indicates (2:1) Jesus Christ, not the Spirit as in Jn; in Jn 8:12 "light" is a title of Christ, but in I John 1:5 it refers to God; only in I John is the expiatory character of the death of Jesus mentioned (1:7, 9; 2:2; 4:10). John says

---

[28] By Howard, Wilson.

[29] Recently Schnackenburg, 35, and Klein, 265 f, have stressed that the linguistic differences do not force one to accept different authorship. E. D. Freed, "Variation in the Language and Thought of John," ZNW 55, 1964, 194 ff, has pointed to the linguistic variations in the works of the same author.

[30] Cf. the assembling of the evidence in Windisch-Preisker, 109 f.

nothing of the new birth through Christ (2:19). On the basis
of these and other differences it has been inferred that Jn and I
John could not have come from the same author, because I John
stands closer to traditional Christianity than does Jn,[31] that I
John is more closely bound to early Catholicism than the Pastorals,[32] and that already it looks back on Jn as part of the tradition.[33] By others it has been proposed that I John represents a
more advanced stage, so that instead of abiding in Christ we have
an abiding in the old teaching,[34] that for I John the opposition is
no longer the non-Christian "world" but the false teachers,[35] or
that I John avoids the potentially misleading statement in Jn about
God's turning to the world.[36] Above all, Klein has attempted to
show that in contrast to Jn, I John considers the eschaton to be
a temporal term (2:8) and, for example, sets chronological limits
for the light. Or he suggests that the "transchronological" οὔπω
of Jn 7:6 is reinterpreted chronologically in I John 3:2. But against
this it must be said in the first place that some of these allegedly
missing concepts are indeed in Jn if these parallels have not been
antecedently removed from the Gospel by excluding them as supposed interpolations or by reinterpretations.[37] That is true for the
futuristic eschatology (Jn 5:29; 12:48; 14:3) as well as for the
concept of the expiatory death of Jesus (Jn 1:29; 3:14 ff; 6:51b;
12:24) or of Christ as παράκλητος (indirectly attested in Jn 14:
16). It is further to be remarked that some differences may be
explained on the basis of the polemic against heretics in I John, as,
e.g., the characterization of the false teachers as ἀντίχριστοι and
the opposition to the false teachers instead of to the hostile world
or "the Jews." It is totally unproved that I John makes reference
back to Jn as to tradition, and it is totally false that I John avoids
mentioning God's turning to the world (cf. I John 2:2; 4:14).
And against Klein's analytical differentiation is to be said that Jn
may by no means be interpreted "transchronologically" and that
Jn rather reflects throughout the future "in the perspective of

---

[31] Dodd.

[32] Marxsen; Haenchen.

[33] Conzelmann, who would like to describe I John as a "Johannine pastoral
letter" (p. 201; thus also Marxsen, Intr., 264; Klein, 268).

[34] E. Schweizer, "Der Kirchenbegriff bei Johannes," StEv I, TU 73, 1959, 375 ff
(=E. Sch., Neotestamentica, 1963, 266 ff).

[35] Bultmann, Comm., 9.

[36] Schottroff.

[37] See above §10 n. 58.

universal history" too (cf. Jn 5:24; 12:31).[88] Thus although it is likely that I John was written some time later than Jn,[89] and although it cannot be clearly proved that I John was written by the author of Jn, there are no cogent reasons for assuming that I John is to be attributed to another author than Jn. In distinction from the strongly charismatic character of the Gospel, the pragmatic character of I John leads necessarily to formulations which are more clearly suitable for achieving this pragmatic goal.

Since there is no adequate reason for assuming that I John was written by someone other than the author of the Gospel of John, we can only maintain for the author of I John what we know concerning the author of Jn.[40]

5. Time of Writing

If I John and Jn come from the same author, then I John would not have been written very long after Jn. Since I John is known as early as the second quarter of the second century,[41] I John cannot have been written later than toward the end of the first quarter of the second century. Between 90 and 110 would therefore be the most probable time for the origin of I John. As to the place of origin we know nothing. If Jn comes from Syria (see §10.7), we could conjecture the same provenance for I John.

§32. The Second and Third Letters of John

Commentaries: see §41. Research: see §31, as well as A. Harnack, "Über den 3 Joh," TU 15, 1897; H. von Campenhausen, *Kirchliches Amt und geistliche Vollmacht in den ersten drei Jahrhunderten*, BHTh 14, 1953, 132 ff; R. Schnackenburg, "Der Streit zwischen dem Verf. von 3 Joh und Diotrephes . . . ," MThZ 4, 1953, 18 ff; G. Born-

---

[88] Against Klein, 314. When Klein characterizes the doubt about the evidence for a profound theological difference between Jn and I John as "exegesis that is timid about making distinctions" and wants to trace the linguistic commonality between Jn and I John to "linguistic mimicry" (p. 269 f), his arguments are not objective.

[39] The reversed sequence assumed by Strathmann; O'Neill, 67, is highly improbable in view of Schweizer's observations (see n. 34).

[40] See above, §10.6. The oldest tradition (in Iren., *Haer.* II. 17. 5, 8; Muratorian Canon, 26 ff) knows no independent account concerning the author of I John.

[41] Polyc., Phil 7:1 presupposes I John 4:2 f; according to Eus., HE III. 39. 17, Papias used texts from I John.

kamm, art. "πρέσβυς," TDNT VI, 1968, 651 ff; A. Kragerud. *Der Lieblingsjünger im Joh*, 1959, 100 ff; R. Bergmeier, "Zum Verfasserproblem des II. und III. Johbr.," ZNW 57, 1966, 93 ff; R. Schnackenburg, "Zum Begriff der Wahrheit in den beiden kleinen Johbr.," BZ, NF 11, 1967, 253 ff; R. W. Funk, "The Form and Structure of II and III John," JBL 86, 1967, 424 ff; J. Heise, *Bleiben. Menein in den Johannesschriften*, Hermeneutische Untersuchungen zum NT 8, 1967, 164 ff.

1. Contents

II John. Without mention of a name the letter is written by "the elder" to the "elect lady and her children." In the prescript (1-3), the author stresses that the bond of love binds those who are addressed with him and with all those who have acknowledged the truth. The real content of the letter (4-11) constitutes an admonition to walk in truth and love and a warning concerning the seducers who do not confess that Jesus Christ has come in the flesh and who preach "progress" (9). With an expression of hope that he may soon personally be with them (12), and with greetings from the "children of the elect sister" of the lady addressed (13) the letter comes to a close.

III John. The elder writes to an individual person, Gaius. Following the prescript (1) there is an introductory intercession (2-4), an expression of joy over the good testimony that the itinerant brothers have brought concerning Gaius. The theme of the letter is hospitality toward itinerant brothers (5–12); Gaius is encouraged to extend his proven hospitality (5–8); polemic against Diotrephes because he has offered opposition to the author (9 f); praise of Demetrius (11 f). Conclusion (13-15): explanation for the brevity of the writing on the basis of his hope for a personal meeting soon (13 f); benediction and greeting (15).

2. Form, Destination, and Aim

No other NT letter, not even Phlm has so completely the form of a Hellenistic private letter as II and III John.[1] Both are real letters.[2] But they deal with, not private matters, but matters of the

---

[1] Funk has shown that with regard to formal expressions (e.g., III John 2, 3), both letters follow the profane letter style more strictly than do all the other NT letters.

[2] On this see below, p. 449 f.

faith and life of Christian communities; and as statements by an ecclesiastically authoritative person they bear a certain official stamp.

II John is addressed to a community. κυρία (1, 5) could be either a proper name or a courteous address to a woman,[3] but on the basis of the tone of the letter as a whole, it must be assumed that the word κυρία here has a figurative meaning. Through the bond of love as a mutual obligation this "woman" is bound "with all who have acknowledged the truth" (1, 5); her "children," who are many in number (4), are not physical but spiritual children like "the children of the elder" (III John 4). The letter concerns questions of the common life of the Christian community (5 f, 7 ff, 10). "The lady" is therefore a figurative designation for the community by way of transferring a political verbal image to an ecclesiastical community.[4] As an ecclesiastical community she is designated "the chosen" as well as her "chosen sister" (13, cf. I Pet 5:13), the community in the place from which the "elder" is writing. II John is intended for a specific individual congregation (4, 12 f).

Nothing is known about Gaius to whom III John is written, as with Diotrephes (9) and Demetrius (12). Gaius was converted by "the elder" (4) and is obviously living in a community in which he and his "friends" (15) stand over against the officials of the community, Diotrephes (9 f) and his circle. It is not clear whether Demetrius also belongs to this community and to the friends of Gaius or whether he is the bearer of the letter or one of the "strange brothers" (5). The community is certainly a different one from that of II John, since the figure of Diotrephes would not fit into that harmonious picture. That III John (9) makes reference to II John, which was written earlier[5] is very doubtful in view of the differences between the situations.[6] The similarities of form are the result of the letters' originating from about the same time. It is not possible to determine the place to which III John was sent any more than is true for II John.

The aim of the two letters is different. In II John "the elder" is issuing warnings to the community addressed concerning false teachers who refute the incarnation of Jesus Christ and preach a progressive theory. Thus the warning concerns Gnostics of some

[3] Thus wrongly still Albertz: "the chairlady of a house church," Ross; Guthrie: "elect lady."

[4] See W. Foerster, TDNT III, 1095; F. J. Dölger, "Domina Mater Ecclesia und die 'Herrin' im 2 Joh," *Antike und Christentum* 5, 1936, 211 ff.

[5] Thus, e.g., Dibelius, Jülicher-Fascher, McNeile-Williams; Strathmann, (see §31).

[6] Cf. Schnackenburg; Guthrie; Haenchen (see §31).

kind, like those combated in I John. They are also here equated with the Antichrist, and "the elder" commands the community not to enter into any kind of relationship with such people. The basis of the elder's authority for issuing such instructions to the community addressed cannot be determined.

In III John "the elder" praises Gaius because he has offered hospitality to the missionary brethren. He orders him to continue to do so and not to allow himself to be deterred by Diotrephes. For this Diotrephes rejects "the elder," makes hateful speeches against him (9 f), does not permit the brethren sent by "the elder" to come into the congregation, hinders the members of the community from receiving the brethren, and excludes them from the congregation if they oppose that policy. What sort of situation is presupposed here is debated.[7] Harnack would like to see here evidence of the struggle of the older provincial missionary organization against the monarchic leadership which is consolidating the individual communities;[8] but there really is no trace of a provincial missionary organization or anything like it. Also the attempts to prove that Diotrephes is a Gnostic[9] or to identify "the elder" as a false teacher who had been excommunicated by the orthodox leader of the community, Diotrephes,[10] are untenable, because there is no mention made of false teaching or of excommunication of the elder. More likely is a conflict between a more rigid ecclesiastical organization and the older, freer charismatic mode,[11] but even that the elder represents the freer charismatics is not expressed clearly. All that is clear is that in the view of "the elder," Diotrephes has arrogated to himself an exclusive role to which he has no right, in spite of his actual leadership role in the community. As a result of his stance, the missionary activity is hindered which the elder stands behind and which is supported by some members of the community of Diotrephes. Obviously "the presbyter as spokesman for one community" is directing his attention "to another community."[12] He is thus a community leader like Diotrephes, but the fact that he calls himself "the elder" suggests that his authority is regarded as more than merely local, which is what Diotrephes obviously is denying to him. The his-

---

[7] Cf. the account by Haenchen (see §31), 267 ff, cf. also 283 ff.

[8] Similarly Schneider; Kragerud.

[9] Fuller; W. Bauer, *Orthodoxy and Heresy in Oldest Christianity*, 1971, 93.

[10] Käsemann in agreement with Heise, 106 n. 16, 164. Against Käsemann are Bultmann, *Comm.*, 95, 100; Schnackenburg, 299 f; Marxsen, 226.

[11] Thus Jülicher-Fascher; von Campenhausen, Bornkamm; Michel (see §31).

[12] Haenchen (see §31), 290, cf. also 310.

torical situation could be explained only if we could determine
who the elder was.

3. Author

II and III John were written by the same author. They use the
same language, they agree in their length and in their epistolary
form (address, introduction, conclusion). In the heading they
carry the same distinctive self-designation of the author: ὁ πρεσβύτερος. This position has recently been contested in various ways,
to be sure. No longer championed today is the assertion that these
two small letters of John were artificially produced in conscious
imitation of the Johannine writings.[13] Indeed, significant objections
are being raised against the theory that II John was written by
the same author as III John. It is said that II John is a fictional
letter[14] from early Catholicism dependent on III John, and that
in distinction from I John the concept of truth in II John is no
longer dualistic but indicates, rather, correct doctrine over against
false doctrine[15] and that it cannot be conceptually harmonized with
I John and III John (the idea of rewards, II John 8; punishment
by the church 10 f).[16] But really, the dependence of II John on
III John is scarcely demonstrable, the more so since II John also
shows clearly formal features of ancient private letter writing.[17]
And the concept of truth in II John by no means includes only
correct teaching, but strongly emphasizes correct living as well and
is not distinguished in this way from I John.[18] On the other hand
it is striking that there are in II John some concepts which are
not found elsewhere in the Johannine writings: ἔλεος (II John
3); μισθός (8); the prohibition of χαίρειν λέγειν (10 f). But ἔλεος
is traditional in the prescripts of letters and is attested frequently
in later primitive Christianity,[19] and in spite of points of contact
the prescripts of the three Johannine letters are otherwise not unified. The word μισθός appears in a figurative sense in John 4:36,
and like II John 8, John 6:27 evidences the concept of "given"
reward: (strive for . . . the food which endures for life which the

---

[13] Dibelius, Jülicher-Fascher.

[14] Bultmann, *Comm.*, 10, 103 ff; Heise, 166 f.

[15] Bergmeier.

[16] Heise.

[17] Cf. Funk.

[18] See Schnackenburg, BZ 1967.

[19] I Tim 1:2; II Tim 1:2; Jude 2; cf. Dibelius-Conzelmann, *Comm. on the
Pastorals*, HNT ²13, 1955, 12 f.

Son of man gives you). The prohibition against extending greetings has, of course, no direct parallel in I and III John, but the polemic (I John 2:18-23; 5:16b) is actually not essentially different. So in spite of certain striking features the assumption is most likely that the literarily unpretentious II John is actually a letter which comes from the same author as III John.

But then the question is raised whether this author who calls himself ὁ πρεσβύτερος is identical with the anonymous author of I John. There can be no doubt that II and III John are closely related to I John (and John) in language, style, and conceptuality.[20] The emphasis on the trustworthiness of the author's witness is found in III John 12 as in John 19:35 (21:24). The characteristic Johannine view that basic being is to be inferred from doing is found in III John 11; II John 4 ff shows numerous parallels with I John, and the polemical front against heretical gnosis in II John 7, 9 is the same as in I John. It is true that detailed distinctions in language and mode of expression have been adduced for the thesis that II and III John are to be attributed to a different author from I John:[21] the particular false teacher is designated as "Antichrist" in II John 7, all the "progressives" are to be expelled from the community (II John 9), instead of Jesus Christ as "the one who has come in the flesh" in I John 4:2, he is in II John 7 "the one coming in the flesh," and in contradiction to John 1:18 and I John 4:12a, III John 11 reads, "Whoever does evil has not seen God." But insofar as these differences cannot be explained on the basis of an altered polemical situation, they are too trivial to make probable the assumption of different authors for I John and II and III John.

Since the evidence points to the stronger likelihood that the three Johannine letters come from the same author, the question must be put finally who this author is who simply names himself ὁ πρεσβύτερος. Since the name is lacking and has scarcely been omitted, ὁ πρεσβύτερος is hardly to be translated as "the presbyter" —of whom there were many—but "the old man." The tradition of the early church in tracing the three Johannine letters and the Gospel of John back to the same author, (see below, 32.4) has also assumed that John son of Zebedee is the author of II and III John. Of course, the same arguments against the authorship

[20] Cf. the assembling of the evidence in R. H. Charles, *The Revelation of St. John*, ICC I, xxxiv ff; xli ff.

[21] Bultmann; Jülicher-Fascher; J. Jeremias, "Joh. Literarkritik," ThBl 20, 1941, 43 n. 39. Different authors are considered conceivable by Michl; Marxsen, Schelkle; Klos (see §31), 55 f.

of Jn by the son of Zebedee are in effect for II and III John.[22]
On the other hand, it is a fact that the author of these four writings could call himself ὁ πρεσβύτερος and in so doing be understood. There are therefore two possibilities: either a man unknown
to us who was perhaps a member of a presbyterion (cf. I Tim
4:14) bore this title in some special sense without our being able
to know anything more certain about him, or ὁ πρεσβύτερος is a
reference to the fact that this man belonged to the circle of "those
presbyters" whom Papias and Irenaeus and Clement present as
guardians and bearers of the apostolic tradition.[23] If this second
assumption is more probable because only thus can one really
understand the use of the title by the author of II and III John
as a designation of authority, then it might also be asked further
whether ὁ πρεσβύτερος Ἰωάννης who is mentioned in this manner by
Papias[24] (see §10.6) may not be designated here. But for this question there really is no sure answer.

4. Time of Writing

II and III John are first attested by Clement of Alexandria, who
according to Eusebius wrote commentaries on all the Catholic
letters.[25] But this evidence from Eusebius is not subject to confirmation.[26] Irenaeus quotes only II John, and the Muratorian
Canon speaks of only two of the Johannine letters which found
Catholic acceptance. Since III John was translated independently
into Latin,[27] it is obvious that it came into the canon in the West
later than II John. Origen[28] and Eusebius[29] know that the authenticity of these little letters of John is not generally recognized, and
Jerome[30] reports that II and III John were written by the presbyter
John. Since II and III John were only accepted into the canon
with hesitation and probably became known only at a late date
(certainly this is true of III John), there is scarcely a special tradition concerning the authorship. Rather, the acceptance of both

---

[22] On the lack of antiquity of this tradition and its untenability cf. §10.6.

[23] Haenchen (see §31), 291, cf. also 310.

[24] In Eus., HE III. 39. 4.

[25] Thus Eus., HE VI. 14. 1.

[26] Cf. §30, n. 9.

[27] See the evidence in T. W. Manson "Entry into the Membership of the
Early Church," JTS 48, 1947, 32 f.

[28] In Eus., HE VI. 25. 10.

[29] Eus., HE III. 25. 3.

[30] Jerome, Vir. ill., 9.

letters was hindered by the brief title ὁ πρεσβύτερος which could not be attached to any one apostle. Since the tradition of the letters themselves allows us to infer nothing concerning the time of origin, and since we know nothing concerning the sequence of writing of the letters, we can only propose that they were written about the same time as I John, i.e., *ca.* 90–110.

C. THE APOCALYPTIC BOOK

§33. APOCALYPTIC AND APOCALYPSES

Literature: Survey of research: J. M. Schmidt, *Die jüdische Apokalyptik. Die Geschichte ihrer Erforschung von den Anfängen bis zu den Textfunden von Qumran*, 1969, esp. 171 ff, 215 ff, 277 ff. Comprehensive Studies: W. Bousset–H. Gressmann, *Die Religion des Judentums im späthellenistischen Zeitalter*, HNT 21, [3]1926, 11 ff, 242 ff; J.-B. Frey, DBS I, 1928, 326 ff (lit.); P. Volz, *Die Eschatologie der jüdischen Gemeinde im nt. Zeitalter*, 1934; J. Sickenberger, RAC I, 1950, 504 ff; J. Block, "On the Apocalyptic in Judaism," *Jewish Quarterly Review*, Monograph Series 2, 1952; H. Ringgren–R. Schütz, "Apokalyptik I–III," RGG[3] I, 1957, 463 ff; H. Gross–J. Michl–F. J. Schierse, "Apokalypsen, Apokalyptik," LThK I, 1959, 696 ff; Ph. Vielhauer, "Apocalypses," "Apocalyptic in Early Christianity," in E. Hennecke–W. Schneemelcher, *NT Apocrypha* II, ed. R. McL. Wilson, 1965, 579 ff, 608 ff; D. S. Russell, *The Method and Message of Jewish Apocalyptic 200* B.C.–A.D. *100*, 1964 (lit.); H. H. Rowley, *The Relevance of Apocalyptic* (rev. ed.), 1946 (lit.); H. D. Betz, "Zum Problem des religionsgeschichtlichen Verständnisses der Apokalyptik," ZThK 63, 1966, 391 ff; A. Strobel, *Kerygma und Apokalyptik. Ein religionsgeschichtlicher und theologischer Beitrag zur Christusfrage*, 1967, 124 ff; A. Nissen, "Tora und Geschichte im Spätjudentum," NovTest 9, 1967, 241 ff, esp. 260 ff; M. Hengel, *Judentum und Hellenismus. Studien zu ihrer Begegnung unter besonderer Berücksichtigung Palästinas bis zur Mitte des 2. Jh. v Chr*, WUNT 10, 1969, 319 ff; W. Harnisch, *Verhängnis und Verheissung der Geschichte. Untersuchungen zum Zeit-und Geschichtsverständnis im 4. Buch Esra und in der syrischen Baruchapokalypse*, FRLANT 97, 1969; K. Koch, *Ratlos vor der Apokalyptik*, 1970, 15 ff (Eng. tr., *The Rediscovery of Apocalyptic*, SBT Series II, No. 22, 18 ff); B. Noack, "Spätjudentum und Heilsgeschichte," Franz Delitzsch-Vorlesungen 1968, 1971, 54 ff; E. Lohse, "Apokalyptik und Eschatologie," ZNW 62, 1971, 48 ff. —The Jewish apocalypses in the original text are to be found only in separate editions; translations of most of them are to be found in the following collections: E. Kautzsch, *Die Apokryphen und Pseudepigraphen des AT II*, 1900; R. H. Charles (ed.), *The Apocrypha and Pseudepigrapha of the Old Testament* II, 1913 (and repr., n.d.); P. Riessler,

Altjüdisches Schriftum ausserhalb der Bibel, 1928; J. Maier, *Die Texte vom Toten Meer* I, 1960.

The concept "apocalyptic" is used traditionally to describe a phenomenon within the history of religion, a religious outlook which is defined by a distinctive eschatological thought world and by an otherworldly perspective. Apocalyptic is also a literary genre in which such eschatological ideas are expressed. In many places where religions are concerned with the question of the end of the world and the world beyond, both apocalyptic ideas and their literary precipitate appear, but apocalyptic developed especially on the soil of early Judaism and primitive Christianity. The name is based on Rev 1:1, "Revelation [ἀποκάλυψις] of Jesus Christ, which God gave to him." Here for the first time a book of this sort, a revelation book which discloses the divine secrets of the End-time, is assigned the title Apocalypse. But the origin of the literary genre lies in Judaism. Although the apocalypticists think of themselves as successors of the prophets the origin of apocalyptic literature presupposes the penetration of extra-Jewish, i.e., Iranian Hellenistic, concepts into Judaism, especially of those dualism and demonology. Thus apocalyptic must be characterized as a new religious and literary phenomenon of early Judaism.

In the post-Exilic time the expectation of a near end of the age as a world catastrophe came more and more into the forefront. The kingdom of God of the future took on the features of a kingdom—not of this world—whose stage is the new heaven and the new earth. Predictions of an apocalyptic type had already penetrated into the older prophetic books (Isa 24–27, Zech 9–14, the book of Joel, among others). The apocalypses proper, however, offer complete books of prophecy in pseudonymous form. The first and most important of these which has survived is the book of Daniel, written in 165/164 B.C. at the time of the Maccabean revolt. The period from the Maccabean wars to the turn of the second century A.D. is the heyday of the Jewish apocalyptic (the books of Enoch, the Testaments of the Twelve Patriarchs, the Jewish Sibylline Oracles, the Ascension of Moses, IV Esdras, the Syriac Baruch-Apocalypse, and the War Scroll found at Qumran, among others).[1] The Jewish apocalypticists conceal themselves behind the authority of some great pious man of early times, such as Enoch, Noah, Abraham, the twelve patriarchs, or Moses, Elijah, Daniel, Baruch, Ezra, etc. In predictive form they write history

[1] See the enumeration in I. T. Beckwith, *The Apocalypse of John*, 1919, 178 ff, and Russell, 37 f.

from the time of the alleged author until the end of the world. Often around the time of the actual author—which is described with special exactitude—a break appears between the presentation of the past and the construction of future history which provides an indication of the time of writing. The apocalypticists receive their revelations in ecstatic or dream visions, but the vision also develops into the stylistic form of apocalyptic. The principal means of expression are parable (allegory) and symbol: persons are represented in the likeness of animals, historical events in the likeness of natural appearances; colors and numbers have secret meanings, which with regard to numbers is related to the world view of the ancient East. The images themselves often have a history behind them and originate from mythological, cosmological, and astrological tradition of the East as well as of the West. There are, however, no formal laws which are applicable for all apocalypses, although a series of formal features is found in most apocalypses.[2]

Apocalyptic is dominated by historical-ethical dualism. The present age is evil and stands under the domination of the demons. God has turned aside from the earth, though his will was once upon a time proclaimed in the history of the fathers and it will once again in the End-time be revealed powerfully and finally executed. The world lies in wickedness, but God will help. The age of the godless earthly rule will come to an end, the new age of the transcendental rule of God stands at the door. In an elaborately conceived religious view of history, the course of world history is seen as being predicted according to a firmly set, meaningful divine plan. From past history, apocalyptic deduces laws which will surely be fulfilled as the world comes to its predetermined goal. In the first instance, therefore, interest lies in the last days and in the confrontation between world history as it is fulfilled in the last days and the soon awaited kingdom of God.[3] The apocalypticists "despair of the world that was living without God was coupled with the lively hope that all things work together for good to them that love God." [4] The seriousness of the threatening judgment and the glow of hope for the imminent redemption through the miraculous power of God exercized a strong influence on Jewish piety in the centuries around the turn of our era.

In the most powerful way primitive Christianity was influenced

---

[2] Attempts at assembling the evidence are offered by Vielhauer, 582 ff; Russell, 104 ff; Koch, 24 ff.

[3] See Vielhauer, 591; Nissen, 275; Harnisch, 123, 129 f, 266; Noack, 63, 69, 78; Lohse, 56.

[4] Rowley, 179.

by apocalyptic ideas which were related above all to the inbreaking of the rule of God and the parousia of Christ. In the eschatological words of Jesus, in Paul's expectation of the End, and in I and II John are echoed the ideas of the book of Daniel and the later Jewish apocalyptic. Mk 13 par.; I Thess 4:15-17; II Thess 2:1-12; I Cor 15:20-28; II Cor 5:1 ff; 12:4; Heb 12:22 f are indications that Christianity very quickly employed in an independent way these apocalyptic concepts and developed them further. Still later the development continued and a Christian apocalyptic literature was formed in which Jewish apocalypses were edited from a Christian standpoint (i.e., IV Esdras, Test XII, Ascension of Isaiah, the Christian Sibyllines) and also new apocalypses were written.[5] The oldest and most important of the apocalyptic works by Christians is the Apocalypse of John.

§34. THE APOCALYPSE OF JOHN

Commentaries: see §41. Surveys of research: E. Lohmeyer, "Die Offenbarung des Johannes, 1920–1934," ThR, NF 6, 1934, 269 ff; 7, 1935, 28 ff; A. Feuillet, "L'Apocalypse. État de la question," *Studia Neotestamentica*, Subsidia 3, 1963 (on this see G. Strecker, Gn 36, 1964, 664 ff); J. M. Schmidt (see §33), 87 ff, 280 f. Research (in additon to items mentioned in §33): L. Brun, "Die römischen Kaiser in der Apk," ZNW 26, 1927, 128 ff; H. Windisch, RGG[2] III, 330 ff; R. Schütz, *Die Offenbarung des Johannes und Kaiser Domitian*, FRLANT, NF 32, 1933; H. Strathmann, *Was soll die "Offenbarung" des Johannes im NT?* (1934), [2]1947; G. Bornkamm, "Die Komposition der apokalyptischen Visionen in der Offenbarung Johannis," ZNW 36, 1937, 132 ff (= G. B., *Studien zu Antike und Urchristentum*, BevTh 28, 1959, 204 ff); H. D. Wendland, *Geschichtsanschauung und Geschichtsbewusstsein im NT*, 1938, 49 ff; M. E. Boismard, "'L'apocalypse' ou 'les apocalypses' de S. Jean," RB 56, 1949, 507 ff; A. Farrer, *A Rebirth of Images*, 1949; E. Stauffer, *Christus und die Caesaren*, [3]1952, 160 ff; J. W. Bowman, "The Revelation to John: Its Dramatic Structure and Message," Int 9, 1955, 436 ff; S. Giet, *L'Apocalypse et l'histoire*, 1957 (on this cf. J. Schmid, ThLZ 84, 1959, 428 ff); J. Michl, LThK I, 1957, 690 ff; A. Feuillet, "Essai d'interprétation du chapitre XI de l'Apocalypse," NTS 4, 1957/58, 183 ff; L. Goppelt, EKL II, 1958, 365 ff; G. Delling, "Zum gottesdienstlichen Stil der Johannes-Apokalypse," NovTest 3, 1959, 107 ff; C. C. Torrey, *The Apocalypse of John*, 1958; O. A. Piper, RGG[3]

---

[5] Even before the middle of the second century there had appeared Did 16, the Apocalypse of Peter and the Shepherd of Hermas. See the surveys in LThK I, 698 ff, Vielhauer, 626 ff, and the translations in Hennecke-Schneemelcher-Wilson II, 663 ff.

III, 1959, 822 ff (bibl.); O. Michel, CBL, 957 ff; S. Läuchli, "Eine Gottesdienststruktur in der Johannesoffenbarung," ThZ 16, 1960, 359 ff; E. Lohse, "Die at. Sprache des Sehers Johannes," ZNW 52, 1961, 122 ff; A. Helmbold, "A Note on the Authorship of the Apocalypse," NTS 8, 1961/62, 77 ff; T. Holtz, "Die Christologie der Apokalypse des Johannes," TU 85, 1962; J. N. Sanders, "St. John on Patmos," NTS 9, 1962/63, 75 ff; B. Newman, "The Fallacy of the Domitian Hypothesis: Critique of the Irenaeus Source as a Witness for the Contemporary-historical Approach to the Interpretation of the Apocalypse," NTS 10, 1963/64, 133 ff; A. Strobel, "Abfassung und Geschichtstheologie der Apokalypse nach Kap. 17,9-12," NTS 10, 1963/64, 433 ff; P. Prigent, "Apocalypse et liturgie," Cahiers théologiques 52, 1964; M. Hopkins, "The Historical Perspective of Apc 1–11," CBQ 27, 1965, 42 ff; M. Rissi, "Was ist und was danach geschehen soll." Die Zeit und Geschichtsauffassung der Offenbarung des Johannes, AThANT 46, [2]1965; J. Kallas, "The Apocalypse—an Apocalyptic Book?" JBL 86, 1967, 69 ff; B. W. Jones, "More About the Apocalypse as Apocalyptic," JBL 87, 1968, 325 ff; E. Fiorenza, "The Eschatology and Composition of the Apocalypse," CBQ 30, 1968, 537 ff; idem, GANT, 330 ff; J. Lindblom, "Geschichte und Offenbarungen. Vorstellungen von göttlichen Weisungen und übernatürlichen Erscheinungen im ältesten Christentum," Acta Reg. Societatis Humaniorum Litterarum Lundensis 65, 1968, 206 ff; J. Becker, "Pseudonymität der Johannesapokalypse und Verfasserfrage," BZ, NF 13, 1969, 101 f; J. Lipiński, "L'Apocalypse et le martyre de Jean à Jérusalem," NovTest 11, 1969, 225 ff; L. Thompson, "Cult and Eschatology in the Apocalypse of John," JR 49, 1969, 330 ff; K.-P. Jörns, "Das hymnische Ev. Untersuchungen zu Aufbau, Funktion und Herkunft der hymnischen Stücke in der Johannesoffenbarung," StNT 5, 1971; G. Mussies, The Morphology of Koine Greek as Used in the Apocalypse of St. John, Suppl. NovTest 27, 1971.

1. Contents

Following the introduction in Ch. 1, the Apocalypse is divided into two formally distinct main sections: Chs. 2 and 3 are hortatory words to the church at the time of the writer (the seven so-called letters); Chs. 4–22 disclose the future. It is this second main section which encompasses almost three-quarters of the entire book and which is in the strict sense apocalyptic. But the introductory account of the vision of Christ to the seer John on Patmos (1:9-20), which is preceded by a preface indicating the contents of the book as a divine revelation (1:1-3) and an epistolary introduction (1:4-8), associates the epistolary communications with the leading apocalyptic ideas of the book as a whole, and (22:21) the book closes like a letter. According to 1:4, 11 the book is intended for the seven churches in Asia in the cities of Ephesus, Smyrna, Pergamum, Thyatira, Sardis, Philadelphia, and Laodicea.

The communications (Chs. 2–3) are symmetrically constructed letters with hortatory, comforting, and punitive content which John has been authorized by the heavenly Christ to write to the churches. Each community receives praise and blame according to its condition. Each letter ends with a promise to the "victor" and either before or after that with a warning word: "He who has ears, let him hear what the Spirit says to the churches."

The Apocalypse proper (Chs. 4–22) reveals and interprets the things that are to come in a long series of visions which appear predominantly in groups of seven. The vision of the seven seals (6:1–8:1) is preceded by a prelude in heaven (4:1–5:14): caught up to heaven, John sees God on his throne, surrounded by the twenty-four elders and the four animals (Ch. 4), the sealed book which no one may open (5:1-5), and the Lamb which can loosen the seal (5:6-14). The opening of the first six seals brings to the view of the seer the four apocalyptic riders (6:1-8), the souls of the martyrs under the altar (6:9-11), and the shaking of the structure of the world (6:12-17). Then there is an interlude: the sealing of the 144,000 from the tribes of Israel (7:1-8), and the great band of martyrs before the throne of God (7:9-17). With the opening of the seventh seal quiet descends upon heaven (8:1). But immediately there begins a second group of seven: the seven visions of the trumpets (8:2–11:19). After an introduction (8: 2-6: prayers of the saints at the heavenly altar; the fire thrown down upon the earth) the first four trumpets (8:7-12) bring fearful catastrophies on earth sea, rivers, sun, moon, and stars. The consequence is prepared for by a threefold lament of an eagle. After the fifth and sixth trumpets (9:1-12; 9:13-21) there follow the satanic locusts and an army of wild horses. In an interlude the apocalypticist—who is once more on the earth—receives two visions (10:1-11, 14): an angel descends from heaven who promises that in the days of the seventh trumpet the mystery of God will be fulfilled and gives to the seer, with instructions to eat it, the small opened book which lies in his hand. First it tastes sweet, but then it is bitter (Ch. 10). Then the seer must measure the temple, and he hears the prophecy from the two witnesses who appear as preachers of repentance and are put to death by the animal from the abyss, but rise again and are raised up to heaven (11:1-14). The seventh trumpet (11:15-19) proclaims the heavenly songs of praise, the appearance of the ark of the covenant in the heavenly temple, but also the cosmic disaster. Then in Chs. 12–14 follows a long interruption of the series of sevens: the dragon and the Lamb, warfare and victory. The heavenly woman with a child is threatened by the dragon, the child is taken up to God (12:1-6), Michael triumphs over the dragon (12:7-12), which vainly continues to pursue the woman on the earth (12:13-17). Two animals emerge (12:18–13:18); the first, from the sea, is fatally wounded in the head but is healed and persecutes the Christians (12:18–13: 10). The second, which emerges from the land, is the aggressive propagandizing companion of the first beast (13:11-17). The number of the first animal, which is the number of a man, is 666 (13:18). By contrast there appear the vision of the Lamb and of the 144,000 who have been sealed (14:1-5) and the announcement and the carrying out of judgment (14:6-20). Even the third group of seven, the seven bowl visions (Chs. 15–16), with the horrible plagues which are poured out upon the earth one after another from the bowls of the wrath of God, does not yet bring the end. Only with the fall of Babylon (17:1–19:10) begins the divine judgment which leads to the concluding triumph of the eternal Lord of history: the judgment of the harlot of Babylon and the animal (Ch. 17) with the lament over the fall of Babylon (Ch. 18) and the joy in heaven (19:1-10). The final section: the coming of Christ and the consummation (19:11–22:5) portrays the victory of Christ, who appears on a white horse and whose names are ὁ λόγος τοῦ θεοῦ, "King of kings" and "Lord of lords," over the Antichrist and his followers (19:11, 21); the thousand-year reign in which those whose piety has been proved through death have a share, and the judgment over Satan, who yet again is let loose (20:1-10), the judgment of the world (20:11-15), and the heavenly Jerusalem (21:1–22:5).

The conclusion (22:6-21) contains the confirmation of the Apocalypse as a prophetic witness of divine truth and a repeated promise of the parousia of Christ. It concludes in epistolary form with a benediction.

2. The Apocalypse of John as an Apocalyptic and Prophetic Book

The Apocalypse is closely associated with apocalyptic literature of contemporary Judaism (see §33). The mythical material, the secret numbers, visions and phenomena from heaven as a means of disclosure of otherworldly things, the representation of what has been seen in richly embellished fantastic images, as well as the frequent dependence on the OT, characterize the Apocalypse as a work which belongs to the same literary genre as the Jewish apocalypses. In a string of visionary images is represented what "must soon take place" (1:1; 22:6), "what has happened and must happen hereafter" (1:19): the final phase in the history of God's dealings with man and the universe.

But at more than one point, the seer of the Apocalypse frees himself in a characteristic way from the schema of apocalyptic literature and sketches a historical picture of quite a different sort from Jewish apocalyptic.

Rev is not a pseudonymous book: John writes under his own name (1:1, 4, 9; 22:8). He does not hide himself behind the mask of some worthy from the past in the manner of Jewish apocalyptic.[1] Presumably he was actually a visionary,[2] but if he portrays what he has experienced, he does not write secret wisdom allegedly stemming from primitive times; rather he gives clear eschatological prophecy and exhortation related to the present (22:10). The book is intended for a large circle: the seven churches as *the* church in the perspective of John. The literary framework in which the Apocalypse is placed, including a preface (1:4 ff), and the conclusion (22:21), is reminiscent of the literary form in which early Christian literature appears first and most frequently (see §11). All this allows us to see that Rev was written with the idea of being read aloud in worship, so that here too the practices of early Christian existence had decisively shaped the literary form.

In its view of history, the apocalyptic book of the NT contrasts even more sharply with the Jewish type.

In the history of his time, John sees a mighty drama being played out. The stage is the earth, more exactly the world as dominated by the Roman imperium and particularly the section in which John lives, the province of Asia. The Christian community and the pagan civil power stand in sharp opposition to each other. The Roman state provides the colors for the animal, the bitter enemy of the church (13:1-ff); pagan Rome is the harlot who sits astride the beast (17:1 ff). Rome is taking the offensive against Christianity: the churches of Asia Minor have to suffer under its attack (2:3, 10; 3:8), the blood of the martyrs has already flowed in Pergamum (2:13). Already in the visions of the seals, there

---

[1] It is fanciful to conclude from the character of Rev as an apocalypse that even the name John must be a pseudonym (Becker).

[2] Thus, e.g., Rissi, 26; Lindblom, 220 ff. The latter thinks he can distinguish in individual cases between the portrayal of genuinely ecstatic visions and literary construction—with scarcely convincing results.

appears before the eyes of the seer a multitude of Christian martyrs under the altar in heaven (6:9). But these events of the past and the present are only a kind of prelude to the great decisive battle which the near future will bring, "the hour of testing which is to come upon the whole world populace" (3:10), in which the divinely predetermined number of martyrs will be complete (6:11), in which those Christians who remain true to death will receive the victor's crown (2:10; 3:11; 13:10, among others). The seer already beholds the endless number of martyrs who come out of the great time of temptation in white robes with palm branches, the sign of the victor in their hands, standing before the throne of God by the sea of glass (7:9 ff; 15:2). He hears their praise in the hymn of the angels (12:10 ff); he sees them as participants in the lordship and the joy of the thousand-year reign (20:4, 6). Therefore he summons them passionately to warfare and to victory in this time of temptation: "Blessed are the dead who from now on die in the Lord! Yes, the spirit says, they shall rest from their troubles since their works follow after them" (14:13).

But this drama is played out, so to speak, only on the forestage. With it and behind it there is a still more weighty operation in which heaven and hell are participants: the war of God and Satan (see especially Ch. 12 ff). The animal with the seven heads and the ten horns who ascends from the sea—this apocalyptic symbol of the *Imperium Romanum*—receives his power from the dragon, the ancient snake, the world deceiver. He is the servant of the Devil and executes his will upon the earth (13:2). The Roman Empire is the satanic world power because it promotes and requires worship of the emperor (13:4 ff). The blasphemous activity of the empire is shown still more crassly by the secondary figure of the second animal, which mounts up from the land and misleads the dwellers of the earth into worshiping the image of the first beast (13:12 ff). With good reason, this second animal has been identified as "the false prophet" (16:13; 19:20; 20:10), the imperial priesthood in the provinces (or some individual from their midst) with their fanatical promotion of the imperial cult.[3] The dragon who lay in wait for the heaven-born child [3a] and who attempted

[3] See Beckwith, Bousset, Brütsch, Lohse on 13:11 ff.

[3a] For many reasons the interpretation—widely regarded as self-evident—that the birth of the child (12:5) refers to the birth of Jesus in Bethlehem (see recently Brütsch and Lohse, *in loc.*) is questionable. The interpretation that sees a reference to "the inbreaking of the messianic time of judgment and redemption" (thus H. Gollinger, *Das "Grosse Zeichen" von Apk 12*, StBM 11, 1971, 151 ff, esp. 167) is more convincing on the whole, although the emphasis on a "male son" is not entirely accounted for by this abstract interpretation.

to storm the heavens (12:4, 7) is the driving force behind the persecution of Christians (12:17) who refuse to participate in the worship of the beast. Yet the resisting community of Christians has an even stronger patron: Christ, the Son of man (1:13; 14:14), the Lamb with the fatal wound that is healed (5:6), who as firstborn has been raised from the dead to heaven and as coregnant with God is Lord over the kings of the earth (1:5). He is the conqueror (5:5; 3:21), the Lord of the new age. The omnipotent God has up till now brought to nothing the attacks of Satan. The child of heaven he has saved from him (12:5), and Satan himself together with his angels has plummeted from heaven (12:9). His victory in heaven guarantees the coming victory on the earth. God will so shape the course of history that those warriors will receive the victor's prize "who have not worshiped the beast and his image and have not received his mark on their forehead and their hands" (20:4).

God's unalterable will concerning the last act in the world drama has already been written down in the secret book with the seven seals, which the apocalypticist sees in the right hand of the Majesty on the heavenly throne (5:1). Before the eyes of the seer, Christ receives this book, the testament of God, in order to execute it as quickly as possible, feature by feature (5:7, 9; Ch. 6 ff). In spite of dreadful horrors, its content is the gospel: the consummation of redemption (14:6; 10:7). The power of the empire will be broken by Christ: he conquers and will destroy the two opponents of the faithful, the beast and the false prophet (19:11 ff). There follows the triumph of the martyrs in the thousand-year reign during which the tested warriors are resurrected and rule with Christ while Satan lies bound in the abyss (20:1 ff). Then after Satan is briefly freed for his final fearful fury on the earth, there comes the ultimate destruction of the archenemy of God (20:7 ff). And after the judgment of the world (20:11 ff) there opens up the luminous spectacle of a marvelous new world with a new Jerusalem and the blessed sharing of the conquerors in eternal fellowship with God (21:1–22:5).

What is new here in Rev is a total recasting of the apocalyptic view of history out of the Jewish into the Christian mold. The apocalyptic view of history has received a new substructure through the historical appearance of Jesus. On this the entire weight of the structure rests. In distinction from Jewish apocalyptic there is lacking here any look back into the past and any forward view out of that fictional past into the present. For John, the point of departure for his eschatological hope is rather the belief in the saving act of God in Jesus, and in his redemptive work which signifies victory. In this event, which the first Christians have themselves experienced, the pivotal point of John's confidence lies in the God who shapes history. Although little attention is devoted by Rev to the earthly life of Jesus, his appearance—especially as characterized by his redemptive death (1:5; 7:14; 12:11) and his triumphant exaltation (3:21; 5:5; 7:14; cf. 1:7)—is the eschatological turning point of history, the pledge of history's divine consummation. The idea of *Heilsgeschichte* [redemptive history], in which Jesus Chirst stands in the center, lies at the base of the view of history in Rev and provides it with its stress on the certainty of redemption: the battle in heaven has been won, Satan is cast out (12:7 ff): "Now has appeared salvation and power and the kingship of our God (12:10)." [4]

The prophetic seer who is speaking in Rev is writing a book of consolation for the church which stands at the point of becoming a martyr church. With this in view, he interprets the events of the present and the recent past and predicts the development of things in a short span of time until the end of the world when God's rule is established. A secure base for the interpretation which the Apocalypse itself requires is offered in the specific situation of the primitive Christian communities, which is sure to lead in a very short period of time to bloody persecution of the whole church, as well as in the confidence of victory which provides perspective beyond the coming time of suffering to the near parousia of Christ and the destruction of all the God-opposing powers. Rev is a book of its time, written out of this time and for this time, not for later generations of the future or even for the End-time. It is as much an occasional writing as are the letters of the NT, and has to be understood basically in its own historical setting. With this must be combined attention to the set traditions of apocalyptic and to its own new Christian-prophetic outlook.

3. Sources, Literary Form, and Structure of Revelation

This message is presented in a form which gives rise to many questions. On the one hand Rev conveys the impression of an orderly and careful structure.[5] In the letters, seals, trumpets, and

---

[4] On the view of history in Rev cf. Wendland; Holtz, 95 ff, 212 ff; Rissi, 60 ff.

[5] The oft-advanced assumption that the instruction to the seer, "Write what you have seen, and what is, and what is yet to occur" (1:19) is worked out in turn in 1:10-18; 2,3; 4:1–22:5 (thus, e.g., Bousset, Harrington, Lohse, *in*

bowls, the number seven is given explicit emphasis, but it also has an emphatic role elsewhere in Rev: seven spirits (3:1); seven lamp-stands (1:12); seven stars (1:16); seven heads (5:6; 12:3; 17: 3); seven angels (8:2), etc. The attempt has been made in various ways to explain the structure of the whole of Rev down to details according to the principle of the number seven.[6] In the section which stands between the seven trumpets and the seven bowls (12–14), one can easily separate out seven scenes,[7] but even here there is no perceptible evidence that this division is intentional and thus gives seven parts. A comparison of the proposed structur-ings[8] shows that the different proposals do not agree in any way, so that other divisions have been proposed with their own good reasons.[9] If one looks at the whole of Rev one can more readily say, on the other hand, that "the book does not exhibit any dis-cernible structure." [10] But it must be said, further, that Rev ex-hibits numerous doublets: the seven trumpets and the seven bowls, the judgment of the world in 14:14 ff and 20:11 ff, description of the heavenly Jerusalem in 21:1 ff and 21:9 ff; the visions in 7:1-17 and 10:1–11:14, interrupt the sequence of the seven seals and the seven trumpets. The seventh trumpet in 11:15-19 brings together heavenly hymns, a vision of redemption, and cosmic catastrophes. Any chronological sequence of the things seen can be demonstrated only with great difficulty: 11:1 ff seems to take place before the destruction of the Jerusalem temple, and 17:5 ff belongs at the earliest to the time of Vespasian. Since the time of H. Grotius (1641) many scholars have been led by these numerous contradictions to account for the origin of Rev on the basis of literary conjectures. Some have proposed the blending together of different Jewish or Christian sources by an editor, while others suggest a long string of alterations of a basic writing by redactors.[11] None of these hypotheses is convincing, however, and so in recent

---

loc.; also in this *Intr.*[12]) is scarcely accurate, since the indication of the contents is related rather to the book as a whole (see Beckwith, Caird, *in loc.*; Fiorenza, CBQ, 540 n. 22).

[6] Cf., e.g., recently, Lohmeyer, Lohse, Rist; Albertz, de Zwaan; Bowman, Goppelt, and those mentioned in Feuillet, *Apocalypse*, 24 f.

[7] Thus Bowman: 12:1-18; 13:1-10; 13:11-18; 14:1-5; 14:6-13; 14:14-20; 15:2-4.

[8] Cf. the tables in Bowman, 444.

[9] See most recently, e.g., Hopkins (two sections, 4–11 and 12–20, with three subsections); and Fiorenza (four sections: 1–3; 4–16; 17–20; 21, 22).

[10] Piper.

[11] See the reports in Beckwith, 224 ff; Bousset, 108 ff; Lohmeyer, ThR 1935, 35 ff.

decades some have sought to account for the difficulties by the assumption of sources or of interpolations,[12] assuming above all that Rev in the form handed down by the tradition was put together from two different writings written by the same author at different times.[13] But none of these hypotheses can make clear why an author would have added to or inserted into a later writing an early writing of his own, without correcting it, so that by this route we have no access to a solution of the literary problem of Rev either.[14] There are, then, two facts: (1) that Rev cannot owe its literary form solely to the stylistic intentions of its author, and (2) that neither connected sources nor secondary interpolations can be convincingly demonstrated. These facts lead only to the conclusion that the author has used various kinds of material in an independent manner.[15] In view of the diverse material, the inescapable question, which cannot be answered with certainty but which is unavoidable for the exposition of individual texts, is whether this particular complex of tradition or this conception is of pagan, Jewish, or Christian origin. For our understanding of the origin of Rev as a whole, however, this history-of-religions inquiry is largely meaningless because in any case John found his material already in a Jewish, if not indeed in a Christian, mold and treated it in a completely free way.

Very striking is the linguistic and stylistic form into which the author has reworked the material that he took over on the basis of his personal visionary experience and the situation of the church of his time. The language of Rev is interspersed with numerous verbal echoes of the OT, yet there is not a single word-for-word quotation, and these allusions frequently show links with the LXX and later translations of the OT, though in the majority of cases they reveal idiomatic knowledge of the Hebrew and Aramaic

[12] Charles; McNeile-Williams; Windisch; Giet, 182 ff, considers 19:9–22:21 to be a later addition; according to Rissi, 83 ff, there are later interpolations in a second edition of the book at 13:18b; 15:2; 17:9b-17.

[13] De Zwaan: visions of the years 70 and 79–96. E. Hirsch, *Studien zum 4. Ev.*, BHTh 11, 1936, 156 ff: 1:1-3, 7; 4:2–22:10, 18 f originated in the year 68/69, and 1:4-6; 1:18–3:22; 22:11-17, 20 f come from the end of the reign of Domitian. M. Goguel, *The Birth of Christianity*, 1954, 369 f: 1:4–3:22 is from the years 80–85; 4:1 is from the end of the reign of Domitian. Boismard: two parallel texts have been woven together, the one that begins with 10:2 from the time of Nero, and the one beginning with 4:1 from the beginning of the reign of Domitian; Chs. 1–3 are from a somewhat later time.

[14] Cf. also Michaelis, *Einl.*, 307 f.

[15] Thus Feuillet, *Apocalypse*, 27; Piper; Vielhauer (see §33), 622.

original texts of the OT.[16] As a result not only does the author write in a strongly semiticizing hieratic style—so that his OT mode of expression can be used as a text-critical aid[17]—but also "throughout the entire book are found grammatical and stylistic difficulties of a special kind and in such a quantity as is evident only in the Revelation: mainly, grammatical incongruities which lend to the linguistic character of Revelation its peculiar mold." [18] This form of the Greek language characteristic of Rev is certainly not the result of a "careful" translation from the Aramaic,[19] nor does it seem to be the result of a literary device of the apocalypticist; rather it is to be understood on the ground that "the author thought in Hebrew but wrote in Greek." [20]

In addition to this special quality of the language in the narrower sense, Rev shows in its hymns and songs of praise an abundance of poetically shaped material: 1:5 f; 4:8, 11; 5:9 f, 12 f; 7:10, 12; 11:15, 17 f; 12:10-12; 15:3 f; 16:5 f; 19:1 f, 5-8; 22:13. It has often been assumed that John is quoting liturgical elements from the Christian worship of his epoch,[21] or that in his hymnic texts he is following the liturgy of Asia Minor[22] or a Passover liturgy.[23] But against this assumption is the evidence that the liturgical elements are largely formed from the OT and are used by the author in the interpretation of his visions. Thus they are "responses to the work of God or Christ" and originate with the author of Rev himself.[24] It is not the pattern of earthly or a supposed heavenly[24a] service of worship which determines the structure of Rev. Rather it is the sequence of the expected eschatological

[16] Evidence in Charles, I, lxv ff.

[17] See Lohse, ZNW 1961.

[18] Bousset, 159. See on the language of Rev, Bousset, 159 ff; Charles, I, cxvii ff ("A Short Grammar of the Apocalypse"); Mussies; J. Schmid, *Studien zur Geschichte des griech. Apk-Textes* II, MThS, 1 Suppl. Vol. 1955, 173 ff.

[19] Thus Torrey.

[20] J. Schmid, ThRv 62, 1966, 306. See esp. Mussies' evidence that the unconscious selection of Greek verb categories by the author of Rev is to be explained on the basis of his Semitic mother tongue (pp. 349, 353). Yet it cannot be overlooked that the author of Rev can use typical Greek expressions as well (thus, e.g., W. C. van Unnik, "ΜΙΑ ΓΝΩΜΗ, Apocalypse of John XVII 13:17," in *Studies in John: Festschr. J. N. Sevenster*, Suppl. NovTest 24, 1970, 209 ff).

[21] Thus, e.g., Lohse, Excursus on 7:17; O. Cullmann, *Early Christian Worship* 1953, 7 f; *contra*, Jörns, 180 ff.

[22] Läuchli.

[23] Prigent, 77.

[24] See Delling; Jörns (esp. 167, 168).

[24a] The thesis that the seer took part in a heavenly service of worship is incapable of proof (against Feuillet, *Apocalypse*, 71; Prigent, 10; E. Stauffer, *New Testament Theology*, 1955, 228 ff).

Introduction to the New Testament

events, probably also the visionary experiences of the author, which are determinative for the structure of the writing as a whole. Yet this pattern of expected eschatological events seems to be disrupted by chronological flashbacks and repetitions (see above, p. 463). There is no perceptible one-line logical sequence of eschatological events, so that one can scarcely speak of Rev as "a casting from a single matrix." [25] More plausible is the assumption advanced since the time of Victorinus of Pettau (d. 304) that the repetitions are to be explained on the ground that the same future eschatological events have been described several times, one after the other (recapitulation theory).[26] But in fact the text contains no sort of indication of an intentional repetition; rather, the visions of the bowls clearly represent a movement beyond the visions of the trumpets. Probably Bornkamm's assumption[27] is correct that the sections 6:1–8:1, 8:2–14:12, and 15:1–22:6 follow each other in the relationship of overture, preparatory, and final event, although even this explanation does not resolve all the riddles of the sequence of the predictions (note, for example, flashback into the past, 12:1 ff, and the anticipation of the judgment of the world in 14:14 ff). As the outcome of this discussion about the correct exposition of Rev which has been carried on since antiquity in an ever-changing discussion,[28] it may be concluded that John is seeking to describe by means of traditional conceptual material the time of the End which has begun in his present and is soon to be consummated. But then it must also be said that the real goal of prophetic apocalyptic presentation is not the course of the eschatological events but their significance for the suffering church of its own time. Thus knowledge of external circumstances of the origins of Rev is especially essential for understanding its message.

4. Time of Writing of Revelation

According to the oldest tradition[29] Rev was written toward the end of the reign of Domitian (81–96). The book's own testi-

---

[25] Goppelt, EKL II, 366.

[26] Similarly Rissi, 18 f.

[27] Thus Vielhauer (see §33), 621; Jörns, 177 f, who proposes a different division and speaks of a "prolepsis" and a "realization." Fiorenza, CBQ, esp. 553, 565, 567, stresses that the sequence of cycles of seven is determined thematically, not chronologically.

[28] See the surveys in Beckwith, 318 ff; Bousset, 49 ff. Recently esp. Piper, Fiorenza. The contesting of the apocalyptic character of Rev (Fiorenza, GANT, 331; carried farther by Kallas) is as ill-founded as is the claim that the aim of Rev is anti-Gnostic (Newman; Prigent, 11).

[29] In Iren., *Haer.* V. 30. 3.

mony indicates that it originated in the province of Asia in a time of severe oppression of Christians, which is most readily conceivable under Domitian. In the letters included in Rev, persecutions by the officials are expected (2:10), the blood of the martyrs has already flowed (2:13; 6:9), the whole of Christianity is threatened with a fearful danger (3:10): the immediate prospect is for the outbreak of a general persecution of Christians throughout the Roman Empire. In 17:6 John sees the harlot who is Babylon-Rome drunk on the blood of the saints and the blood of the witnesses of Jesus (cf. 6:10; 16:6; 18:24; 19:2). In 20:4 participation in the thousand-year reign is promised to the martyrs who have been beheaded because of their testimony for Jesus and for the word of God, and who have not worshiped the beast and his image and have not accepted his sign on their forehead and in their hand, i.e., those who have refused divine honors to the emperor (13:4, 12 ff; 14:9, 11; 16:2; 19:20). Christianity has collided with the state and with the state religion, the Christ cult with the imperial cult. In the interest of faith, Rev raises passionate objections to Rome and the imperial cult. That corresponds to the situation under Domitian.

Prior to Domitian, the state religion did not direct itself against the Christians. Nero's mad acts in Rome against the Christians had nothing to do with the imperial cult. Under Domitian, who according to the Eastern pattern laid claim to divine honors for himself as emperor during his own lifetime,[30] there arose for the first time the persecution of Christians by the state on religious grounds. In 96 in Rome members of the imperial household were called to account for the charge of ἀθεότης; i.e., violation of the state religion. And in the Christian tradition Domitian is unanimously regarded as the first persecutor of Christians after Nero.[31] In the province of Asia imperial cult was promoted with special zeal. Under Domitian, Ephesus received a new imperial temple.[32] Thus it was precisely in the province of Asia, the classical land of the imperial cult, that at the time of Domitian all the prerequisites were present for a severe conflict between Christianity and the state cult, which is what Rev has in view (cf. also I Pet). The seer

[30] The title *Dominus ac deus noster* in Suetonius: *Domitian*, 13; and cf. L. Cerfaux and J. Tondriau, *Le Culte des souverains dans la civilisation gréco-romaine*, 1957, 355 ff.

[31] Melito, in Eus., HE IV. 26. 9, among others.

[32] Schütz, 18 ff. That Vespasian should have laid special emphasis on the imperial cult (thus Giet) contradicts everything that we know (Cerfaux-Tondriau [see n. 30], 354).

nowhere points directly to Domitian as the then reigning emperor, and the Antichrist, the "beast" (13:1 ff, etc.), does not bear the features of any specific historical ruler but rather those of the demonic form of *Nero redivivus,* which was still a popular expectation in that time. But the temporal scene which Rev sketches fits no epoch of primitive Christianity so well as the time of the persecution under Domitian.

Unfortunately, on the basis of Chs. 13 and 17 it cannot be calculated which Roman emperor was reigning at the time of the writing of Rev. According to 17:9 f, the seven heads of the beasts (13:1) represent seven emperors: "the five are fallen, the one [sixth] now is, the other [seventh] is not yet come and when he comes he is to remain for only a short time" (17:10). In neither chapter, however, does the interest center on the last in the series: attention is drawn especially in 13:3 to one of the heads of the beast which appears to have been fatally wounded but whose wound is healed. 17:11 goes beyond the number seven and poses the riddle "The beast which was and is not is itself the eighth and one of the seven." Here, as earlier, the idea is that of the demonic figure of Nero who comes back again from the dead:[33] the Antichrist is incarnate in the demonic power figure of Nero, who comes again out of the kingdom of the dead, in a future emperor who has no right to exist, because he violates the rule of the cosmic number seven, but who nevertheless was once in the sequence of seven. The interest of the author, however, is not in the last of the series of but in the still awaited (seventh and) eighth emperor. Yet according to 17:9a he thinks it important that the reader note who is to be considered the sixth emperor. But the difficulty still exists for us that we do not know with which of the emperors we are to begin the enumeration. If one begins counting with Augustus, as seems obvious, then Vespasian is to be accepted as the sixth emperor (Augustus—Tiberius—Caligula—Claudius—Nero—Vespasian; the "military emperors" Galba—Otho—Vitellius in 68/69 drop out of consideration). Others would like to begin counting as early as Julius Caesar,[34] and consider Vespasian to be the seventh or the tenth emperor, but this procedure overlooks the fact that, according to 17:12, the "ten kings" are still completely future. In following the common practice of counting from Augustus, it must be assumed either that Rev was written in the time of Vespasian (though against that is the fact that Vespasian was not a promoter of the imperial cult

---

[33] On the Nero legend see Beckwith, Bousset, Charles on Ch. 17.
[34] Giet, Lipiński.

and no persecutor of the Christians) or that the author incorporated
a fragment that arose in the time of Vespasian without accommodating the numbering to the present (but that is contradicted by
the fact that 17:7 ff is doubtless the author's own interpretation).
A purely arbitrary assumption is that an author writing in the
time of Domitian fictitiously dated his work back into the time
of Vespasian.[35] Only two possibilities remain: either the author
did not trouble himself at all about an agreement between the dogmatically fixed numbering and the historical reality,[36] in which
case he could scarcely have written 17:9a, or John starts his list
of the emperors as enemies of God with Caligula, just as the author
of IV Esdras gives a special numeration to the three Flavians on
account of their hostility toward the Jews.[37] If this supposition is
correct, then Domitian would be the sixth emperor after Caligula
and the numeration of the Roman emperors by the author would
agree with the origin of Rev under Domitian. But likely as it
seems, this supposition remains only a hypothesis and does not make
possible the certain dating of Rev under Domitian. The secret number 666 (13:18) cannot be introduced for dating purposes, since
its solution is completely uncertain, and with good grounds several
imperial names could be proposed.

Also favoring the end of the first century as the time of origin
of Rev is the fact that according to 2:8-11, the church of Smyrna
has been persevering for a long time, while according to Polycarp
(Phil 11:3), at the time of Paul it did not even exist; and 3:17
describes the community of Laodicea as rich, while this city had
been almost completely destroyed by an earthquake in A.D. 60/61.

In all likelihood, therefore, Rev was in fact written toward the
end of the reign of Domitian, i.e., *ca.* 90–95, in Asia Minor,[37a] in
order to encourage the Christian communities threatened by a
destructive persecution to endure and to make them confident of
the imminent victory of Christ over the powers of the Antichrist.

5. Author

The seer of Rev who is the author of the book, gives his name
in four places (1:1, 4, 9; 22:8) as *John*. Since he received his first

---

[35] Feuillet, *Apocalypse*, 78. *Contra*, Fiorenza, CBQ, 547 f.

[36] Thus, e.g., Bousset, Lohse.

[37] Thus Brun, Strobel (who stresses that those emperors who came to power
after Christ are numbered: therefore, Caligula, Claudius, Nero, Vespasian, Titus,
Domitian, for all of whom, insofar as they are already dead, the term ἔπεσαν [17:
10]=violent death, is appropriate).

[37a] Becker would like to date Rev from the time of Trajan.

vision on the island of Patmos, which lies opposite Miletus off the coast of Asia Minor (1:9), and since his book is in the form of a circular letter to the seven churches in Asia (1:4, cf. 1:11) whose condition he knows precisely, as Chs. 2 and 3 show, he himself without question also belongs in this province. He adduces no title to indicate his position to the readers. As "servant" of God (or Jesus Christ, 1:1) and as "brother and companion" of those Christians addressed who are "in the tribulation and in the kingdom and in the patient waiting for Jesus" (1:9), he asks for a hearing. The simple name John indicates a commonly known personality, and the self-evident manner in which he sets forth his claims to be heard points to a man of high authority. The single datum that he communicates out of his own life is that he was on the island of Patmos "for the sake of the word of God and for the testimony of Jesus" (1:9); i.e., he was a preacher of the gospel and as such was obviously prominent, if the old interpretation of his stay on Patmos as exile[38] is correct.

As early as the second century, the apostle John, the son of Zebedee, was mentioned as author, first prior to 160 by Justin:[39] ἀνήρ τις ᾧ ὄνομα Ἰωάννης, εἷς τῶν ἀποστόλων τοῦ χριστοῦ, ἐν ἀποκαλύψει γενομένῃ αὐτῷ . . . προεφήτευσε, and soon after Clement of Alexandria:[40] Ἰωάννου τοῦ ἀποστόλου. As early as Papias Rev is attested as dependable,[41] and Melito of Sardis[42] wrote about it. Thus from the end of the second century on, Rev was considered to be apostolic and canonical without exception in the West, and in the East, by and large, until the middle of the third century.

This opinion, to be sure, was not uncontested. That Marcion rejected Rev as Jewish[43] tells nothing but the fact that the Antimontanist opponents of John in Asia Minor, the so-called Alogoi (see above, §10 n.6), and the Roman anti-Montanist Gaius (ca. 210 could trace back to the Gnostic Cerinthus the Rev so treasured by the Montanists, shows that at the beginning of the third century the apostle John's authorship of Rev was by no means generally recognized. On the basis of this relative uncertainty, we can

---

[38] Tert., Praescr. haer., 36; Clement of Alexandria, Quis dives salvetur, 42. According to Feuillet, Apocalypse, 81 f, and Helmbold, the Gnostic "Apocryphon of John," which is also to be dated from this period, is a witness to the apostolic origin of Rev.

[39] Justin, Dial. 81. 4 (in relation to Rev 20:4).

[40] Clement of Alexandria (see n. 38).

[41] Thus according to the information in the commentary of Andrew of Caesarea, as given by J. Schmid (see n. 18), I Text, 10.

[42] In Eus., HE IV. 26. 2.

[43] According to Tert., Adv. Marc. 4. 5.

understand that about the middle of the third century, Bishop
Dionysius of Alexandria in connection with his polemic against
the apocalyptic false doctrine of Chiliasm denied that Rev was by
the apostle John and traced it back to another inspired man by
the name of John. This position he demonstrated by pointing out
the great linguistic and stylistic differences between Rev on the
one hand and the Gospel and Letters of John on the other.[44] From
this point on, the apostolic origin of Rev was largely contested
in the East. Eusebius wavered between "recognized" and "spurious"
(see below, §36.1). Thus Rev is lacking in several canonical lists
from Asia Minor and Palestine and in most of the Greek manuscripts of the NT until the ninth/tenth century.[45] It was included
in the Syriac NT only by the revision of Philoxenus (see below,
§38.4.a). But after Rev was accepted into the canon lists by
Athanasius in his thirty-ninth Easter festival letter, and by the
Latin church under the influence of Augustine about the end of
the fourth century, it was no longer officially disputed that Rev
belonged to the NT. Since Jerome does not mention in his catalogue
of writers that the canonical value of Rev was disputed, the
Middle Ages was also unaware of it. It was Erasmus who once
more pointed to the considerations which tell against Rev's having
been written by the evangelist John. Luther, who found Rev objectionable on the basis of its content, explained in his "Preface to
the Revelation of St. John" (1522), that he considered the book
"neither apostolic nor prophetic," [46] and in his more positive preface of 1530 also he stood by the same decision concerning the
author. Although Zwingli and Calvin regarded the Rev with some
reserve, J. S. Semler was the first to deny once again, on theological
and history-of-religions grounds, that Rev was by the apostle
John.[47] Since then the view that Rev and John could not come
from the same author has been firmly established,[48] although now,
as earlier, there are many supporters for the assumption that the
apostle John is the author of the Gospel and the Letters as well as
Rev.[49]

[44] In Eus., HE VII. 25. 1 ff; WGK, NT, 16 f.
[45] Cf. J. Schmid (see n. 18), II, 31 ff.
[46] See WGK, NT, 25 f.
[47] See WGK, NT, 63 f, 67.
[48] Thus, e.g., Bousset, Brütsch, Caird, Lohse, Rist; Fuller, Grant, Harrington, Heard, Henshaw, Jülicher-Fascher, Klijn, McNeile-Williams; Feuillet, Mussies, 351 f (where reference is made to the different morphology of the Greek lan-guage); O. Böcher, Der joh. Dualismus im Zusammenhang des nachbiblischen Judentums, 1965, 14.
[49] E.g., Allo, Beckwith, Hadorn; Albertz, Feine-Behm, Guthrie, Harrison, Höpfl-Gut, Mariani, Michaelis, de Zwaan; E. Stauffer, NT Theology, 1955, 40 ff.

As justification for equating the author of Rev with the author of John and with the apostle John are adduced the great age of this tradition but especially the agreements in language and thought world. But on all these points it is evident that the apocalyptist John cannot be identical with the author of the Gospel and the Letters of John. The language is completely different[50] (e.g., in Rev ἀρνίον, Ἰερουσαλήμ, ἔθνος, ἔθνη = the Gentile nations; John: ἀμνός, Ἰεροσόλυμα, ἔθνος = the Jews). More important is the fact that the eschatology of Rev is shaped in the strongest way by futuristic apocalyptic concepts, while that of John has nothing whatsoever of this. Parallel with this is the fact that John is interested in the earthly life of Jesus while Rev has only several references to his death. Rev and John speak and think in such basically different ways that the ancient tradition (which is by no means uncontested) that the authors of John and of Rev are identical, cannot rest on reliable information but must be credited to an early conclusion in connection with the canonization of the two writings.

Thus concerning the author of Rev we know nothing more than that he was a Jewish-Christian prophet named John. He cannot be identified with John the son of Zebedee, since in 18:20; 21:14 the author of Rev speaks of the apostles as of men other than himself. The "presbyter" John mentioned by Papias by no means belongs with certainty to Asia Minor and is more likely to be identified with the presbyter of II and III John (and thus perhaps also with the Gospel of John and I John).[51] The authority of John the author of Rev is due, not to connections with the Palestinian primitive community, but to the fact that he is a former witness to Jesus among the churches of Asia Minor (1:9) and a present witness to Jesus concerning what he has seen and what he is to show to the servants of God (1:1 f).

6. The Theological Problem

Although in the discussion about the historical criticism and canonical authority of James the theological problem concerning

---

Lohmeyer and Farrer assume the same author, though not the apostle; the question of authorship is left open by Schelkle, Wikenhauser; Boismard, Michl, Piper; L. van Hartingsveld, *Die Eschatologie des Joh,* 1962, 184 f.

[50] Cf. esp. Charles, I, xxix ff, and Mussies.

[51] Sanders, 83 f, wants to identify the author with John the presbyter and then with John Mark.

its message was never introduced until the time of Luther, from the very beginning it was the content of Rev that kindled the discussion about it. Dionysius of Alexandria raised questions about the author of Rev because representatives of a hope of an earthly eschatological age ("Chiliasts") whom he was opposing appealed to Rev 20. In order to make a case against the false teachers over the scriptural authority of their doctrine, he denied the apostolic origin of Rev on the basis of historical arguments and added that the book was more than he could take. Closely similar was Luther's explanation at the beginning of the Reformation period that "his spirit could not put up with this book," because Rev was too much concerned with tales and pictures and in it Christ was neither taught nor made known. Based on an appeal to the discussion in the ancient church, he had determined that the book should be regarded as neither apostolic nor prophetic. Once again as conscious historical consideration of the NT was beginning Semler said that he found "the tone in the Apocalypse unpleasant and objectionable," so that he could not regard the book as inspired and had to deny that it was written by the author of Jn (see above, p. 471). Therefore, Rev has been theologically disputed in all epochs of church history on account of its content, which within the framework of the NT is unprecedentedly visionary and figurative, as well as because of the difficulty in comprehending it. That has remained true until the present. While some find in Rev a "genuine apostolic representation of the end of history," [52] for others it is only "a valuable monument from a historical crisis in the history of our faith" [53] and its Christianity is "a weakly Christianized Judaism." [54] Today there is a basic unity as to the proper method for interpreting Rev, at least wherever such interpretation is based on scholarly presuppositions. Rev can only be understood on the basis of the intentions of the author and our historical remove from its time. If inquiries are first made concerning the traditional meaning of the images and concepts (history-of-tradition method), then we must seek to determine what expectations concerning the End were proclaimed by the author (eschatological method). Finally by reference to the immediate past or to present history it must be observed that the End-time is seen as already being actualized in the present (history-of-the-times method). But even if by consciously linking these methods concerning the intended meaning of

[52] Goppelt, 369; cf. A. Vögtle, *Das NT und die neuere katholische Exegese* I, 1966, 164 ("a thoroughly Christian book").

[53] Rist.

[54] Bultmann, *NT Theology*, 175.

the numerous images and concepts we may gain a relatively certain perspective, the theological problem still remains of the degree to which the eschatological view of history proclaimed in Rev is in harmony with the rest of the NT message and what existential significance for us today there is in this apocalyptic portrayal of the future which for us is so strange. In view of the repetitions and contradictions in Rev, and the insertion into the history of the End-time of the past of the appearance of Christ and the present of the experience of the church, there can be no doubt that Rev can offer no "chronology of eschatological dates," [55] however realistically the author wanted us to understand his prophecies. It is rather a "picture of the essence of the totality of events" [56] which is accessible only to faith. This picture of reality is by no means a superficially christianized Judaism, as is shown by the central significance of the present and future Christ for the total view of divine history and for the present situation of the Christian community.[57] But to an unusually high degree the concepts and images which constitute this picture of reality presuppose not only the ancient view of the cosmos but also ideas of Judaism and Hellenism which are in tension with or stand in contradiction to the central message of the NT (e.g., the call for vengeance in 6:10, or the earthly fulfillment of the future hope of the millennial kingdom in 20:2 ff). Insofar as such concepts and images are in irreconcilable contradiction with this message, the theological task of interpreting Rev can only be discharged when the tension between these images and pictures and the central NT message is set forth and theologically evaluated. There is no basis for excluding Rev as a whole from the NT, but detailed theological criticism of this writing is indispensable. Even though some objections, such as those of Luther, may be resolved on the basis of more adequate knowledge of the contemporary conceptual world, there is no doubt that the apocalypticist stands in danger of portraying God's aim in world history in too unambiguous and unified a manner, and indeed he would like to have it at his own disposal. Thus a criticism of the relationship between the canon as a whole and Rev is especially necessary and is constantly indispensable for determining the true message of this book. Like James, Rev can express the full value of its message only within the framework and the limits of the NT.

[55] Thus correctly Michaelis, *Einl.*, 311.
[56] Goppelt, 369.
[57] Cf. Holtz, 212 ff.

PART TWO

The Formation of the Canon of the New Testament

Th. Zahn, *Geschichte des Nt. Kanons* I, 1888/89, II, 1890/92 (incomplete); *idem, Grundriss der Geschichte des Nt. Kanons*, ²1904; A. Harnack, *Das NT um das Jahr 200*, 1889; *idem, Die Entstehung des NT und die wichtigsten Folgen der neuen Schöpfung*, 1914; *idem, Die Briefsammlung des Apostels Paulus*, 1926; *idem*, "Die ältesten Evv.-Prologe und die Bildung des NT," SAB 1928, 337 ff; H. Lietzmann, "Wie wurden die Bücher des NT heilige Schrift?" (1907), in H. L., *Kleine Schriften* II, TU 68, 1958, 15 ff; J. Leipoldt, *Geschichte des nt Kanons* I, II, 1907/8; E. J. Goodspeed, *The Formation of the NT*, 1926; M.-J. Lagrange, *Introduction à l'étude du NT* I: *Histoire ancienne du canon du NT*, 1933; A. Souter, *The Text and Canon of the NT*, rev. C. S. C. Williams, 1954, 137 ff; H. Höpfl–L. Leloir, *Introductionis in Sacros utriusque Testamenti libros compendium*, Vol. I: *Introductio generalis*, ⁶1958; E. Hennecke–W. Schneemelcher, *NT Apocrypha*, 2 vols, ed. and tr. R. McL. Wilson, 1 ff; C. F. D. Moule, *The Birth of the NT*, HNTC, Companion Vol. I, 1962, 178 ff; R. P. C. Hanson, *Tradition in the Early Church*, 1962; E. Flessemann-van Leer, "Prinzipien der Sammlung und Ausscheidung bei der Bildung des Kanons," ZThK 61, 1964, 404 ff; R. M. Grant, *The Formation of the NT*, 1965; *idem*, "The NT Canon," in *The Cambridge History of the Bible* I, 1970, 284 ff; H. von Campenhausen, *The Formation of the Christian Bible*, 1972; A. C. Sundberg, "A Revised History of the NT Canon," StEv IV, TU 102, 1968, 452 ff; I. Frank, *Der Sinn der Kanonbildung. Eine historisch-theologische Untersuchung der Zeit vom I. Clemensbrief bis Irenaeus von Lyon*, Freiburger Theologische Studien 90, 1971.—Most important texts in Preuschen, *Analecta*; Zahn, *Grundriss*; Souter-Williams, *Text and Canon*, 188 ff; F. W. Grosheide, *Some Early Lists of the Books of the NT*, Textus Minores 1, 1948; Hennecke-Schneemelcher-Wilson I, 28 ff; in part also in EnchB.

§35. The Growth of the New Testament Canon to the End of the Second Century

1. The Authorities in Primitive Christianity

G. Schrenk, art. "γράφω," TDNT I, 1964, 742 ff; R. Meyer–A. Oepke, "Canon and Apocrypha," TDNT III, 1965, 978 ff; A. Jepsen, "Kanon und Text des AT," ThLZ 74, 1949, 65 ff; *idem*, "Zur Kanongeschichte des AT," ZAW 71, 1959, 114 ff; P. Katz, "The Old Testament Canon in Palestine and Alexandria," ZNW 47, 1956, 191 ff; A. C. Sundberg, *The Old Testament of the Early Church*, HTS 20, 1964; O. Eissfeldt, *The Old Testament: An Introduction*, 1965, 560 ff; O. Kaiser, *Einleitung in das AT*, 1969, 315 ff.

The twenty-seven writings discussed in the first part were probably preserved exclusively in connection with ecclesiastical collections and thus not by a direct copying of individual originals.[1] The history of the canon seeks to understand how these collections and finally the collection of the NT took form.

Although the NT writings have been handed down to us only as part of a collection by the church, none of them was written with the aim of being incorporated into such a collection. Even if there was perhaps already a collection of the Pauline letters at the end of the first century, that was not regarded as "Holy Scripture." But Jesus and primitive Christianity were never without a Holy Scripture: they had the OT as "the scriptures" (Mark 12:24), which were taken over from Judaism and quoted from all three parts of the later OT canon. The revelation of God was set down in scriptural form, as was self-evident to the primitive church from the very beginning. It is highly questionable, however, whether before the end of the first century there was already a *closed* canon of the OT and therefore whether primitive Christianity could recognize the OT as an exactly defined entity. The Pentateuch was fixed in the third century B.C., and the grandson of Jesus Sirach in the Preface to Sirach (*ca.* 117 B.C.) knows ὁ νόμος and οἱ προφῆται as fixed collections, but for him ἄλλα πάτρια βιβλία are not yet delimited. But though it is certain that in Judaism of the first century B.C. there was a "Holy Scripture," there was no precisely limited "canon." This state of affairs must have obtained for Judaism as a whole until the end of the first century A.D., since both among the Jewish community of Qumran and within the Christian community which developed out of Palestinian Judaism (cf. Luke 11:49; Jn 7:38; I Cor 2:9; James 4:5; Jude 14 f), texts are used as "Scripture" which did not appear in the later canon of the rabbis. Among the NT writers there appears the designation of Scripture, known from contemporary Judaism as well, as "the law and the prophets," [2] but not the division of "Scripture" into

---

[1] It is impossible to decide whether some small papyrus fragments from the second or third centuries (see below, §38.1.b) come from manuscripts which originally contained only one writing.

[2] E.g., Mt 5:17; further evidence in W. G. Kümmel, ZNW 33, 1934, 111 n. 2 (=WGK, *Heilsgeschehen und Geschichte*, MbThSt 3, 1965, 20 n. 23).

"the Torah, the Prophets, and the Writings" that has been customary only since the first century A.D. in rabbinic circles.[3] The definition of the Scriptures which was carried out in the first century A.D. by the rabbis in the "Masoretic" canon of thirty-nine scriptures[4] was not adopted for centuries by the Christian church. The church had rather a much more inclusive "OT" which from the second century on it defined in various ways.[5] Thus primitive Christianity possessed a "Holy Scripture" but did not recognize an unambiguously defined canon or an exclusive norm. For Jesus and the early church too, the evaluation and comprehension of "Holy Scripture" was subject to the critical authority of Jesus or of the Spirit of God who was sent by the risen Lord, although this critical attitude was not always a conscious one[6] (cf., e.g., Mt 5:21 ff; Jn 5:39 ff; 10:35 f; II Cor 3:12 ff; II Tim 3:15; Heb 8:13). It cannot be proved that in Christian worship of the apostolic times OT texts were *regularly* read, so that from this side too it is impossible to perceive whether there was an exclusive normative character of a firmly defined Holy Scripture in primitive Christianity.

Thus it is not surprising that within the church—this is first discernible in Paul—in addition to or superseding the norm of the OT there emerges the new norm of the earthly and the risen κύριος. For Paul, any contested question of doctrine or faith or life is answered by "a word of the Lord" as categorically as by a "word of scripture." In I Thess 4:15, he offers theological instruction on the basis of a word of Jesus. In I Cor 9:9, 13, 14, he places alongside the scriptural proof the authoritative instruction of the Lord. In I Cor 11:23 ff he describes the act and the word of Jesus in the establishment of the Lord's Supper as the norm for the celebration within the community. In I Cor 15:1 ff "the gospel which I have preached to you" is the foundation of primitive Christian faith. In I Cor 7:10, 12, 25, he notes the wide distance between the command of the Lord, which is unconditionally obligatory, and his own instructions as an apostle authorized by the Lord. At the end of the apostolic epoch we find the same unconditional authority of the κύριος as preserved in the church's tradition or as

[3] Babylonian Talmud, Sanhedrin 90b, attributed to Gamaliel II. Lk 24:44 νόμος, προφῆται, ψαλμοί is not counterevidence, since οἱ ψαλμοί cannot indicate the entire collection of "the writings."

[4] The oldest witnesses for this are IV Esdras 14:45 and an inference from the conclusion of the Council of Jamnia concerning the canonical character of Ecclesiastes and the Song of Songs (Mishna Yadaim 3. 5).

[5] See the evidence in Jepsen and Sundberg.

[6] Cf. von Campenhausen, *Formation*, 21 n. 1.

attested by the κύριος himself (John 18:9, 32; Acts 20:35; Rev 2:1, 8, among others).

But at the same time a further development is in progress. If the authority of the κύριος is unconditional, so also Paul when he is obligated to make a decision himself appeals to the fact that he is one "commissioned by the Lord" and that he possesses the Spirit of God (I Cor 7:25, 40), hence that his instruction κυρίου ἐστίν —i.e., that the Lord himself speaks through him. As ἀπόστολος, he has been commissioned διὰ Ἰησοῦ χριστοῦ καὶ θεοῦ πατρός and any other gospel may be placed under a curse as not coming from God (Gal 1:1, 7 ff; cf. II Thess 3:17). Similarly the teachers of the apostolic period later claim authority in their own names (Heb 10:26 f; 13:18 f; III John 5 ff; Rev 1:1-3) or under the authority of one of the earliest apostles (Eph 4:1; I Tim 5:14; 6:13 ff). But this derived authority of an apostle of Jesus Christ is like that of the Lord, a living authority which grows in the act of proclamation, not the authority of Scripture which is placed alongside the "Scripture" of the OT. Even Rev, which is intended for reading in the context of worship, claims only inspiration (22:18 f) and thus invulnerability for the writing of the seer but not, however, "canonical authority." Even though Paul presupposes that his letters will be read in meetings of the community to which he wrote and will occasionally also be exchanged among the communities (cf. I Thess 5:26 f; II Cor 13:12; Rom 16:16—Col 1:1; 4:16; see also the liturgical conclusion to I Cor 16:20-23), and though Heb (11:32) and I Pet (5:14) are obviously intended for public reading, still that is no proof that early Christian writings were placed on an equal plane with the "Scripture" of the OT. Indeed from all these facts it may be inferred that a new living norm was shaped in the church which included in the first place the Lord and then the apostles who bore witness to the message of the Lord.

2. Preliminary Stages in the Formation of the Canon in the Postapostolic Age

The NT in the Apostolic Fathers, by a Committee of the Oxford Society of Historical Theology, 1905; A. von Harnack, "Über das Alter der Bezeichnung 'Die Bücher' ('Die Bibel') für die heiligen Schriften in der Kirche," *Zentralblatt für Bibliothekswesen* 45, 1928, 337 ff; C. Maurer, *Ignatius von Antiochien und das Joh,* AThANT 18, 1949; E. Massaux, *Influence de l'Évangile de saint Matthieu sur la littérature chrétienne avant saint Irénée* (Universitas Catholica Lovaniensis, Dissertationes . . . II, 42), 1950; R. Heard, "Papias' Quotations from the NT," NTS 1, 1954/55, 130 ff; H. Köster, *Synoptische Überlieferung bei den Apostolischen Vätern*, TU 65, 1957; R. Glover, "The Didache's Quotations and the Synoptic Gospels," NTS 5, 1958/59, 12 ff; C. M. Nielsen, "Polycarp, Paul and the Scriptures," ATR 47, 1965, 199 ff; H. Rathke, *Ignatius von Antiochien und die Paulusbriefe*, TU 99, 1967—A. Harnack, *Die Briefsammlung des Apostels Paulus*, 1926; E. J. Goodspeed, *An Introduction to the NT*, 1937, 222 ff; A. E. Barnett, *Paul Becomes a Literary Influence*, 1941; J. Knox, *Marcion and the NT*, 1942, 39 ff, 172 ff; L. Mowry, "The Early Circulation of Paul's Letters," JBL 63, 1944, 73 ff; C. H. Buck, "The Early Order of the Pauline Corpus," JBL 68, 1949, 351 ff; K. L. Carroll, "The Expansion of the Pauline Corpus," JBL 72, 1953, 230 ff; C. L. Mitton, *The Formation of the Pauline Corpus*, 1955; J. Finegan, "The Original Form of the Pauline Collection," HTR 49, 1956, 85 ff; J. Knox, *Philemon Among the Letters of Paul*, [2]1959; idem, "Acts and the Pauline Letter Corpus," *Studies in Luke-Acts: Festschr. P. Schubert*, 1966, 279 ff; W. Schmithals, "Zur Abfassung und ältesten Sammlung der paulinischen Hauptbriefe," ZNW 51, 1960, 225 ff (=W. Sch., *Paulus und die Gnostiker*, ThF 35, 1965, 175 ff; English translation, *Paul and the Gnostics*, by J. Steely, 1972, 239 ff); C. P. Anderson, "The Epistle to the Hebrews and the Pauline Letter Collection," HTR 59, 1966, 429 ff.—O. Cullmann, "The Plurality of the Gospels as Theological Problem," in *The Early Church*, 1956, 39 ff; K. L. Carroll, "The Creation of the Fourfold Gospel," BJRL 37, 1954/55, 68 ff; J. H. Crehan, "The Fourfold Character of the Gospel," StEv 1, TU 73, 1958, 3 ff.

The attitude of Christians toward norms of Christian doctrine and Christian life that we found at the end of the apostolic age (i.e., toward the end of the first century A.D.) may be found at the beginning of the postapostolic age as well, especially in the earliest of the apostolic fathers. Side by side and of equal value are the "Scripture" and the λόγοι τοῦ κυρίου Ἰησοῦ or the "words of the holy prophets" and "the ἐντολὴ τοῦ κυρίου which has been handed down from the apostles" (I Clem 13:1 f, 46:2 f, 7 f; II Pet 3:2). Corresponding to this is the fact that Ignatius of Antioch designates as authorities "the prophets, but above all the gospel" (Sm 7:2), and that above what "stands written" in the "documents" (i.e., in the OT) he places "Jesus Christ," whose cross, death, and resurrection, and the faith which he awakens are "the holy documents" (Phila 8).[7] Concerning the "Lord," however,

---

[7] On the meaning of τα ἀρχεῖα with reference to the OT cf. H. von Campenhausen, "Das AT als Bibel der Kirche," in H. v. C., *Aus der Frühzeit des Christentums*, 1963, 162 n. 51; also C. K. Barrett, *Das Joh und das Judentum*, 1970, 53 f. The linking of γέγραπται to the gospel as read in worship is baseless (against Frank, 40 f).

Ignatius says that he has done nothing without the Father with whom he was united "neither he personally nor through the apostles" (Magn 7:1, cf. 13:1). He shows thereby that the revelation of Christ is transmitted through Christ's own word or through that of the apostles. Alongside the OT as "Scripture" he has thus set forth the authority of "the Lord," which from the beginning was accessible in the words of the Lord exactly in the same way as in the witness of the apostles. But it is significant that in adducing the words of the Lord there is no indication that they are written down, and to the present day there is no unity on the question whether I Clem and Ignatius did[8] or did not[9] know a written gospel. Therefore as "the Lord" and "the apostles" in this epoch are "a purely ideal canon, intangible and not subject to control,"[10] with the dying out of the generation of the apostles and those who heard them directly, sooner or later the necessity was recognized that the authoritative voice of the Lord and the apostles had to be sought in scriptures where it alone could still be heard. Sooner or later therefore the question concerning the authority of these scriptures had to be posed.

The collecting of early Christian writings which was beginning to take place in this period gave a stimulus to this development. In all probability a collection of the letters of Paul was already formed by the end of the first century. Indeed a collection of ten Pauline letters (without the Pastorals) is clearly attested only in Marcion, ca. 140, but it is very unlikely that Marcion was the first to collect these letters. Already I Clem, which originated in Rome, not only utilizes Rom (35:5 f) and Heb (36:2 ff), but also refers the Corinthians who are being addressed to τὴν ἐπιστολὴν τοῦ μακαρίου Παύλου and offers quotations from I Cor (47:1-3, cf. also 37:5; 49:5) of which it must know a copy. Ignatius writes to the Ephesians that Paul mentions them in each of his letters (Ign., Eph 12:2) and shows thereby that he knows a collection of Pauline letters which includes Eph, as well as by his clear references to at least two Pauline letters.[11] And II Pet 3:15 f speaks of "all the

[8] Massaux.
[9] Thus Köster.
[10] Jülicher in Jülicher-Fascher, *Einl.*, 465. Grant too (in *Cambridge History of the Bible* I, 291 f) has determined that Did probably knew Mt, but he adds, "His (=the Didachist's) primary authority must be tradition, whether oral or written rather than documents." Cf. also von Campenhausen, *Formation*, 134 ff. A different view in Frank, 34, according to whom the authority of Christ in Did 9:5; 15:3 passes on to "the literarily fixed gospel tradition concerning him"—which is extremely questionable.
[11] Rom and I Cor; cf. Ign., Sm 1:1; Ign., Eph 18:1; Ign., Rom 5:1. Cf. on this Rathke, 28 ff, 48.

letters" of our beloved brother Paul and presupposes that they are available to the reader. At least by the beginning of the second century, therefore, there was a collection of Pauline letters that was known in Asia Minor, and it is very probable that this collection already contained all ten of the letters that stood in the canon of Marcion. To explain more precisely the formation of this collection the hypothesis has been offered in various forms that the collection of Pauline letters was created at the end of the first century when the appearance of Acts reawakened interest in the completely neglected Pauline letters; and that the collection, which contained seven letters (I and II Cor, I and II Thess, and Col-Phlm respectively were united as one letter), was arranged according to length and Eph was written as an introduction to the collection. The publication of this collection in Ephesus stimulated the writing of numerous Christian letters and the formation of other collections of letters (Rev 2 and 3, Ign.).[12] But we really have no evidence at all for this claim that Eph was ever placed at the head of the collection.[13] That I and II Cor, I and II Thess, and Col-Phlm were originally joined to form a single letter is, in view of the literary conclusions which are bound up with that theory, extremely improbable and nowhere attested. That the Pauline letters were completely forgotten until the beginning of the second century is undemonstrable (cf. rather I Pet and Heb). All that remains of this thesis is the likely conjecture that the Pauline letters were in the first collection arranged according to length[14] and that this collection arose in Asia Minor.[15] The assumption that the oldest collection took place in Corinth *ca.* 80 and that it consisted of seven Pauline letters (without Col, Eph, and Phlm) which a redactor formed on the basis of fourteen original Pauline letters[16] cannot be supported because of the doubtfulness of assuming such a redaction and the arbitrariness of excluding Col, Eph, and Phlm. But even though details remain uncertain, it is certain that from the beginning of the second century a collection of Pauline letters was widely known which enjoyed a high esteem without its being in any way placed alongside the "Holy Scripture" of the OT.

[12] Thus Goodspeed, Barnett, Carroll, Mitton, Knox; *contra,* Grant, *Formation,* 26 f.

[13] Cf. Buck, Finegan.

[14] Finegan. Only by forcing the evidence can F. Renner demonstrate that the Pauline letters were originally arranged in alphabetical order (*"An die Hebräer"* —*ein pseudepigraphischer Brief,* 1970, 50 ff).

[15] Not in Corinth (thus Harnack).

[16] Schmithals.

Much less certain is the answer to the question when a collection of the Gospels developed, especially since it is not even clear whether I Clem and Ignatius knew gospel writings at all (see above, p. 480). Even if Ignatius knew Mt and perhaps also Jn,[17] he does not refer to any written source and evidences no knowledge of any collection of the Gospels. The assertion that the four Gospels were brought together at the beginning of the second century[18] cannot be proved. Toward the middle of the second century, however, the situation seems to have altered. II Clem knows Mt and Lk, as does the main section of the Letter of Polycarp (Chs. 1–12), which originated in the thirties of the second century. The "Unknown Gospel," which originated in the second quarter of the second century, evidences knowledge of all four Gospels,[19] and the same is also probably true for the Gospel of Peter,[20] which comes from some time before the middle of the second century. Not only did Papias express himself on the circumstances of writing of Mt and Mk, but he also compared Mk with another Gospel, probably Mt (see above, §5.3.2); whether he also knew Jn is questionable.[21] A canon of four Gospels could be attested for this time if the likely assumption could be made more than probable that Tatian created his Diatessaron (see below, §38.2.a.1) already before his break with the great church.[22] But even if the existence of a combined arrangement of the four Gospels could be attested with certainty before the end of the first half of the second century, Tatian's bringing together of the texts of the four Gospels into one composite text, as well as Papias' preference for the living tradition of the κύριος (τὰ παρὰ ζώσης φωνῆς καὶ μενούσης) over "what comes from books," [23] shows that these later canonical Gospels had already begun to achieve growing significance and authority as a source of the tradition. They were not yet regarded as an exclusive and unassailable norm, however, and were not considered to be on the same level as the OT "Scripture." In addition to the canonical Gospels, far into the second century there was wide use of the "Apocryphal" Gospels and of oral Jesus-tradi-

[17] Thus Massaux, Maurer, on reasonable grounds.

[18] Harnack, Goodspeed, Crehan.

[19] See G. Mayeda, *Das Leben-Jesu-Fragment Papyrus Egerton 2*, 1946, and J. Jeremias, ThBl 15, 1936, 34 ff.

[20] See C. Maurer in Hennecke-Schneemelcher-Wilson, *NT Apocrypha* I, 179 ff.

[21] Cf. §10 n. 201.

[22] Cf. C. Peters, *Das Diatessaron Tatians*, 1939, 211 f.

[23] In Eus., HE III. 39. 3.

tion by the ecclesiastical writers. There is also no evidence from this period for the reading of the Gospels in worship.

Parallel to these collections of writings from apostolic times, about the middle of the second century there was a development which laid the basis for the rise of a "Holy Scripture." The main section of the Letter of Polycarp, which in addition to the gospel writings (see above, p. 482) also uses the letters of Paul and I Pet, makes explicit reference only to the κύριος (Polyc., Phil 2:3, 7:2) and the commands of the Lord, the apostles, and prophets (καθὼς αὐτὸς ἐνετείλατο καὶ οἱ εὐαγγελισάμενοι ἡμᾶς ἀπόστολοι καὶ οἱ προφῆται οἱ προκηρύξαντες τὴν ἔλευσιν τοῦ κυρίου ἡμῶν, 6:3) and thus places beside the OT the preaching of the Lord and of the apostles[24] but not new Holy Scriptures. A little later so-called II Clem (14:2) names as authorities for the doctrine that the origin of the church is from above τὰ βιβλία καὶ οἱ ἀπόστολοι and in so doing, according to the most likely meaning of the text, he places the apostles as living authorities alongside the OT scriptures.[25] But the same II Clem who often introduces OT quotations with λέγει ἡ γραφή, λέγει ὁ κύριος (14:2; 13:2), etc., also adduces in 2:4—following OT quotations—a saying of Jesus (Mt 9:13b) with the formula καὶ ἑτέρα δὲ γραφὴ λέγει. While it is without doubt the case that here a gospel writing is placed alongside the OT because it contains the witness for words of the Lord,[26] it cannot really be disputed that in this way a gospel writing appears as an authority on an equal with the OT,[27] but we cannot yet perceive from this whether the existence of a new scriptural norm was already clear. At about the same time the Letter of Barnabas (4:14) offers a saying of Jesus (Mt 22:14) with the same formula citation which is often used for OT texts ὡς γέγραπται, without indicating that he is presenting a saying of the Lord. The possibility cannot be excluded in this passage that the author has been deceived about the origin of the quotation; yet there is no necessity for this assumption, and Barn 4:14 could also be adduced as evidence for the fact that a gospel writing is beginning to be assigned equal value with an OT scripture. The same uncertainty exists with regard to the Letter of Polycarp, which at one point (Phil 12:1) introduces a quotation from Eph (4:26) with *ut his scripturis dictum est* ("how it is written in these scriptures"). Since directly before this Polycarp refers to *sacrae literae,* i.e., to the OT,

[24] Cf. also Polyc., Phil 11:2: *sicut Paulus docet.*
[25] Harnack.
[26] Massaux.
[27] See Grant, *Formation,* 84; Frank, 96 f.

it is quite possible that here by *scripturis* he intends a reference to the OT, but the possibility is also not to be excluded—even though it is unlikely—that in this isolated case he refers to a text in Paul as *scripturae*.[28] In any case these texts show the possibility of first steps in the direction of a new Scripture. Since as early as the beginning of the postapostolic period words of the Lord and the living witness of the apostles are quoted in similar fashion as a divine norm (see above, p. 478), the emergence of a bipartite "Scripture" became an inner necessity as the distance in time from the apostolic period grew.

3. The Beginnings of the Formation of the Canon in the Second Half of the Second Century

K. L. Carroll, "The Earliest NT," BJRL 38, 1955/56, 45 ff—G. Klein, *Die zwölf Apostel,* FRLANT 77, 1961, 192 ff (to Justin); O. A. Piper, "The Nature of the Gospel According to Justin Martyr," JR 41, 1961, 155 ff; A. J. Bellinzoni, *The Sayings of Jesus in the Writings of Justin Martyr,* Suppl. NovTest 17, 1967—A. von Harnack, *Marcion. Das Evangelium vom fremden Gott,* TU III 15, ²1924; J. Knox, *Marcion and the NT,* 1942; E. C. Blackman, *Marcion and His Influence,* 1948, 23 ff —R. M. Grant, "Tatian and the Bible," *Studia Patristica* I, TU 63, 1957, 297 ff; *idem,* "The Bible of Theophilus of Antioch," JBL 66, 1947, 173 ff—W. C. van Unnik, "De la règle Μήτε προσθεῖναι μήτε ἀφελεῖν dans l'histoire du canon," VigChr 3, 1949, 1 ff; *idem,* "The Gospel of Truth and the NT," in *The Jung Codex,* ed. F. L. Cross, 1955, 81 ff— G. Bonner, "The Scillitan Saints and the Pauline Epistles," *Journal of Ecclesiastical History* 7, 1956, 141 ff—D. de Bruyne, "Prologues bibliques d'origine Marcionite," RBén 24, 1907, 1 ff; P. Corssen, "Zur Überlieferungsgeschichte des Römerbriefes," ZNW 10, 1909, 37 ff; W. Mundle, "Die Herkunft der 'marcionitischen' Prologe zu den paulinischen Briefen," ZNW 24, 1925, 56 ff; A. von Harnack, "Der marcionitische Ursprung der ältesten Vulgata-Prologe zu den Plsbr.," ZNW 24, 1925, 205 ff; *idem,* "Die Marcionitischen Prologe zu den Plsbr., eine Quelle des Muratorischen Fragments," ZNW 25, 1926, 160 ff; M.-J. Lagrange, "Les prologues prétendus marcionites," RB 35, 1926, 161 ff; H. J. Frede, *Altlat. Paulus-Handschriften,* Vetus Latina. Aus der Geschichte der lat. Bibel 4, 1964, 168 ff; J. Regul, *Die antimarcionitischen Evangelienprologe,* ibid. 6, 1969, 88 ff; K. Th. Schäfer, "Marcion und die ältesten Prologe

---

[28] The first view in Leipoldt, *Geschichte* I, 291; Grant, *Formation,* 105; the second view in Nielsen, 199 ff; Frank, 48 f (but can *scripturae* designate scriptural passages?); I Tim 5:18 undoubtedly cannot mean the Gospel of Luke when it mentions γραφή (see Dibelius-Conzelmann, HNT,[4] *in loc.,* against Frank, 64 f).

zu den Paulusbriefen," *Kyriakon, Festschr. J. Quasten* I, 1970, 135 ff;
idem, "Marius Victorinus und die marcionitischen Prologe zu den Paulus-
briefen," RBén 80, 1970, 7 ff— D. de Bruyne, "Les plus anciens prologues
latins des évangiles," RBén 40, 1928, 193 ff; A. von Harnack, "Die
ältesten Evangelien-Prologe und die Bildung des NT," SAB 1928, 322 ff;
M.-J. Lagrange, review of de Bruyne, RB 38, 1929, 115 ff; B. W.
Bacon, "The Anti-Marcionite Prologue to John," JBL 49, 1930, 43 ff;
R. G. Heard, "The Old Gospel Prologues," JTS, NS 5, 1954, 1 ff; A.
Strobel, "Lukas der Antiochener," ZNW 49, 1958, 131 ff; E. Haenchen,
Comm. on *Acts,* 1971, 10 f—M.-J. Lagrange, "Le canon d'Hippolyte
et le fragment de Muratori," RB 42, 1933, 161 ff; A. T. Ehrhardt,
"The Gospels in the Muratorian Fragment," *Ostkirchliche Studien* 2,
1953, 121 ff (=A. E., *The Framework of NT Stories,* 1964, 11 ff);
G. Bardy, art. "Muratori (Canon de)," DBS V, 1954, 1399 ff; P. Katz,
"The Johannine Epistles in the Muratorian Canon," JTS, NS 8, 1957,
273 f; N. A. Dahl, "Welche Ordnung der Paulusbriefe wird vom
muratorischen Kanon vorausgesetzt?" ZNW 52, 1961, 39 ff; K. Stendahl,
"The Apocalypse of John and the Epistles of Paul in the Muratorian
Fragment," *Current Issues in NT Interpretation: Festschr. O. A. Piper,*
1962, 239 ff—W. L. Dulière, "Le canon néotestamentaire et les écrits
chrétiens approuvés par Irénée," *Nouvelle Clio* 6, 1954, 199 ff; A. C.
Sundberg, "Dependent Canonicity in Irenaeus and Tertullian," StEv III,
TU 88, 1964, 403 ff—J. Ruwet, "Clément d'Alexandrie, canon des
Écritures et apocryphes," Bb 29, 1948, 94 ff, 391 ff.

Shortly after the middle of the second century Justin Martyr reports (*Apol.* 67. 3) that in the Sunday service of worship there are
read τὰ ἀπομνημονεύματα τῶν ἀποστόλων ἢ τὰ συγγράμματα τῶν προ-
φητῶν, and by these "memoirs of the apostles" according to information which he himself gives (*Apol.* 66. 3) he means the Gospels. Corresponding to this are the frequent quotations by Justin
from Synoptic texts as γέγραπται ἐν τοῖς ἀπομνημονεύμασι τῶν
ἀποστόλων or similar expressions (e.g., *Dial.* 101. 3; 104. 1). He
explicitly emphasizes that these memoirs were written "by the
apostles or by those who were their disciples" (*Dial.* 103.8), and in
this manner he also includes the Gospels of Mk and Lk in the
"apostolic memoirs" since according to the tradition they were
written by apostolic pupils. It is uncertain whether Justin knew
Jn, since he does not include Johannine texts in any of the allusions
to the apostolic memoirs. Even though in *Apol.* 61. 4 there is in
fact a quotation introduced by ὁ χριστὸς εἶπεν which echoes Jn, it
could also originate from liturgical tradition.[29] Thus it cannot be

[29] Bellinzoni, 140, 134 ff.

proved that Justin knew a four-Gospel canon,[30] and it is quite possible that some of the harmonizing Synoptic texts quoted by Justin may have come to him from oral tradition.[31] But he also quotes sayings of Jesus from the individual Gospels, and without doubt he places on a par with the OT as normative Scripture a collection of gospel writings for use in worship, so that in any case there begins to emerge alongside the OT a single new canon for use in the reading of Scripture in worship.[32] When Justin goes so far as to include the Rev of John with ἡμέτερα συγγράμματα (*Apol.* 28. 1) and adds to the testimony of the apostle John ἐν ἀποκαλύψει γενομένῃ αὐτῷ the words ὅπερ καὶ ὁ κύριος εἶπεν (*Dial* 81.4), he is clearly preparing the way for the normative evaluation of an "apostolic Scripture," even though it is not yet placed on the same plane as the Gospels. The Pauline letters are not quoted by Justin, however, and he makes no appeal to Paul, though he does not ignore him by design.[33] Thus a bipartite canon alongside the OT is in the process of development.

Shortly before this, Marcion, who already in his homeland of Asia Minor was sharply attacked for his rejection of the OT, came to Rome and there also was excluded from the church (*ca.* A.D. 144). He then organized his own church, and since he completely rejected the OT, he gave to his church a new Holy Scripture consisting of Lk and the ten letters of Paul (without the Pastorals). With the announced aim of restoring the original text, Marcion considerably shortened the text of these eleven writings which he found in the "Western" text tradition. In addition he altered many texts from an anti-Jewish perspective. Marcion's text as a whole has not been preserved, but we can reconstruct it in part on the basis of the polemic of the church fathers.[34] How Paul was regarded exclusively as "the apostle" is to be inferred not only from Marcion himself but from the prologues to the individual letters of Paul which appeared in his church soon after his death. In addition to providing the circumstances of the origin of the letters, the prologues stress the attack of the *apostolus* against the "false apostles" who teach the Jewish Law. It has been proved conclu-

---

[30] Thus correctly von Campenhausen, *Formation*, 169 n. 101; against the 12th ed. of this *Introduction*.

[31] Thus Bellinzoni, esp. 139 f.

[32] This is wrongly disputed by Flessemann-van Leer, 407 n. 13; Piper. Correctly in von Campenhausen, *Formation*, 168, 176 n. 145; Frank, 130.

[33] Against Klein.

[34] See Harnack, *Marcion*, 40* ff.

sively[35] that the prologues serving as introductions to Gal, I and II Cor, Rom, I and II Thess, Col, Phil, and Phlm, which were taken over by the great church and are found in numerous manuscripts of the Vulgate, are of Marcionite origin and thus provide evidence for this sequence of letters. Originally it included still another prologue to the Letter to the Ephesians which was designated as the Letter to the Laodiceans, while the prologues to Eph and the Pastorals were added on the initiative of the Catholic church. The canon of Marcion, which is characterized according to its theological intention by the somewhat later prologues, was undoubtedly an exactly defined Holy Scripture in two parts. Since the days of the church fathers, it has been thought that Marcion selected his canon out of a more comprehensive church canon.[36] In opposition to this view Harnack proposed the thesis that Marcion was the first to promote the idea of a new Holy Scripture as well as its division into two parts, and that the church followed him on both counts.[36a] John Knox went still further and asserted that the church in reaction to Marcion's canon had been persuaded to put the canon of the four Gospels in place of a truncated "gospel" and to establish the collection of thirteen Pauline letters and other apostolic writings in place of his collection of ten Pauline letters,[37] but these theses are very questionable. On the one hand it is not known whether Marcion knew of a collection of the four Gospels and of the Pastorals, and therefore whether he consciously excluded certain writings from his canon. On the other hand the canon of the four Gospels was already in the process of development, and the authority of the apostolic writings was beginning to be placed alongside the gospel writings, when Marcion offered to his church the two-part canon. Marcion's formation of the canon, therefore, scarcely provided the occasion for the church's formation of its canon, but the fact that Marcion had already established the canonical authority of Paul quite exactly without doubt strengthened the tendency which already existed in the church for evaluating the apostolic writings on a level with the gospel writings and

[35] Thus de Bruyne, Corssen, Harnack, von Campenhausen, *Formation*, 154, 245 f, esp. Schäfer; the objections to this in Mundle, Lagrange, Frede, Regul are not convincing. The text of the prologues is in Preuschen, *Analecta*, 85 ff, and in Schäfer, *Festschr. Quasten*, 136 f.

[36] Thus still Feine-Behm; Hanson, *Tradition*, 188. Harnack too defends the hypothesis that Marcion was critical of the fourfold gospel canon of the church; *contra*, von Campenhausen, *Formation*, 184 ff.

[36a] Thus von Campenhausen, *Formation*, 148 ff; esp. 149, 164.

[37] Similarly Carroll: the NT was consciously created in Rome between 170 and 180 as protection against the flood of apocryphal writings.

for delimiting explicitly this new "Holy Scripture." [37a] This development was still further demanded by the necessity of stressing in opposition to Montanism the fulfillment of the New Covenant in Christ and the apostles.[38] Thus the canon of Marcion did not provide the occasion for the church's formation of its canon, but it did further it; and the church adopted not only Marcionite text forms (the doxology of Rom; see above, §19.5) and the Marcionite prologues to the Pauline letters but also the "Letter to the Laodiceans," which originated in the Marcionite church. This letter, which is found in many of the Latin Bibles from the sixth century on, was perhaps already rejected as a Marcionite forgery in the Muratorian Fragment at the end of the second century.[39] On the other hand the prologues to Mk, Lk, and Jn,[40] which for a long time were regarded as anti-Marcionite introductions to the fourfold gospel canon prepared by the early church in the second half of the second century[41] in opposition to the "gospel" of Marcion, undoubtedly did not originate at the same time, but were written individually and at a considerably later time, although the circumstances of their origin cannot now be exactly determined.[42] But in no case do these prologues prove that the church in the second half of the second century consciously proposed a canon which overlapped the canon of Marcion.

From Justin until the end of the second century, to be sure, we are only inadequately informed concerning the development of the NT canon.

Tatian the apologist, born in Syria, pupil of Justin, later head of an ascetic sect, introduces Jn 1:5 with the formula τὸ εἰρημένον, which is the formal way of introducing a quotation from Scripture.[43] In spite of this view of their authority, by omitting the parallels and smoothing out the disagreements Tatian constructed a gospel harmony almost exclusively on the basis of our four Gospels: the Diatessaron, which for centuries was in use in the Syrian church (see §38.2.a.1). The writing of the Diatessaron confirms that there already existed a collection of the four Gospels, even

---

[37a] Cf. F. Hahn, "Das Problem 'Schrift und Tradition' im Urchristentum," EvTh 25, 1970, 464 n. 52.

[38] See Blackman; von Campenhausen, *Formation*, 211, 221.

[39] Thus Harnack, *Marcion*, 134* ff.

[40] The text in Huck-Lietzmann, *Synopse*, viii; Aland, *Synopsis quattuor Evangeliorum*, 532 f; Regul, 16, 29 ff.

[41] Thus since de Bruyne and Harnack defended by many: e.g., Feine-Behm, Michaelis, Wikenhauser; Strobel.

[42] Cf. Lagrange, Bacon, Heard, Haenchen; esp. Regul.

[43] Tatian, *Oratio ad Graecos* 13. 1 (*ca.* 176).

though the text of them was not yet permanently fixed. Tatian also used the letters of Paul, including Heb, and is said to have edited them linguistically,[44] so he also knew the start of a bipartite NT.

The Valentinian Gnostics knew and used the church's Gospels and from the Valentinian Heracleon comes the earliest commentary on the Fourth Gospel. They also used the letters of Paul, thus also following the practice of the church, yet there is no reference among them to the "canonical" authority of the NT scriptures.[45]

The apologist Athenagoras (ca. 180) cites both gospel texts and the OT alike by φησί,[46] but he appeals also to Paul with the formula κατὰ τὸν ἀπόστολον.[47] While almost everywhere Paul and the Gospels are treated as being on the same level, Theophilus of Antioch (end of the second century) quotes Isaiah, τὸ εὐαγγέλιον and ὁ θεῖος λόγος (= Paul) alongside each other and designates Jn as "Holy Scripture." [48] At about the same time the Gnostic Ptolemaeus cites in his Letter to Flora[49] the σωτήρ together with παῦλος ὁ ἀπόστολος. Just as in the East the letters of Paul are placed on the same level of normativeness as the Gospels without being designated as "Scripture," so also in the West a martyr from Scili (in the year 188) responds to the question of the proconsul, *Quae sunt res in capsa vestra?* ("What are those things in your valise?"), *Libri et epistulae Pauli viri iusti* ("Books and epistles of Paul, a just man").[50] In this way he shows clearly that the Gospels were considered together with the OT as "the Books," but that the letters of Paul, in spite of their being of equal value for practical purposes, had not yet actually received the same ranking.

That a new bipartite canon was in the process of development at the end of the second century is shown also by the fact that in the letter of the churches of Vienne and Lyons from the year

[44] According to Eus., HE IV. 29. 6.

[45] The claim that the "Gospel of Truth," which belongs to the documents found at Nag Hammadi, comes from Valentinus himself and that it proves the authoritative evaluation of all NT scriptures before Marcion (thus van Unnik; Hanson, *Tradition,* 189 f) is incapable of proof, since, on the one hand, the origin and time of writing of this Gnostic document are completely uncertain, and, on the other hand, the mere fact that the NT writings were known does not prove they were valued as "canonical." (See von Campenhausen, *Formation,* 140 n. 171.)

[46] Athenagoras, Apology 10. 3; 32. 1; 33. 2.

[47] Athenagoras, *De resurrectione,* 18.

[48] Theophilus, *Ad Autolycum* II. 22; III. 14; cf. Frank, 165 f; 168.

[49] In Epiphanius, *Panarion* 33. 5. 10, 15. Holl.

[50] R. Knopf–G. Krüger, *Ausgewählte Märtyrerakten,* Sammlung ausgewählter kirchen- und dogmengeschichtlicher Quellenschriften, NF 3, ³1929, 29.

177, Rev is cited as γραφή.[51] And when Melito of Sardis (*ca.* 180)
sets forth a list of the books τῆς παλαιᾶς διαθήκης,[52] this designation
implies *e contrario* that the concept of a "NT" is in the formative
stages. It cannot be doubted that the anti-Montanist who wrote
ca. 192[53] meant by the designation ὁ τῆς τοῦ εὐαγγελίου καινῆς διαθήκης λόγος a collection of scriptures which is to be called καινὴ
διαθήκη and from which "nothing may be added or taken away," [54]
even if it is not unambiguously named "the NT." Although the
consciousness was gradually developing of the existence of a new
scriptural norm, this collection was by no means defined everywhere in the same way. Indeed in many places the consciousness
was still lacking that such a limitation was necessary. Thus *ca.* 170
the anti-Montanists who were called "Alogoi" could throw out from
the presumably acknowledged collection of the church's scriptures
Jn and Rev as allegedly works of the Gnostic Cerinthus without
thereby putting themselves outside the framework of the church.[55]
On the other hand Bishop Serapion of Antioch (*ca.* 200) could
permit the reading of the Gospel of Peter even though he did not
know it himself, and had to withdraw his permission when he
learned that its contents were heretical.[56] The circle of permitted
writings of the "New Covenant" was therefore not yet closed.

This is the state of affairs that we find among the great fathers
of the church at the end of the second century and in the earliest
surviving canon list.

Irenaeus, who knew the churches of Asia Minor, Rome, and
Gaul, stressed the authority of the εὐαγγέλιον τετράμορφον, i.e., the
four Gospels which are granted to the church according to the
eternal divine order, not more and not fewer. As there are four
sectors of the world, four chief winds, four divine διαθῆκαι, so
there are four Gospels as the chief pillars of the church.[57] This
canon of four Gospels was expanded by Acts, which shared the
authority of Lk.[58] In addition the thirteen letters of Paul—Irenaeus
is our first witness for this number of Pauline letters—enjoyed un-
limited authority, while the view concerning Heb, the Catholic
letters, and Rev was not yet fixed. Irenaeus quotes Hermas in con-

---

[51] In Eus., HE V. 1. 58.
[52] In Eus., HE IV. 26. 14.
[53] In Eus., HE V. 16. 3 (Polycrates of Ephesus? see von Campenhausen,
Formation, 231 f).
[54] Van Unnik, VigChr 1949.
[55] Cf. Grant, *Formation*, 150 f.
[56] Eus., HE VI. 12. 2 ff.
[57] Iren., *Haer.* III. 11. 11.
[58] Cf. von Campenhausen, *Formation*, 200 f.

nection with Gen, Mal, Mt, Eph as γραφή,[59] but on the other hand, though he prized I Clem highly, he probably did not regard it as "Holy Scripture." [60] Even in Irenaeus there is no comprehensive designation for "the NT." [61]

On the contrary, Tertullian recognizes as a witness for the church of Africa *totum instrumentum utriusque testamenti* ("the complete instrument of each testament"): beside *lex et prophetae* stand *evangelicae et apostolicae litterae* ("the Gospels and the apostolic writings"). Thus there is an OT and a NT. The canon of the Gospels is closed, but the canon of the apostolic writings is not yet closed. Tertullian clearly attests[62] the four Gospels and calls them *scripturae*.[63] For him, the thirteen Pauline letters, Acts, Rev, I John, I Pet, Jude belong to the "Apostolos." Not mentioned from among the Catholic epistles are II and II John, James, and II Pet. On the other hand[64] he quotes Heb as the Epistle of Barnabas and calls it *receptior apud ecclesias* ("more favorably received among the churches"). In his pre-Montanist period he considered Hermas as *scriptura* but in *De pud.* he rejects it as *apocryphus*.

Clement of Alexandria knows "the four Gospels which have been given over to us," [65] and in the second part of the canon he has fourteen Pauline letters (including Heb) and then Acts and Rev. He prepared expositions of I Pet, I John, and Jude, but it is very doubtful whether it is true, as Eusebius states,[66] that Clement expounded all the Catholic epistles in addition to Barnabas and the Apocalypse of Peter. His NT, however, is still more inclusive. From among the Gospels he uses—although not as being of equal authority—the Gospel of the Hebrews and the Gospel of the Egyptians; he regards as apostolic Scripture, and therefore as inspired, also the Apocalypse of Peter, the Kerygma of Peter, Barnabas, I Clem, Didache, and Hermas; i.e., he has "to a certain degree a still 'open' canon." [67]

The three great theologians at the end of the second century therefore recognize a NT that contains the four Gospels and an apostolic section to which belong uncontestedly the thirteen letters of Paul, Acts, I Pet, I John, and Rev, while the canonicity of the

[59] Iren., *Haer.* IV. 34. 2.
[60] Iren., *Haer.* III. 3. 2 f.
[61] Von Campenhausen, *Formation*, 188.
[62] Tert., Adv. Marc. IV. 2. 5.
[63] Tert., *De carne Christi*, 3.
[64] Tert., *De pud.*, 20.
[65] Clement of Alexandria, *Strom.* III. 93. 1.
[66] Eus., HE VI. 14. 1.
[67] Von Campenhausen, *Formation*, 198 ff.

other Catholic letters and of Heb has not yet been determined and occasionally other scriptures are treated as canonical. That this state of affairs also obtained in the Roman community is attested by the so-called Muratorian Fragment or Muratorian Canon. This fragment was dicsovered in 1740 by the librarian L. A. Muratori in the Bibliotheca Ambrosiana in Milan in an eighth-century manuscript. It preserves, in not always comprehensible Latin,[68] a text which was almost certainly translated into wretched Latin from Greek. The beginning and perhaps also the end are broken off. The unknown author wrote toward the end of the second century in Rome.[69] It is unlikely that he was the Roman "counter-bishop" Hippolytus.[70] We are scarcely dealing here with an official Roman document,[71] but rather with an authoritative list of the writings which are to be "received" in the Catholic church and to be read in public, together with explicit rejection of writings to which other Christians within the church or heretics would like to assign equal value. The text begins with the concluding words concerning Mk. Since the fragment describes Lk as the Third and Jn as the Fourth Gospel, the mention of Mt as the First Gospel has obviously been broken off. The information concerning Mk and Lk shows that the role of eyewitnesses was highly valued: thus Mk "was present when some things took place and has narrated them accordingly," while Lk "had not seen the Lord in the flesh" but narrated according to such information as he could obtain. The Fourth Gospel is written by the disciple John by specific invitation of and with approval of his fellow disciples and the bishops. The Johannine letters also offer guarantees that John had seen and heard the Lord, and therefore in his Gospel he offers all the wonderful deeds of the Lord in the proper order. The author of the fragment is aware of the differences between the individual Gospels, but attaches to them no significance for faith, since the major facts in the gospel history "are proved by the sole and dominating spirit" (*uno ac principali spiritu declarata sint*). In the case of Acts the most important thing is that *sub praesentia eius* [Luke] *singula gerebantur* ("there individual events took place in the presence of Luke"). This way the content of the book is guaranteed. Lk does

[68] In addition to the collections mentioned before §35, the text is available in H. Lietzmann, *Kleine Texte* I, ²1933; in English in Hennecke-Schneemelcher-Wilson, 43 ff.

[69] Von Campenhausen's objections, *Formation*, 243 f, are not convincing; Sundberg's fourth-century dating (StEv IV, 458 f) is arbitrary.

[70] Zahn, Lagrange; *contra*, von Campenhausen, *Formation*, 245 n. 198; Frank, 179; H. Merkel, *Widersprüche zwischen den Evv.* WUNT 13, 1971, 57.

[71] Against Erhardt, who also falsely assumes the original language to be Latin.

not recount the passion of Peter and the journey of Paul from
Rome to Spain because he did not participate in those experiences
(cf. §24.2). Like the sevenfold church in Rev, the seven churches
to whom Paul wrote his letters symbolize for the author the totality
of the Christian church and thus the definitive character of the
Pauline letters for the whole church. Paul's battle against heresy
and his understanding of the OT in Rom are held up as being
especially important. The four letters to individual persons who
were especially close to the apostle (Phlm, I and II Tim, Tit)
have achieved canonical authority on account of the instructions
for church order which are contained in them. Spurious Pauline
letters which stem from heretical circles such as the letters to the
Laodiceans or the Alexandrians, among others, are rejected (*in
catholicam ecclesiam recipi non potest*); one cannot mix gall and
honey. Nothing is said concerning the basis for acceptance of
three of the Catholic letters (Jude and the two letters of John).
Astonishingly Wisdom is listed with the Catholics as a canonical
book. Two apocalypses follow—Rev and the Apocalypse of Peter—
but the last bears the supplemental comment *quam quidam ex
nostris legi in ecclesia nolunt* ("which some of us are not willing
to have read in church"). On the other hand he explains that
Hermas may also be read but it should not be read publicly in
the church to the people (*se publicare in ecclesia populo*), since
it does not belong in the prophetic canon of the OT, which is
closed, nor among the apostles who stand at the end of the ages.
Indeed it was written just a short time ago in Rome by the brother
of Bishop Pius. Finally the list mentions the writings of Arsinous,
Valentinus, Miltiades, and a songbook attributed to Marcion, but it
says concerning them: *nihil in totum recipimus* ("we receive absolutely none of these").

The listing of the scriptures "to be received" agrees in essence
with that established by the contemporary Western fathers. It is
striking that I Pet is missing, but the omission of Heb, James, and
III John is not surprising;[72] although the false Pauline letters and
the Shepherd of Hermas are excluded, the Apocalypse of Peter is
nonetheless recognized (the inclusion of Wisdom in this connection
is to be understood only as a mistake). What is more important
is that here we encounter something of the motives for the exclusion and inclusion of individual scriptures. Quite clear is the
consciousness that just as the number of the prophetic writings

---

[72] Katz' conjecture that originally three Letters of John were mentioned
(cautiously subscribed to by von Campenhausen, *Formation*, 246 n. 205) is not
convincing.

is closed, so also the apostolic writings must be exactly delimited and the new canon must be a closed one. Decisive for including a writing is not its content but the fact that it was written by an apostle.[73] Thus the authors of Lk and Mk are authorized by virtue of their being in the relationship of a pupil to an apostle.[74] Acts is characterized as *acta omnium apostolorum* ("acts of all the apostles"), while the Shepherd of Hermas is excluded because its late origin excludes the possibility of its having been written by an apostle. In addition there is a second motive for the ecclesiastical authority of a scripture: its being intended for the whole *ecclesia catholica,* which causes some difficulty for the Pauline letters, but the author triumphs over this by his comparison of the seven letters with those of Rev.[75] Since the direct eyewitness in Jn and Acts is stressed, and indirect eyewitness for Lk (in the case of Mk something similar must have stood in the text), the polemical intention of the list must have been: the sure connection of the canonical scriptures with the apostolic tradition is to be placed over against the apocryphal Gospels and Acts. The limitation of the canon by excluding nonapostolic writings is therefore concluded by the end of the second century so far as the Gospels are concerned, but for the apostolic part it is still in flux. The practical consequence of such inclusion or exclusion was first of all permission or prohibition for being read in worship, and secondly as a consequence of this with the passage of time came the granting of acceptance or the refusal to accept a writing in those manuscripts which were intended for use in worship.

§36. THE CLOSE OF THE NEW TESTAMENT CANON IN THE ANCIENT CHURCH

J. Ruwet, "Les 'Antilegomena' dans les oeuvres d'Origène," Bb 23, 1942, 18 ff—*idem,* "Le canon Alexandrin des Écritures. Saint Athanase,"

[73] The refutation of this view by von Campenhausen, *Formation,* 254 ("he is merely asking for documents which are ancient and reliable") stands in contradiction with lines 78 f: *neque inter prophetas . . . neque inter apostolos* ("neither among the prophets . . . nor in the apostolic writings"). Frank, 183, can adduce no evidence for his assertion that the deeper basis for considering a writing canonical lies for the fragmentist in "a specific theological viewpoint," which sees in "the agreement with the faith" the ultimate standard for canonicity. And for the fragmentist as for Tatian it cannot be inferred that Jn is—even for the letters of Paul—the "canon within the canon."

[74] Cf. the reference to the related arguments in Irenaeus and Tertullian given in Sundberg, StEv III.

[75] See Dahl, 44 f.

Bb 33, 1952, 1 ff—C. F. F. Andry, "'Barnabae Epist. ver. DCCCL,'" JBL 70, 1951, 233 ff—W. Bauer, *Der Apostolos der Syrer*, 1903; M. Gordillo, *Theologia Orientalium cum Latinorum comparata* I, OrChrA 158, 1960, 22 ff.

1. The NT in the Greek Church from Origen to the End of Antiquity

Within the history of the NT canon, the great Alexandrian Origen (253/54) is of vital significance. That is not the consequence of his having participated actively in the course of its development so as to have determined a significantly different compass for the NT than was the case before his time. Rather his service was that he ascertained what the custom was with respect to NT scriptures in his time among the various provinces of the church, and on the basis of this research he carefully drew certain conclusions. His learned studies as well as his periods of residence in different cities and countries (Rome, Athens, Antioch, Arabia, Cappadocia, Palestine) gave him an encompassing knowledge of the practices in the different churches, and on this he based his judgments concerning the canonical authority of the NT scriptures. Because of the great respect which Origen enjoyed, his views continued to be influential in the following period.

The most important thing was that he determined for the first time which scriptures had general ecclesiastical authority, and on this basis it could be inferred how the different classes of ecclesiastical writings were to be differentiated.[1] (1) The first class, according to him, is that of the ἀναντίρρητα or the ὁμολογούμενα ("those which are uncontested in the church of God under heaven"). To this group belong the four Gospels, the thirteen letters of Paul, I Pet, I John, Acts, and Rev. (2) The ἀμφιβαλλόμενα = the doubtful writings: II Pet, II and III John, Heb, in addition to James[2] and Jude.[3] Although he cited Shepherd of Hermas and Didache as γραφή, he does not seem to have included them within the canon, although he does list Barnabas within the NT.[4] (3) The ψευδή: the Gospel of the Egyptians, the Gospel of Thomas, the Gospel of Basilides, the Gospel of Matthias, which are rejected as heretical falsifications. On the whole it is evident that for Origen as well as for his predecessor Clement, the church's use

---

[1] In Eus., HE VI. 25. 3 ff.

[2] Origen, *Tomoi in Johannem* 20. 10. 66.

[3] Origen, *Tomoi in Matthaeum* 17. 30.

[4] Cf. von Campenhausen, *Formation*, 320.

of scriptures in Alexandria was more open-minded than elsewhere. The criterion for distinction between ὁμολογούμενα and ἀμφιβαλλόμενα is, however, the acknowledgement or rejection of a scripture by a majority of the churches, whose judgment offsets the uncertainty concerning individual questions of authorship.[5] The limits of the canon are thus not yet fixed, and by appealing to a majority decision on what is ultimately a historical question, the decision in individual cases still hangs in the air (esp. concerning Heb and Rev), and writings which were later to be excluded are still here and there regarded as canonical.

That is to be seen clearly from other evidence from the third century. An index of the number of lines in the biblical writings stands in Latin in the Codex Claromontanus (D) of the letters of Paul (see below, §38.1.c) between Phlm and Heb.[6] Almost certainly it was translated from Greek and originates from the third century.[7] In this list are enumerated the four Gospels, the thirteen letters of Paul (Phil and I and II Thess are missing, apparently by oversight), the seven Catholic letters, Rev, Acts. Heb, which Origen only indirectly traced back to Paul, is missing; in its stead as part of the NT are mentioned Barnabas,[8] Shepherd of Hermas, Acts of Paul, the apocalypse of Peter. But the fondness for apocalypses which is evident here received a staggering blow when Dionysius of Alexandria in his work *Concerning the Promises*[9] showed on the basis of linguistic, stylistic, and conceptual indicators that Rev could not have been written by the author of Jn and I John. Although Dionysius himself did not dare to reject the book, because "many brothers treasure it highly," it was on the basis of this criticism that the canonical authority of Rev in the East was shaken. While in these witnesses from the third century there is still evident uncertainty concerning the canonical authority of Heb, Rev, some of the Catholic letters, and a few writings which finally were not included in the canon, the development continues which led finally to a fixed point of view concerning the limits of the NT canon. Methodius of Olympus, who was an opponent of Origen in Asia Minor, quotes all the scriptures of the NT as canonical but also the Apocalypse of Peter and perhaps

---

[5] Cf. von Campenhausen, 321.

[6] Text in Preuschen, *Analecta*, 41 f.

[7] Thus Zahn, Leipoldt, Lagrange; Wikenhauser. The later dating by F. Renner, *"An die Hebräer"—ein pseudepigraphischer Brief*, 1970, 26 ff, is not persuasive.

[8] Andry has shown that *Barnabae epist.* cannot mean the Letter to the Hebrews.

[9] *Ca.* 260, in Eus., HE VII. 25; English in WGK, NT, 16 ff.

Barnabas and Didache. And Papyrus 72 (see below, §38.1.b) from the third century includes Jude and the two letters of Peter and specifically designates the second of these letters as "the second letter"; thus it presumably acknowledges all three of these writings as part of the NT canon.

This uncertainty concerning the limits of the apostolic section of the NT is seen clearly in the extended discussion which Eusebius of Caesarea devotes to the NT in his church history (*ca.* 303). He distinguishes[10] three classes of scriptures: (1) homologoumena, (2) antilegomena, and (3) completely senseless and impious (ἄτοπα πάντῃ καὶ δυσσεβῆ) concoctions of heretics that deviate from the true faith. For him the homologoumena are the four Gospels, Acts, fourteen letters of Paul (including Heb), I Pet, I John, and "if one will" (εἰ γε φανείη) Rev. He distinguishes two groups among the antilegomena: writings held in greater or in lesser esteem. The first group he calls the "antilegomena which now, however, are recognized by the majority." These are James, Jude, II Pet, II and III John. The second group are the νόθα, spurious Acts of Paul, Apocalypse of Peter, Shepherd of Hermas, Barnabas, Didache, and εἰ φανείη Rev. There are a few, as he says, who include in this group the Gospel of the Hebrews, which is used by the Jewish Christians. The strange fact that Rev is first listed among the homologoumena, then among the inauthentic antilegomena, is to be explained on the basis of the widespread rejection of the apostolic origin of Rev from the time of Dionysius of Alexandria on, while the earlier church tradition and Origen had acknowledged the book as canonical.

This scholarly classification, however, does not give a complete picture of the state of affairs at the time of Eusebius. To a large extent the Greek church of his day knew seven Catholic letters, as Eusebius himself attests,[11] so that for him if the homologoumena and the first group of antilegomena are grouped together the NT was constituted in its present-day sense. Yet the number seven for the Catholic letters was not generally recognized in his time, although the name "Catholic letters" was familiar to him. Perhaps there was even a definite sequence of these letters: Ἰάκωβον, οὗ ἡ πρώτη τῶν ὀνομαζομένων καθολικῶν ἐπιστολῶν εἶναι λέγεται.[12] But the authority of the four small Catholic letters in his day was not universally fixed, and above all Rev was still disputed. In Cyril of Jerusalem (*ca.* 350), in the fifty-ninth (or sixieth) canon of the

[10] Eus., HE III. 25.
[11] Eus., HE II. 23, 24 f.
[12] Eus., HE II. 23, 24.

Synod of Laodicea (after 360), and in Gregory Nazianzus (d. 390), we have from the fourth century lists of twenty-six books (i.e., without Rev). Amphilochius of Iconium (d. *ca.* 394) too concedes that Rev is widely declared to be inauthentic. On the other hand, Epiphanius, Bishop of Cyprus (d. 403), mentions Rev as the final NT book.

While the canonical authority of a few of the Catholic letters and Rev was still contested, other scriptures also continued to be treated as part of the NT which finally were not recognized as canonical: the Codex Sinaiticus (see §38.1.c) contains after Rev Barnabas and Hermas; the Codex Alexandrinus (see §38.1.c) contains I and II Clem; and the document *Concerning Virginity,* which was written in Egypt in the fourth century and falsely attributed to Athanasius, quotes Didache as γραφή.

This uncertainty concerning the limits of the NT canon was brought to an end for the church in the East by the thirty-ninth Easter festival letter of Athanasius from the year 367,[13] which has been preserved for us almost complete in Greek, Syriac, and Coptic. In this pastoral letter Athanasius for the first time presented a firmly circumscribed canon of the OT and the NT within which were defined the individual classes of the writings and their sequence. He designated the twenty-seven books of our NT as the only canonical ones. They are our four Gospels followed by Acts and the seven Catholic letters (James, I and II Pet, I, II, and III John, Jude), then the fourteen Pauline letters (Heb after II Thess, before the Pastorals and Phlm), and Rev. No one is to add anything to this, and no one is to take anything away. In addition to the canonical writings (κανονιζόμενα) and those rejected by the church (ἀπόκρυφα) he mentions a third class, the books to be read aloud (ἀναγινωσκόμενα), which may be used by the church in baptismal instruction. They are (in addition to Wisdom, Sirach, Esther, Judith, and Tobit) Didache (on account of the Two Ways, Chs. 1–6) and Shepherd of Hermas (on account of the *Mandata*). Athanasius was also the first to name this ecclesiastically fixed collection of Holy Scriptures κανών.[14]

The authority of Athanasius was such that within the Greek church the canonicity of the seven Catholic letters was rapidly established. On the other hand the position concerning Rev re-

---

[13] Greek text in the collections mentioned before §35; English in Hennecke-Schneemelcher-Wilson (see before §35), 59 f.

[14] He indicates Herm. as μὴ ὂν κανόνος in *De decretis Nicenae synodi* 18:3= *Athanasius' Werke* II, 1, 1935 ff, 15. See his Festal Letter XXXIX in Hennecke-Schneemelcher-Wilson, *NT Apocr.* I, 59 f.

mained generally divided. Chrysostom and Theodoret, the great teachers of the Antiochian school, were against it, as were also the three Greek Cappadocians. The Quinisextine Council (692) set up a NT canonical list with Rev and one without it. And a list of scriptures from the ninth century[15] still does not list Rev explicitly among the books of the NT. Of the Greek manuscripts of the NT which have survived until late Byzantine times only a few contain Rev, and most Greek manuscripts of Rev offer its text either as part of a commentary or together with nonbiblical writings. It was not until the tenth/eleventh century that that slowly altered.[16] One may say that the number of twenty-seven canonical writings of the NT in the Greek church finally prevailed for the first time in the tenth century.

2. The New Testament in the Latin Church from Cyprian to the Fifth Century

By contrast, in the Latin church determination of the canon was reached early and was also final. Since the apostolic authority of Rev was already attested in the Muratorian Canon, it was practically never contested. After the third century only occasionally were other apocalypses also cited as canonical. But in the West on the other hand, Heb and five Catholic letters were for a long time unknown or disputed.

Novatian of Rome (*ca.* 250), in addition to the Gospels, Acts, and thirteen letters of Paul, quoted only I John and Rev as "Scripture." From Cyprian (d. 258) we can discern the state of affairs in North Africa about the middle of the third century, since he introduces many biblical references in his *Testimonia*. Of the Catholic letters only I John and I Pet are cited. Heb never appears, but on the other hand Rev is Holy Scripture.

In the Latin church no scholar can be pointed to who, like Eusebius, took the initiative in bringing order into the history of the canon. On the whole the formation of the canon was carried through in a simpler way corresponding to the deeply impressed sense of law and order in the church. Gradually the Greek theological literature gained a strong influence in the West, as is shown especially by Jerome, who contributed fundamentally to the setting aside of the distinction between the Western and Eastern canons. Pope Damasus paid heed to him in establishing the Roman canon,

---

[15] The so-called Stichometry of Nicephorus; text in Preuschen, *Analecta*, 62 ff. Hennecke-Schneemelcher-Wilson, *NT Apocrypha* I, 49–52.

[16] Cf. J. Schmid, *Studien* (see §34 n. 18), II, 31 ff.

and Athanasius also worked in the same direction during his various periods of residence in Rome and in other places in the West.

Especially discernible is the influence of the Greek church on the decision in the West concerning Heb. The letter was originally considered in the Latin church as non-Pauline. Tertullian attributed it to Barnabas. The Roman Christian who *ca.* 370 wrote a commentary on the Pauline letters, the so-called Ambrosiaster, limited himself to the thirteen Pauline letters without Heb, as did Pelagius in his commentary of Pauline letters which was written in Rome *ca.* 400. Both, however, know Heb and quote from it as Scripture but not as Pauline. After the Muratorian Canon the first sure Latin witness to a canon, an African canon from about the year 360 called the Canon of Mommsen after its editor,[17] mentions the four Gospels, the thirteen Pauline letters, Acts, Rev and then *epistulae Johannis III (una sola) Epistulae Petri II (una sola)*: i.e., "three Epistles of John (one only); two Epistles of Peter (one only)." Only one of the two manuscripts from which the canon is known has the words in parenthesis *una sola* in both places. They appear to be a later correction whose originator wants to have only one letter of John and one letter of Peter recognized. Entirely lacking on the other hand are Heb, James, and Jude.

In the second half of the fourth century, however, the influence of the East made itself noticeable. Hilary of Poitiers (d. 367), who was banished for several years to Asia Minor, quotes Heb, James, and II Pet as apostolic. Lucifer of Calaris (d. 370/71), who was also banished to the East, had the same viewpoint concerning Heb, Jude, and II Pet. And Jerome, who already during his stay in Rome (382–85) used the standard of Athanasius for the NT in his revision of the Latin NT (see below, §38.2.b.2), after his move to the East (394) expressly described this canonical standard in a letter,[18] although he did not suppress his doubt about the Pauline authorship of Heb. In his literary catalogue (*De viris illustribus,* 392) he brought together the information known to him concerning the doubts about the apostolic origin of II Pet, James, Jude, Heb, and Rev, and thus they were transmitted to the Middle Ages. It is possible, though debatable, that as early as 382 a Roman synod influenced by Jerome proclaimed under Pope Damasus the canon of Athanasius as the canon of the NT for the

[17] Text in Preuschen, *Analecta,* 37 f.
[18] Jerome, *Ep. ad Paulinum* 53. 9.

Roman church,[19] but it is certain that in 405 Pope Innocent I, in response to a question of the Gallic bishops concerning the Roman canon, named the canon of Athanasius with fourteen Pauline letters and seven Catholic letters.[20] Undoubtedly it was under the influence of Jerome not only that Augustine represented the canon of Athanasius,[21] but that already before that time an African synod of Hippo Regius (393)[22] determined the same extent of the canon and did so with the formula *Pauli apostoli epistulae tredecim. Eiusdem ad Hebraeos una* ("by the apostle Paul thirteen epistles; of the same, one to the Hebrews"), and not until a new synod in the year 419 did it read, *Pauli apostoli epistulae quatuordecim* ("of the apostle Paul fourteen epistles")!

With these decisions of the Roman and African churches the question of the canon in the West was finally settled. The practice did not keep step with this decision immediately: Heb was for a long time occasionally lacking in the biblical manuscripts.[23] Around the middle of the sixth century Cassiodorus does not yet know any Latin commentary on Heb, but on the other hand until the end of the Middle Ages the apocryphal letter of Paul to the Laodiceans is found in manuscripts of the Vulgate. But these variations do not really call into question the fact that the extent of the NT for the Latin church was bindingly fixed from the beginning of the fifth century on.

3. The New Testament in the Eastern National Churches

Deviating from the course of events in the Greek and Latin churches, the history of the canon in the Syrian national church had a distinctive development. The center of this church was in the lands of the Euphrates. In Edessa, the capital of the principality of Osroene, Christianity had established a footing in the last third of the second century. The *Doctrina Addai,* a Syrian legend from

---

[19] This assumption is sound if the first three parts (including the canon index) of the so-called *Decretum Gelasianum,* which in its entirety comes from the sixth century (text in Preuschen, *Analecta,* 52 ff) were in reality determined by the Roman Synod of 382 (thus, e.g., E. Schwartz, "Zum Decretum Gelasianum," ZNW 29, 1930, 161 ff; Hennecke-Schneemelcher-Wilson, *NT Apocr.* I, 46 f).

[20] Innocent I, Epist. 6 (text in Leipoldt, *Geschichte* I, 230 n. 3).

[21] Augustine, *De doctrina christiana* 2. 13 (*ca.* 396).

[22] To be sure, we have only the repetition of the canonical decisions of 393 by the Synod of Carthage in 397 (text in Preuschen, *Analecta,* 72 f).

[23] In a pseudo-Augustinian work, *Speculum,* from the fifth century; in the Codex Boernerianus of the ninth century, see §38.1.c.

the beginning of the fifth century, narrates that the founder of the church in Edessa had in his farewell speech given instruction to his successor Aggai that outside of the OT no other scriptures were to be read in the churches other than the gospel, the letters of Paul, and the Acts, in which the divine truth was contained.[24] The original canon of the Syrians is therefore much more limited than that of the Greeks and the Latins: instead of the four Gospels the Diatessaron was used, and the Catholic epistles and Rev are lacking. Under Greek influence Heb was regarded as Pauline, but on the other hand Phlm was considered to be un-Pauline and was therefore rejected.[25] In its place the Syrian fathers of the fourth century quote as canonical III Cor together with the letter from the Corinthians and a narrative connecting passage.[26]

A Syriac canon list has been preserved from the period around 400, however,[27] which from the NT also mentions only the Gospels, Acts, and the Pauline letters. After Phlm, the last of the Pauline letters, it remarks, "The entire Apostolos [consists of] 5,076 stichoi," i.e., the Pauline letters (including Phlm but without III Cor) form with Acts the entire Apostolos. Yet this canon list now presents the fourth Gospels, although the Doctrina Addai (see above), Aphraates, and Ephraem (both in the fourth century) testify to the church's use of the Diatessaron, as does Eusebius.[28] And Theodoret, Bishop of Cyrrhos on the Euphrates (d. ca. 466), gathered up and laid aside in his diocese more than 200 copies of the Diatessaron, and introduced in their place the four Gospels.[29] Bishop Rabbula of Edessa (d. 436) similarly instructed his priests to take care that in all the churches four "separate" Gospels were available and were read. But initiative of this sort by the bishops could not entirely do away with the Diatessaron. It has been highly valued for a long time, especially among the Nestorians, even though they too had the Peshitta as the Bible of their church, and within it the four Gospels.

At the beginning of the fifth century, through a cooperative effort of the bishoprics, the Syrian church's Bible, the so-called Peshitta, was formed (see §38.2.a.3). It represents an accommo-

---

[24] Cf. Zahn, Geschichte I, 373.

[25] See Leipoldt, Geschichte I, 208 ff.

[26] This apocryphal exchange of letters has either arisen independently (now attested in Papyrus Bodmer X from the third century) or it was taken over from the apocryphal Acts of Paul (cf. Hennecke-Schneemelcher-Wilson II, 326, 374 ff).

[27] Syriac stichometry in A. Lewis, Studia Sinaitica I, 1894, 11 ff.

[28] Eus., HE IV. 29. 6.

[29] Theodoret, Haereticarum fabularum compendium 1. 20.

dation of the canon of the Syrians with that of the Greeks. At its head stand the four separate Gospels. III Cor was rejected; there were fourteen Pauline letters with Heb followed by three Catholic letters, James, I Pet, I John; the others, like Rev, remain excluded. Thus the canon contains twenty-two writings. For a large part of the Syrian church this constituted the closing of the canon, since no further accommodation to the Greek canon followed. There was even less of an opportunity for that to occur when after the Synod of Ephesus (431) the east Syrians separated themselves as Nestorians from the great church. On the other hand among the Monophysite Syrians of the west, who remained in closer connection with their neighboring churches, a further accommodation to the canon of the Greeks did take place. The revision authorized in 508 by Bishop Philoxenus of Mabbug—i.e., the new translation of the NT, the so-called Philoxeniana—and its reworking by Thomas of Harkel in the year 616 (see §38.2.a.4) contained also II and III John, II Pet, Jude, and Rev. Yet in the fifth and sixth centuries James and the four smaller Catholic letters were still not everywhere regarded as canonical in the west Syrian church, and Rev only very slowly won ecclesiastical recognition in Syria too. In the churches of the Copts and Ethiopians, which were also Monophysite, however, other scriptures were added to the canon of Athanasius: among the Copts, I and II Clem and the eight books of the Apostolic Constitutions; among the Ethiopians in addition to these scriptures still other apocrypha.[30]

§37. The Canon in the Western Church since the Reformation and the Theological Problem of the Canon

Das NT als Kanon. Dokumentation und kritische Analyse zur gegenwärtigen Diskussion, ed. E. Käsemann, 1970 (hereafter NTaK; papers from this source in the following bibl. are so noted).

H. J. Holtzmann, *Lehrbuch der historisch-kritischen Einl. in das NT*, [3]1892, 154 ff; J. Leipoldt, *Geschichte* II; H. Strathmann, "Die Krisis des Kanons der Kirche," ThBl 20, 1941, 295 ff (=NTaK, 41 ff); W. G. Kümmel, "Notwendigkeit und Grenze des nt. Kanons," ZThK 47, 1950, 277 ff (=NTaK, 62 ff); *idem*, "Das Problem der 'Mitte des NT,'" *L'Évangile hier et aujourd'hui, Festschr. F.-J. Leenhardt*, 1968, 71 ff; E. Käsemann, "Begründet der nt. Kanon die Einheit der Kirche?" EvTh 11, 1951/52, 13 ff (=NTaK, 124 ff), Eng. tr., "The NT Canon and the Unity of the Church," in *Essays on NT Themes*, SBT 41, 1964, 95 f; *idem*, "Kritische Analyse," NTaK, 336 ff; H. Diem, "Das Problem

---

[30] According to Gordillo: *Testamentum Domini*, Didaskalia, Senodon.

des Schriftkanons," ThSt 32, 1952 (=NTaK, 159 ff); O. Weber, *Grundlagen der Dogmatik* I, 1955, 274 ff; O. Cullmann, *Die Tradition als exegetisches, historisches und theologisches Problem*, 1954 (p. 42 ff = NTaK, 109 ff); H. Bacht, "Die Rolle der Tradition in der Kanonbildung," *Catholica* 12, 1958, 16 ff; H. Braun, W. Andersen, W. Maurer, "Die Verbindlichkeit des Kanons," *Fuldaer Hefte* 12, 1960 (H. Braun= NTaK, 219 ff); W. Marxsen, "Das Problem des nt. Kanons aus der Sicht des Exegeten," NZSTh 2, 1960, 137 ff (=NTaK, 233 ff); *idem*, "Kontingenz der Offenbarung oder (und?) Kontingenz des Kanons?" NZSTh 2, 1960, 335 ff; *idem, Das NT als Buch der Kirche*, 1966; C. H. Ratschow, "Zur Frage der Begründung des Kanons aus der Sicht des systematischen Theologen," NZSTh 2, 1960, 150 ff (=NTaK, 247 ff); P. Lengsfeld, *Überlieferung. Tradition und Schrift in der evangelischen und katholischen Theologie der Gegenwart*, 1960, 71 ff (p. 104 ff = NTaK, 205 ff); K. Aland, "Das Problem des nt. Kanons," NZSTh 4, 1962, 220 ff (=NTaK, 134 ff); E. Schweizer, "Scripture—Tradition—Modern Interpretation," in E. S., *Neotestamentica*, 1963, 203 ff; *idem*, "Kanon?" EvTh 31, 1971, 339 ff; H. Küng, "Der Frühkatholizismus als kontroverstheologisches Problem," in H. K., *Kirche im Konzil*, 1963, 125 ff (=NTaK, 175 ff); G. Ebeling, " 'Sola scriptura' und das Problem der Tradition," in G. E., *Wort Gottes und Tradition*, 1964, 91 ff (=NTaK, 282 ff); F. Mussner, " 'Evangelium' und 'Mitte des Evangeliums,' " *Gott in Welt, Festschr. K. Rahner* I, 1964, 492 ff (=F. M., *Praesentia Salutis*, 1967, 159 ff); N. Appel, "Kanon und Kirche. Die Kanonkrise im heutigen Protestantismus als kontroverstheologisches Problem," *Konfessionskundliche und kontroverstheologische Studien* 9, 1964 (on this cf. W. Marxsen, ThLZ 92, 1967, 604 ff); W. Joest, "Erwägungen zur kanonischen Bedeutung des NT," KuD 12, 1966, 27 ff (=NTaK, 258 ff); A. Stock, *Einheit des NT. Erörterung hermeneutischer Grundpositionen der heutigen Theologie*, 1969; F. Hahn, "Das Problem 'Schrift und Tradition' im Urchristentum," EvTh 30, 1970, 449 ff; K.-H. Ohlig, *Woher nimmt die Bibel ihre Autorität? Zum Verhältnis von Schriftkanon, Kirche und Jesus*, 1970.

For the Catholic church of the Middle Ages there was no problem about the extent of the NT. The NT canon of the ancient church which had been taken over was the undisputed authority. Even when Thomas Aquinas and especially Nicholas of Lyra (d. 1340) discussed the question whether Heb has a rightful place in the canon, that occurred precisely in order to defend the canonical authority. And on the occasion of the union with the west Syrian Jacobites at the Council of Florence in 1442, the canon of Athanasius was once more established as undisputed.[1] Although on the basis of reports in Jerome, humanists practiced historical

[1] See EnchB, §47, p. 21 f.

criticism on Heb, a few of the Catholic letters, and Rev (Erasmus, Cajetan), no one dared seriously to dispute their canonicity. The Council of Trent[2] declared that the entire Bible of the Old and New Testament was canonical as it was comprised in the Vulgate, and enumerated all the individual books, among them Heb as the fourteenth letter of Paul, and James as a letter of the apostle James. It declared every part of the whole to be of equal value. At the same time, however, it demanded that there were to be received *sine scripto traditiones pari pietatis affectu ac reverentia* ("the unwritten traditions with equally pious affection, and reverence").

In spite of the objections which the Reformers raised against individual books, the Protestant churches also confirmed the canon of the NT in the same compass which it had received in the ancient church. For Luther (see esp. *Prefaces to the German NT,* 1522)[3] what is apostolic is canonical. The expression "apostolic," however, he understands in a twofold sense: at times apostolic is what the apostles wrote; at other times what has about it the apostolic quality, even though it was not written by the apostles. "The proper touchstone by which to find out what may be wrong with all the books is whether or not they treat of Christ. Whatever does not teach Christ is not apostolic, even if Peter or Paul teaches it. On the other hand whatever preaches Christ, that is apostolic, even if it is done by someone like Judas, Annas, Pilate or Herod" (Preface to James). From this point of view Luther placed at the end of the NT four of the seven writings which were disputed in antiquity and by the humanists (Heb, James, Jude, and Rev), and he did not number them in with the rest. In this way he made it clear that these four books which "in earlier times had received a different estimate" he would not count among "the really certain chief books of the NT," because only the later "clearly and purely present Christ to me." The intermingling of theological criticism and historical questions concerning the authorship resulted in Luther altering his attitude somewhat with the passage of time, and from the outset he was explicit in stressing that he did not want to force anyone to accept his own point of view. Just as the extent of the canon was in no way altered by this theological criticism, the fundamental question concerning the theological justification of the

---

[2] Session 4 on April 8, 1546: *Decretum de canonicis scripturis;* text in EnchB, §47, p. 25 f.

[3] WA, Deutsche Bibel VI and VII. Eng. tr. in *Luther's Works,* Vol. 35, ed. E. T. Bachmann, 1960, 357 ff. Cf. also W. G. Kümmel, "The Continuing Significance of Luther's Prefaces to the NT," *Concordia Theological Monthly* 37, 1966, 573 ff.

limits of the canon as established in the early church was posed, but for some time was not dealt with. There was just as little practical significance to the historically understood distinction between "canonical" and "apocryphal" or "protocanonical" and "deuterocanonical" writings of the NT among Lutheran theologians from J. Brenz to L. Hutter. They were expressly combated by J. Gerhard and then abandoned, while in the Reformed church such distinctions never surfaced at all. The placing of Heb, James, Jude, and Rev at the end of the printing of the Luther Bible survived from Reformation times—but not in any other of the Reformation translations!—and in the Reformed confessional writings there is a difference in the classification of Heb: *The Confessio Belgica* (1561) presents it as the fourteenth Pauline letter, while the *Confessio Gallicana* (1559) and the *Westminster Confession* (1647) place it among the Catholic letters. But nowhere were the contents of the NT altered.

Although the external history of the NT canon was at an end, from the time of the Enlightenment theology the justification of this ecclesiastical limitation of the canon and the binding force of the canon for Protestant theology became a problem. J. S. Semler[4] was the first to point out that the closing of the canon in the ancient church had taken place only "with regard to the clerics" and "that these dare not use any other books for public reading and for obligatory instruction." From this he concluded that investigation of the canon remains completely open for "all thoughtful readers." For Christian readers the fact that a writing belongs to the canon is not the standard for evaluation; "the only evidence which is wholly satisfactory to a sincere reader is the inner conviction by truths which are encountered in the Holy Scripture (but not in all parts, nor in individual books)." By means of this insight the strictly historical investigation of the origin of the individual writings of the NT, as well as of the collection as a whole, was recognized as a theological task which scholars then for a long time wrongly sought to carry out either by means of historical criticism of the canon through verification of the apostolic origin of its individual parts (J. D. Michaelis, F. C. Baur), or as historical defense of the canon by proof of the apostolic origins of these writings (Theodore Zahn). This approach, whether of historical dispute or of defense of the propriety of the limits of the canon as set by the ancient church, was wrong because the

---

[4] *Abhandlung von freier Untersuchung des Canons* [Treatise on the free investigation of the Canon], 1771/75; excerpts in WGK, NT, 63 f.

rightness of fixing the canonical authority of certain scriptures while excluding others cannot be historically verified, and thus the consequence of this false approach was either the demand to abandon the dogmatic concept of the canon completely[5] or the effort to prove the complete unity and equal value of the NT scriptures.[6] These mistaken conclusions show, however, that the *history* of the canon points up the historical circumstances and the motives for the rise and the fixing of the canon but cannot render a decision concerning the substantive necessity of forming the canon and the justification concerning its limits.

It is this insight, gained since the time of Semler, into the historical development and the centuries-long wavering over the limits of the canon which leads to a consideration of the reasonableness and value of this formation of the canon. The history of the canon shows that the two-part canon composed of the Gospels and the apostolic writings had formed spontaneously in the course of the second century within the life of the church. But the limitation of the canon of the gospels to four and, above all, of that part of the Apostolos which goes beyond the Pauline letters, was carried out by the church according to definite grounds consciously and with the exclusion of other points of view. Thus it is very true that in the decisions of the church concerning the ultimate limits of the canon, the spiritual experiences of the churches in using certain scriptures in connection with worship played a role,[7] but the oft-repeated assertion is not true that the church only determined which scriptures had already established themselves as canonical and therefore indeed were already canonical.[8] From the middle of the fourth century on, by its official decisions, the church rather determined that a part of the scriptures of the NT which had been recognized as canonical here and there from the end of the second century on, but whose canonical value had been repudiated elsewhere, were indeed to be regarded as canonical.[9] In the course of the second century the canon of the NT took its place alongside the OT, which was already more broadly recognized as Holy Scrip-

---

[5] G. Krüger, *Das Dogma vom NT,* 1896; W. Wrede, *Über Aufgabe und Methode der sog. Nt. Theologie,* 1897; see WGK, NT, 303 f.

[6] "I possessed a unified NT," A. Schlatter, *Rückblick auf seine Lebensarbeit,* 1952, 233 f (cf. on this WGK, NT, 194 f and n. 251).

[7] Joest, 29, cf. also 261; Ohlig, 83.

[8] Thus, e.g., Lagrange; Diem, 6/7, cf. also 162; Ohlig, 91, 208; K. Barth, *Church Dogmatics* I, 2, 1956, 599 ff; *contra,* Käsemann, "Canon," 95 f.

[9] That implies not that "the formation of the canon is a conscious creation of the growing church" (Frank, 204), but that the church consciously set only the ultimate limits of the canon.

ture, because from the very beginning, the basis of the church was the witness to and the preaching of the ultimate eschatological redemptive act of God in Jesus Christ. As a result of the dying out of the generation of the eyewitnesses and those who heard them, this witness and this preaching must assume written form in order to be protected against disappearance or alteration, and thus the canon of the NT as guarantor of the primitive witness to Christ must be limited to writings which come from the time of primitive Christianity even though these chronological limits might not be strictly set.[10] But from this there results a double consequence: (a) It was fundamentally necessary for the canon to remain closed; it could not be relativized by the equally justifiable juxtaposition of the apostolic rule of faith[11] or by the superimposition of the *sensus quam tenuit et tenet sancta mater ecclesia* ("the meaning which has been held and is held by the holy mother church").[12] (b) The possibility must be acknowledged, which up to this point has not yet entered the picture, that newly found primitive Christian writings had to be added to the canon as it was handed down, which requires us to consider that in the ultimate determination of the canon the chronological factor no longer played a decisive role: Hermas was excluded in the Muratorian Canon on chronological grounds, but I Clem, in spite of its having originated in the first century, was not included. The question of substantial agreement with the chief witnesses of the NT could in such a case not remain out of consideration, quite apart from the question how there can today be an ecumenical agreement concerning such an expansion of the NT.

The opposite question concerning the justification and enduring authority of the limits of the canon as established by the church in the fourth century is on the other hand not simply a theoretical problem. The view that the limits of the canon are unassailable because Holy Scripture "has God himself as its real originator and author," which guarantees[13] "the unconditional inerrancy of all its parts" is, in view of the indisputable contradictions between the two Testaments and within the NT itself, just as untenable as the "self-evident dogmatic dowry" that "the true NT is the

---

[10] The thesis that "basically it was not necessary to limit the canon to the witness of primitive Christianity" (so Käsemann, "Canon," 102; similarly Schweizer, EvTh, 345 n. 10) overlooks the necessity of the coherence of the canonical scriptures with the historical Christ event.

[11] Thus Cullmann.

[12] *Professio fidei Tridentina* (1564), EnchB, §73, p. 31. Modern Catholic formulations for the tradition *in addition to* scripture in Ebeling, 117, cf. also 308 n. 47.

[13] Bacht.

whole NT." [14] Rather, the decisions of the ancient church concerning the limits of the canon, which deal for the most part with the question of apostolicity,[15] are fundamentally in need of reexamination,[16] and the criterion of apostolicity has proved itself to be historically and dogmatically useless.[17] "It is in accordance with the course of the history of the canon, as has often been said, that the necessity of its form cannot be proved in the abstract. Rather the canon is essentially much more a factual reality than the realization of a theological concept." [18] Accordingly the ancient church's limitation of the canon, which was carried through in some parts of the church only hesitantly, and the acknowledgment of which in the ancient church was never a question of orthodoxy, cannot be regarded as unconditionally obligatory: the canon was "never . . . unambiguously closed" and "the absolutizing of the limits of the canon would be the absolutizing of an element of tradition." [19] It is with reason, therefore, that the Lutheran confessional writings have never set the limits of the canon.

But in spite of this, on two grounds there cannot be for us any serious possibility of improving on the decision of the ancient church concerning the extent of the canon by excluding individual scriptures. (1) The question favored because of the discussion within the ancient church and in the Reformation period, whether those writings whose canonicity was long disputed ought not rather to be excluded[20] has been justly abandoned, not only because the question of "apostolic" origin has been posed, unjustly and inappropriately, for *these* writings alone, but above all because also in writings whose canonical authority has never been seriously contested there are parts which stand in direct contradiction to the central message of the NT. Thus on historical grounds it is not possible, by the exclusion of a few scriptures, to fix the limits for a NT that uniformly and in all its parts is a suitable witness to

[14] Stock, 125; Küng, 143, 149, 153, cf. also 192, 198, 203; Ohlig, 183, 211. Further references in Kümmel, *Mitte*, 79 ff.

[15] Ohlig's analysis of apostolicity into four dimensions ("apostolicity is . . . a dynamic concept," 60) can indeed appeal to individual decisions in the ancient church in which canonicity was affirmed in spite of doubt about the apostolic authorship, but it does not correspond to the decisive argumentation of the fourth century.

[16] Käsemann, "Canon," 99 f; Marxsen, *Buch der Kirche*, 30.

[17] See Kümmel, "Notwendigkeit," 250 ff, cf. also 86 ff.

[18] Weber, 285.

[19] Schweizer, "Kanon?" 350; Weber, 283. Cf. also Käsemann, "Canon," 103 f; Marxsen, *Buch der Kirche*, 26.

[20] Cf. Kümmel, "Notwendigkeit," 252 f, cf. also 89 f.

the apostolic message concerning Christ. (2) What is still more important, however, is that such a new limitation of the NT canon would spring from a misunderstanding of the essence of the NT canon. Luther evaluated the books of the NT according to the degree to which they "show us Christ and teach us everything that it is necessary and blessed for us to know," but alongside this he also placed the warning "but only take care that you do not make a Moses out of Christ, nor a law or a book of doctrine from the gospel." [21] Thus Luther recognized that the books of the NT are canonical in the full sense only insofar as they make audible the witness to God's historical act of redemption in Christ in such a way that it can be promulgated by preaching. This means that what is really canonical can only be recognized by critical listening to the voices which resound in the canon of the NT, and that exegetical interpretation can explain the greater or lesser proximity of a scripture or a portion of scripture to the underlying message of Christ but cannot decide in some generally valid way on the normative character of this particular portion of scripture only. The indispensable question concerning the "canon within the canon" or the "inner limits of the canon" [22] leads to the insight that a new determination of the external limits of the canon would be nonsense, but it also frees us to raise the basic question which is posed again and again and must be answered, what it is in the NT that "preaches Christ and makes him real." [23] The factual delimitation and the actual openness of the limits of the canon correspond to the historicity of the revelation of God in Jesus Christ.

[21] Luther, German NT of 1522: "Welches die rechten und edelsten Bücher des NT sind"; Vorrede auf das NT, WA, Deutsche Bibel VI, 10, 8. Eng. tr. (see n. 3), 363, 360.
[22] "Canon within the canon does not signify exclusion, but criterion for exposition" (Käsemann, "Canon," 105 f; cf. Kümmel, *Mitte*). Where the question of "canon within the canon" is abandoned and the canon is regarded only as "the beginning of the history in which the Lord has asserted himself," the normative value of the canon is lost (*contra*, Schweizer, "Kanon?" 351, 355; similarly Marxsen, *Buch der Kirche*, 65).
[23] Luther, Preface to the Epistles of Saint James and Jude, WA, Deutsche Bibel VII, 384; Eng. tr. (see n. 3), 396.

PART THREE

The History and Criticism of the Text of the New Testament

Editions of the text: see §1.—Introductory works: E. Nestle–E. von Dobschütz, *Einführung in das Griech. NT*, ⁴1923; F. G. Kenyon, *Handbook to the Textual Criticism of the NT*, ³1926; *idem*, *The Text of the Greek Bible*, rev. A. W. Adams, ²1961; H. Lietzmann, "Einführung in die Textgeschichte der Plsbr.," HNT 8, ⁴1933 (=H. L., *Kleine Schriften* II, TU 68, 1958, 138 ff); K. and S. Lake, *The Text of the NT*, ⁹1933; C. S. C. Williams, *Alterations to the Text of the Synoptic Gospels and Acts*, 1951 (good introduction with examples); E. C. Colwell, *What Is the Best NT?* 1952 (good introduction); A. Souter–C. S. C. Williams, *The Text and Canon of the NT*, 1954; H. J. Vogels, *Handbuch der nt. Textkritik*, ²1955 (cf. *idem*, *Übungsbuch zur Einführung in die Textgeschichte des NT*, 1928); O. Stegmüller, "Überlieferungsgeschichte der Bibel," in *Geschichte der Textüberlieferung der antiken und mittelalterlichen Literatur* I, 1961, 165 ff; H. Greeven, "Textkritik II. NT," RGG VI, ³1962, 716 ff; J. H. Greenlee, *Introduction to NT Textual Criticism*, 1964 (good examples); B. M. Metzger, *The Text of the NT: Its Transmission, Corruption and Restoration*, 1964 (good introduction with good examples); J. N. Birdsall, "The NT Text," *The Cambridge History of the Bible* I, 1970, 308 ff.—Comprehensive works: F. H. A. Scrivener, *A Plain Introduction to the Criticism of the NT*, ⁴1894; C. R. Gregory, *Textkritik des NT* I–III, 1900/1909; Herm. von Soden, *Die Schriften des NT in ihrer ältesten erreichbaren Textgestalt* I, 1902/10; M.-J. Lagrange, *Introduction à l'étude du NT II: Critique textuelle 2: La critique rationelle*, 1935.—Surveys of criticism and bibliographies: F. G. Kenyon, *Recent Developments in the Textual Criticism of the Greek Bible*, 1933; J. Jeremias, "Der gegenwärtige Stand der nt. Textforschung," ThBl 17, 1938, 10 ff; W. G. Kümmel, "Textkritik und Textgeschichte des NT 1914–1937," ThR, NF 10, 1938, 206 ff, 292 ff; II, 1939, 84 ff; K. et S. Lake, "De Westcott et Hort au Père Lagrange et au-delà," RB 48, 1939, 497 ff; E. Massaux, "État actuel de la critique textuelle du NT," NRTh 85, 1953, 703 ff (good overview); B. M. Metzger, *Annotated Bibliography of the Textual Criticism of the NT 1914–1939*, StD 16, 1955; *idem*, "The Textual Criticism of the NT," ExpT 78, 1966/67, 324 ff, 372 ff; J. Duplacy, *Où en est la critique textuelle du NT?* 1959; *idem*, "Bulletin de critique textuelle du NT," I,II, RechSR 50, 1962, 242 ff, 564 ff; 51, 1963, 432 ff; 53, 1965, 257 ff; 54, 1966, 426 ff; *idem*, in collaboration with C. M. Martini, "Bulletin . . . III," Bb 49, 1968, 515 ff; 51, 1970, 84 ff; IV, Bb 52, 1971, 79 ff (these very careful surveys of research are henceforth to appear regularly); K.Th. Schäfer, "Der Ertrag der textkritischen Arbeit seit der Jahrhundertwende," BZ, NF 4, 1960, 1 ff; H. H. Oliver, "Present Trends in the Textual Criticism of the NT," *Journal of Bible and Religion* 30, 1962, 308 ff; R. Kieffer, *Au delà des recensions?* Conjectanea Biblica, NT Series 3, 1968, 5 ff (clear survey).—Survey of NT manuscripts: C. R. Gregory, *Die griech. Handschriften des NT*, 1908, K. Aland, *Kurzgefasste Liste der griech. Handschriften des NT I. Gesamtübersicht*, ANTF 1, 1963; *idem, Materialien zur nt. Handschriftenkunde* I, ANTF 3, 1969 (esp. 22 ff: "Fortsetzung zur 'Kurzgefassten Liste' "). Cf. also K. W. Clark, *A Descriptive Catalogue of Greek NT Manuscripts in America*, 1937; B. Botte, "Manuscrits grecs du NT," DBS V, 1957, 819 ff; K. Treu, *Die griech. Handschriften des NT in der UDSSR*, TU 91, 1966.—Illustrations of NT MSS are presented in: (introductory works) Nestle-von Dobschütz, Greenlee, Metzger, Birdsall; (reference works) LThK II, after Col. 352; BhHW, after Col. 320; (general presentation) W. Ekschmitt, *Das Gedächtnis der Völker*, 1964, 333 f, 405 f. See further: H. J. Vogels, *Codicum Novi Testamenti specimina*, 1929; W. H. P. Hatch, *The Principal Uncial Manuscripts of the NT*, 1939; *idem, Facsimiles and Descriptions of Minuscule Manuscripts of the NT*, 1951; O. Paret, *Die Überlieferung der Bibel*, [3]1963; H. Zimmermann, Nt. Methodenlehre, 1967, suppl.; V. Salmon, *Quatrième évangile* (see below), suppl.—Research on the entire field of textual criticism: B. H. Streeter, *The Four Gospels*, 1924, Part I; *NT Manuscripts Studies*, ed. M. M. Parvis and A. P. Wikgren, 1950; E. Fascher, *Textgeschichte als hermeneutisches Problem*, 1953; G. Zuntz, *The Text of the Epistles*, 1953 (on this see W. G. Kümmel, ThLZ 83, 1958, 765 ff); K. W. Clark, "Textual Criticism and Doctrine," *Studia Paulina, Festschr. J. de Zwaan*, 1953, 52 ff; *idem,* "The Effect of Recent Textual Criticism upon NT Studies," in *The Background of the NT and Its Echatology: Festschr. C. H. Dodd*, 1956, 27 ff; *idem,* "The Theological Relevance of Textual Variation in Current Criticism of the Greek NT," JBL 85, 1966, 1 ff; P. Sacchi, *Alle Origini del Nuovo Testamento*, 1956; M. Karnetzki, "Textgeschichte als Überlieferungsgeschichte," ZNW 47, 1956, 170 ff; B. M. Metzger, *Chapters in the History of NT Textual Criticism*, NTTS 4, 1963; G. D. Kilpatrick, "Atticism and the Greek NT," *Nt. Aufsätze, Festschr. J. Schmid*, 1963, 125 ff; *idem,* "The Greek Text of Today and the Textus Receptus," *The NT in Historical and Contemporary Perspective: Festschr. G. H. C. Macgregor*, 1965, 189 ff; K. Aland, "Glosse, Interpolation, Redaktion und Komposition in der Sicht der nt. Textkritik," *Apophoreta, Festschr. E. Haenchen*, Bh. ZNW 30, 1964, 7 ff (=K. A., *Studien zur Überlieferung des NT und seines Textes*, ANTF 2, 1967, 35 ff); J. Duplacy, "Histoire des manuscrits et histoire du texte du NT," NTS 12, 1965/66, 124 ff; V. Salmon, *Quatrième évangile. Histoire de la tradition textuelle de l'original Grec*, 1969.—On ancient books and writing: W. Gardthausen, *Griech. Paläographie*, [2]1911/31; W. Schubart, "Griech. Paläographie," *Handbuch der Altertumswissenschaft* I, 4, 1925; *idem,*

Das Buch bei den Griechen und Römern, [3]1961; R. Devreesse, *Intro- duction à l'étude des manuscrits grecs,* 1954; C. H. Roberts, "The Codex," *Proceedings of the British Academy* 40, 1954, 169 ff; *idem, Greek Literary Hands,* 1956; *idem,* "Books in the Graeco-Roman World and in the NT," *The Cambridge History of the Bible* I, 1970, 48 ff; H. Hunger, "Antikes und mittelalterliches Buch- und Schriftwesen," in *Geschichte der Textüberlieferung der antiken und mittelalterlichen Literatur* I, 1961, 27 ff; B. A. van Groningen, *Short Manual of Greek Palaeography,* [3]1963; A. Dain, *Les manuscrits,* [2]1964; T. C. Skeat, "Early Christian Book-Production: Papyri and Manuscripts," in *The Cambridge History of the Bible* II, 1969, 54 ff.—On methodology: P. Maas, *Text- kritik,* [3]1956; L. Bieler, *The Grammarian's Craft: An Introduction to Textual Criticism,* Classical Folia, [2]1958; T. Timpanaro, *La genesi del metodo del Lachmann,* 1963; B. H. van Groningen, "Traité d'histoire et de critique des textes Grecs," Verhandelingen der Koninklijke Neder- landse Akademie van Wetenschappen, Afd. Letterkunde, Nieuwe Reeks LXX, 2, 1963; H. Palmer, *The Logic of Gospel Criticism,* Chs. 5 and 6 ("Choosing the Readings"), 1968, 55 ff.

§38. THE MANUSCRIPT TRADITION OF THE NEW TESTAMENT

No NT writing has been preserved in the original, yet on the basis of the oldest papyrus manuscripts of the NT it can be con- jectured that the originals of the NT writings were written on both sides of papyrus sheets ("notebook form").[1] What we possess are more or less exact copies of the originals and copies of them, and quotations in early Christian writers. To reconstruct from these copies and quotations the original text of the NT is the task of textual criticism.

The text of current editions is based on (1) Greek manuscripts, (2) ancient versions, and (3) NT quotations in the church fathers.

1. The Greek Manuscripts

a. General Observations

The manuscripts are differentiated primarily according to the writing material used, secondarily according to the mode of writing employed.

The writing material is either papyrus or parchment. Papyrus, which is manufactured from the pith of the papyrus plant, was

---

[1] Cf. Roberts, *Codex.*

predominantly used for NT writings until the beginning of the fourth century, but only rarely thereafter. Until the fourth century the book form was used exclusively for NT manuscripts, though the practice was otherwise for the literary papyri! From the fourth to the thirteenth century the customary writing material was parchment (*membrana,* made from the skins of sheep, goats, calves, or other animals). Parchment was occasionally written on twice: one washed off or scraped off the old writing and superimposed a new writing. Such a manuscript, the original text of which today can once again be read either by chemical or photographic means, is called a palimpsest (*codex rescriptus*).

The manuscripts are grouped according to the style of writing into large-letter or capital-letter manuscripts (Majuscules or uncial manuscripts)[2] and small-letter manuscripts (minuscule manuscripts). In majuscule manuscripts the text is written throughout without separation of words, and in earlier times there was no separation according to meaning at the end of the lines. In addition to this "book script" there is also a more flowing majuscule cursive in which several letters are linked together. Presumably the NT originals were written in such majuscule cursive.[3] From the majuscule cursive there developed gradually the minuscule writing which resembles the script which is customarily used in writing Greek today. Majuscule manuscripts are found until the tenth century. From the ninth century on, they appear together with the minuscule manuscripts, but by the eleventh century the minuscules have achieved absolute dominance. In the oldest manuscripts accents, breathing marks, and punctuation are largely lacking. It is only from the eighth century on that they are regularly used. From the second century on, biblical manuscripts employ abbreviations for the *nomina sacra* (e.g., $\overline{\Theta\Sigma}$ for θεός, $\overline{IH}$, $\overline{IH\Sigma}$, or $\overline{I\Sigma}$ for Ἰησοῦς, etc.).[4]

[2] On the basis of the letter size: 1 *uncia*=1 inch.

[3] See the table of scripts in BhHW III, 1723 ff, and the examples of profane "majuscule-cursives" in Hunger, *Buch- und Schriftwesen,* 87 (first century); also E. G. Turner, *Greek Papyri,* 1968, table VII (second century) and the NT papyrus of the third century, $\mathcal{P}^{53}$ in *Quantulacumque, Festschr. K. Lake,* 1957, tables following pp. 152 and 156.

[4] Cf. A. H. R. E. Paap, *Nomina Sacra in the Greek Papyri of the First Five Centuries A.D.,* Papyrologica Lugduno-Batava 8, 1959 (on this see H. Gerstinger, Gn 32, 1960, 371 ff); J. O'Callaghan, " 'Nomina Sacra' in papyris graecis saeculi III neotestamentariis," AnBibl 46, 1970; S. Brown, "Concerning the Origin of the Nomina Sacra," *Studia Papyrologica* 9, 1970, 1 ff. The origin of the *nomina sacra* is unclear. Contrary to the thesis that Christian scribes first introduced $\overline{K\Sigma}$ in order to differentiate—by way of analogy with Jewish usage —the name of God from the rest of the text (Brown) is the fact that the

According to the most recent list[5] the number of known manuscripts includes 85 papyri, 268 majuscules, 2,792 minuscules, and 2,193 lectionaries. It is the Gospels which are most frequently copied. Then there follow by a considerable margin the Pauline letters; only a few manuscripts contain Rev.[6] The whole NT contained originally ℵ, A, B, C, ψ (?), and about 56 minuscules (part of them today with gaps).

The designations for the manuscripts are not uniform. Most are still known today according to the system which was introduced by J. J. Wettstein (d. 1754), in to which the majuscules were designated by Latin, Greek, and Hebrew capital letters (A, B, C, Ξ, ℵ, etc.), and the minuscules by arabic numbers (1, 2, 3, etc.). Gregory introduced a new method which should now be used exclusively. It is the basis for the list which is being continuously developed by the Institute for NT Text-critical Research of the Westfälische Wilhelms-Universität in Münster, Westphalia: the majuscule manuscripts for which the letters of the alphabet are no longer sufficient are to be designated by the consecutive arabic numbers with a 0 placed in front (01, 02, etc.). For the most common of the 45 majuscules it is customary now to employ the designation by letter followed by the arabic numeral in parentheses preceded by a 0: ℵ (01), A (02), B (03), etc. The designation with letters alone is still used, however. The minuscules have the numbers 1, 2, etc. The papyri are designated by a bold print 𝔓 with an arabic number as an exponent: $𝔓^1$, $𝔓^2$, etc. The lectionaries (see §38.1.e) are indicated by a lowercase 1 with an exponent in arabic numbers: 1^1, 1^2, etc. Other sigla were proposed by Hermann von Soden and used in his work which is mentioned on page 23. He abandoned the distinction between majuscule and minuscule manuscripts and simply numbered the manuscripts consecutively with

---

contractions for Ἰησοῦς appear with the greatest frequency (O'Callaghan). As early as the beginning of the third century the contraction σϸος=σταυρός is attested; see K. Aland, "Bemerkungen zum Alter und zur Entstehung des Christogrammes anhand von Beobachtungen bei $𝒫^{66}$ und $𝒫^{75}$"(=K. A., Studien . . . ,ANTF 2, 1967, 173 ff).

[5] Cf. the treatment going beyond K. Aland, "Materialen . . ." I, ANTF 3, 1969, 22 ff, in Bericht der Stiftung zur Förderung der nt. Textforschung für die Jahre 1970 and 1971, Münster 1972, 10 ff (information kindly supplied by K. Aland).

[6] Five papyri, 10 majuscules, 235 minuscules (see J. Schmid, Studien zur Geschichte des griech. Apk-textes II, MThSt, Suppl. Vol. 1, 1955, 13 ff, with supplements in ZNW 52, 1961, 82 ff; 59, 1968, 250 ff); final figures kindly supplied by K. Aland.

arabic numbers. The system is very complicated, however, and has not been widely used.[7]

The sequence of the various parts of the NT is the same in almost all the Greek manuscripts: Gospels, Acts, Catholic letters, Pauline letters, Rev. A few of the newer editions of the NT have followed this order,[8] but other sequences are represented as well, e.g., in ℵ and A (Gospels, Pauline letters, Acts, Catholic letters, Rev)[9] or the Muratorian Canon (Gospels, Acts, Pauline letters, Catholic letters, Rev).[10]

Frequently the manuscripts contain other kinds of information for orienting the reader and for the use of the manuscript, at the beginning either of an entire volume or of individual books, in the margin or in the text or at the end of individual books, or at the end of the volume as a whole. Along with the Gospels there often appear the Letter of Eusebius to Carpianus and the Canons of Eusebius, which are synoptic tables of similar sections.[11] The individual books are introduced by prefaces (ὑποθέσεις) with information concerning the contents of the writing, the author, the number of chapters, etc. There follows the *titulus,* which is the superscription of the book. In the margin are found superscriptions for the chapters, information concerning the beginning and the end of pericopes, etc. In addition there sometimes appear scholia (explanatory notes) in the form of marginal comments. In part, there are complete commentaries or commentaries on selected portions (catenae) in the margin. Appendixes contain information concerning the names of the copyist or the patron of the manuscript, the time and place of writing, etc. Frequently the manuscripts also exhibit corrections in the hand of the scribe or of later editors. In our editions of the text these are distinguished from the original text by an * (ℵ*, B*) or by exponents (ℵ^2, B^2, or ℵ^a, B^a, etc.). An example of the introduction of such a correction into the text is found in the words ἐν Ἐφέσῳ (Eph 1:1) by the correctors of ℵ* and B*.

---

[7] Concordances of the different numerations are offered by B. Kraft, *Die Zeichen für die wichstigsten Handschriften des griech. NT,* [3]1955, and by K. Aland, *Kurzgefasste Liste,* 321 ff.

[8] E.g., von Soden, Tischendorf, Westcott-Hort.

[9] Thus also B. Weiss.

[10] Thus also the Vulgate, Erasmus, and the present manual editions of the Greek NT.

[11] In Nestle's *NT Graece* both are printed in the Prolegomena; for convenience the appropriate numbers are printed on the inner border of the Nestle edition. On the purpose of these tables see H. K. McArthur, "The Eusebian Sections and Canons," CBQ 27, 1965, 250 ff.

The division of the text into chapters, which is in common use today, first appeared soon after 1200. The tradition goes back to Stephen Langton, Archbishop of Canterbury (d. 1228). The division into verses originated with the Parisian bookseller Robert Stephanus (Estienne) and appears for the first time in his edition of the NT from the year 1551.

b. The Papyrus Majuscules

On papyri in general: W. Schubart, *Einführung in die Papyruskunde*, 1918; K. Preisendanz, "Papyruskunde," *Handbuch der Bibliothekswissenschaft* I, 1952, 50 ff; K. Treu, RGG³ V, 1961, 91 ff (lit.); E. G. Turner, *Greek Papyri: An Introduction*, 1968.—On NT papyri in general: G. Maldfeld, "Die griech. Handschriftenbruchstücke des NT auf Papyrus," ZNW 42, 1949, 228 ff; B. Botte, "Papyrus Bibliques," DBS VI, 1960, 1109 ff; K. Aland, "The Significance of the Papyri for Progress in NT Research," BMS, 325 ff; *idem*, "Das NT auf Papyrus," in K. A., *Studien*, ANTF 2, 1967, 91 ff; *idem*, "Die Konsequenzen der neueren Handschriftenfunde für die nt. Textkritik," *ibid.*, 181 ff.

The NT manuscripts on papyrus are of special importance, since they are older than the preserved parchment manuscripts, and only to this extent can their special treatment and designation be justified.

𝔓⁵² is the oldest preserved fragment of the NT (early second century).[12] A fragment the size of the palm of the hand, it contains in fragmentary form Jn 18:31-33, 37 f in agreement with the Nestle text.

𝔓⁶⁴ and 𝔓⁶⁷ have proved to be fragments of a single manuscript of Mt from about the year 200, the text of which does not differ essentially from the Nestle text. If the conjecture (which is not yet finally ascertained) is sustained that 𝔓⁴ with a text from Lk also belonged to the same manuscript—this text does not diverge significantly from the Nestle text either—then we would be dealing here with a manuscript which contained at least Mt and Lk.[13]

---

[12] Papyrus Rylands Greek 457 (Manchester). Ed. C. H. Roberts, *An Unpublished Fragment of the Fourth Gospel in the John Rylands Library*, 1935. Cf. J. Jeremias, ThBl 15, 1936, 97 ff.

[13] On the homogeneity of these three fragments see K. Aland, NTS 9, 1962/63, 309; 12, 1965/66, 193 f. 𝒫⁴ = Paris, Bibliothèque Nationale, Suppl. Gr. 1120, published in RB 1, 1892, 113 ff; 𝒫⁶⁴ = Oxford, Magdalen College, Pap. Magd. Greek 18, published HTR 48, 1953, 233 ff; 𝒫⁶⁷ = Barcelona, Fundación San Lucas Evangelista, P. Barc. 1, published by R. Roca-Puig, *Un Papiro griego del evangelio de San Mateo*, ²1962.

From the second and third centuries, in addition to important fragments, there have been preserved six extensive manuscripts which enable us to have a view of the form of the Greek text of the NT a century before the great majuscules. Three of these ($\mathfrak{P}^{45-47}$) are found for the most part in the collection of the late Englishman A. Chester Beatty in Dublin, while three are in the possession of the Geneva collector M. Bodmer.

$\mathfrak{P}^{45}$, $\mathfrak{P}^{46}$, $\mathfrak{P}^{47}$ (Chester Beatty Papyri) contain 126 leaves, in part severely damaged, from three papyrus books: $\mathfrak{P}^{45}$ (one leaf in Vienna) contains fragments of all four Gospels and Acts. $\mathfrak{P}^{46}$ (a part of the manuscript belongs to the University of Michigan in Ann Arbor) offers the Pauline letters in the sequence Rom (from 5:7 on), Heb, I and II Cor, Eph, Gal, Phil, Col, I Thess. $\mathfrak{P}^{47}$ presents Rev 6–17. $\mathfrak{P}^{45}$ is dated in the third century, and $\mathfrak{P}^{46}$ ca. 200. These manuscripts offer the oldest consecutive text of the four Gospels and the *Corpus Paulinum*. While $\mathfrak{P}^{45}$ evidences a different text form for each of the Gospels, for Acts it is the oldest witness of the "Short," "Egyptian" text. $\mathfrak{P}^{46}$ is a valuable witness for the "unrevised" text of Paul from the second century and thus of the old constituent elements in all later textual forms. $\mathfrak{P}^{47}$ (second half of the third century) offers certainly the oldest but not the best text of Rev.[14]

$\mathfrak{P}^{66}$ (Papyrus Bodmer II) encompasses the whole of Jn, although Chs. 1–14 contain a few gaps, and 15–21 are found only in fragments. This codex, which was probably written before 200,[15] offers a text which (similarly to $\mathfrak{P}^{45}$ in Acts) belongs to an early stage of the "Egyptian" text. The numerous corrections of this carelessly written text were obviously for the most part taken over from a manuscript which stood closer to the "Egyptian" text than the original prototype.[16]

---

[14] Edition: F. G. Kenyon, *The Chester Beatty Papyri*, II, III, and III Suppl., 1933–37 (text and facsimile volumes). On the entire find: H. Lietzmann, *Die Antike* 11, 1935, 139 ff (=H. L., *Kleine Schriften* II, TU 68, 1958, 160 ff). On $\mathcal{P}^{45}$: M.-J. Lagrange, RB 43, 1934, 1 ff, 161 ff; C. C. Tarelli, JTS 40, 1939, 46 ff; 41, 1940, 253 ff; H. W. Huston, JBL 74, 1955, 262 ff. On $\mathcal{P}^{46}$: H. Lietzmann, SAB 1934, 25 (=H. L. *Kleine Schriften* I, TU 68, 1958, 170 ff); K. W. Clark, *Studia Paulina*, Festschr. *J. de Zwaan*, 1953, 56 ff; H. Seesemann, ThBl 16, 1937, 92 ff. On $\mathcal{P}^{47}$: J. Schmid, *Studien zur Geschichte des griech. Apk-textes*, MThSt, 1st Suppl. Vol., 1955, 109 ff.

[15] The dating is not wholly certain: Aland, ANTF 2, 106—ca. 200; H. Hunger, *Geschichte der Textüberlieferung* I, 1961, 82 f (cf. also J. B. Bauer, BZ, NF 12, 1968, 121 f)—not later than the middle of the second century; C. H. Roberts (in Aland)—probably later than 200.

[16] Editions: V. Martin, *Papyrus Bodmer II. Évangile de Jean. chap I–XIV*, 1956; *idem* and J. W. B. Barns, *Papyrus Bodmer II. Supplément. Évangile de*

$\mathfrak{P}^{72}$ (Papyrus Bodmer VII and VIII) contains as one of the components of a mixed manuscript the text of Jude and the two letters of Peter. It was probably written in the third/fourth century by a scribe whose mother tongue was Coptic. The manuscript offers the oldest preserved text of these three letters. In I Pet it is in agreement with the "Egyptian" witnesses, but in Jude it is in part similar to an old text which has only scattered attestation. The text of $\mathfrak{P}^{72}$ confirms by and large the value of the text of the three letters which is witnessed in B. In a few places, however, it contains a better text than B.[17]

$\mathfrak{P}^{75}$ (Papyrus Bodmer XIV–XV) includes in one quire the Gospels of Lk and Jn. It contains Lk 4:34–18:18; 22:4–24:53, and Jn 1:1–13:10 with some small omissions and a remnant of other sheets. Jn begins on the same page where Lk ends, so the manuscript presumably presupposes a canon of four Gospels and was written at the end of the third century. The text agrees extensively with B, so that the two manuscripts must depend on a common prototype which dates back to the end of the second century. Thus it is proved that the text of B does not originate from a recension of the third or fourth century, but rather was already in existence in the second century. In addition to the contacts with B there is kinship with $\mathfrak{P}^{45}$ and $\mathfrak{P}^{66}$ and with the Sahidic version (Jn 10:7

Jean. chap. XVI–XXI, Nouvelle édition augmentée et corrigée avec réproduction photographique complète du manuscrit (chap. I–XXI), 1962. Lists of variants: H. Zimmermann, BZ, NF 2, 1958, 214 ff; M.-E. Boismard, RB 70, 1962, 120 ff; K. Aland, NTS 10, 1963/64, 62 ff. Research: A. F. J. Klijn, "Papyrus Bodmer II (John I–XIV) and the Text of Egypt," NTS 3, 1956/57, 327 ff (very uncertain reconstruction!); E. Massaux, "Le Papyrus Bodmer II (P^{66}) et la critique néotestamentaire," *Sacra Pagina* I, Bibliotheca Ephemeridum Theologicarum Lovanensium 12/3, 1959, 194 ff; J. N. Birdsall, *The Bodmer Papyrus of the Gospel of John,* The Tyndale NT Lecture 1958, 1960; E. C. Colwell, "Scribal Habits in Early Papyri: A Study in the Corruption of the Text," BMS, 1965, 370 ff, esp. 386 f; G. D. Fee, "The Corrections of Papyrus Bodmer II and Early Textual Transmission," NovTest 7, 1964/65, 247 ff; *idem,* "Corrections of Papyrus Bodmer II and the Nestle Greek Testament," JBL 84, 1965, 66 ff; *idem, Papyrus Bodmer II (P^{66}): Its Textual Relationships and Scribal Characteristics,* StD 34, 1968 (on this see G. D. Kilpatrick, ThLZ 96, 1971, 747 ff); E. F. Rhodes, "The Corrections of Papyrus Bodmer II," NTS 14, 1967/68, 271 ff; A. F. J. Klijn, *A Survey of Recent Researches into the Western Text of the Gospels and Acts,* Suppl. NovTest 21, 1969, 38 ff.

[17] Edition: M. Testuz, *Papyrus Bodmer VII–IX,* 1959. Good list of variants in F. W. Beare, JBL 80, 1961, 253 ff (for I Pet), and E. Massaux, *Le texte de l'épître de Jude du Papyrus Bodmer VII,* AnLov III, 24, 1961. Studies: E. Massaux, *Le texte de la Iᵃ Petri du Papyrus Bodmer VIII (P^{72}),* EThL 39, 1963, 616 ff; J. N. Birdsall, "The Text of Jude in P^{72}," JTS, NS 14, 1963, 394 ff; S. Kubo, P^{72} *and the "Codex Vaticanus,"* StD 27, 1965 (on this see E. J. Epp, JBL 85, 1966, 512 ff; C. M. Martini, Bb 51, 1970, 94 ff).

ὁ ποιμήν instead of ἡ θύρα), therefore 𝔓⁷⁵ belongs without doubt to the prior form of the "Egyptian" text.[18]

Three papyrus fragments from the third or fourth century are of especial importance on account of their text form:

𝔓³⁷ a codex leaf with Mt 26:19-52 in majuscule cursive (University of Michigan, Ann Arbor; third/fourth century). By reason of its variation between B and D it proves the early existence of this mixed text in Egypt.[19]

𝔓⁴⁸ a codex leaf with Acts 23:11 ff, now found in Florence (Bibliotheca Mediceo-Laurentiana; end of the third century) attests the broad "Western" text of Acts in the third century in Egypt.[20]

𝔓⁸¹ a codex leaf with I Pet 2:20–3:1, 4-12, now in Barcelona (Seminario de Papirología; fourth century) evidences the most contacts with 𝔓⁷², B, and the Sahidic version.[21]

A later papyrus manuscript is important because of the extent of its contents: 𝔓⁷⁴ (Papyrus Bodmer XVII) consists of fragments of a papyrus book from the seventh century which contains Acts and the Catholic letters. Only about half of the text of Acts is well preserved, the beginning and end of Acts are severely damaged, and from the Catholic letters only small fragments have survived. In Acts, the text shows a strong relationship with ℵ and to a lesser degree with A, but there is no contact with the "Western" text and the special readings of B and the Koine.[22]

[18] Edition: V. Martin and R. Kasser, *Papyrus Bodmer XIV–XV*, 1961. List of variants: K. Aland, "Neue nt. Papyri II," NTS 11, 1964/65, 5 ff. Research: K. W. Clark, "The Text of the Gospel of John in Third-Century Egypt," NovTest 5, 1962, 17 ff (shows that P^{75} offers the best text of Jn in the third century); J. A. Fitzmyer, "Papyrus Bodmer XIV: Some Features of our Oldest Text of Luke," CBQ 24, 1962, 170 ff; C. L. Porter, "Papyrus Bodmer XV and the Text of Codex Vaticanus," JBL 81, 1962, 363 ff; *idem*, "An Analysis of the Textual Variation Between P^{75} and Codex Vaticanus in the Text of John," *Studies in the History and Text of the NT: Festschr. K. W. Clark*, StD 29, 1967, 71 ff; E. Haenchen, *Apg*=Meyer III,[14] 667 ff; C. M. Martini, *Il problema della recensionalità del codice B alla luce del papiro Bodmer XIV*, AnBibl 26, 1966 (fundamental; cf. on this J. N. Birdsall, JTS 18, 1967, 462 ff [good review]; J. Schmid, BZ 11, 1967, 133 ff; K. Treu, ThLZ 92, 1967, 895 ff [good review]; J. Duplacy, Bb 51, 1970, 87 ff); K. Aland, "Die Bedeutung des P^{75} für den Text des NT," *Studien zur Überlieferung des NT und seines Textes*, ANTF 2, 1967, 155 ff.

[19] Edition: A. H. Sanders, HTR 19, 1926, 215 ff; on this see M.-J. Lagrange, *Critique textuelle* II, 1935, 157 f.

[20] Edition: *Papiri Greci e Latini* 10, 1932, 112 ff; on this see M.-J. Lagrange (see n. 19), 406 ff.

[21] Edition: S. Daris, "Un nuovo frammento della Prima Lettera di Pietro (I Peter 2,20–3,12)," *Papyrologica Castroctaviana* 2, 1967.

[22] Edition: R. Kasser, *Papyrus Bodmer XVII*, 1961; on this see Ph.-H. Menoud, RThPh 12, 1962, 112 ff.

c. The Parchment Majuscules

From the third century only a few fragments of parchment manuscripts have been preserved, of which the most important are 0189 (a leaf with the "shorter" text of Acts 5:3-21 from the second or third century)[23] and 0212 (a Greek witness for the Diatessaron of Tatian; third century, see §38.2.a.1). From the fourth century on, we have in addition to numerous fragments the great majuscule manuscripts, the most important of which are:

B Vaticanus (03 Gregory) which since the end of the fifteenth century has been in the Vatican Library. It contains the OT with two gaps, and the greater part of the NT. From the NT is lacking Heb (from 9:14b on) I and II Tim, Titus, Phlm, Rev. B comes from the early fourth century and is thus the oldest of the great biblical manuscripts. Its home is likely Egypt. Since its ink had faded out, sometime before or around 1000 the entire text was traced over with new ink furnished with accents and breathing marks. At the same time the restorer undertook a kind of revision, in that words and letters which seemed to him to be wrong he left untouched. Already before his time two correctors had worked on the text.[24]

א Sinaiticus (01 Gregory, S in Lietzmann, HNT, among others) was rediscovered by C. Tischendorf in 1859 in the monastery of St. Catherine on Mount Sinai after a part of it had been found in 1844. Tischendorf presented the manuscript to Tsar Alexander II. Whether this transfer of the manuscript to Russia took place in a really irreproachable manner is, according to recent research, very doubtful.[25] The manuscript remained in Leningrad until 1933 and was then sold by the Soviet government to the British Museum in London for £100,000. The OT is nearly complete, and

[23] Edition: A. H. Salonius, ZNW 26, 1927, 116 f; on the date, K. Aland, "Das NT auf Papyrus," *Studien zur Überlieferung des NT und seines Textes,* ANTF 2, 1967, 92.

[24] Photographic reproduction: *Bibliorum SS. Graecorum Codex Vaticanus 1209 (Cod B) denuo photypice expressus . . . : Pars altera, Testamentum Novum,* 1904. On the history of the codex see C. M. Martini (see n. 18), 1 ff; on its origin in Alexandria, see J. N. Birdsall in *The Cambridge History of the Bible* I, 1970, 360. W. H. P. Hatch, JBL 72, 1953, xviii f, proposes that it comes from Upper Egypt.

[25] Cf. on this *The Mount Sinai Manuscript of the Bible,* 1934; W. Hotzelt, "Die kirchenrechtliche Stellung von Bistum und Kloster Sinai zur Zeit der Entdeckung der Sinaibibel," ThLZ 74, 1949, 457 ff; I. Ševčenko, "New Documents on Constantine Tischendorf and the Codex Sinaiticus," *Scriptorium* 18, 1964, 55 ff.

the NT is preserved complete. At its end stands Barnabas and part of the Shepherd of Hermas.[26] The manuscript was copied not later than the middle of the fourth century in Egypt, or more probably in Palestine (Caesarea).[27] Tischendorf differentiated—probably too sharply—six or seven different hands which had later effected corrections in the codex. According to the research in the British Museum[28] the document is probably the work of three scribes and several later correctors. Although as a whole ℵ is to be associated with the "Egyptian" text form, occasionally it also has close associations with the "Western" form of the text.[29]

A Alexandrinus (02 Gregory) was once a complete Bible. From the fourteenth century on, it was in the library of the Patriarch of Alexandria. In 1627 it was presented as a gift to the King of England, and since 1751 it has been in the British Museum in London. The manuscript is newer than the two previously mentioned and was probably written in the fifth century in Egypt.[30] It has larger gaps in Mt, Jn, and II Cor, and also contains 1 and 2 Clem (up to 12:5). The character of its text is not unified: in the Gospels it uses the Koine text; elsewhere it belongs to the "Egyptian" text.[31]

C Codex Ephraemi Syri Rescriptus (04 Gregory) is in the Bibliothèque Nationale in Paris and is the most important of the palimpsests, written in the fifth century, erased in the twelfth century, and written over with thirty-eight treatises of the Syrian church father Ephraem (d. 373). Little of the OT has been preserved, but five eighths of the NT is in the manuscript. The wearisome task of deciphering it was first completed by Tischendorf.[32]

[26] Photographic reproduction of the NT part: K. Lake, *Codex Sinaiticus Petropolitanus, The NT, the Epistle of Barnabas and the Shepherd of Hermas,* 1911.

[27] See M.-J. Lagrange, "L'origine médiate et immédiate du Ms. Sinaïtique," RB 35, 1926, 91 ff.

[28] H. J. M. Milne–T. C. Skeat, *Scribes and Correctors of the Codex Sinaiticus,* 1938.

[29] B. M. Metzger, *The Text of the NT,* 46; G. D. Fee has demonstrated these links for Jn 1:1–8:38 in "Codex Sinaiticus in the Gospel of John: A Contribution to Methodology in Establishing Textual Relationships," NTS 15, 1968/69, 23 ff.

[30] T. C. Skeat, "The Provenance of the Codex Alexandrinus," JTS, NS 6, 1955, 233 ff, considers Constantinople more probable.

[31] Photographic reproduction: F. G. Kenyon, *The Codex Alexandrinus in Reduced Facsimile, NT and Clementine Epistles,* 1909.

[32] C. Tischendorf, *Codex Ephraemi Syri rescriptus sive fragmenta Novi Testamenti,* 1843; R. W. Lyon, "A Reexamination of Codex Ephraemi Rescriptus," NTS 5, 1958/59, 260 f.

D designates two remarkable manuscripts from the fifth/sixth century[33] which were once in the possession of Calvin's friend and pupil Theodore Beza. Both manuscripts are bilingual (Greek text and Latin translation on facing pages); accordingly the manuscripts come from a region of the church where Greek was still spoken (South Gaul and South Italy have been proposed, but also Egypt and Syria). The text is written in lines of unequal length according to the meaning. The first manuscript contains the Gospels (in the sequence Mt, Jn, Lk, Mk) and Acts (D[ea]). The second contains the letters of Paul (D[p]). D[ea] was originally in Lyons in the monastery of Irenaeus, and is called Codex Bezae Cantabrigiensis (05 Gregory) because in 1581 it was given by Beza to the University of Cambridge, where it is now in the University Library. D[p] is the Codex Claromontanus (06 Gregory), named after the monastery of Clermont, near Beauvais, where it was originally; now it is in the Bibliothèque Nationale in Paris. D[ea] offers for Lk and Acts a text differing sharply from the older manuscripts, which is related to the Old Latin and Syriac texts and has been designated as the "Western" text (see below, §40). The Latin text of D[p] agrees with that of Lucifer of Calaris (fourth century).[34]

Of the remaining majuscules there remain to be mentioned:

G Codex Boernerianus (012 Gregory), a Greek-Latin bilingual (interlinear translation) manuscript of the ninth century from St. Gall, now in Dresden. It represents the "Western" text of the Pauline letters (without Heb).[35]

W Freer Gospels (032 Gregory), a gospel manuscript of the fifth century from Egypt, in possession of the Freer Collection in Washington. The character of the text varies considerably and shows in part relationship with the "Western" text and elsewhere with the "Caesarean" text (see below, §40). The sequence of

[33] Other datings in Epp, *Theological Tendency* (see n. 34), 7.

[34] Facsimile of D[ea]: *Codex Bezae Cantabrigiensis quattuor Evangelia et Actus Apostolorum complectens Graece et Latine. Phototypice representatus*, 1899. Cf. J. D. Yoder, *Concordance to the Distinctive Text of Codex Bezae*, NTTS 2, 1961. On the text type of D[ea]: E. J. Epp, "Coptic Manuscript G 67 and the Rôle of Codex Bezae as a Western Witness in Acts," JBL 85, 1966, 197 ff; *idem, The Theological Tendency of Codex Bezae Cantabrigiensis in Acts*, SNTSMS 3, 1966 (full bibl.); J. N. Birdsall (see n. 24), 353 f. D[p] only in the edition of C. Tischendorf, *Codex Claromontanus sive Epistulae Pauli omnes Graece et Latine e codice Parisiensi celeberrimo nomine Claromontani . . .* , 1852; cf. H. J. Frede, *Altlat. Paulus-Handschriften*, Vetus Latina, Aus der Geschichte der lat. Bibel 4, 1964, 15 ff.

[35] Photographic reproduction: A. Reichardt, *Der Codex Boernerianus der Briefe des Apostels Paulus*, 1909. Cf. H. J. Frede (see n. 34), 50 ff.

the Gospels (Mt, Jn Lk, Mk) corresponds to D^{ea}. Important is an insertion after Mk 16:14 which was also known to Jerome (Freer Logion, see §6.5).[36]

Ⓚ Koridethi Gospels (038 Gregory), earlier belonging to the monastery of Koridethi in the Caucasus, is now in Tiflis. The manuscript, which was probably written in the ninth century at Sinai in late majuscules, shows in Mk relationship to minuscule group 1, etc. (the Lake group), 13, etc. (the Ferrar group), and the minuscules 28, 565, 700, and is thus a major witness for the so-called "Caesarean" text (see below, §40).[37]

d. The Minuscules

Since the minuscules are the most recent textual witnesses (the oldest dated manuscript is from 835), only a few of them are important for the recovery of the original text: namely, those which may be traced back to a valuable old prototype. Most of these manuscripts are important only as witnesses for the medieval history of the NT text, but little is known for certain on this subject, in spite of the useful preliminary work of Hermann von Soden and numerous researches, especially by Americans.[38] Two groups of minuscules have been recognized as important witnesses for the so-called "Caesarean" text; the first of these is the Ferrar group,[39] discovered by W. H. Ferrar and attested in minuscule 13, and the second is the Lake group,[40] which was demonstrated by K. Lake on the basis of minuscule 1. The "queen of the minuscules," 33 (ninth century is a witness of the "Egyptian" text. Minuscule 1739, from the tenth century, is in Rom a witness for the text of Origen, but in the rest of the Pauline letters it is the witness for

[36] Edition: H. A. Sanders, *The NT Manuscripts in the Freer Collections* I: *The Washington Manuscript of the Freer Gospels*, 1912.

[37] Edition: G. Beermann and C. R. Gregory, *Die Koridethi-Evangelien*, 1913. Cf. B. Botte, DBS V, 1957, 192 ff (bibl.).

[38] On the remaining tasks see K. and S. Lake, "The Byzantine Text of the Gospels," *Mémorial Lagrange*, 1940, 251 ff, and E. J. Epp, "The Claremont Profile-Method for Grouping NT Minuscule Manuscripts," *Studies in the History and Text of the NT: Festschr. K. W. Clark*, StD 29, 1967, 27 ff.

[39] In Nestle: φ. K. and S. Lake, *Family 13 [The Ferrar Group]. The Text According to St. Mark*, StD, 11, 1941; J. Geerlings, *Family 13—The Ferrar Group. The Text According to Matthew, . . . to Luke, . . . to John*, StD 19-21, 1961/62.

[40] In Nestle: λ. K. Lake, *Codex 1 of the Gospels and its Allies*, TSt 7,2, 1902.

a still older Egyptian text. And 2053, which is a manuscript of Rev written in the thirteenth century, offers together with majuscules A and C the best text for Rev. These and some other minuscule manuscripts should therefore not be neglected in the reconstruction of the original text of the NT.

e. The Lectionaries

The practice of reading from the Scriptures in worship led to the compilation of church readers (lectionaries) which offered specific sections of the NT appropriate to the order of the church year. Lectionaries with pericopes from the Gospels were called in the Greek church *Evangelion* (in Latin *Evangeliarium* or *Evangelistarium*); lectionaries the contents of which were selected from Acts, the Catholic letters, and Paul were called Apostolos or Praxapostolos. The lectionaries contain the greater part of the NT, even if it is divided in small sections. Up to the present we know 2,193 lectionaries. Since Gregory they have been designated by lowercase l with an Arabic exponent (l^1, l^2, etc.). The oldest fragments of these biblical lectionaries go back to the fifth century. From the text-critical standpoint the lectionaries are much less studied than the minuscules, but in Chicago a carefully planned project has been begun which has shown that the individual pericopes have their own text history and to some degree show the influence of the old text forms.[41] What is not yet clear, however, is the degree to which this special tradition of the text can aid in the achievement of the primitive text.[42]

2. The Versions

B. M. Metzger, "The Evidence of the Versions for the Text of the NT," in *NT Manuscript Studies*, 1950, 25 ff; *idem*, "A Survey of Recent Research on the Ancient Versions of the NT," NTS 2, 1955/56, 1 ff; *idem*, "Recent Contributions to the Study of the Ancient Versions of the NT," BMS, 347 ff; A. F. J. Klijn, *Bible Translator* 8, 1957, 127 ff,

---

[41] See the account in A. Wikgren, "Chicago Studies in the Greek Lectionary of the NT," *Biblical and Patristic Studies: Festschr. R. P. Casey*, 1963, 96 ff.

[42] Cf. on the lectionaries: H. Greeven, "Die Textgestalt der Evangelienlektionare," ThLZ 76, 1951, 513 ff; H. Vogels, *Handbuch der Textkritik*, 69 ff; J. Duplacy, "Les lectionnaires et l'édition du NT Grec," *Mélanges Bibliques, Festschr. B. Rigaux*, 1970, 509 ff.

(warns against inferences from versions concerning an unattested Greek text); A. Vööbus, "Early Versions of the NT," *Papers of the Estonian Theological Society in Exile* 6, 1954 (see on this W. Nagel, ThLZ 84, 1959, 750 ff); B. Botte, L. Leloir, C. Van Puyvelde, "Orientalis de la Bible (versions)," DBS VI, 1960, 807 ff. See also RGG I, ³1957, 1196 ff; LThK II, 1958, 380 ff.

As Christianity spread among various ethnic groups in regions which were not dominated by the universal language of Greek, the necessity arose of translating the NT into the languages of the several lands. Thus corresponding to the course of the spread of Christianity there arose first the Syriac, the Latin, and the Coptic versions. Among the translations of the NT they have the greatest significance for the history of the text because they go back to Greek prototypes which are older than the more inclusive Greek manuscripts which have come down to us. The oldest more nearly complete Greek manuscripts of the NT which we have, $\mathfrak{P}^{45}$ and $\mathfrak{P}^{46}$, come from the beginning of the third century. The oldest manuscript of almost the entire NT, the Vaticanus (B), comes from the fourth century. The oldest Syriac and Latin translations, however, arose as early as the second century, and the Coptic ones reach back in part to the beginning of the third century. Even the more recent versions of the NT can be of great value for textual criticism if they indirectly reproduce a Greek text which is otherwise not preserved or only weakly attested, though that is rarely the case. For the most part these versions have at their base the later Greek texts which we know, or they are derivative versions based on the Syriac, Latin, or Coptic versions. They need therefore be mentioned here only briefly. But even the older translations are only to be used with caution as witnesses for the Greek text: no translation exactly corresponds to the original even if it is literal. Nuances and special features of the Greek language (imperfect, aorist, perfect; subjunctive, optative; middle voice; the multitude of prepositions, etc.) cannot be reproduced exactly in a translation. Often a translation variant is only the consequence of an interpretation of a difficult Greek text. Added to that, the textual history of the versions themselves is studded with problems. In any case the oldest versions lead us back to a form of the NT which chronologically reaches as close as almost any other does to the original text, and they permit cautious conclusions concerning the Greek text which was in use in the lands where they were written.

a. The Syriac Versions

Of the oldest translations into Syriac (i.e., in the language of the ecclesiastical district of Edessa in Mesopotamia), we have direct witnesses only for the Gospels.[43]

1) *The Liège Diatessaron*, ed. with a Textual Apparatus by D. Plooij, C. A. Philipps, A. H. A. Bakker, Part I–VIII, Verhandelingen der Koningklijke Akademie van Wetenschappen te Amsterdam, Afdeeling Letterkunde, Nieuwe Reeks 29–31, 1929–1938. 1963–1970 (complete ed. with comprehensive parallel apparatus); A. S. Marmardji, *Diatessaron de Tatien*, 1935 (Arabic text with French tr.); C. H. Kraeling, *A Greek Fragment of Tatian's Diatessaron from Dura*, StD 3, 1935; A. Baumstark, "Die syr. Übersetzung des Titus von Bostra und das 'Diatessaron,'" Bb 16, 1935, 257 ff; W. G. Kümmel, "Textkritik . . . ," ThR, NF 11, 1939, 84 ff; C. Peters, "Das Diatessaron Tatians," OrChrA 123, 1939 (suppl.: Bb 23, 1942, 68 ff); B. M. Metzger, "Tatian's Diatessaron and a Persian Harmony of the Gospels," JBL 69, 1950, 261 ff (=B. M. M., *Chapters in the History* . . . , 97 ff); G. Messina, "Diatessaron Persiano," BeO 14, 1951 (criticism in B. M. Metzger, JBL 71, 1952, 47 f); H. Vogels, "Der Einfluss Marcions und Tatians auf Text und Kanon des NT," SStW, 278 ff; L. Leloir, *Saint Éphrem, Commentaire de l'évangile concordant, Version arménienne* (with Latin tr.), CSCO 137/145, 1953/54; *idem*, "Le Diatessaron de Tatien," *L'Orient Syrien* I, 1956, 208 ff; *idem*, "L'original syriaque du commentaire de S. Éphrem sur le Diatessaron," Bb 40, 1959, 959 ff; *idem*, "Le Diatessaron de Tatien et son commentaire par Éphrem," RechB 5, 1962, 243 ff; *idem*, *Le Témoignage d'Éphrem sur le Diatessaron*, CSCO 227, Subsidia 19, 1962; *idem*, *Saint Éphrem, Commentaire de l'Évangile concordant, Texte syriaque édité et traduit* (Latin), 1963; *idem*, *Éphrem de Nisibe, Commentaire de l'Évangile concordant ou Diatessaron. Traduit du Syriaque et de l'Arménienne*, Sources Chrétiennes 121, 1966; J. Duplacy, "Où en est . . . (see preceding §38), 77 ff; I. Ortiz de Urbina, *Vetus Evangelium Syrorum et exinde excerptum Diatessaron Tatiani*, Biblia Polyglotta Matritensia, Series IV, 1967 (see on this J. Assfalg, BZ, NF 14, 1970, 143 ff); J. Molitor, "Tatians Diatessaron und sein Verhältnis zur altsyr. und altgeorgischen Überlieferung," OrChr 53, 1969, 1 ff; 54, 1970, 1 ff; H. Merkel, *Die Widersprüche zwischen den Evv.*, WUNT 13, 1971, 68 ff.

1. *The Diatessaron of Tatian* (see §35.3) is possibly the oldest Syriac text of the Gospels. To be sure, everything here is highly debated. We know for certain that the Syrian Tatian, who had lived in Rome for a long time, was excluded from the great church

[43] Cf. on this A. Vööbus, *Studies in the Gospel Text in Syriac*, CSCO 128, 1951.

there because of his extreme ascetic ("encratitic") views, and that *ca.* 172 he returned to the East. In the second half of the second century he wrote a compilation of the Gospels in a single narrative which, according to Eusebius, was called τὸ διὰ τεσσάρων (= harmony?).[44] This gospel harmony as a whole was lost and can be inferred only from secondary and tertiary sources. A parchment fragment of the passion narrative in the Greek language from the beginning of the third century[45] is possibly a portion of the original text of Tatian, but because it is so small it does not permit any adequate conclusions. The indirect tradition splits into eastern and western branches. The main witnesses of the eastern branch are the commentary on the Diatessaron by Ephraem Syrus (d. 373), only half of which is preserved in the Syriac language and the whole of which is found only in the Armenian translation; a translation of the Diatessaron into Arabic from the Syriac; similarly a translation of the Diatessaron into Middle Persian from the Syriac; and finally there are quotations in the Syriac writers and the lectionaries.[46] Among the witnesses to the western branch is the Codex Fuldensis of the Vulgate, which follows only Tatian's *order,* a Middle Dutch harmony of the Gospels, several Old High German, Upper and Lower German, Middle English, and two Old Italian harmonies.[47] The eastern witnesses go back as a whole to a lost Syriac prototype, while the western witnesses go back to a lost Latin prototype, the text of which had already been accommodated to the customary later Syriac or Latin text, with the result that some of the witnesses give only Tatian's order and some give only his text. As a result the reconstruction of the original of Tatian's Diatessaron can only be carried out in a very conjectural way, and it is debated whether Tatian wrote his work in Rome or in Syria, whether the original

---

[44] Eus., HE IV. 29. 6. F. Bolgiani, *Vittore di Capua e il "Diatessaron,"* Memorie dell' Accademia delle Scienze di Torino, Classe di Scienze Morali, Storiche e Filologiche IV, 2, 1962, 22 ff, has shown how very likely it is that Tatian has used as a designation for his harmony a musical term which indicates by "fourth" the meaning "harmony."

[45] On the discussion about the original language of this Greek fragment see ThR, NF 11, 1939, 95 f, and DBS VI, 863.

[46] Ortiz de Urbina has collected the quotations from the Diatessaron from the Syriac fragment of Ephraem's commentary on the Diatessaron and from the Syriac literature as a whole down to the fifth century; Molitor offers a Latin translation with annotations of this hypothetically achieved reconstruction of the text of the Diatessaron.

[47] Precise information in Vööbus, "Early Versions" (see above, p. 526), 6 ff.

language was Greek [48] or Syriac,[49] whether Tatian's work is the
source of the so-called "Western" text of the Gospels[50] or, as is
more probable, is only one of its oldest witnesses,[51] and whether
in addition to the four canonical Gospels Tatian also used the
"Gospel of the Hebrews" [52] or the Infancy Gospel of James and
a Hebraic gospel.[53] What is certain, however, is that the Syriac text
of the Diatessaron is at least as old as the Old Syriac text of the
Gospels and is closely related to it and remained in use until the
fifth century in the East Syrian church.

2. *The Old Syriac Versions.* Perhaps even before the end of the
second century, the four individual Gospels were translated into
Syriac. The Syrian designation makes a distinction between *Evangelion Da-Mepharreshe* (the "Gospel of the Separated") and the
Diatessaron (the "Gospel of the Mixed"). The Old Syriac Gospel
of the Separated, the so-called Vetus Syra, is preserved in a double
manuscript tradition: the Curetonian Syriac (syr^cur or sy^c) and
the Sinaitic Syriac (syr^sin or sy^s). Syr^cur was found in 1842 in
an Egyptian monastery, is now in the British Museum, and was
published in 1858 by W. Cureton. The manuscript, which is not
quite complete, comes from the fifth century. Syr^sin was discovered
in 1892 by the sisters A. S. Lewis and M. D. Gibson in the monastery of St. Catherine on Mount Sinai, where it still is. It is a
palimpsest manuscript from the fifth or fourth century.[54] Although
the two texts probably go back to a common basic text, on the
whole the syr^sin seems to be older.[55] Important are the many points
of contact between the Old Syriac and the so-called "Western" text
of the Gospels (Old Latin versions, D, etc.; see §40). The question
of the connections between the Diatessaron and the *Vetus Syra* is,
in spite of individual disagreements, to be answered as follows: the
text of the Gospel of the Separated arose *ca.* 200 or later under the
influence of the text of the Diatessaron and continued in ecclesiasti-

---

[48] Most recently Lagrange, *Critique Textuelle* II, 27 ff; Vogels, *Handbuch,*
112; Kraeling.

[49] Most recently Vööbus, Van Puyvelde; Peters, Leloir, Merkel.

[50] Herm. von Soden, Vogels.

[51] Most recently Merkel, 91 ff.

[52] Baumstark, Peters.

[53] Messina. See with relation to nn. 52 and 53 A. J. F. Klijn (*A Survey . . . ;*
see n. 16), 5 ff.

[54] Editions of both texts: F. C. Burkitt, *Evangelion Da-Mepharreshe* I (text
and tr.), II (researches), 1904; A. S. Lewis, *The Old Syriac Gospels or Evangelion Da Mepharreshe,* 1910. Facsimile edition of syr^sin by A. Hjelt, 1930.
A. Merx, *Die vier kanonischen Evv, nach ihrem ältesten bekannten Text* I, 1897;
II-IV, 1902/11, offers a well-informed but very one-sided commentary.

[55] Otherwise Lagrange, Vogels.

cal usage until the fifth century. From the sixth century on, it was suppressed, though readings from the Old Syriac still are evident until the twelfth century.[56]

For Acts and Paul also the existence may be shown of an Old Syriac translation on the basis of quotations in the Syriac writers and of the Armenian translation of commentaries of Ephraem Syrus.[57]

3. *The Peshitta* (syr[pesch] or sy[p]). Since the works of F. C. Burkitt[58] it has been taken as proved that in the later Syriac manuscripts of the NT the astonishingly unified translation of the NT which has been handed down is the work of Bishop Rabbula of Edessa (d. 436), and that this ecclesiastical Bible very quickly replaced the Diatessaron and the Old Syriac versions in public usage. Through the research of Vööbus and Black[59] this assumption has been shaken without a clear explanation having been found for the new material brought forward by Vööbus. What stands firm is that since the tenth century the Peshitta (= "common [translation]," a designation in use since the tenth century), which was a revision of the Old Syriac version, and in which the four smaller Catholic letters and Rev (see §36.3) were lacking, enjoyed growing acceptance from the end of the fifth century on, and remained the Bible of the church for the two separated branches of the Syrian church. On the other hand it is debated whether the Peshitta was already in existence before Rabbula and arose in Antioch as the work of several revisions which aimed at an accommodation to the Greek text, and whether this translation only prevailed some centuries later in Syria proper, especially among the monks.[60] Or it may be that Rabbula was indeed not the author of the revision but participated in its beginnings at the opening of the fifth century ("Pre-Peshitta"), while the majority of the ecclesi-

---

[56] Vööbus. An edition of the complete Old Syriac material for the Gospels has been prepared by Vööbus but has not yet been published. See his "Completion of the Vetus Syra Project," RB 7, 1962, 49 ff.

[57] On Acts cf. F. C. Conybeare in J. H. Ropes, *Beginnings* III, 380 f; J. Kerschensteiner, "Beobachtungen zum altsyrischen Acta-Text," Bb 45, 1964, 63 ff. On Paul: J. Molitor, *Der Paulustext des hl. Ephraem*, MBE 4, 1938; J. Kerschensteiner, "Neues zum altsyr. Paulustext," *Studiorum Paulinorum Congressus Internationalis Catholicus* I, AnBibl 17/8, 1968, 531 ff.

[58] Esp. *Evangelion Da-Mepharreshe* (see n. 54), II, 100 ff.

[59] A. Vööbus, *Studies* (see n. 43), 46 ff; *idem*, "Das Alter der Peschitta," OrChr 38, 1954, 1 ff; M. Black, "The NT Peshitta and its Predecessors," SNTS 1950, 51 ff; *idem*, "Rabbula of Edessa and the Peshitta," BJRL 33, 1950/51, 203 ff; *idem*, "The Text of the Peshitta Tetraevangelium," *Studia Paulina, Festschr. J. de Zwaan*, 1953, 20 ff.

[60] Thus Vööbus.

astical manuscripts reproduce a later developed form of this revision.[61] The Greek prototype of the oldest form of the Peshitta also has not yet been explained.[62]

4. *The Philoxenian and the Harklean Versions.* In the year 508 in Monophysite circles a revision of the Peshitta—including a new version of those writings of the NT which were still lacking —was undertaken. The Philoxenian version (sy[ph]) is named after Philoxenus, Bishop of Mabbug (Hierapolis) on the Euphrates, who authorized one of the bishops in his territory to carry out the work for which the Koine type of the Greek text was used.[63] A century later, in 616, the Philoxenian version underwent a new revision in Egypt by Thomas of Harkel (Heraclea). He strove for a still more exact agreement of the Syriac wording with the Greek Koine text, but he also used good manuscripts of the so-called "Western" text. As a result there is found in the marginal comments of his translation, the Harklean version (sy[h]), important material for textual criticism, especially on Acts. The scholarly work of the more recent translations did not, however, suppress the Peshitta for use in the churches, even among the Monophysites.[64]

5. The version of the NT in *Palestinian Syriac* (West Aramaic; sy[pal]), which is preserved in only a fragmentary way, and which arose in the fifth or sixth century, cannot be treated with assurance with respect either to its text-critical character or to its origin, and thus for textual criticism it plays no essential role.[65]

b. The Latin Versions

S. Berger, *Histoire de la Vulgate pendant les premiers siècles du moyen âge*, 1839; F. Stummer, *Einführung in die lat. Bibel*, 1928; H. J. Vogels, *Vulgata-Studien. Die Evv. der Vulgata untersucht auf ihre lat. und*

[61] Thus Black; similarly Kerschensteiner (see n. 57).

[62] Critical editions of the Gospels: G. H. Gwilliam, *Tetraevangelium Sanctum juxta simplicem Syrorum versionem*, 1901; edition of the entire NT: *The NT in Syriac* (British and Foreign Bible Society), 1905/20.

[63] See A. Vööbus, "New Dates for the Solution of the Problem Concerning the Philoxenian Version," *Spiritus et Veritas*, Festschr. K. Kundsin, 1953, 169 ff.

[64] The text edited by J. White (*Sacrorum evangeliorum . . . Actuum apostolorum et epistolarum tam catholicarum quam paulinarum versio Syriaca Philoxeniana*, 1778–1803) is really concerned with the Harklean version. Of the Philoxenian version we know for certain only the four small Catholic letters and Rev, which are lacking in the Peshitta; these are printed in *The NT in Syriac* (see n. 62). Bibl. on the two more recent Syriac versions in DBS VI, 875 ff.

[65] Index of the fragments of text in C. Perrot, "Un fragment christopalestinien découvert à Khirbet Mird," RB 70, 1963, 506 ff (esp. 510 f).

griech. Vorlage, NTA 14, 2/3, 1928; C. H. Turner, *The Oldest Manuscript of the Vulgate Gospels,* 1931 [Codex Sangallensis]; W. G. Kümmel, ThR, NF 10, 1938, 306 ff; A. F. J. Klijn, *A Survey of the Researches into the Western Text of the Gospels and Acts,* 1949, 152 ff; *idem, A Survey . . . , Part Two 1949–1969,* Suppl. NovTest 21, 1969, 51 ff; B. M. Metzger, "The Evidence . . ." (see p. 525), 51 ff; T. A. Marazuela, *La Vetus Latina Hispana I Prolegomenos,* 1953, 65 ff, 530 ff (bibl.); B. Fischer, "Der Vulgata-Text des NT," ZNW 46, 1955, 178 ff (for criticism of the Vulgate ed. of Wordsworth-White-Sparks); *idem, Die Alkuin-Bibel,* 1957; *idem,* "Ein neuer Zeuge zum westlichen Text der Apg," *Biblical and Patristic Studies: Festschr. R. P. Casey,* 1963, 33 ff; K. Th. Schäfer, *Die altlateinische Bibel,* 1957; H. Zimmermann, *Untersuchungen zur altlat. Überlieferung des 2 Kor,* BBB 16, 1960; F. H. Tinnefeld, *Untersuchungen zur altlat. Überlieferung des I Tim,* Klassisch-Philologische Studien 26, 1963; H. J. Frede, *Altlat. Paulus-Handschriften,* Vetus Latina, Aus der Geschichte der lat. Bibel 4, 1964; E. Nellessen, *Untersuchungen zur altlat. Überlieferung des I Thess,* BBB 22, 1965; W. Thiele, *Die lat. Texte des I Petr,* Vetus Latina, Aus der Geschichte der lat. Bibel 5, 1965; U. Borse, *Der Kolosserbrief-Text des Pelagius,* diss. Bonn, 1966; R. Loewe, "The Medieval History of the Latin Vulgate," *The Cambridge History of the Bible* II, 1969, 102 ff, 514 ff.

1. *The Old Latin Versions.* Since the end of the seventeenth century (R. Simon) the fact has become known again that, before the widespread use of the Vulgate from the end of the fourth century, there were Old Latin versions of the NT which were only quite gradually replaced by the Vulgate. The origin and history of these Old Latin versions has never yet been adequately explained, because no unmixed text is preserved, and because the material from manuscripts and the church fathers has not been presented in its complete compass in a dependable way, nor has it been fully studied. A beginning has been made, however. After the Maurist P. Sabatier had in 1749 in the third volume of his work *Bibliorum sacrorum Latinae versionis antiquae seu vetus Italica* brought together all the known manuscripts and quotations from the church fathers, at the end of the nineteenth century publication began of the Old Latin manuscripts and fragments which had become known up to that time.[66] A. Jülicher prepared the comprehensive

[66] From the fifth century on; the most important editions until 1954 are indicated by Vogels, *Handbuch der Textkritik,* 83 ff. The complete index of all MSS and their editions in *Vetus Latina* 1, 1949, 11 ff ("Index of Sigla for Manuscripts and Church Fathers") is now to be replaced by an improved new edition (*Vetus Latina* 1:2 "Index of Sigla for Manuscripts"). Cf. provisionally *Vetus Latina* 24:2, 1971, 14 ff; 26:1, 1969, 11* ff; *Itala* (see n. 67) 11, vii.

edition of the manuscripts of the Gospels, which after his death W. Matzkow edited anew under authorization of the Commission on the Church Fathers of the Berlin Academy of Sciences. This offers a dependable text of all the manuscripts. It is divided into a European and African form of the text, though the reconstruction of the European text remains problematic.[67] Based on a collection of the entire tradition in the manuscripts and the church fathers which was begun by J. Denk, the archabbey of the Beuron under the leadership of B. Fischer began an edition of the Vetus Latina of which three volumes of the NT part have appeared up to now.[68] In the text (which is arranged according to two to four text forms) one finds the readings of the total manuscripts and the complete citations of all the church fathers. The Old Latin manuscripts are usually designated by lowercase Latin letters. The Beuron edition unfortunately uses a new numeration.

The decision concerning the age of the Latin version of the NT is dependent on the still debated question whether already at the end of the second century Tertullian knew the Catholic Latin texts of the Bible, which is, after all, likely.[69] What is certain is that in the middle of the third century in Africa and Italy Latin texts of the NT were in use and mutual influence between them occurred. Unity has not yet been achieved either on whether there was one original translation (which would then have had to originate in Africa) which became differentiated by revision from the Greek text,[70] or on whether from the outset several translations arose alongside each other. It is likely that the history of the individual parts of the NT run along different lines. But it is certain that we can determine at least three different text forms: an African one, a "European" one, and a Spanish one, and that the African text form (which is without doubt the oldest) is most clearly in agreement with the witnesses of the so-called "Western" text. Knowl-

---

[67] A. Jülicher–W. Matzkow–K. Aland, Itala. Das NT in altlat. Überlieferung nach den Handschriften hg. (I, Mt, 1938; II, Mk, ²1970; III, Lk, 1954; IV, Jn, 1963).

[68] Vetus Latina. Die Reste der altlat. Bibel, nach Petrus Sabatier neu gesammelt und hg. von der Erzabtei Beuron. 1:1, B. Fischer, Verzeichnis der Sigel für Kirchenschriftsteller [Index of sigla for the church fathers], ²1963 (with suppl. leaves until 1970); 24:1, H. J. Frede, Epistula ad Ephesios, 1962; idem, Epistulae ad Philippenses et ad Colossenses, 1966/71; 26:1, W. Thiele, Epistulae Catholicae, 1956/69. Two new texts are edited by Fischer, Festschr. Casey, and Frede, Paulus-Handschriften, 121 ff.

[69] Thus Klijn, A Survey . . . Part Two, 53; Thiele, I Pet, 35 f; skeptically Frede, Vetus Latina 24:2, 9.

[70] Thus Zimmermann, 65; Frede, Vetus Latina 24:1, 29*; Thiele, I Pet, 215; idem, Vetus Latina, 26:1, 66, 73, 78, 86, 97.

edge of the Old Latin version is therefore of great importance for illuminating this text which is so important for the second century. The designation of the Old Latin text as "Itala" is mistaken, since by this designation Augustine probably meant only one European form of the Old Latin version.[71]

2. *The Vulgate.* On account of the hopeless confusion of the text of the Old Latin, Pope Damasus (366–84) commissioned Jerome to prepare a uniform translation of the Bible. Jerome used a different method for the NT, which he undertook first, than he did later for the OT, which he retranslated into Latin almost entirely from the Hebrew. As he states in the foreword with which he published his version of the Gospels in 384,[72] he used as the basis for the Gospels a Latin text and then corrected it according to older Greek manuscripts. But in this he sought only to alter *quae sensum videbantur mutare* ("whatever seemed to change the meaning"), and leave everything else as he found it. Accordingly in the case of the Gospels the Vulgate is Jerome's revision of the Old Latin text, based on Greek texts (he has made alterations in about 3,500 places!), but he has retained many of the Old Latin readings. On the other hand for the rest of the NT it is very questionable whether the revision has anything at all to do with Jerome and when it was carried out.[73] Similarly for individual parts of the NT it is only conjecturally that we can answer the question which Latin text and which Greek text forms were used as the basis.[74] For the recovery of the original Greek text of the NT the Vulgate comes into the picture only as a witness for the Old Latin prototype, and must be used with caution at that. In the year 405 the translation of the OT and NT was completed, and it prevailed only very slowly, since at the outset there was no official authority

[71] Augustine, *De doctrina christiana* II. 15. 2: "In ipsis autem interpretationibus Itala caeteris praeferatur" ("with regard to the translations, the Itala should be preferred to the others"). Cf. J. Schildenberger, "Die Itala des hl. Augustinus," *Colligere Fragmenta, Festschr. A. Dodd,* 1952, 84 ff.

[72] *Ep. ad Damasum* (see *NT Latine,* ed. E. Nestle, XIV-XVI); and *Biblia Sacra iuxta Vulgatum versionem* (see n. 80) II, 1515 f.

[73] That Jerome is the author of the revision of the text of the letters of Paul and the Catholic epistles is disputed, e.g., by Zimmermann, 257; Thiele, *I Pet,* 220 f. Thiele, *Vetus Latina* 26:1, 100* f, proposes the Pelagian Rufinus the Syrian as author of the Vulgate for the second half of the NT. It is much debated also whether Pelagius used an existing Vulgate text for the letters of Paul (thus, e.g., H. J. Frede, *Vetus Latina* 24:1, 36*; *idem, ibid.,* 24:2, 14; Loewe, 110) or a text which represents the final stage prior to the Vulgate (see Tinnefeld, 102 ff; Nellessen, 249 ff; Borse, 192).

[74] For the Gospels the probable Latin prototype has been reconstructed by Vogels.

behind it and the exclusive authorization of the Vulgate was not assured until the eighth century. This honorific title meaning "generally in use" was first received by the translation at the end of the Middle Ages.[75]

The text of Jerome was not preserved with purity, however. The Vetus Latina was so firmly fixed and so familiar that in practical use expressions from it penetrated back into the improved text. Conversely the Old Latin text was itself accommodated to the Vulgate. New recensions were repeatedly required in order to bring the confusion to an end. More or less thorough attempts at correction were undertaken, among others, by Alcuin, on instructions from Charlemagne *ca.* 800, by Lanfranc of Canterbury in the eleventh century, and by theologians of the University of Paris in the thirteenth century. Nevertheless the text remained a mixed text. The Council of Trent in its fourth session of April 8, 1546, determined *ut haec ipsa vetus et vulgata editio, quae longo tot saeculorum usu in ipsa ecclesia probata est, in publicis lectionibus, disputationibus, praedicationibus et expositionibus pro authentica habeatur, et ut nemo illam reicere quovis praetextu audeat vel praesumat* ("that this ancient and common edition, which by long use over so many centuries has been approved in the church itself, is to be taken as the authentic one in public readings, in disputations, in preaching, and in expositions, and that nobody should dare or presume to refuse it by any pretext whatsoever"). However, the authentic edition established by the council had to be waited for. In 1590 Pope Sixtus V authorized an official edition, the so-called Sixtina. But it contained so many errors that by the commission of Pope Clement VIII in 1592 it was replaced by the so-called Clementina, which, however, in subsequent reprints itself had to be improved. Down to the present day the text of the third edition of the Clementina of 1598 is the official Latin text of the Bible for the Catholic church.

The number of manuscripts of the Vulgate having NT texts is unknown.[76] The oldest manuscript (Sangallensis) comes from the fifth century. The best manuscript is the Amiatinus from the eighth century (Florence). The official Vulgate text has been frequently reprinted.[77] A large critical edition which seeks to reconstruct the

---

[75] Faber Stapulensis; cf. A. Allgeier, Bb 29, 1948, 353 ff.

[76] The estimate is more than 8,000 (Vööbus; Metzger).

[77] Readily available in the edition *NT Latine. Textum Vaticanum cum apparatu critico . . . curavit E. Nestle,* [8]1954.

text of Jerome appeared in Oxford beginning in 1889.[78] In 1907 Pope Pius X entrusted to the Benedictine order the same task of reconstructing the Vulgate text of Jerome. In this work,[79] which is in preparation in the abbey of San Girolamo in Rome and is to provide the basis for a new revision of the Vulgate, no part of the NT has as yet appeared. On the other hand there is now available a manual edition for the entire Bible, edited by a group of specialists from several confessions, which offers for the NT a critically improved text of the Oxford edition with a selected apparatus.[80]

c. The Coptic Versions

In the different dialects of the Egyptian colloquial language comprehensively called "Coptic" (the designation originated through the Arabic from Αἰγύπτιος), several translations of the NT were probably undertaken. Since we have only a few witnesses for translations in the less important dialects,[81] we can only have anything like certainty about the two chief versions.

1. The Sahidic (south or upper Egyptian) version (sa or sah) probably came into being bit by bit in the third century, and preserves in fragments almost the whole of the NT. The oldest manuscript comes from the fourth century. The text agrees in the main with 𝔓 75 and B, but "Western" readings are also found, especially in the Gospels and the Acts.[82]

---

[78] J. Wordsworth, H. J. White, H. F. D. Sparks, *NT Domini Nostri Jesu Christi Latine secundum editionem Sancti Hieronymi*, I-III, 1889/1954. An *Editio minor*, ed. H. J. White (1911), ²1920, was based on this large edition.

[79] *Biblia sacra juxta Latinam versionem . . . edita*, 1926 ff.

[80] *Biblia Sacra iuxta vulgatam versionem adjuvantibus B. Fischer, J. Gribomont, H. F. D. Sparks, W. Thiele recensuit et brevi apparatu instruxit R. Weber*, I, II, 1969. The NT is found in Vol. II, 1513 ff.

[81] On the fragments in Middle Egyptian, Akhmimic, and Fayumic, cf. Metzger, "Recent Contributions," 358; Vööbus, "Early Versions," 237 ff; Botte, DBS VI, 820. A Middle Egyptian MS, not yet published, of Acts 1:1-15:2 from the fourth/sixth century is—probably not unambiguously—a homogeneous witness for the "Western" text of Acts; see on this T. C. Petersen, "An Early Coptic Manuscript of Acts: An Unrevised Version of the Ancient so-called Western Text," CBQ 26, 1964, 225 ff; E. J. Epp, "Coptic Manuscript G 67 and the Rôle of Codex Bezae as a Western Witness in Acts," JBL 85, 1966, 197 ff; E. Haenchen and P. Weigandt, "The Original Text of Acts?" NTS 14, 1967/68, 469 ff.

[82] Edition of the texts known up to 1924: G. W. Horner, *The Coptic Version of the NT in the Southern Dialect, Otherwise Called Sahidic or Thebaic* I-VII, 1911/24 (text and tr.). Since then, H. Thompson, *The Gospel of John According to the Earliest Coptic Manuscript*, 1924; idem, *The Coptic Version*

2. The age of the Bohairic (bo or boh) (northern or lower Egyptian) version is debated. But since we now know two manuscripts from the fourth/fifth century, the origin of this version before the end of the fourth century is certain. The Bohairic version also has contacts especially with the text of B ℵ, and the "Western" readings are more rare than in the Sahidic version.[83]

Both versions seem to have been translated directly from the Greek, but they have influenced each other mutually;[84] however, the history of their origin is still completely unclear.[85] Both versions are in the main important witnesses for the "Egyptian" text.

d. Other Versions

The rest of the versions of the NT which come from antiquity are in almost every case not translated directly from the Greek, and therefore do not serve as direct attestation for the Greek text of the NT. An exception is made only by the Gothic version of the fourth century. But its text-critical value is small because the Greek prototype must already have belonged essentially to the Koine type (the numerous "Western" readings probably go back to subsequent Latin influence). From among the secondary translations into Arabic, Armenian, Ethiopic, Georgian, and Sogdian, the Armenian and Georgian versions have proved to have text-critical significance. For the Old Armenian version, which can only be reconstructed inferentially on the basis of quotations, goes back to the Old Syriac text of Tatian, and the Old Georgian text, which is preserved in manuscripts, goes back to this Old Armenian one.

---

of the Acts of the Apostles and the Pauline Epistles in the Sahidic Dialect, 1952; R. Kasser, Papyrus Bodmer XIX. Évangile de Matthieu XIV, 28–XXVIII, 20. Épître aux Romains I,1–II,3 en sahidique, 1962; cf. also the reference to an unpublished early MS with the text of I Pet in Metzger, "Recent Contributions," 359.

[83] Edition of the texts known up to 1905: G. W. Horner, The Coptic Version of the NT in the Northern Dialect, Otherwise Called Memphitic and Bohairic I-IV, 1898/1905. Since then, P. E. Kahle, "A Biblical Fragment of the IVth–Vth Century in Semi-Bohairic," Le Muséon 63, 1950, 147 ff (fragment of Phil); R. Kasser, Papyrus Bodmer III: Évangile de Jean et Genèse I–IV, 2 en bohaïrique, CSCQ 177/8, 1958 (Jn is from fourth/fifth century; Gnostic origin is assumed by Massaux, NTS 5, 1958/59, 210 ff).

[84] J. L. Koole, Studien zum kopt. Bibeltext, BhZNW 17, 1936, has shown that this is true for Paul and Acts; idem, Bulletin of the Bezan Club 12, 1937, 65 ff.

[85] Cf. recently R. Kasser, "Les dialectes coptes et les version coptes bibliques," RB 46, 1965, 287 ff; P. Weigandt, "Zur Geschichte der kopt. Bibelübersetzungen," RB 50, 1969, 80 ff.

Nevertheless here no unity has been achieved concerning details; e.g., was the oldest Armenian version of the Gospels a Diatessaron[86] or fourfold Gospels? [87] For the recovery of the oldest Syriac text and its Greek prototype, the Old Georgian and Old Armenian versions are in any case important.[88]

3. The Quotations in the Early Christian Writers

The adducing of parts of the NT text in the Christian writers of the first centuries is important on three grounds for textual criticism: (1) these quotations reproduce in part a NT text from a time from which we have no, or only scattered, direct manuscript tradition; (2) the quotations in the Fathers can in almost every case be located geographically, and when compared with the text of the manuscripts they make possible the pinning down of their geographical provenance as well as the determination of local text groups; (3) the text-critical discussions of the Fathers give an insight into the form of the text of that time as it was influenced by various currents. The evaluation of these quotations is difficult, however, because on the one hand in the manuscripts of the works of the Fathers, the quotations themselves may have already undergone alteration, so that one must work with critical editions of the writings of the Fathers, and on the other hand the Fathers by no means always quoted with verbal exactitude and always from the same text.

According to some scholars, Marcion and Tatian have strongly influenced the oldest text of the Gospels and the Pauline letters.[89] But according to the more probable assumption, both Fathers are only witnesses for the "Western" text widely used in the second century, and only in scattered details have alterations based on Marcion's text penetrated orthodox texts.[90] On the other hand, Justin and Irenaeus are without doubt witnesses for the early

[86] Lyonnet.

[87] Vööbus.

[88] See on these versions: Metzger, "Recent Contributions," 361 ff; Vööbus, "Early Versions," 133 ff; L. Leloir, DBS VI, 810 ff, 829 ff; Kieffer, *Au delà . . . ,* 26 f n. 119; S. Lyonnet, *Les Origines de la version arménienne et la Diatessaron,* BeO 13, 1950; J. Molitor, "Die Bedeutung der altgeorgischen Bibel für die nt. Textkritik," BZ, NF 4, 1960, 39 ff.

[89] Herm. von Soden; H. Vogels, "Der Einfluss Marcions und Tatians auf Text und Kanon des NT," SStW, 278 ff.

[90] C. S. C. Williams, *Alterations* (see bibl. preceding §38), 10 ff; E. C. Blackman, *Marcion and His Influence,* 1948, 42 ff, 128 ff.

"Western" text,[91] as are Tertullian and Cyprian. Clement of Alexandria, on the other hand, in spite of some "Western" readings, is not a witness of the "Western" text, but offers probably an Egyptian local text which is related to $\mathfrak{P}$ 45, [92] while Origen, first in Alexandria and then in Caesarea, varied between using the "Egyptian" and the so-called "Caesarean" text.[93]

Research into these quotations from the Fathers is thus an important aid for the grouping of the NT textual witnesses (see §40). Indeed, M.-E. Boismard has attempted to show that from the text of the Fathers before the period of the great manuscripts of the fourth century, a form of the text (in many cases a shorter form) can be reconstructed which has been lost in the Greek manuscripts, so that the original text can only be gained on the basis of the quotations in the Fathers.[94] Although Boismard's researches have produced extremely rich material, they have not proved that the text which is reconstructed on the basis of many quotations ever existed, and that it is in fact the primitive text. They show only that the texts from the Fathers must be taken into account more seriously and that they should not simply be incorporated into the text groups which can be perceived in the fourth/fifth century.[95] But the question is completely open whether the NT text in the manuscripts was ever so freely handled as in the quotations in the Fathers.[96]

Critical editions of the patristic literature, which as a whole are still incomplete, are offered in the following series: *Die griechischen*

[91] K. T. Schäfer, "Die Zitate in der lat. Irenäusüberlieferung und ihr Wert für die Textgeschichte," *Festschr. M. Meinertz*, NTA, Suppl. Vol. 1, 1951, 50 ff; E. Massaux, "Le texte du Sermon sur la Montagne utilisé par S. Justin," EThL 28, 1952, 411 ff.

[92] M. Mees, *Die Zitate aus dem NT bei Clemens von Alexandrien*, Quaderni di "Vetera Christianorum" 2, 1970.

[93] See K. W. Kim, "Origen's Text of John in his 'On Prayer,' Commentary on Matthew, and 'Against Celsus,'" JTS, NS 1, 1950, 74 ff.

[94] M.-E. Boismard, "À propos de Jean 5,39," RB 55, 1948, 5 ff; *idem*, "Critique textuelle et citations patristiques," RB 57, 1950, 388 ff; also "Lectio brevior, potior," RB 58, 1951, 161 ff; *idem*, "Problèmes de critique textuelle concernant le quatrième évangile," RB 60, 1953, 347 ff; *idem*, "Les traditions johanniques concernant le Baptiste," RB 70, 1963, 10 f.

[95] Cf. M. J. Suggs, "The Use of Patristic Evidence in the Search for a Primitive NT Text," NTS 4, 1957/58, 139 ff.

[96] See on this A. F. J. Klijn (*A Survey* . . . ; see n. 16), 165; R. Schnackenburg, *Joh*, HThK IV, 1, 1965, 160 f; M. Mees, "Lectio brevior im Joh und ihre Beziehung zum Urtext," BZ, NF 12, 1968, 111 ff, esp. 116 ff; G. D. Fee, "The Text of John in the Jerusalem Bible: A Critique of the Use of Patristic Citations in NT Textual Criticism," JBL 90, 1971, 163 ff (methodologically important!).

christlichen Schriftsteller der ersten drei Jahrhunderte [The Greek Christian writers of the First Three Centuries] edited by the Berlin Academy, 1897 onward, now extended to the fourth–sixth centuries; *Corpus ecclesiasticorum Latinorum*, edited by the Academy of Vienna, 1866 onward; *Corpus scriptorum christianorum orientalium*, 1903 onward; *Patrologia orientalis*, 1903 onward, Reprints and to some extent new editions too are offered also in the following series, which are still in the course of publication also: *Corpus Christianorum, Series Latina*, 1954 onward, and *Sources Chrétiennes, Series Graeca* and *Series Latina*, 1941 onward (with French translation). Much to be desired is the edition of the NT text of individual Fathers.[97]

In addition to the writings of the Fathers which are preserved in their complete form, there are also the fragments which are preserved in catenae, i.e., in collections of quotations from the Fathers written in chainlike fashion in the margin of biblical manuscripts.[98]

§39. The Printed Text

From the fifteenth century, the century in which the art of printing was discovered, there is no printed edition of the Greek NT. It was not until the beginning of the sixteenth century that the Greek NT was edited: this occurred in a double *Editio princeps*:

1. *The Complutensian Polyglot*, so called after the place in which it appeared: Complutum (=Alcalà in Spain). The text is given in Greek and Latin, and for the OT also in Hebrew. Commissioned by Cardinal Ximenes (d. 1517), it was prepared by

---

[97] The following are mentioned as examples: H. Roensch, *Das NT Tertullians*, 1871; Hans von Soden, *Das lat. NT in Afrika zur Zeit Cyprians*, TU 33, 1910; *The NT in the Apostolic Fathers*, 1905; O. Bauernfeind, *Der Römerbrieftext des Origenes*, TU 44, 3, 1923; W. Sanday–C. H. Turner–A. Souter, *NT S. Irenaei*, 1923; A. Harnack, *Marcion*, [2]1924; C. H. Milne, *A Reconstruction of the Old Latin Text or Texts of the Gospels Used by St. Augustine*, 1926; G. J. D. Aalders, *Tertullianus' Citaten uit de Evangelien en de Oud-Latijnsche Bijbelvertalingen*, 1932; H. Vogels, *Das Corpus Paulinum des Ambrosiaster*, BBB 13, 1957; B. M. Metzger, "Explicit References in the Works of Origen to Variant Readings in NT Manuscripts," *Biblical and Patristic Studies: Festschr. R. P. Casey*, 1963, 78 ff; M. Mees (see n. 92); G. D. Fee, "The Text of John in Origen and Cyril of Alexandria: A Contribution to Methodology in the Recovery and Analysis of Patristic Citations," Bb 52, 1971, 357 ff.

[98] Texts: K. Staab, *Pauluskommentare aus der griech. Kirche*, NTA 15, 1933; J. Reuss, *Matthäuskommentare aus der griech. Kirche*, TU 61, 1957; bibl. in LThK VI, 1961, 57.

capable Spanish scholars, beginning in 1502. It is still not clear
which manuscripts of the Greek NT their text was based on. The
printing of the NT was completed in 1514 and that of the remaining parts in 1517, but it was not until 1520 that Pope Leo
X gave permission for its public distribution. The work does not
seem to have reached Germany before 1522. Luther did not use
it for his *NT Deutsch* published in September, 1522.

2. *The Edition of Erasmus.* The Basel printer Froben wanted to
anticipate the work of Ximenes, which he knew about, and in
1515 asked Erasmus to assume responsibility for an edition. Erasmus
agreed, and in March of 1516 he published the first NT in the
Greek language with his own Latin translation. This hasty edition,
of which Erasmus himself said in a letter[1] in 1516, *praecipitatum
verius quam editum* ("more precipitated than edited"), reproduces
in the main, with slight corrections, the text of two Basel minuscule manuscripts, and four other minuscules were used only occasionally. Erasmus had only a single manuscript for Rev, which
broke off at 22:16; the missing verses he translated—with many
mistakes—from the Vulgate back into Greek. In four subsequent
editions Erasmus made improvements, but the basis of his text remained the same throughout.[2] It was on a reprint of the second
edition (1519) that Luther based his translation of the NT.

The later printings of the NT from the sixteenth century conformed to the Erasmus text, into which were introduced a number of corrections according to the *Complutensis* or manuscripts
which were compared. Famous are the four editions of the Parisian
printer Robert Stephanus (Estienne), especially the third (1550),
the *Editio Regia,* which for the first time offered in the inner
margin a critical apparatus (its siglum ϛ = text of Stephanus). The
fourth edition (1551) introduced the division of the text into
verses which is still in use today. The editions of the Greek NT
which Theodore Beza brought about in Geneva in 1565–1604,
and which achieved normative significance in Calvinist circles, did
not tie in significantly with the text of Stephanus, although
Beza drew upon manuscript material—but surprisingly not upon
both the great majuscules, D, which he himself possessed!

In the printings of the seventeenth century the text which had
been worked up in the sixteenth century was finally fixed. This

---

[1] P. S. Allen, *Opus epistolarum Des. Erasmi Roterodami* II, No. 402.

[2] Cf. K. W. Clark, "Observations on the Erasmian Notes in Codex 2," StEv
I, TU 73, 1959, 749 ff; B. Reicke, "Erasmus und die nt. Textgeschichte," ThZ
22, 1966, 254 ff; E.-W. Kohls, *Die theologische Lebensaufgabe des Erasmus und
die oberrheinischen Reformatoren,* ATh I, 39, 1969, 13 ff.

text represents a form of the Koine text of late antiquity (see §40) which had developed over hundreds of years and thus become corrupt. The service performed by the famous editions from the printing house of the Elzevier family in Leiden, and later in Amsterdam (seven editions from 1624 to 1678), lay essentially in the masterly printing and the beautiful editions. The text, however, was hardly distinguishable from the Beza text of 1565. In the preface to the second edition (1633) stands the sentence, *textum ergo habes nunc ab omnibus receptum, in quo nihil immutatum aut corruptum damus* ("thus you now have the universally received text in which we present nothing that has been changed or is corrupted");[3] for this reason the text from Stephanus to Elzevier, which prevailed for nearly four centuries and was valued by old Protestant orthodoxy as inspired, was called the *textus receptus*.

The editions of the eighteenth century did not assail the *textus receptus*, but they added a critical apparatus and the principles for a scholarly textual criticism founded on the progressive research into manuscripts, versions, and quotations from the Fathers, and the growing insight into the history of NT text. After J. Mill (1707) for the first time printed the readings of all the accessible manuscripts and versions under the *textus receptus*, J. A. Bengel (1734), under the *textus receptus*, which was scarcely altered, mentioned the readings which seemed to be preferable to those in the text. J. J. Wettstein (1751/52), who introduced the sigla which are still commonly in use today for the majuscles and the minuscules (see §38.1.a), indicated in his text those places which should be altered; and J. J. Griesbach (1774/75) altered the text itself very cautiously on the basis of methodological principles.

But not until the nineteenth century was the dominance of the *textus receptus* broken. C. Lachmann (1831) applied the tested principles of classical-philological textual research to textual criticism of the NT. For the recension of the NT text he laid down the principle that one should not start with the *textus receptus*, but with the text which was read in the church *ca.* 380, which can be reconstructed on the basis of the oldest Greek manuscripts, the Latin versions, and the quotations from a few of the

---

[3] H. J. de Jonge, *Daniel Heinsius and the Textus Receptus of the NT*, 1971, has shown that the foreword as well as the text of the Elzevier edition of 1633 are to be credited to the Leiden philologian Daniel Heinsius.

church fathers.[4] Thus for the first time there was a critical text of the NT based on the best witnesses.

C. von Tischendorf discovered a large number of the manuscripts of the NT, and for the first time compared them or newly edited them and thus made available a substantively richer body of material for textual criticism. The first edition of his *NT graece* appeared in 1841, but the most complete collection of material was contained in the eighth edition: *Editio octava critica major* I, 1896; II, 1872 (III: *Prolegomena*, 1894, edited by C. R. Gregory). The importance of this work did not lie in its text, which lacked any formation according to firm principles and gave too much preference to the text of א, which Tischendorf himself had discovered, but its incomparably rich critical apparatus makes it an indispensable tool for any text-critical work to the present day.

Contemporary with Tischendorf was the work of the Englishman S. P. Tregelles, who worked on the text of the NT for decades. His edition of 1857/72[5] is to be preferred methodologically to that of Tischendorf, but because it is skimpier in its apparatus and has not used א (in part also B) it has not prevailed over Tischendorf's.

The first edition of the Greek NT formed along strict methodological principles was presented in the edition of the Cambridge professors B. F. Westcott and F. J. A. Hort.[6] Manuscript B was most highly valued as a representative of the "neutral" text and is the standard for the reconstruction of the text (see §40). The edition of B. Weiss[7] also has a preference for B while engaging in extensive comparisons with the other older majuscules.

The last great critical edition of the NT comes from Hermann von Soden.[8] In taking upon himself this great task he opened new avenues, above all by adducing the more recent manuscripts in which he found witnesses of old recensions. The core of his theory was formed by the assumption that there were three recensions to

---

[4] See WGK, NT, 146 f.

[5] See P. Tregelles, *The Greek NT, ed. from Ancient Authorities with their Various Readings in Full and the Latin Version of Jerome* I-VI, 1857/72.

[6] B. F. Westcott and F. J. A. Hort, *The NT in the Original Greek* I (text [2]1898; II (basic principles of textual criticism and documentary evidence) (1882), [2]1896, repr. 1953.

[7] B. Weiss, *Das NT. Textkritische Untersuchungen und Textherstellung* (1894–1900), [2]1902/5.

[8] Herm. von Soden, *Die Schriften des NT in ihrer ältesten erreichbaren Textgestalt hergestellt aufgrund ihrer Textgeschichte* I (studies), 1902/10; II (text and apparatus), 1913; manual edition, 1913.

which the whole of the manuscript tradition could be traced back,[9] and by the claim that the confusion of the text of the Gospels must be attributed essentially to the influence of Tatian. The results of von Soden are still fiercely debated, especially since his collations and the apparatus are not unqualifiedly dependable. The chief achievement of von Soden was the opening up of new material, especially a very large number of later Greek manuscripts.

What Tischendorf achieved for his time in his *Editio octava,* an edition with a critical apparatus bringing together the whole text tradition, the great new Oxford edition of the Greek NT (*NT Graece secundum textum Wescotto = Hortianum*) sought to achieve on the basis of today's advanced knowledge of the tradition. But since the editions of Mk and Lk by S. C. E. Legg (see p. 23) have been found to be inadequate, this plan has been abandoned. Instead there are two undertakings of editions of a comprehensive overview of the known manuscript tradition of the NT, which are only loosely connected with one another. On the one hand there is a group of scholars—first English and now English and American—who since 1942 have been at work on an International Greek NT Project according to which the readings of the manuscripts, versions, and quotations from the Fathers are registered in comparison with the basic text, the *textus receptus.* For a long while nothing was heard from the project,[10] then a sample of the planned edition was sent out in 1965 and was subjected to strong criticism.[11] It now appears that the gathering of material for the edition of Lk is far advanced,[12] but apart from information concerning the method of selection for the minuscules to be cited, nothing precise is known concerning the form of the edition.

Since it will obviously be quite a while yet before some volumes of this English-American project are published, beginning in 1968 group of Continental scholars have made firm plans to prepare

[9] Lucianic text (=Koine or Byzantine text; siglum: K); Hesychian text (=Egyptian text; siglum: H); Pamphilian text (or Jerusalem text; siglum: I).

[10] Cf. J. Duplacy, "Une tâche importante en difficulté: l'édition du NT Grec," NTS 14, 1967/68, 457 ff.

[11] K. Aland, "Bemerkungen zu Probeseiten einer grossen kritischen Ausgabe des NT," NTS 12, 1966, 176 ff (=K. A., *Studien zur Überlieferung des NT und seines Textes,* ANTF 2, 1967, 81 ff).

[12] E. C. Colwell, J. A. Sparks, F. Wisse; P. R. McReynolds, "The International Greek NT Project," JBL 87, 1968, 187 ff; E. C. Colwell, "International Greek NT Project," NTS 16, 1969/70, 180 ff. The Institute is located in Claremont, Cal., in connection with the Institute for Antiquity and Christianity; editors are E. C. Colwell, J. M. Plumley, K. W. Clark.

a *Novi Testamenti Graeci editio maior* in collaboration with a series of existing research centers. In order to avoid any competition, it has been decided to begin with the Catholic letters, starting with James. The exact plans for the arrangement of this edition and a sample page indicate that here, with the help of a complicated but very clear system, a text that is to be critically constructed will be accompanied by exact information concerning the readings from all the papyri, majuscules, and old versions, and a systematically selected number of minuscules and quotations from the Fathers.[13]

These projected large multivolume editions will take the place of Tischendorf's *Editio octava,* and will provide an inexhaustible resource for further text-critical research. On the other hand the manual editions will serve for practical use; of these only the two most widely used will be mentioned here.[14] The edition of Eberhard Nestle[15] (first published in 1898)᾿ offered no new text, but a cross section based on the editions of Tischendorf, Westcott and Hort, and Bernhard Weiss which was developed by a majority decision. Since the thirteenth edition of 1927 the attestation of the manuscripts has been reworked in the apparatus, and by the introduction of recently found materials it has been kept up to date (up to the twenty-fifth edition in 1963, edited by Erwin Nestle and K. Aland). The twenty-sixth edition, which is now in preparation, will not only constitute anew the text on the basis of the manuscripts which are known today and present-day text-critical insights, but the new apparatus will be so completely rearranged and so comprehensive that all normally necessary information can be derived from it.[16] In addition to the edition of Nestle, which remains basic for scientific work in the NT, in 1966 there appeared

[13] Cf. K. Aland, "Novi Testamenti Graeci editio maior critica. Der gegenwärtige Stand der Arbeiten an einer neuen grossen kritischen Ausgabe des NT," NTS 16, 1969/70, 163 ff; J. Duplacy, Bb 51, 1970, 125 ff; 52, 1971, 111 f. Editors responsible for the project are K. Aland, J. Duplacy, B. Fischer. On the question how broadly a computer can assist in the collecting and sorting of data, cf. the circumspect account by B. Fischer, "The Use of Computers in NT Studies with Special Reference to Textual Criticism," JTS, NS 21, 1970, 297 ff.

[14] On the editions mentioned on p. 23 (Vogels, Merk, Bover) and the relationship of these manual editions to each other, cf. K. Aland, "Der heutige Text des griech. NT. Ein kritischer Bericht über seine modernen Ausgaben," in K. A., *Studien* (see n. 11), 58 ff.

[15] *Novum Testamentum Graece cum apparatu critico curavit Eb. Nestle* (1898), [25]1963 *novis curis elaboraverunt Erw. Nestle et K. Aland.*

[16] See on this "The New Nestle Greek NT," NTS 6, 1959/60, 179 ff; *idem,* (see n. 14), 77 ff. In the new edition, the siglum 𝔎 is replaced by 𝔐 =majority text, and the siglum 𝔥 has unfortunately been dropped.

an edition developed by several Bible societies,[17] the text of which was based on the majority decision of the editors, but which does not deviate significantly from the text of Nestle.[18] It is intended to serve above all for translators of the NT into living languages and thus records essentially fewer variants. But for these it offers a richer attestation and records in a second apparatus the differences in punctuation between the modern editions and the most important translations in the major world languages. Furthermore by letters the editors have indicated what value they attach to individual variants for the achieving of the original text. This edition is therefore useful for supplementing Nestle, but cannot by any means replace it.

§40. THE PRESENT STATE OF NEW TESTAMENT TEXTUAL CRITICISM

W. H. P. Hatch, *The Western Text of the Gospels*, 1937; F. G. Kenyon, *The Western Text in the Gospels and Acts*, 1939; *idem*, "Hesychius and the Text of the NT," *Mémorial Lagrange*, 1940, 245 ff; K. and S. Lake, *The Byzantine Text of the Gospels*, ibid., 251 ff; *idem, Family 13 (The Ferrar Group): The Text According to Mark . . .* , StD 11, 1941; C. C. Torrey, *Documents of the Primitive Church*, 1941, 112 ff; B. M. Metzger, "The Caesarean Text of the Gospels," JBL 64, 1945, 457 (=B. M. M., *Chapters . . .* [see bibl. preceding §38], 42 ff); *idem*, "Recent Spanish Contributions to the Textual Criticism of the NT," JBL 66, 1947, 401 ff (=*ibid.*, 121 ff); *idem*, "The Lucianic Recension of the Greek Bible," NTS 8, 1961/62, 189 ff (=*ibid.*, 1 ff); A. F. J. Klijn, *A Survey of the Researches into the Western Text of the Gospels and Acts*, diss. Utrecht, 1947; *idem, A Survey of the Researches into the Western Text of the Gospels and Acts, Part Two 1949–1969*, Suppl. NovTest 21, 1969; R. V. G. Tasker, "An Introduction to the Manuscripts of the NT," HTR 41, 1948, 17 ff; P. Glaue, "Der älteste Text der geschichtlichen Bücher des NT," ZNW 45, 1954, 90 ff; H. Greeven, "Erwägungen zur synpt. Textkritik," NTS 6, 1959/60, 281 ff; J. Geerlings, *Family 13—The Ferrar Group: The Text According to Matthew, . . . to Luke, . . . to John*, StD 19–21, 1961/62; S. Jellicoe, "The Hesychian Recension Reconsidered," JBL 82, 1963, 409 ff; K. Aland, "Die Konsequenzen der neueren Handschriftenfunde für die nt.

---

[17] *The Greek NT*, ed. K. Aland, M. Black, B. M. Metzger, A. Wikgren, 1966. See on this R. P. Markham and E. A. Nida, *An Introduction to the Bible Societies' Greek NT*, 1966.

[18] Cf. K. Aland (see n. 14), 78 f. On the characteristics and criticism of this edition cf. I. A. Moir, NTS 14, 1967/68, 136 ff; C. M. Martini, Bb 49, 1968, 133 ff.

Textkritik," NovTest 9, 1967, 81 ff (=K. A., *Studien zur Überlieferung des NT und seines Textes*, ANTF 2, 1967, 180 ff); *idem*, "Die Bedeutung des $\mathfrak{P}^{75}$ für den Text des NT. Ein Beitrag zur Frage der 'Western non-interpolations,'" *Studien* . . . , 155 ff; *idem*, "Bemerkungen zu den gegenwärtigen Möglichkeiten textkritischer Arbeit," NTS 17, 1970/71, 1 ff; R. Kieffer, *Au delà des recensions? L'évolution de la tradition textuelle dans Jean VI,52-71*, Conjectanea Biblica, NT Series 3, 1968; K. W. Clark, "Today's Problems with the Critical Text of the NT," *Transitions in Biblical Scholarship*, ed. J. C. Rylaardsdam, 1968, 7 ff; J. G. Griffith, "Numerical Taxonomy and Some Primary Manuscripts of the Gospels," JTS, NS 20, 1969, 389 ff; E. C. Colwell, *Studies in Methodology in Textual Criticism of the NT*, NTTS 9, 1969 (contains "Method in Grouping NT Manuscripts," 1 ff=NTS 4, 1957/58, 73 ff; "Method in Establishing the Nature of Text-Types of NT Manuscripts," 45 ff=*Early Christian Origins: Festschr. H. R. Willoughby*, 1961, 128 ff; "Method in Establishing Quantitative Relationships Between Text-Types of NT Manuscripts" [with E. W. Tune], 56 ff=*Biblical and Patristic Studies: Festschr. R. P. Casey*, 1963, 25 ff; "Method in Classifying and Evaluating Variant Readings" [with E. W. Tune], 96 ff=JBL 83, 1964, 253 ff; "Hort Redivivus: A Plea and a Program," 148 ff=*Transitions in Biblical Scholarship*, ed. J. C. Rylaardsdam, 1968, 131 ff); M. M. Carder, "Evidence for a Caesarean Text in the Catholic Epistles," NTS 16, 1969/70, 252 ff; J. Duplacy, review of C. M. Martini, *Il problema della recensionalità* (see §38 n. 18), Bb 51, 1970, 87 ff. See also bibl. preceding §38.

Lachmann, who overthrew the *textus receptus* (see p. 542), did not cherish the illusion that he could recover the original text of the NT, but resigned himself, by the reconstruction of the fourth-century text, to recovering the "oldest among those texts which were demonstrably in wide use, to the extent that this information could be inferred from the manuscript tradition as it was known at the time. As a result of the discovery of further old manuscripts, or their becoming known, and by an improved method of inquiry, the question shifted—as early as the second half of the nineteenth century but especially since the papyrus discoveries of the last four decades—to how close an approximation to the original form of the text could be achieved on methodologically assured grounds.

The point of departure for the discussion of this question today is still formed by the theses of Westcott and Hort (see p. 543). According to them all the material on the earliest history of the Greek text of the NT falls into three main groups and a secondary group of text types:

1. *The "Syrian" Text*. It is offered by most of the majuscules

and almost all the minuscules, by the versions which originated after 300 and the great mass of the church fathers from the end of the fourth century on, and is the basis of the *textus receptus*. It goes back to a recension by the presbyter Lucian in Antioch (d. 311). From there it spread to Constantinople and to the entire East. As a mixed text based on other texts, it was considered by Westcott and Hort to be of lesser value.

2. *The "Western" Text*. It is to be seen in D, a few minuscules, the Old Latin and the Old Syriac versions, and the quotations from the oldest Fathers of the West (Justin, Irenaeus, Tertullian, Cyprian, among others). Its home is also Syria; it is called the "Western" text by Westcott and Hort after the precedent of Semler and Griesbach, because its distinctiveness was first noted in the textual tradition of the West. Characteristic of it are the tendency to circumlocution, clarification, embellishment, harmonization in the text of the Synoptics, etc. For this reason Westcott and Hort consider it degenerate in spite of its great age (second century).

3. *The "Neutral" text*. Its prime representative is B. It appears in somewhat less pure form in א; Origen and the Coptic versions belong to this type, as well as a few other secondary witnesses (the majuscules C, L, P, Q, R, T, Z, Δ, Θ [though some of these represent it in only a few writings], a few minuscules, especially 33, and Alexandrian Fathers such as Clement and Dionysius). B and א, independently of each other, go back to a superior text which stands close to the autographs, and which B represents in pure form and א in an occasional mixture with readings from other origins. It is called the "neutral" text because it has survived unaltered and uninfluenced by any mixture. For this reason Westcott and Hort see in it the oldest and most valuable type.

3a. *The Alexandrian text* is attested in various ways by such manuscripts as H, א, C, L, R, X, Z, Γ, Δ, and in part also in Origen and the Coptic versions. In reality it is only a variation of the "neutral" text, from which it deviates only through smaller stylistic and substantive variations, thus indicating that the Neutral text underwent a slight recension in Alexandria.

In keeping with their views concerning the text types, Westcott and Hort constructed their critical text on the basis of the Neutral text, especially B. The "Syriac" and "Alexandrian" texts remain out of consideration, as well as the "Western" text as a whole. In a few places only where the "Western" text, contrary to its general inclination toward expansion, retains a shorter reading than the Neutral text, it is noted and regarded as the preserver of the original.[1]

The Westcott and Hort version of the history of the text has at one point achieved universal acceptance, namely, the insight into the inferiority of the "Syrian" text type (usually better called Antiochian text, Lucianic text, Byzantine, or Imperial text, or, because of its widespread use, Koine Text [$\Re$]). This text form, from which the *textus receptus* of the sixteenth and seventeenth centuries was developed, is the result of the work of revisers who smoothed out the language of the traditional text and harmonized the variant readings of the texts as they found them (cf. Rom 6:12), and in the interest of a unified text they made supposed improvements in the form of additions and omissions. Nevertheless more recent research has shown that even Koine readings *can* be old and good, especially when the reading can be shown to be old on the basis of individual additional attestation.[2] The characteristic features of this text are apparent from the fourth century on, yet it is questionable whether there was ever a unified form of the Koine text which could be reconstructed,[3] and the assertion that most of the readings of the Koine text were already in existence before 200[4] is completely unproved.

On a second point the theory of Westcott and Hort has recently proved once more its essential correctness after being under attack for a long time. The various efforts to determine whether, on the basis of individual writings or individual sections of texts, the most important manuscripts and versions belong to specific text types have led to the widespread recognition that already *ca.* 200 there was a text type of which the oldest representatives are $\mathfrak{P}^{45}$ (for Acts), $\mathfrak{P}^{46,47,66}$, $\mathfrak{P}^{72}$ (for I Pet), $\mathfrak{P}^{75}$ B, C, $\aleph$ (in part), and the Coptic versions, and that without doubt it was widely used in Egypt.[5] Since in his letter to Damasus about the submitting of his

[1] The "Western non-interpolations" (placed in brackets by Westcott and Hort) are: Mt 27:49; Lk 22:19 f; 24:3, 6, 12, 36, 40, 51, 52.

[2] Examples in Zuntz, *Text* (see bibl. preceding §38), 50 ff, 150; Greeven; Metzger, "Lucianic Recension," 202 f = 38; J. Duplacy, "Une Variante méconnue du texte reçu: '. . . Η ΑΠΟΛΥΣΗΤΕ' (Lk 22:68)," *Nt. Aufsätze, Festschr. J. Schmid,* 1963, 42 ff; G. D. Kilpatrick, "Some Problems in NT Text and Language," *Neotestamentica et Semitica, Festschr. M. Black,* 1969, 198 ff.

[3] See K. and S. Lake, *The Byzantine Text.*

[4] Kilpatrick, *Macgregor Festschr.* (see bibl. preceding §38), 190; similarly K. Treu, ThLZ 92, 1967, 897. *Contra,* Colwell, *Studies . . . ,* 52 = *Festschr. Willoughby,* 135 f.

[5] Cf., e.g., Klijn *Survey . . . , Part Two,* 37 ff; Aland, "Konsequenzen," 90 = 188; *idem,* "Bemerkungen," 3; Kieffer, 214 ff, 244 f; Griffith, 401; Colwell, "Quantitative Relationships," 59 = 28.

version of the Gospels[6] Jerome mentions a certain Hesychius as
the originator of the Septuagintal text which was in customary use
in Egypt, ever since W. Bousset (1894) this text type has often
been characterized as Hesychian (Nestle: $\mathfrak{H}$); but to trace this
text type back to a bishop of this name of whom almost nothing
else is known, is extremely dubious, since the text is without doubt
earlier than the bishop himself.[7] This text, to be sure, was not the
only one used at the end of the second century in Egypt (see
below), and it is debatable whether we are dealing here with a
"neutral" text—i.e., more or less unspoiled in transmission—or
a text which has been revised on the basis of sound principles. That
the Egyptian text which is attested in B, ($\aleph$), C from the fourth
century is not based on a recension of the third/fourth century
according to good critical principles,[8] but was already in existence
around 200, has been proved for certain.[9] But on this basis it cannot be decided whether the Egyptian text that existed *ca.* 200 was
a well-preserved local text,[10] or whether it goes back to a recension
which was completed before 200,[11] or whether at this early period
in Egypt there were two different forms of the text, of which one
($\mathfrak{P}$ [75] and B) is a recension of the "wild" text of the other ($\mathfrak{P}$ [66],
$\aleph$).[12] If at the moment this question still cannot be answered with
certainty, it ought by no means to be overlooked that Papyri 46
and 66 have been corrected in such a fashion that almost throughout "Western" readings are replaced by "Egyptian" readings. Thus
it cannot be denied that in the course of the early tradition of the
"Egyptian" text, revisional activity also played a role, so that old
readings based on good prototypes were brought back into the
commonly used text.[13] Even if it is accordingly questionable

---

[6] See §38 n. 72 and the references in Kieffer, 28 f.

[7] In spite of Jellicoe; cf. Kenyon, "Hesychius"; Kieffer, 28 f.

[8] Cf. the history of research in C. M. Martini, *Il problema della recensionalità* (see §38 n. 18), 27 ff; also recently Tasker; Colwell, "Method in Establishing the Nature of Text-Types," 54=137; and "Hort Redivivus," 167 f=151 f.

[9] See Martini (see n. 8), *passim,* esp. 149; and C. L. Porter, "Papyrus Bodmer XV" (see §38 n. 18), 18; further in Birdsall, *Cambridge History* (see bibl. preceding §38), 328; Aland, "Bedeutung des $\mathcal{P}^{75}$," 155; also *"Novi Testamenti Graeci Editio Maior,"* NTS 16, 1969/70, 168; Duplacy, review, Bb 1970, 90.

[10] Thus Aland, "Konsequenzen . . . ," 90=188; J. Schmid, review of Martini's *Recensionalità,* BZ 11, 1967, 133 ff; G. D. Fee, "Codex Sinaiticus" (see §38 n. 29), 44.

[11] Thus, questioningly, J. Duplacy, review, Bb 1970, 90 f.

[12] Thus Kieffer, 221 f; Klijn, *Survey . . . , Part Two,* 48 f, who would like simply to establish these two texts side by side.

[13] Cf. G. Zuntz, *The Text of the Epistles,* 1953, 252 ff; A. F. J. Klijn, "Papyrus Bodmer II" (see §38 n. 16), 333 f; G. D. Fee, NovTest 7, 1964/65, see *ibid.,* 256 f; E. F. Rhodes, see *ibid.,* 279 f.

whether at any time there was one "Egyptian" text in one manuscript, and whether accordingly the "Egyptian" text may be equated
with the primitive text, still it is once more certain that the
"Egyptian" text can already be demonstrated before the end of the
second century, and that the readings of its witnesses have the
greatest weight for the recovery of the primitive text.

Although the judgment of Westcott and Hort concerning the
Koine text and the "Egyptian" text has thus proved to be essentially
correct, their opinion concerning the so-called "Western" text is
no longer tenable. That this is an erroneous designation may be
inferred from the fact that the text may be shown to have been
in use not only in Egypt ($\mathfrak{P}^{38}$, $\mathfrak{P}^{48}$, in part $\aleph^{14}$), but also in
Syria (the Old Syriac version of the Gospels and the Diatessaron),
and above all in the West (Vetus Latina, Irenaeus, Tertullian),
whereas the geographical home of both Greek chief witnesses ($D^{e,a}$
and D^p, see p. 523) is uncertain. What we are dealing with, then,
is a text which is attested from the second century onward
throughout the entire region of the church (Marcion, Tatian,
Irenaeus), for which no better name has been found, but at the
same time the origin and the text-critical value of this text type
has not yet been explained convincingly. Just as certain as the fact
that this text type does not represent the original text[15] is the fact
that it does not simply represent an editing of the primitive text
in the early second century.[16] But the repeatedly represented view
that the "Western" text is simply the uncontrolled text of the
second century that had grown wild,[17] is also scarcely adequate.
One cannot overlook the fact that an essential part of the variants
of the "Western" text, especially in the Gospels and Acts, arise
from a smoothing out, an expanding, and in part a tendentious
editing.[18] It is, however, extremely questionable whether one can
even regard the "Western" text as a unified text type,[19] and thus

[14] See above, p. 522, with n. 29.

[15] Thus P. Glaue.

[16] Thus W. H. P. Hatch, C. C. Torrey.

[17] Thus, e.g., G. Zuntz (see n. 13), 263 ff; E. C. Colwell, "Method in Establishing the Nature of Text-Types," 53=137.

[18] See the lists in F. G. Kenyon, *The Western Text in the Gospels and Acts*,
1939, 4 ff, and above, §9.6, with the bibl. given there, esp. E. J. Epp, *The
Theological Tendency of Codex Bezae . . . in Acts*, SNTMS 3, 1966 (p. 175 ff,
bibl.). The stylistic revision of Mk in the second century conjectured by O.
Linton, "Evidences of a Second-Century Revised Edition of St Mark's Gospel,"
NTS 14, 1967/68, 321 ff—if it really occurred—also belongs in the context
of the "Western" text.

[19] *Contra*, e.g., Kieffer, 245; Colwell, "Hort redivivus," 166=149 ff. Cf.
also the special position of $D^{e,a}$ in Griffith's calculations, 397 ff, 400 f, 403 f.

the age and the geographical distribution of a "Western" reading must be tested in individual cases if one wants to differentiate old readings which are still considered basic for the recovery of the primitive text from readings which are later or which have only isolated attestation.[20]

For a long while it was thought that this task was aided by the discovery of a third text type, which does not belong to the Koine text: the "Caesarean" text. The thesis that in Mk a special text type can be demonstrated,[21] which fluctuates between "Egyptian" and "Western," but also manifests isolated readings of its own,[22] was expanded by Streeter, who showed that Origen had already found this text in Caesarea when he moved there (hence "Caesarean" text). However, new research, especially on the basis of $\mathfrak{P}^{37}$ and $\mathfrak{P}^{45}$, has shown that Origen used such a text in Alexandria and in Caesarea in addition to the "Egyptian" text, and that within the witnesses which were claimed for the "Caesarean" text a development toward the Koine text took place.[23] Although such a text was obviously used for a long time in Palestine,[24] up to now the age of this text has not been determined, and it is also not possible to demonstrate it with any certainty outside of Mk.[25] Thus if on the basis of recent research one probably cannot speak of a "disappearance" of this text form,[26] still it is not sufficiently tangible to serve as an aid for deciding between older and recent tradition within the "Western" text.

One must therefore be content to assert that for the earliest period of the text tradition there existed the two text types: the "Egyptian" and the "Western." [27] But since, as far as we can perceive, no manuscript of the NT text represents one of these text types with complete purity, all that can be accomplished is

[20] E.g., there no longer exist convincing grounds, based on the thesis of the so-called "Western non-interpolations" (see n. 1), to exclude from the primitive text on principle these extra elements of the "Egyptian" text (in contrast to the "Western" text). Cf. Aland, "Bedeutung des $\mathcal{P}^{75}$. . . ," 157 f, 167 ff.

[21] In the majuscules Θ, W (in part), the minuscules 28, 565, 700, and the minuscule groups 1 and 13 (see p. 523 f), and the Old Georgian version.

[22] Examples in W. G. Kümmel, ThR, NF 11, 1939, 104 n. 1.

[23] On the history of research cf. Metzger, "Caesarean Text," and "Recent Spanish Contributions," and Kieffer, 25 ff.

[24] For the gospel text of the fourth century in Jerusalem this has been shown by J. H. Greenlee, The Gospel Text of Cyril of Jerusalem, StD 17, 1955.

[25] M. M. Carder's attempt to demonstrate this for the Catholic epistles is unsuccessful (cf. Aland, "Bemerkungen").

[26] Thus Kieffer, 245, 247.

[27] A strict local text theory is therefore no longer tenable; cf. Birdsall, Cambridge History (see bibl. preceding §38), 353.

to determine better and worse witnesses for a text type[28] and on the basis of this grouping to recognize certain specific readings as characteristic for one text type. The more strongly a reading is attested in one or both of the old text types, the more its witness is to be regarded as certain, and the "Egyptian" text now as earlier must be regarded as being on the whole a better text type. But since now as earlier our knowledge of the earlier history of the text is inadequate, when we raise the question of the primitive text in individual cases, we must keep in view besides the external attestation the old rules of internal criticism: *proclivi lectioni praestat ardua; brevior lectio potior* ("the preferred reading is the difficult one, the shorter reading is the more significant"). Also to be kept in mind are the sources of errors in the manuscript tradition,[29] intentional alterations of the text,[30] and the fact of assimilation of related texts to one another, especially in the Synoptics.[31] Important too is the observing of connections between adjacent variants which can only be judged together.[32]

Of course, in observing all these rules some uncertainties remain, but that is scarcely the basis for designating "thoroughgoing eclecticism" as the single possible method.[33] On the one hand one should not overlook the fact that the agreement between the modern critical text editions is astonishingly great, while the number of seriously contested variants is relatively small.[34] And even if a new edition of the text, such as the twenty-sixth edition of Nestle which is already in preparation, varies in some details from the modern *"textus receptus,"* the twenty-fifth edition of Nestle,

---

[28] Good survey of the grouping of manuscripts is offered by W. H. P. Hatch, *Facsimiles . . . Minuscule of Manuscripts* (see bibl. preceding §38), 60 ff, and the list of F. Hahn in the German tr. of F. G. Kenyon–A. W. Adams, *Text of the NT = Der Text der griech. Bibel,* [2]1962, 191.

[29] See the examples in Metzger, *Text of the NT,* 186 ff.

[30] Cf. C. S. C. Williams, *Alterations* (see bibl. preceding §38), 1 ff; J. N. Birdsall, *Cambridge History,* 337 ff; K. W. Clark, "Textual Criticism and Doctrine" (see bibl. preceding §38), 52 ff.

[31] Greeven, "Erwägungen," 281 ff; H. Zimmermann, *Nt. Methodenlehre,* 1967, 47 f.

[32] Examples in Vogels, *Handbuch* (see bibl. preceding §38), 182 ff; Zimmermann, (see n. 31), 48 f.

[33] Thus Kilpatrick, "The Greek Text of Today" (see bibl. preceding §38), 205. Similarly Birdsall, *Cambridge History,* 376; Duplacy, *Histoire des Manuscrits* (see bibl. preceding §38), 139; Fee, "Corrections" (§38 n. 16), 257; Epp, JBL 85, 1966, (§38 n. 17), 513; more limited, Clark, "Today's Problems . . . ," 166 f; *contra,* Klijn, *Survey . . . , Part Two,* 70; Colwell, "Hort Redivivus," 154 f = 136 f.

[34] See Aland, "Der heutige Text . . ." (§39 n. 14), 62 ff.

the newest finds and researches have shown that our critical text of the Greek NT must come very close to the primitive text of the NT writings which were taken up into the canon. And, on the other hand, in spite of all the existing unclarity, we know so much concerning the history of the text that a largely objective decision is possible in most of the contested cases through careful observation of the witnesses of the readings and full recognition of the sources of errors. The number of contested texts which we are not able to explain by this method is thus relatively small. And even though in these cases a decision must be reached by subjective means—critically tested—this responsibility can hardly be completely evaded. The skeptical question whether the primitive text "remained stable long enough to hold a priority" [35] is unjustified. Even if the oldest text that has been found on the basis of attestation and inner criteria should prove to be factually untenable in individual cases, the exegete ought not to shrink from a discreetly handled conjecture; but these cases will not be numerous.

[35] K. W. Clark, "The Theological Relevance" (see bibl. preceding §38), 16.

APPENDIX

§41. Commentaries on the Individual Books of the New Testament

Dates given here are those of the latest revised edition of the commentaries. Those published as part of a series have been cited first, alphabetically according to the abbreviations given for the series' names in the List of Abbreviations. Individual commentaries follow, cited alphabetically according to author's name.

Matthew

HNTC: F. V. Filson, 1960; CNT: P. Bonnard, [2]1970; Ét. bibl.: M.-J. Lagrange, [4]1927; HNT: E. Klostermann, [2]1927; ICC: W. C. Allen, [3]1912; IntB: S. E. Johnson, 1951; Meyer: B. Weiss, [10]1910; E. Lohmeyer, 1956 (ed. W. Schmauch; incomplete); Moffatt: T. H. Robinson, 1928; NTD: J. Schniewind, 1937; RNT: J. Schmid, [5]1965; Torch: G. E. P. Cox, 1952; Ty: R. V. G. Tasker, 1961; UB: J. Wilkens, I,II, 1934/37; Zahn: Th. Zahn, [4]1922; ZüB: W. Michaelis, I, 1948, II, 1949 (up to 17:13).

P. Gaechter, 1964 (Ger.); G. Gander, *L'Évangile de l'Église*, 1970; A. Loisy, *Les évangiles synoptiques I,II*, 1907/8; C. G. Montefiore, *The Synoptic Gospels II*, [2]1927: B. Rigaux, *Témoignage de l'évangile de Matthieu*, 1967; A. Schlatter, *Der Evangelist Matthäus*, 1929; J. Wellhausen, [2]1914 (Ger.).

Mark

HNTC: S. E. Johnson, 1960; CGTC: C. E. B. Cranfield, 1959; Ét. bibl.: M.-J. Lagrange, [4]1929; HNT: E. Klostermann, [4]1950; ICC: E. P. Gould, 1896; IntB: F. C. Grant, 1951; Meyer: E. Lohmeyer, [10]1937 (with supplement ed. G. Sass, [2]1963); Moffatt: B. H. Branscomb, 1937; NTD: J. Schniewind, 1936; E. Schweizer, [11]1967: RNT: J. Schmid, [5]1963; ThHK: F. Hauck, 1931; W. Grundmann, [5]1971; Torch: A. M. Hunter, 1949; Ty: A. Cole, 1961; UB: G. Dehn, [6]1953; Zahn: G. Wohlenberg, [3/4]1930.

P. Carrington, 1960; E. Haenchen, *Der Weg Jesu. Eine Erklärung des Mk und seiner synpt. Parallelen* (1966), [2]1968; A. Loisy, *Les évangiles synoptiques* I,II, 1907/8; *idem, Marc*, 1911; C. G. Montefiore, *The Synoptic Gospels* I, [2]1927; A. E. Rawlinson, 1925; B. Rigaux, *Témoig-*

nage de l'évangile de Marc, 1965; A. Schlatter, *Markus, der Evangelist für die Griechen,* 1935; V. Taylor, 1952; J. Wellhausen, [2]1909 (Ger.).

Luke

HNTC: A. R. C. Leaney, 1958; CB: E. E. Ellis, 1966; Ét. bibl.: M.-J. Lagrange, [4]1927; HNT: E. Klostermann, [2]1929; HThK: H. Schürmann I, (Chs. 1–9), 1969; ICC: A. Plummer, [5]1922; IntB: S. M. Gilmour, 1952; Meyer: B. Weiss, [9]1901; Moffatt: W. Manson, 1930; NIC: N. Geldenhuys, 1950; NTD: K. H. Rengstorf, [9]1962; RNT: J. Schmid, [4]1960; ThHK: F. Hauck, 1934; W. Grundmann, [2]1961; Torch: W. R. F. Browning, 1960; UB: L. Fendt, 1937; Zahn: Th. Zahn, [3/4]1920.

H. W. Bartsch, *Wachet aber zu jeder Zeit!* 1963; J. M. Creed, 1930; H. Gollwitzer, *Die Freude Gottes,* [2]1952; A. Loisy, *Les évangiles synoptiques* I,II, 1907/8; *idem, L'évangile selon Luc,* 1924; C. G. Montefiore, *The Synoptic Gospels* II, [2]1927; B. Rigaux, *Témoignage de l'évangile de Luc,* 1970; A. Schlatter, *Das Ev. des Lukas,* 1931; J. Wellhausen, 1904 (Ger.).

John

Anchor: R. E. Brown, I,II, 1966/70; HNTC: J. N. Sanders, completed by B. A. Mastin, 1968; Ét. bibl.: M.-J. Lagrange, [5]1936; HNT: W. Bauer, [3]1933; HThK: R. Schnackenburg, I,II (Chs. 1–12), 1965/71; ICC: J. H. Bernard, I,II, 1928; IntB: W. F. Howard, 1952; Meyer: R. Bultmann, [10]1941 (supplement, [2]1957); Moffatt: G. H. C. Macgregor, 1928; NIC: M. C. Tenney, 1948; NTD: H. Strathmann, [6]1951; RNT: A. Wikenhauser, [3]1961; Torch: A. Richardson, 1959; Ty: R. V. G. Tasker, 1960; UB: W. Brandt, [3]1940; Zahn: Th. Zahn, [5/6]1921; ZüB: G. Spörri, I,II, 1950.

C. K. Barrett, 1956; E. C. Hoskyns, [2]1947; R. H. Lightfoot, 1956; A. Loisy, [2]1921 (Fr.); H. Odeberg, I, 1929 (incomplete); A. Schlatter, *Der Evangelist Johannes,* 1930; J. Wellhausen, 1908 (Ger.).

Acts

Anchor: J. Munck, 1967; HNTC: C. S. C. Williams, 1957; Ét. bibl.; E. Jacquier, 1926; HNT: H. Conzelmann, 1963; IntB: G. H. C. Macgregor, 1954; Meyer: E. Haenchen, [14]1965 (Eng. tr., 1971); Moffatt: F. J. Foakes-Jackson, 1932; NIC: F. F. Bruce, 1954; NTD: G. Stählin, 1962; RNT: A. Wikenhauser, [3]1956; ThHK: O. Bauernfeind, 1939; Torch: R. R. Williams, 1953; Ty: E. M. Blaiklock, 1959; UB: O. Dibelius, [5]1951; Zahn: Th. Zahn, I,II, [3/4]1922/27.

A. Loisy, 1920 (Fr.); K. Lake and H. J. Cadbury, "English Translation and Commentary," and "Additional Notes to the Commentary," *Beginnings* I, Vols. 4 and 5, 1933; F. Stagg, *The Book of Acts: The Early Struggle for an Unhindered Gospel,* 1955.

Romans

HNTC: C. K. Barrett, 1957; CNT: F.-J. Leenhardt, 1957 (supplement, 1969); Ét. bibl.: M.-J. Lagrange, [2]1930; HNT: H. Lietzmann, [4]1933; ICC: W. Sanday–A. C. Headlam, [5]1902; IntB: J. Knox, 1954; Meyer: O. Michel, [12]1963; Moffatt: C. H. Dodd, 1932; NIC: J. Murray, I,II, 1960/65; NTD: P. Althaus, [9]1959; RNT: O. Kuss, 1950; ThHK: H. W. Schmidt, 1963; Torch: A. M. Hunter, 1955; Ty: F. F. Bruce, 1963; Zahn: Th. Zahn, [3]1952 (rev. F. Hauck); ZüB: E. Gaugler, I,II, 1945/52.

H. Asmussen, 1952 (Ger.); K. Barth (Eng. tr., from 6th Ger. ed., E. C. Hoskyns, 1933); P. Boylan, 1934; E. Brunner, 1938 (Ger.); Th. Haering, 1926 (Ger.); J. Huby–S. Lyonnet, [2]1957 (Fr.); E. Kühl, 1913 (Ger.); O. Kuss, 1. and 2. Fascicles, 1957/59 (Ger.); A. Nygren, 1949; A. Schlatter, *Gottes Gerechtigkeit,* 1935.

I Corinthians

HNTC: C. K. Barrett, 1968; CB: F. F. Bruce, 1971; CNT: J. Héring, 1949; Ét. bibl.: E.-B. Allo, 1934; HNT: H. Lietzmann–W. G. Kümmel, [5]1969; ICC: A. Robertson–A. Plummer, [2]1914; IntB: C. T. Craig, 1953; Meyer: J. Weiss, [9]1910; H. Conzelmann, [11]1969; Moffatt: J. Moffatt, 1938; NIC: F. W. Grosheide, [2]1954; NTD: H. D. Wendland, [12]1968; RNT: O. Kuss, 1940; Torch: W. G. H. Simon, 1959; Ty: L. Morris, 1958; UB: O. Schmitz, 1939; Zahn: Ph. Bachmann, [4]1936 (addition by E. Stauffer); ZüB: W. Meyer, I, 1947, II, 1945.

K. Barth, *Die Auferstehung der Toten,* 1924; A. Schlatter, *Paulus, der Bote Jesu,* 1934.

II Corinthians

CB: F. F. Bruce, 1971; CNT: J. Héring, 1950; Ét. bibl.: E.-B. Allo, 1936; HNT: H. Lietzmann–W. G. Kümmel, [5]1969; ICC: A. Plummer, 1925; IntB: F. V. Filson, 1953; Meyer: H. Windisch, [9]1924 (1970 reprint with foreword and bibliographical supplement by G. Strecker); Moffatt: R. H. Strachan, 1935; NIC: P. E. Hughes, 1962; NTD: H. D. Wendland, [12]1968; RNT: O. Kuss, 1940; Torch: R. P. C. Hanson, 1954; Ty: R. V. G. Tasker, 1958; Zahn: Ph. Bachmann, [4]1922.

K. Prümm, *Diakonia Pneumatos* I, 1967; A. Schlatter, *Paulus, der Bote Jesu,* 1934.

Galatians

CB: D. Guthrie, 1969; CNT: P. Bonnard, 1953; Ét. bibl.: M.-J. Lagrange, [2]1925; HNT: H. Lietzmann, [3]1932; ICC: E. D. Burton, 1921; IntB: R. T. Stamm, 1953; Meyer: H. Schlier, [12]1962; Moffatt: G. S. Duncan, 1934; NIC: H. N. Ridderbos, 1953; NTD: H. W. Beyer–P. Althaus, [9]1962; RNT: O. Kuss, 1940; ThHK: A. Oepke, [2]1957; Torch: J. A. Allan, 1951; Ty: R. A. C. Cole, 1965; UB: G. Dehn, [3]1938; Zahn: Th. Zahn, [3]1922 (rev. F. Hauck); ZüB: C. Maurer, 1943.

H. Asmussen, *Theologisch-kirchliche Erwägungen zum Gal,* 1935; R. Bring, 1961; J. B. Lightfoot, 1865; A. Loisy, 1916 (Fr.).

Ephesians

CB: G. Johnston, 1967; CNT: Ch. Masson, 1953; HNT: M. Dibelius–H. Greeven, [3]1953; ICC: T. K. Abbott, 1897; IntB: F. W. Beare, 1953; Meyer: E. Haupt, [2]1902; Moffatt: E. F. Scott, 1930; NIC: E. K. Simpson, 1957; NTD: H. Conzelmann, [9]1962; RNT: K. Staab, [3]1959; Torch: J. A. Allan, 1959; UB: K. Mittring, 1936; Zahn: P. Ewald, [2]1910. E. Gaugler, *Auslegung nt. Schriften* VI, 1966; A. Klöpper, 1891 (Ger.); H. Schlier, [3]1962 (Ger.).

Philippians

HNTC: F. W. Beare, [2]1969; CB: G. Johnston, 1967; CNT: P. Bonnard, 1950; HNT: M. Dibelius, [3]1937; HThK: J. Gnilka, 1968; ICC: M. R. Vincent, 1897; IntB: E. F. Scott, 1955; Meyer: E. Lohmeyer, [8]1930 (supplement by W. Schmauch, 1964); Moffatt: J. H. Michael, 1928; NIC: J. J. Müller, 1955; NTD: G. Friedrich, [9]1962; RNT: K. Staab, [3]1959; ThHK: W. Michaelis, 1935; Torch: F. C. Synge, 1951; Ty: R. P. Martin, 1960; O. Schmitz, [5]1934; Zahn: P. Ewald, [4]1923 (rev. G. Wohlenberg).

K. Barth, 1928 (Ger.) (Eng. tr., J. W. Leitch, 1962); A. Klöpper, 1893 (Ger.); J. B. Lightfoot, [6]1881.

Colossians

CB: G. Johnston, 1967; CGTC: C. F. D. Moule, 1957; CNT: Ch. Masson, 1950; HNT: M. Dibelius–H. Greeven, [3]1953; ICC: T. K. Abbott, 1897; IntB: F. W. Beare, 1955; Meyer: E. Lohmeyer, [8]1930 (supplement by W. Schmauch, 1964); Meyer: E. Lohse, [14]1968; Moffatt: E. F. Scott, 1930; NIC: F. F. Bruce, 1957; NTD: H. Conzelmann, [9]1962; RNT: K. Staab, [3]1959; Torch: F. C. Synge, 1951; Ty: H. M. Carson, 1960; Zahn: P. Ewald, [2]1910; ZüB: W. Bieder, 1943.

A Klöpper, 1882 (Ger.); J. B. Lightfoot, [6]1882.

I and II Thessalonians

CB: A. L. Moore, 1969; CNT: Ch. Masson, 1957; Ét. bibl.: B. Rigaux, 1956; HNT: M. Dibelius, [3]1937; ICC: J. E. Frame, 1912; IntB: J. W. Bailey, 1955; Meyer: E. von Dobschütz, [7]1909; Moffatt: W. Neil, 1950; NIC: L. Morris, 1959; NTD: A. Oepke, 1933; RNT: K. Staab, [3]1959; Torch: W. Neil, 1957; Ty: L. Morris, 1956; UB: J. Schneider, *I Thess*, 1932; G. Helbig, 2 Thess, [2]1955; Zahn: G. Wohlenberg, [2]1909.

Philemon

CB: G. Johnston, 1967; CGTC: C. F. D. Moule, 1957; HNT: M. Dibelius–H. Greeven, [3]1953; ICC: M. R. Vincent, 1897; IntB: J. Knox, 1955; Meyer: E. Lohmeyer, [8]1930 (supplement by W. Schmauch, 1964); E. Lohse, [14]1968; Moffatt: E. F. Scott, 1930; NIC: J. J. Müller, 1955; NTD: G. Friedrich, [9]1962; RNT: K. Staab, [3]1959; Torch: A. R. C. Leaney, 1960; Ty: H. M. Carson, 1960; Zahn: P. Ewald, [2]1910; ZüB: W. Bieder, 1944.

J. B. Lightfoot, [6]1882.

Pastoral Epistles

HNTC: J. N. D. Kelly, 1964; Ét. bibl.: C. Spicq, I,II, [4]1969; HNT: M. Dibelius–H. Conzelmann, [3]1955; ICC: W. Lock, 1924; IntB: F. D. Gealy, 1955; Meyer: B. Weiss, [7]1902; Moffatt: E. F. Scott, 1936; NTD: J. Jeremias, [8]1963; RNT: N. Brox, [4]1969; ThHK: G. Holtz, 1965; Torch: A. R. C. Leaney, 1960; Ty: D. Guthrie, 1957; UB: W. Brandt, 1941; Zahn: G. Wohlenberg, [3]1923.

B. S. Easton, 1947; A. Schlatter, *Die Kirche der Griechen im Urteil des Paulus*, 1936; E. K. Simpson, 1954.

Letter to the Hebrews

HNTC: H. W. Montefiore, 1964; CNT: J. Héring, 1954; Ét. bibl.: C. Spicq, I,II, 1952/53; HNT: H. Windisch, [2]1931; ICC: J. Moffatt, 1924; IntB: A. C. Purdy, 1955; Meyer: O. Michel, [12]1966; Moffatt: T. H. Robinson, 1933; NIC: F. F. Bruce, 1964; NTD: H. Strathmann, [6]1953; RNT: O. Kuss, [2]1966; Torch: W. Neil, 1955; Ty: T. Hewitt, 1960; UB: W. Loew, [3]1941; Zahn: E. Riggenbach, 2/[3]1922.

A. Vanhoye, *Situation du Christ. Hébreux 1–2, Lectio Divina* 58 1969.

James

Anchor: B. Reicke, 1964; CB: E. M. Sidebottom, 1967; HNT: H. Windisch–H. Preisker, [3]1951; HThK: F. Mussner, 1964; ICC: J. H. Ropes, 1916; IntB: B. S. Easton, 1957; Meyer: M. Dibelius, expanded by H. Greeven, [11]1964; Moffatt: J. Moffatt, 1928; NIC: A. Ross, 1954; NTD: J. Schneider, [9]1961; RNT: J. Michl, [2]1968; Torch: E. C. Blackman, 1957; Ty: R. V. G. Tasker, 1956; UB: H. Rendtorff, 1953; Zahn: F. Hauck, 1926.

J. Marty, 1935 (Fr.); J. B. Mayor, [3]1910; C. L. Mitton, 1966; A. Schlatter, 1932 (Ger.).

I Peter

Anchor: B. Reicke, 1964; HNTC: J. N. D. Kelly, 1969; CB: E. Best, 1971; HNT: H. Windisch–H. Preisker, [3]1951; HThK: K. H. Schelkle, 1961; ICC: Ch. Bigg, [2]1910; IntB: A. M. Hunter, 1957; Meyer: R. Knopf, [7]1912; Moffatt: J. Moffatt, 1928; NTD: J. Schneider, [9]1961; RNT: J. Michl, [2]1968; Torch: C. E. B. Cranfield, 1960; Ty: A. M. Stibbs–A. F. Walls, 1959; UB: H. Rendtorff, [7]1951; Zahn: G. Wohlenberg, [3]1923; ZüB: E. Schweizer, [2]1949.

F. W. Beare, [2]1958; A. Schlatter, *Petrus und Paulus nach dem I. Petrusbrief*, 1937; E. G. Selwyn, [2]1947.

II Peter

Anchor: B. Reicke, 1964; HNTC: J. N. D. Kelly, 1969; CB: E. M. Sidebottom, 1967; Ét. bibl.: J. Chaine, 1939; HNT: H. Windisch–H. Preisker, [3]1951; HThK: K. H. Schelkle, 1961; ICC: Ch. Bigg, [2]1910; IntB: A. E. Barnett, 1957; Meyer: R. Knopf, [7]1912; Moffatt: J. Moffatt, 1928; NTD: J. Schneider, [9]1961; RNT: J. Michl, [2]1968; Torch: C. E. B Cranfield, 1960; Zahn: G. Wohlenberg, [3]1923.

Jude

Anchor: B. Reicke, 1964; HNTC: J. N. D. Kelly, 1969; CB: E. M. Sidebottom, 1967; Ét. bibl.: J. Chaine, 1939; HNT: H. Windisch–H. Preisker, [3]1951; HThK: K. H. Schelkle, 1961; ICC: Ch. Bigg, [2]1910; IntB: A. E. Barnett, 1957; Meyer: R. Knopf, [7]1912; Moffatt: J. Moffatt 1928; NTD: J. Schneider, [9]1961; RNT: J. Michl, [2]1968; Torch: C. E. B. Cranfield, 1960; Zahn: G. Wohlenberg, [3]1923.

I, II, III John

Ét. bibl.: J. Chaine, 1939; HNT: H. Windisch–H. Preisker, [8]1951; HThK: R. Schnackenburg, [2]1963; ICC: A. E. Brooke, 1912; IntB: A. N. Wilder, 1957; Meyer: R. Bultmann, 1967; Moffatt: C. H. Dodd, 1946; NIC: A. Ross, 1954; NTD: J. Schneider, [9]1961; RNT: J. Michl, [2]1968; ThHK: F. Büchsel, 1933; Torch: N. Alexander, 1962; Ty: J. R. W. Stott, 1964; UB: H. Amussen, [8]1957.

E. Gaugler, *Auslegung nt. Schriften* I, 1964.

Apocalypse of John

HNTC: G. B. Caird, 1966; Ét. bibl.: E. B. Allo, 1933; HNT: E. Lohmeyer, 1926 ([2]1953, expanded); ICC: R. H. Charles, I, II, 1920; IntB: M. Rist, 1957; Meyer: W. Bousset, [6]1906; Moffatt: M. Kiddle–M. K. Ross, 1940; NTD: E. Lohse, [10]1971; RNT: A. Wikenhauser, [3]1959; ThHK: W. Hadorn, 1928; Torch: R. H. Preston–A. T. Hanson, 1949; UB: H. Lilje, [5]1958; Ty: L. Morris, 1969; Zahn: Th. Zahn, I,II, 1924/26; ZüB: Ch. Brütsch, I-III, [2]1970.

I. T. Beckwith, 1919; W. J. Harrington, *Understanding the Apocalypse*, 1969; A. Loisy, 1923 (Fr.).

INDEX OF PASSAGES

A. New Testament

The index does not cover the paragraphs listing the contents of the individual books in §§6–10, 14–25, 27–32, and 34, the tables (pp. 58, 59, 65, and 66), or the section dealing with the contents of the manuscripts (pp. 515–25).

B. Early Judaism and the Ancient Church

INDEX OF PERSONS

Items listed in the Index of Passages are not repeated here.

INDEX OF SUBJECTS

Items which can readily be located by consulting the Table of Contents
and the Index of Passages are not listed here.